European Integration as an Elite Process

Routledge Advances in Sociology

7 Day

University of Plymouth Library
Subject to status this item may be renewed
via your Voyager account
http://voyager.plymouth.ac.uk
Tel: (01752) 232323

European Integration as an Elite Process

The Failure of a Dream?

Max Haller

Routledge
Taylor & Francis Group
New York   London

First published 2008
by Routledge
270 Madison Ave, New York, NY 10016

Simultaneously published in the UK
by Routledge
2 Park Square, Milton Park, Abingdon, Oxon OX14 4RN

Routledge is an imprint of the Taylor & Francis Group, an informa business

© 2008 Max Haller

Typeset in Sabon by IBT Global.
Printed and bound in the United States of America on acid-free paper by IBT Global.

Library of Congress Cataloging-in-Publication Data

Haller, Max, Dr.
European integration as an elite process : the failure of a dream? / by Max Haller.
     p. cm. — (Routledge advances in sociology ; 40)
   Includes bibliographical references and index.
   ISBN 978-0-415-40390-0
   1. European Union.   2. Elite (Social sciences)—European Union countries.
3. Supranationalism—European Union countries.   4. European Union countries
—Politics and government.   5. European Union countries—Economic integration.
I. Title.
   JN30.H348 2008
   341.242'2—dc22   2007049055

Published thanks to a contribution of the Department of Sociology and Social Research
of the University of Trento and the MUIR, in connection with the project 'Rientro dei
Cervelli'.

ISBN10: 0-415-40390-1 (hbk)
ISBN10: 0-203-92730-3 (ebk)

ISBN13: 978-0-415-40390-0 (hbk)
ISBN13: 978-0-203-92730-4 (ebk)

For Martha
(23.3.1948–5.6.2006)

Contents

List of Figures

List of Photos

List of Tables

Preface

THE PROBLEM

In referenda on May 29 and June 1, 2005, the French and Dutch population rejected the new *Constitution for Europe*. These events in two founding members of the European Community have been perceived like a drumbeat all over Europe. They have irradiated a phenomenon that was evident to critical observers long since: A considerable split has arisen between elites and citizens in the process of European integration. In practically all earlier decisions about access to the Union at the national levels, and about further decisive steps of institutional integration, approval was much stronger in the national parliaments than among the general population. In two of the most wealthy and democratically stable Western European nations, Norway and Switzerland, the population has rejected joining the EU, in spite of strong recommendations by their political elites. Participation at the European elections is much lower than participation at national elections and decreases significantly in most member states.

Thus, the enthusiasm about European unification and integration, spread over all Europe in the aftermath of the Second World War, has disappeared and given way to disenchantment and even a sceptical attitude after far-reaching steps of institutional integration and deepening. In this period, the Union has also been enlarged from the original six to now twenty-seven member states, accepting twelve new member states in East Central Europe and the Mediterranean, and beginning to make negotiations about further inclusion of several states, including Turkey. In view of the aforementioned signs of crisis, however, leading politicians and commentators agree that something must have gone wrong in the way the European Union has been integrated and enlarged.

The central thesis of this study is that it is the increasing split between elites and citizens which lies at the base of the current impasse in which the European Union finds itself. One central element of this impasse is that it is suffering from a serious deficit of democratic legitimation. Another one is that a considerable hiatus exists between the boastful speeches and high aspirations of the EU concerning its aims and achievements and real social and economic development. This is so particularly in those areas which affect great parts of the population, such as in employment and standards of living. In connection with, and partly out of these two problems, others follow—like the widespread feeling that powerful organisations and groups have much more influence in Brussels than ordinary citizens, or that neoliberal principles of economic policy are guiding the integration process, thus undermining the European model of a welfare society, developed in different variations in North and South, West and East.

THEORETICAL APPROACH AND EMPIRICAL BASIS

Starting from the Weberian idea of sociology as a "science of social reality," and from the principles of "democratic elite theory" (Etzioni-Halevy 1993), this study argues that an understanding of the problems of European integration must include a systematic consideration of four levels and issues: (1) The basic values and principles that have guided the integration process since its beginnings in the 1950s; (2) the specific institutional form which integration has taken in the half century since then; (3) the interests of the elites—political, bureaucratic, professional, and economic—their size, privileges, and interrelations; and (4) the perceptions and evaluations of the populations, particularly as they concern the structure and behaviour of the elites and the consequences of the integration process. The thesis of this study is that today significant discrepancies exist between the elites and citizens as far as all these aspects are concerned: About the basic values and aims of integration; about the institutional structure which the European Union has developed over the decades; about the factual and perceived interests, interrelations, and behaviours of the elites; and about the relation of the elites to the interests of the population in general and the weaker social classes and groups in particular.

How did these discrepancies come about? This study argues that the process of European integration has undergone significant changes since it started in the aftermath of World War II. At this time, economic recovery and reconstruction and the securing of peace in Europe were in the forefront; the "founding fathers" of the European Community were highly respected political personalities, many of them having been expelled from their countries by fascist governments. In the course of the 1970s and 1980s, integration became a central concern also to big enterprises, of the rising powerful European bureaucracy in Brussels, and of a new type of politicians, promoting their careers by close networks with a broad clientele in public, semipublic, and private enterprises and organisations. At the same time, efforts at introducing democratic elements into the Union were started, leading to a European Parliament directly elected by the citizens in the member states. However, these and other measures were not able to contain the rising split between elites and citizens. One main reason for this was that politics at the level of the Union works as a "consociational system" making it difficult to see who is responsible for what. In addition, economic development in the Union, and especially so in the "Euro zone," began to lag behind that in other regions of the world, such as in the United States or in East Asia—thus disproving the prognoses of continued strong growth as a consequence of integration.

This study includes a broad array of qualitative and quantitative data. Extensive oral interviews have been carried out with national and European politicians (particularly with members of the European Parliament), with Commissioners and officials of the EU Commission in Brussels, and with national officials working on EU affairs; with the representatives of member states who participated in the access negotiations with the EU; and with representatives of business and labour organisations. Biographies of leading political personalities have been analysed concerning their basic value orientations and political strategies. The social characteristics of the members of the European Parliament have been compiled from the homepage of the EP and reanalysed. Large, representative population surveys are used to grasp the perceptions and attitudes of the general population; these data sets include the Eurobarometer series, the International Social Survey Programme, and some national surveys. Two smaller, special surveys have been carried out in nine member countries of the EU around the European elections of 2004. Statistical data from Eurostat and national statistical offices were reanalysed or produced anew particularly for the aim of this study (e.g., on the "European substitute bureaucracies" in some member states); extensive texts have been analysed, including historical writings about European integration, media and press reports, the full text of the EU constitution, and a TV discussion of president Chirac with youth people of his country. Each of these sources of data has been consulted in order to investigate specific hypotheses of the study. They will be described in detail in the sections where they are introduced and analysed.

This is the first comprehensive study of the new European elites and their networks of influence and power at the level of the European Union and their perception by the general public in the twenty-seven member states. Its theoretical approach and empirical design are much broader than usual elite studies, which typically limit themselves to the description and analysis of the social characteristics and attitudes of the elites. It places the analysis of the elites into a systematic consideration of the institutional context within which they are working, and of their relation to and perception by the citizens. In addition to the original empirical research carried out for this study, it also contains summaries of existing pertinent research from the most recent relevant studies carried out by economists, political scientists, sociologists, and experts of international and European law.

The study presents an interpretation of the character of the political system of the EU which is compatible with its achievements but explains also its shortcomings and failures. Based on this interpretation, it also includes proposals for a strengthening of the democratic and social elements in the European Union. The book fills in a serious gap in the literature. Some of the few books which have covered the issue of elites and power in the European Union (Galtung 1973; Holland 1980) are now outdated. They have also focussed primarily on economic and political issues and elites, which is true also for some insightful recent studies (Bornschier 2000a; van Apeldoorn 2002). It is a central thesis of this study, however, that professional and bureaucratic elites (the new "Eurocracy") also play a decisive, independent role in the development of integration. The bulk of the now immense literature on European integration is written by jurists, students of (European) law, and by political scientists in the tradition of comparative government theory (*vergleichende Regierungslehre*). Many of these works, however, have either a normative orientation (proposing certain constitutional models for the European Union, such as federalism) or a scientific-practical orientation analysing the workings of multilevel government in Europe. Missing is an orientation which combines both approaches and which was considered as central by Montesquieu in his classic *Spirit of Laws* (1748): It is not enough to devise ideal models of constitutions but one must also take into consideration the social conditions which make a constitution really "work."

OVERVIEW ON THE CONTENT

This book is divided into eight chapters. The first two chapters set out the framework for the study; Chapters 3 to 5 analyse the role of the new European elites; and Chapters 6 to 8 investigate the perceptions and attitudes of the citizens, the historical-intellectual ideas of integration, and the problem of the character of the Union and the finality of integration.

In the first chapter, the central problem of the book, the split between the elites and citizens is documented. It analyses the negative outcomes of the referenda on the Constitution for Europe in France and the Netherlands, the split in the results of parliamentary votings, and popular referenda about important steps of integration, and it documents the quite divergent view of the elites and of the citizens about the aims and workings of the EU. It shows that scepticism concerning integration is spread out, particularly in the democratically most developed member countries of the EU. The second chapter presents the concepts and theoretical principles of the book and develops a series of concrete hypotheses. Its central theses are that the different elite groups all have their specific interests in integration and further this process in particular ways. The political and economic elites are of decisive influence when great single steps are taking place; the bureaucratic and professional elites provide for a continuous advance of integration, even in phases of seemingly stagnation ("Eurosclerosis"). The intellectual elites are important as providers of basic ideas, but they are also used by the powerful elites to legitimate integration. Thus, ideas play a significant role in the integration process, and it is essential to look at them from the critical perspective developed by the sociology of knowledge.

Chapter 3 investigates the European political elites. Following the thesis of the book, that charismatic political personalities can have a decisive impact on the course of history, it starts by sketching out significant social characteristics of the three "founding fathers" of integration, Adenauer, Degasperi, and Schuman, and of its decisive "spin doctor," Jean Monnet. Then, it is shown that the values and strategies of these men clearly anticipated both positive and problematic characteristics of later integration. It is shown that political life in some of the founding member states underwent a significant change in the next decades, leading to widespread clientelism and corruption; this may have contributed to the increasing distrust against politics both at the national and the European level. Finally, the present-day "European politicians" are investigated. They include the elected governments of member states, the members of the European Parliament, and the members of the European Commission and the European Court of Justice. It is shown that all of them have often varying interests in the continuation of integration. Chapter 4 investigates the role of the economic elites connected with European integration. The interests of the corporation owners and managers in integration are well known, as are those of agrarian producers. However, it turns out that multinational corporations are not as dependent on integration as it is sometimes asserted; there is also no indication of the emergence of a European business (or capitalist) class. Nevertheless, business interests are closely interwoven with the process of integration and provide it in certain periods with a particular speed and with a direction which is partly neoliberal, partly neocorporatist. It is also shown that the integration of the post-Communist central East European countries was molded by this logic with the consequence of a (momentarily) massive deterioration of the living standards of the population and a (long-lasting) predominance of Western capital. Chapter 5 analyses the structure and growth of the "Eurocracy," the new large European bureaucracy in Brussels and elsewhere. It criticizes the predominant view of this bureaucracy as a small and highly efficient apparatus by pointing to its dynamic, hitherto undamped, expansion and the growth of an EU "substitute bureaucracy" in the member countries. It also summarizes research on practices of mismanagement and clientelism in Brussels. Data on the material and other gratifications of the Eurocracy indicate its rather powerful and privileged position.

In chapter 6, the attitudes of the citizens as well as those of the elites toward integration in the different member countries are investigated. In this regard, a split exists not only between elites and citizens but also highly divergent views in different countries. A sociological typology of such attitudes is developed, showing that integration is altogether rejected or seen very critical in some countries, while in others it is seen as a means to advance national goals which seem unattainable by remaining outside the EU. It is also shown that the frequently quoted idea of the EU as a "community of values" does not withstand a closer scrutiny. Given these discrepancies, a clarification of the issue of the character of the EU and the finality of integration become of paramount importance. This issue is taken up in the two final chapters. Chapter 7 investigates the ideas of European integration as it has been developed through the centuries. Two main results arise. First, there was not only one but many different ideas of European integration; some of them have been much less noble than it is usually assumed. Present-day political elites, however, refer only to the positive ideas (securing of peace, furthering of prosperity) as means to legitimate the process of integration. Second, there was one central idea, expressed most clearly by Kant, which seems valid up to the present day. It says that peace in Europe (and the world) will be secured first of all when all European countries will become democratic; an "ever closer integration" (Treaty of Rome) is simply not necessary from this point of view. This view is supported by a multitude of recent empirical studies. Based on these findings, Chapter 8 takes up the issue of the character of the European Union. It argues that an understanding of it as a "social community of law" provides a coherent solution to the dilemma between the aims that integration should enhance economic and political efficiency (which it does only to a limited degree), that it should preserve (if not strengthen) the democratic quality of politics and provide for a balanced pattern of social integration and development. As a social community of law, the EU should renounce acting as a "government" (which it now claims to a considerable degree) and focus on the enactment of general rules whose implementation should be left to the member states. At the same time, however, the range of EU law should be widened to also include definite individual social rights. This would lead to a more balanced development of economic integration and social integration. It would also reduce the high but often utopian expectations concerning its democratic quality to a realistic level.

Acknowledgments

This work grew out of my long-standing interest in European integration, problems of local, national, and European identity, and of democratic attitudes and participation at these different levels in political communities. The impetus for writing this book came from a research project of the same title, funded by the University of Trento (Italy), in the context of the programme MUIR (*Incentivi per la mobilità di studiosi impegnati all'estero*). I was teaching at this university from autumn 2002 till summer 2005. I am very grateful to the Facoltà di Sociologia and in particular to its dean at this time, Prof. Antonio Scaglia, who endorsed my work all the time. Substantive support was given also by the other members of that faculty: Renzo Gubert, Antonio Chiesi, Sergio Fabbrini, Gaspare Nevola, Gabriele Pollini, and Riccardo Scartezzini.

Several colleagues have read and commented on significant parts of the manuscript. David Lane (University of Cambridge) provided important general recommendations about the structure of the book and has read carefully several chapters. Important ideas and repeated encouragement were also provided by Mattei Dogan (Paris). During her visit to Graz in June 2005, I had the possibility to discuss the elite-theoretical framework of this study with Eva Etzioni-Halevy (Israel). Several chapters of the book have been carefully read and commented on by my colleagues at the University of Graz: Markus Hadler, Franz Höllinger, Helmut Kuzmics, Manfred Prisching, and Dieter Reicher (Department of Sociology), Peter Koller (Department of Philosophy of Law), and Klaus Poier (Department of Public Law and Political Science). Albert Reiterer (Vienna) read several chapters of the book and elaborated very useful special studies. Several chapters of the book have been commented on by Reinhard Blomert (Berlin), Hermann Strasser and Gerd Nollmann (Duisburg), Stefan Immerfall (Schwäbisch Gmünd), Harald Greib (France), Anders Hellström (Lund, Sweden), Paul Michael Lützeler (Washington), John Meyer (San Francisco), Robert Jackall (New York), Vittorio Olgiati (Urbino), Bernhard Plé (Graz), and Bastian van Apeldoorn (Netherlands).

I am very grateful also to a number of young sociologists and students of sociology who assisted me in the collection and analysis of specific materials and data. Dott.[essa] Liria Veronesi (Trento) carried out statistical analyses of the Eurobarometer surveys, collected biographic materials of leading European political personalities, and helped to organise the special "European election survey" in June 2004. Mag. Regina Ressler (Graz) carried out many statistical analyses and is a coauthor of several articles and research reports whose results have entered partly into this book. Mag. Gerd Kaup and Florian Haller provided very helpful assistance of many kinds. Mag. Theresa Hofbauer (Vienna) provided data about the EU bureaucracy in Brussels and commented on Chapter 5. Special country informations about the EU elections in 2004 have been provided by Bogdan Mach and Krzysztof Zagorski (Warsaw), Gyorgy Lengyel (Budapest), Therese Jacobs (Brussels), Laura Suna (Riga), and Viera Uhlárová (Bratislava).

As part of this work, a small survey in nine countries was carried out around the European elections in June 2004. In this endeavour, the following young researchers assisted me by translating the questionnaire and by carrying through the interviews and collecting media reports about the elections: Beatriz Diez-Hernando (Madrid), Antje Springer (Mannheim, FRG), Laurent Tessier (Paris), Tina Burret (Cambridge, UK), Calle Hanson (Umea, Sweden), Marcin W. Zielinski (Warsaw, Poland), and Zsombor Vasvari (Budapest).

In the academic year 2006/07, an important input to this work came from a course about European integration at the Department of Sociology of the University of Graz, whose topic was *The European Union Seen by the Elites and Citizens*. The twenty-seven students participating in this course made rather comprehensive empirical researches both in Austria and Brussels, interviewing politicians and citizens, surveying press reports, statistics and relevant literature, and writing a final report which resulted in a fine book (edited by Haller and Ressler 2006). Their enthusiasm has been a source of inspiration and encouragement for my own work as well.

At this place, I would like to thank also all those politicians and high officers who provided their time for extensive and exciting interviews about problems of European integration, carried out by the author. They include members of the European Parliament in several countries: Hans-Peter Martin, Hannes Swoboda and Johannes Voggenhuber (Vienna), former Prime Minister Michel Rocard and Bernard Lehideux (Paris), Peter Olajos (Budapest), Giuseppe Gargani (Rome), and Sepp Kusstatscher (Brixen, Italy); in addition, the Polish vice-minister of Foreign affairs, Jan Truszczynski, and Tomasz Nowakowski (both in Warsaw) were interviewed. In Brussels, interviews were carried out with the MEPs Jo Leinen (Germany), Jens Peter Bonde (Denmark), Dr. Edeltraud Böhm-Amtmann, head of the German *Bundesland* Bavaria in Brussels; and several officers of the commission. The Italian MEPs Armando Dionisi, Antonio Panzeri, Francesco Speroni, and Mauro Zani were interviewed by Liria Veronesi. I very much hope that they all appreciate the basically critical spirit of this book. I am convinced that such a spirit and the research questions and analyses arising out of it will in the end be much more helpful for political leaders than any adulation could be.

The work on the book also profited a lot from the possibility to present first results of it at international conferences and other colloquia. Here, I have to mention in particular the "International Network Study of Elites and EU Enlargement" (sponsored by the British Council), which organised a series of conferences in Trento, Italy (June 2002), Budapest (September 2004), Prague (2005), and Kiev, Ukraine (October 2006) at which I could present sections of this book. This network was founded by David Lane (Cambridge), and the meetings were co-organised by Olga Kutsenko (Kiev), Gyorgy Lengyel (Budapest), and Jochen Tholen (Bremen). Lectures on different parts of the book were also presented at the International Workshop "Sociological Perspectives on European Integration," organised by Josef Langer at the University of Klagenfurt (Austria) in September 2006; at a conference on "Repräsentation und Verfassung" in December 2004, organised by the Austrian Political Science Association in Vienna; and at internal lecture series of the Department of Sociology and the Department of Economics of the University of Graz, organised by Gerald Angermann-Mozetic and Heinz Kurz, respectively. Also one negative consequence of the rather long work on the book must be mentioned. This was the fact that some of the chapters may be too long, while other topics (e.p. participation in European elections, the "output legitimation" of the EV, public relation activities of the EV) can only be presented in a shortened way. In several parts of this book, I could also rely on earlier publications (a summary of the main theses has been presented in Haller 2003b); they are quoted in the respective parts. However, all chapters and sections of this book have been written wholly anew. Last but not least I would like to thank the publisher, Routledge, for including this book into the series "Routledge Advances in Sociology"; Ben Holtzman and Eleanor Chan have been very competent and constructive collaborators during the process of preparing the final manuscript.

This book is dedicated to Martha, my wife and mother of our three sons. She who has supported me since over thirty years passed away during the work on this book—far too early.

Graz, January 2008

1 Living in Two Different Worlds?
The Increasing Split Between Elites and Citizens About European Integration

INTRODUCTION

Scientific research begins with problems (Popper 1972). For some time, the European Union has had a big problem: a deep and increasing split between its elites and citizens. This split emerged most sharply in May/June 2005, when clear majorities of the French and Dutch population rejected the Constitution for Europe. In reality, however, the split has existed long since. It had become evident in the early 1990s, when the ratification of Maastricht Treaty faced much more difficulties than expected. The European parliament deemed the treaty inadequate; it was approved only by marginal majorities of the French electorate and rejected by the Danes. Only small minorities of the Swedes and Finns voted for joining the EU, and the Norwegians and Swiss rejected membership altogether. For Diez Medrano (2003:2), the "surprising rejection of the Maastricht Treaty by the Danish population . . . represented the people's triumphant entry onto center stage of the European integration process." It was described as "a shock to the Community."[1] The split between elites and citizens could also be observed in the fact that significant differences existed in the majorities that European issues got at parliamentary votings and at popular referenda. Empirical data proving it shall be presented in the first section of this chapter. Even in the cases where popular referenda about integration got large majorities, the results do not show an overwhelming approval of the population; in most of these cases, turnout was rather low. This shall be shown in the second section. Finally, it will be shown that the split between elites and citizens appears also when looking at findings from opinion polls and qualitative researches.

1.1 The French and Dutch reject the Constitution for Europe: A shock for the political establishment

The elaboration of the Treaty Establishing a Constitution for Europe was rightly seen as one of the most significant steps forward in the process of European integration since the 1950s. The European Council in Nice in 2001 had failed in the effort to find a solution for the institutional reform necessary because of the imminent enlargement with ten new central-east European member states. As a consequence, a special convention (later called "Constitutional Convention") was installed with the task to develop proposals. This convention was very efficient and elaborated a comprehensive, several-hundred-pages-long text. This text contained important new elements making the Union more efficient and democratic and included all the earlier treaties into one single document, making them much more readable.

The negative outcomes of the referenda in France and the Netherlands were the most obvious manifestations of the aforementioned split between the political elites in the EU and its citizens. Let us therefore first look at the results of these two referenda. We will look also at the levels of turnout and at the results of a Eurobarometer survey in autumn 2005. In addition, we compare the results in these two countries with those in the two other countries which held referenda about the constitution, namely, Spain and Luxembourg. In their case, we can compare the results of the referenda also with the results of the successive parliamentary votings. Such referenda were mandatory by constitution only in Denmark and Ireland. In others, they were proposed voluntarily by the governments in order to provide more legitimacy to the constitution; this was the case in Luxembourg, the Netherlands, Portugal, Spain, France, Poland, the Czech Republic, and the United Kingdom. Up to now, such referenda have been carried out only in the four aforementioned countries. All the others seem to renounce carrying out referenda at all, after the fact that the European Council in June 2007 has decided to change the "Constitution for Europe" in some minor regards and to submit them only to parliamentary votings. We will come back to this rather problematic strategy in the final chapter.

A compulsory exercise in democracy with a feeble outcome. The constitutional referendum in Spain

The referendum in Spain was ordered voluntarily by Premier Zapatero (of the socialist party PSOE) and the parliament; it was the first such referendum since democracy had been established anew in Spain. A large majority of the voters participating in the referendum were in favour of the constitution (77%). This was no surprise since all the major parties had supported it, and the Spaniards generally have a rather positive attitude toward integration. The Spanish result was perceived as a very positive start of the ratification process throughout the EU. However, there was a serious flaw in this result: Only 42.3% of the electorate participated in the referendum; this was the lowest turnout in any election or referendum held in the history of democratic Spain. Particularly disturbing was that the turnout was lowest among the youngest groups of the electorate.[2] Several reasons were responsible for this low turnout, such as a low start of the campaign for the referendum. More problematic, however, was that in Spain there was "widespread apathy surrounding the constitutional treaty, and ignorance of its contents":[3] In a government

Table 1.1   Results of Polls, Referenda, and Parliamentary Votes About the EU
Constitution in Spain, France, the Netherlands, and Luxembourg (2005)

| Country | Referenda | | | Parliamentary voting | | | Euro-barometer 64 (Autumn 2005) |
	Date	Turnout (%)	Yes/No (%)	Date	Institution	% yes	(%) pro
Spain	(20.2.)	42,3	76,2/23,8	(28.4.)	Parliament	94,2	62
				(19.5.)	Senate	97,4	
France	(29.5.)	70,0	45,1/54,8		—		67
Netherlands	(1.6.)	63,3	38,4/61,6		—		62
Luxembourg	(10.7.)	86,2	56,5/43,5	(28.6.)	Parliament	100,0	69
				(25.10.)	Parliament	98,2	

Sources: Centrum für angewandte Politikforschung (CAP), München. See http://www.cap-lmu/themen/eu-reform/ratifikation/index.php; http://en.wikinews.org/wiki/France_votes_no_in_EU_referendum; and many other Internet sources.

poll, 90% of the voters admitted having little or no knowledge of its content.[4]
It is interesting to compare the results of the referendum with those of opinion
polls and parliamentary votings.

Table 1.1 shows that a clear majority of the Spaniards—62% according
the Eurobarometer survey in autumn 2005—in principle are in favour of the
constitution. High proportions of Spaniards voted neither in the European
elections of 2004 nor in this referendum. Thus, " . . . it seems that Europe
remains a political and institutional entity from which many electors feel
distant, even though they recognize the advantages of Spanish membership
in the EU."[5] The percentage of those who said yes in the referendum among
the electorate as a whole is only about one third (32%). A very different
result was obtained in the parliamentary ratification held in the parliament
and the senate after the referendum. Here, 94.2% and 97.4% of the deputies voted in favour of the constitution. Thus, a rather deep cleavage turns
out: While only one third of the Spanish citizens have taken the opportunity to give a positive vote to the constitution, their political representatives
have nearly unanimously agreed to it.

Political leaders who trusted in their citizens for a moment: Great Britain and France

In France, the ratification of the European Constitution proceeded in a
very different way. Also in France, the referendum was not obligatory by

Photo 1   The heads of state or government and ministers of foreign affairs of the twenty-five EU member states, after having signed the Constitution for Europe, Rome, October 29, 2004. The constitution was also signed by the candidate countries Bulgaria, Romania, and Turkey.

Source: European Community, Audiovisual Service

constitution but ordered personally by President Chirac. He did so in his traditional national holiday interview on July 14, 2004. "I trust in my people," he said in this interview; citizens are affected directly, therefore they should also be asked directly. The expectation was that a solid majority would approve it.[6] One of the first reactions came from London: British Foreign Minister Denis MacShane said he was glad about Chirac's courage. Aside from personal interests—Chirac expected that a positive vote would gain him personal prestige and stature and split his political adversaries—Britain had in fact influenced his own decision. It seems indicated, therefore, to have a short look at the British situation.

Prime Minister Tony Blair had announced a referendum on the Constitution for Europe already two months before, on April 20, 2004. With this decision, he had executed a U-turn in his opinion; the time before he had downplayed the importance of the constitution and considered a referendum as unnecessary. Blair himself was in favour of the constitution—in fact, one of his main political aims as PM was to make the British feel more like Europeans. He claimed that many false myths were prevalent in the UK so that "it is right to confront this campaign [of mythmaking] head-on."[7] Another main motive of Blair certainly was the fact that the constitution—as membership in the EU in general—is a highly contested issue in British public and politics. Supporters and opponents can be found in both major political camps. Therefore, Blair's announcement, "Let's people speak," was also a strategy of taking the bull by the horns, so that the discussion would be solved once and for all.

After Chirac's announcement of an EU referendum, a very vivid public debate developed in France, both in the printed media and in television. Over one million books about the constitution were printed and sold; at least thirty-nine books on the constitution were printed.[8] The constitution itself was printed and spread in 420,000 copies; at the time of the referendum, it was sent to every person entitled to vote by post.

The result of this debate was a very high turnout rate of 70%—in fact, one of the highest of all referenda in the Fifth Republic. A clear majority of 54.8% of the voters rejected the proposed constitution. President Chirac was personally shocked; he fired his prime minister, Raffarin, and replaced him with D. de Villepin—contrary to the announcement in the TV discussion analysed next. A very hot debate was aroused in France, and also in many other EU member states, about the reasons for this rejection. The main arguments of the proponents of the constitution were that the referendum was mainly an object lesson, a personal vote against President Chirac and the French political elite in general. They were blamed for having been unable to solve the deep-going problems of the country, such as its persistent high unemployment rate. It must be said, however, that such an argument is basically problematic from the normative democratic point of view. Has a political party ever opposed the outcome of an election because the voters had the wrong motive for their decisions? It was also argued that the no-voters were instigated in their decision by parties and groups at the extreme left and right who are in principle against European integration. This argument is partly true, partly false. It is true insofar as the major political parties all had supported the constitution (although a minority of the PS and the UMP opposed it), and only smaller parties, like the French Communist Party, Trotskyite movements, and other far left groups, as well as the right-wing Front National, were against it. However, this thesis is false in regard to the voters. It would be difficult to argue that over half of the French voters are tending toward the extreme left or right. Moreover, opinion polls show a solid majority for the constitution. As in the other four countries compared here, also in France two thirds of the population are in favour of a constitution (see Table 1.1).

Knocking out the European Constitution? The case of the Netherlands

The referendum in the Netherlands took place only three days after the French referendum, and its outcome was certainly influenced by the negative vote of the French citizens. Not less than 61.6% of the voters rejected the constitution—also in this country at a rather high turnout rate of 63.3%. One could compare the sequence of these two successive referenda with the outcome of a boxing fight: While the French voters executed a strong blow which made the adversary stagger in the ropes, the Dutch fought back with a blow which produced the knockout for the constitution. After the Dutch rejection, politicians throughout Europe drew the conclusion that the ratification process could not go on further as planned, and that even the constitution was "dead." Several countries, therefore, decided to postpone their own ratification process and eventually planned referenda, first of all Tony Blair for Britain.

Also in the Dutch case, the process of ratification disclosed a deep split between the elites and the citizens. The referendum was only optional. Its realisation was obtained by three leftist parties in the parliament which were supported also by some small parties (among them the Greens and the list of the right-wing populist leader Pim Fortuyn, who had been murdered for political reasons in 2002). In a parliamentary vote on November 25, 2003, it was decided that only with a turnout of at least 30% would the result be binding. (There remained disagreement on this, however.) All major governing and opposition parties, as well as the major newspapers, supported the constitution. They did not engage very much, however, in the pro-campaign, and equal financial support was given to supporters and critics of the constitution. This was a clear difference to Spain, where 20 million euros had been spent for the governmental pro-campaign, and even the famous Dutch football star Johan Cruyff was engaged as a popular advertising medium. In the public discussion, the leftist opponents of the constitution dominated. Their campaign was also quite populist: They warned against political centralisation in Brussels and a declining influence of the Netherlands in the EU; they mobilized the fear of being dominated by the large states; fears in relation to foreign infiltration, immigration and increasing labour market competition, and the entry of Turkey into the EU; and about the rising inflation because of the euro. But also the yes camp designed horror scenarios in the case of a rejection of the constitution. The relative unpopularity of the government in power at the time of the referendum had also played some role. Also in the case of the Netherlands, it is not possible to argue that the citizens were against the constitution in principle. Table 1.1 shows that 62% are in favour of such a constitution. In an online survey of a Dutch research institute in which 800,000 persons participated, even 75% were in favour of a constitution.[9] In this survey, 73% were for more transparency in the workings of the European Council, and 70% were in favour of the right of a citizen's petition (as foreseen in the constitution). Thus, we must conclude that also the Dutch, critical about the European Constitution, did not vote for its putting away. Contrary to the political elites, they wanted it to be reworked and renegotiated (see also the following section). Thus, we should see the rejection of this version of the constitution as a chance, not as a catastrophe, for the further process of integration (Kühnhardt 2005).

A model pupil revokes the "permissive consensus" toward integration: The constitutional referendum in Luxembourg

A fourth referendum about the constitution was held in Luxembourg on July 10, 2005. Also in this country, the referendum was not obligatory by constitution, but proposed by its premier, Jean-Claude Juncker. He is very popular and a respected personality throughout the EU. It was the first referendum in the grand duchy about matters of European integration. Premier Juncker connected the referendum with his personal political fate, threatening that he would retire from office in the case of a negative outcome. The mainstream political elite "formed a united front in favour of the text."[10] Later on, Juncker also warned that only a positive vote would guarantee the country's national interests. The opposition was led by a specially organised committee, composed of groups such *Action pour la Démocratie*, the social movement *Attac*, some unionists, and by two parties of the extreme left, not represented in the parliament. The outcome did bring the result the political leaders and elites had wished for: 56.5% of the voters said yes to the constitution. This, however, was a rather low percentage given their strong involvement and the many advantages which EU membership has for Luxembourg. Also, the turnout of 86.2% cannot be considered as being very high since participation in the referendum was obligatory.

Also in Luxembourg, the now familiar split between citizens and elites emerged. Among the voters, here at least 48.7% (86.2 × 56.5%) approved the constitution, and opinion polls also confirm a clear majority of the supporters (see Table 1.1). In the two parliamentary votings, however, the outcomes were overwhelmingly pro, with percentages known only from election procedures of party leaders or from the former state-socialist countries: 100% and 98.2%, respectively, of the deputies voted in favour of the constitution. The result in Luxembourg confirms also that "the 'permissive consensus' that had for a long time enabled governments to deal with European affairs freely had come to a rather abrupt halt in even the most Europhile states."[11] Even in this country, the referendum turned out to be a "much riskier affair than originally intended." The main arguments of the pro-voters were the general positive EU attitude and the popularity of PM Juncker. The arguments of the nonvoters were more concerned with the constitution itself: That the constitution was "too complicated" and too liberal, and that it needs renegotiation, and opposition to further enlargement of the EU.

Differences between opinion surveys and outcomes of elections and referenda

Many argue that the outcomes of the referenda in France and the Netherlands were determined mainly by home-made political issues; therefore, opinion polls reflect more accurately the true attitudes toward integration.

In referenda about accession to the EU or about the constitution, very complex issues are concerned, and many pros and cons are at stake; the final decision, therefore, may in fact be a matter of chance. Furthermore, in referenda, often political issues other than those related to the concrete text are at stake. Both of these arguments contain some truth. Nevertheless, the conclusion is unwarranted that opinion polls are more valid as an indicator of the "true will" of people. There are significant differences between the results of opinion surveys and of elections or referenda. Both are valid indicators of people's opinions and political wishes but of a different kind.

An opinion survey catches the attitudes of the population at one point in time. We know, from research on the survey method, that it is very easy to get answers to nearly any question; that the formulation of questions and their context influences the answers given; and that the subjective mood of the respondents at the time of the interview can have significant effects on the opinions expressed (Rossi et al. 1983; Diekmann 1995). While these facts do not invalidate the usefulness of surveys in general, they invalidate them as reliable indicators for real behaviour (Ajzen and Fishbein 1980; Markard 1984). The situation is different in the case of an election or a referendum. Voting implies a real decision from the viewpoint of the individual voter. It requires that he/she makes up his/her mind and goes to the polling station to vote. Voting is also a time-related process in which a process of opinion formation in the public sphere and among individuals occurs; it includes information collection, discussion among friends and acquaintances, and personal thinking and consideration. In a real decision, which is both a rational and emotional process, the person involved will also think about alternative lines of action as well as about its costs. Before an election or referendum, a process of public discussion and opinion formation is going on, and the individual voter has time to form his own opinion and decision accordingly (Luthardt 1995; Hadler 2005). Thus, we can say that the outcomes of elections and referenda have much more weight in political terms than those of opinion surveys, not only because only the former has factual legal-political consequences.

Two further arguments point particularly to the political importance of the outcomes of referenda. One is the high level of participation which occurs if a referendum touches an important issue and is felt as being relevant by the citizens. This was the case in both the French and Dutch referendum, where large proportions of the electorate took part. In both countries a very intense public discussion was going on before the referendum, as we have shown. The other fact is pointing to the relevance of the outcome. In France, the voters very seldom say no to a proposal made to them by their political elites. In the nine referenda which were held in the Second Republic (between 1958 and 2000), only one was rejected by the citizens; in six cases, the proposals got a majority of two thirds or more (Perrineaux 2005:233). Thus, it seems that the citizens must have fundamental objections in order to give a negative answer in a referendum.

1.2 Do parliamentary delegates represent their citizens?
An analysis of the outcomes of referenda and parliamentary
votes on European integration, 1972–2005

What we have seen in the foregoing section shall now be shown for the EU as a whole: The fact is that there exists a deep split between elites and citizens when we look at the results of parliamentary votings and the outcomes of referenda. For this aim, the results of all referenda about European integration since the early 1970s have been compiled in Table 1.2a and Table 1.2b, including turnout and votes in favour of integration. For the decisions from 1992 (Maastricht) till 2003, we included also the outcomes of the precedent or following votes in the respective parliamentary assemblies.[12] Three issues shall be investigated here: The overall number of referenda and the proportions of positive and negative outcomes; the difference in the positive results of the referenda and parliamentary votings; and the relations between levels of turnout and outcomes of referenda.

The positive outcomes of referenda as indications of a general consent to integration

A first observation concerning the referenda is that a much higher number had positive outcomes, that is, were in favour of accession to the EU or an

Photo 2a "To be allowed to sign the Constitution for Europe is a dream which has been dreamed by many of us; now it is reality." German Chancellor Gerhard Schröder (left), signing the constitution, together with Foreign Minister Joschka Fischer.

Source: Reuters

Photo 2b. Young people in Paris, celebrating a triumph after the rejection of the Constitution for Europe by the French citizens, May 29, 2007.

Source: Associated Press, Frankfurt.

institutional deepening, than negative ones (23 versus 8). Accession to the EU (or a close cooperation with it) was rejected two times by the Norwegians and by the Swiss. One political community even decided to leave the European Union. This was the island of Greenland, an autonomous province of Denmark. The negative outcome of the referendum in 1982 was the result of a population movement which had agitated against an overfishing of the seaside around Greenland and the exploitation of the natural resources of the island by enterprises from the EU.[13] Since its exit from the EU in 1985, Greenland has the status of an associated overseas EU member.

Institutional deepenings of the EU were rejected by the Danes and Swedes (Maastricht Treaty, euro). The negative vote of the Irish on the Treaty of Nice must be more considered as an accident at work, since turnout was very low (34.8%), and the Irish accepted the treaty in the successive year. We might well interpret these findings as indicating a generally positive attitude of the citizens toward the process of European integration.

The important finding in Table 1.2 a and b, however, concerns the relation between the popular votes positive to integration in referenda and in the parliamentary votings. The latter have always been much higher than the former. Figure 1.1 presents the discrepancies in a graphic form for six cases. The difference was highest in the case of the French ratification of the Maastricht Treaty: A marginal proportion of 51.1% of the voters agreed to

Table 1.2a   Results of Referenda and Parliamentary Votes About Joining the
EC/EU and Ratification of Treaties With Positive Outcomes,
1972–2005

Country and topic	Year and kind of voting	Turnout %	Result % pro
Ireland: Joining the EC	10.05.1972: Referendum	70,9	83,1
Denmark: Joining the EC	02.10.1972: Referendum	90,1	63,3
Great Britain: Remaining in the EC	05.06.1975: Referendum	64,0	67,2
Denmark: Single European Act	27.02.1986: Referendum	75,4	56,2
Ireland: Single European Act	26.05.1987: Referendum	44,1	69,9
Ireland: Ratification of Maastricht Treaty	19.06.1992: Referendum	57,3	69,1
France: Ratification of Maastricht Treaty	23.06.1992: Congress		89,0
	20.09.1992: Referendum	69,7	51,1
Denmark: 2nd Ratification Maastricht Treaty	18.05.1993: 2nd Referendum	85,5	56,8
Austria: Joining the EU	05.05.1994: Nationalrat		80,0
	12.06.1994: Referendum	82,4	66,6
Finland: Joining the EU	16.10.1994: Referendum	70,4	56,9
	18.11.1994: Eduskunta		77,0
Sweden: Joining the EU	13.11.1994: Referendum	83,3	52,7
	15.12.1994: Riksdag		88,0
Ireland: Amsterdam Treaty	22.05.1998: Referendum	56,3	61,7
Denmark: Amsterdam Treaty	28.05.1998: Referendum	76,2	55,1
Switzerland: Special contract with the EU	21.05.2000: Referendum	48,0	67,2
Malta: Joining the EU	08.03.2003: Referendum	91,0	53,6
	14.07.2003: Parliament		58,6
Slovenia: Joining the EU	23.03.2003: Referendum	60,3	89,6
	28.01.2004: Parliament		100,0
Hungary: Joining the EU	12.04.2003: Referendum	45,6	83,8
	15.12.2003: Parliament		100,0
Lithuania: Joining the EU	10./11.05.2003: Referendum	63,4	91,0
Slovakia: Joining the EU	16./17.05.2003: Referendum	52,2	92,5
	01.07.2003: Parliament		92,1
Poland: Joining the EU	07./08.06.2003: Referendum	58,9	77,5

(continued)

Table 1.2a   Results of Referenda and Parliamentary Votes About Joining the EC/EU and Ratification of Treaties With Positive Outcomes, 1972–2005 *(continued)*

Country and topic	Year and kind of voting	Turnout %	Result % pro
Czech Republic: Joining the EU	13./14.06.2003: Referendum	55,2	77,3
Cyprus: Ratification of accession treaty	14.07.2003: Parliament		100,0
Estonia: Joining the EU	14.09.2003: Referendum	63,0	66,8
	21.01.2004: Parliament		100,0
Latvia: Joining the EU	20.09.2003: Referendum	72,5	67,0
Bulgaria: Ratification of accession treaty	11.05.2005: Parliament		99,2
Romania: Ratification of accession treaty	17.05.2005: Parliament		100,0

Sources: See Table 1.2b.

Table 1.2b   Results of Referenda and Parliamentary Votes About Joining the EC/EU and Ratification of Treaties With Negative Outcomes, 1972–2003

Country and topic	Year and kind of voting	Turnout %	Result %
Norway: Joining the EC	26.09.1972: 1st Referendum	79,2	53,5 against
Greenland: Remaining in the EC	23.02.1982: Referendum	74,9	54,0 against
Norway: Joining the EU	1992: Parliament		67,0 pro
Denmark: Maastricht Treaty	1992: Parliament		72,6 pro
	02.06.1992: Referendum	82,9	52,1 against
Switzerland: Joining the EEA	1992: Ständerat		85,0 pro
	1992: Nationalrat		62,0 pro
	06.12.1992: Referendum	78,0	50,3 against
Norway: Joining the EU	28.11.1994: 2nd Referendum	89,0	52,2 against
Denmark: Joining the EMU (Euro)	28.09.2000: Referendum	87,5	53,1 against
Ireland: Nice Treaty	07.06.2001: Referendum	34,8	53,9 against
Sweden: Joining the EMU (Euro)	14.09.2003: Referendum	81,2	56,1 against

Sources: PFETSCH (1997:290ff.); FISCHER WELTALMANACH, several volumes; Switzerland: RUST (1993:31); Initiative and Referendum Institute Europe: "List of all 29 referendums on European integration, 1972–2001"; see http://www.iri-europe.org/?page_name=referendums (2006-02-04).

the treaty, but 89% of the members of the congress (the common assembly of the parliament and senate)—a formidable 38 percentage difference. A similar high difference existed in Switzerland between people's vote and the vote of the *Ständerat* where the issue was the joining of the European Economic Area. The smallest difference came up in Austria in 1994: Here, 66% of the voters and 80% of the parliamentary deputies consented to the accession to the EU. However, this difference must be considered as having been distorted. The high popular consent to the accession was also the result of a massive propaganda campaign of the Austrian government and all major interest groups, which included quite problematic threats by government members in the case of nonaccession (see Heschl 2002). Opinion polls shortly before the referendum had indicated only a marginal preponderance of the proponents of accession to the EU against the opponents. In most other cases, the parliamentary voting percentages in favour of integration are about 20% higher than those among the general population.

In those countries, where only parliamentary votes were taken on the European constitution, the following percentages in its favour resulted: 95% and more in Austria and Germany; 90–93% in Greece, Italy, and Lithuania; 80–89% in Belgium and Slovenia; 70–79% in Hungary and Slovakia. It is unthinkable that similar overwhelming majorities would have been attained in popular referenda.

One could object that these discrepancies are not due to a lack of representation of the interests of the citizens among the parliamentary deputies but simply to the mechanism of representation. This argument could

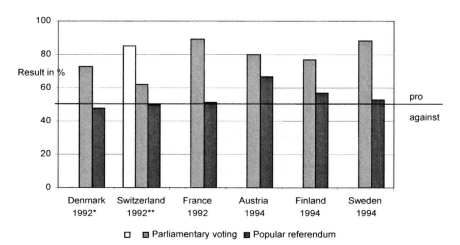

Figure 1.1 Results of parliamentary votes and popular referenda about European integration in six countries, 1992–1994.

*Denmark 1992, popular referendum: 47,9% pro = 52,1% against
**Switzerland 1992, Ständerat: 85% pro; Nationalrat: 62% pro; popular referendum: 49,7% pro = 50,3% against

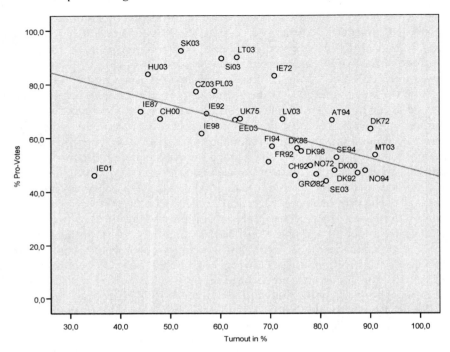

Figure 1.2   Scatter diagram of turnout and proportions of results of national referenda about European integration in 30 countries, 1972–2003.

Note: Norway 1992, Cyprus 2003, Bulgaria and Romania 2005: no referenda.
Sources: Tables 1.2a, 1.2b.

be valid in cases when election procedures are based on a clear majority principle, that is, if the winning party gets an overproportional number of seats in the parliament. This, however, is hardly true for the countries compared. Therefore, the only conclusion to be drawn from the findings is that the political parties represented in the parliamentary bodies of these countries in fact do not represent the attitudes of considerable fractions of their voters as far as the process of European integration is concerned. It must be assumed—and in fact everybody who watches political processes can see it all the time—that within the political parties a process of streamlining is going on. Its consequence is that a uniform opinion on the issue of European integration (as on all issues of high importance) is formed which has to be followed by all members of these parties. In this way, both political parties as a whole and also those individual deputies who might have dissenting opinions are pursuing a line which diverges from the opinion of many of their voters. To give just one example: The Austrian Greens have been for a long time decided opponents of an EC/ EU membership; since Austrians' access to the EU, they are among the most fervent supporters of further integration. It is quite improbable that their voters—whose social structure did not change—have changed their opinion so strongly.

The split in the results of parliamentary votes and popular referenda

The second important finding concerns the relation between levels of turn-out and outcomes of the referenda. Here, a very significant fact can be observed: The higher the level of turnout, the lower the consent to integration. The relation between these two dimensions is shown in Figure 1.2. What the visual inspection of the scattergram shows is confirmed also by a statistical calculation: The correlation between the two dimensions is not less than −.51. If we take turnout as the independent variable, it determines not less than 26% of the dependent variable, the outcome.

Let us have a look at the extreme cases in this scattergram. On the left side—indicating low turnout and high consent to integration—we find cases such as the Irish vote of 1987 (44% turnout—70% consent), and the Hungarian and Slovak votes about accession to the EU of 2003. At the other side of the picture—high turnout, low consent—we find cases such as the accession referenda in Denmark 1972, Norway 1994, and Malta 2003. Thus, we can confirm fully the finding obtained in the foregoing section. In countries in which a very vivid debate about integration took place, the result was negative concerning the EU Constitution (France, Netherlands), but in Spain, where this decision was much less discussed in public, the outcome was positive. The split between elites and citizens was most pro-nounced (a) in countries where an intense discussion was going on, and (b) in countries with a well-established democratic tradition.

That the citizens of the EU in general have a positive attitude to the idea of a constitution is shown also by the Eurobarometer survey. In autumn 2005, 63% were in favour of a European Constitution, in spring 2006 61%.[14] In the Netherlands and France, quite a similar high approval could be found. Very significant was the finding in the survey that awareness of the constitution was highest exactly in those countries where a refer-endum with a vivid public debate had taken place (France, Luxembourg, Netherlands). Thus, the finding is corroborated that there exists a signifi-cant gap between voters and their political representatives. This problem is aggravated in the case of the European Council because here only govern-ments in power are represented, but not the oppositional parties and their voters. In the member states of the EU, common trends exist concerning the strength of political parties, and in the last decades centre-right par-ties have dominated. They were able, therefore, to constitutionalise their political preferences in the EC/EU (Schäfer 2006:195; Manow et al. 2006). Since also national parliaments are less and less able to control the execu-tive, a cleft emerges which could threaten the legitimacy of integration: "Voters and their representatives are living in two different worlds, and the positions of those voters who are sceptical or opposed are almost totally ignored" (Bartolini 1999:49; quoted in Schäfer 2006, p. 196).

Elites who mistrust their citizens? Countries which never held a referendum on European integration

In how many member countries of the EC/EU do citizens have the opportunity to express their views on the far-reaching process of European integration? Also in this regard, two surprising results emerge.

First, by far not all member country governments have opened up such an opportunity to their citizens. Looking at the "old" fifteen EU member states, in five of them—Belgium, Germany, Greece, Italy, and Portugal—the citizens have never had such a possibility. This is quite remarkable since membership in the EU has doubtless changed the political system of these countries in a fundamental way. In three others—Luxembourg, Netherlands, and Spain—they could do so only in 2005, and in France, only in 1992, twenty-five years after the establishment of the EEC. Only in all ten new member states which entered into the Union in 2004 were referenda held. This corresponds to the extensive anchoring of referenda also in their national constitutions (Adam and Heinrich 1987). Only in the two post-Communist countries, Bulgaria and Romania, which entered into the EU in 2007, no referenda were held. These are also the countries with the least developed political systems in terms of democratic maturity.

Second, it is evident that there exists a definite connection between the political-democratic history of a country and the possibilities of its citizens to decide in a referendum about European integration. Among the countries which organized referenda, we find two groups: (a) the old and well-established West and North European democracies, France, Great Britain, and the Scandinavian countries. Here, we have to mention also Switzerland and Norway, whose citizens rejected membership. In Chapter 7, we will show that this rejection was motivated to a considerable degree by the fear of citizens that the quality of national democracy would be undermined: (b) the new democracies in Central East Europe, mentioned before.

The countries which have never or only very recently held a referendum also include two groups: (a) the Benelux countries. In their case, the consent of the population to integration seems to be given anyway, in fact of the high interdependence of these countries with their neighbour states, the direct advantages from the accommodation of the EU offices (Belgium, Luxembourg), and a certain fear of being dominated by the big neighbour Germany; (b) the second group contains countries which have had a history of fascist government in the twentieth century, namely, Germany, Italy, and Greece. Also in Spain, only in 2005 was a referendum held, that is, nearly two decades after its entry to the EC.

From the perspective of referenda as an important element of democracy, it appears particularly remarkable that the citizens of Germany have never got the possibility to decide in a referendum about their membership in the EEC/EU. The political elites of this country evidently did it not find it necessary, and they may have believed to have good reasons for this attitude. "We need the European Union in order to protect Germany from itself—before its history," said a German manager (quoted in Newhouse 1997:115). Thus, the distrust of Germans of their political elites seems to be confronted by a similar distrust of the elites against their citizens. The immediate reason for this distrust is certainly the fear that the German population would have rejected certain steps of integration if it were asked directly. A large majority of the Germans and many of its economists were against the substitution of the deutsche mark by the euro, since the DM had become a symbol of the German economic miracle and of its stability and prosperity.[15] Surveys of the Institute for Demoscopic Research Allensbach have shown that in 1994 58% of the Germans were against, and only 22% in favour, of the introduction of the euro; in 1999, shortly before its introduction, support increased (40% in favour, 31% against); till September 2001, however, it dropped again (29% in favour, 45% against); in March 2001, 60% of Germans considered the introduction of the euro as a "bad," only 23% as a "good" decision.[16]

It is not surprising, therefore, that the Constitutional Court of the Federal Republic of Germany (*Bundesverfassungsgerichtshof*) had to be concerned two times (1993 and 1998) with constitutional challenges of German EU membership. In the first judgement it stated that the EU could not yet be considered as a state but only as an association of states since the member states continued to determine the degree of integration and to own significant rights of sovereignty.[17] In this case a legal authority has defined by an official decree a matter which in most modern democracies is considered as being an object for asking citizens directly. This is a typical case for Germany, where political matters are often reformulated as legal issues (Münch 2008a). It is true that the German constitution does not provide for referenda on the national level, except the issue of the creation of new *Bundesländer*.[18] However, this would not prevent Germany from carrying through a referendum, according to many experts on constitutional law. A large majority of the Germans, 81%, were in favour of carrying through such a referendum.[19] Also, many German deputies have asked to carry out such a referendum. The same was true in Austria.

From this point of view, the refusal to allow the citizens to decide themselves directly about the process of integration can be seen as a further example of the typical relation between political and state authorities and citizens in Germany, which is characterized by a certain arrogance and patronizing among the former and subservience among the latter. This was noted by many historians and political writers (Jaspers 1966; Dahrendorf 1968; Greiffenhagen 1979; Engelmann 1993; Haller 1999b; see also Heinrich Manns's novel *Der Untertan*). It might be no accident that there exists no English counterpart of the German word *Untertan* (the subservient citizen). It must also be seen, however, as part of the memory of National Socialism, which has engraved a deep sense of guilt into German collective consciousness (Haller 1999b). This fact turned out very clearly in the extensive interviews carried out by Juan Diez Medrano (2003) with ordinary citizens and local elites, as well as from his analysis of newspapers and novels. He finds that the Nazi regime was "a major conditioning factor of West German national and foreign policies" for most of the second half of the twentieth century; it also provided the main arguments for European integration (Diez Medrano 2003:179). One respondent said that Germany should be a member of the EU "to protect itself against its demons" (ibid., p. 39). German elites, therefore, feel that such important decisions cannot be left to the citizens who once in the twentieth century gave their votes to the dictator Hitler. However, also in this regard, the reality was more complex, as will be shown in Chapter 7. There was never a majority of citizens who voted for Hitler and his NSDAP; in the German parliament (Reichstag), however, he got in fact such an overwhelming majority. Thus, in this crucial historical phase, exactly the same pattern could be observed as that which we noted for many member states of the EU in the last two decades: strong support among the political elites, but a rather modest one if not an outright rejection among the population. In the long run, the avoidance of any popular referendum on such a basic issue could well lead to the accumulation of an engrained and dangerous resentment among significant subsections of the German population.

1.3   Pride and fears about European integration among elites and citizens

In concluding this chapter, we present three further sources of empirical evidence on the increasing split between elites and citizens concerning European integration: findings from a large survey on attitudes among political elites and citizens throughout Europe; findings from qualitative interviews with EU politicians in Brussels and ordinary people in Austria; and an analysis of the television discussion of President Chirac with youth people of his country.

Pride in Europe: The gap between populations and political elites

A group of German and English political scientists have published a large, informative study on *Political Representation and Legitimacy in the European Union* (Schmitt and Thomassen 1999). Two sources of data were used: (a) population surveys in connection with the elections to the European Parliament from 1979 till 1994 in all member states of the EU/EU plus the candidate countries Austria, Finland, and Sweden; (b) surveys of all candidates and members of the national parliaments and the European Parliament. Out of the many findings of this study, the pride of being European, is reported in Table 1.3, comparing the general population with the candidates and representatives of the parliaments.

Table 1.3   Proud to be European, among Voters, Members of National
Parliaments (MNP), and Members of the European Parliament
(MEP) in Fifteen Countries (1994)

	% proud of Europe			Differences voters–	
	Voters	MNPs	MEPs	–MNPs	–MEPs
South West Europe					
France	65	72	64	+7	–1
Italy	80	86	80	+6	0
Spain	66	92	86	+26	+20
Portugal	64	76	69	+12	+5
Greece	47	58	82	+11	+35
Gross Mean	*64*	*77*	*76*	*+12*	*+12*
Central Europe					
Germany	42	62	83	+20	+41
Austria	46	—	70	—	+24
Luxemburg	70	50	100	–20	+30
Belgium	60	66	78	+6	+18
The Netherlands	45	42	86	–3	+41
Gross Mean	*53*	*55*	*83*	*0,7*	*+31*
Northwest Europe					
Denmark	49	—	38	—	–11
Sweden	37	—	64	—	+27
Finland	41	—	73	—	+32
England	51	—	68	—	+17
Ireland	64	81	89	+17	+25
Gross Mean	*48*	—	*66*	—	*18*
Overall gross Mean	*55*	*68*	*75*	*+8*	*20*

Source: Schmitt and Thomassen (1999), p. 37, Table 2.2. Representative population surveys
(N ca. 1000) in all countries; members of national parliaments: N = 1367; candidates for the
EP: N = 1726; MEPs: N = 314.

Three findings are of interest here. First, we can see significant differences in the pride of being European: It is very high in Italy and Luxembourg, high in Belgium, France, Spain, Portugal, and Ireland, and lower in Scandinavia, Great Britain, Austria, and Germany. Second, it turns out that the political elites are by far prouder to be Europeans than their voters. This is true in particular for the deputies for the European Parliament

(MEPs): In twelve of fifteen EU members states, the difference is positive; in nine states, it is rather large. Over the EU as a whole, somewhat more than half (55%) of the voters are proud to be Europeans, but two thirds (68%) of the members of national parliament, and three fourths (75%) of the MEPs!

Third, we can see significant differences between countries. The gap between voters and their political representatives is much smaller in South and Southwest Europe than in Central and Northwest Europe. The largest gap exists in Germany, the Netherlands, and Luxembourg: Here, the mean difference in pride in Europe is 31%. Between 80% and 100% of the members of the European Parliament are very proud of Europe in these countries, but only between 40% and 70% of the populations. In Northwest Europe (Scandinavia, Great Britain, Ireland), the general population is least proud of Europe (about 40–60%), but also the political elites are less enthusiastic here. Thus, the mean difference between elites and their populations is somewhat smaller, but still 18%. A very low or no split in pride about Europe exists in France, Italy, and Portugal; in Denmark, voters are more proud than their deputies—but both on a rather low level. It is quite probable that the split between elites and citizens is mainly typical for the political elites. If one compares (using the Eurobarometer) the attitudes toward integration between elite groups in general (managers, academic personal) and the whole population, no strong difference comes up.

The authors of this study draw quite a sober conclusion from their findings: "One might wonder whether the governments and politicians responsible for the Maastricht Treaty were living in the same European world as the people they were supposed to represent. A possible lack of agreement between political elites and the mass public on the future of Europe might reveal not only an ineffective system of political representation but also a lack of legitimacy of the institutions on the EU" (Schmitt and Thomassen 1999:4).

*How top decision makers see European integration
and their distance to the general population*

There exist two recent studies comparing elites' and citizens' view which confirm the deep split between them. One has been carried out by the *Centre for the Study of Political Change* (CIRCAP) at the University of Siena, Italy.[20a] The other has been made by EOS Gallup Europe on behalf of the European Commission (D.G. X – Information, Communication, Culture) in 1996 among 3778 top decision makers in the 15 member states of the EU.[20] The study investigated the opinions of members of the top elites concerning European integration. The sample included five groups: Elected politicians; high civil servants; industry and business leaders; top media persons; and cultural, academic and religious leaders. Based on a specially compiled list of 22,000 of such leaders throughout the EU, in each of the smaller and middle-sized countries 30-40 leaders, and in the four larger ones 90 leaders were interviewed (mostly by telephone); total samples per country varied between 150 for the smaller, and 450 for the larger countries. The realized sample included 3.778 members of these five political elites. In this survey, a few questions were asked in the same way as in the Eurobarometer. The mean age of the respondents was 52,5 years, the large majority (89%) were men. The survey gives an excellent information about the opinions of the elites compared to the citizens of their respective countries.

Two general questions were asked: "Generally speaking, do you think that (OUR COUNTRY's) membership of the European Union is a good thing/ a bad thing/ neither good nor bad/ don't know"; and: "Taking everything into consideration, would you say that (OUR COUNTRY) has on balance benefited or not from being a member of the European Union?" The findings are stunning (see Table 1.4): Among the elites, there exists practically unanimity concerning integration and its positive effects: 94% believe that their country's membership is a good thing, and

Table 1.4   The evaluation of EU membership among Top Decision Makers and the general population (EU-15, 1996)

	(1) Top decision Makers	*(3)* General population	*(3)* Difference *(1) – (3)*
(OUR COUNTRY's) membership in the EU is ...	%	%	%
... a good thing	94	48	+46
... a bad thing	2	15	-13
... neither good nor bad	4	28	-24
Total	100	100	
Perceived benefit from membership for (OWN COUNTRY)			
Benefit	90	43	+57
No benefit	8	36	-28
Don't know	2	36	-19
Total	100	100	

Source: Top Decision Makers: The European Union. A View from the Top. EOS Gallup Europe 1996. Decision Makers: N=3.778. General population: Eurobarometer: representative population surveys.

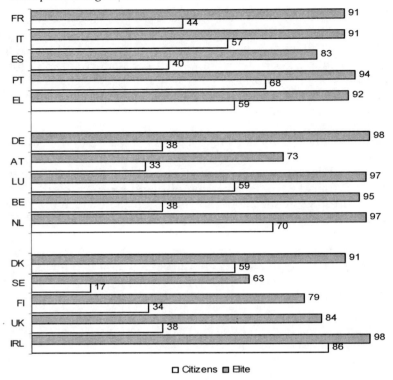

Figure 1.3   Perceived benefit from the European Union by country and by Top Decision Makers and Citizens, 1996 (in %).

Source: Top Decision Makers and the European Union, p. 5.

90% think it has benefitted from integration. Only 8% of Top Decision Makers think his or her country has not benefitted, and a tiny minority of 2% that EU membership is a bad thing. Among the general population, quite a different image exists: Here, less than half (46%) think that the country's membership is a good thing, and just somewhat more than half (57%), that the country has benefitted from EU membership. 13% of the citizens consider membership outright as a bad thing, and even 36% believe that it has not brought any benefits. Thus, in this fundamental evaluation of EU membership, an opinion difference between 46% and 57% exists between the political, economic, bureaucratic and cultural elites – a split that must be considered as very deep, as a striking contrast. Between the different elites, there exists nearly unanimity about European integration. Contrary to the expectation, that intellectual and cultural elites could be more critical about integration, the differences are minor: 92% of the civil servants, 91% of the industry and business elites, 90% of the politicians, 89% of the cultural and intellectual elites, and 86% of the media elites think that their country has benefitted from EU membership. Additional findings show, however, that the industry and business leaders were most in favour of integration. The only socio-demographic characteristic which has some effect is gender: 91% of the male elites believe in the beneficial effects of membership, but "only" 80% of the female top elites.

Also quite telling are the differences between the member countries in the elites' and citizens' perceptions of the effects of integration. Figure 1.3 shows the results in this regard. Here, we can see that the split between elites and citizens is largest in Germany (difference elites-citizens in perceived benefit 60%), followed closely by Belgium (57%). Then come six countries in which the difference is between 40% and 47%: France, the United Kingdom, Sweden, Finland, Spain and Austria; in four countries, the difference is between 32 and 38%: Luxembourg, Italy, Greece, and Denmark; in the Netherlands and Portugal, it is 27 and 26%. The lowest split between elites' and citizens' evaluation of integration can be observed in Ireland: 21%; normally, one would consider even such a difference as an indicator of quite a problematic split.

These differences can well be interpreted, taking into consideration the findings that will be presented in this study (see particularly chapter 6): In Germany, membership in the EU is seen as a means to overcome the weak national identity and pride by the elites, and it is one of the few countries where the citizens have never had the possibility to express their consent or dissent with integration in a referendum; many opinion polls have shown that important steps of integration were taken by the elites, in spite of majorities of the citizens being against them. In the United Kingdom, the Scandinavian countries and Austria, the EU and Brussels is seen by many, if not the majority of the citizens, as a distant, bureaucratic apparatus which interferes into national autonomy and independence. Even in France and the Netherlands, motors of integration since the beginning, evidently a deep split exists between elites and citizens. The negative outcomes of the referendum on the Constitution for Europe in 2005 proved that these survey results are very hard and consequential facts. It may appear rather surprising that even in countries like Belgium and Luxembourg which evidently profit directly from European integration (by hosting the main institutions of the EU) such a large split does exist between the elites and citizens. Taking into consideration the different effect which integration has on elites and citizens, it is much less surprising. In both these countries, it is mainly the capital and the people employed directly by the many EU offices which profit directly from integration. The rest of the population and the country may even be affected negatively; in Brussels, for instance, by rising prices for accommodation and food, strong influx of foreign workers and employees etc.

The further results of this survey confirm the enthusiasm of the top elites for European integration: 85% of them are in favour of the EURO (again a striking contrast to citizens where scores are half of this value);

they believe that the EU does not play a big enough role in the world, and they show strong support for a common defence and foreign policy.

The European Union seen from above and from below: Qualitative results about perceptions and evaluations of elites and citizens

As outlined in the introduction, a group of sociology students of the University of Graz (Austria) made a series of studies on the perception of the European Union among political, bureaucratic, and economic elites in Brussels and in the Austrian province of Styria (see Haller and Ressler 1996a). The studies included, among others, a population survey (N = 329), in-depth interviews with MEPs from Austria and other countries, and with officials and representatives of nation-states and lobby groups in Brussels; and focus group discussions with citizens. A central question of these studies was to investigate the view of integration by the elites and by the citizens. In the following, some exemplary findings are reported.

One topic seen critical throughout the EU is the role of lobbying in Brussels. The Austrian population showed that this is true also for citizens: The statement "In general, the influence of lobbies on the political processes in the EU can be evaluated positively" was rejected by 75% of the respondents in the population survey; 23% said "agree partly," and only 3% "agree very much." The EU elites and experts interviewed expressed opinions which correspond to those 3% of the citizens who had a rather positive view. An Austrian MEP from the centrist-conservative *Volkspartei* argued that lobbying is an indispensable positive element of the process of opinion formation and decision in the EU: "[Expressed] shortly, concisely: Lobbying is professional, connected with proposals, includes the build-up of networks, the establishing of personal contacts . . ." (Haller and Ressler 1996a:163ff.). Less surprising is that the director of the Austrian Federal Economic Chamber sees it the same way, as an indispensable method, and as a mutually fruitful dependence of business, administration, and politics. Particularly the EU Commission needs the lobbyists in order to develop concrete proposals for directives and regulations—a fact which corresponds to reality in all modern democracies (see Chapter 5). The political elites and interest-group representatives argue that among the general population many misperceptions and prejudices about lobbying exist. They distance themselves strongly from problematic methods associated with lobbying, such as invitations to dinners, bribery, and the like. The aforementioned MEP said: "Should I come into a situation where somebody tries to make 'good will' with financial means—without argument—then he will have never seen the door of my office so fast." A deputy director in the bureau of the commissioner for agrarian affairs said that lobbyism is practically irrelevant in the allocation of subsidies and their local distribution because this is fully in the hands of national and local administrations. Methods like gifts and bribery are not used anymore; the intent is only "to bring the right idea at the right point in time to the right person [in the Commission]." Lobbying, he said, is not the reason why the lion's share of EU budget goes to the agrarian sector; large countries do not have more influence in this regard than small ones. In the TV discussion of French President Chirac, which will be analysed in the next section, he confirmed exactly that this is the case: "Today, they have one single idea, that is, to stop the Common Agricultural Policy which benefits essentially France . . . It will be impossible that the president of France will at sometime not defend this Common agricultural Policy."[21] He also said in this interview quite openly: "Today . . . 80% of the subsidies for French farmers come from Europe. This represents ten and a half billion Euros per year, and we have accomplished it that this will be maintained until 2013, we have been the only ones to ask for this. How did we get it: simply, in connection with a global negotiation, we have agreed with our German friends . . . we have decided, the chancellor [Schröder] and I, that in the future every time as it will be necessary we will arrange us, even if we will not have the same interests."

In Chapter 4, we will show in detail that lobbyism is in fact a very important way for large enterprises and powerful agricultural business organisations to get influence in Brussels. The point that is relevant here, however, concerns the perceptions and evaluations of the elites. One must say that they simply do not recognize the main problem: This is not, or not mainly, if bribery, corruption, and other forms of semi-illegal or illegal practices actually exist in Brussels. They might well be right in refusing that such practices are typical or that they themselves are using them. The main problem, however, is if business and powerful organisations have an influence in Brussels which is not transparent to the public and which is much stronger than that of other social groups.

A president alienated from his youth: Analysis of a TV discussion of Jacques Chirac

As part of the campaign for the French referendum on the proposed Constitution for Europe, on April 14, 2005, President Chirac conducted a TV discussion with 83 young French people between the ages of 18 and 30, from all regions of France and all social and professional backgrounds and political camps. The discussion was directed by four TV journalists. The discussion, aired by the private channel TF1, lasted two hours and was seen by not less than 7.4 million people.[22] Thus, this discussion was an important public event in the decisive period before the French referendum on the European Constitution. It provides also a significant insight into the problem discussed in this section, the relation between political elites and citizens. The discussion shall be analysed here from two points of view: first, in regard to its formal characteristics and, second, in regard to the substantive issues discussed.[23]

First, let us look at the social dynamics of the discussion. It was intended as a dialogue, as presented by the moderator Patrick Poivre d'Arvor: "Here we are gathered for two hours in a broad cast which is very unique and

Table 1.5   Analysis of the TV Discussion of President Chirac with Young
People, April 2005

		Moderators	President Chirac	Young People	Total	(n)
Number of requests to speak	%	42.3	33.5	24.1	99.9	(340)
Number of interruptions ...						
... made himself/herself	%	47.4	32.2	20.3	99.9	(59)
... experienced from others	%	39.6	32.1	28.3	100	(53)
Length of speaking time (number of words)	%	27.4	47.5	27.1	100	(10.870)

very much expected since the dialogue of a head of state with young adults
is really rare. Now, everybody should dialogue and not monologue, for
this I ask you to be as concise and precise as possible in your answers and
questions . . ." (p. 1). If the discussion was really a dialogue, the chances
for speaking should have been similar for all participants. Table 1.5 gives
some simple figures in this regard. We can see that it was true only in part:
The young people, although 83 in numbers, were those who had the few-
est number of occasions to speak; when they were speaking, they were
often interrupted. Speaking most often and also interrupting others were
the journalists. This may be understood, given their role as moderators
who must take care that speaking time is distributed not too unequally.
However, they exerted also some patronizing, by introducing first at length
a problematic, posing themselves questions to the president, and interpreting or giving answers to the youth themselves. The young speakers were
clearly underrepresented also in the total time of speaking (as measured in
number of words); they had just about one fourth of total speaking time
(27%), little more than half of the time of Chirac (47%).

If one reads the transcript of the discussion, the impression is that the
youth people served mainly as the presenters of catchwords which were
then used by the president (and sometimes also by the journalists) for rather
long monologues.

The substantive statements made by the president are not very peculiar. They are of interest here mainly because they come up again and
again in the speeches of leading politicians all over the EU. The difference
between such speeches—after which usually no discussion is held—and
this TV discussion, however, is the fact that in the framework of the latter
it became much more evident that the arguments and answers were quite
diffuse and vague and dissatisfying for the questioners. Six main kinds of

arguments of President Chirac are remarkable: (1) very general values are invoked as the main arguments for the necessity of a constitution; (2) the difference between general values and specific constitutional rights is not recognized; (3) if the French will vote with no, this will impair its influence in Europe; (4) the constitution is necessary to enforce the role of the EU as a powerful actor in the world; (5) the constitution has been imprinted very strongly by France and is opposed to Anglo-Saxon "ultraliberalism"; (6) negative effects of integration are hardly recognized.

(1) Very general arguments are given for the necessity of the constitution. Alexandra from Marseille asked why a constitution—which was difficult to understand, in her opinion—was necessary at all. The answer of President Chirac: "One must regard the state of the world and what the future will be. I would like that everybody understands the world how it is nowadays. These powers, we cannot cope with them alone. France does not have the means . . . We must get a framework. Europe must be strong and organized in order to oppose this evolution. We have two possible solutions: The solution of 'laissez faire' i.e. an ultraliberal-driven Europe and let's say an Anglo-Saxon, Atlantist Europe. That it is not what we would like. The second way is a humanist Europe, that, in order to implement its humanism, its values, has to be organized and strong" (p. 3). Later on, a questioner reproaches the president for holding a "double discourse" concerning ultraliberalism: In France, his prime minister, J. P. Raffarin, carries through such a policy by privatizing many public services; on the world level, the president argues against it (p. 8). Chirac answers that the European Constitution guarantees the public provision of basic services; but, on the level of Europe and the world, "we are on a road junction. On the one side, there is the international ultraliberal current, on the other side, the organised and humanist current. And this we would like to defend." Later, he adds: "Would you prefer an organized Europe that matters in the future, a Europe in which France keeps its essential role . . . Or would you prefer to let Europe in its current state, which is obviously not dramatic but which cannot nevertheless promote our values and our interests nowadays in the entire world as well against the emerging great powers as (against) the ultraliberal stream?" (p. 9).

(2) A journalist asks the president to mention "three small, concrete things" which would change if the constitution were adopted. J. Chirac: "A certain number of things: First a few points. First of all, all the major principles contained in our values are from now on defined as the basic of every European policy. For example, equality between men and women, fight against all forms of discrimination. Protection of civil service. Strengthening of the Eurogroup and our monetary power. Cooperation to fight against terrorism, international criminality and unauthorized immigration. Environmental issues" (p. 10). A young lady, working as nurse, asks if minimal standards in the health sector will be maintained. The president answers that the health services will remain national, that nobody must have fear. This topic is taken

up by another questioner: "Mister President, you have spoken of fear. I beg your pardon, but this is not about fear. Because in fact we do not live in the same reality. What I mean in practice is that we all feel Europeans. We ask for something concrete. We ask for concrete changes because it is a constitution and thus a milestone" (p. 12). President Chirac: "What is concrete, Miss, is that all our values on which our national and European ambition is based are clearly affirmed, recognised, officially agreed for Europe. That means that for the first time all the values which I have mentioned . . . become constitutional values" (p. 12). It will be argued in Chapter 8 that the definition of Europe as a "community of values" is rather questionable and that a clear distinction must be made between the declaration of basic, general values on the one side, and the formulation of concrete rights and duties in a constitution on the other side. A main weakness of the European Constitution, particularly in regard to the social aspects of integration, is that it limits itself to first issue, the declaration of values.

(3) Another typical argument brought up by Chirac is that in the case of a rejection of the constitution, fatal consequences will follow. In connection with agricultural policy, Chirac says that in an enlarged community, if all other 24 members vote yes, the probability is high that the black sheep which has blocked everything will not count more something in the Europe of tomorrow (p. 8). Later on, he speaks of an "operation boomerang" (p. 18) in connection with the possibility that the French reject the constitution as a whole. This would mean that the weight of France and its capacity to defend its interests would be weakened significantly. Shortly before the end of the discussion, he confirms this again: " . . . this constitution is necessary in order to organise Europe and to preserve the essentially French values which are imprinting themselves on Europe since two centuries. And on the other hand, if France randomly rejected this constitution, it would cease to exist politically inside Europe at least for some time" (p. 25). It was, in fact, one frequently formulated thesis in the public after the French no to the constitution. Practically nobody among the influential elites argued that the no could also have been perceived as a big chance for a rethinking the form and content of the constitution and a renewed, more broadly based EU-wide discussion on the constitution (Kühnhardt 2005).

(4) A central argument for the constitution in Chirac's view is that it enables Europe to become a big power able to defend its values. In connection with the issue of Turkey's EU membership, the following dialogue of Chirac with a journalist is illuminating. The latter asked why Turkey should become an EU member. Chirac: "For two reasons. First, if Europe wants to be enough powerful in regard to the great others it must have enough peoples and size." Patrick Poivre d'Arvor: "We are 450 millions already at the moment, this is not quite bad . . ." Chirac: "Absolutely, but if we want to preserve this power, it is necessary to continue [with enlargement]" (p. 21). Toward the end, he comes back to this argument in connection with his wish that the constitution will be supported by the French:

"Europe must be powerful enough in order to be able to impose or to resist to the pressures of the great blocs . . ." (p. 25).

(5) It is very interesting in this regard that the constitution for Chirac has essentially been inspired by France, and this is a main reason why the French should affirm it: "The European Constitution is the heir of French thought. It has not been supported at random by several French from its origins, to the Convention president Giscard d'Estaing. This is simply because the whole inspiration of this text . . . is essentially French" (p. 25). These statements are probably true, as will be shown in Chapter 6, where we look at the aims connected with European integration in the different members states and their relative influence. The problem is, however, that a Constitution for Europe has no chance of being accepted on a broad basis and in all member states, if it is imprinted so strongly by the particular spirit of one country. In Chapter 8, we will make proposals how the constitution should be reworked in order to be acceptable also to the Britons, as well as those new member states in East Central Europe which are also quite liberal minded.

(6) Finally, Jacques Chirac denies negative consequences of integration and he argues that the constitution has nothing to do with them. This concerns issues such as the privatization of public services in France, the splitting of labour markets, the increase in precarious forms of part-time labour, and the increase in organised international crime. European integration is not the only or maybe not even the main factor responsible for these problems. It is out of the question, however, that it has to do with the rise of these problems. An answer which would be felt as more adequate by the citizens would be that (a) these negative effects must be accepted as by-products of other, very important aims (such as a catching up of the poor countries in Europe), and that (b) at the level of the old member states certain measures are taken or will be taken in order to alleviate their negative effects for specific groups.

The feelings of the young discussants—as those of the TV watchers—after this discussion might not have been very positive. One evaluation of the discussion reads as follows: Chirac "could not give adequate answers to the authentic concerns of the young people. Immediately after the discussion, poll results about the percentage of voters against the Constitution have been skyrocketing for a moment from 52% to 56%; his performance was criticized by the French media as 'escapist,' 'indoctrinating' and, thus, counterproductive; his papal counsel *Do not have fears* was probably rather the expression of his own fear before the result of the referendum than it could convince the opponents."[24]

Thus, we may conclude also in this case that this influential political leader was thinking and speaking about a different world and ideals than his young compatriots. It again turns out as an essential task of social science to investigate the reasons why citizens are so much less enthusiastic about European integration than their political leaders.

CONCLUSION

Looked at from the outside, European integration has been a highly successful process. Since 1945, there was no major war on this continent, and it is highly unlikely that there will be one in the future; overall economic growth has been spectacular in this period; and the introduction of the common currency euro marks the last innovation, significant both from the substantive and the symbolic point of view, concerning the creation of an "ever closer Union," the aim set forth in the Treaty of Rome. In spite of all these facts, the citizens of France and the Netherlands have rejected in spring 2005 a new Constitution for Europe which would have consolidated all the previous steps of integration and added to them some innovative institutional reforms designed to increase the transparency and efficiency of the political system of the EU. In this chapter, we have documented the circumstances of this highly surprising rejection. We found that it was only the most recent manifestation of a rather deep split between elites and citizens concerning the approval of integration which was developing already since the early 1990s. This study is based on two general assumptions why this split between the elites and the citizens was coming about. One is that the elites have promoted the integration process without involving the citizens. As a consequence, the new institutions they have created do not foresee a substantial cooperation of the citizens; in fact, even the possibilities for democratic participation at the level of the member states have been undermined because their competences are transferred more and more to the Union. The other reason is that also in terms of social and economic development, elites and citizens profit quite differently from the process of integration. This has become most clear in the last decades, after the breakdown of the Iron Curtain and the accession of the former state-socialist countries into the EU. These processes opened up immense possibilities for investment and profits for West European business companies and corporations but did not lead to a corresponding rise of employment opportunities and incomes among the population at large. In the following three chapters of this book, the motives, strategies, and actions of the three powerful groups of elites—the political, economic, and bureaucratic elites—are investigated. In chapters 6 and 7, the perceptions and evaluations of the citizens in the different member states and the ideas of the intellectuals connected with European integration are presented. Considerable discrepancies turn out between the latter and the factual process of integration how it took shape since the 1950s. Based on these findings, in the last chapter some proposals are developed for the further institutional development of the Union which departs from the elitist way prevalent up to now.

2 European Integration as an Elite Process
Theoretical Approach

INTRODUCTION

The rejection of the Constitution for Europe by the French and Dutch in May 2005 manifested a deep split between elites and citizens in the process of integration. Contrary to what one could expect, consent to integration among the citizens does not increase over time but seems to stagnate or even to decrease.

In this chapter, we present a sociological approach to the understanding and explanation of this split, which is a puzzle, given the dominant view of European integration as a process securing peace and democracy and guaranteeing prosperity and welfare in Europe. Our approach assumes that the process of integration must be understood as a continuous interaction between (a) the decisive actors, "political and economic elites," who react to (b) changing societal and political circumstances by devising new forms of cooperation and institutions, and (c) the interaction between elites and citizens. From the normative side, this approach is inspired by democratic elite theory which posits that elites must have transparent relations between each other and be responsive to the citizens. This approach is sketched out in the next two sections. Ideas and values play a strategic role in the relations between elites and citizens as instruments of legitimation, as shown in the third section; intellectuals critical of dominant ideologies and able to develop alternative visions are also essential in this regard. The final section constitutes a first application of this sociological framework by sketching out the historical contexts at the time of the foundation of the ECSC and the EEC.

2.1 Elites and democracy

In this section the two general approaches underlying this study are sketched out. The first is democratic elite theory, the second the perspective of sociology as a science of social reality.

Some insights from classical elite theory

The theory of elites is concerned with the issue of power distribution in society; its central thesis is that in every political community there exist relatively small groups who dispose of disproportionate power. Elites usually comprise only a restricted number of people; their counterpart is the population at large, in classical elite theory called the "mass." Because elites are fewer in numbers, they can organize themselves easily; the nonelites usually are much less organized.[1] Empirical research for the United States has shown that there exists a considerable degree of direct social interaction and communication between the different elites (Mills 1959; Domhoff 1990). Let us shortly consider the basic tenets of elite theory before developing some hypotheses on the connection between elites and European integration.[2]

Elite theory has been founded by the well-known trio of Vilfredo Pareto, Gaetano Mosca (1966), and Roberto Michels.[3] Pareto's theory of elites states that every society contains a small group of elites or "aristocrats"—persons who are the most able and efficient in their respective category. The fight between and the replacement of one elite by another is the essence of history; if an elite becomes inefficient, it is thrown out by another elite. For Gaetano Mosca, every society is divided into those who govern and those who are governed. The small "political class" is able, due to its stronger organization, to exercise all political power functions and to enjoy all the privileges. Robert Michels' famous "iron law of oligarchy" states that all parties and organizations are characterized by an internal dichotomy between a minority of leaders, who have the necessary skills to manage large and complex organizations, and the rank-and-file members, who just have to carry out the orders. The thinking of these elite theorists can be considered as a kind of "bourgeois Marxism": They recognize a deep-going inequality of power distribution in society, but—contrary to Marx—they envisage no way out of this situation. Their basic ideas have been taken over also by some recent sociologists. Most notably among them is C. Wright Mills (1959); he contends that American society is dominated by a "power elite," composed of a tight network between the members of the upper class, composed of the members of the corporate, political, and military elites.

The general perspective elaborated by classical elite theory is still relevant today; not all of its theses, however, can be accepted. Three critical points must be raised: (1) there exists no simple dichotomy of those who govern against those who are governed. The pervasive transformations of the social structures in Europe since 1945—rising levels of education and income, transition to postindustrial economies, and so on—have led to a very differentiated social structure (Guttsman 1990; Hoffmann-Lange 1992:310). Modern culture has increased the possibilities to organize many different concerns and social groups (Meyer and Jepperson 2000). The manifold political offices in modern democracies produce a complex structure of political stratification (Putnam 1976:8f.). Democratic constitutions have established mechanisms by which the power of the elites is restricted, and citizens can take part in the selection and dismissal of political elites. Consequently, elites do not dispose of all the power; they must share it with subelites; also the elites of different sectors control each other. Political elites are controlled in various ways by the citizens. The population at large is no undifferentiated "mass" but has many ways to announce and exert their interests.

Elites are not per se power-driven, egoistic, and ruthless or even corrupt. However, they are also not inherently efficient and working in the common interest (as the elites themselves and conservative elite theory would have it). Their actions are guided by a combination of utilitaristic-rational, value-based, and emotional components in correspondence to the situation in which they find themselves. As holders of the most influential positions, elites have a particular responsibility to uphold the most important values of their society (Lasch 1995). Empirical research in Germany has shown, in fact, that political elites support basic democratic values more strongly than the general population (Faelcker 1991). What is also missing in the classical approaches is a consideration of the constitutional framework within which elites operate. In a modern society, this is the institution of democracy, which has been devised explicitly in order to come to grips with the problem of the control of political power.

Propositions deduced from democratic elite theory

Some classical and present-day social theorists have provided us with a framework for a more detached and critical view of the role of elites in modern societies (see Etzioni-Halevy 1993:53ff.; Haller 1995). One of the first was the great French political philosopher Montesquieu (1689–1755). He argued that political power must be limited in the interest of individual rights and liberties (Montesquieu 1955). As the main instrument for this, he devised a clear separation between the legislative, executive, and judicial political powers as the essence of democracy. If these functions are united in one person or group, absolute power or tyranny results; if they are separated, the holders of the different powers will control each other. This idea has been taken up by social scientists of the twentieth century such as Joseph Schumpeter (1962), R. Aron, S. Eisenstadt, and others. They draw together "the liberal idea of the separation of powers within the state with the notion of the independence of elites outside the state as well, in what has come to be known as democratic elite theory" (Etzioni-Halevy 1993:60). Liberal thinkers like Mill and Bentham argued that societal institutions and rights (must) exist which contribute to the check of power, such as freedom of the press, speech, and association; and the accountability of the governors must be checked by periodic, free elections. The German sociologist Max Weber focused on the power of the modern bureaucratic elites—a highly important topic also concerning the European Union today (see Chapter 5). For Weber, bureaucracy is the most rational and effective means of domination in modern societies. State bureaucracies, however, tend to become very powerful; therefore they must also be checked by other institutions and actors.

Democratic elite theory is based on two perspectives. One is exemplified by political philosophers like Montesquieu or Hannah Arendt (1951, 1963), who investigate the essential characteristics of democratic systems from a normative point of view. Social-scientific elite theorists and researchers ask how democracy really works. This distinction is reflected in the main focus of the different social-scientific disciplines concerning European integration: While jurisprudence is focusing mainly on normative questions, economics and sociology are asking how the EU institutions really work and which effects integration has. Political science may stand in the middle, including research both from the normative perspective (as in comparative government) and from the empirical-explanatory perspective (as in research on elections and public opinion).

In the present work, it is assumed that social-scientific analysis must include both a normative and an empirical-analytical perspective. Empirical research on the actual working of institutions, on the interests of the actors involved and so on, can be carried out in a much more "informed" way and has more practical-political relevance if it is related systematically to normative principles (see also Wiener and Diez 2004:244). The distinction between the normative and the empirical-analytical perspective must be made very clear in social-scientific research. It is not done adequately in the two dominant theories of integration. Functionalist theory, which holds that integration begins in the economic sector and then spills over to other sectors, "was imbued from the outset with pro-integration assumptions" (Jensen 2003:81; for summaries of integration theories see Rosamond 2000; Cini 2003a, Part 2; Wiener and Diez 2004; Faber 2005). It is also true for intergovernmentalism and in particular federalism, where integration is seen as the outcome of deliberate actions of governments, and which expects that its final state will be the United States of Europe. (For critical reviews, see Burgess 2003; Dehove 2004; Faber 2005.)

Ideas and institutions, actors and social structures in the process of European integration. The sociological perspective

The theoretical assumptions and hypotheses on European integration, presented in this and the following section, are based on the idea of sociology as a science of social reality.[4] This approach provides us with a general framework wherein specific political and macrosocial processes, such as European integration, can be located. Four principles are basic for this perspective.[5]

The first concerns the *distinction between four levels or areas of social reality and corresponding types of sociological analysis* (see *Figure 2.1*). These are (1) the level of ideas and values; (2) the level of social and political institutions; (3) the level of concrete actors and social processes; and (4) the level of social-structural and historical conditions of action (Weber 1973, 1978a; Popper 1972; Meleghy 2001; Haller 2003a:487ff.). The basic idea is that processes at all these levels follow their own logic, but are influenced by those at other levels in two ways: First, the higher level "determines" the processes at

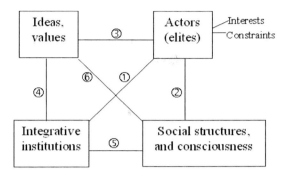

Figure 2.1 The central components of sociological analysis and the relations between them.

the lower level. An example is the value of equality: Once it is recognized that this value applies also to gender relations, there can be no return to an ideology which denies the principle of equality between men and women; people in countries where it is not realized can appeal to it. Second, certain conditions at the lower levels are necessary in order that processes at higher levels can work. The functioning of democratic institutions, for instance, presupposes a certain level of education and knowledge among the electorate. Only specific kinds of institutions will work efficiently in societies with certain social structures and patterns of relationships. Democracy, for instance, is incompatible with unmasked forms of slavery (see also Montesquieu 1965:90).

Let us illustrate some of the main problems and theses in regard to European integration as they will be investigated and advanced in this study. The research questions correspond to the encircled numbers in *Figure 2.1*.

1. European integration and the creation of the EC/EU has been initiated and pushed mainly by the (political) elites. Why were the elites ready to start such a far-reaching enterprise? In functional and intergovernmental theories of integration, there often are no concrete actors. Governments, societal sectors, and the like remain rather shadow figures and units. The frameworks within which elites act are the new European institutions. These institutions, once established, constitute a new environment for political action, and they even create new kinds of elites. The two most important among them are the "Eurocrats" and the European political and juridicial elites.
2. The general public in Europe has attended the process of integration for a long time with a "permissive consensus." In recent times, however, it became more and more critical about this process. Why has this been the case, given the seemingly high success of integration? After the rejection of the European Constitution by the French and

Dutch, a deadlock has been reached. The way out pursued by the elites—to implement the "Constitution for Europe" with some minor linguistic-cosmetic changes—is clearly a return to the old pattern of "elitist integration."

3. This standstill seems hard to comprehend since elites argue that they have been inspired only by universal and progressive ideas and values. An investigation of their role from the viewpoint of a critical sociology of knowledge, however, reveals that most of these values are often only as legitimating devices. Elites speak much less about the interests and the less "noble" ideas behind their actions.

4. Ideas and values such as peace, democracy, and human rights are usually invoked as the steering principles for the elaboration of the integration treaties and the institutions of the European Union. The analysis of the most relevant ideas in the Constitution for Europe gives surprising results in the regard, showing a strong weight of other ideas and interests.

5. The constitution of the EU will be investigated also in relation to its internal structure. Here we will ask to what degree it is able to come to grips with the high internal differentiation of the Union in socioeconomic and cultural terms, and the extreme size and power differentials between its member states.

6. Finally, we will investigate the relation between the basic ideas and values, guiding the process of integration, and the social-structural situation, perceptions and attitudes of the general public. It will be shown that there exist considerable contradictions and conflicts in these regards. The implication is that integration cannot continue to proceed in a direction which is rejected by the majority of people in some and considerable minorities within many other countries.

A second central principle is that social-scientific explanation must combine *understanding (Verstehen)* and *causal-statistical explanation*. Understanding includes a rational reconstruction of the situation within which an actor found himself when he carried out his action. The concept of the "problem situation" and of *situation analysis* requires reconstructing how the actor himself has perceived the constraints, conflicts, and opportunities within which his action has been performed; thereby, it is assumed in the first instance that the actor has acted out of rational considerations (Popper 1972; Farr 1985; Haller 2003a:560). We will apply situation analysis in Section 2.4 following, where we investigate the economic and political situation of the "motors" of integration, France and Germany, after World War II.

The third general principle of sociology as a science of social reality concerns the use of "ideal types" in order to explain social processes and human actions. This concept is especially useful for working out the characteristics of the European Union, the role of its member states, and its specific character as a new, multilevel system of "government." The EU is composed of member states with very different kinds of industrial relations, educational and cultural systems, and welfare-state institutions. They can be compared to each other and in their relation to the common institutions. The success of European integration is crucially dependent on finding compromises between the preservation of nationally inherited and effective social and political institutions and the development of a common institutional framework. In Chapter 8 we will argue that law is the central institutional instrument in this regard. The European Union itself, however, can also be compared in a fruitful way to other complex and/or large political communities in the world, like Switzerland, the United States of America, and India. The relevance of the principle to develop and compare ideal types of social and political institutions to elite analyses is obvious. Elite studies "seem to be shut in a conceptual Tower of Babel where scholars gamble with non-specified words" such as governing class, ruling class, power elite, leadership group, upper class, and so forth . . ."It would be more promising to have recourse to typologies and to configurations" (Dogan 2003:6).

The fourth methodological principle concerns the underlying theory of action. Here, we do not start from a view of humans as being rational "calculating machines" which confront costs and benefits of different lines of action and then decide. Rather, the main concept is that of "identity," which presupposes that the concrete actions of individual and collective actors are always guided by their overall self-image. This includes a bundle of basic values, a certain estimation of one's own abilities, and an ordering of the different aims of life. Identity is closely related to the social context within which one lives; an identity must also be recognized by others. One of the central aims of political leaders is to win public recognition and stature. For ordinary people, it is to win a respected social and political status. The political system plays a decisive role in this regard, first of all, by granting or not granting citizenship to certain categories of people. Also entitlements to influence and power are granted in a different extent to certain categories of persons. This happens both through the shape of the formal legal and political institutions, as through informal practices of social and political inclusion and exclusion (Hoover 1997:6). Issues that are relevant from this point of view include national identity and its relation to European identity. It will be a central question how citizens' possibilities for participation enable or inhibit the development of a European consciousness (see also Haller and Richter 1994; Haller 1999; Haller and Ressler 2006b; Nissen 2006). In this regard, the sociological approach is closely akin to the anthropological perspective (Wallace and Young 1997; Bellier and Wilson 2000; Shore 2000). In his focus on concrete individual personalities and concrete elites (seen from an ideal typical perspective), it clearly goes beyond the dominant theories of integration.

Table 2.1   The Normative-Functional and the Empirical-Analytical Perspective in the Analysis of the Elites: Areas to be Investigated by Social-Scientific Analysis

Area to be investigated	Normative-functional perspective (Aims and values and functional pre-requisites for elite action)	Empirical-analytical perspective (Actual values, interests and behaviour of the elites)
Aims and values	- Basic consensus about main societal values and aims	- Unauthorized definition of basic values and aims
	- Disclosing of basic values and aims	- Opportunistic emphasis of noble and popular, hiding of other values and aims
	- Adequate value consensus between elites and population	- Lack of correspondence between the values of elites and people
Functional differentiation	- Adequate functional differentiation between the elites	- Usurpation of as many competencies as possible
	- Relative autonomy of the different elites	- Making of decisions without due inclusion of all groups concerned
	- Adequate disclosure of competencies and restriction to the respective sphere	- Interfering into the competencies of other groups and elites
Network Structure	- Adequate and transparent interconnections with other elites	- Establishment of efficient network structures based on self-interest
	- Disclosure of relevant interconnections with other elites	- Concealment of network structures
Recruitment	- Recruitment based on criteria of functional aptitude and achievement	- Social exclusiveness in recruitment rules and practices
	- Adequate recruitment from all large segments and strata of society	- Concealment of extrafunctional criteria of recruitment
Recognition and remuneration	- Functional and societal adequate forms of recognition and remuneration	- Usurpation of as many and large remunerations as possible
	- Adequate size of material remuneration	- Concealment of certain forms and of the size of remunerations and privileges
	- Disclosure of all forms and amounts of remuneration	

2.2 European integration as an elite process

Let us now turn to a discussion of the role of elites in the process of European integration. Three general questions are relevant in this regard: the definition, composition, and size of the elites; the functional differentiation and network structures between them; the process and recruitment and election of the elites, as well as their remunerations; the relation between elites and citizens. An overview of these problems and the main questions in the case of the EU from the normative-democratic and empirical-analytical perspective is given in *Table 2.1*.

The definition, composition and size of the different elites

A delineation of the elite must consider two dimensions, the horizontal differentiation within different elite groups and the vertical differentiation between elites and nonelites. First, let us look at the *horizontal distinction* between different societal sectors and their elites. Corresponding to the main subsystems of society, we can distinguish—in functional terms—between social, economic, political, and cultural elites. Elites are differentiated from each other and—in the *vertical dimension*—from the nonelites by the possession of specific societal resources, such as control of physical force and means of coercion (e.g., police and army), administrative-bureaucratic resources, economic-material resources, and symbolic resources (knowledge, information, and the ability to influence the opinion of others). On the basis of these resources, two groups of elites can be distinguished; the first includes the political, economic, and bureaucratic elites who have original sources of power; the second includes all other groups such as cultural and intellectual elites (Etzioni-Halevy 1993:94ff.).

European integration has in the first instance been a political process; *political elites* must therefore be at the core of our considerations. The political elite, at the European level, includes the heads and members of the national governments who, as members the European Council and the Council of Ministers, decide about the most fundamental political issues. The European political elite includes, furthermore, the members of the European parliament, the European Commission, and the European Court of Justice. One group highly important for the integration process is the new European bureaucratic elite, the Eurocracy. The European Commission is a true supranational authority which has been equipped with a high degree of independence and power. Its competencies and staff are increasing continuously—a fact which has been underestimated strongly by many social scientists, as will be shown in Chapter 5.

A further, very powerful but also frequently neglected group in the process of European integration are the *economic elites*. Since its beginning, integration was focused on economic market integration; the introduction of the common currency was the last significant step in this regard. In all these steps, economic elites have played a significant, sometimes even the decisive, role. Economic elites are quite differentiated internally, as will be shown in Chapter 4. However, in the process of European integration, the owners and managers of large corporations and the leaders of agrarian and business interest groups have been most influential.

Also, *intellectual* and *cultural elites* play significant roles in the integration process, but they can exert only influence, because they do not dispose of political, administrative, and economic-material resources. An exception is the *media elite*; it includes the owners of large media corporations and the less powerful, even if sometimes quite influential, journalists known to the general public.

Another group are the *academic elites* in and outside universities, and *intellectual and cultural elites* which comprise all those persons who participate in the public dialogue about the ideas and aims of integration. These two groups are important as the providers of scientific-technical knowledge (which is also important as an instrument of legitimation) but also of new ideas and critical analyses connected with the process of integration. In Chapter 6, we will discuss the role of the academic and intellectual elites since the beginning of European integration in the aftermath of World War II, and in Chapter 7 we will look back at the idea of European integration developed by intellectuals through the centuries.

Furthermore, active representatives of the less advantaged groups must be considered when we look at the role of elites in modern societies (Etzioni-Halevy 1993:95). Here, we have to consider the *representatives of labour* at the national and at the European level and the leaders of social movements, extraparliamentary opposition groups, NGO's, and the like.

The vertical differentiation within the elites and the role of charismatic leaders

In regard to the vertical distinction between the more and less powerful segments of the elites, it seems reasonable to make a distinction between three subgroups: leading or charismatic elite personalities, the elite core or nucleus, and the subelites (see also Putnam 1976:8).

The *elite core* or *nucleus* includes a restricted number of persons who occupy the most powerful positions in a member state or at the level of the EU; most of them are known to the general public in more than just one country. They include some heads of member state governments (in particular those of large countries), some leading parliamentarians and top commissioners, and, maybe, a few influential entrepreneurs, corporation managers (who are also active politically), and representatives of large interest groups. Thus, the elite nucleus comprises the members of the elites who occupy the top positions at the "apex of power" (Dogan 2003) in the different sectors of the complex, multilevel system of European politics. The *subelite* includes all those political and economic actors who are theoretically independent from, but practically subordinated to, the elite core. These are the rank-and-file members of legislatures, managers of enterprises, less known members of national governments and of the European Commission, and the like.

At the center of the elite core, there are outstanding *charismatic elite personalities*. These are considered here as a highly important and sociologically relevant category. Charismatic authority rests "on devotion to the exceptional sanctity, heroism or exemplary character of an individual person, and of the normative patterns or order revealed by him" (Weber 1978a:215,1111ff.; Bendix 1960:298ff.; Zingerle 1981:130ff.; Nippel 2000). Extraordinarily, mission-oriented motivated and energetic personalities also play an important role in political life today. Research on elections shows that the top candidates play a decisive role for the decisions of the voters (Gabriel 2000; Hadler 2005). Also, the personal moral integrity of the candidates for a top political office is an important element in this regard. Charismatic leaders were decisive, for instance, in the dissolution of old and the building of new nations in Central and East Europe in the 1980s and 1990s (Haller 1996a). In Chapter 3, we will show that the same was true in the process of European integration. The sociological analysis of elites does not try to give a comprehensive historical account of elite personalities and their actions; this is done much better by historians. Rather, the aim is to look at such personalities from an ideal-typical perspective and to relate their characteristics and actions systematically to the specific periods and political constellations in which they operated.[6]

The following hypothesis is advanced concerning the role of elite personalities in the process of European integration:

> *(2.1) Influential political personalities, such as the heads of the governments of large member states and the holders of top offices in the EU, often determine the course of integration to a decisive depree. It is essential, therefore, to look at the social characteristics and action strategies of these personalities in order to understand the dynamic of European integration.*

The European political elites

Where does the unquestioned and often enthusiastic participation of the political elites in the process of European integration come from? If we believe established theories of integration, they act mainly in the interest of their states and peoples. This is a rather incomplete explanation, both from the viewpoint of a realistic theory of politics and from that of a theory of identity. First, the interests of a state are manifold and difficult to define. Behind the asserted national interest, often only the interests of specific groups are hidden. A relevant example is the purported pressure from globalization. The reference to its seemingly irresistible power is frequently used as an argument for adopting neoliberalist policies or for claiming a speedup of European integration.

Also, personal political aims may constitute a motivation for leading national politicians to participate enthusiastically in the process of integration. Two of the strongest motives for politicians are the striving for power and prestige. These motives can be satisfied by participation in the process of integration (Vaubel 1995:36ff.). It is probably felt that the participation in the central decisions of this huge new political community balances more than the giving up in part national independence. Moreover, heads and members of national governments often use the decisions made at the level of the EU to arrive at a policy at home which they alone would not have been able to realize. The relevance of prestige is also evident. The participation in the ever-recurring summits of the heads of the member state governments bestows upon all participants the positive feelings accompanying the participation in grand ceremonies (see Collins 2005 about the importance of such rituals). The group pictures of the summits show this quite clearly. Out of these considerations, the following hypothesis is advanced:

> *(2.2) The political elites see their participation in process of integration as a means to advance political goals which they would not be able to enforce alone. Moreover, the striving for prestige and power are important motives for their participation in the process of integration. They feel that membership in the EU provides them with grandeur and world-political influence, but also with more weight and prestige at home.*

A central topic in this regard are the patterns of recruitment, composition, and behaviour of the political elites. Here, a significant change has taken place in Europe. Today, the selection of political personalities occurs mainly through the party system. This system has changed substantially over the last decades. On the one side, all large parties have become less "ideological" and have developed all-purpose political programs suited for a majority of the voters. On the other side, politicians became involved more and more into interests and decisions related to the expanding state functions. In this way, the character of many political leaders changed from that of a representative of certain political orientations (conservative, liberal, socialist, etc.) to a person who has to be an efficient "networker," a successful manager of election campaigns, a person who can provide his followers with diverse gratifications (Scheuch 1992; Klages 1993); we can call such a person a "political maker." The expansion of the welfare state strengthens these trends: While the citizens depend more and more on government, confidence in political institutions and personalities is decreasing (Dogan 1997; Lipset and Schneider 1983). However, since European politics is concerned much less with direct welfare-state administration and redistribution, its image may be better than that of politics at the national level. Out of these trends, the following hypothesis is developed:

(2.3) We can observe a shift in the dominant type of political leaders in Europe from that of the representative of certain political camps to successful "political makers." This shift was associated with an increasing distance between elites and citizens and distrust of the general public toward politics and politicians. This mistrust translates itself also into attitudes toward the EU. In general, however, there may be less mistrust against the EU than against national politicians because European politicians in Brussels have less possibility to distribute directly money and benefits in kind to individual recipients than national governments and parties have. In addition, the distance from Brussels of the citizens of most member states reduces public attention to and knowledge of affairs in Brussels.

The economic elites

European integration offers undoubted advantages also to economic elites. The EU and its enlargement provide them with a large and secure internal market which is continuously expanding in size—a central element for the growth of capitalism since its origins (Luxemburg 1923; Wallerstein 1974). Within the economic elites, the owners and managers of multinational corporations will be the most fervent advocates of integration; they are also interested in deregulation but also in the establishment of new market regulations and in the obtaining of financial support for expensive technological research and development. The support of integration among other sectors of the entrepreneurial classes, as well as among the representatives of labour, may be less enthusiastic. Their consent is won, however, by several strategies, including the introduction of significant elements of corporatism which are established to provide a certain protection of the EU internal market against worldwide competition. Such strategies have been most necessary and effective in the case of agriculture. Labour organizations have been weakened by the process of integration and by the trend toward postindustrial employment structures and increasing labour-market competition. Their efforts to include elements of social protection into the integration process will not be very successful, however, for several reasons (lack of organizational power on the European level, resistance from certain countries and from employers, etc.). An important question in this regard is if the owners and managers of the large EU corporations merge into a new global business class (Sklair 1997). In Chapter 4 we will show, in accordance with recent comparative research on values and orientations of managers, that this is not the case (M. Hartmann 1999; Bauer and Bertin-Mourot 1999; Wasner 2004:217ff.; Axt and Deppe 1979:199). Concerning the economic elites, the following thesis is proposed:

(2.4) The core of economic elites, the owners and managers of large, multinational corporations, are among the most determinate supporters

of integration because they profit directly from it. They are particularly eager to promote further integration in periods of increasing external competition as a consequence of globalization and in periods when the opening up of new markets becomes possible because of fundamental political changes at the international scene (e.g., breakdown of the Iron Curtain). The consent of other economic elites (such as agricultural producers and leaders of farmers' association), is won by providing massive subsidies to them. However, due to their internal divergences of interests and to persisting national systems of ownership, organization, and management, the economic elites at the European level will not merge into one cohesive, closed capitalist elite (or class). This does not undermine their decisive political influence, however, also because countervailing economic elites (such as the representatives of labour) are much weaker at the European than at the national level.

The new European bureaucracy and the EU Service class

Quite a different situation exists in the case of the bureaucratic elite. It is a central thesis of this book, and will be documented extensively in Chapter 5, that a truly new European elite (the "*Eurocracy*") is on the rise which is mainly responsible for the seemingly irresistible process of continuous further integration. The functioning of the complex political system of the EU presupposes the existence of a bureaucratic elite or "service class" which is much larger than usually assumed. Due to the fact that the EU authorities (Council, Commission, Parliament, Court of Justice) carry out mainly legislative functions, a large number of additional staff (an EU "*substitute bureaucracy*") is needed both in the EU "capitals" and at the level of the nation-states to implement this legislation (see also Burley and Mattli 1993). Due to the continuous increase of these legislative activities, the EU "service class" is growing continuously without a parallel reduction of staff at the level of the nation-states. The consequence is that integration is increasing substantially the power of bureaucracy, the "Moloch en Europe" (Dogan and Pelassy 1987).

Here, the following hypothesis is advanced:

(2.5) The "Eurocracy" (in particular the commission and its administrative apparatus) provides the strongest factor of continuity to the process of integration. It is primarily interested in a checkless expansion of its own competences and power. In this endeavour, it is strongly supported by the European Court of Justice and by an EU "substitute bureaucracy" in the member states. Due to the strength of its institutional position, its distance from the national capitals, and the lack of an effective European public sphere, this Eurocracy has been able to secure considerable material privileges.

The functional differentiation and the relations
between the different elites

As far as the relation between the different elites is concerned, we may distinguish five areas of differentiation (*Table 2.1;* see also Putnam 1976; Etzioni-Halevy 1993). They concern the ideas and values of the elites (this issue shall be treated in the next section), the functional differentiation and the relations between the different elite groups, the patterns of election, appointment and recruitment, and the remuneration structures.

A basic normative requirement of a well-functioning democracy is an adequate functional differentiation between the elites. This concerns the relations within the governing elites of the EU (members of the Council, the Commission, the Parliament and the ECJ) and the relations between these and other, mainly economic, elites. These relations are shaped by the highly complex political system of the European Union.[7] The complexity of this system is also the main reason why there exists no closed "dominant class" or "power elite" in the EU, but rather a complex network of elites (see also Risse-Kappen 1996). A main characteristic of the multilevel system of government of the EU is that it does not distinguish clearly between the legislative, executive, and judicial functions. The Commission is a worldwide unique hybrid, exercising in part all three functions; the council carries out functions of political steering and of legislation; both these institutions are not elected directly by the citizens throughout Europe. The European Parliament, while gaining continuously in competences, still has far less power than a national parliament; it can only change or reject, but not initiate legislative proposals. The elections to this parliament follow quite different rules in different countries and turnout at these elections is declining. It dropped from 63% in 1979 to 45,6% in 2004. An additional important characteristic of the political system of the EU is the weakness (if not nonexistence) of a Europe-wide public sphere (Kleinsteuber 1994; Gerhards 2000).

Overall, the political system of the EU can be characterized as a *consociational system,* that is, as a system where decisions are the result of complex deliberations and are accepted only if all major involved parties agree. The concentration of competences in the EU commission will enable this compact institution to advance the process of integration in a continuous way while the actions of the council will be more related to changing outcomes of national elections, international political changes, and so forth. The institutional weakness of the European parliament, as well as its large size, will reduce its function as an opposition but will also induce it to deal with a myriad of problems even if it does not have much real decision power in them. The absence of an open competition between government and opposition makes it difficult for the media elites to produce "exciting" reports which could activate Europe-wide public interest; moreover, they may often be captivated by the political elites in order to report in a favourable way about EU affairs.

A main problem concerning *elite network structures* exists in regard to the relation between the political and economic elites. The development of the central EU authorities in Brussels has led to the emergence of a mass of lobbyists who try to influence the processes of legislation. While the phenomenon of lobbyism is also well known in some other nations (particularly in the U.S.), in the EU it has a peculiar character. This is so because there exists little transparency about the exact number of lobbyists, their sponsors, and the ways in which they influence the decision processes. We can assume that the strong presence of lobbyists in Brussels will provide large enterprises and powerful economic and political interests groups an overproportional amount of influence. Several consequences will result from this: an overproduction of regulations which often are in the interest of only very small groups; a one-sidedness of the legislative activity in favour of interests of these interest groups; a relative neglect of interests of population groups which have little resources and are weakly organized. The general public will recognize these facts and develop critical attitudes about them—a fact which will also have negative consequences for the general attitudes toward the EU.

As far as the *patterns of election, appointment, and recruitment* of the elites are concerned, several problems are relevant. One is the fact that the members of the central political-decision institution, the Council and the European Council, are not elected directly EU-wide by the citizens concerning their European role. Another one is that the elections to the European Parliament are considered by both national politicians and by the general public as "second order elections" where no "hot" European issues are at stake.

Finally, also in regard to recognition and remuneration, specific problems exist at the European level. European politicians and bureaucrats will be highly qualified and they have to work under complicated work conditions insofar as they have to resettle in Brussels. At the same time, a public is lacking which controls their activities and remunerations, and the particular context of the EU enables it to develop special privileges concerning employment conditions, taxation, and the like. The consequence will be that the material privileges of EU politicians will be rather high but are not matched in a corresponding degree of social recognition.

Out of these considerations, the following hypotheses are advanced:

> *(2.6) The complex political system of the EU has the consequence that the European political elites are at the same time rather strongly differentiated from each other and interwoven in a complex manner. There exists no tightly knit European "power elite" as in more homogeneous nation-states. Nevertheless, the economic, political, and bureaucratic European elites are closely interacting, although often in a rather nontransparent way. Also, the processes of election and recruitment, and of remuneration, are affected by these new problems, making them less transparent and impersonal than those of the level of the member states.*

*The influence of the different fractions of the elites
on the speed of the process of integration*

The varying speed and often contradictory form of integration in different periods must be seen as the outcome of a complex interaction between the interests and strategies of the different elite groups. European integration has been induced by political elites, but backed by economic elites and later on furthered continuously by the steadily increasing new European bureaucratic elites. The interests, resources, and strategies concerning the integration process of these groups, however, diverged in different periods and in different aspects. The political elites were responsible for the most decisive single steps toward further integration, but also for the moments of disruption and crisis. Political elites can act out of their own ideas and values concerning integration, but they are also exposed to manifold expectations and pressures from other forces inside (e.g., economic elites, voters) and outside of their own country. The economic elites are also strong supporters of integration, influencing its direction sometimes in a way which becomes problematic from the viewpoint of politics. An example is the pressure toward enlargement. After some time, however, the new bureaucratic European elites have become a continuous and very strong motor of integration. Out of these considerations, the following hypothesis is proposed:

> *(2.7) European integration as a whole is a discontinuous process in which moments of dynamic integration are followed by periods of stagnation and moments of crisis. The political elites are the force of acceleration, but also of slowdown of the integration process; the economic and the new European bureaucratic and professional elites are the forces continually furthering integration. As a consequence of the different forces, the speed and direction of integration often are quite contradictory and often produce problematic results.*

2.3 Ideas, values, and the role of the intellectuals in the process of European integration

The systematic consideration of ideas and values for the process of integration is essential from the sociological perspective. Social and political integration of a society would be impossible if it were based only on political and bureaucratic control or on pure utilitarian economic interests (Kluckhohn 1951; Parsons 1951; Münch 1982; Wolfe 1989). However, the values of a society do not form ever-existing, permanent, and coherent systems. Even in the course of a few generations values can change substantially; there exist serious contradictions and conflicts between different values and their bearers; all positive values have their negative antipole; values do not persist without some degree of social

control (Cancian 1975; Inglehart 1977; Etzioni 1988; Haller 1987; Coleman 1990; Bourdieu 1999).

A critical sociological analysis of ideas and values and their function in
social and political processes is based on two principles (see also Mannheim
1970; Lepsius 1988; Lieberman 2002:709; Boudon 1986, 2004; Camic and
Gross 2004; Haller 2003a:485ff.). First, the values involved must be identified
very concretely, and it must be shown how specific institutions are related to
these values. Second, the relative importance of values has to be determined in
particular in connection with *interests*. We can never assume that the values
which social actors invoke as the reasons for their behaviour are the "true"
reasons of behaviour; they can always be advanced in order to legitimize certain kinds of behaviour, in order to mask certain interests.

Explicit and implicit values in the process of European integration

In the process of European integration, the invocation of values abounds.
Not only political actors, but also historians, social scientists, philosophers, journalists, and commentators of all sorts, stress the relevance of
values for integration. In fact, the European Union is characterized by
many as a *community of values*—a rather surprising characterization
whose rationale shall be investigated in Chapter 6. In view of this fact, it
appears strange that "so far, the EU literature has largely ignored ideas
. . ." (Risse-Kappen 1996:59). However, the ideas and values invoked for
the process of European integration are often quite contradictory. In different parts of Europe, different values and expectations are connected
with integration (see Chapter 6). There exist hardly particular values
which are distinguishing Europe from people in other advanced Western
countries and regions such as North America or Australia (Heit 2005).
Therefore, this ideology-critical approach can (and must) be applied
extensively to the process of European integration, "bringing Europe
down to earth," as the apt phrase in the book of a young Swedish sociologist says (Hellström 2006). Four general questions are relevant in this
regard: (1) How many and which were the values that have guided the
process of European integration according the statements of the actors
(political elites) themselves? (2) Where did these values come from? (3)
What relevance did these values have for the behaviour of the actors in
the integration process? (4) What relevance did the values have for the
design of the European institutions?

Statements about the importance of values in the process of integration abound both in political and scientific speeches and writings.
Values are implicit also in social-scientific theories of integration. Federalist theories, for instance, "are rooted in what is intrinsically a moral
imperative which is drawing its intellectual bases from the German
Bundestreue ('federal comity' or federal arrangement made for mutual
benefit) . . ." (Burgess 2003:67). The concept of "European citizenship"

implies the ethical-moral principle of solidarity between the people of the EU member states (Poferl 2006). Anthropologist Douglas R. Holmes (2000:94) notes a contradiction in this regard: The EU project is "predicated on a broad-based societal theory blending a complex moral vision and technocratic practice, yet lacks virtually any formal constitutional theory of its own."

Values are also related to *social conflict*. Values can be used by the elites to hide interests and social cleavages with the intent to reduce the level of (overt) conflict in a society. Subordinated or deprived groups can appeal to values in order to get a moral legitimation for demands for changes in the distribution of power and privilege (Moore 1978). Many believe that only a highly integrated society, a society with little or no conflict, is a "good society" (Shils 1982). To build such a society has always been the object of governments and rulers. For this endeavour, they also tried to increase societal homogeneity in regard to values.

The tendency to adduce common values to the EU seems to increase parallel with the growth of the size and heterogeneity of the community itself. In the first contract about the European Steel and Coal Community, settled in 1952 between six countries, rather homogeneous in cultural terms, only two values have been mentioned explicitly: Peace, economic growth and prosperity. Half a century later, with 25 member states and a population of nearly half a billion, the Constitution for Europe listed about a dozen basic values (see Chapter 7). Furthermore, the EU generally uses a language focusing on integration rather than on conflicts of interests. For instance, instead of social inequality relating to social structure as a whole, the concept of "social exclusion" is used, which is focusing mainly on deprived groups and on technocratic strategies of social policy (Heschl 2003). Given the highly differentiated internal structure and differentiation of ideas concerned with integration, the elites make use of extensive strategies of persuasion in order to convince the citizens throughout the EU about the blessings of integration (see Chapter 6). These are necessary, particularly because the "myth of success" of the 1960s (Etzioni 2001:254) became quite fragile in more recent times.

However, the focus on integration may not be in the long-term interest of the Union itself. Conflict often brings into public awareness norms and rules that were dormant before and may lead to innovation and reform (Coser 1956:127; Simmel 1971). In this way, conflict is essential to produce a type of integration which is not only superficial but which rests on a truly common value system. If there is no public "moral dialogue" in which the basic values are formulated and discussed explicitly, some of people's deeply held values can be offended and the legitimacy of the whole integration process may be undermined (Etzioni 2001:xxxvi; Heit 2005).

Especially in situations where no clear-cut problem definitions exist, general ideas are indispensable to provide definitions of a problem and legitimation to practical strategies and measures (Jachtenfuchs 1996b).

Also, transnational communities are dependent on "collectively shared values and consensual knowledge" (Risse-Kappen 1996:59). European integration is based on a bundle of values (Münch 1993). The integration literature in jurisprudence, political science, and economics, however, has either ignored the role of values or taken an implicitly normative, even apologetic, stance. Specific "European myths" were invented about past and future accomplishments of integration and imminent threats in the case of nonintegration (Etzioni 2001:252). The huge *Cecchini Report*, which tried to show the economic losses from nonintegration, can be characterized as a politically commissioned report used to legitimize the process of integration. References to values can serve as a legitimation device for political strategies and decisions; they may also be invoked retrospectively as justifications for certain courses of action (Bourdieu 1999). It also happens regularly that critical opinion and voices about integration are denounced. In his extensive analysis of official documents, public declarations, and arguments raised during the EU referenda in Ireland, Denmark, and France, Anders Hellström (2006:217) was able to find eight criteria by which "good" and "bad" Europeans were distinguished from each other. Thus, integration has become a dominant value in the sense of Kluckhohn (1951:415) in postwar Europe.

A final point to be made here concerns the misleading equation of the concept of "Europe" with the European Union as is done every day. Countries which want to become EU members are said to be on the "way to Europe." The concept of "Europe" includes, however, an extremely broad and rich array of historical, geographic, cultural, and political images and connotations, but it is also rather vague and indefinite (Kaelble 1987; Jordan 1988; Therborn 1995; Haller 1990; Hellström 2006). It should not be confounded with that of the "European Union," which denotes a historically and geographically specific political entity. Out of these considerations, the following hypotheses are proposed:

(2.8) Ideas and values are highly relevant for the process of European integration. Their role, however, is often more implicit. There exist a hiatus between abundant official ("solemn") declarations of values and their actual relevance for political strategies and decisions. The appeal to common values may be a deliberate strategy of the European political elites to deflect from potential cleavages and conflicts and overcome the existing divergences in values, interests, and lifestyles between the different social, cultural, political-territorial subgroups, and subunits. Contradictions and conflicts between different values are downplayed by the elites through strategies of "depoliticization" (Hoffmann-Lange 1992:312). European integration will in general be presented by the elites driving the process as positive and beneficial and as being guided by rationality and the idea of progress (Hansen and Williams 1999). Persons and groups which are critical

of this process will be stigmatized as being one-sided "anti-Europe-ans," inimical to the ideas of modernity and progress.

The role of intellectuals in the process of European integration

In this context, we have also to look at the role of intellectuals in the development and propagation of ideas and values about European integration. Intellectuals are persons who are engaged in public discourses about important social and political issues; they usually belong to the scientific, artistic, or literary professions. They are analysing and commenting on social and political developments and situations on the basis of universal values such as freedom, equality, social justice, and other characteristics of a "good society" (Mannheim 1970; Lepsius 1988; Charle 2001). This brings them typically, but not necessarily, in opposition to the powerful. In fact, it is the central aim of intellectuals to attract public attention and to gain influence among the powerful (Boudon 2004). In modern history, intellectuals have played a decisive role for major social transformations by developing ideas and visions about a better society and new political institutions. This was the case in the age of civil and social revolutions from the mid-seventeenth to the early twentieth century, and it was also the case in the movements for national independence in the nineteenth century. Even in the last European revolution, the transition from state socialism to democracy and market societies in East Europe in the 1980s and 1990s, intellectuals were those who propagated the changes and fought for them long before they actually took place. In many cases, however, the actual changes and transformations did not take place in the way they had been envisioned by the intellectuals. The same was the case with European integration. The "idea of Europe," foreseeing the peaceful unification of the continent, has been propagated long since by thinkers and intellectuals (see Chapter 7). The real process of integration after World War II, however, occurred in a way not foreseen by many of these intellectuals.

Out of these considerations, the following hypotheses are proposed:

(2.9) Intellectual elites have played a significant role in developing the idea of a peaceful and "united" Europe through the centuries. The political elites are referring frequently to these ideas in order to legitimate their efforts. They do so, however, in a rather one-sided and selective way; emphasis is placed only on those historical ideas which seem to confirm the concrete realization of European integration since 1945. Since then, intellectuals became rather silent because of two reasons: First, because the concrete form of European integration did not correspond to some of the historical visions; and second, because many of the academic and professional groups from which intellectuals typically are recruited were co-opted by the political elites for their specific project of European integration.

2.4 The historical-situational context of the origin and further expansion of the EU

A central element of the sociological approach is the consideration of the situational context within which European integration began and the changes in this situation over time. This context includes two elements, the *international or global situation* and the *internal situation* within the Union. Both of these aspects have been relatively neglected in integration research. By considering them it is possible to give a convincing explanation for the start of the process of integration and to understand some of the puzzles in the development of this process till the present day.

The formation of federations as a reaction to external threat

If we look at the emergence of federations between independent states, the consideration of the *international situation* is indispensable. Elisabeth Fix (1992/93) has investigated the history of the emergence of such federations from the times of ancient Greece up to Europe in the nineteenth century. In all cases, the reason for the alliance was to gain security against a foreign, large and strong, mostly despotic state. Usually, such alliances were formed in times of internal crisis and external threat.

Let us apply these ideas to the situation of Europe and its position in the international system after World War II. The received thesis is that the European countries, in particular France and Germany, had become convinced that the most important thing to be secured was the avoidance of any further war between them. Therefore, they developed the idea of close economic cooperation as a base for a later political cooperation and integration, which should inhibit a war forever. A closer look at the historical circumstances and the real forces operating at this time, however, gives a somewhat different picture.

"S'unir ou perir." Western Europe after World War II

Three aspects had changed fundamentally as a consequence of World War II (Lipgens 1974; Elias 1985; Kuzmics 2001; Loth 1996). First, the Soviet Union and the United States emerged as new world powers, and the former large European states were relegated to second-order political and military powers. This aspect alone would have made futile any further war between France and Germany. In fact, the situation of these two countries after World War II was one of profound weakness. This was most evident in the case of Germany, which was devastated economically, divided internally into military occupation zones, and dishonoured morally due to fascism and the Holocaust. For Germany, nationalism appeared as an ideology compromised once for all. The overarching aim of its politics after the war was to regain international respect and political autonomy. Participating in European integration was and is seen, till today, as an undisputed strategy of German politics toward this aim. For the other large Western states, it was also a problem how to treat defeated Germany and to make impossible a repeated German aggression. This was particularly a problem for France, which also tried to gain control of the contested core industrial area Ruhr (Gillingham 1987). However, France found itself in a quite weak situation after the war (Italy might have been in a similar situation). It was also a defeated nation, with a weak economy, and a damaged moral reputation due the collaboration of many with the Vichy regime (Wolton 2004).

The new bipolar structure of the world produced new actors and interests and they decided the course of events in postwar Europe (Waltz 1979; Mearsheimer 2001; Siedschlag 2006). The Soviet Union was not ready to give up its grip on central east Europe, and the United States decided to integrate Western Europe into their domain of influence. Through the Marshall Plan, their starving economies would recover and Western Europe—including Germany—become an ally of the United States. Thus, the East-West conflict had the function of a midwife for European integration (Lipgens 1974:522): Cooperation between the old enemies France and Germany was seen as the only way out of their common weakness, expressed in the dictum, widespread at this time: "S'unir ou perir." The United States actively supported West European integration, and exerted even pressure in this direction by making conditional the financial aid through the Marshall Plan on cooperation between the recipient states (Hyde-Price 2006:225; Loh 1996:48ff.). The explanation of the origins of European integration as an outcome of the emerging rivalry between the two world powers gets support also by a simple consideration concerning the role of the Soviet Union. If in fact the prevention of future wars had been the main rationale for European integration, it would be hard to understand why there were no efforts to include the Soviet Union. This was the country which had experienced the most pervasive blood tribute in World War II.

Rise to world power? The situation and prospects of the EU at the beginning of the twenty-first century

During the postwar decades, the situation in Western Europe changed substantially, due to the fact that the process of integration was seemingly successful in economic terms. The continuing process of institutional integration and enlargement led to a rising self-consciousness of the EC/EU also in terms of its role in the world. Competitive economic pressure from the other leading world economies (U.S., Japan) led to a new coalition in the 1980s between transnational business interests and the European Commission, and to the ideas of enlarging the home market and furthering technological-industrial development (Bornschier 1998; Ziltener 2000). A landmark was the breakdown of the Iron Curtain in 1989/90, which changed the world-political situation, displacing the bipolar system with a unipolar world in terms of military power, dominated by the United States.

These changes had four consequences for Europe (Hyde-Price 2006:226f.): Broad agreement persisted that also the reunited, larger Germany should remain embedded closely into the EU in order to address security concerns of its neighbours; the Maastricht Treaty on the European Union established the economic aim of driving Europe faster toward competitiveness with the U.S.; and the EU gained a new role as a factor promoting political stability and economic prosperity in post-Communist Eastern Europe; it facilitated the access to the EU of politically neutral states, such as Austria and Switzerland, where this access had long been demanded by the representatives of TNCs (Bieler 2002).

At the background of these changes, the EU began to develop a new role on the international scene by two potentially contradictory strategies: One was the development of the European Common Security and Defence Policy (ESDP), the other the insistence on representing a new kind of "civil power," guided less by power politics than by "soft" forms of international negotiations and actions. However, in both regards some reservations are in place. First, as far as the ESDP is concerned, the record of the EU has been quite negative. Its indecisiveness and internal discord in the case of the war in Yugoslavia, and the deep cleavage between two camps in the EU in the case of the second war in Iraq, are in fresh remembrance. Nevertheless, the EU continues to act and speak as if it were on the way to become a global player. Most of this, however, up to now is not much more than "rhetoric and shop-window type activism" (Siedschlag 2006:5).

What about the possibility of the EU to play a wholly new role in international politics, as a civil power, basing its claims mainly on ethical and moral precepts? Also in this regard, questions have to be raised. If we apply the ideology-critical approach, introduced in the foregoing section, it is easy to understand why this view is much liked in European policymaking circles. In this way, the EU can be portrayed as following an approach based on "soft" strategies of "diplomacy, persuasion, negotiation and compromise," in contrast to the (American) military and coercive approach (Hyde-Price 2006:217ff.). Such an approach, however, may tend to neglect the role of power. It is also intrinsically contradictory assuming that civilian, normative power is always a "good thing." From a realistic perspective, we should start from the following two assumptions: (1) Like any actor at the international scene, the EU will also be motivated to a high degree (although certainly not exclusively) by bold interests of security, influence, and power. (2) It will behave quite differently in relation to other actors on the world scene, depending on their power. If these are very strong, the EU will act quite cautiously (one can think here of countries such as the U.S., Russia, or China); if they are weak, it will not shrink away from using its power if necessary (see also Galtung 1973).

Out of these considerations, the following theses are proposed:

(2.10) The origins of European integration and its further evolution cannot be understood by looking only at the stated intents of the leading actors in Europe but must also consider changes in the world-political constellation. Integration must also be seen as means to (re-)gain national autonomy and prestige, and security and influence at the international level. These motives were decisive for the integration takeoff in the 1950s, and for the increasing speed of institutional integration and enlargement since the late 1980s. Today, the EU is characterized as an economic giant that should also assert its political weight on the world scene. Two contradictory aims and visions exist in this regard, however: that of a new global power, equipped with its own military forces; and that of a new kind of "civilian power," achieving international influence through forms of "soft" diplomacy and economic incentives.

The increasing gap between elites and citizens in the attitudes toward integration

At the centre of this study is the problem of an increasing gap between elites and citizens in regard to the process of integration. The former see it as a world-historical unique accomplishment; the latter are more and more sceptical in this regard. This is in fact a formidable conundrum since one could expect that in the course of time attachment and attitudes toward the new political community should become more positive. There are two lines of development which help us to understand and explain this central problem.

First, there are the developments and strategies at the level of the elites and the political system of the EU, indicated in the foregoing sections. Until the 1980s, European integration had been a rather elitist process, with very little discussion and participation among the citizens. This situation has changed for several reasons: Integration has covered more and more areas of social and political life; the empowerment of the new European institutions has undermined possibilities for democratic participation at the level of member states; in recent decades, the socioeconomic success of integration was more modest than expected.

Second, significant changes have also taken place at the level of the populations and citizens in the member states of the EU. They included: social-structural changes which increased mean levels of education of the population; the redistribution of the economically active population from the first and second sectors (agriculture and industry) toward the third sector (services), and knowledge-based occupational activities (Bell 1999; Mendras 1988; Castells 1997, 1999). Also, fundamental changes in the values and styles of life of the people trade places, away from tradition-based forms of thinking and behaviour toward more individualistic and secular ones occurred (Beck 1986; Inglehart 1997). These trends have been enforced by the accession of northwestern countries to the EC, whose social structure has been quite advanced and whose populations have high standards in terms of democratic participation. In the political realm, participation in traditional forms (party membership, voting at elections) has declined, and more critical attitudes toward politics and the political elites have emerged. European integration has contributed to these trends in several regards. Out of these considerations, the following hypothesis is developed:

> *(2.11) Half a century of European integration has not led to increasing positive attachments of the citizens toward this project and the European Union, but rather to a stagnation and even partial decline of such attitudes. The reasons were (a) the behaviour of the political elites, which often seems not to correspond to their stated aims; (b) the institutional development of the EC/EU, which reduced possibilities for citizens' participation; (c) changes in social structures and value orientations, which have raised citizens' political standards and expectations.*

CONCLUSION

We may conclude this chapter by pointing out shortly the main differences of our approach to the two established theories of integration, the (neo-) functional and intergovernmental approach. *Functional integration theory* holds that integration between hitherto separate units emerges because this leads to gains in productivity and welfare. Once integration has been initiated in one sector, it spills over to other sectors and from the economic to the political sphere. Thus, integration processes acquire a logic of their own and reinforce themselves with increasing international exchange and division of labour. The newly established supranational agencies play a crucial role in this process. The final stage will be a highly integrated economic and political community (Deutsch 1957; Haas 1958; Taylor 1993; Jensen 2003; Schmitter 2004; Faber 2005). For the intergovernmental theory of integration, integration is a strategy pursued by national governments in order to gain security in a changed international situation, and to be able to come to grips with the forces of globalization. Integration strengthens the position of national governments both within their own state and at the international level (Hoffman 1966; Milward 1992; Moravcsik 1998; for reviews see Faber 2005:86ff.; Burgess 2003).

The approach pursued in this study diverges from these approaches in several regards. First, it avoids equating functional explanations with causal ones. The function of integration can be quite different from the causes which have led to its emergence. A corollary of the functional imagery is teleological thinking, which assumes an inherent logic of development and a well-defined final stage. Such a kind of thinking is also inherent in federalism, a variant of the intergovernmental approach, which foresees the emergence of the "United States of Europe." Second, our approach does not speak only about "systems" or about "national governments" but differentiates clearly between different kinds of actors and their manifold interests. Besides governments and political elites, the economic, bureaucratic, professional, and intellectual elites are also considered as decisive actors. A third focus of our approach, which is underexposed or wholly missing in the established theories, is the focus on the role of citizens and their interests which are different from those of the elites and which are also diverging in different member states. Fourth, our approach considers systematically the role of ideas and values in the process of integration, both in their positive function as motivating forces and in their legitimate function, when the powerful elites use them in order to conceal certain interests.

In the next three chapters, the role of the political, economic, bureaucratic, and intellectual elites is investigated. In Chapter 6, the perceptions and attitudes of the populations toward integration are investigated, including the strategies of the elites to win their consent. In the last two chapters, the issue of the finality of European integration is taken up. Chapter 7 investigates the vision of historical and present-day elites and confronts them with the actual course of integration. In Chapter 8, it is proposed to understand the EU as a "community of law." This opens up a conclusive way to reconcile national autonomy with the necessary amount of cooperation and integration, as well as an efficiently working elite with an informed and participating public.

3 The Political Elites
How Integration Has Opened Up a Wide Field of New Political Careers

INTRODUCTION

In this chapter, the European political elites shall be analysed. Political elites are defined as the occupants of the central political power positions; thus, they include particularly the members of governments and parliaments. The "European" political elites include the members of the nation-state governments who participate directly in European politics through the European Council, the members of the European Parliament and the Commissioners. While they are not politicians in the strict sense of the word, we include here also the members of the European Court of Justice because de facto they have contributed significantly to the process of integration.

The concept of political elites suggests that we focus our attention also on the personal characteristics, interests, and motives of political actors. From this point of view it seems to be a puzzle why national political elites were ready to give up considerable power to the EU. Our elite-theoretical perspective provides a solution to this puzzle.

In the first part, we give a sociological portrait of those few political personalities who have shaped the beginnings of the process of European integration in a decisive way. These include the three "founding fathers" of the European Community, Adenauer, Degasperi ,and Schuman, and the "political-bureaucratic entrepreneur," Jean Monnet. Then, the changes in the national political systems of several large member states are investigated; with particular focus on the rise of party clientelism and corruption in some member countries and at the level of the EU. In the third and fourth section, we investigate the three most important groups of "European politicians," the members of the European Parliament, the commissioners and the members of the European Court of Justice.

3.1 How the charismatic founders of the EEC left their mark on later integration

After Second World War, three different ways of the recovery and further development of Europe were open (Loth 1996:9ff.). The first and most comprehensive was to try to develop Europe as a whole economically—with the inclusion of the central European countries occupied by the Soviet Union into the process of economic recovery. This was the core of the proposal of John Foster Dulles in 1947, which foresaw to support Europe with a massive financial program (the famous Marshall Plan). The second idea was to establish an integrated Europe as a "third force" between the new superpowers, the United States and the Soviet Union. This idea was proposed by West European Social Democrats, including the British Labour Party; its core would be an alliance between Britain and France. The third idea was to unite only those continental European countries which were not under Soviet occupation. This implied an acceptance of the new East-West division of Europe and to abandon Poland, the Czech Republic, Hungary, and all other east European countries to Soviet rule. This was the idea which in the end was realized. Today, it is often asserted that this was the only realistic way open. However, collective memories of this sort—to be differentiated from historical knowledge—are always connected with political power interests (J.-W. Müller 2002). Like every nation-state, the EU has also developed its "founding myth," which serves to legitimate present-day policies.

Four leading European politicians contributed definitely to this decisive position of points. A sociological analysis of their ideological, cultural, and political background and their decisions and actions is therefore of interest here, for several reasons: It helps to gain a more critical, historical-objective view of their positions and actions, and it throws a more comprehensive light on the origin and development of European integration.

Common characteristics of the three Catholic "founding fathers of Europe"

The first three political personalities or statesmen who were of decisive importance for the breakthrough of European integration through the establishment of the European Coal and Steel Community (ECSC) in 1952 were: French Foreign Minister Robert Schuman (1886–1963), German Chancellor Konrad Adenauer (1876–1967), and Italian Prime Minister Alcide Degasperi (1881–1954). Four characteristics are common to them: (1) They had been born between 1880 and 1890 and had experienced themselves the terrors of fascism during their adult age; (2) they all were Catholics; (3) they were fervid anti-Communists; (4) even if in principle democratic, they also showed considerable autocratic tendencies. These characteristics are closely related to each other. Since the formation of the socialist and Marxist movements in the nineteenth century, the Catholic Church was among their most fierce adversaries. This was so not the least because Marx and Engels had declared religion as the "opium for the people," that is, as an ideology which helps to mask and legitimize capitalist exploitation. After World War II, Christian Democratic parties rose to leading positions in many West European countries mainly because they were able to fill in the ideological vacuum which emerged after the fall of fascism and the proscription of communism in many western countries (Greschat and Loth 1994). All these parties were supporting West European integration, as was Pope Pius XII in a series of speeches and writings.

Catholicism contains two further components which help to understand its positive attitude to European integration but also the specific elitist form of this integration. One can be considered as rather positive; it is a universalistic stance which is contrary to narrow-minded nationalism and parochialism. Catholicism is usually not associated as closely with state authority as the protestant and orthodox Christian churches are; it is a truly universal religion, spread out over the whole world (Höllinger 1996). Another characteristic of Catholicism may. be considered as being less positive. It is the tendency of Catholic thinking to focus on tradition and dogma, hierarchy, and authority. The Christian dogma sees continuity between all institutions on earth; while the state as a secular institution is clearly subordinated to the holy church, it nevertheless derives its existence from God and part of the hierarchical structure of the cosmos (Hauser 1949). In Catholicism, this general stance expresses itself in the claim for absolute truth (infallibility of the pope), the distinguished position of the priest, the duty of the church members to believe and obey, and the rigid church hierarchy (Krämer 1973). Up to the nineteenth century, the Catholic Church was a definitive supporter of the old monarchical dynasties and estate structures (Maier 1983:23). Even in the first part of the twentieth century, the position of Catholicism toward the fascist dictatorships remained ambiguous. The rigid vertical structure of the Catholic Church and the insistence of the Vatican on being the final, definitive authority in all matters of social ethics and morale reflect this characteristic till today. All these characteristics are relevant for the form in which European integration took shape and developed later.

The oldest of the three political personalities was Konrad Adenauer (1876–1967), chancellor of the Federal Republic of Germany between 1949 and 1963. Already in the Weimar Republic, Adenauer had considerable political influence in German politics, as long-term major of Cologne (1917–1933), leading member of the catholic *Zentrumspartei*, and head of the Prussian *Staatsrat*[1] (Planitz 1975:47ff.). Since his youth, he was an opponent of Bismarck's great power politics. The National Socialists dismissed Adenauer from his offices, took away his properties (although he received a considerable state pension), and later on he could survive the regime only in Swiss exile. Already in the 1920s, Adenauer had developed the idea of a "West German Republic," which would establish lasting peaceful relations with France. This idea originated from his deep aversion toward Prussia, which dominated the Catholic Rhineland (Maier 1983). Abhorred characteristics of Prussia included its militarism, deification of the state, nationalism, and materialism (Greschat and Loth 1994:239).

The second most important political personality in the first phase of European integration was Robert Schuman (1886–1963). He was also engaged for a reconciliation between the states and peoples of Europe already in the interwar period as he was active in the Resistance against Hitler and his collaborators in France. Schuman, born in Luxembourg, had been a German citizen and soldier till the end of World War I; in 1919 he became a member of the French Assemble Nationale, in World War II vice state secretary for refugees. He was deported to Nazi Germany and could only evade his murder by escaping. The famous Schuman-Plan, sketched out by Jean Monnet, which intended the integration of French and German basic industries, laid down the basis for European integration. Schuman can be considered "more than the De Gaulle, even more than Adenauer and Degasperi," as the "father of Europe" (Debus 1995:28).

A third leading political personality of the immediate afterwar years was Alcide Degasperi (1881–1954), Italian prime minister 1945–1953. Originating from the Trentino, a former part of Tyrol and Austria, he had been parliamentary deputy already in the *Reichsrat* of the Habsburg monarchy in Vienna. After World War I, he became a member of the new catholic Partito Popolare of Don Luigi Sturzo. After its ban by Mussolini, he survived fascism as librarian in the Vatican. During Word War II, Degasperi cofounded the Democrazia Christiana (DC), which became the decisive political force in Italy till the early 1990s, when it was dissolved after the disclosure of a quagmire of corruption (Chubb and Vannicelli 1988). Degasperi was the first to support fully the Monnet-Schuman Plan, because he felt it necessary for Italy to take part in the process of European integration. This stance is typical for Italy till the present day (see Chapter 6).

It is often stated that the terrible experiences of fascism, National Socialism, and World War II have fundamentally changed the minds of the elites and peoples of Europe and made clear for them the necessity of a peaceful cohabitation and cooperation. From the viewpoint of the three political personalities presented before, this thesis is wrong. All of them had realized this necessity already in the interwar period. Given the circumstances at that time (deep economic crisis, unemployment, rise of fascist governments to power in Italy and Germany), their ideas came, so to speak, too early.

Let us now look more closely at the four characteristics shared by these three men. The first was their Catholic worldview. That this was a decisive determinant is very clear for Robert Schuman. He was much more than just a practising Catholic (Debus 1995:12ff.): He was active

Photo 3a   Two architects of European integration: Jean Monnet (left) and Robert Schuman.

Source: European Community, Audiovisual Service.

Photo 3b   April 18, 1951: The foreign ministers of the six founding countries sign the Treaty of Paris (ECSC): Paul van Zeeland, Joseph Bech, Carlo Sforza, Robert Schuman, Konrad Adenauer (German Chancellor and Foreign Minister), Dirk Uipko Stikker (from left to right).

Source: European Community, Audiovisual Service.

as leader of diocesan youth and co-organiser of the meeting of Catholics in Metz in 1913. After the death of his beloved mother in 1910, he considered exchanging his lawyer robe for that of a priest; in his old years, he followed a monastic way of life, dedicated to reading and praying. As a man, Schuman was extremely modest and engaged in social affairs (he remained unmarried). However, he avoided letting his religious views influence his political actions, as he tried to avoid political games of power and intrigue.

Also, Alcide Degasperi was a decided Catholic religious person. Coming from a very Catholic province, he became member and cofounder of the two influential Catholic parties, as mentioned before. Since his youth, Degasperi maintained close personal connections with church leaders, including the pope. In his student time, he was president of the Associazione Catholica Universitaria Trentina. Finally, Konrad Adenauer was also a practising Catholic who conducted a life without any scandals, connected closely to his wife (who died much earlier) and his large family. Like Schuman, he also tried to distinguish clearly between the religious and the political sphere and rebutted attempts by church leaders to intervene into politics. An important success of Adenauer was the political reconciliation between Catholics and Protestants in Germany by establishing the new, inclusive party Christlich-Demokratische Union (CDU). This was probably one of the main reasons for the much higher countability and stability of the political life in the Federal Republic of Germany compared to the Weimar Republic.

There exist also indirect confirmations for the thesis that the Catholic background was decisive for the aims of European integration at this period. One was the attitude of a second leading German politician, the popular minister for economic affairs in Adenauer's government, Ludwig Erhard. Erhard, educated as a protestant, was an outspoken opponent against the form of integration which was foreseen by the four politicians mentioned before (Hentschel 1996:228ff.; Bandulet 1999:45). Direct market regulations, subsidies, and anything which smelled of a "planned economy" were condemned by Erhard (see Erhard 1957). In fact, such elements were clearly present both in the ECSC and the EEC, as will be shown in the next chapter. The other indication for the fact that Catholicism was central in this first phase was that serious reservations about political integration came from that country where Protestantism has been very influential, namely, the Netherlands (Greschat and Loth 1994:109).

Adenauer and Degasperi shared a second characteristic, that is, their autocratic attitudes and behaviours, sometimes problematic from a democratic point of view. About Adenauer, this characteristic is well-known. His inclination toward making decisions alone and often in an autocratic way once almost cost him his reelection as mayor of Cologne. He showed the same behaviour as chancellor, which led a biographer to call the Federal Republic under his leadership an "autocracy" (Planitz 1975:134; Maier

1983:338 ff.). The highly respected German philosopher Karl Jaspers wrote that Adenauer's style of leadership contributed significantly to the continuity of an authoritarian and submissive way of political life in postwar Germany (Jaspers 1966).

Adenauer's counterpart in Italy, Alcide Degasperi, was very successful insofar as he led the Democrazia Christiana (DC) to become the leading political party in postwar Italy (48% of the votes in 1948). This, however, was achieved at the cost of a rather aggressive and spiteful election campaign in which the Italian Communist Party PCI (which had large support among the population) was slandered as paving the way for a Soviet-style Communist regime (Procacci 1983:386ff.). At the same time, also critical and liberal forces of the political centre who were ready to support reforms were more or less excluded. Thereby, the foundation was laid for the political dominance of the DC for decades, which ended abruptly in 1992 when its deep involvement in clientelism and corruption was uncovered. (We will come back to this below.) Very negative consequences had also the fact that the unitarian labour union CGIL was smashed; also in this regard, Catholic Italian circles and American forces cooperated (Alf 1977:96). By creating three labour unions distinguished along confessional-political lines (a Communist, socialist, and Christian union), the basis for the "Italian sickness" of excessive industrial strikes was established.

In these events, a third characteristic came to the fore which was typical for Adenauer and Degasperi. In Germany, militant anticommunism had a long tradition since the times of World War I. In 1919, the Communist leaders Karl Liebknecht and Rosa Luxemburg were murdered in Berlin, not the least because of their agitation against Germany's participation in the World War I. The fight against the Communist Party continued during the Weimar Republic when it was outlawed by all bourgeois parties. In Chapter 6, it will be shown that the inability of the German centre and right parties to cooperate with social democrats and Communists was the main cause for the seizing of power by the National Socialists. After 1945, Adenauer continued this hard politics against the Kommunistische Partei Deutschlands (KPD), which had been reestablished in all four occupied zones with the consent of the occupying forces.[2] Adenauer denounced also the Social Democrats, which he declared to be the ideological brothers of communism. In 1956, the Bundesverfassungsgericht, after Adenauer's insistence, forbade the KPD. The consequence of the sentence was an estimated 150,000 to 200,000 judicial procedures against persons who often had only very peripheral or no relations at all to the KPD. The public, the media, and critical intellectuals criticised the verdict strongly as contradicting democratic principles, and Adenauer personally was accused of having exerted pressure on the BVG.

The fight against communism was a decisive element also of Alcide Degasperi's politics as prime minister (1945–1953). In the immediate postwar years, the Communists—distinguished by their resistance against fascism—had become part of the government and contributed to the elaboration of a quite revolutionary constitution. (See Chapter 8, where some elements of it are compared with the proposed Constitution for Europe.) In 1948, however, and under American pressure, Degasperi—by pointing to the "terrible threat" of the Volksfront (Malgeri 1982:103) and the suppression of people in the USSR—was able to win the elections by a wide margin (Procacci 1983:387). In this period, he continued his efforts to bring the DC into a hegemonic position. He saw this as necessary and he used all tactical means "without complexes and hesitations" (Malgeri 1982:109).

The following conclusions can be drawn from this short sketch of these three European politicians of the "first hour." On the one side, Adenauer, Degasperi, and Schuman can really be considered as outstanding, charismatic politicians due to their resistance to fascism, their personal integrity, their firm political-ideological convictions, and their far-reaching political decisions. At a time when the blockade of Berlin by the USSR showed the threat of a third world war, and when considerable mistrust between the former war adversaries (France and England against Germany) persisted, it was certainly a historical achievement to create trust and a close cooperation between them. Thus, it was deserved that Adenauer, Degasperi, and Schuman all were awarded the *Karlspreis* of the city of Aachen. However, there are some other sides of these politicians (this is true more for Adenauer and Degasperi than for Schuman) which have to be evaluated critically and which have paved the way also for the problematic, elitist way of further European integration. One was their often rather authoritarian and discriminatory-exclusionary behaviour in regard to leftist parties. The other was their decision to accept and to consolidate the East-West division of Europe along the Iron Curtain and to integrate Western Europe firmly into the western part of the new bipolar power blocs. From this point of view, the highly praised "reunification of Europe" 1989/90 and 2004 in fact has not restored some old "unified Europe" (which has never existed in history). Rather, it has only abolished a division which was created just by the process of integration of West Europe itself.

Jean Monnet: An elitist political-bureaucratic entrepreneur and spin doctor

Quite a different kind of political personality was the French Jean Monnet (1888–1979), who was probably not less decisive for the successful "takeoff" of European integration than the three political personalities presented in the foregoing section (Morgan 1992).[3] Monnet was a very successful "spin doctor" for many politicians in the first half of the twentieth century. Also, his personality, ideas, and action strategies exhibit several characteristics which became highly relevant for the character which the new community would assume in the decades to come.[4] The analysis of these characteristics can also explain why Jean Monnet was much more successful than other "Europeanists" of the time, including count Couden-hove-Kalergi with his older and more broadly based Paneuropa movement. Monnet kept distance to these movements and had some disdain for their populism. He was no "visionary" but "an elitist and pragmatist," without any party affiliation, motivated only "by the remorseless ideology of efficiency" (Dinan 1999:11). Monnet was also capable of "inspiring incredible devotion among those who worked with him" (Spierenburg and Poidevin 1994:78), as he himself was a very hard worker.

Monnet was born in 1888 in Cognac, a small French town, famous for its unique alcoholic product. In his family, two ideological influences were present: His mother and a sister were devout Catholics; the father was a "radical socialist," which means that he was rather liberal and anticlerical. It seems that the son took more after his father than his mother. Quite relevant is Jean Monnet's experience as an independent businessman connected with extensive travels and stops abroad. Early, at the age of 16, he went for two years to London for an apprenticeship. Here, he got firsthand knowledge of English language and life—certainly quite untypical for a young Frenchman of this time. In his youth he continued his father's business. Later, between 1922 and 1932, he acted as managing partner of the European branch of the American bank Blair & Co. and as a financial adviser for American firms. Until World War I, he continued to travel to England and the United States, to Scandinavia, Russia, and Egypt. These travel experiences and an extensive knowledge of foreign countries, especially of the Anglo-Saxon world, were certainly a significant incentive for the political interests and activities of Jean Monnet; nearly all of them were aiming toward establishing international reconciliation and cooperation. At the beginning of World War I, he developed the idea of a cooperation in the provision of military equipment between France and England. He also helped to establish a connection of France to the Hudson Bay Company for the import of vital civil goods (e.g., grain) from North America. Later on, he took part in the establishment of the Allied Maritime Transport Council. After the war, Monnet became a vice secretary general of The League of Nations. Later, in the face of the Second World War, Monnet resumed his activities of international political coordination: First, he organised the rearmament of the French air force; then, he became president of a French-English Committee of Coordination of resources. Toward the end of war, he developed the Plan Monnet, which aimed at the economic reconstruction of France and became institutionalized in the Commissariat General du Plan with Monnet as president. Then, in 1950, he developed, together with French Foreign Minister Robert Schuman, the most successful and momentous Schuman Plan[5] which proposed that France and Germany integrate their coal and steel industries. This plan was realized in 1950— together with the Benelux countries and Italy—as the European Coal and Steel Community (ECSC). Jean Monnet became the first president of the directorate, the "High Authority"—the nucleus of the bureaucracy of the

European Community. Even after his voluntary demission as president of the High Authority in 1955, he founded the "Action Committee for the United States of Europe"—a movement which operated under Monnet's direction for twenty years (see also Middlemas 1995:31). Monnet never held a formal political office as an elected politician or as a bureaucrat (except the four-year period as ECSC president). The foregoing short sketch of the personality and the action strategies of Jean Monnet exhibits five characteristics which characterize the European Union till today. Let us look shortly at each of them.

First, European integration and the establishment of the ECSC were clearly an elitist "creation from above" with no involvement of the people and only a post hoc involvement of their elected representatives, the parliaments (see also Dinan 1999:14). After World War II, manifold movements for peace and integration all over Europe were active (Jost 1999:49–60). All these movements, however, were a matter of the better educated and politically active people. Monnet's plans and actions had a clearly elitist character. He developed his plans with carefully selected, small and closed, sworn groups of advisers and fellow combatants. The plans were then proposed directly to leading political personalities to whom Monnet had developed personal contacts. As long as he did not have the support of these politicians, the plans were strictly kept as a secret in order to avoid a negative public discussion. This strategy is stressed again and again in his biography (Monnet 1988:375ff.; Spierenburg and Poidevin 1994:10). Democratic procedures played only a secondary, corrective function in the Monnet-Schuman plan (if any at all). In this regard, he had a stance similar to Adenauer and Degasperi. Also, the parliamentary ratification process for the ECSC, which lasted somewhat more than a year in the member countries, does not show him as a highly committed democrat: "I don't believe that the claim for democratic control justifies the fuzziness or toughness of parliamentary procedures which have their own rites and their own rhythms" (Monnet 1988:458). In all these regards, Monnet's project appeared as an heir to his great compatriot Saint-Simon as he aimed at "a kind of Saint-Simonean modernization of Europe" (Siedentop 2001:33). There are also surprising similarities with his compatriot Jacques Delors, the outstanding later president of the European Commission.

The second characteristic of Monnet is closely related to the first. Maybe as an alternative to democratic procedures, Monnet saw a main strategy for pursuing far-reaching political reforms and innovations in the *strategy of persuasion*. It was said explicitly about him that he was a "conjurer" (Monnet 1988:418). He stresses that persuasion can be a very strong and efficient strategy if "the force of simple ideas is at stake and if these ideas are repeated again and again" (ibid.). Also in this regard, Monnet anticipated a central and very important strategy of the EC/EU up to this day. By distributing vast quantities of brochures and booklets, by carrying out public relations campaigns before important elections and referenda, by supporting information bureaus in all member states, the EU tries to compensate for the low interest of people in its affairs and the lack of direct contact between citizens in the member states and the EU offices in Brussels.

The third characteristic of Monnet is that he developed many different plans of international cooperation and integration. This *flexibility and inventiveness* was one of the keys for the eventual success of the plan for the ECSC. Monnet was often in a position to be able to present a plan if circumstances were favourable: "To be frank, our initiatives were often successful because there were no competitors" (Monnet 1988:420). One reason why the plan for the ECSC was successful was also because it proposed only a modest clearly circumscribed economic cooperation with a small administrative unit. Thus, it was much more easily acceptable by the governments than a plan of a far-reaching political integration. This flexibility in developing many different plans, adapted to the circumstances (in terms of economic and political situation, public opinion, and the like), is a basic characteristic of the working of the European Union till today. The Union usually does not develop broad and coherent plans for integration but operates in a piecemeal fashion, proposing some new measure, looking at public reactions, and realising it if no serious critique is coming about, as the premier of Luxembourg, Jean Claude Juncker, once remarked. In this way, many innovations are realised without much discussion of or even without acknowledgment by the public.

Fourth, with the High Authority, a *bureaucratic, independent agency* was installed whose competences were superimposed upon national governments. The establishment of this authority and the securing of its independence vis-à-vis national governments was the central point of the Monnet-Schuman plan. By establishing this authority as a stable institution, the process of integration would acquire its own, irreversible dynamic, independent from the goodwill and action of individual personalities Monnet correctly expected (Fontaine 2000:19; Salmon 2002). The establishment of this High Authority was in fact the most consequential feature of the Monnet-Schuman plan; as will be shown in Chapter 5, its successor, the European Commission, is developing continuously, to a size hardly imagined by Monnet. He wrote in this regard: "I was determined to develop the High Authority into an apparatus as slight as possible. The first nucleus would grow only to the extent that the tasks traced it out" (Monnet 1988:469). However, here Monnet hardly was aware of the momentum which such a bureaucracy can develop (Mazey 1992:31; Page and Wouters 1995). Most illuminating is a story which he reports in his autobiography. At the time of his voluntary demission as president of the High Authority, he was reminded that he had lost a bet; a colleague told him that he had said after assumption of office: "If one day we [the High Authority] will be more than 200 persons, our endeavour was a failure" (Monnet 1988:515; Page and Wouters 1995:191). In fact, the size of the High Authority had increased already by sixfold!

A fifth important characteristic of Monnet's plan (as of all of his earlier political activities) was its focus on *economic cooperation*. The proposal to put the coal and steel industries of France and Germany under a common administration was also in the interest of the enterprises of these industrial sectors; the large French coal-mining sector needed the strong German steel industry as a cooperation partner and vice versa (see Chapter 4). A central element of this narrow and modest focus, however, is the idea of a functional "spillover" of integration from one area—the production of coal and steel—to other areas of economic and later also noneconomic areas and life. This spillover, Monnet argued, would take place only in a very slow and unspectacular way. However, in the long run it would lead to comprehensive integration and to the rise of a new Europe-wide feeling of solidarity (Monnet 1988:382). However, Monnet had no concrete vision of how the final state of this integrated Europe would look, except from the general aim of an ever closer integration (Middlemas 1995:615f.).

3.2 Changes in the structures and workings of politics in western Europe, 1950–2000

The early 1950s, when the foundations for European integration were laid in some way, still represented an "old world" with politicians who had been active already in the decades before. However, in the erstwhile fascist countries, new political institutions and parties were established which laid the basis for a more democratic and ordered political life than had existed during the 1920s and 1930s. Moreover, most people were fully engaged with restoring their possessions and enterprises or with building up new ones for which the *Wirtschaftswunder* opened up ample opportunities. In this climate, the charismatic political personalities sketched out before and their political actions and strategies were not challenged. The situation changed fundamentally in the course of 1960s and 1970s. The student revolts were only the beginning of deep-going changes and a process of transformation of the old sociocultural and political system. A look at these changes helps us to understand better the relations between the elites and citizens today, both in the national and the European context.

Erosion of confidence in political institutions and elites

In many countries, political majorities shifted from the Christian and conservative parties to the left; new parties at the far left and right spectrum, and some with wholly new programs—such as the Greens—appeared; the traditional form of the political party—ideological committed to a certain program, equipped with an extensive apparatus and anchored in particular segments of voters—began to dissolve itself. This was a consequence of changes among the electorate (rise in the levels of education and women's employment, transition to postindustrial society) and of the rise of radio and TV as the new, dominant media of mass communication (Gellner and Veen 1995). Most evident was this change among the large parties of the left; the socialist parties eliminated the militant vocabulary of class conflict from their programmes and made them acceptable for the large political centre (Giddens 1998). The voters became more discriminating in their decisions; many became *Wechselwähler,* who change their votes from election to election, depending on personalities and programmes offered. As a consequence of all these changes, citizens today are much more critical of their political elites and the workings of the democratic systems. An "erosion of confidence" in public institutions took place, including all large-scale organisations and associations, such as unions and churches, but in particular the political institutions and parties. This phenomenon is persistent and international; it has structural reasons concerning all important institutions, and it has not only an emotional or ideological but a rational-pragmatic character (Dogan 2005:4ff.; Brechon 2004).

European integration, which after 1992 acquired more and more a political character, was certainly affected by these trends. In the reconciliation between the European states, the transition from national mistrust to mutual confidence was certainly a very positive trend, compensating in some way for the increasing distrust of politics within the nation-states (Dogan 2005:31). However, increasing trust between the European peoples did not translate itself into an increasing trust into the EC/ EU institutions (Reichel 1984:292ff.). The way in which the process of European integration itself was framed might have contributed to an increasing critical stance of many citizens toward the political institutions and elites both at home and in Brussels. European politics today cannot be separated neatly anymore from national politics. People's satisfaction or dissatisfaction with national politics can also be determined by political measures coming from Brussels.

At the background of these general considerations, we will document in the following the emergence of political scandals in many EU member countries and at the level of the EU Commission in Brussels itself. Three general arguments shall be substantiated with this presentation: (1) The European Union and particularly the European Commission is open to political misbehaviour and corruption not less than many of their member states, in spite of frequent assertions to the contrary (see Chapter 5); it is also to be expected given the fact that corruption is a worldwide phenomenon, by far not restricted to the less developed countries (Roniger and Günes-Ayata 1994); (2) EU membership of a country with a badly functioning political system and administration will not automatically abolish these practices; rather, bad practices at the level of the member states frequently spill over to the EU; (3) the increasing distrust of the citizens of their political institutions is not only a negative fact, and the emergence of political scandals also opens up a way for a reform of the political systems at the national and the EU level.

Rise of party clientelism and corruption in Catholic south and central Europe

In the course of the 1990s, in all large EU member states of Catholic Central and South Europe, massive scandals of political parties were uncovered with high political personalities involved. These facts have certainly contributed to the decreasing trust in politics and politicians at the national but possibly also at the European level. These scandals are shortly sketched out in the following not only in order to show how badly many politicians behave today. Rather, from the sociological point of view, we look at political corruption and scandals from a more differentiated, even "constructive," point of view (Markovits and Silverstein 1988). Newspapers, TV-networks, and others may have an interest in detecting and "producing" scandals because it increases their sales. So may the enemies of a political group or institution because it provides them with ammunition. We cannot argue that the occurrence of political scandals will necessarily undermine the legitimacy of a political system. A political scandal is the revelation of corruption and its denouncing in public. The way in which scandals come into being gives a special insight into the workings of a political system, both from the macro- and microperspective. In order to get such insights, we have to take into account the two social functions and meanings of scandals (Markovits and Silverstein 1988:2ff.).

From a Durkheimian perspective, the detection and public impeaching of norm-breaching behaviour strengthens a community's *conscience collective,* its common moral norms; it also helps to create scapegoats and enemies needed by all communities, and it aids social processes of legitimation and mass mobilization. Corruption and its detection through scandals are also closely related to the political system and the power structure of a society. In liberal democracies, there is a tension between the liberal pole—which aims at restricting state power as much as possible—and the democratic pole, which aims at providing possibilities for participation and equality of all. Scandals can occur only in liberal democracies, and their essence consists in a transgression of the distinction between the private and the public, which is essential to democracies. The critical feature of a scandal is not the absolute level of corruption, the personal gain, or the normative merit of the ends, but "the presence of any activity that seeks to increase political power at the expense of [democratic, transparent] process and procedure" (Markovits and Silverstein 1988:5).

Italy got off to a dramatic start in 1992, when legal authorities in Milan opened investigations against several thousands of politicians, businessmen, managers, judges, and district attorneys because of corruption and the illegal financing of political parties. One of the main personalities accused was the prime minister Bettino Craxi; against him investigations were started in 40 cases of corruption; he was convicted, as were two former ministers (Fischer Weltalmanach 1996:360ff.). In 1994, over 6,000

persons were under judicial investigation, including 335 deputies, 100 sen-
ators, 453 regional and provincial, and 1,524 municipal councillors, 973
entrepreneurs, and 1,373 civil servants (Dogan 2005:40). Nearly a whole
political class, the well-established partitocrazia, had been decapitated.
As a consequence of this scandal, the two largest parties, the Democrazia
Cristiana (DC) and the Partito Communista Italiano (PCI), were dissolved.
The scandal and its solution, however, were also the beginning of the rise
of the elusive personality, businessman, and media owner Silvio Berlusconi.
He twice became Italian prime minister (1994–1995 and 2001–2006),
for the second time in spite of the fact that massive accusations had been
made against him because of his democratically suspect media power and
his dubious business relations, which included persons in the orbit of the
Mafia. Berlusconi was accused several times of offering bribes to public
officers and illegal party financing. In many of them, he could ward off further accusations and convictions only by using his parliamentary majority
to change the corresponding laws (Veltri and Travaglio 2001). While these
events were unique in Europe, they were not so surprising in Italy. This is
one of the European countries most highly susceptible to corruption, as
captured in the Italian term *tangentopoli* (bribe republic), and it was closely
connected with the penetration of party influence in many sectors of public life, as expressed in the book title *La Repubblica dei Partiti* (Scoppola
1991). The deterioration of the political system had been accelerated since
the 1960s; the proportion of Italians who had a negative opinion of the dignity and honesty of their rulers rose from 33% to 70% within a few years
(Dogan 2005:50). Since the mid-seventies, links between the Sicilian Mafia
(which at this time gained a dominant position in the international drug
trade) and certain sectors of the Italian political elite were strengthened
(Chubb and Vannicelli 1988; Ginsborg 2004).

Another EU member state long characterised by a high level of political
corruption is *France*. Already in the course of the 1990s, thirty persons
were accused of corruption, including top managers and ministers.[6] Massive
political scandals came to light in this country in 2000. After continuous
accusations, seldom pursued by the courts, judicial inquiries were opened
in connection with financial machinations involving the state-owned petroleum enterprise Elf. The foreign minister, Roland Dumas, the governor
of the Banque Nationale de France, J. C. Trichet, and the former prime
minister and EU commissioner, Edith Cresson, were impeached because of
the suspicion of fraud.[7] Dumas and three other persons were convicted in
2003, in addition to thirty-seven managers and intermediaries involved in
the scandal. The state corporation Elf was founded by de Gaulle in 1963 in
order to secure France's independence in the provision with petroleum. The
company established close relations particularly with Africa, by supporting
also dubious political-military operations of the president. Later on, President Mitterrand reestablished political control of the company, which continued to interfere in politics by financing political parties and candidates

with his approval. Documents of a deceased estate agent and politician also aroused a high degree of suspicion of President Jacques Chirac because of illegal financing of his party. It was stated that during Chirac's long-standing office as mayor of Paris, money destined for public building works was diverted on a large scale to party coffers; through bank accounts in Switzerland, more than 600 billion FF allegedly went to party caches.[8] Jacques Chirac is the person most "representative" for the more recent French system of clientelism and corruption. Since his early career, when he established close relations with industrialists, he was involved in politically dubious activities, including support of criminal potentates in Africa, and business activities, including the delivery of equipment for atomic power plants to dictators like Saddam Hussein. The author of a comprehensive work on these activities asks: How was it possible that the French have elected and tolerated a president who was "a personality responsible or accomplice of so many delicts and crimes, of economic and political nature, at the national and international level?" (Verschave 2002:267).

In the mid-nineties, the long-standing socialist government of Felipe Gonzales in *Spain* came under strong political pressure because of involvement in many affairs and scandals.[9] Among them was an affair around a case of state terrorism (a dirty underground war) in the context of the public fight against the militant Basque underground movement ETA; secret service, high public officials, and politicians were involved.

Finally, even in the politically rather stable and much less corruption-inclined *Federal Republic of Germany*, a scandal related to party financing came to light which laid the long-standing chancellor, Helmut Kohl, open to suspicion.[10] In connection with investigations against the former treasurer of the Christlich-Demokratische Union (CDU) for tax evasion, it was found that Kohl had maintained accounts of illegal money for the party. Kohl resigned as honorary president of his party; the CDU was sentenced to pay a restitution of 42 billions DM. Compared to accusations against top Italian and French politicians, the misconduct of Kohl was rather minor. In fact, French newspapers sharply criticized this scandal but not Kohl's actions as such but rather their bagging by the media. However, this inglorious end of an outstanding political career appears also significant from the viewpoint of the legitimacy of the political elites in Germany and Europe. Kohl, with his often propagated basic virtues of "fatherland, sense of duty, love for the home country, diligence" (Leydendecker et al. 2000:21), had been the epitome of the new, reliable, and serious German statesman for decades. However, he was already suspected in the early 1980s. Then, it became known that he was one of the main receivers of illegal donations from the businessman Friedrich Flick (the largest shareholder of the Daimler Benz Company). Three critical biographies described Kohl as a power-hungry man since his first political steps; already as party leader and minister president of the *Bundesland* Rheinland-Pfalz he had established a tight personal political network (Leydendecker et al. 2000).

But the problem was not only the Kohl System which was so problematic but the whole development of the political parties in Germany. All over Europe, but particularly in Germany, political parties needed more and more money for their administrative apparatuses, expensive public relations, and election campaigns. Since the contributions of members were declining, other sources of income had to be sought: They were found in public financing and in contributions of strong financial groups and corporations. Public financing of parties has been established early by law in Germany and is particularly important there (Nassmacher 1982, 1992). At the same time, the influence of political parties was increasing during the 1980s and 1990s in the allocation of public contracts and top jobs. The parties reacted toward the tightening up of laws concerning the financing also "with refined methods of laundering illegal donations and with continuous unscrupulousness" (Leydendecker et al. 2000:21). Sociologists Erwin and Ute Scheuch (1992) diagnosed, based on an empirical study, a "feudalisation of the political system": Successful politicians rally around them large clans of vassals, and they see that they get what they need (jobs, offices, subsidies, etc.; see also Scholz 1995; Rudzio 1995; von Arnim 2000). It becomes less and less important whether a party takes part in government or not since in a proportional democracy also opposition parties can take parts of the cake. It is not surprising, therefore, that not only the German Christian Conservative Party, but also the Liberal and Social Democratic Parties in earlier times, were involved in scandals of illegal party financing and money laundering. This issue was taken up by the German weekly magazine *Der Spiegel* in a recent cover story giving their country the same title as Italian journalists gave to theirs: "The Republic of Bribery."[11]

Earthquake in Brussels. The disclosure of clientelism and corruption in the EU Commission

Most relevant for the split between elites and populations concerning European integration, however, may have been a scandal which rocked the leaders and institutions of the Union directly. For years, accusations of nepotism and corruption against particular members of the EU Commission had been made. In 1999, the European Parliament set up an independent investigating committee. Its report was a shock for the commission: It revealed massive irregularities in several development programmes (for instance, in the programme *Leonardo da Vinci* for further education) and cases of nepotism and favouritism. It also showed that in cases of irregularities, which had become known internally, no investigations had been initiated; instead, the officials involved were honourably discharged with generous compensations. The main excuse of the commission—not to have known anything about these affairs—itself came under attack; the committee argued that these assertions themselves were proof of the fact that the commission had lost control over administration (Bandulet 1999:224).

Also, the European Audit Office again and again had denounced short-comings in the administration and control of the EU budget. In the Annual Report of 1998 it stated that about 5% of all payments were erroneous due to administrative errors and fraud; this was true particularly in the areas of agriculture and structure policy (Fischer Weltalmanach 2001:1080).

As a consequence of this report, the whole commission was forced to resign on March 16, 1999. Most remarkable in this affair was the fact that all the commissioners directly involved in cases of mismanagement and nepotism originated from the southwest Catholic EU members states. The commissioner most incriminated was the French Edith Cresson, formerly prime minister of France under President Mitterand. She had instructed, for instance, her dentist to carry out well-paid scientific expertises for which he did not have any qualifications. Cresson felt in no way guilty, which is understandable since she did nothing other than transplant a piece of French political culture to Brussels (Bandulet 1999:22). Two further commissioners accused were the Spaniard Manuel Marin and the Portuguese Joao de Deus Pinheiro. The thesis that in this case the "political culture" of the southwest European, Catholic countries had been transplanted to Brussels is also proven by the fact that less than 15% of the Italian, Spanish, and Portuguese members of the European Parliament opted to vote out the whole commission, but 65–76% of those from Denmark and Sweden, and 93% of those from Germany. The person who deserves most credit for the disclosure of the whole affair was the Dutch EU officer Paul van Buitenen; as a consequence of his integrity, he was put under heavy pressure by his superiors (Bandulet 1999:16ff.).

This scandal was only the most spectacular among many other, less spectacular incidents of fraud and corruption at the level of the central offices of the EU and in the member states in their function as receivers and distributors of EU subsidies. Particularly in the area of agricultural subsidies, many kinds of misuse of means, of false informations provided in order to get subsidies, of exports to countries which serve only as formal receivers, fraud and corruption are a continuous problem which creates a lot of work for the EU Court of Audit and the newly created Anti-Fraud Office OLAF. In its 2005 report, this office found a total number of 12,076 irregularities, with a financial impact of 1.042 billions of euros.[12] In the most recent report (2006), a further increase is noted.[13] An additional billion euros disappears at the level of member states.

What can we conclude from these analyses? It seems that the three theses proposed at the beginning of this section have been fully confirmed. First, it is out of question that the phenomena of clientelism and corruption are spreading out not only among some of the oldest and largest member states of the EU, but also at the level of the EU institutions in Brussels and elsewhere.

Second, also the thesis that the phenomena of clientelism and corruption are spreading out from the countries more accessible to them to the EU has been confirmed fully. However, what is evidently also happening is that bad practices are spreading out from these countries to Brussels itself. This problem will become aggravated in the years to come. In 2004, many states became members of the EU which are characterized by rather high levels of corruption at home. The 2006 *Corruption Perception Index* shows that EU member countries like Poland and Bulgaria, and candidate countries like Croatia and Turkey, have a higher level of corruption than Tunisia or Namibia, the Dominican Republic or Costa Rica.

Finally, this neglect of a very important political problem among students of the EU is not only a problem of a scientific bias, but has also negative practical implications in two regards. The detection of scandals has also positive aspects; it can—and usually does—initialise a reform process. This has in fact happened in many member countries of the EU. Businessmen, politicians, and bureaucrats are now much more careful in the relations to each other; legal prescriptions have been decreed in many countries concerning donations to political parties, their size, obligations to publication, and the like. Also, at the level of the EU, such reform processes have been initiated. The most important was the establishment of an independent Anti-Fraud Office (OLAF), which investigates cases of fraud and corruption within the EU institutions. Another serious consequence of the neglect of the problems of fraud and corruption among social scientists is that the high level of dissatisfaction with European integration among the general public cannot be explained adequately. That these two problems are correlated closely to each other shall be shown in the following section.

Clientelism as a main factor reducing citizens' satisfaction with the workings of democracy

It can be expected that phenomena of clientelism, corruption, and fraud in connection with politics and public services have a significant impact on the judgement of the citizens about the quality of their democracies. People in countries with high levels of corruption could expect that the EU brings an improvement in this regard; those in countries with low levels of corruption might see more problems at the level of the EU. The rather high scepticism regarding European integration in the United Kingdom, the Scandinavian countries, and Austria could well be connected with this problem; people could expect that the bad practices of some countries are taken over also by the EU.

We can test this hypothesis more or less directly. In the Eurobarometer, a question is asked about the satisfaction with democracy at the level of one's own state and at the level of the EU. The question was: "On the whole, are you very satisfied, fairly satisfied, not very satisfied or not at all satisfied with the way democracy works in [our country/the European Union]." In all twenty-seven member states, the proportions very satisfied with democracy in one's own country were 9%, satisfied 47%, not very satisfied 30%

and 11% not satisfied at all. Concerning satisfaction with democracy at the level of the EU, the corresponding figures were 6%, 44%, 26%, and 8%. Thus, a majority (56%) is satisfied with democracy at home and half with democracy at the level of the EU. Thus, satisfaction with democracy at the national level is higher than that at the EU level. There are significant differences between the old and new members, however. Among the fifteen old member states, 59% were satisfied with their own democracy (including the two categories "very satisfied" and "satisfied"), at the level of the EU only 49%. In the ten new member states, the situation is quite different: Here, 49% are satisfied with their own democracy, but 60% with that at the level of the EU. This is a first confirmation of the hypothesis presented before. It can also be confirmed when we look at the single countries.

Although, in general, there seems no clear connection between the two variables,[14] this emerges, however, rather clearly if we look at specific groups of countries. In Table 3.1, the countries have been grouped according the level of satisfaction in the two dimensions; also, the candidate countries Croatia and Turkey have been included. Here we can see that eight groups are distinguished by specific patterns; in addition, two countries (Italy and Portugal) show a particular pattern. The country groups are: (1) People in the three Benelux countries and Ireland are characterized by a very high level of satisfaction with their own democracy, as well as with that of the EU. However, also in these cases, satisfaction with national democracy is clearly higher than that with the EU democracy, particularly so in Denmark and Luxembourg. (2) The two Scandinavian countries, Austria and the Netherlands, show a rather high satisfaction with democracy, but a satisfaction with the EU which is below average; the difference between national and EU satisfaction with democracy is the largest in this group among all twenty-nine countries compared. (3) The three largest member countries, the United Kingdom, France, and Germany, show an average level of satisfaction with democracy at home (it is higher in the UK, but lower in France), and a satisfaction with the EU, which is clearly below average. (4) The next group includes three Mediterranean countries (Spain, Malta, Cyprus); here, satisfaction with national democracy is above average, but so is that with the EU; still, the first is higher than the latter. (5) This pattern changes from this group on. In Malta, Estonia, and Turkey, satisfaction with national democracy and with the EU is at about the same (intermediate) level. (6) Next come the more developed east central European countries (Czech Republic etc.); here, there exists clearly a higher estimation of the quality of democracy at the level of the EU than at home. (7) The same is true, even more marked, for the last two groups, Lithuania, Slovakia, and Croatia and Romania and Bulgaria. In these countries, the quality of the national democracy is evaluated very negatively (only about one fourth are satisfied with it), but satisfaction with EU democracy is much higher (between 43% and 55% satisfied). (8) Finally, there are two exceptional cases. Contrary to all other old member countries, the Italians and the Portuguese are more satisfied with democracy at the level of the EU than at the level of their home

Table 3.1.   Satisfaction with Democracy in One's Own Country and in the EU and Levels of Corruption in the EU Member and Candidate Countries (2006).

Countries	Satisfaction with democracy (% satisfied)			Corruption index 2006
	Own country	EU	Difference	
Denmark	93	65	28	9.5
Luxembourg	83	63	20	8.6
Ireland	75	65	10	7.4
Belgium	68	67	1	7.3
Finland	78	42	36	9.6
Sweden	74	45	29	9.2
Austria	75	45	30	8.6
Netherlands	75	47	18	8.7
United Kingdom	60	40	20	8.6
Germany	55	43	12	8.0
France	45	40	5	7.4
Spain	71	60	9	6.8
Cyprus	63	54	9	5.6
Greece	55	52	3	4.4
Malta	48	49	−1	6.4
Turkey	50	49	1	6.4
Estonia	43	47	−4	6.7
Italy	53	58	−5	4.9
Czech Republic	58	64	−6	4.8
Slovenia	54	65	−11	6.4
Hungary	46	60	−14	5.2
Latvia	41	53	−13	4.7
Poland	38	62	−24	3.7
Portugal	30	39	−9	6.6
Lithunia	23	47	−24	4.8
Slovakia	25	43	−18	4.7
Croatia	22	43	−21	3.4
Romania	27	55	−28	3.1
Bulgaria	22	54	−32	4.0
Mean value	56	50		

Source: Eurobarometer 65 (Spring 2006).

country. This is not very surprising in the case of Italy, taking into account the facts presented earlier.

It is also quite evident that that there exists a close correlation between levels of corruption and the satisfaction with democracy. In Table 3.1, also objective levels of corruption in the EU member countries and candidate countries are reported. If we go from the upper to the lower part of the table—which implies a decreasing satisfaction with one's own democracy—levels of corruption are increasing more or less regularly. Corruption is significantly lower in all West European countries—except Italy—where satisfaction with democracy is rather high, but satisfaction with democracy in the EU is significantly lower. In the east and southeast European EU member and candidate countries with high levels of internal corruption, satisfaction with the way democracy works at home is extremely low.

3.3 The new European political elites: I. Elected politicians

There is consensus among political scientists that the European Union represents a complex, multilevel system of governance in which both national and European politicians, bureaucrats, and professionals participate. When we analyse the new European political elites, we have to look, therefore, also at the national elites which participate in this process. This shall be done in a short discussion in the following section. In the next section, a more detailed analysis is given of the new European elites proper, the members of the European Parliament.

(a) National political elites as European politicians

The decisive impulses for European integration have always been given by leading national politicians, the heads and members of governments. Why have they been ready to give off a considerable part of their power to supranational institutions? It is not possible to carry out a systematic investigation of their motives, strategies, and actions here. However, it seems appropriate to give at least a sketch of an explanation at the basis of the elite-theoretical perspective developed in this book. This is necessary also because the actions of these national elites and the European elites proper, which we shall investigate in the next section, are closely related to each other. Two general questions have to be answered in this regard: How much power did national political elites in fact dispense when they established the supranational organisations? What did they lose, but also, what did they gain by doing so?

How much power did the national elites give up when they established the European Commission, the ECJ, and—later—the European Parliament? There are two answers to this question. One is that they in fact did not really give up so much of power. In this regard, we can refer to Alan Milward's (1992) book *The European Rescue of the Nation State*. He has argued convincingly that

European integration can be seen as a means to preserve or restore national autonomy and independence in times of superpowers and globalisation. This was obvious at many critical turning points of recent European history: After the war, when both France and Germany were in bad economic and political circumstances and when Schuman and Adenauer gave the decisive impulse by establishing the ECSC; in the 1970s, when troubling economic and currency problems led Giscard d'Estaing and Helmut Schmidt to establish the European Monetary System; in 1989, when the breakdown of the Soviet system opened up a unique opportunity to reunify Germany; this was caught by Helmut Kohl and connected with a decisive step of further European integration (common currency) to which (after having put aside serious concerns) also François Mitterand consented. The persistence of the importance of the member-state governments is reflected in the institutional development of the Union. Not the least as a consequence of Charles de Gaulle's early resistance to centralising tendencies by a further enforcement of the commission and the EP, in 1974 the European Council had been established, which guarantees that the heads of member-state governments have the last say in all decisive political matters of integration policy. Here, probably the most fundamental difference between the EU and USSR exists (which in some other regards shows astonishing parallels, as Boukovsky [2005] shows): Even the prime minister of a ministate has the possibility to say no if he feels that some vital interest of his country is violated. Accession to the EU and participation in it is a freely chosen decision and strategy.

What do the national political elites—individually and as a collective—win by participating in integration? From an elite theoretical point of view, very different kinds of aims and gains are relevant. We have to distinguish here between collective-political and personal-individual aims. In political terms, the heads of governments often may be convinced that it is in the interest of their own countries to join the Union. This may have been so certainly also in the case of the accession of the leading politicians of less developed countries to the EC and EU, in South and East Europe. For the latter, a main motive of this kind was surely the expectation to participate in economic growth and to gain political autonomy and security, after half a century of heteronomy; we will show in Chapter 8 that security is a very important yet underestimated concern of the EU. Moreover, being a member of the EU provides new opportunities for national political elites to pursue political goals: They can codetermine important common European goals; and they often pursue political aims at the level of the Union, which they are unable or unwilling to pursue in their home countries, using decisions at the EU level as pretense (by doing so, they certainly contribute to the negative image of the EU at home). Third, since European integration produces immense new fields of political, bureaucratic, and professional jobs and careers, it provides national politicians with an additional important source of influence and power by giving them the possibility to codetermine who gets these jobs. (Often, national politicians themselves cross over to jobs in European institutions.) Finally, participation in European integration provides also additional gratifications for individual political leaders. Both for those of large and small nations, the participation in meetings of the Council and other big and festive summits provides immediate gratification, as does participation in all kinds of such rituals (Collins 2005). It confers prestige abroad and at home and this particularly, if some proposal of a prime minister has been accepted by the others. This is also one of the mechanisms which keep the process of integration running; every country and government which takes over the half-year presidency of the council is eager to develop an ambitious program of furthering integration.

Thus, European integration cannot be understood without taking into account the decisive influence and actions of national political leaders and elites. Important and influential leaders of large member states—some of them have been mentioned before—have often gained historical stature by promoting decisive steps of European integration. But also the proposals and actions of leaders of smaller countries have been of considerable importance in this regard, although often only after some time. We could mention here personalities such as Henri Spaak (Netherlands), Pierre Werner (Luxembourg), or Leo Tindemans (Belgium).

An interesting difference can be observed as far as the temporal impact of the actions of national political leaders is concerned, compared with those of the European political and bureaucratic elites. The latter promote and further European integration continuously, even if their representatives are by no means outstanding personalities. National political leaders act more erratically, contingent upon time and historical circumstances. The influence of these two categories of elites can well be compared to the wonderful "cooperation" between the two font rivers of the longest stream on earth, the Nile: While the White Nile throughout the year provides a steady amount of water to the lower Nile (from Khartoum to the river mouth in the Mediterranean), the Blue Nile provides the seasonal flood which fecundates the soil in the Egyptian river valley. Normally, the White Nile provides only 31% of the yearly Nile water discharge; in the dry season, however, the White Nile contributes approximately 80–90%.[15] Exactly the same pattern can be observed in European integration: Even in phases of an apparent political standstill, the EU institutions proper, the commission, the EP, and the ECJ continue with their work and keep it going on all the time, as we shall document in the following.

A final remark concerns the explanation of the whole process of integration. Here, we have to distinguish between three kinds of effects: the motives of the actors, the causal forces, and the consequences of actions. The individual motives of the actors involved are very important, but they should not be confounded with the causes of their behaviour. To secure the peace in Europe was certainly an important motive for the "fathers" of integration; however, as we shall argue in Chapter 7, it is wrong to think that integration was necessary for the maintenance of peace. A similar case are the expectations connected with economic growth as an effect of integration; also, they may be an important motive for many leaders to pursue access to the Union, but empirical data show that the real effect of integration on economic growth is quite debatable. On the other side, there are causes and consequences of integration which the political elites and leaders hardly see or mention openly. One of the causes is that the European institutions provide a new level of political and administrative steering and, thereby, an ample field for new jobs and careers. There are also consequences not foreseen by the political elites; not the least among them is the fact that integration often goes much further than foreseen or wished for.

(b) The members of the European Parliament

The members of the European Parliament (MEPs) can be considered as the core of the new European political class. Although the competencies of the EP and the real power of its deputies may leave quite a lot to be desired, the MEPs are the only group which is elected directly by the citizens and which devotes its work primarily to the Union. From the perspective of the formation of a new elite it is essential, therefore, to look more closely at this group. Here, a short characterization of the MEPs shall be presented concerning their social background, education, and careers; their working conditions and workload; their income and remunerations; the motives for their political activity and their view of the aims of European integration.

We can investigate these issues at the background of three opposite hypotheses concerning the role of a member of the European Parliament (EP). One hypothesis says, given the still limited competencies of the EP, that a career in the EP usually is not a full political career. It is only a temporary stepping stone to the real political ambitions (Katz and Wessels 1999:89), Another says that it is a possibility for providing a lucrative job to merited personalities which cannot be placed elsewhere. A third thesis says that it is a possibility to provide a political party with an attractive name. The possibility of a job in the EP as a "consolation prize" (Feron et al. 2006) for deserved older politicians seems to be confirmed by the fact that many candidates at the European elections are older national politicians whose careers seem to come to end. The third thesis gets support by the fact that often actors, sportsmen, or TV speakers are appointed as candidates whose publicity seem to be the main asset for their political job.

In the following, we first present an analysis of basic social characteristics of the members of the European Parliament in July 2007. The data have been taken out of the homepages of the MEPs at the Web site of the European Parliament. In most cases these pages also contain, in addition to political affiliation and membership in EP committees, a short curriculum, including year of birth, education, earlier jobs, career, and awards. These data give us already some interesting insights. Afterwards, we present results of extensive personal interviews with 22 MEPs in seven member countries of the EU.[16]

Social characteristics of the MEPs

A first interesting social characteristic of the MEPs concerns their *age structure* (*Table 3.2*). The large majority of MEPs is in the age group 50–59 years (41%); next come the groups 30–39 and 60–69 years. This age structure can be interpreted in two ways. One is to say that one becomes a mem-

Table 3.2 Age Structure and Education of the Members of the European Parliament by Gender (2007)

Characteristics		Men %	Women %	All %
Age in years	–29	0.4	0	0.3
	30–39	8.5	14.9	10.4
	40–49	19.3	21.9	20.1
	50–59	38.5	46.7	41.0
	60–69	27.2	15.7	23.8
	70 +	5.5	0.8	4.3
Highest level of education	Academic	82.7	81.0	82.1
	Other	10.4	9.5	10.1
	No information	7.0	9.5	7.8
Field of education	Legal sciences	19.3	14.5	17.8
	Economics, business	13.1	8.7	11.8
	Social sciences	9.8	7.9	9.2
	Humanities	9.8	21.5	13.4
	Natural sciences	12.2	9.5	11.4
	Medical sciences	6.5	3.7	5.6
	Other academic education	6.6	11.6	8.2
	No academic education, not specified	22.8	22.7	22.8
Total		100	100	100
(N)		(543)	(242)	(785)
%		69.2	30.8	100

Source: Homepage of the European Parliament (www.europarl.europa.eu), July 2007, special analysis.

ber of the EP after having acquired quite a lot of occupational experience, but still in an age cohort in which capacity to work is high.

In terms of gender, the EP is characterized by a remarkable high female proportion—nearly one third of the deputies are women. Since the early years of the EP, this proportion has grown continuously (Katz and Wessels 1999:99). These proportions vary significantly by countries (*Table 3.3*): They are considerably higher (43% and more) in the Scandinavian countries, in the Netherlands, Luxembourg, and France, and in parts of Europe (Estonia, Slovenia, Bulgaria). On the other side they are rather low (20% and less) in Italy, the Mediterranean isle states (Malta, Cyprus), but also in some east European countries (Czech Republic, Poland, Latvia). This corresponds, by and large, to the well-known differences between countries in terms of female labour-force participation, which is higher in Protestant countries with a strong welfare state (Scandinavia) and in countries which provide ample support for employed mothers (France). Quite remarkable also is the difference between the proportions of women in the different political groups in the EP. The Socialists, the Liberals and Democrats, and the Greens/European Free Alliance show an overproportional number of women, the European People's Party, the more nationalist and EU critical groups (Europe of the Nations, Independence/Democracy Group) a proportion below average.

An important characteristic of the social structure of the political elites is their level and kind of education. The trend toward professionalisation of politics demands that politicians acquire a high level of knowledge and expertise. However, there is also the normative requirement that deputies should not differ too much in their social composition from their electorate. *Table 3.2* shows that the overwhelming majority (82%) of the deputies to the European Parliament have an academic education. This is certainly far above the level among the general population, where at maximum 20–30% have an academic degree. The proportion is not very different, however, from the composition of members of national parliaments.[17]

In terms of field of study, the legal sciences are on top with about 18%; next come the humanities, economics, and natural sciences. Thus, in the EP the legal sciences also have an important place as a base for European politics—although among the deputies its dominance is much less than among the European bureaucracy, as will be shown in Chapter 5. In general, these data confirm Katz and Wessels's (1999:92 ff.) finding that a high proportion of the MEPs are coming from "brokerage occupations." These are jobs which facilitate a full-time political career, because they have flexible hours and require relevant skills, such as in the sectors of law, the media, and party offices. There exists a significant difference between men and women in the most frequent fields of study: Men have more frequently a degree in legal, economic, social, and natural sciences, women more frequently in humanities. This corresponds quite well to the preferences

Table 3.3 The Proportion of Women by Countries and Political Groups in the European Parliament (2007)

Proportion of women among MEPs of selected countries			
Bulgaria	44%	Cyprus	0%
Estonia	50%	Malta	0%
Slovenia	43%	Italy	17%
Denmark	43%	Poland	13%
Sweden	47%	Czech Republic	21%
Netherlands	48%	Latvia	22%
France	43%		
Luxembourg	50%	All countries	30.8% (N = 785)

Proportion of females by political groups		
European People's Party (Christian Democrats) and European Democrats (PPE-DE)	24%	(278)[1]
Socialist Group in the EP (PSE)	40%	(216)
Alliance of Liberals and Democrats (ALDE)	38%	(104)
Union for Europe of the Nations Group (UEN)	11%	(44)
Greens/European Free Alliance (VERTS/ALE)	48%	(42)
European United Left/Nordic Green Left (GUE/NGL)	29%	(41)
Independence/Democracy Group (IND/DEM)	12%	(24)
Identity, Tradition and Sovereignty Group (ITS)	22%	(23)
Nonattached members	15%	(13)

[1] Total number of deputies.

Source: Homepage of the European Parliament (www.europarl.europa.eu), July 2007, special analysis.

of male and female students in most countries. A degree in legal sciences is also more typical for deputies of the People's Party, a degree in economics and social sciences for the deputies of the Socialist Group.

Another relevant information is the occupational experience of the MEPs. Here, the question is if they have been politicians for most of their life, or if they have also acquired other occupational experiences. The data show a high level of professionalisation among the MEPs. The proportion of those who have not been in politics before entering the EP is below 10% in most countries. In Italy (less distinctively also in

France), an exclusive political career is much more typical than in north-west Europe (the UK, the Benelux, and the Scandinavian countries). Also among the Socialist Group, an exclusive political career is more frequent than among the other party groups in the EP. *Table 3.4* gives some general informations on the kind of nonpolitical functions and positions before (or parallel to) the EP activity. The two most frequent were a legal profession (lawyer etc.) and teaching at university; then, many MEPs have worked in lower/intermediate white-collar jobs, as managers in private business, and in other academic professions. Female MEPs have more frequently worked in intermediate white-collar jobs (which shows that European politics offers good opportunities for them), men somewhat more frequently in private business. Another specific finding here is that East European MEPs have been more frequent (28% versus a mean of 18%) university teachers.

The proportion of those who have devoted their whole career exclusively to politics is not high—between 15% and 30%—depending on country and region. However, some 60–75% of the MEPs have spent their earlier working life combining political and nonpolitical occupational activities. The range of occupational activities covered by the MEPs is very wide; most of them require an academic education. To mention just some of them: receptionist, bookbinder, laboratory technician, parish priest, wine grower, director and manager of different sorts of enterprises (public and private), lawyer, interpreter, teacher and university professor, journalist, doctor, veterinary surgeon, engineer, concert pianist, and other musicians. *Table 3.4* also shows in which kind of political position or function the MEPs have been, or still are active, besides their activity in the EP:[18] The highest proportion (about two thirds) has been active in some association, interest organisation, or lobby group. Many of these positions or functions are of a semipolitical nature, in partly autonomous organisations working in the interest of particular groups. Functions of this kind usually are far less demanding in terms of responsibility and time demand than a private entrepreneurship, for instance. Also, the political activities include many different positions and activities: councillors in municipal and provincial councils, mayors, deputies to national parliaments, collaborators in bureaus of ministers, and state secretaries. The same is true for the associations and organisations for which the MEPs have worked (associations of youth, of women, environmental groups, unions, political parties, etc.). There exist some clear differences between groups of countries in the frequency of these activities: Scandinavian MEPs earlier have been more frequent national deputies; east European MEPs have occupied more frequently the position of a minister and or another high political position; Germans have been most frequently been functionaries of some organisation or association; among the British, the proportion of exclusive political careers is the lowest.

Table 3.4 Earlier (and Parallel) Political and Occupational Activities of the
MEPs (2007)

Earlier (parallel) political activity/position	%
Minister, state secretary, and other top positions	9.9
Deputy, councillor, mayor	6.1
Functionary of interest or lobby organisation	65.7
Other political function (secretary of party, assistant of deputy, etc.)	3.9
No political function	10.4
Not specified	3.8
Other occupational/professional functions	
Only political function	18.1
Public service, higher position	5.4
Private business: manager, higher position	12.0
Lawyer and other legal profession	7.6
University teacher and professor	17.7
Other academic profession (doctor, engineer, etc.)	10.1
Lower/intermediate employee/officer	16.8
Self-employed entrepreneur	4.8
Other (worker, farmer)	7.5
Total	100 (N = 785)

Source: Homepage of the European Parliament (www.europarl.europa.eu), July 2007, special analysis.

Relevant is here also the length of office in the European Parliament. The analysis of the MEPs in the present, sixth EP shows the following: 54% of the delegates are the first time in the EP, 46% the second time, 20% the third time, that is, already over 15 years. Eight persons are members since 1979/80, about twenty-eight years (Jens-Peter Bonde, Elmar Brok, Ingo Friedrich, Klaus Hänsch, Marco Pannella, Hans-Gert Pöttering, Karl von Wogau, Francis Wurtz). The fact that most of them have occupied or are occupying important offices (two are chairs of a political group, Hänsch and Pöttering parliament presidents) seems to indicate that a career in the EP is to a considerable matter a degree of a good *Sitzfleisch* (steadiness) and not only a matter of outstanding political qualities. This is at least the definite opinion of critical members of the EP which we have interviewed. Given the fact that an MEP neither within nor outside the parliament has ample opportunities to prove political abilities as they are required on the national level—rhetorical qualities, popularity, ability to prosecute an aim also against massive resistance, etc.—such a conclusion seems not absurd. If it is true it would constitute a serious problem because a parliament is the main institution in which gifted and charismatic political personalities can gain experience (Weber 1988:348).

Work challenges, gratifications and strains

How do the members of the EP themselves evaluate their political career at the level of Europe? Was becoming a member of the EP felt as a personal vocation, or was it more a continuation of a "normal" political career? The statements of the MEPs show definitively that the latter was the case. We asked the MEPs how they went into European politics. The answers were quite uniform and only of a very general nature. "It was the completion of a political experience. In the Sixties and Seventies, when I started my political activity, Europe was only very far . . . Then, at the end of the 1990s, beginning of the 2000s, the new role of the European parliament—which is strengthening today—brought me to this choice. This choice is a very concrete and effective benchmark for me. Today, there exists no national politics without the European dimension," said Mr. Giuseppe Gargani, in the EP since 1999, member of the PPE and chair of the committee on legal affairs. Born in 1935 and graduated in law, he started his political career in the youth movement of the DC in 1960, was its regional councillor, then member of the Italian national parliament, and a high officer in the Italian ministry of justice. A similar statement was given by his compatriot Armando Dionisi (PPE group in the EP): "After a long political experience on the regional level, I made the choice to become a candidate for the European elections because I thought it would be appropriate to represent the interests of this region also on the European level." Some said that they had been occupied with EU matters already in their earlier political activity. The Austrian MEP of the Greens, Eva Lichtenberger, was interested in problems of traffic already in the parliament in Vienna (the transit traffic is a hot issue in Tirol, the province from where she comes): "Traffic policy without the EU is a non-sense today." A typical career is that of the former Austrian MEP Dr. Maria Berger (PSE group), born 1956. She started as university assistant for public law, with a focus on European law, then worked in two ministries in Vienna, where she got the task to prepare Austria's entry to the EU; she has been a member of the EP since 1996; in 2007, she left the EP to become minister of justice in the new Austrian government. Another, quite simple and authentic rationale for becoming active in European politics was given by several others: I was appointed as a candidate by my party.

Thus, it is evident that the EP offers new opportunities for a continuation of a political career which has commenced at the local, regional, or national level. But this is an opportunity not only for the MEPs themselves but also for many other people. Johannes Voggenhuber, MEP of the Austrian Greens and an influential member of the Constitutional Convention, made this quite clear: "Each of us [MEPs] has at least two collaborators. A political group (Fraktion) with 50 members has 6 scientific collaborators. This means that this constitutes a highly intensive labour market . . ." That most MEPs did enter European politics not out of a sense of mission but just in order to continue and secure their political career does not mean that they are motivated only by individual material and other personal interests. The Austrian MEP Paul Rübig (EPP) said in this regard: "In the same way as my compatriots [in Austria] fight for their budgets, we are fighting for the European citizens. In European politics, we are not fighting for us but fight for programmes, such as Leonardo, or Socrates." This sentence could probably be subscribed by any MEP. The fact that the position of an MEP offers a good income and an interesting job is taken for granted—maybe except in those few parliamentary sessions when the MEPs decide about their own income and remunerations.

The work and career of an MEP is also personally quite interesting, desirable, and worthwhile. This comes out in most interviews. (It could also be shown by analysing the way the candidate lists for the European elections are established. One can seldom read that a political party has difficulties finding enough candidates. The reverse, an intensive fight for the available posts, is the usual impression.) For Maria Berger, work in the EP "is very exciting, because in the area of legal policy . . . a lot of political virgin soil exists. For instance, new biotechnological inventions meet with complex, legal problems. Or the process of elaborating a new constitution for 480 million citizens of different nationalities and this in a multi-cultural parliament with very bright and engaged colleagues from many countries and in a debate which as a rule is more businesslike than in internal politics." A similar statement, with some interesting additional elements, was made by the Italian MEP Francesco Speroni, member of the *Lega Nord* and the Group Independence/Democracy in the EP: "A political activity has the disadvantage of being exposed, private life suffers somewhat particularly if you are at the top and people look how you are vested, how you eat and the like. The advantage is that you are a person who decides, who not only has ideas but the possibility to transform the ideas in norms. In fact, I have always understood myself in the first place as political legislator . . . The satisfaction is if you see your designed law becoming a norm and published in the Gazzetta Ufficiale. It makes it also possible for you to configure your activities in a free way; in fact, the parliamentary duties are not very heavy because with two, three days a week you can manage them . . ." Quite a nice characterisation of an MEPs work was given by Mauro Zani (PSE group), a member of the Commission on Development. It is impossible, he said, to follow everything going on in the EP, but one must concentrate oneself on specific topics: "I am researching at the moment, not for a particular urgent reason, the situation of the great lakes in Africa and I think that we need some years to understand the real situation. In comparison with the work of a national deputy which is more operative, where a direct relation to the voters exist and every week you have to be present in your constituency, the work of an Eurodeputy is more a work of study and research. These two components, study and research, are central . . .”

The statement of Speroni, quoted before, about the modest time pressure seems to contradict the frequent complaint of politicians about the high time investment and stress of their work. Such statements were frequently made by the MEPs and they are certainly credible. Answering the question if they feel that the incomes of MEPs are a privilege, several of them pointed to the fact that their working week is between seventy and eighty hours; some also referred to the burden of having to travel all the time and to the long-term absence from their families. The explanation of this contradiction seems not too difficult: Most politicians are not only active for their parliamentary (or other) duties proper, but try to be present in their constituencies at public meetings of all sorts, give public speeches regularly, become honorary presidents and the like in associations of all kinds, and—in the case of the EP—also travel around Europe and even the whole world to see the places and groups whose problems are on the agenda of the EP.

Political activity, exercised in this way, can well become a greedy occupation which only physically and psychologically very robust personalities can sustain. One outstanding representative of a “political man” of this kind was Otto Habsburg, the senior member (born 1912) of the EP for twenty years (1979–1999). He continues to travel, give lectures, visit ethnic minorities, and so on, all over Europe up to his present advanced age. Other MEPs, and maybe particularly those with a very high political ethos, may also suffer under such a burden. A tragic example was Alexander Langer, an Italian representative and copresident of the Greens in the EP 1989–1995; after a tireless political life which saw him busy all the time and travelling around Europe continuously, he committed suicide in 1995. One of the reasons was doubtless a deep-going physical and psychic-spiritual exhaustion (see Kronbichler 2005).

Most MEPs also referred to their long working hours when asked if they consider their generous incomes and expense remunerations as just or not. It turned out that, particularly, MEPs from countries with a generally very positive attitude toward the EU (Hungary, Italy) did not see problems in this regard. Several of them, as well as others, definitely stated that their incomes are quite adequate; they referred to judges in the ECJ whose incomes are even much higher; they charged that the media tend to exaggerate this issue; and they pointed to the fact that they have to deliver a substantial proportion of their salary to the political party for which they ran in the election. It seems necessary, here, to look shortly at the objective income situation of the MEPs.

The basic salary of the MEPs is paid by the member states and corresponds to that of deputies to national parliaments; from this point of view, they are not very high. This implies that the basic salaries vary extremely by countries and are much lower for MEPs of the new member countries (in some countries they are less than 1,000, in Italy nearly 10,000 euros). In addition, however, MEPs get reimbursements for their expenses, and these are the same for all deputies (so they outbalance somewhat the differences in the basic salaries). In countries with a rather critical attitude toward the EU, these regulations have come under heavy attack, particularly because they often have no meaningful relation to real expenses. In Austria, MEP Hans Peter Martin made this his main topic in the European election campaign of 2004 and won (with massive support of the tabloid *Kronenzeitung*) not less than 14% of the votes.

These reimbursements include (see von Arnim 2006:268ff.) a fixed sum (268 euros) for participation in a plenary or committee session which, in a month, can add up to 3,500 euros per month; fixed reimbursements for travel costs, including economy-class flights (the MEP can in fact take a flight which costs much less); a monthly allowance of 2,785 for costs in their home constituencies; a generous health insurance and a pension insurance which usually does not restrict national pension claims. In addition, an MEP can get up to 14,865 euros per month for collaborators. These costs must be documented, but the MEP alone decides about the person whom he employs (it is not forbidden to employ kinsmen). Looking at all these additional reimbursements, it is out of question that MEPs are quite privileged in the whole compensations available to them. This judgement seems to be divided everywhere, even in the EP, which for decades has tried to develop new rules in this regard. In May 2005, the EP was able to pass a reform.[19] The new statute, which will come into force in 2009, establishes the basic salary as 38.5% of the salary of a judge at the ECJ; at present, this would be 7,000 euros; travel reimbursements will provided only according the actual expenses.

Evaluation of the EP as an institution

How efficiently is the European Parliament working? Several MEPs stress that work in the EP is much more factual than in national parliaments because the political constraints by party groups are less strong. The EP was denominated as an efficient "working parliament" as the most influential parliament in Europe (Voggenhuber). The influence of single deputies is considered as considerable by some interview partners, particularly if an MEP is the *rapporteur* in a certain matter. However, most express also critical comments. The characterisation of the EP as a "huge voting machinery" (Voggenhuber) is probably quite appropriate. On some days, 300 to 400 votes are taken, often in a few blocks which include very different matters. The rest of the time, speech after speech is given in the plenary with very little discussion or response. As any visitor can see, in a normal plenary session, only some 50 EPs—5% of all—are participating, practically only those who wait their turn to speak; every speaker addresses his/her words mainly to the president, who stoically presides over the session. Only if a vote is coming up, hundreds of MEPs pour into the hall.

Three problems are most remarkable concerning the work of the EP. First, the sheer size of the EP makes it very difficult that all deputies play some appreciable part. Therefore, MEPs tussle to get the duty of *rapporteur;* in order to make this possible for many, topics are separated into several subtopics as told by the MEP Hans Peter Martin. The Italian deputy of the Greens, Sepp Kusstatscher from South Tyrol, observes: "If there are maybe 50 people in one committee, the one more diligent than the other, it has the consequence that motions become longer and longer, and many subtlenesses are integrated all of which results in far too detailed regulations." This leads to the second problem, namely, that the European Parliament is occupied or occupying itself with a myriad of highly specialized technical topics, or with world-political issues which are far out of the competences of the EP (resolutions on problems in many places around the world). Most of our interview partners agreed that this is the case. For the MEP Michel Rocard (PSE), former French prime minister, this is a remnant of the first years of the EP when it had little competences and therefore devoted itself to such resolutions. The third problem is that for a single deputy it is impossible to look personally at all the points and problems which are on the agenda, even of the sessions of the committees. Answering to the question if he can follow the many products of the EP, MEP Mauro Zani (PSE group) said: "I am not able to follow it. For me it is an extremely complex matter, because the mass of paper is enormous." The voting behaviour of single MEPs, therefore, cannot but follow in most cases just the line provided by the political party group to which he or she belongs.

An interesting side effect of this high degree of specialization is that members of the EP are quite open to the influence of lobbyists. Some MEPs (mainly those of the PPE) see only positive aspects in lobbying (we will come back to this in the next chapter); some argue that they would have voted anyway in the direction which was wished for by a lobby group. Others, however, report massive instances of such kinds of influence. Ona Jukneviciene, a Lithuanian MEP, educated as an economist and working earlier for the IMF, reported this: "I was lobbied quite strongly by the UK Federation of Industrialists where they worked on the working time directive because British were promoting much longer hours for a week. I have contacts from other organisations . . . for instance tobacco companies in relation to the Budgetary Control Committee because there are different restrictions for tobacco industries, so they are pushing ahead. The lobbying in the European parliament is much stronger than in our national parliament, and I would say very strong, very strong indeed."

It was surprising, at least at first sight, that none of the interview MEPs saw any serious problem in the relations with the Commission: "There are conflicts (in the EP) but not with the Commission" (Voggenhuber); "the Commission is a daughter of the parliament" (Gargani). Most said that the Commissioners or high officials are quite well accessible if they want to approach them. What is the reason? One maybe is that the principle of "one does not hurt each other" (Martin) operates. However, it is the common interest of both parliament and commission to further European integration and to strengthen the European institutions proper (EP, Commission, ECJ) against the intergovernmental institutions, like the European Council. MEP Voggenhuber made a distinction here between the Commission (and the EP, implicitly), which represents the *Gemeinschaftseuropa,* and the intergovernmental institutions, which represent the national governments: " 'Gemeinschaftseuropa' was successful and intergovernmental Europe has been a failure." This statement contains a lot of truth if one thinks of the highly controversial Common Agricultural Policy where the EU spends most money and which belongs clearly to the Council (see Chapter 4).

We may conclude this preliminary portrait of the MEPs by mentioning their views about necessary reforms of the EP and about the future of the EU (see also Blondel et al. 1998). Most saw the necessity of reforms, mentioning, for instance, a strengthening of the personality element in the European elections; a tightening of its agendas; the providing of the power to make legislative initiatives of its own; the necessity to improve the communication politics of the EP (see also Scully and Farrell 2003; Anderson and McLeod 2004). Nearly all (except, the French) agree that the three seats of the EP—Brussels, Strasbourg, and Luxembourg—are an incredible wastage and a serious handicap for the work of the EP. Approached about the existence of a democratic deficit in the EU, most agreed that is does exist, but they also pointed to the fact that it became reduced significantly in recent times. Some firmly believe that the EU must become a global player, acting on an equal footing with new rising powers such as China. (The proponents of these theses are more on the conservative side, and more frequently Italians.) Others—mainly from left and green parties—see the main deficit of the EU in its weak social dimension; a common tax system "would be a dream" (Jörg Leichtfried, Austrian MEP of the PSE group). For the Hungarian MEP Peter Olayos (PPE group), a serious weakness of the EU is that it neglects the issue of minorities. Given the large Hungarian minority in Romania, this is understandable; the MEP Michl Ebner from South Tyrol (which is a minority province within Italy) complains about the same problem (Ebner 2004). Several of the interviewed MEPs agree with the thesis that European integration for a long time has been a bureaucratic elite project (Swoboda). Only MEPs from political groups quite critical toward integration express some doubts in this regard. Enrico Speroni member of the Lega Nord and EP group Independence/Democracy, answers as follows to the question what the principal advantages and disadvantages of membership in the EU are: "If I must explain to a voter what the advantages for being in the EU are

I have difficulties, aside from the convenience that you must not change Liras in Schilling when you go from Milan to Graz . . . it is difficult to see advantages if one thinks of a Swiss or a Norwegian who also are well off and have a good standard of life without being in the EU . . ."

The findings of this small study of the MEPs have clearly shown that here a large area of new career possibilities for the political elite has been created. It is certainly legitimate that politicians—like any other professional group—also follow their own interests. However, in some regards (e.g., compensations) the situation seems rather problematic from the normative democratic point of view, sketched out in the preceding chapter. Moreover, the workings of the EP show some highly problematic aspects. One is the fact that MEPs feel themselves wedged into a huge "voting machinery"; another one is the extreme fragmentation and specialisation of the work. The EP itself seems not to be innocent in the modest image the EP has among citizens in Europe. That this is so is clearly indicated by the decreasing levels of turnout at European elections (Blondel et al. 1998). Carrubba et al. (2004) found that in the EP "party groups hide the vast majority of legislative votes from the eyes of voters, therefore obfuscating legislative behaviour." There is no question that the majority of the MEPs take their role quite seriously. (Scully and Farrell 2003:286). However, given the fundamental problems in the legitimacy of the EU in general, and the EP in particular, rigorous reforms seem necessary. We will come back to this issue in Chapter 8.

3.4 The new European political elites:
II. Political bureaucrats and professionals

The Commissioners between member state
governments and the Eurocracy[20]

The European Commission occupies a central position in the political process of the Union. It is the institution mainly responsible for the task of promoting the interest of integration: " . . . its multinational civil service, its exclusive right to initiate legislation in the first pillar, and its quasi-executive authority, the Commission epitomizes supra-nationalism and lies at the center of the EU system. Not surprisingly, the Commission and the Berlaymont, its headquarters building in Brussels, are synonymous with the EU itself" (Dinan 1999:205; see also Donnelly and Ritchie 1994). At the top of the EU bureaucracy are the commissioners and their presidents. Their political background and personalities, careers and behaviours provide us with a particular insight into the nature and the workings, the power and the flaws of the Eurocracy. Commissioners have a very broad array of tasks. They have, in fact, "six professions," as Jacques Delors once said: "Policy innovator, law maker, law enforcer, manager of community policies, diplomat and political broker" (Shore 2000:143). Three issues shall be discussed in this section: the character of the members of the Commission; their social characteristics, careers, and profiles; and the power of the Commission as a collective agent.

Politicians or bureaucrats?

A first important question concerning the position and role of the Commission members is: Are they politicians or bureaucrats? This is not only an academic-defining question but leads us to heart of the issue of the character of the European Union, the question if it is a state or only an "intergovernmental regime" (see also Edwards and Spence 1994:6). This question can be answered from two perspectives. First we can look at the characteristics of an ideal-typical politician and bureaucrat and at the relevant characteristics of these two roles (Weber 1973b, 1978a,b; Jarass 1975:126ff.; Dogan 1975:4).

As we can see in *Table 3.5*, the Commissioners share two out of four characteristics with the politician: They usually come from political or professional backgrounds, and their appointment is limited in time although they enjoy a remarkable security of tenure in office (Donnelly and Ritchie 1994:34). The former Dutch Commissioner Karel van Miert (2000:46), for instance, reports that during his four-year term of office he had to deal with four different ministers for traffic in France and the United Kingdom. On the other hand, Commissioners are appointed to their office (by the heads of national governments), and they have collective responsibility for their work. Thus, the role of the Commissioners is a hybrid or "bridge role," sharing characteristics of both politicians and bureaucrats (see also Page and Wouters 1995:201).

Table 3.5   The Commissioners of the EU—Politicians or Bureaucrats?

Characteristics	Politician	Bureaucrat	EU Commissioners
Typical occupation and career	Varying occupational backgrounds, although politics as profession predominates	Steady professional-bureaucratic career	Varying backgrounds, but mainly political
Access to the office	Election	Appointment	Appointment
Duration of office	Limited in time, unpredictable	Unlimited, tenure	Limited in time, predictable
Responsibility	Personal responsibility	Collective responsibility	Collective responsibility

As politicians, Commissioners can in fact have a considerable impact on the development and politics of integration. Probably most of them have a high level of ambition when taking up their office (see, e.g., van Miert 2000), and in every Commission there are some determined and forceful and highly successful personalities. Jaques Delors was an outstanding example in this regard. From this point of view, it is right that "a Commission president's performance depends not as much on the attributes of the office itself as on his personality, country of origin, national political experience and prospects" (Dinan 1999:205ff.). However, their other "role" as bureaucrats is at least of similar, if not higher, importance. This bureaucratic side of the Commissioners is often overlooked. As bureaucrats, the Commission president and his colleagues must not play forceful political roles and be well known in public. They just have to coordinate and further the workings of the vast Eurocracy internally and in relation to the other actors in the EU governing system. This may happen in a quite unspectacular, but nevertheless very efficient, way. In this way, the Commission and their apparatus dispose, in fact, of a large power. This factual power of the Commission is often obscured by the frequent use of the concept of *"competencies"* instead of power: "The word 'competence' assigns power to those deemed 'competent' to act. This abstract noun thus harkens back to the Monnet method of benign bureaucratic expertise, and therefore ultimately tends to obscure the need for democratic legitimation . . . A discussion about the allocation of 'competences' suggests an apolitical conversation about relative expertise. Deciding on the allocation of 'powers,' in contrast, emphasizes the politics of debating the relative jurisdictions" (Halberstam 2003). The bureaucratic-political character of the commissioner's role is strengthened by the fact that nearly all members of their own cabinets (specially appointed officials) are career officials, usually from their home countries (Page and Wouters 1995:201). These cabinets, originally including only a handful of persons, have grown in recent times to formidable bureaus, often through the method of hiring officials from home administrations for temporary attachments (Donnelly and Ritchie 1994:43). This proliferation of cabinet members had also the negative side effects of lowering the morale of the civil service and creating barriers between the Commissioners and the DGs.

Social characteristics and careers. A sociological profile

The second possibility to answer who the EU Commissioners are and what their "true" political power and influence may be is to look at the process of their appointment, their social characteristics, and political behaviour. At the background of the hypothesis of the double role of the EU Commissioners both as politicians and bureaucrats, many of the otherwise paradoxical characteristics and processes in this regard become intelligible.

This applies in particular to the "abstruse politics of choosing a EU Commission" (Dinan 1999:208; see also Donnelly and Ritchie 1994:33; Middlemas 1995:214ff.; Pollack 2003:107ff.). As bureaucrats, Commissioners will be selected by their "masters," the heads of the national governments, in such a way as to guarantee not only an optimal role, but also that the main interests of the powerful member states are not threatened (Hartmann 2001:101). Thus, even Jaques Delors, the highly respected Commission president, became "the subject of greatest hostility by member states" (Middlemas 1995:218) at the end of his office terms, not the least because he was so determined and successful.

Table 3.6 presents some information about the social characteristics of the Commission presidents since 1958. Five general characteristics and tendencies are instructive: (1) Nearly two thirds of the Commission presidents (seven out of eleven) have been jurists by education. This clearly underlines the strong influence of this profession and the character of the EU as a *"community of law,"* as we shall argue in Chapter 8. (2) There exists a heavy overrepresentation of the Francophone world; five out of the eleven presidents came from France, Belgium, or Luxembourg. Also, this fact contributes to a particular influence of the French political system and culture on the Eurocracy. (3) We may hypothesize that the role of the Commissioners is influenced significantly by their national background. A Commissioner from a large nation-state will be in a much better position to develop a powerful role if he has the backing of his home government. In fact, the only three "strong" Commissioners came from France, Germany, and England. In other cases—most notably that of Italy—we can see that the instability of national politics is reflected also in a modest role of its Commission presidents: Franco Malfatti (1970–1972) and Romano Prodi (1999–2004). (4) Practically all Commission presidents have been politicians before taking on their office in the EU. Up to the early 1980s, the typical Commission president had been a state secretary, sometimes only a deputy to the national parliament. Since that time, however, only former prime ministers have been appointed to this office. This trend indicates that the Commission presidents are gaining more and more in political stature. However, a look at their political power and influence shows that only few of them have been able to capitalize on this possibility. Up to now, only two or three Commission presidents have been really "strong" political personalities (Hallstein, Jenkins, Delors; see also Hartmann 2001:109f.). This fact is in itself significant because it underlines the "mainly" bureaucratic character of the office. (5) Finally, it is interesting to look at the activities of the Commission presidents after the end of their term. Here, we can see that three of them took over leading positions in private business, mostly in enterprises under strong political influence (F. X. Ortoli, G. Thorn, and J. Santer). Such careers are certainly not an evidence that politics was a true vocation (Weber 1973b) for them.

Table 3.6   Presidents of the EU Commission and their Social and Political
             Characteristics.

Name (Nationality) (Period/years in office)	Academic education	Occupational activity		Strength of leadership*
		before	after EU office	
Walter Hallstein (G) (1958–1967/10)	Jurisprudence	State secretary, university prof.	Parliament deputy	Strong
Jean Rey (B) (1967–1970/3)	Jurisprudence	Lawyer, politician	Minister	Weak
Franco Malfatti (I) (1970–1972/2)	None	Journalist	Parliament member	Weak
Sicco Mansholt (NL) (1972/1)	None	Farmer, minister	Voluntary political activities	Weak
Francois-X. Ortoli (F) (1973–1977/4)	Jurisprudence, ENA	Minister, deputy	President of oil company	Weak
Roy Jenkins (UK) (1977–1981/5)	economics, p. lit. science	Minister	Party founder	Strong
Gaston Thorn (Lux.) (1981–1985/5)	Jurisprudence	Prime minister	Bank president, TV-president	Weak
Jacques Delors (F) (1985–1995/10)	No formal (jurid., econ.)	Minister	Honorary positions and activities	Strong
Jacques Santer (Lux.) (1995–1999/5)	Jurisprudence	Lawyer, prime minister	MEP, president of TV network	Weak
Romano Prodi (I) (1999–2004/5)	Jurisprudence, economics	Univ. prof., prime minister	Politician, prime minister	Weak
Manuel Barroso (Port) (2004–)	Jurisprudence, polit. science	Minister, prime minister	—	Weak

*Up to Santer taken from Dinan 1999:207; for Prodi and Barroso my own estimation, based on press reports.

From a sociological point of view, we can distinguish between three types of Commission presidents: the *neutral broker,* the *forceful political agent,* and the *deselected prime minister.*

   The neutral broker is a Commission president who comes from a small and old member state (that is, the Benelux countries). It can be expected that he will carefully try to find political compromises between the diverging interests of the large and influential member states. From this point of view, it is easy to understand why the ministate of Luxembourg has been so prolific in providing Commission presidents. Politicians from this ministate are not connected personally with the interests of some large member state. Already two Commission presidents (Thorn, Santer) came from this country (more than from Germany!). Also one of the "founding fathers" of the EU, Robert Schuman, had been born in Luxembourg and was fluently speaking German. In addition, in the last round of appointment in 2004, the present premier of Luxembourg, Jean Claude Juncker, was considered throughout the Union as the ideal candidate for this office.

The thesis that prime ministers from small states are preferred because they are the optimal "compromise" candidates can be proved by looking at the process of their appointment. In the case of Jacques Santer, this has been described aptly by D. Dinan (1999:208ff.). According to the unofficial rota, in 1995 the turn for the president was a Christian Democratic candidate from a small country to succeed the French socialist J. Delors. Ruud Lubbers, the molded Dutch prime minister, seemed to be the obvious choice. However, his candidacy soon ran into difficulties. Due to Lubbers's earlier resistance to German unification, Chancellor Kohl opposed his candidacy. With the support of French President Mitterand he proposed another candidate, Jean-Luc Dehaene, also a conservative prime minister of a small state (Belgium). Among the other states, reluctance arose because of the predecision by these two states, but Britain was decisive in the rejection of Dehaene; Prime Minister John Major wanted to gain internal political profile by "caricaturing Dehaene as rabid Eurofederalist." Only at a special summit and in the last minute, a compromise candidate was found in the person of the premier of Luxembourg, Jacques Santer (also a Christian Democrat and from a small country), even if he was at least an Eurofederalist," as was Dehaene. This highly politicized nature of the appointment process had a strong negative impact on the European Council as well as on Santer's own reputation (Dinan 1999:209).

The *forceful political agent* is a commission president who has shown a high personal political profile in his office. So far, only two of the eleven Commission presidents—Walter Hallstein and Jacques Delors—can be considered to have played such a role. It is interesting that none of them has been a prime minister in his country of origin; their strength evidently was based on a combination of personal visions, ambition and energy, and decisive support by one or more large nation-states. The first, Walter Hallstein (president 1958–1967), was jurist and university professor by education and profession (see Hallstein 1979; Loth et al. 1995; Middlemas 1995:216f.). He took part in the Schuman conference in Paris in 1950 which led to the establishment of the ECSC. From 1951 to 1958 he acted as state secretary for foreign relations in Adenauer's cabinet and was proposed by France and Belgium as the first candidate for the Commission of the new EEC. Hallstein was a definite supporter of integration; under his leadership, important steps were taken, such as the publication of the Hallstein-Plan for a common market (1959) and the development of the CAP. Hallstein was "unashamed to include 'theory, doctrine, utopia, forecasts, planning, futurology (and) vision' in his writing, nor to admit that for him the final stage was 'full and complete federation' " (Spence 1994:64). Hallstein's influence came to a halt through de Gaulle's politics of restricting the power of the Commission. Hallstein's proposal of giving to the EEC a financial base of its own was rejected and he had to resign from office in 1967.

The other outstanding Commission president was Jacques Delors (1985–1995; see also Delors 1993; Edwards and Spence 1994:13ff.; Middlemas 1995:218f.; Schneider 2001). Delors can be compared to Jean Monnet in several regards (Grant 1994:272ff.): He came from a Catholic family background; he did not attain a formal academic degree (although he began to study jurisprudence during the war and later economics); his political orientation was liberal, but with elements of leftist Catholicism and Social Democracy. Like Monnet, he also was directly involved in socioeconomic reform and planning processes in France, as a member of the French Economic and Social Council and the General Planning Committee in the 1960s and minister of economics and finance under President Mitterand. The EU career of Delors started in 1979, when he became a member of the European Parliament and the chairman of its Economic and Monetary Committee. Under his three terms as president of the Commission (1985–1995), very important steps of integration were taken: the completion of EMU, the Single European Act (1987), and the Treaty of the European Union (the Maastricht Treaty, 1992); the enlargement of the Union toward the south and the north (Spain and Portugal 1985; Austria, Finland, and Sweden 1995). Delors's personal engagement for European integration is confirmed also by his continued activities after the end of his office in 1995: He became president of the administrative board of the Collège d'Europe in Brussels, director of the research group Notre Europe, and president of the Conseil de l'Emploi, des Revenus et de Cohesion Sociale. Delors's achievements have been widely recognized; he got many international awards, including two dozens honorary doctorates. However, also in his case the institutional backing and the favourable opportunities at the time were equally decisive (Ross 1995). After a prolonged period of "Eurosclerosis," many throughout Europe were asking for renewed efforts toward integration; the European multinational corporations asked for the establishment and enlargement of the Common Market. In fact, Delors took over his proposals in this regard to a large degree from the Round Table of Industrialists (see Chapter 4).

Since the late 1990s, a new pattern of recruitment for presidents of the Commission emerged insofar as now also two former ministers of large nation-states became presidents. However, both have a common characteristic, which again proves that the political stature of the Commission president did not grow very much. They both lost their posts as premier in national elections before becoming presidents of the commission. The first of them was Romano Prodi. Prodi studied jurisprudence in Milan and economics at the London School of Economics and became university professor of economics; later, he acted as minister and manager of the large state holding IRI. In 1995, he became leader of the liberal-leftist electoral alliance Ulivo, and in 1996 Italian premier minister. However, already in 1998 he had to resign due to a lost vote of confidence in the parliament. Prodi was welcomed with sympathies as the new president of the European Commission in 1999 but he was not able to come up to the expectations. After his return to Italian politics in 2004, he was able to overthrow the right-wing regime of Silvio Berlusconi and again became Italian prime minister.

The second former prime minister from a larger country appointed as president of the EU Commission is José Manuel Barroso. He studied jurisprudence and political science. Barroso's political activity began early; as a student, he was one of the leaders of a Maoist students' movement. Later on, he joined the Portuguese Social Democratic party, which had a centre-right political orientation. Barroso also worked as an academic scientist in Lisbon and Washington. In 1987, he became state secretary for foreign affairs—a post in which he could distinguish himself in the peace process in Angola. In 1992, he became minister of foreign affairs. He was elected as the leader of his party in 1995, and in 2002 he became Portuguese prime minister. At the European elections in 2004, his party, however, again lost votes. At home, Barroso was rather unpopular both because of his support of Bush's war against Iraq (he had invited Bush, Blair, and Aznar to a summit on the Azores before the war) and because of this austerity programme for the reduction of the country's budget under the Stability and Growth Pact of the EU. About the process of his appointment, a renowned German newspaper wrote: "The piece with the title 'Second-rate quality' has been performed ten years earlier at the same place. Only the actors were different . . . Wringing hands, the Christian Democrats had looked long for the right candidate. But he who was wanted by everybody . . . could not be retuned, the prime minister of Luxembourg Jean-Claude Juncker . . . It seemed plausible, therefore, that the liberal Verhofstedt could make the race . . ."[21] However, a veto came from the British premier, Tony Blair, not in the last instance because Verhofstedt had opposed the war against Iraq. Finally, Barroso was accepted not the least because he seemed to be no person who rubs people up the wrong way. International commentators characterized him as "the smallest common denominator" and a "compromise candidate," as a career man with little charisma but with the ability to grasp a good opportunity when it does arise.[22] This is a perfect characterization of the behaviour and the secret of success of the Eurocracy in general (see also Chapter 5).

The power of the Commission as a collective agent

The commissioners are responsible as a collective group for the politics of the European Commission—a fact which reinforces its character as a bureaucratic unit. The deliberations of the Commission are explicitly kept a secret; dissenting opinions of commissioners are not published (Verheugen 2005:44). Thus, the important principle of bureaucratic secrecy (Weber 1978a) is fully effective here—a principle whose origins go back to the time of the absolute monarchs, in the eighteenth century (Beninger 2004:37). Therefore, the weakness of individual presidents and members of the Commission may not be a big problem. It is sufficient that there are a few innovative and strong personalities in any commission. This is in fact what is happening all the time. In nearly all commissions, there are a few imaginative and influential commissioners who are able to put forward new ideas and to accomplish their realization. However, also the less innovative commissioners are in a position to further the process of integration. They have only to take up the many new proposals that are elaborated continuously in the departments assigned to them. This bureaucratic character of the Commission has long been criticized (Edwards and Spence 1994:6). In this way, practically every Commission could further the process of European integration in a significant way. Here, the ingenuity of Monnet's idea that the Commission as a whole should be the responsible agent turns out most clearly. Let us give some examples for influential single Commissioners and bureaucrats.

An influential early Commissioner was the Dutch Sicco Mansholt (1908–1995). He was Commission president for only two years (1972–1973), but he was a central element of politics of the European Community as the first long-term commissioner for agriculture (1958–1972). Mansholt came from a rather unconventional background; his parents were farmers and socialists. He was active in the resistance against German occupation, worked in a tea plantation in Indonesia, and later started his own farm in the Netherlands. After the war, he served for thirteen years as Dutch minister for agriculture. Under Mansholt's aegis as commissioner, the EEC agricultural policy, focussing on extensive subsidies for agricultural products, led to large overproduction in many areas. Thus, its reform became urgent. The "Mansholt plan" intended to reduce the working population in agriculture and to further the development of larger and more efficient farms (here, certainly, his social democratic background had an influence); as such, it was rightly seen as a threat to small farmers throughout Europe.[23]

An influential early member of the commission was also the Italian Altiero Spinelli (1907–1986). Born the son of a socialist father, he became a member of the Italian Communist Party in his youth and participated in the fight against fascism. He was incarcerated in 1927; during imprisonment, he wrote (with Ernesto Rossi) the famous *Manifesto di Ventotene,* an important early document asking for a united Europe, organised according the federal principle. In 1943 he founded the Federal Movement of Europe, whose secretary he remained until 1962. In the immediate postwar years, he participated in the European movement and supported the development of a European Defence Union (declined by the French parliament in 1954).

He was a member of the European Commission (1970–1976) and an MEP (1976–1989). His central idea about European integration was that nation-states have to pass on some of their competencies to the Union, and that also the peoples must participate in the process of integration—an idea whose relevance is coming out ever more clearly today. After his initiative, the European Parliament in 1984 passed a declaration about the establishment of a "European Union," which was an important step toward the Maastricht Treaty in 1992.

Another influential member and vice-president of the commission (1977–1985) was the Belgian Etienne Davignon (born 1932), trained as jurist, philosopher, and economist. Before his work for the EC, he was chef d'office of Belgian Foreign Minister P. H. Spaak and president of the International Energy Agency. As commissioner, he drafted the *Davignon Report* (1975), which investigated possibilities for furthering the process of integration and proposed a mechanism of consultation in matters of foreign relations. After his term on the Commission, Davignon became a member of the Société Générale de Belgique and supported the establishment of SN Brussels Airlines (successor of failed Sabena).

One could mention in this regard also Commissioners from liberal parties who, because of their basic political orientation, should have had serious reservations against an extension of the steering political activities of the European Union. However, even these commissioners, such as the German sociologist Ralf Dahrendorf (commission member 1973–1976) or Martin Bangemann (1989–1999), former leader of the German Liberal Party (FDP) and minister of economics, contributed their part to the consolidation and amplification of the integration process. Under Dahrendorf's term, for instance, for the first time matters of education and science were brought up in the commission. Martin Bangemann initiated the *Bangemann-Report* (1994), which explored the perspectives for a European "information society" and gave extensive policy recommendations for its promotion. During his terms of office, his "apparent economic liberalism soon melted to reveal a bent towards protection for key sectors" (Middlemas 1995:248; van Miert 2000:63).

One could mention in this regard also Commissioners coming from the Christian Democrat and from the Socialist and Social Democratic camps. Among the first was the Austrian Franz Fischler, influential commissioner for agriculture 1995–2004. The agricultural directorate is one of the largest, including a staff of 5,000 persons already in the early 1990s (Donnelly and Ritchie 1994:38). Fischler was a son of a small farmer in Tirol, studied agricultural sciences, became director of the Austrian Farmers' Association and minister for agriculture. As a member of the Commission, he was successful in achieving the first steps of a transition from product-oriented agricultural subsidies to farm- or person-oriented subsidies. Others that could be mentioned here are the Dutch socialist Karel van Miert, commissioner for competition (1989–1999), who had a quite critical attitude toward the interests and actions of European multinationals (see van Miert 2000). The former British Labour Party leader Neil Kinnock (commissioner 1995–2004) was responsible for transport, and later, as vice-president, for personnel and administration. Also, this and other British commissioners, such as Leon Brittain, Chris Patten, or Peter Mandelson, were—despite the very EU-critical climate in their home country—quite ready and successful to advance European integration. A good example is the commissioner and vice-president Leon Brittain (1989–1999), former minister of the Conservative British government. In a speech entitled "A pro-European policy for conservatives"[24] on 21.7.1999, he criticized the widespread belief in Britain that support of the EU is wrong in any case and the single currency a "serious disease."

We can draw a clear lesson from this short sketch of the orientations and actions of these different commissioners: Even if many of them had rather narrow aims and areas of competencies, each was able to further the process of integration in a considerable way in his particular sector of policy. Differing personal and political backgrounds seem to be irrelevant. None of them ever made proposals to check or even reduce EU engagement in his or her area of competence. Thus, one thing is clearly achieved by the commission as a collective body over the decades, namely, that the process of integration is going on all the time and the trend toward an "ever closer Union" is never interrupted.

It is quite interesting in this regard that commissioners often develop a much more critical attitude toward the EU after than during their terms of office. The former Dutch Commissioner Frits Bolkestein, a liberal responsible for the internal market, said in an interview in June 2005: "The European Union does too much . . . All things which a member state can do by himself, should be handled there . . . Austria pays in and gets money back. I am against this money recycling."[25] The Austrian commissioner for agriculture, Franz Fischler, after his term as Commissioner made the proposal to restitute to the nation-states considerable parts of this policy.[26]

(c) A silent revolution through law: Jurists and the European Court of Justice

There is one institution and elite whose acting has been highly consequential for the process of integration but nevertheless has been working rather unobserved from the public and underestimated often also in scientific accounts of the political system of the EU. The institution is the European Court of Justice (ECJ), and the professional group are the legal experts. Although it is not possible here to give an extended presentation of the ECJ and the role of the legal profession, it is nevertheless essential to present some relevant aspects for two reasons: First, it will be argued in Chapter 8 that the best way to understand the nature of the EU and the finality of integration is by denoting it as a "community of law"; second, it will be argued here that the elite-theoretical approach of this work can contribute significantly to an understanding of the high influence of the ECJ in the process of integration.

As an introduction, let us shortly characterize the genesis and working principles of the ECJ. (For overviews, see Dinan 1999:301–312; Arnull 1999, 2003:179–92; Nicoll and Salmon 2001:143–56; Pollack 2003:155–202; Chalmers 2004.) The ECJ was established in 1952 together with the ECSC, with the seat in Luxembourg, and integrated into the Treaty of Rome, establishing the EEC (Art. 177). Since the treaties of the European Community were formulated only rather generally, an institution was necessary to arbitrate in cases of differing interpretations. It was determined that each member country appoints one judge to the ECJ (therefore, it has twenty-seven judges today); the judges are appointed for a renewable term of six years. They are chosen from among lawyers whose independence is beyond doubt and who possess the qualifications required.[27] They elect one president for three years among them. The ECJ includes, in addition, eight advocates general and a registrar. The main activities of the ECJ are references for preliminary rulings; in these cases, courts of the member states bring cases related to community law with which they are concerned before the ECJ in order that he gives a judgement (which then is binding throughout the EU); actions for failure of a member state to fulfil obligations under community law; actions for the annulment (as well as for failure to act) of a measure implemented by a community institution.

In the first years, the ECJ's work was rather unobtrusive, but with time it acquired more and more importance. The reason was that the ECJ—through is specific decisions on individual cases—established principles which have changed the legal situation throughout the community in a fundamental way. Two of these principles are of paramount importance: The principle of *direct effect,* established in the case *Van Gend en Loos* (1963), says that any EU regulation (and partly also directives) can be directly applied to individuals in all member states; the principle of *supremacy of community law* (first stated in the *Costa vs. Enel* case [1964]) says that EU law supersedes national law in all cases. Out of these principles, the ECJ unfolded a vast activity in putting through and realizing the supremacy of community law over national law in many cases. Between 1967 and 1995, the cases before the ECJ concerning preliminary references have grown steadily from less than ten to about 250 per year (Pollack 2003:187). Also, the workload of the ECJ has grown correspondingly; its total number of personnel in 2006 included 1,757 persons (see *Table 5.1*). One can say that it was the ECJ which to a considerable degree materialized the process of integration, by establishing concrete rules and by putting through the validity of EU law and regulations in many detailed areas of economic and social life throughout the Union. Its working was a real "silent revolution" through law (Dehousse 1994:32). Through its activities and decisions, the ECJ in fact achieved a "constitutionalisation" of the legal order of the community.

Where did this widely recognized and discussed judicial activism (Arnull 2003:188f.) come from? There were two main sources for it: the specific character and aims of legal work and the professional-elite interests of the legal profession in the widest sense.

It is a central principle of legal work to develop systems of norms which are as coherent and comprehensive as possible. This principle has also inspired the judges at the ECJ, as it has been pointed out succinctly in the following characterisation of the "policy" of the judges: "By policy is meant the values and attitudes of the judges—the objectives they wish to promote. The policies of the European Court are basically the following: 1. Strengthening the Community . . . ; 2. increasing the scope and effectiveness of Community law; 3. enlarging the powers of the Community institutions" (Hartley 1998:79 as quoted in Pollack 2003:189; Rasmussen 1986). Thus, the court was always activist and interpreting the treaties in a "teleological" way, that is, in the direction of strengthening integration, toward "an ever closer Union." But how did the nation-states and the national courts consent to this far-reaching interpretation and acting of the ECJ, which certainly was restricting their own discretion? Here, an interpretation based on the professional-elitist interest of the legal profession seems to be very fruitful. In fact, the national courts of justice are clearly among the supporters of these activities of the ECJ. By addressing themselves directly to the ECJ, they can circumvent the constitutional courts of their own country and gain autonomy. Moreover, there are not only the national judges but the whole legal profession, which is interested in enforcing and enlarging European law. At most universities throughout Europe, new departments of European law have been established; the researchers and teachers employed there may well be several thousand people. There exists also a close connection between universities and the ECJ; outstanding professors of European law are frequently recruited as members of the ECJ.

These hypotheses are confirmed by an outstanding student of European law, Joseph Weiler (1999:203). He finds it surprising that among academics no critique of the elite-driven process of European integration emerged. He attributes it, to two facts: (1) to a theoretically based neglect of the legal aspect of integration among political scientists and economists; (2) to the fact that the law professorate historically has had an outstanding place in the legal discourse in Europe, much more than in the United States. Among legal scientists, there was no neglect of this dimension but rather a tendency to overemphasize it; there exists an "almost unanimous non-critical approach and tradition . . . towards the Court of Justice" (Weiler 2003:205). The reason for this is that "Community law and the European Court were everything an international lawyer could dream about: The Court was creating a new order of international law in which norms were norms, sanctions were sanctions . . .."

From the sociological, elite-theoretical point of view, we may only add that this wonderful new world of law was not only a huge intellectual challenge but provided also ample opportunities for new jobs and careers. These jobs are highly rewarding not only in terms of income (the incomes of the ECJ-judges are among the highest in the EU system) but also in terms of a challenging and powerful new professional role. Membership in the ECJ or expert work carried out for it makes it possible for lawyers to take over a quasi-political role. Court decisions, as any legal act, everywhere have some political sides to them. In the EU and the ECJ, this aspect of the legal role has become essential. This is true even if we might concede that the ECJ is constrained in its decisions by the treaties, and it would damage its own reputation and the validity and implementation of its judgements if it would not respect these limits (Pollack 2003:188). The European legal expert is a paradigmatic example for the thesis well-known in the sociology of professions that new institutions and organisations often also create new professions (Abbott 1988).

A further important aspect of this development of the ECJ is its relations to other bodies in the EU political system, particularly the Commission and the EP. Here, all observers agree that these relations are, despite occasional conflicts, very positive in principle. The reason is quite simple: All these institutions have the same ultimate aim—to further European integration. If some governments may have expected that they could limit or retard the activism of the ECJ, this was "a foolish hope . . . central judicial institutions invariably have centralizing rather than particularist tendencies . . ." (Chalmers 2004:63).

We may conclude these sketchy remarks by a short prospect. Today, a more critical attitude against the activity of the ECJ is spreading out, both among scientists and politicians. It is obvious that its work has favoured centralization, economic integration, and here in particular a liberalistic economic order, mainly in the interest of corporations and enterprises. It would be foolish, however, to criticize the role of the ECJ in a fundamental way, and to negate its legitimacy at all. Rather, what seems necessary is that its role and workings should be redefined in some way, together with general reorientation of the whole EU. One could here think of a reform of the appointment and the workings of the ECJ, but—more fundamentally—also of a stronger focus on individual social rights in the whole Constitution of the EU. By doing so we can maintain the fruitful interpretation of the EU as a "community of law" and the important role of the ECJ, but take into account the critics of many that the EU is lacking a social dimension. This issue shall be taken up more concretely in Chapter 8.

CONCLUSION

It seems paradoxical that the political elites have promoted European integration which deprives them of power at the level of their own state. The explanation usually given to this paradox is that they have been ready to do so because—after the rise of the superpowers and in the era of global-ization—in this way they can preserve their autonomy or regain influence. Thus, elites act in the interest of their nations. This interpretation, however, is not compatible with the increasing split between elites and citizens concerning the consent to integration. The analyses of this chapter have started from the assumption that integration is favoured by the elites also out of personal interests and gains. Here, we have to consider the establishment of many new political positions and careers in the European Parliament, the Commission, and the European Court of Justice. These positions open up possibilities for new career opportunities for national politicians also outside their own state. The participation of the members of national governments in regular meetings and decisions at the European level carries high symbolic value and opens up many possibilities to pursue political aims unpopular at home. In this regard, also a close look at the values, interests, and strategies of single, charismatic political leaders is revealing. We have shown that the characteristics and strategies of the "founding fathers" of integration have significantly shaped the form in which integration later on developed: This includes both the rather autocratic behaviour of the Catholic politicians of the first hour (Adenauer, Degasperi, Schuman) and the elitist style of thinking and acting of the main "spin doctor" of integration, Jean Monnet. Changes in the political culture in the last decades, particularly in Catholic member states such as Italy and France, have led to an increasing distrust in politics and the political elites among the general public. Clientelism and corruption have also encroached on the EU institutions in Brussels. All this has contributed to the rise of scepticism against integration among the general public. However, it would be a mistake to ascribe these problems only to individualistic interests or personal misbehaviour of specific members of the political elites. Rather, also the form in which the political system of the EU itself has developed has created them. A parliament which is perceived by many deputies as a big "voting machine," commission presidents and members who are appointed by the heads of national governments through a kind of bazaar trade, and jurists who have to make decisions of far-reaching political importance on the basis of treaties which focus mainly on economic-liberalistic integration will be in a very difficult position when it comes to develop a position which is both independent and balanced in terms of differing social interests. It is important, therefore, to look more closely at the basic ideas and aims of integration and their perceptions among the population at large. This shall be done in Chapters 6 and 7. Out of this analysis, we can then also draw some concrete conclusions about the necessary reform and further development of the political institutions of the EU.

4   The Economic Elites
Between Global Capitalism and European (Neo-) Corporatism

INTRODUCTION

In modern societies, politics and the economy are closely intertwined. This is particularly so in the process of European integration, which began as a coordinated administration of a few basic industries, extended into a free trade area, and still today—even if called a "Union"—is characterized in the first instance as a large, common market. This market is characterized not only by intense internal trade relations but also dominated increasingly by large multinational "European corporations." About 40% of the 100 largest corporations of the world belong to the EU.[1] But also other economic groups and associations, such as those of agriculture, have played a decisive role in the process of integration. In spite of ever-recurring criticisms, the bulk of the EU budget (55%) still goes into agriculture. Thus, it is obvious that economic interests and their proponents, the economic elites, have played an important role in the process of integration. It seems that established theories of integration clearly underestimate the role of economic elites,[2] while they cannot be neglected in social-historical accounts (see Middlemas 1995 as an example).

In this chapter, the role of the economic elites is investigated in four steps. First, some general hypotheses are developed about their composition, interests, and actions in the process of European integration. It is also discussed what the dominant ideology of integration has been. Second, it is asked if European integration has in fact led to a fully integrated economic space. This question is crucial because it is argued that economic integration is the most dynamic and basic among all forms of integration. It sheds also light on the degree of the integration of the "European" economic elite. Third, the concrete role of the economic elites in the establishment and further development of integration and enlargement of the EEC, EC, and EU are investigated. Next, we look at the agricultural policy of the EU, an area where the split between elites and citizens is particularly evident. Fifth, we investigate the role of the economic elites in the process of enlargement of the EU toward Central East Europe. Finally, the implications of this theoretical perspective and findings on the relation between economic and political integration of Europe are discussed.

4.1 The European economic elites and their role in the integration process

Three issues shall be discussed in this section: economic elites and elite theory; the definition and interests of the economic elites in the integration process; and the issue of the dominant ideology of integration.

The influence of economic elites from the perspective of elite theory

Political and economic elites are the only elite groups which dispose of their own independent bases of power. The power base of economic elites are financial means, the ownership of means of production, and the control of large organisations. Owners of large enterprises and top managers dominate work organisations which employ tens or even hundred of thousands of people and control budgets which are larger than those of many nation-states around the world. Thus, it is obvious that these elites have a huge influence in modern societies. This applies particularly to the European Union given its well-known democratic deficit. In the following, three points are made and investigated: (1) The economic elites have played highly significant roles in all stages of the European integration process; in different stages of this process, different subgroups of elites have been particularly influential. (2) The exertion of this influence mostly occurred unrecognized in public and even by scientific observers. (3) The development of the EU institutions and the consequences of integration, however, have led to a rising public scepticism and distrust of large corporations and the economic-political system of the EU among the general public.

Composition and interests, strategies, and actions of the economic elites in connection with the development of the Common Market

Usually, when speaking of economic elites, today one thinks only of the owners and managers of large corporations since they are the most powerful and can exert direct influence on politics. However, we have to consider also small and medium-sized enterprises. They can become relevant for politics in two regards: first, because their dependents represent significant fractions of voters; second, because some of them have strong interest organizations. A distinction between the following three economic pressure groups and elites might be sufficient for the purposes of the following discussion: (1) Farmers and their associations; (2) small and medium-sized enterprises (with up to hundreds or a few thousands of employees) and their organisations; today, also, these enterprises often operate on a world scale; (3) large enterprises, active on the national and international level, the so-called multinational corporations (MNCs). It will be shown that not only the MNCs but also the other enterprises and their pressure groups have been quite active and influential in the process of European integration. Among the farmer, in particular to the so-called big linkers among top managers of banks and industrial corporations are important; they hold many positions in different boards, and they are often also engaged in formulating broad business strategies for economic and political problems in the interest of large sections or the whole business community (Fennema 1982:207).

In order to understand the attitudes and actions in regard to integration, we have to ask what the main interests of these economic elites have been and are today. A least three kinds of interests are relevant in this regard:

- The interest or motive to attain an *adequate income and profit;* this is generally the commonly recognized motive. The term *adequate income* seems better suited than the usually mentioned motive for profit, which is associated only with the returns from invested capital and, therefore, seems hardly adequate for the case of a farmer or shopkeeper. The term *adequate* refers to the sociologically important notion that expectations concerning an adequate return for one's efforts vary highly between social strata, economic sectors, countries, and so on. This issue is particularly important for agricultural policy; the relatively low income of farmers was always one of the main reasons for the extensive state intervention in this sector.
- The *interest of security.* Security means the expectation that an enterprise will be able to overcome problems and difficulties that emerge from the invention of new technologies, the enlargement of markets, the intensification of competition, and so forth. Motives of this sort are central for small and large enterprises. For these, they may even be more important. For a large firm it is more difficult to adapt in a short time to problems of underutilization of capacities, of decline of profit margins, or even losses.
- The interest to gain *power, influence and prestige.* This interest may be most important among large enterprises; the more a firm controls a specific market, the more it can exert influence on price setting, exert pressure on furnishers, and so forth (Arndt 1980). Also, the interest to gain prestige, which cannot be dissociated neatly from that of power (power itself grants prestige and vice versa), is often relevant for large firms. Every week one can read in the newspapers that this or that firm has been able to swallow one of its rivals, thus becoming the largest (or second or third largest) firm of its sector in Europe or in the world. A deep-going study of managers has concluded that a great deal of their "work consists of ongoing social struggles for dominance and status. Real administrative effectiveness flows . . . from the prestige that one establishes with other managers . . . (from) the socially recognized ability to work one's will, to get one's way . . ." (Jackall 1989:195).

A sociological explanation of the actions of the economic elites (as of any other actors) must take into consideration also the situational circumstances within which they operate. In this regard, three general theses are proposed; the first relates to the situation at the end of World War II, the second to developments inside the EC/EU, and the third to new challenges from globalization since the 1980s. (1) The problem situation and the political actions taken in the postwar period by the states founding the EEC were to a large part inherited from the past or a continuation of earlier, traditional policies. This idea runs counter to the widely established view that the EC/EU is a totally new "invention." It is congruent, however, with the idea of *path dependency* in political and social theory, which says that new institutions cannot be (and usually are not) created out of nothing but build on the inherited institutional structure of a society. (2) Two factors played a specific role in the situation in the immediate postwar years: on the one side, an economic and political weakness of the main actors (enterprises, governments); on the other side, the existence and strengthening of economic interest organisations and pressure groups. This can be shown clearly both for the interests of the coal and steel industries and for the agricultural policy of the EU. (3) In the course of the postwar decades, new problems emerged which to a considerable degree were consequences of the strategies and actions taken. In the 1980s, the establishment of the full free market and the common currency were an answer to increased global competition; in the 1990s, the breakdown of the Iron Curtain opened up big new markets for capital, and politics answered by a speedy admission of many central East European countries to the EU. (4) The public throughout the EU, however, is becoming more and more aware of the influence of powerful economic interests and of the close networks between the economic and the political elites. This critical perception is one of the main reasons for the sceptical attitude toward integration which is spreading out in many EU member countries.

The dominant ideology of economic integration

European integration has been based on and legitimized always by economic theories and arguments. A widely established thesis says that neo-liberalistic economic theories were dominant in this regard. The main thesis proposed here is, however, that this ideology has never been that of an unconditional (neo-) liberalism, aiming toward a fully free market. Rather, from the beginning both the leaders of the industrial corporations and the political elites were aiming toward establishing the EU and its large enterprises as a "big player" on the world political-economic scene. Let us look at some important steps in this regard.

The decisive takeoff of European integration was the establishment of the European Steel and Coal Community (ESCS) in 1952. Through the fusion of French and German basic industries, which also were essential for the production of arms, a war between the two countries should be made impossible once and for all. This well-established story, however, is true only to a limited degree. First, it is not true that integration was the essential factor preserving peace in Europe since 1945 in Chapter 7. Second, while it is true that economic integration was a means for political aims, it diverts attention from the fact that the interests and networks of industrialists played a decisive role. The Treaty of Rome (1957), which established the free market among its member states, also established a common agricultural policy and created a European social fund. Nevertheless, the treaty was not welcomed everywhere and by all. The main opposition from the French side was that it would remove the protection which French industry enjoyed (Dinan 1999:31). These reservations could be overcome with two measures. First, parallel to the establishment of the EEC, the EURATOM Treaty was concluded, which established a common industrial policy in the area of atomic energy. Second, also the EEC Treaty was perceived as being a means for strengthening the position of the industrial corporations of the member states by providing them a big home market. This was the reason why the liberally minded German economic minister Ludwig Erhard was against the EEC: He argued that the abolishment of trade restrictions on the world scale would be the better strategy.

The intent to make Europe to a strong economic and political player on the world scale emerged even more clearly in the 1960s and 1970s. In the influential book *The American Challenge* Jean-Jacques Servan-Schreiber argued that the EEC cannot be content to establish a free market but must develop its own industrial policy. It should support the creation of large firms, particularly in strategic areas such as aviation, space, and the electronic industry, in order to make these firms and sectors competitive with American firms. Rather similar arguments were put forward in the 1980s by Jacques Delors in favour of his successful plan for the single market. This plan was based to a large degree on proposals made by the European Round Table of Industrialists (ERT). The intents of this influential business elite group have been described by an in-depth study as follows: "The ERT was not interested in merely 'unblocking' legislation on non-tariffs to trade. Nor was the group promoting a Thatcherite deregulatory programme. Rather, the group called for a restructuring of the regulatory framework of the European Community, and a recalibration of the social and economic political relations to create a unified market that would be conducive to 'the reindustrialization of Europe' " (Green Cowles 1995:503).

The basic thrust of these arguments concerning the furthering of the economic strength of the EC/EU by supporting strategic industrial sectors and enterprises was retained in all later treaties. Its recent actualization took place in the Agenda of Lisbon in March 2000, when the heads of the member states governments agreed to make the EU "the most competitive and dynamic knowledge-driven economy [of the world] by 2010 capable of sustainable economic growth with more and better jobs and greater social cohesion." The measures foreseen included:[3] the support of knowledge and innovation in Europe; the reform of state aid policy;

the simplification of the regulations for business operations; completion of the internal market for services, and so on. Central, although not highlighted openly, for this strategy were measures aimed at strengthening entrepreneurs and firms, particular in strategic sectors, such as information technology) reductions of company tax levels and establishing an EU-wide standard corporate tax system, and measures to attract more investment.

What can we conclude about the dominant economic legitimation of the European integration process? From a leftist perspective, it is a transfer of the U.S. model of *neoliberal capitalism* to Europe. For Pierre Bourdieu (2000), for instance, such a model includes the following basic axioms: The market is the best means to achieve efficient and just production and distribution; globalisation requires the removal of all barriers to free international trade and the reduction of state social expenditures; social rights are ineffective and should be kept at a minimal level. For Bourdieu the worldwide enforcement of these ideas constitutes also a case of symbolic domination; Europeans have entered into a kind of colonisation by submitting themselves to the ideological domination of the neoliberal model. A very different interpretation of European integration has been given by critics from the liberal side. For the Czech president Vaclav Klaus, a trained professor of economics, European integration has turned, especially since Maastricht, into *unification,* which implies political centralisation, loss of freedom, and curtailing of democracy.[4] As other EU critics with a personal experience with state socialism (e.g., Boukovsky 2005), Klaus sees considerable similarities between the former Soviet system and the EU; both show(ed) that regulation becomes the more necessary the more complex a system is.

Both these strains of arguments contain some truth but are not sufficient per se. The thesis presented here is that European integration contains both elements, that of a liberalization of market forces, of deregulation and privatization, but at the same time the reintroduction of well-known older European forms of supranational cooperation and concerted action. This can also be shown in the area of trade policy as such. While the EU in many regards supports international trade liberalization, it was said that the exceptions it has to free trade are enough to refute the view that it is fundamentally liberal (a concise summary of these critical arguments is given in Vaubel 1995:16ff.). The most significant of these exceptions is agricultural policy, which imposes huge costs both for the EU itself (through the high budget expenditures) and acts as a "virus" which makes more difficult free trade also in other areas. Also in manufacturing and services, a myriad of tariffs, antidumping measures, and the like exists; this fact hardly corresponds to the principle of an unrestricted liberalism. The possibilities to implement restrictions on free external trade have been made easier since 1994; besides this, defensive trade policy and instruments for an active industrial policy have been strengthened with France as its strongest supporter (Borrmann et al. 1995:161ff.).

4.2 Does the EU constitute a closely integrated economic community?

It might look far out to ask if the European Union really constitutes an integrated economic space after half a century of integration. However, the answer to this question cannot be taken for granted. In the foregoing section, we have alluded to politicians who have argued that worldwide establishment of free-trade principles would be preferable anyway to regional economic integration. From the sociological point of view, it is questionable if the abolishment of trade barriers in a certain region will automatically lead toward a process of "growing together in a natural way." Nation-specific patterns of industrial organization and management, linguistic barriers, religions, and other cultural traditions do not coincide with geographic propinquity. It is interesting to investigate, therefore, to which degree it can be said that the EU today really constitutes a fully integrated economic space. If this is the case, it would support the functional interpretation of integration. If this is not the case, we must conclude that the process of integration has been pushed also by particular economic and political interests.

Three issues shall be discussed in this section: first, the role of economic integration for economic growth and welfare; second, the specific relevance of economic considerations for the process of European integration; third, the interests and actions of the economic elites.

International economic integration as a way to stimulate economic growth and welfare

Among economists, it is widely agreed that free trade and intense economic relations between different regions and states have positive effects (Lipsey 1972:591; Kleinert 2004; Ingham 2004; Farmer and Vlk 2005). This applies in particular to relations between nations with comparable levels of development. In line with the arguments in favour of free trade, during the 1950s and 1960s, economic integration was seen as an important measure for economic progress; also, the United Nations supported such efforts (El-Agraa 2004a:18). However, it turned out that negotiations about worldwide free trade were slow and inefficient, and the realisation of these intentions very difficult. As a consequence, the idea of regional free-trade areas between fewer, more homogeneous, neighbouring groups of countries was developed.

International economy, a new branch of economics, distinguishes between five degrees of economic integration (El-Agraa 2004a:1f.): (1) *Free-trade areas*, with free trade inside, but nationally determined policies concerning relations with the outside world; (2) *Customs unions*, with common external commercial relations; (3) *Common markets*, which also have free internal mobility of all production factors (capital, labour, enter-prises, goods and services); (4) *Complete economic unions* with integrated monetary and fiscal policies, exercised by a central authority; and (5) *Political unions* or states.

The European Union today certainly represents a common market but possesses also some elements of steps (4) and (5). From the viewpoint of potential free trade between all countries in the world, the European Union evidently is only a second-best solution (Scitovsky 1962:15; Smeets 1996:48). Economic integration in general increases trade competition and specialisation among its members and is beneficial for them. It may have the opposite effect on trade and specialisation between the Union and other countries, however, because integration diverts or even suppresses trade with the outside world. Moreover, internal economic policies may have negative effects on external trade. A case in point are the extensive EU sub-sidies for the agricultural sector which provide cheap agricultural products to the world market, undersell the products of farmers in poor countries of the Third World (Smeets 1996:63), and run counter to the opening of the EU markets for other products of these countries (Matthews 2004). Several measures of EU foreign trade violate the principles of international free trade (Ingham 2004:87). From all these points of view, it is essential, therefore, to ask what the role of free trade was for European integration.

"Unity via the back door": The strategic role of the economy in the process of European integration

The positive effects of trade integration were one important motivation to pursue European economic integration. However, a declared intent of European integration was not only to initiate and promote economic inte-gration but also to initiate a *spillover* of economic integration to social and political integration. The functionalist explanation of integration takes this spillover process as the main reason for the successful and seemingly irresistible process of integration since the establishment of the ESCC in 1952 (see Chapter 2). The economy had to play a decisive instrumental role in the general process of integration: "In the short and medium terms the goal should be overall economic integration. Experience gained in working together would then pave the way for the achievement of political unity, i.e., *political unity should be introduced through the 'back door'* " (El-Agraa 2004b:29).

In this section, we shall investigate how far the factual integration pro-cess has gone in economic terms. If we find that it has proceeded very far, European integration was in fact a process developing "from below," as Carl J. Friedrich (1969:47) wrote in his classic book *Europe: An Emergent Nation:* " . . . it is the businessman who has had the largest share in building the new European community after the framework of institutions had been erected by the politicians." If no such deep-going economic integration can be observed, however, European integration must be seen mainly as a politically induced process. In this case, we may suppose that it has been also or even more in the interests of political and bureaucratic elites.

The development of a European economic space and the rise of the "European corporation"?

Four issues shall be discussed in this section: the development and intensity of EU internal trade; merger and acquisition activities within the EU and over its borders; the rise of the "Eurocorporation" and the "Euromanager"; and the development of the patterns of labour mobility within the EU.

Let us first look at the patterns of exchanges of goods and services, of exports and imports. The question is how much of these exchanges are taking place within the EU and how much not. Given the huge size of the EU, we should certainly expect that the largest share of exports and imports is internal exchange; neighbour states have always more trade with each other (Farmer and Vlk 2005:21). The crucial question is if the proportion of EU internal exchange is growing over time. Let us look at some findings in this regard.[5]

First, it is true that the largest part of exports and imports remains within the EU: In 2005, between 60% and 79% of the exports and between 55% and 78% of the imports came from other EU member states. There are considerable differences between countries. It is not surprising that some smaller countries (Austria, Netherlands, Portugal) show the highest shares of EU internal exports, and countries situated at the geographic periphery (Ireland, United Kingdom, Sweden, Greece, Italy) show a relatively lower share. Looking at imports, the pattern is similar. Quite interesting is that the non-EU member states Switzerland and Norway are integrated very closely with the Common Market: Switzerland has the highest share of EU imports (80%) of all countries compared, and Norway the highest share of EU exports (81%). There exists a related, interesting fact which fully corresponds to these findings about the limited relevance of the EU frontiers for economic relationships in Europe. The founder of the highly influential European Round Table of Industrialists (ERT), Pehr Gyllenhammar, was a Swedish manager, and four out of the seventeen first members of this group came from non-EC member states (Switzerland and Sweden; see Green-Cowles 1995:504ff.).

The second issue concerns the development of these patterns over time. In all countries, the level of exchange with other EC/EU member countries increased strongly during the 1960s and 1970s but slowed down later. In the mid-1950s, in most countries less than half of the exports and imports went to other EC member states. In most countries, already since 1980 no further increase can be observed. In two countries (Ireland and Greece) even a decrease of the EU share in exports and imports can be observed since 1990. All this seems surprising, given the fact that several of these countries became EU members only in the mid-1990s and that the full single market became effective in 1992. However, from the viewpoint of economic theory it is not surprising. If in a region a certain level of integration has been reached (with or without an economic union), a further expansion of intraindustrial trade brings only little additional advantages (Smeets 1996:67). Thus, we must conclude that European integration through the EEC/EC and EU has not been the main factor for the growth of intra-European trade since the 1950s. The strongest increase in intra-European trade took place in a period when the EEC contained only few members; at this time, also, the EC and the EFTA were intertwined by strong trade flows between them (Borrmann et al. 1995:23); till today, the "Europeanisation" of trade patterns can be observed among some non-EU member states to the same degree as among the EU member states.

Second, let us investigate if a new type of "*Eurocorporation*" is coming into being. Here, we look at two aspects: first, at the patterns and the development over time of merger and acquisitions (M&A) activities; second, at trends in management. A merger means that two firms enter into a very close relationship with each other—in fact, they intend to form a new single enterprise. This will be a very ambitious undertaking, since this makes it necessary to develop one single new unit with a coherent organisational identity and culture (Siegwart and Neugebauer 1998; Lucks and Meckl 2002; Kleinert 2004). The more different the original cultures of the two firms are, the more difficult this process will be. Extensive research has shown that for these and other reasons a high proportion (maybe half or more) of mergers turn out as failures (Tichy 2002; Seldeslachts 2005). If the European Union is a closely integrated economic union, the merging of firms within the EU should be easier than the merging of EU firms with firms outside the EU.

Merger activities have attracted the attention of the EU Commission since the beginning since they can have negative effects on competition within the relevant markets. A system of merger control was installed, therefore, already in the early 1980s. In 2004, this system was replaced by a new regulation which also recognizes the possibility of efficiency gains through mergers. (In practice, this means to allow more mergers.) First, let us look shortly at the general development of merger activities.

Merger activities are not a new phenomenon of postwar economic history (Siegwart and Neugebauer 1998). They typically come in waves, usually after significant technological breakthroughs, in connection with periods of economic growth and after changes in political parameters relevant for the economy (Mayes and Kilponen 2004:321). M&A activities have increased massively throughout the world. In the EU, a first wave occurred in the 1980s, which reached its peak in 1991. In this year, 10,653 mergers took place involving a total value of 164 billion euros. Until the mid-1990s, the number declined to around 9,400, but then rose again to a peak of 14,294 mergers in 1996, involving 1,860 billions of euros; thereafter, the number declined again to 9,811 (627 billions) in 2004 (Meiklejohn 2006:11; Fligstein 2001:147ff.; Molle 2001:347). Most mergers involved the larger member states, with the United Kingdom by far on top, followed by Germany, France, and the Netherlands

Table 4.1 Total M&A Activities in the EU-15, 1991, 1995, 2000, and 2004, Divided by Domestic, Community, and International Mergers

		Domestic	Community*	International mergers			Overall
				EU target*	EU bidder**	total	total
1991	%	54.4	11.9	26.3	7.3	33.6	100
1995	%	58.6	12.8	17.0	11.6	28.6	100
2000	%	54.8	15.2	13.2	16.9	30.1	100
2004	%	56.4	13.4	17.5	12.7	30.2	100
Average***	%	56.4	13.4	17.5	12.7	30.2	100

*Mergers between firms based in different EU member states.
**Mergers between EU-15 and non-EU-15 firms.
***Including all years between 1991 and 2004.

Source: Meiklejohn (2006), p. 13.

(see *Table 4.2*, first column). Relatively speaking, however, smaller countries, such as the Netherlands, Finland or Sweden, had a higher share of mergers.

The question relevant in this context is to which countries the merged firms belonged. Two kinds of data are relevant in this regard. The first are merger activities by domestic, EU, and international operations. The findings tell a rather clear story (*Table 4.1*): (1) More than half of all mergers are taking place within the single member states of the EU. This means that the national context is still the most important unit of economic transactions and relations. This is also an indication of the fact that globalization does not eliminate the relevance and autonomy of the nation-states (Weiss 1998; Heismann 1999). (2) The next most frequent constellation are mergers between EU firms and firms outside the EU. These mergers are about one third of all—double the proportion of mergers within the EU. (3) A weak increase of mergers within the EU occurred in the 1990s; since 2000, this type of mergers has decreased, however (Mayes and Kilponen 2004; Molle 2001).

A second relevant information concerns the direction of those mergers which involve firms within and outside the EU. Are these distributed more or less equally over different other countries, or can we see some specific patterns in this regard? *Table 4.2* shows that definitely the latter is the case. Looking at these data, it could even be deduced that the EU does not exist at all. The main direction of merger activities follows historical and cultural criteria—mainly language—but not EU borderlines. Four clearly distinguishable groups of countries exist between which mergers are most frequent: (1) The Anglo-Saxon countries, including the United Kingdom, Ireland, and the United States. Twenty-four percent of British mergers involved U.S. firms, but only 9% French firms (the next most frequent target country); quite similar is the proportion of mergers of Irish with U.S. firms. (2) The Scandinavian countries Denmark, Finland, and Sweden; in this cluster, non-EU member Norway is also included as the second most frequent target of Danish and Swedish acquisitions. (3) The French-speaking countries Belgium, Luxembourg, and France. (4) The German-speaking countries Germany and Austria; after Germany, the next most frequent country where Austrian firms find partners for merging is Hungary. (4) The Iberian countries Spain and Portugal, which have most close relations with each other, and then to Argentina and Brazil, respectively. Rather similar patterns emerge if trade patterns between European countries (Tichy 1994) and between countries worldwide (Borrmann et al. 1995:21) are analysed. The clear division of Western Europe into these different groups of countries has led many economists to argue that the EC/EU does not constitute an "optimal currency area" since there exists no full mobility of all production factors between the member countries. Similar findings have been reported in analyses of international networks of banks and industries in the 1970s: They also showed close networks between groups of American and European banks and industries (Fennema 1982).

Table 4.2   Cross-Border Merger Activities of EU-15 Firms 1991–2004: Most Frequent Target Countries

Bidder Country	Total cross-border M&A by country of bidder	Community operations		International operations	
		Total number	Most targeted country (number)	Total number	Most targeted country (number)
Ireland	1,114	697	UK (494)	417	USA (224)
UK	10,660	4,437	France (977)	6,223	USA (2,557)
Denmark	1,345	778	Sweden (212)	567	Norway (155)
Finland	1,343	717	Sweden (279)	626	USA (126)
Sweden	2,752	1,577	Finland (403)	1,175	Norway (311)
Netherlands	3,921	2,321	Germany (596)	1,600	USA (419)
Belgium	1,694	1,134	France (398)	560	USA (151)
Luxembourg	503	344	France (77)	159	USA (26)
France	5,118	2,760	Germany (626)	2,358	USA (600)
Germany	6,191	3,125	France (608)	3,066	USA (742)
Austria	1,194	575	Germany (331)	620	Hungary (110)
Italy	1,775	1,031	France (284)	744	USA (155)
Spain	1,446	570	Portugal (172)	876	Argentina (133)
Portugal	329	182	Spain (132)	147	Brazil (72)
Greece	346	114	UK (32)	232	Romania (33)

Source: Meiklejohn (2006), p. 13.

The economic fragmentation within the EU is evidently a matter of deep-rooted social, cultural, and political divisions. The close relations between the United Kingdom and the United States, for instance, are highly relevant also from the political point of view. In 2003/04, when the U.S. began their second war against Iraq, Britain joined them. By doing so, it caused the most serious crises of the EU foreign policy because France, Germany, and other member countries strongly opposed this war. In Chapter 7, it is shown that the British ideas and expectations concerning European integration diverge substantially from those of most other EU member states. Thus, the European cultural macroregions, defined along linguistic-cultural and religious lines and different political institutions and histories (Haller 1990), are by far more important than the European Union. Countries like Ireland and the United Kingdom, but also Spain and Portugal, fulfil a potentially very important "bridge function" (Haller 2003c) between Europe and the outside world.

A third issue concerning the question of the emergence of a European economic space is related to the development of a new type of *"Euromanagers."* That this is a real possibility is evident from several points of view: International work mobility is typically high among the professions; the role of the managers has become professionalized in the last decades, for instance, by the development of international business schools (Hartmann 2003); English becomes the *lingua franca* throughout Europe. An empirical study carried out by Michael Hartmann (1999, 2002) about the composition of top managers in the large corporations of several European countries showed, however, that a new type of Euromanager did not emerge. The top managers of the 100 largest enterprises in Germany, France, and Great Britain are recruited nearly exclusively from their home universities. Very few managers had longer periods of working abroad during their careers. A French study found similar patterns and its author concluded: "The dominant classes have no interest to forgo the national bases of their social superiority but they can limit themselves less and less to these relations" (Wagner 2004:139). The new European business schools will not change these patterns; MBA degrees usually are seen only as a refinement but not as an essential part of education. Thus, we do not see the emergence of an Euromanager or a "world manager" (Kanter 1995).

Similar findings turn out if we look at patterns of *labour mobility*. In a fully integrated market, all four productive "factors" (goods, services, capital, and labour) must be mobile in order that imbalances between the different national economies are cleared. The creation of such a market also in the realm of employment is a declared aim of the EU policy. The EU argues that labour mobility is not only beneficial for the EU economy as a whole but also for the single worker as the responsible commissioner for this issue, Vladimir Spidla, recently wrote a newspaper article entitled, "Praise of labour mobility."[6] However, extensive social-scientific research has shown that also considerable social costs are associated with geographic labour mobility. It does not only imply a giving up of many close social ties, but often is associated even with significant losses of qualifications and an occupational descent. The low inclination of citizens of the EU to migrate to other countries is not surprising from this point of view. Economic considerations lead to the expectation that labour mobility from countries and regions with low income levels or high unemployment to those with better conditions should take place. A sociological study of the intents to become mobile geographically has shown that economic push-and-pull models work only within countries but not between them (Hadler 2006). Many social and cultural factors play a significant role, such as the personal and familial situation, local, regional, and national affiliations, language barriers, and the like (Brinkmann 1981).

The empirical findings prove that these factors work strongly against the emergence of an integrated economic space. First, EU citizens show a rather low level of geographic mobility, half of the rate of U.S. citizens. Only 38% of EU citizens change residence in the course of ten years; and only 4% move across national borders.[7] Less than 1% of EU residents migrate in the course of a year to another EU state; in the U.S., this number is six times as large. Furthermore, there is no indication of an emerging EU labour market over time. Already in the first wave of postwar European migration, from the 1960s to the early 1970s, this migration was one from outside into the EEC/ EC, namely from South European countries (at that time not members) and from North Africa, Yugoslavia, and Turkey to the central and north European countries, or from the commonwealth into Great Britain (Münz and Seifert 2001; Mayes and Kilponen 2004:326ff.). Since 1990, the switch to immigrants from outside Europe is rather pronounced. Also, a new stream of immigration from East to West Europe began after 1989. Today, we can even observe seemingly strange patterns of labour mobility from poor countries east of the EU (Romania, Ukraine) to the south European periphery (south Italy, Portugal), in spite of rather high levels of unemployment in these regions. Work conditions and wages at the large farm plantations in Spain and in service jobs in the booming tourist centres are so bad that it is difficult to find domestic workers for them. The influx of illegal migrants from Africa contributes to this modern form of a bondagelike exploitation (Milborn 2006). However, also East-West migration will diminish in the future, when wage levels will rise in the East. Already now, in some of the more developed regions in the East European member countries, a shortage of workers is emerging.

Two conclusions emerge from all these findings: First, the European Union does not constitute a fully integrated economic space, clearly detached from the outside world. Two factors prevent the emergence of such a space: On the one side, the historically inherited, internal social and cultural barriers between the different language and culture areas; on the other side, the new forces of globalization which have led to an increasing interconnection

between all macroregions of the world, both in terms of economic relations (capital investments, corporate mergers, trade patterns) and in terms
of migration. Globalisation seems to be a stronger force of integration than
Europeanisation (Beck and Grande 2004:173). These interconnections are
also clearly influenced by inherited cultural affinities and economic-political relations between subsets of EU member states and the outside world.
The second conclusion concerns the degree of integration of the European
economic elites. Our findings do not support the thesis of the emergence of
a new "European business class" (van Apeldoorn 2000, 2002) or even a
transnational global capitalist class (van der Pijl 1989; Holman 1992). These
authors rightly point to the importance of power and influence of international big business and its elites. However, they underestimate the internal
differences between its different subgroups and fractions, the autonomous
power of the political and bureaucratic elites, and also that of ideas and
institutions, such as democracy.

4.3 The role of the economic elites in the establishment
and further development of integration

In the following, the role of economic elites in the different stages of the
process of European integration shall be discussed. These stages are the
establishment of the European Coal and Steel Community (ECSC); the revi-
talisation of integration in the 1980s; the process of marketisation of corporate control and the influence of lobbying in Brussels. Finally, we present
some findings on the public perception of the power of the economic and
political elites.

Corporate economic interests in the establishment of the
European Steel and Coal Community (ECSC)

A well-established story is told about the origins of European integration and
the strategic role of the Monnet-Schuman plan for the establishment of the
ECSC in the early 1950s: In order to break once and for all with the history of
bloody wars in Europe, Monnet and Schuman proposed to put German and
French coal and steel industries of the Ruhr and Lorraine, the backbones of the
armament industries, under a common administration. The idea of European
integration was "in the air" already since the 1920s and had inspired numerous efforts and plans; it was only Jean Monnet's ingenious, practical proposal
which really became successful (see, e.g., Dinan 1999:11ff.). However, this
"Monnet-myth" does not withstand closer examination. The formal cooperation between the French and German steel and coal industries, initiated by the
ECSC, was not new at all and it was consistent with postwar efforts of many
other French politicians of the time. Their intent was to reintegrate Germany
into Europe under French conditions and to subsume the Ruhr industry to an
"organic control" (Gillingham 1986, 1987, 2004; Schäfer 2005).

The idea of a close cooperation between French and German basic industries dates back to the International Steel Cartel (ISC), founded in 1926, which involved comprehensive agreements between producers and governments and served as a vehicle for diplomatic cooperation and factual economic integration. In Germany, a policy of competition was not known before. In the late nineteenth century, cartelization was recognized as legal; until the early 1930s, the number of cartels increased to about 3000–4000 (Nollert 2005:165). The ISC, born out of the emergency of the world economic crisis, had in fact been established as a new form of "functional" international integration. Ninety percent of world steel exports were controlled by the cartel. The Nazi period and the Second World War did not destroy this kind of cooperation. In fact, the big German producers of coal and steel did not suppress the French, Belgian, and other coproducers but tried to preserve the ties that they had socialised before. During the war, the German type of "organised capitalism" was expanded to the occupied territories. After four years of German administration, "the producer associations of France and the other West European countries adopted characteristics which to an amazing way were similar to the Ruhr models" (Gillingham 1986:382). In spite of strict U.S. bans of cartels, the producers of France and Germany quite early after the war began to reach out their antennas to achieve a restoration of the old connections and forms of organisation. From this point of view, we can understand somewhat better the surprising fact that industrialists, not politicians, were the first to show the necessity of an intact German and French mining industry for European economic recovery. In 1947, the German banker Pferdmenges offered, on behalf of Ruhr iron and steel industries, to cede a 50% share of this industry to French interests (Gillingham 1985:166). It was after this idea that experts in the French Commissariat au Plan, including Jean Monnet, began to draft a proposal for a new steel and coal authority.

The idea of economic cooperation in Europe dates back already to 1915–1920. Then, Etienne Clémenceau established a system of state-directed management of the whole economy by a small group of "unbureaucratic bureaucrats"; his *directeur de cabinet* was Jean Monnet (Holmes 2000:99, 405). After the Second World War, the power of the national associations of producers increased, the concentration in the sectors of coal and steel accelerated, and many kinds of subsidies and other market-alien elements were retained. French foreign minister Georges Bidault already in 1948 proposed to change from a politics of compensation toward a policy of cooperation with Germany (Gillingham 1987). Many other French high officials and politicians joined this idea of looking for an agreement with Germany. Pressure by Britons and Americans finally paved the way for the Monnet-Schuman plan (Loth 1996). In Germany, the acceptance of all political groups and the unions to the new Franco-German cooperation was achieved by strengthening social partnership, extending the principle of codetermination to the coal industry, and providing investment incentives for coal and steel. In this process, new "cooperative" supranational institutions were created with the "musty odor of the old cartels" (Gillingham 1987:22).

The rise of the modern corporation and the contribution of the EU to the marketisation of corporate control

Let us now look at the role of business interests in the further process of European integration. The postwar economic boom in Western Europe was associated also with a strong process of industrial concentration. To give just one example: In the 1960s, there existed dozens of independent producers of automobiles in all larger countries. At the turn to the twenty-first century, only five big firms produced half of all European cars; most of the smaller firms had disappeared or had been absorbed by the large firms. We have pointed already in the introduction to the fact that 40% of the world's largest corporations belong to the EU. Comparing total GDP of nation-states with total sales of the largest corporations, S. Anderson and J. Cavanagh show that half of the largest units are corporations. General Motors, Daimler-Chrysler, and three other corporations have larger sales (about $160 billion) than the GDP of states such as Poland, Norway, or Greece.[8] These authors conclude that large corporations are more powerful today than many nation-states around the world. This conclusion has been challenged by others.[9] However, it is out of question that big corporations, which employ hundreds of thousands of workers and often have fifty and more production and distribution sites around the world, have massive economic and also considerable political power and influence.

Why did these large corporations emerge at all in Western capitalism?[10] The dominant explanation in this regard is efficiency, as put forward in the historical study of Alfred Chandler (1977): "Modern multiunit business enterprise replaced small traditional enterprise when administrative co-ordination permitted greater productivity, lower costs, and higher profits than co-ordination by market mechanisms" (Chandler 1977:6; here quoted after van Apeldoorn and Horn 2005). This explanation, in line with the transaction cost approach in economics, has been questioned both out of systematic and historic reasons. In historical terms, it has been shown that the development of the modern corporation was also shaped by the dynamics of power and property, and by political struggles involving class interests and the state (Roy 1997). This fight involved considerable opposition from small business and from workers who felt threatened by the power of the new corporations. Furthermore, the rise of large corporations, as of all large organisations, does not always increase efficiency but often leads also to rising inefficiencies, bureaucratic waste, and extra profits due to the large power of these firms (Schumacher 1973; Kohr 1978). Empirical economic research has shown that small and middle-sized firms are more productive than large ones (Aiginger and Tichy n.d.).

A consequence of the rise of economic corporations was the separation of ownership and control. The rise of the managers who run most large private corporations, instead of the owners themselves, has been the object of much debate. Today, we can say that what happened was not a separation of ownership and control (as maintained in the thesis of Berle and Means) but a separation of ownership and management, especially with the expansion of the financial markets in recent years. Ownership in the firms was itself transposed into a commodity, separated from the social context in which it was embedded, the firm (van Apeldoorn and Horn 2005). As a key "auxiliary institution," stock markets have developed; they work as mere markets for the circulation of property rights as such, as mechanisms of liquidity. Thereby, money capital itself became an independent power. In West Europe, large blockholders of corporations (such as banks, entrepreneurial families, etc.), several decades after World War II, still dominated capitalism. This could be considered as an "organised capitalism" around a stable coalition or "community of interests" of blockholders, managers and workers. Since the early 1990s, a "marketisation of corporate control" has taken place whereby the managers and the purposes of firms are increasingly dependent on the stock market (van Apeldoorn and Horn 2005; Windolf 1994). In this market, the evaluation of company performance is based primarily on shareholder value. Therefore, managers also care increasingly about this shareholder value and less about the real productive capacity of the firm. In markets where this principle dominates, shareholders receive larger net profits from their shares, and the incomes of managers are higher than those in more traditional corporations. Even trade unions within these companies become increasingly oriented toward efficiency and performance (in financial terms) and less toward traditional unionist macrosolidarity (König 1999; Hartmann 2002; Höpner 2003).

The process of European integration has contributed (Windolf 1992; significantly to the emergence of this shareholder capitalism in Europe (van Apeldoorn/Horn 2005:20ff; Coen 1997). The basics for this process were laid by the internal market programme, activated to a large degree by the *European Round Table of Industrialists* (ERT) in the 1980s (Bornschier 2000a). The role of the ERT and its leading personalities is also an excellent example showing that decisive personalities and coherent and determined networks of elites can have decisive impact on historical events. The ERT was promoted in the early 1980s by Pehr Gyllenhammar, chief executive officer of the Swedish automobile manufacturer Volvo. He argued that a comprehensive "Marshall Plan for Europe" was necessary to override economic and industrial stagnation in Europe. (Green Cowles 1995:504; see also van Apeldoorn 2000). Gyllenhammar was a "political man"; he spoke fluent French and English, entertained close ties to leading businessmen and politicians (including the French President Mitterand), and liked to speak to the media. He was able—in close cooperation with the EC industry Commissioner Etienne Davignon—to establish the ERT as an informal, yet well-organized

Photo 4a   Pehr Gyllenhammar (born 1935), CEO of Volvo (1970–1990), and other Swedish corporations; founder of the European Round Table of Industrialists.
Source: ERT.

and highly influential group of leading European businessmen. From 1983 to 1985, this group developed a comprehensive plan (formulated also in a paper of Wisse Decker, CEO of Philips), called "Europe 1990." His aim was not only to create the fully integrated market but also to concentrate and stimulate efforts to strengthen strategic sectors of industry and research in Europe. The ideas of the ERT found strongest support among French politicians and were later formally established as an aim of the EC/EU in the Single European Act and the Maastricht Treaty; the latter included (in Title

XIII "Industry") the aim of enforcement of the competitivity of the European industry on an equal footing with the aim of securing a fully competitive market. This aim led to a "strategic industry and trade policy" which is used by the EU to support "European champions," even if this runs counter to the preservation of competition (Berthold and Hilpert 1996:81ff.). Examples of efforts to strengthen and protect European industries from foreign competition included the automobile industry (here, self-restraint contracts with Japan and the EU are supplemented by national import quotas); microelectronics (chip production); and the aircraft industry, where huge amounts of money were spent (often in the form of subsidies for research; see also Feldmann 1993). It is not surprising from this point of view that the American Chamber of Commerce, after widespread complaints from American companies about EC industry standards, border formalities, and export licences, expressed concerns in this regard (Egan 2003:35). It seems

Photo 4b   The EURO, the 2002 winner of the "Karlspreis," funded by citizens of the German town of Aachen, as "a recognition for *personalities and bodies* which help to overcome borders and establish friendship between the peoples of Europe."

Source: European Community, Audiovisual Service.

that they became increasingly alarmed about the high subsidies of the EU for the aircraft industry, which amounted to 15 billion euros in the last years (according U.S. sources); in 1992, the EU and the U.S. had concluded a treaty to tolerate such subsidies.[11]

In the second half of the 1990s, the pretended neoliberal project of market integration was furthered by a number of new initiatives to create also a single financial market. The Cardiff Council called for the Commission to develop an action plan for removing the remaining obstacles to an integrated financial market; the Commission subsequently issued a Financial Services Action Plan. The Commission's 2003 action plan for "Modernising Company Law and Enhancing Corporate Governance" further extends this line of policy. A milestone was certainly the earlier establishment of the European Monetary Union (EMU) and the euro. The EU Commission attributed great importance to cross-border mergers, whose number was very high throughout the 1980s and 1990s, as shown in the first section. However, there was only a very low number of cases which were involved in merger control activities of the commission. In the period 1991–2004, there were about 152,000 mergers in the EU; only 2,336, that is, 1.7%, were notified to the commission. Of these, only about 5% raised serious competition issues that could not be resolved in the first phase of the procedure. This means that only a tiniest proportion of all M&A activities was seen as problematic (Ilzkovitz and Meiklejohn 2006:11, 22ff.). Thus, "the Community Merger Control does not suggest that the merger regulation places a very heavy burden on business, nor that the Community is exceptionally severe in its application of the regulation" (ibid., p. 29).

The actual influence and lobbying of economic actors in Brussels

A central issue when speaking about the influence of economic elites in Brussels today is lobbyism. The relevance of this topic is quite evident: There is no other capital in the world where in recent decades so many lobbyists have been settled as in Brussels. It is estimated that today about 15,000 persons in Brussels are engaged directly or indirectly with lobbying activities for large enterprises, business and labour associations, national and regional political communities, states and local governments, and so forth (König 1999:204ff; Attac 2006:58ff.; Balanya et al. 2000). Exact data about the number of lobbyists do not exist. In 2005, 2,030 organizations with 4,007 persons were accredited at the European Parliament, and some 2,180 organizations in the *European Affairs Directory*.[12] Lobbying is no new invention at the level of the EU—it is quite important also in Washington, and it cannot be discredited as a whole because it fulfils also important functions of reciprocal information between business, politics, and public administration. The form in which it has developed in Brussels, however, is problematic for three reasons. First, there are no strict rules about lobbying, including the registering of the persons and organisations active, their working procedures, and the like. There is often an interchange between positions within the Commission and the career as a lobbyist. Second, the EU Commission itself has a positive general attitude toward lobbying and uses the lobbyists extensively when new regulations are proposed. The ways in which this information is used, however, are rather intransparent to the public. Third, powerful social groups and organisations, such as business and professional associations, are overrepresented among the lobbyists, while the unions are underrepresented (Kirchner 1977; Kirchner and Schwaiger 1981; Kohler-Koch 1996; Greenwood 1998; Eising 2004; Michalowitz 2004). Given the democratic deficit of the EU, this strong influence of lobbying evidently is a serious problem in terms of an equal representation of all groups and interests in the EU member states.

We cannot assume that all lobbyists and lobbying activities in Brussels will be highly successful. Many smaller enterprises and associations may be induced to use lobbyists just in order to "stay on the ball." Investigating a series of political decisions at the level of the EU, political scientist Irina Michalowitz (2004:269) concluded that lobbying does not seem to matter a lot in many cases. It is only when lobbyists are in line with the main aims of political actors that they are likely to score. One of the reasons is that most lobby bureaus are rather small, composed of only a few (one to three) persons. How can this surprising finding be interpreted? Does it show that economic elites in fact do not have so much influence on European integration as it is often proposed? On the one side, it may in fact be true that the economic elites do not interfere so much and directly into the political process as it is often maintained by leftist thinkers and anticapitalist NGOs. It would be a wrong conclusion, however, to say that lobbyism in Brussels is no problem at all. First, lobbyism in its present form doubtless works in favour of large enterprises and powerful groups. Multinational corporations and business organizations have many informal ways to influence important decisions. An example was the EU directive on bank balances (1987), which was influenced in a significant way by the *Bundesverband Deutscher Banken* (Coen 1997; König 1999:200ff.). A similar picture emerges from a case study about the creation of EADS, the European Aeronautic, Defence and Space Company, a joint venture of large firms in Germany (Daimler Chrysler), France (Aérospatiale-Matra), and Spain (CASA) which produces the Airbus and the "Eurofighter." EADS was established as a close network between the participating firms. The European Commission and the respective national governments, however, played a decisive role (Bockstette 2002). The involved firms used their financial means for massive public relations activities; they were unimpeded by any counterlobby. Also, single managers, such as Jürgen Schrempp and Jean-Luc Lagardère, played a decisive role.[13] Second, the essence of much lobbying consists in acting without much publicity. Often, it is essential for success to know one specific, decisive person in the commission or the parliament, and to intervene at the right time (Hörmann 1997). Third, the public throughout Europe is well aware of this fact. Therefore, as long as lobbyism in its present form continues to operate in Brussels, it will contribute significantly the high level of scepticism toward integration among the general public in Europe. Let us look a little bit closer at the problem that exists in this regard.

The public perception of corporate power and influence in Brussels

We can use two kinds of sources about the public perception of lobbyism in Brussels in the member countries of the EU. The first is a small Austrian population survey[14] and interviews with politicians and commission officials in Brussels in spring 2006 (Haller and Ressler 2006a). The intent was to investigate differences in perception and attitudes between elites and citizens. Both groups were asked the same questions about the influence of powerful groups in Brussels. In the population survey, nine groups were mentioned in a standardized question and the respondents had to say if they considered the influence of these groups as very high, just right, or too weak. We have shown already in Chapter 1 that a deep split emerged between citizens and elites in regard to the meaning and importance of lobbying in Brussels: While the interviewed citizens were quite critical in this regard, representatives of the political elites (EU deputies and officials) saw only positive aspects in lobbying. Lobbying, in their view, is an indispensable and necessary instrument for politicians and officials to get relevant information for new political initiatives, regulations, and laws. Problematic aspects of lobbying from the viewpoint of transparency and democratic accountability were hardly mentioned.

The second source is a small survey carried out for this study among about 250 people in nine member countries of the EU in connection with the European elections in June 2004. Here, a question was asked about groups in Brussels which have a lot of influence and power and groups which do not have enough influence (see *Figure 4.1*). The result shows a sharp and deep split between those groups which are considered to be very powerful and groups which are seen as being too weak in the political arena of Brussels. The powerful actors comprise large member states, multinational enterprises, and political elites. Too little influence is ascribed to small nation-states, small and medium-sized enterprises, to the unemployed, and to ordinary citizens. If we assume that the ordinary citizen "has the greatest need of democracy to advance his interests and aspirations" (Fabbrini 2003:126), then it is a startling result that less than 1% of our respondents ascribe a high influence to these citizens in the political system of the European Union. A rather similar picture emerges out of an open-ended question, asked before the closed one. Here, on top of the groups with too much influence in Brussels the following three groups emerged: Large member states (27%), multinational companies (17%), and politicians (9%); only 13% stated that there are no such groups.

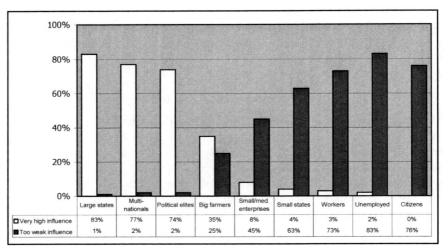

	Large states	Multi-nationals	Political elites	Big farmers	Small/med. enterprises	Small states	Workers	Unemployed	Citizens
☐ Very high influence	83%	77%	74%	35%	8%	4%	3%	2%	0%
■ Too weak influence	1%	2%	2%	25%	45%	63%	73%	83%	76%

Figure 4.1   Belief about powerful and powerless groups in Brussels.

Source: Special European Survey 2004, carried out in 9 EU member states.

Concerning groups whose interests are not represented enough in Brussels, on top were poor, small member states (21%) followed by poor and disadvantaged people (10%). In addition, many other groups were mentioned, such as workers, pensioners, consumers, minority groups, immigrants, and disabled. Only 8% believe that there are no groups underrepresented in Brussels.

The findings of this small study are confirmed by a recent EU-wide survey of the organization *Open Europe*: Here, among 17,443 persons interviewed in 2007, 56% said that the EU does not represent ordinary people. (The findings are reported in detail in Chapter 6.)

European political elites seem hardly aware of this highly critical—and realistic—perception of the power structure in the European Union by the public. A few days after the European elections of 2004, French President Chirac and German Chancellor Schroeder, both defeated strongly in the elections, met at Aquisgrana in France and announced the creation of a German-French group of industrialists whose task would be to meet regularly with the governments and to develop new strategies for industrial politics.[15] No comparable proposal was made by the political elites giving a stronger voice to workers, to the unemployed, or to ordinary citizens.

4.4 A reverse redistribution: The agricultural policy of the EU

The Common Agricultural Policy (CAP) is one of the basic pillars of European integration. It is also an area where the preponderance of sectional interests, the collusion between the interests of economic, political, and bureaucratic elites at the expense of those of citizens, but also the ideological appeal to ideals and values, masking particular interests, can be shown very clearly. In fact, "the CAP is an excellent example of what happens when there is no real link between the EU institutions and the EU's citizens" (Fouilleux 2003:251). The issue debated among economists and political scientists today is not any more about the success or failure of this policy—the majority considers it, in spite of partial successes, as a failure—but about the reasons why it could not be reformed in a radical way. Therefore, it seems necessary here to devote a section to the CAP for two reasons: first, because it is the largest area of spending in the EU budget; second, because it is a paradigmatic case for the split between EU elites and citizens. Three issues shall be dealt with: the weight of the farm expenses in the EU budget; the historical and ideological background and the present-day workings of the CAP.

The strange distribution of the expenses in the budget of the EU

The budget of a political community provides a condensed information about its true political priorities from the viewpoint of finance sociology (Goldscheid and Schumpeter 1976; Ardi and El Agraa 2004).

A look at the budget of the EU (see *Table 4.3*) shows a very strange situation, and it runs counter to the self-presentation of it by the EU with the title "Investment in growth and more & better jobs. Meetings today's needs—building a foundation for the future." In 2006, the bulk of the EU budget of 121 billion euros—54.8% or 66 billions—went to the agricultural sector, and the largest part of it to "direct aid and market measures." The proportion of these expenditures has not been reduced compared to the year before. The size and weight of the agrarian expenses cannot be relativized—as it is usually done—by referring to the fact that the budget as a whole constitutes only 1% of the gross national income of all member states. The EU expenses for agriculture alone have exactly the same size as the total budget of Austria—a middle-sized member state. Thus, the EU spends more for agriculture alone that about half of its member states have to spend altogether. This is really a strange situation at a time when agriculture is less than 5% of the employed population in most member states and contributes only about 1% to 3% to the gross national product. The characterisation of this budget as a "historic relic" by internationally recognised experts may be close to the truth.[16]

How did this situation come about? The following issues shall be discussed: the historical-institutional background of the CAP; its original aims; the decision-making processes in the CAP; and the outcomes of it in different aspects.

The historical and ideological origins of the CAP

After World War II, agriculture in Europe was a very important sector, but also a problem area: In the early 1960s, about 20–25% of the employed

Table 4.3   The EU Budget 2006 (Expenditure Estimates in Billions of Euros)

	Budget 2006	Change from 2005
Competitiveness including	7.9	4.4%
Education and training	0.7	7.8%
Research	4.2	4.1%
Information society	1.2	3.3%
Energy and transport	1.1	5.7%
Cohesion—Prosperity including	39.8	4.5%
Regional development	21.9	2.6%
Cohesion Fund—Investment for environment and transport	6.0	17.5%
Employment and social affairs	11.7	3.0%
Natural resources including	56.3	4.4%
Environment	0.2	4.2%
Agriculture including	54.8	4.4%
Rural development	11.8	11.6%
Direct aid and market measures	42.9	2.6%
Health & consumer protection (animal welfare & plant health)	0.3	4.6%
Fisheries	1.0	2.0%
Citizenship, Freedom, Security, and Justice including	1.1	4.5%*
Freedom, Security, and Justice	0.5	0.1%
Citizenship (including Culture, Health and Consumer Protection, Employment, and social affairs)	0.5	10.4%*
EU as a global partner including	8.3	9.5%
External relations (ex. cooperation with Asia, Latin America, the Mediterranean, aid to victims of human rights violations)	3.2	8.9%
Cooperation with African, Caribbean, and Pacific (ACP) countries	1.0	5.5%
Enlargement	2.1	16.4%
Humanitarian aid	0.5	0.0%
Administration including	6.7	5.8%
The European Commission	3.1	6.6%
Other institutions	2.5	5.3%
Compensations to new EU countries	1.1	−17.7%**
TOTAL	121.2	4.5%

*Does not take into account certain transition funds for the new EU countries, which are fixed at €77 million for 2006 by the accession treaties.

**Amounts fixed by the accession treaties.

Source: http://ec.europa.eu/budget/library/publications/budget_in_fig/dep_eu_budg_2006_en.pdf#sear%20ch=%22eu%20budget.

in the EEC worked in the farm sector, and it contributed 10% or more of gross value added; however, a strong rural exodus began in the course of the 1960s, and farm incomes were falling behind of those in other sectors; in most member states, small and inefficient forms predominated and a myriad of regulations existed in regard to agriculture (Fennell 1987:1ff; Tracy 1989:215ff.). Thus, given the aim of creating a common market, it was unavoidable to establish a common institutional framework also for agricultural production. The following targets were set for this policy: Provide for a secure supply of food; guarantee the stability of markets for agricultural products; guarantee an adequate income for farmers; raise the efficiency of farming. Later on, concerns such as food safety and preservation of the environment were added (El-Agraa 2004b:355).

However, the fathers of European integration did not only look forward towards an achievement of this aim; they were also constrained by social, political, and cultural factors given at the time. Already, at the end of the nineteenth century, challenges from overseas competition produced a first wave of protective measures (particularly in France and Germany) which "left a heavy legacy to Europe" (Tracy 1989:32). Only Denmark and the Netherlands responded with constructive reforms which strengthened their agriculture and laid the base for its productivity till today. Interventions in the farm sector rose strongly during the economic crisis of the 1930s, and even more during the Second World War—in spite of continued international efforts to liberalize the farm markets.[17] In this period, not only National Socialists in Germany but also leading French politicians (such as Pétain) proclaimed the aim of self-sufficiency in food supply and a philosophy of a *retour à la terre*. In France, also, a corporatist, all-encompassing farm organisation (the *Corporation Paysanne*) was established, quite similar to Hitler's *Reichsnährstand* in Germany. At this time, throughout Europe, the ideology of the family farm as a pillar of society and democracy was influential. Two consequences of these actions were decisive: First, the measures introduced were not removed (as originally foreseen) but were retained and persisted, throwing world markets into still greater chaos (Tracy 1989:143). Second, influential farm organisations and unions began to emerge—a trend which was strengthened in the years after the Second World War.[18] These organisations were instrumental in obtaining income and price guarantees; due to their ideological affinity to the conservative Christian-democratic governments in power at this time, they had privileged access to governments. In addition, the farmers also adopted efficient extraparliamentary tactics for putting through their interests, such as demonstrations and invasions of EU offices and meetings, often with considerable violence involved.

The mechanisms responsible for the redistribution toward the strong

Three main instruments are used in the EU agricultural sector (see Koester and El-Agraa 2004:371ff.[19]): (1) *Import regulations and tariffs* for the main agricultural products (grain, sugar, milk, and beef) and many other specific kinds of products; here, "threshold prices" are set up, usually far above the world market prices. (2) *Domestic market regulations,* such as intervention prices and purchases of goods by the EU if the market price falls below it; direct payments to farmers growing particular crops—a most important element; production quotas, introduced in 1984 in order to come to terms with the rising production and the emergence of extreme high differences between internal and world market prices; consumption subsidies for specific food stuffs. (3) *Market regimes:* For the important products (most of all: grain), detailed intervention prices, premium payments, and so on, are set. (4) *Export regulations and subsidies:* These became important when the EC/EU developed from an importer to an exporter of many products. However, due to pressure from the U.S. and the GATT and WTO agreements in the Uruguay round (1986–1994), subsidies had to be reduced.

How does the decision process in the EC/EU concerning agricultural issues work? Most analysts agree that this process clearly favours the interests of the farm sector at the expense of the general population. First, it is usually a very difficult process with a complicated structure. Since the beginning, the CAP was considered as problematic and there were recurring efforts of reforms (Fennell 1987:vii). It is much more difficult to criticise something which is very complicated. To give just one example: Alone for the different kinds of prices, which are necessary in order to grant specific supports, ten different terms exist.[20] Second, there exists a structural difference between the interests of farmers and those of the general public—consumers and taxpayers—who have to pay for the subsidies to the agricultural sector: For the first, the support measures are direct and sensible; for the latter, they are only small. The first, moreover, are well organized and politically influential. Citizens and voters are unable to make clear their preferences because they lack the relevant information; the opposite is the case for agricultural producers (Koester 1977:154ff.). Third, the decision processes in the political system of the EU favours the agricultural producers at the expense of the public (Tracy 1989:333ff.; Koester 1996): The agriculture ministers have a considerable latitude in their decisions, and they use this to favour the agricultural sector while neglecting the broader public interest; the practice of unanimity in the Agricultural Council leads to complicated "package agreements," which gives something to everybody but is often far removed from commission proposals; the commission tends to acquiesce too readily in compromise settlements; even the European Parliament is often swayed by the farm lobby. An important party in favour of a continuation of this policy is the European bureaucrat who "may promote his career more easily by maintaining good relations with representatives of the sector in which he is employed, rather than pressing for unpopular reforms" (Tracy 1989:362f.). With about 5,000 officials, the General Directorate Agriculture and Rural Development constitutes a huge bureaucratic apparatus, by far the largest of all GDs (see Chapter 5). Particularly, payments for export subsidies cause heavy administrative work for the collection of the relevant information (Koester and El Agraa 2004:375).

What was the outcome of this policy which in its structural principles is considered as "a crucial policy failure" by an economist who is very sympathetic to the EU (El-Agraa 2004b:365)? On the one side, the CAP did achieve some of its main objectives: Food supply was secured; market prices were stabilized; the incomes of farmers are certainly higher than they would be without the CAP; and maybe the most important of all: the agricultural problem did not impede the overall integration process. Some of these achievements, however, were not due to the CAP. For instance, the increase in the supply of food was mainly the result of technological advances and of the "dynamism of individual farmers in a free enterprise system" (Tracy 1989:335). However, the direct costs and inconsistencies of the CAP are considerable. We have already mentioned the costs for consumers and taxpayers. But further unforeseen consequences resulted, particularly regarding the distribution of costs and benefits. Four kinds of consequences are most noteworthy.

First, the increase in the productivity of agriculture, connected with the ample EU subsidies, led to an overproduction in many areas. The first responses to it were strange and caused disgust throughout Europe, such as the annihilation of full-fledged agricultural products. Later, foods were stored ("butter mountains") and quota systems introduced. These are usually opposed by economists, because they contradict the basic idea of a customs union (that production should move to regions and enterprises which are the most efficient). They are preferred, however, by politicians and bureaucrats, because "the higher the bureaucratic burden, the better the prospects for job promotion" (Koester and El-Agraa 2004:378).

A second consequence is that different countries profit quite differently from the CAP: The widespread argument that the first impetus for integration was a compromise between French farmers and German industrialists is not true; rather, both countries are net contributors to the CAP, while Denmark, the Netherlands, and Ireland are major gainers; also, the South European countries get less subsidies for their products than these (Buckwell et al. 1982:136).

Third, the change in the structure of farming—decline of small farmers, rise of "agribusinesses"—has led to a rather strange kind of redistribution. Price subsidies favour the large producers since food consumption accounts for a larger share of expenditures of poor households. Therefore, the "transfer from consumers to producers is regressive, that is in greater proportion from the poor [consumers] and in greater proportion to the rich [producers]" (Buckwell et al. 1982:166). *Table 4.4* shows the distribution of farms by size in the EU-15, the mean payment that a farm in each

Table 4.4   Inequity of Direct Payments to Farms in the EU-15 (Receipts per Farm by Farm Size, 2000)

Farms size class (in hectares)	Payment per farm (in euros)	% of EU-15 farms in size class	Number of farms in size class	% of EU-15 payments to size class
0–1.25	405	53,8	2,397,630	4.3
1.25–2	1,593	8.5	380,000	2.7
2–5	3,296	16.3	726,730	10.7
5–10	7,128	9.2	409,080	13.0
10–20	13,989	6.8	303,500	19.0
20–50	30,098	4.1	184,100	24.8
50–100	67,095	0.9	41,700	12.5
100–200	133,689	0.2	10,720	6.4
200–300	241,157	0.1	2,130	2.3
300–500	376,534	0.03	1,270	2.1
Over 500	768,333	0.01	610	2.1

Source: Baldwin 2005, p. 17 (data source: European Commission, Agriculture in the EU—Statistics and Information, 2002).

size class gets, and the whole payments to the different size classes. Here, we can see that more than half of the farmers are in the lowest size class (53.7%), but each of them gets only 405 euros, altogether only 4.3% of all payments. At the upper end, a tiny fraction of 610 farms (0.01% of all) get 768,333 euros per farm. The 56,430 very large farms (size classes 50 and over), 12.1% of all farms, get 25% of all EU subsidies. Thus, "almost any large landowner in the EU gets a big cheque. The 4,000 largest farms get about the same proportion of the EU subsidies (6%) than the 2.7 million smallest farms. Since the owners of the biggest farms are some of the wealthiest citizens in the EU, the CAP is a Robinhood-in-reverse policy" (Baldwin 2005:17). Also, the big agricultural and food processing and distributing businesses in Europe are recipients of large sums of money from the CAP. This issue has been discussed in public in recent times throughout Europe and it has led the EU to ask their member states to disclose the figures of the major recipients of such subsidies. Up to now, these figures were considered as "top secret" by the national governments and the EU, a fact which proves that interests of the economic elites and their relations to the political elites are at stake. Recently, the share of the top ten receivers of agricultural subsidies has been published for four EU member states.

In the Netherlands and Denmark, two of the main producers of agricultural products in the EU, the "top ten receivers" get not less than 35% (NL) and 22% (DK) of all supports; in Sweden and Portugal, the proportions were about 9% and 5%. Among the list of large firms, receiving subsidies from different EU sources, the first four are multinational agricultural businesses.[21] They include (in parenthesis the sums that they received from the CAP in 2005 in euros): *Tate & Lyle*, a UK-based firm with a turnover of 5.5 billion euros and production facilities in 29 countries (160 million); *Campina Hilversum*, a Dutch company with a turnover of 3.5 billion euros and 7,000 employees (111 million); *ARLA Foods*, a Danish firm, with a turnover of 6 billion euros and 20,000 employees (95 million); *Danisco*, also a Danish food producer, with a turnover of 21 billion euros and 10,000 employees in 46 countries (68 million); *Czarnikow Sugar*, a multinational corporation (world leader in sugar market services) based in London, established by a Russian (58 million).[22] These are only the very top receivers. Overall, it is clear that the larger part of the EU agricultural subsidies goes to very large farms and agricultural firms and not to the venerated small family farms. For France, it has been estimated that the biggest fifteen recipients get a massive 60% of all direct CAP payments, but the small French farmers—70% of all—get only 17%.[23]

Fourth, the CAP contributes to the problems associated with the concept of the *Fortress Europe*. With their high subsidies of agricultural products, the EU contributes to unfair competition on the world market. Also, this is very problematic because it leads to a similar perverse redistribution between the rich and poor on the global scene, increasing Third World poverty. According to the *Human Development Report 2003*, in 2000 an average dairy cow in the EU received subsidies of $913, but one person in sub-Saharan Africa, the poorest region of the world, $8.

In their comprehensive and balanced overview, Koester and El-Agraa (2004) bluntly conclude: "Thus, the CAP has failed badly in trying to achieve the policy objectives set for it." Many argue that proposals for a substantial reform have to be based more on an analysis of political decision processes than on an analysis of the immanent weaknesses of the CAP. Such reforms have been felt as necessary from the beginnings. While the first of them—the Mansholt plan of the 1960s—failed, from the 1980s on they became more successful. At this time, the influence of the farming bloc decreased, environmentalists got more influence, over-production became wasteful and expensive, and pressure from external trade partners increased. In 1992, limits to subsidies for agrarian production (especially grain) were introduced. In 2003, Commissioner Franz Fischler initiated a major reform which "decoupled" subsidies from particular crops and established "single farm payments." These consider also environmental, food safety, and animal-welfare standards, set limits on the subsidies for large producers, and incentives for the development of the agricultural land. A further major incentive for reform comes from the EU expansion in 2004, which increased the number of farmers in the EU from 7 to 11 million and the agricultural land area by 30%. As a consequence, the high level of support cannot be maintained, and it has been agreed that the farmers in the new member states will get lower payments than the old members until 2013.[24] It is remarkable, and in line with the general observations at the beginning of this chapter, that these changes in the CAP were more often responses to external pressures on the Union than a genuine and spirited response to the various CAP-critical groups within the EU.

4.5 EU enlargement toward the East: Reunification of Europe or conquest settlement of eight new member states?

In 2004, the European Union was enlarged by ten new member states, comprising eight former state-socialist countries of the Communist bloc from the Baltic States down to Slovenia. This was doubtless a historical event. The European Union glorified it as a historical breakthrough, as the "reunification of Europe," in the words of Romano Prodi, then president of the European Commission. The integration of these countries into the EU would consolidate their transition to freedom and democracy, and it would bring them back on the way to prosperity and wealth, on which they had been retarded for half a century. However, the way in which this "reunification" came about and its concomitants and consequences offer also an exemplary case of the role of economic interests and economic elites in the integration process. Five aspects shall be investigated in this regard: (1) the ideological justification for the strategy of transition from state socialist to market societies; (2) the strategies and actions of the economic elites in post-Communist East Europe; (3) the accession process; (4) socioeconomic development since the access to the EU; (5) the new structure of economic and political power in East Europe today.[25]

The theory and ideology of transition

The dominant story of the transition of the Central East European countries from state-socialist command economies to capitalist economies and democratic polities reads as follows: The system of state socialism broke down because of its inherent weaknesses; the transition process would have to be fast and drastic in order to avoid that old sectional interests could organize themselves, which would inhibit a thorough reform. But after "going through the valley of tears," the countries would recover and turn onto a path of strong economic growth. Thus, quite a similar process was foreseen as that which involved the accession of the new South European member states in the 1970s, which also were lying behind the old both in terms of democratic maturity and economic development. The successful process of integration of the South European countries and the positive economic development of several the post-Communist countries in the last decade seem to confirm this picture.

However, the process of transition was not so predetermined or inescapable, and the consequences of the integration were not so positive as it is depicted in the preceding characterization. The following theses are proposed in this regard: (1) The "shock therapy" prescribing a fast and painful process of transition was a rather problematic strategy; (2) West European transnational corporations and capital had a massive interest in such a process of transition; (3) the access to the EU of the post-Communist countries must to some degree be seen as an "annexation," even if no direct pressure was exerted upon them; (4) for the general population, and the political systems of these countries, this elite-driven transformation process has also had some serious negative consequences.

Let us look shortly at the different stages of the process, beginning with the difficult period of transition. Poland was a paradigmatic case for the economic "shock treatment" (Hofbauer 2003:47ff.). The theoretical proponent of this strategy was the U.S. economist Jeffrey Sachs, a student of the neoliberal economist Milton Friedman. It was realized by finance minister Leszek Balcerowicz in 1989 and implied a rigorous privatisation program: the selling of profitable parts of state enterprises to foreign companies, the release of thousands of workers, a disempowerment of the unions, and a restrictive monetary policy. In some cases, such as the weapons industry, restrictions for exports were imposed; state sector enterprises were discriminated by the imposition of an extra tax. This austere policy was not taken freely. On the one side, a hyperinflation of 600% in 1989 more and more restricted the room for maneuver for the government. On the other side, Poland (like Hungary) had large debts toward Western banks; therefore, the International Monetary Fund exerted pressure on the government to take on a rigid course of belt-tightening. The consequence of the hyperinflation was an expropriation of savers, a drastic reduction in industrial output, and massive losses in real incomes of workers and employees. These were also due to a stabilisation pact finalized in 1989 between Lech Walesa's union *Solidarnosc* and Balcerowicz in which it was agreed that wages should rise 20% less than prices. In this way, the national economies of the post-Communist Central East European countries were "affiliated" to the Western markets in a rather brutal way and within a short period of time.

In this process, the structure of production and exports changed significantly: While many of these countries had exported manufactured goods to other COMECON countries, in the exports to West Europe, the proportion of raw materials and semifinished goods became predominant, and the balance of trade deteriorated. The social consequences of the shock therapy were massive: The level of employment precipitated, and the rate of unemployment exploded, as did social and economic inequality. Overall, a massive deterioration of the life situation of the population took place which expressed itself in a significant reduction of the birthrate, of life expectancy, and a sharp increase of the mortality rate. The transition process was similar in all post-Communist countries, although in a few (such as Slovenia or the Czech Republic) it could be controlled better; in others (such as Romania and Bulgaria, and most successor states of the CIS), however, it had even more devastating consequences. At the turn of the century, only four (Hungary, Poland, Slovenia, and Slovakia) among twenty post-Communist countries had a GDP which was at least as high or higher than that of 1989. In eight of them (Moldova, Georgia, Ukraine, Turkmenistan, Kazahkstan, Tajikistan, and Latvia), GDP was less than half of that ten years before (Ingham 2004:254). In a survey about the level of life satisfaction and happiness among the general population, the post-Communist East European countries scored lowest around the world (Haller and Hadler 2006).

Given these devastating experiences, even leading economists, such as the former chief economist of the IMF, Joseph Stiglitz, today admit that this form of transition was a "bitter and disappointing failure" and the so-called *Washington Consensus* (transition through liberalization, stabilization, and privatization) was "a misguided recipe for successful transition" (Roland 2001; quoted in Ingham 2004: 243, 251). Some analysts refer to China in this regard, arguing that this country has shown a possible alternative strategy which did not try to undertake the economic reforms simultaneously with the political reforms (Ingham 2004:244). This reference is hardly appropriate. The changes in East Europe—also in Russia—included a true political revolution for democracy, supported by the intellectuals and the population at large. The abandonment of the political reforms has never been an alternative for the post-Communist East European countries. What would have been a true alternative, however, was a smoother transformation of the economic sphere and a more controlled process of integration to the EU.

The successful fight of West European capital for the East European enterprises

One clear indicator for the great importance of economic considerations in the transition process in East Europe is the fact that Western capital was extremely interested in the possibilities for investment in this region. Already since the early 1990s, a real "buyout fight" for enterprises was setting in. Every week newspaper headlines appeared such as "Thrust toward East Europe" (*Handelsblatt* 5.2.1997), "Poland: A magnet for investors" (*Süddeutsche Zeitung* 14.9.1999), "There, were large profits allure" (*Die Welt* 4.11.2003), "Austrian banks won fight for xxx" and the like appeared. Such a kind of fight unfolded not only in regard to alienable enterprises in East Europe. A scientific conference in Vienna took place in 2006 with the title "The Battle for Ukraine." Participants discussed the prospects for Ukraine's political and economic developments with the general question of whether the West, the EU and NATO, or Russia would be the winners in the fight for economic and political influence in this large country. Thus, we have here a clear instance where we can see that economic competition can take on the character of a "battle without weapons," as Weber (1978a:38f.) calls it.

The profitability of investments in the post-Communist countries has also been raised by the fact that those countries provided formidable "tax oases" for Western capital. While enterprises in Germany, for instance, have a tax burden of over 30%, in many East European countries it is only between 10% and 15%; the mean level in the new member states was 19.7% in 2004.[26] In addition, they offer many additional incentives and benefits for foreign companies, such as: total or partial wavers of corporation tax up to ten years; subsidies for investments and for the employment of specific categories of workers; special economic areas with very low or no taxes at all; fully free possibility of capital and earning transfers from the subsidiary companies of foreign enterprises to the West.[27]

Western capital has profited enormously from the opening of the East European markets and the takeover of significant parts of the East European economy. Today, a considerable share of the large private enterprises in East Europe is owned by Western capital (maybe 30% or more). Already in the mid-1990s, 74% of all Hungarian banks, for instance, were owned by foreign capital—a proportion two to three times as large as in West Europe (Várhegyi 1998). The share of foreign capital in Ukrainian banks was 29.3% in May 2007; it was expected to rise to 40–45% by the end of the year.[28] According recent press reports, in six East European countries, the share of foreign banks in the total assets of the banking sector is 90% and more; in five other countries it is between 70% and 89%.[29] Luca Kristóf and András Csite (2004) have carried out a survey among the largest 492 Hungarian companies and found that 31% of them were in the hands of foreign capital. Sixty-five percent of the largest supplier and 50% of the first customer of these companies was a foreign-owned firm.[2] The exports to this region have exploded in the past years. German export balance, for instance, rose strongly since 1995, and corporate profits expanded much stronger than GDP growth (Reimon and Weixler 2006:101ff.). Western corporations can make enormous profits in the post-Communist countries. The total income that foreign investors got from their investment in the more developed countries was about 7–10%, in Slovakia 17%, in Russia 15%; about 50% of the earned capital was repatriated to the West, and the other 50% was reinvested in the new member states (Hunya 2006).

It is quite interesting in this regard, however, that the EU accession of the Central East European countries was no decisive event for Western capital and enterprises. The association treaties between the EU and the post-Communist countries created a large free-trade area already in the 1990s (Donges and Schleef 2001:15). West European firms and banks have become very strong in Central East Europe already since then. Large investments took place also in countries which only later became EU members (Bulgaria, Romania) or are not members till today (Ukraine, Russia). A multinational enterprise, such as the German corporation Volkswagen, was not dependent on the "conquest" of East Europe; rather, the main orientation of this corporation is the world market as a whole (Donges and Schleef 2001:35ff.).

Thus, the process of the penetration of the economies of Central East Europe since the transition in the early 1990s can well be described as a further stage in the process of "capitalist conquest settlement." Geographic expansion and the opening up of new markets has been a central strategy of capitalist expansion since its early days (see Luxemburg 1923; Wallerstein 1974; Bohle 2000). Such an expansion took place also after the Second World War in Germany and other continental European countries where capitalist development had been delayed for several decades (Lutz 1984), today it is the case in those parts of the Third World which show high levels of economic growth.

Certainly, foreign investment in the post-Communist countries is not detrimental to them. In fact, these investments play a positive role by creating new jobs, enabling transfer of technical and managerial know-how, and contributing to growth (Breuss 2002; Zschiedrich 2004; Zarek 2006). The problem was, however, the speed and brutality in which this process took place. This time aspect of speed and pace is often as equally important as the substantive aims toward which a reform or a change is directed. Negative consequences of the externally enforced, fast transition process in east Europe include the creation of split labour markets, rising income inequality and unemployment, increasing regional inequalities, and reduced autonomy of economic policy in those countries. Negative consequences arose also from the fact that the expansion of Western capital in the East was often directed mainly toward a conquering of the sales markets in these countries. A German economist (Hankel 1993) sees this as a paradigmatic case of the creation of a dependent economy because local industries (and their workplaces) are destroyed in such a process. An exemplary case of this kind was also the reunification of East and West Germany. In spite of the transfer of billions to the East, economic growth was much weaker there than foreseen.

The accession to the EU: Return to Europe or violence-free annexation?

As outlined previously, the EU welcomed and praised the breakdown of the Iron Curtain, the "reunification of Europe." However, the thesis proposed here is that the accession of these countries had less the character of a "return to Europe" than that of a "peaceful annexation" (*Anschluss*; Roesler 1999). In this process, the interests of economic and bureaucratic elites in the EU, as well as those of the new economic and political elites in the post-Communist countries, played a significant role. Two kinds of arguments underline this thesis: (1) The difference in size and power between the old EU and the new member states; (2) The fact that the EU took a series of measures to accelerate the transition and integration process.

First, it is quite evident that the weight of all the new EU member countries of the post-Communist area regarding size, economic and political strength in relation to the EU of the 15 was rather small. The EU negotiated separately with each of the candidate countries about all the thirty-one chapters which comprised the *acquis communautaire*, the extensive legal and political regulations valid in the EU which had to be taken over fully by the candidate countries. The so-called Copenhagen criteria of 1993 stated that the onus was on the accession countries to adapt their economic and political institutions to the conditions of a free market, guaranteeing of human rights, institutional stability, and so forth (see Glenn 2003:219ff.; Ingham 2004:243ff.). In some regards, the EU requested even adaptations in areas (such as social policy) where it had no or little competences in the old member states (Bohle 2000:316). Thus, East Europe could be used as a testing ground for reforms which later could be introduced also in the West.

In this process, the different candidate countries were often pitted against each other. Hannes Hofbauer (2003:83ff.) has compared the reports in the West European press about the progress of the accession negotiations with those of a regatta race: One month, this country, the next month another country was able to "conclude a chapter" and thus put itself at the front of those to be accepted soon as a new member. The personal experience of the chief negotiators in this process confirmed that this often was a truly painful process.[30] The main intent of the EU negotiators was that the accession countries had to consolidate their progress along the lines of the IMF conditions; resulting internal economic and social problems of these countries were seldom discussed (Hofbauer 2003:76). It is also more than evident that West European economy and enterprises were much stronger than their counterparts in the East. In fact, private enterprises had to be created anew after half a century of state socialism, and there existed no "capitalist class" at all in these regions after the breakdown of the communist systems (Eyal et al. 2000). A direct indicator of the extreme differences in this regard are the incomes of people employed in industry and services. In 2002, their annual gross income was 34,622 euros in Germany, 32,434 in Austria, and 25,808 in Italy. The corresponding figures for East Europe were Poland 7,065, Czech Republic 7,212, and Hungary 5,906.[31]

Third, the EU was very interested in a fast transformation process and quite early took measures to support the post-Communist countries in the establishment of the new institutions. The Phare program was established for this aim. Through this program, in the second half of the 1990s, about 1,200 managerial and legal experts were trained to help the East European countries in the establishment of the new legal order and the putting through of privatization programs. Between 2000 and 2006, 1.5 billions of euros were available through Phare (and the additional programs ISPA and Sapard; Hofbauer 2003:73). However, compared to the 30 billion euros spent through the structural funds in the EU-15, this is a small sum. In 2005, all eight East Central European new member states together received around 4 billion euros, compared to 6 billion for Spain alone, or 13.4 billions of Euro of the "old" cohesion countries (Ireland, Portugal, Spain, Greece) together.[32] But the new member states were not able to make use of money provided. In fact, the sums mentioned before represent only 26% of those promised by the EU; about 30 billion available have not been used. The reasons are that the EU means for development usually are connected with the obligation of the receiving countries to cofinance the projects with 50% of the total amount granted. These are quite high sums which the public households may not have been able to take over. Furthermore, the administration of the projects connected with the use of these sums requires a considerable amount of know-how and expertise. For this task, a new group of project experts has developed in these regions who specialize in giving advice to local authorities and enterprises on how to make use of the EU funds. This "project class" (Kovách/ Kucerová 2006:4) includes "experts, designers and administrative staff of the EU, national, rural and regional development projects, holders of intellectual power, representatives of non-governmental organisations and other practitioners."

There exists one further indicator for the high interest of the EU in the enlargement process toward the East. In fact, the EU supported the governments of the accession countries with public relation campaigns before they hold their referenda about the accession in order to win the support among the populations. In one of the Baltic states, the EU Commission even opened a bureau which managed the whole referendum campaign (see also Chapter 6).

The development of east central Europe 1990–2005 and its perception by the population

Finally, let us take a short look at the factual development of the East European countries since their revolutions and accession to the EU. The overall socioeconomic development, the political development, and the attitudes of the population toward the EU and the further prospects of their countries are considered.

First, we can see that after the painful transition these countries have developed rather positively in economic terms. Economic growth was about 3% and 4% in most East Central European countries; GDP rose by 60–70% from 1990 to 2004 in the Czech Republic and Hungary, but even by 228% in Poland; in all new member states by 170% (*WIIW Handbook of Statistics* 2005). Most post-Communist countries have been able to increase their exports and to raise the proportion of manufactured goods from 70% to 80%; however, the share of high-tech goods still is at most one tenth, except Estonia and Hungary with one fourth (Ingham 2004:259f.). Also, the composition of their exports is changing toward a higher share of high-quality goods (Zarek 2006). In terms of consumer

possibilities, the situation in the present-day central East European countries looks much better than a few decades ago. In fact, consumerism in
the widest sense may have been one of the main attractions of the Western
economic model for the people, as in all less developed countries (Sklair
1991:75ff.). However, this positive development still does not reflect itself
in social terms. Population growth declined in practically all countries,
and unemployment was still 6–8% in 2004 in most countries, in Poland
even 19%. Economic analyses show an impressive rise in productivity, but
a significant lag of wages; in some countries, wage increases are weaker
than growth of GDP. The trade unions were not able to influence significantly the process of transition (Schroeder 2006). An important side
result of the transition to capitalism, therefore, was a massive increase of
economic and social inequality.

A second characteristic of the development in these regions is the high
degree of political instability in most of the countries. Practically none of
the governments since 1990 was reelected. On September 23, 2006, two
large headlines were printed side by side in an Austrian newspaper: "Now
also Poland sinks into chaos" and "The East, a political pile of shards."[33]
Also the Czech and Slovak governments have only unstable party coalitions
which might not remain in office for long. There are several explanations
for this political instability. One is that the EU accession of the post-Communist member states was too early. One could argue that without accession to the EU, political instability in this region could even be higher.
However, in view of the facts presented in this section, the explanation
referring to the pace and form of the transition and EU accession may also
be valid. It refers to the (fast) pace of the process and the extreme hard-
ships which the "shock-therapy" transition has caused. Given the massive
disequilibria and inequalities which have resulted, it is extremely difficult
for interest organisations and political parties to develop coherent political
reform programs, and for the citizens to provide stable support to them.

Finally, let us take a short look at the perceptions and evaluations of
the general public of the process of transition, the access to the EU, and
the future prospects of their countries. A first indicator of the attitude of
East European population toward the accession of their countries are the
figures on participation in referenda and European elections. We have
shown in Chapter 1 that the outcome of the referenda was clearly positive in most countries, but levels of turnout were often very low. Thus,
a considerable indifference or even scepticism of the citizens can be supposed. The same fact exists in regard to the turnout at the elections to
the European parliament in 2004. Here, nearly in all post-Communist
countries, less than half of the population participated; in several countries only about one third, in Poland only 21%, in Slovakia 17%. Thus,
the democratic character of the enlargement process is doubtful to some
degree, since the process was negotiated by the elites without much public
discussion (Glenn 2003:223).

Which are the perceptions of the population about their life situation at the beginning of the twenty-first century? There exist many national and EU-wide surveys which show a high level of feelings of uneasiness and even anger. The Public Opinion Research Center (CBOS) in Warsaw regularly carries out surveys on general attitudes among the population in Poland, the Czech Republic, Hungary, and Russia. In January 2003, one year before the accession of Poland to the EU, it was asked how people evaluate the present economic situation of their country.[34] The mood was most pessimistic in Poland, with 64% of the respondents saying that the situation is bad, 56% neither good nor bad, and only 4% good; the percentages evaluating the situation as bad were 46–46% in the Czech Republic and Russia and 31% in Hungary. In all these countries, less than 10% considered the economic situation of their country as good. Seventy percent of the Poles saw corruption as a big problem in their country. Rather modest expectations were concerned with the EU accession of Poland. Thirty-two percent of the respondents expected that it will bring more losses than gains; those who expected gains for Poland as a whole were 42%, personally 28%. A clear majority—44%—of the respondents expected that Poland's accession to the EU will bring more gains to the latter than to Poland. Among the optimists, young people, people with higher education and the highest incomes were overrepresented; among the pessimists, those living in the countryside, older people, pensioners, and persons with low income or no employment.

The Eurobarometer polls give a good picture of the general mood among the population in East Europe. Results in spring 2005 showed the following:[35] Between 30% and 46% of citizens of most East European member countries are not satisfied with their present life; in the old member states, these proportions are only 10% to 15%. Asked how they estimate the present situation compared to that of five years ago, about 40% see an improvement, but 20% to 30% see a worsening; the expectations for the next five years are somewhat more positive (40–50% expect an improvement), but also in this regard between 10% and 20% expect a worsening. However, not only among the general population there was no enthusiasm for accession to the EU. A survey among elites at the regional and local levels in these countries showed that many of these were rather disengaged from the enlargement process (Hughes et al. 2001).

Rise of a new "power block" in post-communist Europe?

Finally, we have to discuss the role of the intellectual, political, and economic elites in the post-Communist countries themselves. Which were the groups and persons who contributed decisively to the overthrow of the old Communist regimes and to the building up of democratic institutions and capitalist economic structures?

A theory which considers mainly the actors in the transformation countries themselves has been proposed by Ivan Szelenyi and collaborators (Eyal et al. 2000). They build on theories of the rise of the intellectuals to class power under socialism and argue that what has been created in Hungary, the Czech Republic, and Poland in this transition period was "capitalism without capitalists." Contrary to the rise of Western capitalism, where capitalists were the decisive class, in state socialism no private capital and capitalists existed. In this situation, the members of the newly rising, well-educated classes, including technicians, scientists, and higher state officials, fought for the establishment of a bourgeois society and a capitalist economic order. In this undertaking, which started already in the last stage of communism, the intellectuals were continuing an old East European tradition in which the bourgeoisie traditionally had been rather weak. Former cadres, who possessed also cultural capital, were able to remain in their positions or to climb into leading positions in the new private economy. This group entered into "an alliance with the new politocracy and the opinion-making intellectual elite, many of whom are former dissident intellectuals." Eyal et al. (2000:13) conclude that "post-communist capitalism has been a product of the intelligentsia" which today dominates in a "power bloc," backed by a managerialist ideology.

The thesis proposed here is that the role of the intellectuals (who mainly can exert influence on public opinion, but have no real "power") on the one side, and the political and economic power elites on the other side, was quite different in the transition process. (For an overview see also Bozóki 2003.)

First, it is quite evident that the intellectuals played a crucial role in the "velvet revolutions" which led to the fall of the Communist regimes. Many of these intellectuals were men educated in the liberal arts or were literary writers—quite similar to the fighters for national independence in Germany, Italy, and other European countries in the nineteenth century. The intent of these men, however, was, in the first instance, to fight for freedom and democracy and also for social equality, but not for capitalism and bourgeois society. In this fight, they were strongly supported by broad strata of the population. It is true that some of the dissidents of the Communist system later became influential members of the new political class. Yet these were exceptions rather than the rule, and they typically ended up on political positions more of a honorary-symbolic nature, such as state presidents. Lumir Gatnar (2004) found that in Czechoslovakia almost a total exchange of the political elites took place. In the first stage of transition, dissidents and people from the underground culture were frequent actors, but most of them left the political scene later on. The typical successful politician in the post-Communist countries was quite another type: It was either a person already active under the former system (albeit not in a prominent position) or a political newcomer well experienced in the power game; therefore, often also quite rude but successful private entrepreneurs were able to pursue political careers. Thus, it is quite doubtful if "the alliance of dissident intellectuals and reform communist technocrats" formed a "hegemonic power bloc" as proposed by Eyal et al.

Eyal et al. (2000) also underestimate the influence of foreign capital. Two facts are evident which confirm the massive influence of the interests of Western private capital: First, it was shown before that the transition from state socialism to capitalism followed widely the requirements set by international capital. The new holders of the political offices in the post-Communist countries had to be very sensitive to the wishes of foreign investors in their countries. Second, the relative weight of foreign capital may in fact have been low until the late 1990s, but in recent years its share has increased massively, as was shown earlier.

Finally, empirical findings of East European sociologists concerning the relation between the economic and political elites clearly disconfirm the idea of a "new power bloc." For Hungary, Gyorgy Lengyel (2004) found that there are clear differences in the patterns of recruitment of managers and politicians; the members of economic elites did not want to be involved in political party membership. Similar findings of a rare transition from business to political careers have been reported for the Czech Republic by Lumir Gatnar (2004). In his analysis of the characteristics of the 100 richest Poles, Wlodzimierz Wesolowski (2004) found high levels of interchange; moreover, he found a high level of professionalisation of the top managers of public companies; most of them did not have similar positions in the Communist period. For Russia, David Lane (1997) concludes that there exists a *"fragmented elite structure."* This might well be an apt description of the elite structure in all post-Communist countries.

CONCLUSION

The following general conclusions can be drawn from these analyses. On the one side, it is out of the question that liberal market reforms and economic integration in East Europe have had significant positive effects on economic growth and prosperity. However, the main factor for growth has been the extension of the free market to Central East Europe, not the supporting political measures of the EU. It may be mainly the growth associated with private entrepreneurship and the free market which explains the attractiveness of the EU for most of its neighbour states and which makes it appear as a model for similar efforts at regional economic integration elsewhere in the world (Müller 2002:150). Contrary to widespread arguments from leftist critics, it is also not true that European integration has been a pure "neoliberal" project. Rather, in some regards a new kind of "regulated capitalism" has been institutionalized in the EU which includes also elements of a new, large-scale corporatism. A surprising finding of Coen's

(1997) survey of ninety-four large European firms was that there was a high increase of collective action on the European level. "Transpersonal business organizations such as UNICE have increasingly gained corporate actor qualities . . . (and) the same holds true for agricultural interests" (Risse-Kappen 1996:66). This element is obvious in the concerted effort of politicians, of large corporations, and of Eurocrats who aspire to promote the establishment of "Eurocorporations" and to subsidize research and development in sectors strategic for technological progress and political-military independence. European business organizations have gained corporate actor qualities already in the 1980s and 1990s (Risse-Kappen 1996:66). A strong new and powerful elite coalition has emerged and dominates the policy of the EU not only in economic matters. It consists of a coalition between large members states favouring the protection and support of national industries and businesses, multinational corporations and powerful business organisations, and the increasingly powerful Eurocrats and lawmakers in the European Commission and in the European Court of Justice. A trend toward an "inward-looking orientation" among enterprises and politicians within the EU exists which may strengthen tendencies of interventionism and protectionism (Borrmann et al. 1995:78; Forder 1999).

5 The Eurocracy
The Irresistible Growth of a New and Powerful Supranational Bureaucratic Elite

INTRODUCTION

If we want to understand the dynamics of European integration, it is of utmost importance to look at the bureaucracy of the European Union. The bureaucracy is the main supporting pillar of the Union; "Eurocrats" are the "driving motor" of integration. It is also a unique construction in world-historical terms. In all modern nation-states, bureaucracies are powerful institutions working "behind the windows" of government and parliaments. In the European Union, the bureaucracy has been authorized explicitly to enact lawlike regulations and decrees. To investigate the EU bureaucracy from a social-scientific and critical point of view is necessary because its central role has not been recognized adequately in scientific research. (For exceptions, see Edwards and Spence 1994; Puntscher-Riekmann 1998; Bach 1999; Shore 2000; Nugent 2002.) The role of the EU bureaucracy is strongly underestimated, if not ignored altogether,[1] and the significant role of their "founders" is left over to the work of historians and biographers.

The chapter is structured as follows: First, we discuss the concept of bureaucracy and the special situation of the Eurocracy. Then, hypotheses are developed concerning the interests of the different elites as well as of the general public concerning the EU bureaucracy. In the next sections, empirical data are presented about the size and numerical development of the Eurocracy, on their remunerations and much-discussed privileges, and its internal structure and workings.

5.1 Bureaucracy as an instrument of domination and the specific character of the Eurocracy

Any bureaucracy is an institution of political steering and domination. This is indicated by the meaning of the term, which denotes "domination of (or by) the bureau (and its employees)." This aspect, strongly emphasized in the path-breaking work of Max Weber, has been downplayed or even lost in many present-day tracts on bureaucracy.[2] Issues of interests and conflicts within and about bureaucracies are underexposed in these approaches.

This aspect has also been rather neglected in the social-scientific litera-ture on the EC and EU bureaucracy.[3] Some have criticized that Weber's bureaucratic elements cannot be found empirically in concrete, present-day forms of administration and that he exaggerated the growth of bureaucracy (Swedberg 1998:42, 226). However, taking into consideration the massive growth of all national bureaucracies since the beginning of the twentieth century (when Weber wrote) up to date, his thesis turns out as one of the best sociological forecasts ever made.

The rise of state bureaucracies as powerful instruments of steering in continental European capitalism. The theses of Max Weber

Although the phenomenon is very old, the term *bureaucracy* has been invented only in the eighteenth century in France (Albrow 1972:13). From France, the term *Bürokratie*s pread to Germany. France and Germany were the first countries which developed an elaborated system of education and qualification for entrants to the public service. A new science—*Kamer-alwissenschaft*—was established in 1720 in Prussia, focussing on public administration and finances (Mayntz 1985:4). Later, it was split up into the disciplines of law and economics. Bureaucratic "reform from above" pursued by enlightened absolutism, became the equivalent of the bourgeois revolution (Stürmer 1977:10). Also, English authors wrote about bureau-cracy but mainly in a critical sense, referring to continental state adminis-trations (Albrow 1972). In the late nineteenth century, the first systematic works on bureaucracy appear, such as Gaetano Mosca's *The Ruling Class* (1895) and Robert Michels's *Political Parties* (1915; see Mitchell 1968:21.) For both, bureaucrats are a central component of the "ruling elites" which are able to preserve and reproduce their power in all societies.

The character of bureaucracy varies by nations and cultures; the French and German models of bureaucracy certainly have played an exemplary role for the EU (Shore 2000:179; Bourricaud 1958:460). Since the late Middle Ages, the power of state institutions has grown continuously here, at the expense of other autonomous bases of political power. At the end of the nineteenth century a new kind of "organized capitalism" was evolv-ing, with a close integration of private corporations, large interest orga-nizations, public bureaucracy, and a governmental policy aiming toward national strength and autarky (Stürmer 1977:18f.). For the period since World War II, Dogan and Pelassy (1987) have shown the further explosive growth of the bureaucratic state "Moloch" in Western Europe.

The German sociologist Max Weber (1864–1920) clarified the concept and developed strong theses about the functions of bureaucracy in mod-ern societies. For Weber, bureaucracy has two meanings (see also Bendix 1960:423–57; Schmid and Treiber 1975: 21ff.). On the one side, it is the most efficient form of administration, which is used both by governments and by private enterprises as a means of domination. In this sense, it is a very old invention, going back to ancient high cultures. In modern times, the French and the Germans "perfected the rational, functional and specialized bureaucratic organization of all forms of domination from factory to army to public administration" (Weber 1978b:1400; Peters 1995:136ff.).

On the other side, bureaucracy is closely connected with the rise of the modern state. This state is characterized in general as a system of "legal authority with a bureaucratic administrative staff" (Weber 1978a:217). Weber mentions three causes for the spread of large state bureaucracies; it is evident that also the emergence of the Eurocracy is directly related to them. The first is the spread of capitalism itself (Weber 1978a:224). Capitalism provides the means for the expansion of bureaucracy, by supplying the necessary money resources out of increasing fiscal revenues. Second, technical inventions in the fields of communication and transport make the working of the bureaucracy much more efficient and precise. In the EU, these means have gained particular importance: The bringing together of thousands of officials from the national bureaucracies to meetings in Brussels or elsewhere (Bach 1992) would not be possible without an extensive air traffic all over Europe. Finally, bureaucratization grows as a consequence of increasing wealth, demands on consumption goods, and the expansion of social welfare policies (Weber 1978a:972; see also de Tocqueville 1976:787ff.).

In spite of their parallel rise, a potential conflict between bureaucracy and democracy arises (see also Bendix 1960:438ff.). The issue of the control of the bureaucratic apparatus emerges. High-level bureaucrats may become more powerful than their political "masters" (Weber 1978a:224). We will show that this is true also for many of the EU General Directors (bureaucrats) vis-à-vis their Commissioners (the politicians). The power of the bureaucrats over the politicians is due to their superior technical knowledge and to the specific invention of "bureaucratic secrecy"—a principle "defended fanatically" by the bureaucracy (Weber 1978b:929).

All these characteristics have one consequence: Bureaucracies have an extremely strong power of persistence (Weber 1978a:987, 991). Even the French revolution did not weaken the bureaucracy. Rather, the opposite took place, as Alexis de Tocqueville (1988) has shown in his study *L'ancien Régime et la Révolution*.

The power of the Eurocracy

At this point, we may ask what the power and influence of the European bureaucracy—in the following also denominated as *Eurocracy* (without implying negative undertones)—is and how it can be analyzed from a sociological point of view, but also from that of the normative theory of democracy. We have to look in this regard both to the formal-institutional rights granted to the Commission and to its concrete workings. If we speak of the "Commission" (or the Eurocracy) in the following, we mean both the small group of the 27 politically appointed commissioners and their large bureaucratic staff. Four characteristics are relevant in this regard.[4]

(1) First and most importantly, the European bureaucracy has a privilege which has never been granted to any other bureaucracy, namely, the exclusive right to initiate legislation. This right—and the power emanating from it—is very important even if the decrees and regulations formally must be enacted by the European Council and Parliament. The Commission is well aware of this extraordinary power: "By virtue of the Treaties, the Commission has a virtual monopoly on legislative initiative within areas of Community competence."[5] The Commission describes itself as the EU's "executive body," as the "dynamo" (Shore 2000:128) or "powerhouse of European integration" (Müller 1994:58). The key of the Commission's power is that it "has the sole right to initiate proposals. It has a 'monopoly.' This fact alone gives the Commission's right of initiative greater significance than the customary right to initiate legislation that we know in our national constitutions."[6] (2) The European Commission is responsible for the monitoring of the implementation of the EU laws in the member states. From this point of view, the Eurocracy is something like the supervisor or warden of the member states. (3) The European Commission is responsible collectively for its politics. Hence, there exist only limited possibilities for individual commissioners to distinguish themselves by specific political aims or programs. The moderate political profile of many single commissioners, however, does not prevent the commission as a whole to achieve an ever deeper integration, as will be shown next. (4) Members of the Eurocracy, below the commissioners, are not elected but appointed to their offices. This reinforces the nonpersonal, faceless character of the Commission and of the Eurocracy in general.

The European bureaucracy as an expert work organization and network structure

The bureaucracy of the EU is a specific case. First, it is mainly concerned with the preparing and enacting of laws, regulations, and recommendations but not with their direct practical implementation; it can be denoted as a "regulating bureaucracy" (Bach 1992). "The kind of education and knowledge required will be at the highest level available (typically academic), and it will be closely related to the main activity of enacting decrees. Only the expert knowledge of private economic interest groups in the field of 'business' is superior to the expert knowledge of the bureaucracy" (Weber 1978a:994).[7] The expert knowledge of the commission is judicial, and it may be also economic and technical. From this point of view, the Commission is first of all a "profoundly legalistic" institution. "Everything it does must have a legal basis which can be traced back to, or justified in terms of its Treaties" (Shore 2000:132). Therefore, the legal service plays a central role in the Commission's work and an extraordinary large proportion of its staff has a legal background. "European law and European institutions . . . support each other through a self-reinforcing system of bureaucracy and law" (Shore 2000:138).

A further relevant aspect is the fact that the Eurocracy employed in Brussels, Luxembourg, and Strasbourg is only a part of the whole bureaucratic machinery which operates throughout the EU. The Eurocracy relies also upon extensive networks of officials from the member states, and experts from private institutions. Moreover, specialized "European departments" are concerned with the maintenance of contacts to Brussels and the implementation of EU regulations throughout the continent. We call this the "EU-substitute bureaucracy." In this chapter, for the first time an empirically based estimation of its size of is given.

Work relations, practices and outputs: "Bureaucratism" in Brussels and elsewhere

The charge of "bureaucratism" can have two meanings: First, it relates to the work and behaviour of the bureaucrats which is characterized as impersonal and obscure; second, it relates to the outcome of bureaucratic work which is described as over-regimentation, as the production of myriads of laws and decrees which, in the best case, may be superfluous or, in the worst case, will be obstructive for entrepreneurial activities and patronize citizens and customers.

The Eurocracy may be compared to the administrations of other international organizations, such as the UN, the OECD, the ILO, and the like. In comparisons between the EU bureaucracy and their national counterparts, the former is often depicted as being less "bureaucratic" and characterized rather by function-oriented work processes, transnational networks, and a functional legitimacy, based on accomplishment of tasks and instrumental problem solving (Bach 1992:27). However, "international bureaucracies, typically, are far cry from the nicely adjusted, self-contained, and hierarchically ordered models of organization theorists" (Haas 1964:98). Why should we assume that the Eurocracy is so highly effective and oriented only toward the aim of promoting the European welfare (*Gemeinwohl*) as it is depicted in the self-image of the Commission officials (Shore 2000:178)? At least three arguments cast doubts on this assumption.

First, what is the "ethos" of the Eurocracy? The main difference between the ethos of the politician and the entrepreneur and that of the bureaucrat lies in the responsibility which they can take for their actions (Weber 1978b:1404). The first two promote their own aims and goals; they both struggle for personal power in order to realize these goals and incur a risk if they are unsuccessful. The bureaucrat has to fulfil his duty, that is, implement the orders of his legitimate (political or private) chief. He has a lifetime appointment in his job; the highest risk to which he is exposed is that of being displaced to another office or being retired. Also, the Eurocracy has to follow directives and political decisions of its ultimate "masters," the member state governments. However, it has been endowed with an authority of its own as the "guardian of the contracts" and as the promoter of the truly supranational "European interests." What are these interests? Since there exists no strong public sphere and only a limited democratic political process at the level of the EU, its definition remains to a considerable degree in the hands of the Eurocracy itself (see also Shore 2000:135ff.).

Second, is it plausible that the organization structure and work processes at the EU level are significantly different from those of national bureaucracies? Also, this thesis is questionable for at least three reasons: (a) Even national bureaucracies are not really nicely structured and well-ordered. The French state administration has been characterized as a "fragmented machine" where functional and hierarchical lines often cross each other; at the ministerial level, they "are always in turmoil and constitute a bewildering structure" (Luc Rouban 1995:42ff.). In the German ministerial bureaucracy, a high level of autonomy of low-level operating units exists in the practical development of new programmes (Schmid and Treiber 1975). (b) The formal structure of the European bureaucracy is following closely the hierarchy of educational degrees; moreover, Eurocrats enjoy the same job security (lifetime tenure) as national bureaucrats. As a consequence of this, formal degrees and organizational hierarchies will be very important also within the Eurocracy. (c) The relevance of such formal prerequisites and structures is increasing in any bureaucracy as it grows older (Downs 1967:158ff.).

Third, and finally, how is it possible to measure the output efficiency of the Eurocracy? One possibility is to ask if the European Union has reached the fundamental goals it has set for itself, such as economic growth, full employment, and the like. As it will be shown in Chapter 6, the balance sheet in this regard is rather mixed. The other possibility is simply in terms of regulations and decrees enacted. In this regard, the Eurocracy is certainly highly effective as will be shown below. However, serious doubts are appropriate if this kind of productivity can really be considered as a success. This is indicated by the fact that politicians and the commission itself aim toward reducing the output of EU decrees and regulations already for twenty years, as we will show in Section 5.4.

Actors and interests in the development of the Eurocracy

It is a central thesis of this study that concrete individual and collective actors play a central role in the emergence and development of social institutions. In the case of European integration, we must consider five categories of actors: political elites; economic, bureaucratic, and academic elites; and the general population. All of them have an interest in the expansion of the European bureaucracy although some of them have also contradictory expectations and critical attitudes.

Political entrepreneurs and political elites: Anthony Downs (1967:5ff.) has argued in his theoretical study *Inside Bureaucracy* that a new bureau usually is established by a small group of charismatic leaders in order to fulfil a new specific social function. A particularly important role in this regard is played by innovative and forceful personalities (zealots) who advocate its establishment (Downs 1967:5f.). Also in the case of European integration, the role of such a "political entrepreneur," Jean Monnet, has been extremely important, as we have shown already in Chapter 3.

Second, we have to consider the influence of national politicians, particularly the heads and members of governments. All their proposals and actions which are motivated by the idea of promoting European integration sooner or later lead also to an increase of the Eurocracy. Often, national politicians have a direct interest in the establishment of EU regulations. In this way, aims can be realized which they are unable to accomplish at the level of their nation-state.[8] (For the case of Austria, see Heschl 2002.) The same argument was used in many other countries and in particular in the case of the post-Communist states (Hofbauer 2003). National politicians also have interests in opening up new positions and career prospects for their political clienteles. The thousands of higher positions in the institutions of the EU provide ample opportunities in this regard, particularly for academics. Some national politicians, such as Charles de Gaulle and Margaret Thatcher, been very critical about the Eurocracy. However, it seems that they have not been more successful than Ronald Reagan or George Bush senior in the U.S. in this regard; everywhere around the world, the public sector is "difficult to control and even more difficult to roll back" (Peters 1995:17).

An interest in a strong and growing European bureaucracy is clearly evident among the new "European politicians" proper such as the members of the European Parliament. A parliament becomes more powerful if it is part of an extended political system with a broad array of functions and competences. The main functions of a parliament, legislative and controlling activities, can be exerted only in cooperation with a bureaucracy. Therefore, the European parliament will de facto be one of the main actors favouring the extension of this bureaucracy. The EP and the Commission increasingly see themselves as allies in the quest for more union power and competences against national governments.

Self-interests of the Eurocrats: Once a bureaucracy has been created, its members develop definite and manifold interests in the preservation and upgrading of their positions. Economic theorists of bureaucracy see bureaucrats as "utility maximizers" who rationally pursue their own goals. These include not only narrow self-interests and "egoistic" aims, for instance, in terms of job security and income, but a broad array of valued social goods: power, money income, prestige, convenience in the work efforts, personal loyalty to one's own work group or the bureau as a whole, desire to serve the public interest, commitment to a specific program of action, public reputation, and patronage (Downs 1967:84, Niskanen 1971:38). In international bureaucracies, additional challenges come from working in a stimulating multicultural environment. Niskanen (1971:36ff.) argues that all these individual goals of bureaucrats "are a positive monotonic function of the total *budget* of the bureau during the bureaucrats' tenure in office" (Niskanen 1971: 38; see also Peters 1995:213). Thus, all bureaucrats in leading positions, including those with altruistic goals or with goals fully in accordance with the aims of their institutions, will be inclined to fight for an increasing budget.

All these aspects may contribute to the fact that nearly all bureaucracies tend to grow over time. This tendency has been condensed in "Parkinson's Law," which states that in any work organization everybody tries to expand his work so that the time available is filled out (Parkinson 1957). A corollary of this law is that the staff of any public administration department will continually increase (Parkinson postulates a relatively exact proportion: 5% to 6% per year). Downs (1967:17) mentions five concrete reasons why bureaus seek to expand: (1) An expanding organization can attract and retain more capable personnel; (2) it provides its leaders with increased power, income and prestige; (3) it reduces internal conflicts by avoiding zero-sum games; (4) it may increase the quality of its performance; (5) the usual incentive structure provides greater rewards for increases than for reductions of the expenditures. In the case of the Eurocracy, these tendencies are reinforced by an important constitutional characteristic of the EU: The Treaty of Rome was, as all of its successor treaties, an "outline treaty," as pointed out by Walter Hallstein in 1965: "In such immense fields as agriculture, transport, external trade, social policy, competition policy, and so on, the Treaty therefore provides a framework for continuous action."[9]

Economic elites: Bureaucracy is an indispensable instrument of coordination and steering in advanced capitalism. The increase of the division of labour, the growing technical complexity and interdependence of the different economic sectors, and the process of globalization all require more and more general regulations whose enactment must be assigned to a public authority. As a consequence, entrepreneurs and corporations themselves are interested in laws and regulations valid throughout the EU—contrary to their usual opposition against governmental interference into the "free market." Thus, it is not surprising that multinational enterprises, representatives of business organizations, and their lobbies employ nearly 15,000 people in Brussels. The Commission, with its manifold directories and departments, is their main contact partner.

The general public: The European bureaucracy is far away from the horizon of the general population throughout Europe. However, their attitudes and expectations are highly significant in this regard as well. Generally, however, quite contradictory expectations exist among the public: "A large part of our population wants to expand the role of government . . . A correspondingly large part our population is exasperated by the methods of bureaucracy and dissatisfied by its performance" (Niskanen 1971:3; see also Schmid and Treiber 1975:13). Citizens express rather low levels of support for government, bureaucracy, and taxation, but these negative attitudes vanish if specific categories of public activity or expenditure are at issue (Peters 1995:37; Haller et al. 1990). The expectations of the population concerning the European Union are clearly relevant because they enter into the political programs of European and national politicians. As it will be shown elsewhere (see Chapter 6), citizens expect that the European Union plays a significant role in nearly every area of politics. Also, this attitude provides a favourable background for the expansion of the competences and the staff of the Eurocracy.

5.2 The personnel: Size, growth and social characteristics of the Eurocracy

Data on the size and development of the Eurocracy are certainly basic for an adequate estimation of its influence. The data are mostly taken from official statistics of the EU and from special studies carried out either on behalf of the Union or by independent researchers. Many of these data are not really "new." Their systematic presentation and interpretation from the theoretical perspective developed in this work, however, sheds a rather new light on the development and the functions of the Eurocracy.

The small size of the European bureaucracy— a rather misleading argument

It is a standard objection against the thesis of a bureaucratisation of the European Union that its bureaucracy is very slim compared with the public administrations of nation-states. According to the present vice-president of the commission, Günter Verheugen, the charge of "bureaucratism" is the first among six "unfounded myths" in connection with the EU: "If I will believe to German media, the European Commission disposes of a huge army of officers which stretches his octopus arms until the last municipality. In fact only a little more than 20,000 officers work in the European Commission, less than the employees of the public transportation services of Berlin, less than the municipal administration of Cologne, less than the British Highway Authority" (Verheugen 2005:11). Many commentators and scientists repeat the thesis that the European Commission and its bureaucracy is "a surprisingly small organisation" (Spence 1994:62; for similar statements see Peters 1995:149; Bach 1999:23; Shore 2000:8; Hartmann 2001:127).

In fact, most of the above-quoted numbers cannot be questioned; from such a point of view, the Eurocracy is indeed a very slim organization. Yet the frequently repeated argument about the small size of the EU bureaucracy is nevertheless extremely misleading. Three reasons make a comparison between the EU bureaucracy and national or regional/local administrations rather meaningless. First, the European Union is no state, and it is wholly unrealistic to expect that it will become a kind of state in the foreseeable future. Also, the comparison of the Eurocracy with a typical big-city administration "is odious because the functions of the two organizations are disparate" (Nicoll and Salmon 2001:129). The EU administration is in the first place a law- and decree-producing machinery but it has no direct executive functions. The bulk of the officials of state and local administrations, however, are working in this area (such as tax collectors, judges, policemen, teachers, etc.). Second, the argument about the small size of the EU bureaucracy rests only on a static view. The development of this bureaucracy over the past decades provides a very different picture (see also Page and Wouters 1995:191; Vaubel 1995:36). Present-day state administrations in Europe had more than two centuries to develop. An adequate comparison of the Eurocracy with the national bureaucracies would have to look at the size of the latter around the end of the eighteenth century. Third, the exclusive consideration of the administration in the central offices of the EU overlooks the fact that there are ten thousands of officers working mainly for the EU also in the national governments at the state, provincial, and local levels; we call them *EU substitute bureaucracies*.

The personnel of the Eurocracy and the dynamics of its development

Let us look first at the number of the officials of the European Union, as they are reported in the official statistics of the commission. *Table 5.1* shows that the EU employed around 40,000 persons in 2006; the staff of the commission, the heart of the EU bureaucracy, amounted to 24,583 permanent and some additional 3,000 temporary employees. About 11% of these are translators and interpreters (4,000 in 2003).[10] Compared to the size of national administrations, this is in fact a rather small number. All in all, in 2003 the public sector employed between 200,000 and half a million people in smaller countries like Austria, Sweden, or Belgium, 1.9 million in Italy and the United Kingdom, 2.4 million in France, and 2.9 million in Germany and the United States.[11] However, these are the employees in the whole category "public administration, defence, and compulsory social security." If we look only at civilian employees of the central government (Bund, federal government), the figures are much lower: 111,000 in Austria, around 200,000 in the United States, and 300,000 in Germany.[12]

Table 5.1.   Officials of the European Union 2006 by Type of Institution.

	EU Officials			
	Permanent	*Temporary*	*Total*	
	N	N	N	%
European Commission	24,583	3,045	27,628	68.0
Operation	*18,205*	*366*	*18,571*	*45.7*
Technological R & D	*3,792*		*3,792*	*9.3*
Other	*2,586*	*2,679*	*5,265*	*13.0*
European Parliament	4,883	918	5,801	14.3
Council of the EU	3,393	47	3,440	8.5
Court of Justice	1,346	411	1,757	4.3
Court of Auditors	657	134	791	1.9
Economic and Social Committee	642	29	671	1.7
Committee of the Regions	425	32	457	1.1
European Ombudsman	13	44	57	0.1
Data Protection Supervisor	24	0	24	0.1
Total N	35,966	4,660	40,626	100.0
%	88.5	11.5	100.0	

Source: Data received from Eurostat/European Statistical Data Support (ESDS). For the following tables, which are related to earlier periods (smaller total numbers), see also *Bulletin Statistique* published by Commission Européenne–Direction Générale du Personnel et de l'Administration.

The personnel employed directly by the EU is not the whole story. For decades, the EU has established legally independent agencies which carry out special functions. A recent list enumerates thirty-one such agencies, whose task is "to accomplish very specific technical, scientific or managerial tasks."[13] They are concerned with such issues as security of sea and air traffic, food safety, railways, environment, and even "Education, Audiovisual, and Culture"—matters clearly belonging to the member states in the first instance. If we make the modest assumption that each of these agencies employs thirty people, an additional thousand employees are working here.

Forty thousand officers may appear as a "small" number compared to the size of the EU. The picture looks quite different, however, if we look at the dynamics of the development of the EU bureaucracy (see *Figure 5.1*). Here, we see an impressive and steady, nearly linear growth: In the early 1970s, the number of 10,000 was reached and surpassed; in the mid-1980s, 20,000; in the mid-1990s, 30,000; and in 2005, 40,000. Thus, the

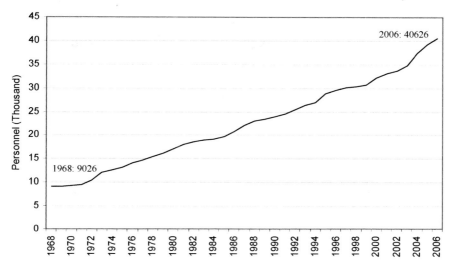

Figure 5.1 The development of the EC/EU employees,* 1968–2006 (absolute numbers).

*In all institutions, including decentralized units and officials with fixed-term contracts.

Source: Data received from Eurostat/European Statistical Data Support (ESDS).

number of EC respectively EU officials has increased more than the four-fold between 1968 and 2006. None of the authors mentioned before has taken notice of this permanent increase! One could argue that an increase of the EU personnel is obvious and necessary since the size of the European Union has expanded over these three decades from six to twenty-five countries (in 2006), or, in terms of population, from about 185 in 1968 to over 450 million. Yet there are no particularly strong increases in the number of EU officials in the years when new countries joined the Union (see also Page and Wouters 1995:191; Oldag and Tillack 2005:94).

This trend can be compared with the development of the administrations at the national level, although a neat distinction of the public sector from the private economy is very difficult (Peters 1995:18). Here, the unique expansion of the Eurocracy turns out even more clearly. Since 1990, the number of employees in the public administration has increased in a few countries (see *Figure 5.2*). It increased, in particular, in France in the early 1990s, and in the United Kingdom in the late 1990s; afterwards, it remained stable in both countries. In other countries—including paradigmatic welfare states such as Sweden and Denmark—sharp drops can be observed in the 1990s; the later increase reached only the level that already existed earlier. Overall, the picture is one of relative stability of public-sector employment in most member states of the European Union. This deceleration or even growth stop corresponds to the increasing questioning of the public sector since 1980 (Pierre 1995:2f.).

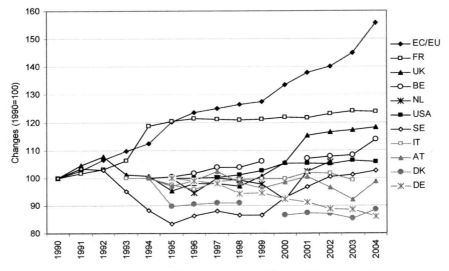

Figure 5.2   The development of the number of public employees in selected countries and in the EC/EU, 1990–2004 (relative changes).

Sources: ILO Yearly data, Table 2B (total employment by economic activity) and 2E (France) under http://laborsta.ilo.org (2006–03–15); USA: ILO Public Sector Data under http://laborsta.ilo.org (2006–03–16); EC/EU: Data received from Eurostat/European Statistical Data Support (ESDS).

Over a longer time period, we can even observe marked decreases in many countries. Employment in the public sector had reached a peak in the 1980s and decreased later, for instance, in Sweden, the Netherlands,[14] Germany, and the United Kingdom. In the United States, a decrease from 18.1% to 14.3% took place since 1970.[15]

Thus, the overall picture is that one main aim of the European Union— to reduce public employment in favour of private activities—has in fact been realized at the level of the nation states, but not at the level of Union itself. The Eurocracy has continuously grown—also in phases of "Euro-sclerosis" (Shore 2001: 138).

Does the buildup of the EU reduce national bureaucracies? The EU substitute bureaucracy

Since the central EU bureaucracy is concerned mainly with the enacting of general guidelines, laws, and decrees, a considerable number of public officials in the member states must be concerned with the implementation of these laws. In this section, we will show for the first time that the development of the EU was accompanied directly by the parallel development of a "substitute EU bureaucracy" outside the main seats of the EU offices in Brussels, Luxembourg, and Strasbourg. The existence of the development of this bureaucracy has escaped nearly completely the attention of all observers of the Eurocracy. I will present here data on the number of bureaus (departments, units) and employees at the level of the nation-states, their provinces, and communes which are concerned exclusively with EU agenda at the local level. These tasks include the implementation of EU directives, the distributing of money from EU funds, the advice of local governments and enterprises in getting access to EU funds, the collection and archiving of data, and the dissemination of information about the EU.

For this aim, special small surveys have been carried out in six regional/local units of four member states by collaborators in these countries.[16] The researchers first collected comprehensive information about the offices within the respective governmental, provincial, and local administrations that were concerned with EU affairs. Then they went to these offices and carried out personal interviews with their heads or another informed person in order to find out how many of the collaborators were concerned with EU affairs. The regional units were the Italian provinces of Trento (466,000 inhabitants) and Roma and Regione Lazio (ca. 5 million); the Austrian *Bundesland* Styria (1.2 million); the German *Bundesland* Baden-Württemberg (10.7 million inhabitants); and the Swedish Län's (counties) Stockholm (1.8 million), and Skane (1.1 million).

One first finding of this in-depth research was that it was very difficult to get an exact estimation of the size of these bureaucracies. The reason was that—in addition to those who were concerned fully with the EU agenda, also many other (if not nearly all) officials had to consider EU-related matters in their work. This fact was expressed most clearly by two Swedish officials interviewed for this purpose. "EU-affairs are completely interwoven with the daily work of the municipal and regional authorities," said Louise Carle of the "Region Stockholm." Karl Löfmark, head of the International Bureau, Commune of Malmö, said that "the distinction between Eurocracy and national bureaucracy has become redundant. There are (also) many local initiatives that are beyond central control. Not even the smaller municipalities know about all the EU-projects going on under their jurisdiction."[17]

Nevertheless, it was possible to find out in a rough way the number of officials in the local and/or regional units selected who are mainly concerned with EU issues. The figures are shown in *Table 5.2*. We can see that in the different units between seven and forty-eight persons are concerned mainly with EU affairs. The province of Trento is an outlier with its high number of eighty-three; this may be due to its special status as an autonomous province and the many activities it is carrying out (also in cooperation with the University of Trento) for international and intercultural contacts. In the case of the *Regione* Lazio, only the offices situated in Rome have been registered. If we extrapolate these figures to the four countries as a whole (taking into account the number and size of their provinces), we get a rough estimation of about 500–1,200 officials concerned with EU affairs in Austria and Sweden, and between 1,500 and 2,500 in Italy and

Table 5.2 EU Substitute Bureaucracies in Five Regions of Three EU Member States

Country	Region/Province/Commune	Number of officials concerned with EU matters
Italy	Comune and Provincia di Trento	83
	Comune di Roma	25
	Provincia di Roma	20
	Regione Lazio	22
Austria	Comune of Graz	7
	Bundesland (province) Steiermark	23
Germany	Bundesland Baden-Württemberg	40
	40 larger cities	48
	Association of communes (Gemeindetag)	4
	Universities, technical colleges	48
	Regierungspräsidien	20
	Ministerial offices	25
Sweden	Län (county) Skane	16
	Län Stockholm	22
	Region Stockholm	10
	Region Skane	15

Source: Special Surveys, carried out 2005–2006.

Germany. Looking at the EU as a whole, we could assume that in the eight smaller member states (less than 5 million inhabitants) between 300 and 700 officials are mainly occupied with EU affairs, in the 13 middle-sized (5 to 29 million) 500 to 1,200, and in the 6 large (30 million and more) member states 1,500 to 2,500. Then, we get an estimate of the whole EU substitute bureaucracy varying between 17,900 and 36,200 persons. Thus, we could say that an additional EU bureaucracy exists in the member states which is of about the same size as the "official" Eurocracy in Brussels. We have to keep in mind, however, that these are by far not the only member-state officials who are concerned with EU affairs. A multiple of them is in fact concerned with EU affairs every day, although not exclusively. The presentation of these figures clearly illustrates a general point made also by some critical analysts of the EU. Chryssochoou et al. (1999:217) write in this regard: "Little doubt exists that European integration has strengthened the executive branches of the member polities . . ."

Growth of the expenditures for administration and of the legislative output

Let us shortly look at two further indicators for the growth of the Eurocracy, the development of expenditures for administration, and the legislative output.

Figure 5.3 presents the basic data about expenditures. We can see that both general EU expenditures and expenditures for administration have increased massively between 1958 and 2004: The first from 82.3 million euros to 114,955.6 million (114.9 billion), the latter from 7.3 to 6,292,4 million. Thus, general expenditures increased by a factor of 1,400, administrative expenditures somewhat less, by 861. Even if we consider a shorter period (1968 as the base year), these increases are much larger than those in the personnel where we have seen an increase by the factor 40. The following two reasons may explain the large difference: (1) The expenditures are given in absolute figures, not considering inflation; the increase in inflation-adjusted terms was certainly considerably smaller; (2) with increasing "age" of the Eurocratic administrative apparatus, an increasing number of officials are becoming pensioners, which also contributes to administrative expenses.

Another quantitative and reliable but also politically relevant indicator for the development of the Eurocracy is its output in terms of regulations

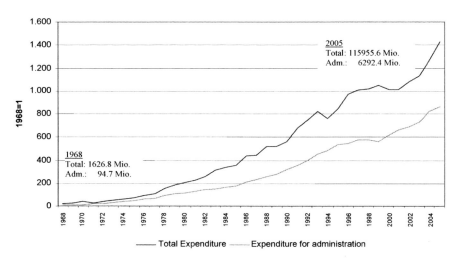

Figure 5.3 Total EC/EU expenditure and expenditure for administration from 1968 to 2005.

Sources: 1958–2000: Financial Report 2004, pp. 146f., table 7; available under http://europa. eu.int/comm/budget/publications/fin_reports_en.htm (2006–04–28). 2005: General budget of the European Union for the financial year 2006, p. 7, table 2.1; available under http://europa. eu.int/comm/budget/publications/budget_in_fig_en.htm (2006–04–28).

Table 5.3   Legislative and Regulating Activities of the EC/EU, 1971–2000

Numbers of . . .	1971–1975	1976–1980	1981–1985	1986–1990	1991–1995	1996–2000
Directives	108	264	330	537	566	532
Regulations	1,788	4,022	6,106	9,124	7,752	5,583
Decisions	716	2,122	2,591	3,251	4,242	5,299
Total no. of "domestic" legal acts	2,612	6408	9,027	12,912	12,560	11,414
Court decisions	693	1,155	1,760	2,127	2,027	2,487
International agreements	454	488	517	542	852	1,223
Recommendations and opinions	68	114	95	143	1,246	1,505
White and green papers	0	0	1	9	28	37
EU expenditure as % of EU GDP*. . .	0.4	0.7	0.8	0.9	1.0	1.1
Governmental expenditure	1.0	1.5	1.6	1.8	2.0	2.4

*Last year of 5-year period only.

Source: Alberto Alesina et al. (2001), *What Does the European Union Do?*

and decrees produced. Two data are given in this regard. *Table 5.3* shows the number of "domestic" legal acts—regulations, decisions, and directives (which are binding for all or parts of the member states)—of the Commission and the decisions of other institutions of the EC/EU from the period 1971–1975 up to 1996–2000 (Alesina et al. 2001). Here, we can see the same dynamic as in the personnel and financial areas: a continuous and strong increase up to the last period. The number of these decisions increased from 2,612 in the first half of 1970 to 11,414 in second half of 1990, that is, by a factor of 4.3. A somewhat less strong increase has occurred in decisions of the European Court of Justice and international agreements. However, the nonbinding recommendations and opinions exploded almost (increase by a factor of 22 from 68 to 1,505); the *White* and *Green Papers* were invented in 1980. Comparable findings emerge if we look at the development of the size of the official Journal of the Community where all its binding legal acts must be published. While the number of volumes per year did not increase very much (from 285 to 349) between 1970 and 2005, the number of pages and of words per year increased by more than the threefold (the number of pages from 6,300 to 21,200, the number of words from 1,890 to 6,360).

The increase of the legislative output is certainly not a phenomenon confined to the EU. Already in the 1970s, for instance, representatives of the German Federation of Cities and Communes complained about the "flood of laws" (Waffenschmidt et al. 1979:84). The reasons for this trend are highly relevant also for the EU: (1) The ambition of parliamentarians and governments to present to the voter a maximal number of new laws; (2) the tendency of the highly skilled officers in the ministerial bureaucracies toward perfection and systematisation; (3) an increasing distrust of the public in the competence and loyalty of administration. This latter fact may be even more relevant for the Eurocracy, whose directives have to be implemented in twenty-five states with very different administrative cultures. Also, the negative consequences of the inflation with laws and regulations mentioned in this German analysis may be relevant for the EU: increasing confusion of the whole legal order; alienation of the citizen from it; excessive demands on public administration and increasing bureaucratisation of public life (Waffenschmidt et al. 1979; see also Rasmussen 1986).

Personal and social characteristics of the Eurocracy. The dominance of the French model of public administration

The officials of the EU are divided into statutory and nonstatutory or external personnel (see Spence 1994:65ff; Dinan 1999:218ff). For the statutory staff, a bulky handbook of 167 pages entitled *Staff Regulations and Rules* determines their rights and obligations, career structures, pay scales, social security provisions, and pension arrangements.[18] Statutory employees are appointed on a permanent basis (tenured) and amount to about 88% of the whole EU staff in 2006. Two thirds of all officials work for the Commission, 14.3% for the European Parliament, and the rest for other EU institutions, such as the Council, the Court of Justice, and the different committees (see *Table 5.1*). The staff is divided into four categories or grades: Category A comprises officials with a university education, dealing with autonomous administrative and advisory duties; they are subdivided into twelve steps. Steps A13–A16 are distinguished from those below by their management responsibilities. Category B comprises officials with executive duties and an advanced secondary education; the further subdivision is into nine steps. Category C includes secretarial and clerical staff with secondary education, subdivided into nine steps. Category D includes officials with a primary education, employed mainly in manual or simple service duties (such as porters, chauffeurs, and the like).

Thus, also in the Eurocracy, a very close relation between levels of schooling obtained and positional categories exists. It clearly indicates that the organizational structure of the EU is mastered after the traditional structure of the public service in continental Europe. In the last decades, some of these countries try to relieve the strict correlation between

Photo 5a   The Berlaymont Building in Brussels, seat of the EU Commission and the "Eurocracy."

Source: Markus Würfel.

educational certificates and careers in the public service in favour of more achievement-oriented promotion systems. Again, we can note here that the EU itself is adhering more closely to older models than its member states. Entry into the higher levels of service in the EU bureaucracy is by a *concours*, modelled after the French system of recruitment, an EU-wide competitive exam. New entrants are usually appointed to the lowest steps in the respective grades. This practice has been introduced because of a negative attitude of the unions toward hiring for middle and higher levels from outside, which reduces chances for internal promotion (Spence 1994:67).

A graphic picture of the distribution of the officials by grades shows a kind of inverse pyramid (see *Figure 5.4*): The second highest grades—officials at the levels A5–A12—constitute the single largest category (44.3%), followed by the two lower grades (B and C) whose size is only about as half as large. Thus, it comes clearly out that the highly educated academics form the core of the staff of the EU Commission. At the highest and lowest level, we find two rather tiny groups.

Photo 5b   The European Commission, 2007.
Source: European Community, Audiovisual Service.

Let us look at the composition of all members of the EU bureaucracy in terms of some additional social characteristics. One important issue in this regard are the processes of recruitment. The dominant normative principle today is that of merit recruitment, which should ensure that the most able and efficient personnel are employed. Moreover, there is also the idea of "representative bureaucracy," which means that a bureaucracy should represent the characteristics of the population in whose name it administers policy (Peters 1995:92). How does the Eurocracy look like from these two points of view? Let us first look at gender and age.

In terms of *gender*, females are only weakly underrepresented in general; 48.3 % of all officials are females. It seems that the decisive policy of the EU to promote women's employment has had some effects here. However, the highest levels in the commission are a "male bastion" (Spence 1994:83). Less than 10% of the seventy-two general directors in 2006 are females. It is quite interesting, however, that the same is true also at the lowest level of the D grades (80% men). These grades include persons with elementary education, working in manual or simple service jobs, such as chauffeurs, porters, and so on. The main reason may be that also these jobs are highly privileged compared to similar jobs in the labour market of Brussels (see following). It is quite revealing that the EU considered it necessary to limit the absolute number of these jobs to eighty-five in total.

In terms of *age*, the EU personnel show a strong overrepresentation of the age groups thirty-eight to fifty-five. Younger but also older age

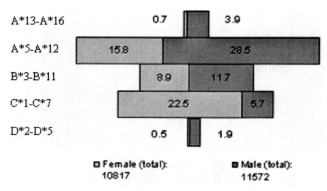

Figure 5.4   Personnel in the EU Commission by gender and grade (in %).

Note: Personnel (employees and temporary employees) without external personnel; intermediate grades, valid from May 1, 2004, until April 30, 2006.

Sources: See table 5.10.

groups are underrepresented. The underrepresentation of the younger may be a consequence of the fact that the preconditions for getting access to an EU job usually are a high level of education and previous work experience. The underrepresentation of the older age groups may be, first, a result of the strong expansion of the EU bureaucracy over the last decades (see also Shore 2000:174). It could become a problem in the future if this expansion cannot continue at the same rate; then, the underrepresentation of younger officials could lead to a decreasing dynamic of the whole bureaucracy. A second factor for the weak presence of employees over sixty may be that EU officials can retire at the age of sixty. This is also a fact which clearly contradicts the general political aim of the EU to increase the duration of the working life in its member states in order to solve the problem of the increasing mean age of the populations.

We have compiled detailed data on the distribution of the EU officials by grades and *member countries*; due to reasons of space, they cannot be presented *in extenso* here. In general, all member states are well represented among the Eurocrats. This shows that the selection procedure for EU jobs is based also on implicit yet effective national quota. This fact is certainly an important matter of political compromise between the member states. It may be "necessary" from this point of view. However, this fact again proves that the EU is not a "better" institution than any other political community; they all have also "political" criteria for appointments (Peters 1995:91). Such criteria, certainly run counter to the ideal of merit recruitment. The implementation of national quotas has several dysfunctional consequences for the process of personnel management. For several reasons—in order to attain an adequate proportion of nationals in the commission, the wish to have conational staff around the senior positions, and the wish to retain staff in certain key policy areas—"brokerage and package deals are part of a round of new appointments made necessary when one or two staff leave or are promoted" (Spence 1994:80). Often, external staffs are recruited in order to bypass the strict recruitment rules of the EU—a fact which can undermine the ethics of the European civil service. Members of *cabinets* often seek and get extra promotion, particularly if their commissioner departs. When the access of new member states makes it necessary to create new jobs, older staff members are often invited to resign and go into early retirement. In the period 1986–1988, for instance, when the Commission recruited 1,320 new officials from Spain and Portugal, 446 officials choose early retirement, and 939 extra posts were created (Spence 1994:82).

However, some countries are overrepresented, others underrepresented. Among the higher-level officials (grades A13–A16), the French are clearly overrepresented (16.8% of these are French, compared with 12% from the UK, 10% from Germany, and 8.6% from Italy); this points again to the overproportional influence of French bureaucracy. Related to population size, Britons and Germans are underrepresented. At the middle and lower levels (B to D grades), however, the Belgians stand out with representing one third of all employees. In relative terms, the same is true for officials coming from Luxembourg, although their absolute numbers are modest. This is natural, on the one side, since less qualified personnel must not be hired all over Europe; however, it reinforces the influence of French "administrative culture" in Brussels.

The dominance of French administrative culture in Brussels has been described in detail by Cris Shore (2000:179ff.; see also Spence 1994). This administrative model is characterised by selecting highly specialised expertise and technocrats from the elitist *grandes écoles*, by a highly politicised senior management, a powerful "cabinet system" (private offices of the commissioners), and, in general, by a combination of rather rigid bureaucratic rules and structures with a pervasive informal system based around personal networks and flexible working methods (see also Crozier 1967; Shore 2000:180). Hierarchy plays an important role for careers in the Eurocracy. It is said that some DGs resemble "feudal systems" where supervisors act like "barons." Advancement to higher levels is frequent within the four grades. Among the A categories, however, there exists a clear barrier restricting access to the highest managerial positions where political and social network criteria play a decisive role. Demotion, the counterpart of promotion, is practically unheard in the Eurocracy; this is partly a result of national protection. Together, these factors cause considerable frustration among middle-level A-grade officials, as an internal (but never published) study showed (Spence 1994:69).

5.3 Material gratifications and lifestyles:
The rise of a new "Euroelite"?

The income and other material remunerations of the members of the Eurocracy are highly important from the viewpoint of an elite-theoretical perspective. First, work income should reflect, from a normative point of view, individual efforts and achievements. These, however, cannot be measured objectively in a simple way but are determined also by social and normative expectations. Empirical research has shown that there exist shared norms of what constitutes a fair or equitable payment for any given level of work (Jaques 1967). Second, income is related to power which arises from the demand for certain qualifications, the level of union organisation, and the power of the organisation or corporation to which somebody belongs (Brinkmann 1984). Third, level of income per se has a high symbolic value, indicating occupational and social status and making possible a certain style of life. All these aspects apply particularly to public employment, where productivity of individual work is not measurable and work often does not have equivalents in the private sector (Peters 1995:108).

At the basis of the elite-critical approach developed in this book, we should expect that the specific situation and power of the Eurocracy should reflect itself also in high incomes, remunerations, and privileges. There are at least six reasons for this; the first three are characteristic for all public bureaucracies, the next three for the special situation of the Eurocracy. These are: (1) A large proportion of public officials are highly educated and professionally trained specialists. (2) The employer, the state, cannot go bankrupt as a private firm can go if it pays "too high" wages over a longer time. (3) Public employees are strongly organized collectively in most continental West European states. (4) Working in Brussels implies for most EU officials having been mobile and living in a foreign country; it is certainly justified to recognize this in terms of a higher salary. (5) The European bureaucracy practically determines by themselves the size of their incomes; in this regard, their members are comparable to top managers of large enterprises where the supervisory board usually accepts the proposals of the managers. (6) The incomes and privileges of the Eurocracy are seldom discussed in public since a European "public space" is still in its infancy and the Eurocracy working in Brussels, Luxembourg, and Strasbourg is very remote from the national capitals of the member states.

The income of the EU officials in comparison with those of other bureaucrats

First, let us look at the official income tables for the members of the EU bureaucracy (see *Table 5.4*). We can see that the monthly gross income goes from 2,325 per month up to 16,000 euros. Thus, a person with elementary education, working as a porter or janitor (category D), earns between 2,325 and 4,252 euros per month; this corresponds to the income of a young university graduate in the member states. The monthly salaries of secretaries and persons in similar jobs with a lower or intermediate vocational education (grades C1–C5) go from 2,325 to 5,444 euros; those of persons with a high-school diploma vary between 3,810 and 9,045 euros. Academics and/or persons in higher qualified positions begin their work career with an income near 5,000 euros a month and can end up with 10,000 euros and more. Directors Generals (A1) have salaries between 14,822 and 16,094 euros per month. Also, these are surprisingly high figures. In addition to these basic gross salaries, the EU official gets each month in addition:[19] (1) A family allowance, comprising a household allowance (150 euros plus 2% of the basic salary), a child allowance of 328 euros per month for each dependent child (up to the child's eighteenth year of life, or twenty-sixth year, if he or she is receiving education); and an education allowance equal to the actual education costs up to 223 euros per month for each child who goes to a school (double is paid in specific situations). (2) An expatriate allowance equal to 16% of the basic salary plus household and child allowance. In addition, EU officials get an installation allowance (equal to two months' basic salary) when they move to Brussels (which is obligatory), a resettlement allowance, travel expenses once a year (they can use business-class flights), removal expenses, and so forth. If we add these additional monthly payments (family allowance, etc.), the income of an official in grade D1, step 4 increases (assuming he/she has 1 child) from 4,252 euros to 5,585 euros; that is, by 31%. This increase is higher in absolute but lower in relative

Table 5.4 Basic Gross Monthly Salaries of EU Officials by Grades and Steps (Categories), 2005 (in Euros)

Grades*		Selected Steps (categories)		
		1	*4*	*8*
A1	(A*16)	14,822	16,094	16,094
A4	(A*12)	9,045	1,094	11,579
A8	(A*7)	4,878	5,444	—
B1	(B*11)	7,994	8,921	9,045
B5	(B*5)	3,810	4,252	4,878
C1	(C*7)	4,878	5,444	5,519
C5	(C*1)	2,325	2,595	—
D1	(D*5)	3,810	4,252	4,311
D4	(D*1)	2,325	2,595	—

*Old grades; in parenthesis: new grades.

Source: Staff Regulations of Officials of the European Communities 1.1.2005, pp. I–106f.

terms the higher the position. In grade A1, step 1, the factual income is not 16,094, as shown in Table 5.4, but 19,584, that is, 21% higher.

Thus, it is evident that the incomes of the Eurocrats are in fact very high. Let us compare them with those of other groups.[20] First, we look at the annual incomes of public officials in Germany, France, and Italy. We can rely in this regard on a report commissioned by the EU itself.[21] Moreover, our own extensive inquiries of national income statistics for officials in a few countries (Austria, Germany, Italy, United Kingdom, United States) show that they are rather reliable. The incomes of the Eurocrats are indeed much higher than those of national public officials. The income of a routine secretary or a porter in Brussels is about 80% higher than that of the corresponding employee in a German public office, between 94% and 143% higher than those of French officials, and 161% and 325% higher, that is, the about two- or threefold that of an Italian official. Among top officials, differences are also larger. A director general in Brussels earns about double that of a corresponding top national official in Germany and France, and more than the threefold of that in Italy.

A comparison of the net annual income of the members of the Eurocracy with that of three comparable groups of other international organisations in Brussels (national representatives of member states in Brussels, international organisations, private multinational organisations) shows that EU officials earn about the same as the employees of other international organisations in Brussels; they are lower compared to managers of multinational corporations. From this point of view, it is right to say that the salaries of the EU are not particularly high (Spence 1994:70). In this sense, a young and very bright personal assistant of a GD, of German origin and educated as a jurist, stated in an interview that he considers his income as adequate since an occupational alternative for him would be to work for a private international consulting organisation.[22] However, EU officials enjoy some special privileges which are unknown in private business. These include the additional payments mentioned before as well as lower taxes, lifetime appointment (tenure), a tolerable workload and stress, and a favourable pension scheme (von Arnim 2006:181ff.; Spence 1994:70). The workload and work efforts of EU officials may not always be very high. The average EU official is certainly quite diligent and fulfils his duties well. Many officials in higher positions work more than the regular hours and often outside regular working times than their national counterparts.

Also, retired EU officials have quite good conditions[23] both in regard to the age of retirement and the level of pensions. Probably a unique regulation of the EU pension scheme is "retirement in the interests of service" (Art. 50). In this case, the official gets—up to the normal pension age 63—an allowance which is first 100% of the salary for three months, then goes down to 70% for the next five years and 60% thereafter. The reasoning behind this measure is certainly the necessity to create new jobs for applicants who have to get a job because of political considerations such as the access of new member states who want to get their share of EU jobs.

In this regard, also the symbolic meaning of incomes and income relations is relevant. The large differences between the salaries of national and of EU officials indicate also a relation of subordination between the two. We can compare similar income relations in the member states with federal constitutions, between civil servants of the central government and those of regional and/or provincial units. In Austria, for instance, the income of a civil servant in the central government in Vienna is clearly not persistently higher than that of an official of governments or administrations at the level of the nine *Bundesländer* (provinces). The second possibility is to ask national civil servants about their relations and experiences with Eurocrats. Interviews of this kind indicate quite clearly that the interaction is often felt as occurring not on an equal footing. Certainly, in many of the committees and expert groups, composed of EU and national officers, the relation may be more equal (see Wessels 1996).

What can be said about the transparency of the incomes of EU officials? It is well known, from studies on national state bureaucracies, that public officials, besides their officially declared incomes, enjoy a myriad of other benefits (see, e.g., Beninger 2004). The reason is that through such additional, often noncash benefits, the "true" size of the income can be concealed in order to avoid criticism from parliament deputies and the media. Many additional components of the remunerations of EU officials fall under this category, such as extra cash payments at several occasions (for instance, at Christmas); dismissal payments; holidays and financial support for further education and language courses; additional payments and fringe benefits, such as access to cheap meals, access to tax-free supermarkets, special housing and travel subsidies, subsidies for family and children, support for further education, language courses, and so forth. Certainly some of them, such as language courses, are appropriate, but often the distinction between a language course in Southern France and a free holiday may be diffuse.

Another regulation, probably unique to the EU Commission, is the "nonactive status" of an official. If an official "has become supernumerary by reasons of reduction in the number of work in his institution" (Staff Regulations, 2005, Art. 41, Appendix IV), he ceases to perform work for the commission and to get a salary. However, he/she gets an allowance which corresponds to that in the case of "retirement in the interests of the services." Again, one is amazed how EU officials can become "supernumerary," given the frequently complained inadequate accoutrement of this apparatus on the one side and the high qualifications and many-sided work experiences of its staff on the other side. One can speak of a "golden handshake" for EU officials when the EU offers to its employees to retire by the age of fifty or after twenty years of service, in order to open up new posts for applicants from the new member states.[24] Members of the Eurocracy who do not work enough are unlikely to be confronted with disciplinary action because the staff is very litigious and soon goes before a court where he usually wins against the commission. Voluntary abandonment and staff turnover are extremely low (Shore 2000:195).

Thus, many observers agree and conclude that employment, work, and income of the Eurocracy are in fact very advantageous: "EU officials are reputedly among the most privileged public officials in world" (Shore 2000:193; Dinan 1999:221; Vaubel 1995:37); they "live in a Cockaigne" (*Schlaraffenland*), given their opulent salaries, allowances, pension schemes, and tax system. Two British political scientists wrote: "A position in the European civil service has been termed a 'bureaucrat's paradise' partly because of the alleged power of bureaucrats. . . . the pay level of the EC civil service is considerably higher than that of the member states" (Page and Wouters 1995:188–89). The salaries and privileges of the EU officers are also the object of repeated criticisms in the national media. These were raised already at the time of the establishment of the *High Authority* in 1952 (Spierenburg and Poidevin 1994:77). Newspapers, particularly influential tabloids in the UK and Germany, take up this issue ever again. Their reports may contribute significantly to popular distrust against the EU.

These high salaries have also negative consequences. The head of a unit in the EU bureaucracy spoke of a "gilded cage" in which many Eurocrats find themselves captured (Shore 2000:195): "Out here people are well paid and very protected. They tend to take things for granted . . . The lifestyle is much more comfortable. Because everyone is so well paid promotion is not so important: it would mean a lot more work for not much more money . . ." The high salaries of the EU officials may not be the main motivation to seek a job in Brussels. Once they have settled there, they may become crucial, however.

The demand for jobs in the Eurocracy. An indicator for its relative standing and privilege

As argued before, it is very difficult to determine if a certain level of income is adequate or "just" from a normative point of view (see Jaques 1967; Brinkmann 1984). However, there exists an indirect indicator which gives a clear indication of the relative deprivation or privilege of a certain group. This is the relation between the number of applicants for job openings and the number of available positions. Taking this criterion, we must again conclude that jobs in the EU bureaucracy are highly privileged.

The recruitment of new personnel for jobs in the Eurocracy is a multistage selection process. In the first steps, a screening is taken among all applicants if they fulfil the formal requirements; in the second step, a self-selection occurs (some of the applicants do not show up at the tests); the third step, after a test, is the invitation to a formal application; the fourth step is an oral interview with the candidates. The successful candidates do not directly get a job but are put on a waiting list; from this list, any EU office can take people if they need some and have a vacancy. The whole procedure has been consigned to a special new, independent office, the European Personnel Selection Office (EPSO), in 2003.

If we look at the numbers of persons involved in this selection process, the following figures turns out for the year 2003: 37,647 applied for a job; 36,647 were invited to the preselection; 18,222 passed the first test; 5,774 were invited to apply formally; 3,538 took an oral test; and 2,904 also passed this last stage successfully. Thus, it turns out very clearly that the run to EU jobs is very strong. Only 7.7% of those who applied at the beginning were selected at the end. The selection was most acute in the highest category (A), somewhat weaker in the middle (C), and lower in administrative categories (LA). This process of recruitment, while probably not subject to clientelism, constitutes a big "elimination machinery" whereby the tens of thousands of applicants have to be whittled down to a few thousand for real consideration, and to some hundred available posts.

The selection procedure may be objective and neutral by usual standards of screening procedures. However, mass screening procedures of this sort (comparable to games like Trivial Pursuit; Spence 1994:67f.) have clear limitations. They are able to sort out those who lack easily measurable capacities. At the same time, a high degree of chance influence operates if some ten thousands of people have to fill out such tests. The final result may be that very good applicants have been eliminated, while others who have been very bright and perseverant in the preparation and carrying out of the tests finally are successful.

The rise of a new Euroelite: Resocialisation and self-isolation of the EU personnel in Brussels

From the viewpoint of an elite-theoretical approach, it is of interest how the EU politicians and bureaucrats see themselves and behave in their daily life in Brussels and elsewhere. It was a central assumption and hope of Monnet that the establishment of a new supranational agency responsible for the furthering of the integration process would be accompanied by a process of resocialisation of their personnel toward a new European consciousness. Such a process has in fact taken place, as it has been shown by the in-depth anthropological study of the EU Commission by the British anthropologist Cris Shore (2000:147ff.). A very telling concept to describe this process is the French word *engrenage,* which denotes an experience of being linked as an element in a chain of a wheel. It means that, once somebody works in Brussels, sooner or later he or she is "caught up in the system" and develops a deep loyalty to the Community issues. The process of *engrenage* involves much more than just a professional or organisational loyalty to the European cause; it includes a new way of thinking and style of life. Much more than EU parliamentarians who often turn to their nation-states to continue their political careers there, EU bureaucrats "have a powerful vested interest in the advancement of the European Union: having opted for a career in the service of the European Union, their prospects and status, and often their personal identity, become inextricably bound to its fortunes" (Shore 2000:152). However, resocialisation has the consequence of an identification with the institutions of the EU, not so much with "Europe." This turned out quite clearly in the interviews with the Director Generals of the Commission, carried out by the Identity Foundation, and it was confirmed in our own personal interviews with EU officials.

Among the structural conditions of the lifestyles of the Eurocrats in Brussels which contribute to their deep-going resocialisation is the character of Brussels as the new, self-styled "capital of Europe" (Shore 2000:147ff.). Such a capital has it in fact become since decades; Brussels acts as a magnet for governments, businesses, lobbyists, and many other interest groups from around the world struggling to influence the decision-making process that directly affects nearly half a billion people. Already in early 1990, Brussels housed over 160 embassies, 90 offices of regional units, 2,000 NGOs, about 10,000 lobbyists, 800 press people, 2,000 multinational companies, and many international schools, conference sites, and the like. These offices are concentrated in one particular area along three large roads (rue Belliard, rue de la Loi, av. Courtenberg). In this area, a wholly new building infrastructure has been created. The people working there have few contacts with the older parts of the city and indigenous Belgians. Eurocrats have long working days, use cafeterias and lunchrooms inside their buildings, usually reside in new living quarters, and spend their weekends often outside Brussels (many also fly back to their home countries). Thus, residential enclaves or "ghettos" of rich diplomats, Eurocrats, and foreign businessmen have been created, while "old Brussels" has remained a rather provincial town. Within Brussels, a dual economy emerged with high rents and housing prices, and very high prices for everyday services, such as car repairs, for the European and international personnel.

The lifestyle of the Eurocrats is quite different from that of local residents of Brussels: "They enjoy diplomatic privileges which make them relatively immune from the hassles faced by most local residents in dealing with the Belgian authorities; their salaries are often two or three times those of people in equivalent jobs in Belgium ... Like colonial officers or European diplomats in some Third World countries, their occupation and status places them in a social category outside and above the moral universe of Brussels society" (Shore 2000:162). Among old citizens of Brussels, considerable resentment against the Eurocrats exists.[25] Many EU officials themselves feel that they are living in a kind of "exile." All these factors contribute, on the one side, to the development of a strong *esprit de corps,*"a palpable sense of 'European identity' and consciousness among EU-officials" (Shore 2000:166). At the other side, however, this process of *engrenage* "increases the social and psychological distance between EU officials and citizens in the member states, thereby creating a new kind of core-periphery relationship between Brussels-based elites and the people(s) of Europe" (ibid.). "Eurocrats need a reality check" was the title of a letter to the editor of the Brussels-based weekly *European Voice*[26] in which the writer told his observations of some EU civil servants in a canteen of the Commission, complaining about the high cost of the "disgusting meal." The EU-staff is becoming, in the words of Shore (2001:32), "a self-recognising 'community' with its own distinctive identity and ethos. Various factors . . . reinforce the important sense of 'distinction' and *esprit de corps* that is transforming the EU administrative elite into a bureaucratic caste."

5.4 Eurocratic processes and practices

The constitution of a "bureaucratisation of the EU" does not only refer to the size of the EU administration and the number of its officers, but also—or even in the main instance—to the workings of this bureaucracy. It implies that a large amount of its work is due to very complex internal divisions, to an adherence to overdetailed working rules and regulations which often are useless from a functional point of view, to an overproduction of laws, regulations, and decrees. We find this critique even in a recent publication of the influential German Commissioner and vice-president Günter Verheugen: "As far as the Commission is concerned, it must be admitted that it becomes ever more difficult to be managed. With 25 Commission members and a corresponding number of departments it is unavoidable that friction losses and coordination shortages result. In the area of international politics, five Commissioners share the responsibilities, in the economic area at least ten. The layout of the departments in many cases is due to the necessity to find adequate tasks for the respective offer of Commission members. The system is doubtless arrived at the limits of his capacities. Without being able to quantify it exactly, *I am sure that more than fifty percent of the whole activity of the Commission are only internal coordination.* This is too much, even for a supranational office, because it means in plain language that the Commission is kept busy too much with itself" (Verheugen 2005:53; my translation and emphasis)

Thus, it seems to be in the interest of the Eurocracy itself to subject their work processes to an independent, critical social-scientific analysis. Five topics shall be dealt with in this concluding section: the highly complex internal structure; the role of the General Directors; the system of "comitology"; bureaucratic waste, clientelism, and corruption; and, finally, the ability of the Eurocracy to reform itself.

The complex and tangled internal organisational structure

The intent of this section is not to give a detailed outline of the internal structure of the commission; rather, we will discuss only three main problems in this regard, which have to be considered in order to get a rounded picture of the Eurocracy.

The first issue concerns the horizontal division of labour between Commissioners, General Directorates, and their subunits. At the level of the Commissioners, similar processes are at work as in national states when it comes to the definition and distribution of portfolios between the ministers. This is usually a difficult process of bargaining which is guided not only by functional considerations but also by the necessity to consider the interests of the different parties supporting a government. In the EU, this process is even more complicated: The selection of Commissioners has to consider an intricate bundle of prerequisites related to the member countries, the strength of the political currents and parties in the EP, gender composition, and so forth. The final outcome of the negotiation packages often lacks coherence; one main area can fall into the responsibility of several different Commissioners with ensuing problems of coordination. This fact is noted in reports of Commissioners (van Miert 2000:38ff.; Verheugen 2005) as well as in social-scientific accounts (Middlemas 1995:232).

A serious problem is the extensive size of the Commission: twenty-seven members, one from each member state (von Arnim 2006:197ff.). Such a large body is hardly able to work in an efficient manner, and many proposals have been made to reduce its size. Apart from the fact that the Commission itself decides only about a tiny fraction of all decisions, it also leads to a proliferation of new activities, since each Commissioner likes to prove the importance of his agenda and show his/her ability to assert himself/herself. The meetings of the Commission itself must be regulated in a formal way (e.g., by delimiting the allowed speech time), which chokes any vivid discussion and makes most sessions a bit of a yawn for many participants (see van Miert 2000).

Problems exist also in regard to the delineation of the functions and tasks of the different General Directorates. The implementation of directorates follows three reasons: administrative-functional logic, the politics of the commission, and the politics of the member states. The first aspect would lead to the expansion of the DGs according the accretion of new tasks. But this is not always the case (Spence 1994). Also, the accession of new countries plays some part in the creation of new GDs in order to provide them with high-status jobs. The consequence is that often GDs are not clearly assigned to single responsible Commissioners, and rivalries exist between the several Commissioners and GDs involved in common subject matters (Spence 1994:105). Also, workload and work capacities are distributed unevenly over the different GDs and units (Dinan 1999:222). The consequence is that same officials are overloaded with work while others may have a comfortable way of life (van Miert 2000: 373).

How does the principle of hierarchy, a central component of any bureaucracy, work in the Eurocracy? According to the ideal-typical, positive characterisations of the Eurocracy mentioned earlier, we should expect that this principle should not be as relevant in the EU as in classical bureaucracies. This may also be the case, because of the atypical shape of the EU bureaucracy, which does not show the picture of a pyramid but shows a bulge at the second highest level, that of highly qualified, relatively independent academic officials (see *Figure 5.4*). Nevertheless, also in this case the hierarchical principle of any bureaucracy takes its toll. An emphasis on hierarchical distinctions and detailed rigid procedural rules comes particularly from the French administrative tradition. Some administrative acts and papers must have ten signatures—a fact which was complained about by Commission President Prodi and it induced him to ask: "Who has really read the paper?" Thus, also in this regard the principle of multiple responsibilities prevails—a principle which produces rather negative outcomes in terms of final responsibility (Oldag and Tillack 2005:95).

Sociological research on organisations has shown that formal structures in practice are supplemented—and often thwarted—by informal structures. This is the case particularly in the French bureaucracy, and it extends also to the Eurocracy (Crozier 1967; Oldag and Tillack 2005:91ff.). Also, in view of the flat organisational structure, informal relations and networks may often be more important than the formal ones. The reliance on informal networks is enforced by the practice of the Commissioners' employing sometimes large personal "cabinets," and by the possibility, foreseen by the staff regulations, to employ "temporary staff." *Table 5.1* shows that the Commission employs 4,460 persons (11.5% of all) as temporary staff. Criteria along which personal networks are formed and influence communication patterns include: national belonging; political party lines; class and elite networks (particularly among the graduates from the French *Grandes Écoles*); diffuse networks, such as the members of the Opus Dei, the Freemasons, and others (Oldag and Tillack 2005:82ff.; Shore 2000).

A further central criterion of the workings of a bureaucracy is to document all decisions in a written form. In this way, decisions can later be reconstructed, if another official has to follow them, or if they are contested by clients or citizens. However, the writing down of protocols and files may often degenerate into an end of itself. How does this principle work in the Eurocracy? On the one side, the production of writings is important in the case of the EU as well. Since the Commission and its administration is mainly an institution which produces laws, directives, and regulations, the putting into writing is a main task of its officials. Furthermore, it produces a myriad of writings, booklets, and brochures for specialists and for the general public throughout the EU in order to communicate their decisions and achievements. On the other side, there exist also serious problems in this regard. Oldag and Tillack (2005:92ff.) found that the EU bureaucracy has no explicit system of archiving, knows no file reference number, and does not certificate all entrances. Also, the proceedings of the hundreds of committees, ad hoc working groups, and so on, are sparsely documented. As a consequence, slouchiness, even manipulation, frequently occurs. Such kinds of mismanagement occur particular in those areas where the commission has to administrate programs which redistribute billions of euros. The shortage of personnel is felt particularly in these areas.

The General Directors of the Commission: Clandestine wrights of Europe?

The bureaucratic apparatus of the European Commission is internally divided into thirty-six directorates, managed by directors general.[27] Below this level, there exist directorates, managed by directors, and below them, units. One Director General usually cares for up to three directorates. A director cares for 3–7 units. Thus, there exists a clear hierarchical structure within each DG, which includes several hundred and in a few cases several thousands of highly qualified civil servants.

The top management of the Eurocracy—the thirty-six Directors General and the thirty Deputy Directors General—occupy very important positions (see also Middlemas 1995:242ff.; Egeberg 2003:140ff.). In several regards, they are even more powerful than the Commissioners. They are appointed for life and the description of their role includes, in fact, political tasks and duties. A GD must be, as stated in the official Web site of the EU, a "high-calibre manager, with the highest standard of ability, efficiency and integrity." His or her competencies include the ability to develop a global mission, vision, and strategy for the directorate; to achieve the Commission's objectives; to organise and structure the work in the DG; he must be open to innovative and creative ideas, but also be able to analyse data, generate alternatives, and draw conclusions from them; he is responsible for staff management and must lead people in a hierarchical context and direct multidisciplinary and multinational teams; his duties include interpersonal management and the establishment of relations and networks inside and outside the organisation. The Directors are not staying all the time in the same directorate but rotate between them about every five years. Considering all these characteristics, it is evident that the GDs can be well compared to French top civil servants (Bourricaud 1958:466). This is the level "where political power and administrative action merge" (Dogan 1975:3).

It seems necessary, therefore, to give a short characterisation of this group in terms of their national origins, their qualification and prior careers, the duration of their affiliation with the EU, as well as the process of their recruitment and appointment. Besides statistical data, provided by the EU, we can rely here on a very informative recent survey of the German Identity Foundation among thirty-three of the thirty-six Directors General (Identity Foundation 2003).[28]

First, let us look at some basic social characteristics of the general directors and the deputy GDs. Practically all of them have an academic education; the majority originate from higher middle- or upper-class families; half of them have grown up in households of public employees. Many have attended international schools or have studied abroad. The field of education clearly reflects the character of the EU as an economic and legal community: 39% have a degree in economics or business administration and 25% in jurisprudence; together, two thirds have graduated in these two academic fields. According to Dogan (1975:4), it is natural that most of the top civil servants are jurists, because a training in law "is necessary in order to formulate a political decision in administrative terms." Such an education is related particularly to the legalistic character of the commission and the economic-technocratic orientation of the EU (Shore 2000:135). The analysis of the occupational careers of the GDs shows that 31% of them worked in the civil service before entering the EU, and some more (15%) in different fields closely related to politics (diplomatic service, international organisations, politics); next come academic positions and private business.

Very remarkable is the composition in terms of national origin: Two countries stand out in the number of GDs, Germany and France (twelve and eleven of the 72 GDs, respectively); next come—with seven GDs each—Italy, the United Kingdom, and Spain.[29] In the survey of the thirty-three GDs interviewed by the Identity Foundation (2003), 21% were of French origin. It is also quite interesting that the majority of the GDs are Catholic. The next largest group are GDs without a religious denomination (42%); only 6% are Protestant or Jewish. Not less than 90% of the GDs are men—a fact which clearly contradicts the otherwise definite policy of the EU to support women's career perspectives. Three fourths of the GDs have already worked twenty years or more for the commission. Thus, most of them must have a very intimate knowledge of the workings of the Commission and a high level of identification with it.

This fact is again proved by the survey of the Identity Foundation (2003) in which a two-hour interview was carried out with thirty-three of the thirty-six general directors. The findings show that nearly all GDs estimate their ranges of power and competencies as very large; they see themselves as idea givers for European integration and feel a high responsibility for it. They see themselves as members of a positional elite with vast privileges. One GD, interviewed by the Identity Foundation (2003, p. 72), bluntly stated: "Yes, we belong to the European ruling class." The title of this study—"Considerations About the Clandestine Wrights of Europe"—seems to be quite accurate. These findings correspond to those of the anthropological study of the commission by Cris Shore (2000:199). A Director-General with almost forty years of service compared the bosses of the DGs to "medieval barons."

The real power of the bureaucratic apparatus of the Commission, embodied by the DGs and their staff, can be seen in the amount of discretion they have in issuing legal acts of the EU. For the year 2004, Commissioner Verheugen reported very interesting facts in this regard. In the decisions about legal acts, a distinction is made between A-points which, are passed by the Commission (and the Council of Ministers) without discussion, and B-points, which are discussed because they concern important political issues or contested topics. By far the largest proportion of authoritative acts or decisions of the Community—97.4% out of a total of 9,275—were taken by the bureaucratic apparatus and did not turn out in the political directing body, the appointed Commissioners. Only 244 of them appeared at the Commissioner's agenda. However, also among these written procedures are a much-used strategy of decision making; the request for such a procedure is called a "greffe" (Spence 1994). Only about eighty topics (B-points) were discussed directly by the Commissioners; about 160 (A-points) were decided by a "greffe" and not discussed at the meetings of the Ccommissioners. The proportion of the latter was less than 1% of all decisions made by the whole Commission and its bureaucratic apparatus (see also Oldag and Tillack 2005: 79; von Arnim 2006: 199). In fact, however, also national bureaucrats, particularly the Committee of Permanent Representatives (COREPER) of the member states, participate in the formulation of these decisions (Müller 1994:58).

Thus, the General Directorates and their top officials, the "barons of the commission" (Oldag and Tillack 2005:79), incarnate the power of the Eurocracy. In several instances GDs have overruled their commissioners. In this way, the political responsibility of the commissioners before the European Parliament is undermined. Commissioner Verheugen remarked that the high influence and staying power of the top officials makes reform attempts of the appointed commissioners very difficult (Verheugen 2005:45).

Comitology—The "long arms" of the Eurocracy

The comitology is a central feature of the political system of the EU. This term denotes the hundreds of committees composed of representatives (officials and experts) of the member states which assist the Commission in their daily work of proposing administrative and legislative measures. The existence and working of these committees is one of the explanations why the "slim" Eurocracy is able to unfold such far-reaching activities. In the scientific literature, this system is rightly considered as one of the most peculiar features of the EU (see Docksey and Williams 1994:117ff.; for general discussions, see Müller 1994:52ff.; Puntscher-Riekmann 1998:167ff.; Bach 1999:51ff; Hartmann 2001:124ff.). Here, only some of its most relevant features shall be summarized.

The system of committees was not planned in the original treaties establishing the European Economic Community. It was established in connection with the management of EU agricultural policy in the early 1960s and formally legitimized in 1970 by the European Court of Justice (Bandulet

1999; 88). Its workings were considered quite early as problematic; it was reformed in 1987 and then again in the late 1990s. Its intent was to assist the Commission in the handling of the new redistribution programs and subsidies and to provide the member states with a possibility to control the distribution of agricultural funds by the Commission.

There exist three kinds of committees, here sketched out only in abbreviated form: (1) *Advisory committees*, which can make proposals; (2) *management committees* involved in decisions implementing the day-to-day management of policies of the Union; (3) *regulatory committees* with the task to propose certain measures to the commission, which then must implement it. The committees have several categories of members (Docksey and Williams 1994:122): representatives of member states, of professional and economic milieux, and scientists and scientific experts or other highly qualified persons. The number of committees is very large. Already in 1986, the European Parliament identified 310 such committees divided into thirty-one categories of procedure; in 1993, 361 committees (Docksey and Williams 1994:122f.). In the mid-1990s, between 35,000 and 40,000 national officials and experts travelled between their capitals and Brussels; per year, these were about 360,000 such travels (Bach 1999:54). At the end of the 1990s, about 450 to 500 committees existed (Bandulet 1999:88; Hartmann 2001:124). A core institution is COREPER, the Committee of the Permanent Representatives of the national governments in Brussels consists of the ambassadors of the member states in Brussels and their staffs, including high-status national bureaucrats on assignment in Brussels. Its tasks are to prepare the council's agenda and to set up and monitor legislative working groups of permanent representations and other national officials. It is "extremely powerful and even more secretive than the Council . . . in certain cases, COREPER is the EU's real legislature" (Dinan 1999:261).

Two issues are relevant here. The first relates to their power: Do they seriously contest the power of the Eurocracy described in this chapter? On one side, the committees ensure that the viewpoints and positions of the different member states, as well as those of experts of all sorts, are taken into account in the decision processes. However, its members can only make proposals, but it remains with the Commission or the Council what they do with them. The committee sessions are chaired by members of the Commission. Thus, in general, the comitology may enhance the power of the Commission (Hartmann 2001:126; Puntscher-Riekmann 1998:173; Greib 2006).

A second issue is related to democratic elite theory. Here, we have to ask if the system of comitology changes the bureaucratically dominated decision procedures in the European Union. Maurizio Bach (1999:52ff.) argues that the whole complex of the European bureaucracy and its associated comitology system can be characterized as a kind of "supranational technocracy." It may foster a kind of "European consciousness," but the interests of all those involved are primarily of a technocratic nature focussing upon clearly delimited, special areas of competence. The consequence is an isolation between different areas of policies and kinds of rationality. We must add a further problematic aspect: Most of the work of the committees is carried out secretly, without any public participation. Thus, the real influence and power structure remain hidden, and democratic accountability is lacking (Bach 1999:103).

A concomitant of the comitology system of the EU is that often very small units have an extraordinary influence. In this way, small circles of bureaucrats, politicians, and lobbyists are able to impose fundamental new directions of the EU policy (see also Page and Wouters 1995:192; Michalowitz 2004:63). How this happens in practice has been shown in a case study of the EU family and gender policy by Nora Fuhrmann (2005). In the late 1990s, only three small bureaus (one in the commission, one at the EP, and the European Women's Lobby) have been able to put through the principle of "gender mainstreaming" for the EU as a whole, in spite of the fact that in different member states quite different "gender regimes" and related policies existed (Esping-Andersen 1990; Sainsbury 1999; Haller, Höllinger, and Gomilschak 2000; Hakim 2001). This was possible because the three units used all available strategic means and coalitions, without involving the general public. Fuhrmann (2005) writes that they often proceeded in a "tricky way."

Political bureaucratism and mismanagement, clientelism and corruption

Bureaucratism and mismanagement, clientelism, and corruption are phenomena existing throughout the world. They cause serious economic adversities for the persons and institutions concerned and also undermine the functioning of social and political processes (Roniger and Günes-Ayata 1994). Given the size and characteristics of the EU bureaucracy, we should be surprised to find no such phenomena there. In fact, they have great relevance also in this case, and their forms shed a significant additional light on the specific weaknesses of the Eurocracy. Also in this case, we must note a surprising neglect of this topic among social-scientific analyses of the EU bureaucracy.[30] If at all, journalists and other writers (Bandulet 1999; Oldag and Tillack 2005) or critical EU insiders (van Buitenen 2000, 2004; Greib 2006) have raised the issue.

We have to distinguish between three different forms of such misbehaviours. The first and most severe form includes violation of existing laws in order to obtain personal advantages and gains, such as fraud, bribery, and so forth; if disclosed, such forms of behaviour fall under criminal law. Second, there exist many "lighter" forms which do not constitute direct breaches of law but which nevertheless have to be considered as "unethical" behaviour; their detection is certainly difficult. Many forms of clientelism, nepotism, patronage of offices, and formally "legal" use of administrative means in order to obtain personal profits can be subsumed under this group. The German sociologist Erwin Scheuch (1992) has coined the term *benefit utilisation* (*Vorteilsnahme*) for these forms. Eva Etzioni-Halevy (1999:114) uses the term *semi-corruption* to denote all kinds of "exchange of resources accruing from public office for other resources in semi-legitimate ways." Third, there are many diverse forms of "mismanagement" and "bureau-cratism" which constitute fully legal forms of organisation and behaviour which do not produce socially valuable outcomes and must be considered as wasteful. Fourth, there exists a type which we could call "political bureau-cratism." Here, costly but needless bureaucratic expenditures exist because of political considerations.

In advanced societies, all these forms are widespread due to the growing size of the public sector, an intricate entanglement of the public and private sector, and an increasing influence of political parties and interest groups. From this point of view, even present-day Germany has been character-ized with concepts such as "scandal republic" (Scheuch 1992; Scholz 1995; Leydendecker 2003). In democratic societies, corruption causes not only material damages; it undermines trust in political institutions and, thus, contributes to a general delegitimation of politics. An empirical illustration of this fact is that political parties, or even single personalities (like Hans Peter Martin in Austria or Paul van Buitenen in the Netherlands), were able to get large fractions of votes in elections to the European Parliament 2004 only by concentrating on mismanagement and corruption in the EU. The specific nature of corruption in the EU has to do with two sets of factors: on the one side, the internal structure of its institutions and the workings of the Eurocracy; on the other side, the relation between the EU and its member states.

Three aspects of the internal structure of the EU directly contribute to the rise of mismanagement and corruption. First, the complexity of the tasks and the size of the financial means which have to administered by the Commission. Because the Commission frequently takes over tasks for which it has not enough qualified personnel, it must delegate the concrete implementation to outside, private agencies and institutions. This was a central point of the critique of the expert group in 1999, namely, that the Commission often took over new, politically important and costly tasks without disposing of the necessary personnel to administrate them (Müller 1994; Bandulet 1999:226; Shore 2000:176; Oldag and Tillack 2005:93).

A second aspect is the number and complexity of the regulations valid in the EU. This point is rightly made by Vladimir Boukovsky (2005:49ff.) in his provocative comparison between the former Soviet Union and the EU. The argument is quite simple: The more rules and prohibitions exist, the higher the number of possibilities for breaking some of them. This applies in particular to rules which try to change well-established forms of social practice. Boukovsky mentions the case of the U.S. legislation on prohibi-tion of alcohol in the 1920s, which only assisted the American mafia to establish lucrative channels of forbidden distribution and selling of alcoholic beverages. In the EU, there exist nearly identical cases. As the commission reports in its "Anti-Fraud Report 2005,"[31] the two products most affected by financial irregularities were cigarettes (cigarette smuggling) and sugar—both products highly regulated by the Commission. The problem of fraud in connection with too complex regulations has been recognized also by the former Commissioner Karel van Miert (2000:381): "Already since many years the European Commission is afflicted by multiple forms of cheating and fraud. It is in particular the highly complex agricultural policy which is predestined for the most diverse bogus manipulations." Also, the European Court of Auditors mentions in its annual report agriculture as the area where still considerable failures in the expenses exist and controls have to be improved.[32]

A third aspect of the EU system favouring corruption is the absence of strong media and of an EU-wide critical public opinion. Local media in Brussels, Luxembourg, and Strasbourg may not be particularly interested in detecting irregularities in the Eurocracy since it is the cow from which they get their milk. The complexity of the Eurocracy, the density of regulations, the international character of the processes, and the linguistic problems all contribute to the fact that mismanagement and scandals are usually not disclosed by critical journalists or deputies but—if at all— mainly by EU internal agencies (Müller 1994:75). These, however, may not always be very eager to do so. If the EU Audit Court or OLAF—the European Anti-Fraud Office, established in 1999—discloses irregularities, it is up to the Commission to take the consequences. These are often taken with considerable delay and without the necessary strength. That the EU institutions themselves have not a very positive attitude toward the revelation of cases of mismanagement has clearly been shown in the case of the Dutch EU officer Paul van Buitenen, who acted as a "whistleblower," that is, informed EU members and the media about irregularities. As a reaction, he was suspended from office and exposed to severe mobbing with the argument that he had betrayed internal information to outsiders (van Buitenen 2000, 2004). The same happened to nine other EU officials (van Buitenen 2004:241 ff.).

The other side relevant for the rise of mismanagement, clientelism and corruption in the Eurocracy, concerns the relation between the EU and its member states. Here, we have to distinguish four kinds of problems: the slop-over of corruption from member states to the EU; the direct interventions of member states in Brussels; the autonomy of the member states in the administration of EU funds; and "politically induced bureaucratism," arising from political wishes of some large member states explainable only by considerations of national prestige.

As we have seen, the Eurocracy is frequently portrayed as a wholly new, modern and highly efficient kind of supranational administration. However, we cannot assume that persons and officials who switch from their home countries to Brussels leave behind their familiar ways of thinking and behaving. Administrative procedures in Brussels will not only reflect the best practices existing in the member states. Rather, the political and administrative "culture" in Brussels will also be influenced by the bad practices in the less developed member states (as well as those in Belgium). In order to get a first hint to this possibility we can look at the level of corruption in the individual member states of the EU as it is reported in the *Transparency International Corruption Perception Index* (CPI).[33] This index shows the degree of corruption as perceived by businesspeople and risk agencies; it varies from one (very high) to ten (very low corruption). We can divide the 158 countries contained in the Table for 2005 into five groupings: very high (1–2.9), high (3.0–3.9), intermediate (4.0–5.9), low (6.0–7.9) and very low corruption (8.0–9.9). Among the countries with very low corruption, it is rather surprising to find here first all three West European countries which are not EU member states (Iceland, Norway, Switzerland); and second, all those member states of the EU whose population shows rather critical attitudes to the EU (Denmark, Sweden, Austria, United Kingdom). In the group with intermediate levels of corruption we find member states like Hungary, Italy, the Czech Republic, Slovakia, Greece, and Latvia; in the same category there are countries like Botswana, Taiwan, Uruguay, or Colombia. In the group with high corruption we find three EU members, Poland, Bulgaria, and Romania, but also the candidate country Turkey; in the very high corruption country group with thirty-six countries, mostly from the Third World, three more European countries are contained which probably will become candidates in the future (Bosnia-Herzegovina, Serbia, Ukraine). The mean value of the old EU-15 member states was 7.4 in 2005, of the 12 new member states 5.7 (2005). However, two old members, Italy and Greece, had more corruption than several of the new member states (such as Malta, Estonia, and Slovenia).

Two conclusions can be deduced from these facts: First, an effective and transparent public administration in the home country may lead many people to suspect that the system of the EU is not very clean; this perception may contribute to a critical or even negative attitude toward the EU. Second, it is quite probable that mismanagement, clientelism, and corruption are prevalent to a considerable degree in some of the old (particularly South European) EU member countries, and particularly in many of the new Central East European members. Their practices will be transfused to some degree also to the EU in two ways: Through the behaviour of EU officers coming from those countries and through misallocation and misuse of EU means going to them and administrated locally.[34]

These theses have been proven by historical facts. When the Commission led by Jacques Santer came under heavy attack by the media and the European Parliament in 1999, the Commissioners involved in cases of mismanagement and clientelism all came from member states where such practices are quite common. They included the French Commissioner Edith Cresson, who employed her dentist and friend as a scientific adviser; the Portuguese Pinheiro, who engaged his wife as a national expert; the Spanish Manuel Marín, who provided his wife a high-status job (Bandulet 1999:19ff.; van Buitenen 2000, 2004). The most heavily involved French Edith Cresson—formerly even French premier—affirmed until the end of her office term that she did not feel guilty and that her behaviour was quite usual in French politics. The vote in the European Parliament about this case showed a deep split between "two Europes": Only 14% of the Portuguese, 13% of the Italian, and 4% of the Spanish delegates voted for the deselection of the Commission, but 65% of the Swedish, 75% of the Danish, and 93% of the German deputies did (Bandulet 1999:13).

There are two further aspects where the member states can contribute to mismanagement, clientelism, and corruption in the EU system. First, they often intervene directly in Brussels when it comes to allocate jobs and experts into committees, offices, and contracts of different kinds and to distribute the huge financial sums from the Agrarian Policy and the Regional Structural Funds of the EU. Second, the member states are themselves responsible for the distribution of the EU funds. The control of the adequate use of these funds will depend directly on the efficiency and the correctness of national public administrations. One could enumerate hundreds of evident cases of misuses of EU funds (see Müller 1994:75ff.; Bandulet 1999:49ff.; van Miert 2000; von Arnim 2006:128ff.). Furthermore, the member states are hesitant to make public information on misuses because this could lead to reduction of means for the funds.[35]

How does the EU try to come to terms with these problems? In 1988, an internal Commission Unit for the Coordination of Mismanagement (UCLAF) was established (van Miert 2000:381ff.). Its work was not without success but suffered from a lack of personnel and clear working rules. Particularly the EP and its Committee for Budgetary Control (chaired by Herbert Bösch, Austrian MEP) were anxious to give to this institution more independence and power and proposed to establish a new institution wholly independent of the commission. This happened in 1999 with the establishment of OLAF, the European Anti-Fraud Office. This is a wholly independent office, with a director appointed for five years, and about 350 collaborators. It works in a quite transparent way, presents information on the Internet, and publishes an annual report (Draxler 2002; Haller and Ressler 2006a:257ff.). In 2005, 12,076 cases of irregularities were detected by OLAF with a total financial impact of 1,042 million euros.[36]

Finally, there exists the phenomenon of *"political bureaucratism."* One obvious example are the three seats of the European Parliament: Strasbourg, where most of the plenary sessions are held; Luxembourg, with the general secretary and some offices; and Brussels, where the meetings of the parliamentary committees are held. It is recognized by all observers—including the majority of the MEPs—that its splitting-up has only negative functions. First, because it produces high additional costs for buildings and infrastructure; in Strasbourg, a very expensive new parliamentary edifice has been built, in spite of the fact that such a building existed already for the Council of Europe. This building is not used most of the year; its main "users" are tourists and pupils. Second, because it produces a high wastage of time for the members and employees of the EP, who have to travel twelve times a year between Brussels and Strasbourg together with an autocade of camions which transport documents and materials forth and back. Repeated attempts of several groups of MEPs to change this situation have been without success, mainly because France insists on keeping Strasbourg as an official site of the EP.

Another example is the language policy of the EU. Here, the principle is to grant to any national language—as small as it may be—an official status in the EU. This means that thousands of official documents have to be translated into twenty-three official languages, myriads of sessions have to be translated simultaneously, and so on. Therefore, the EU employs a staff of translators and interpreters of over 5,000 persons[37]—the single largest language service in the world. The principle to grant to each national language an equal status is certainly well-founded. However, it is also evident that a trade-off must be found between this principle and that of an economic use of personnel and financial means. So it may be doubted if it makes sense to declare languages like Maltese or Irish (Gaeilge) official EU languages. Both of them are spoken by rather small groups of people (300,000 in the case of Maltese, less than 100,000 in the case of Irish), and it can be assumed that all speakers (especially MEPs and Commission officials) also speak English well or another official EU language. This situation appears even stranger, considering the fact that large subnational languages—such as Catalan, which is spoken by over 7 million people—are not recognized as official EU languages. Some recent decisions correct this strange situation a little bit, by defining a few "working languages" (English, French, and German) in the internal communication of the commission.

A third example concerns the persistence of national institutions whose *raison d'être* has evidently disappeared after the establishment of a corresponding and encompassing EU institution. A case in point are the national central banks in the countries of the euro zone. With the implementation of the euro, the main task of national banks—the provision of the economy with the national currency, currency policy, and control of all related matters—has been taken over by the European Central Bank in Frankfurt. However, no national central bank has been closed down, and probably few—if any at all—have significantly reduced their staff. A certain inclusion of the member states into the policies of the ECP would certainly be possible also without this highly expensive "European System of National Banks." It is very costly also because the salaries of the officials of all these in the national banks are very high.

In this context, it is also interesting to look at some findings concerning the knowledge and attitudes of the population about mismanagement and corruption in the EU. A small Austrian survey (n = 327), including persons from all social strata, carried out in autumn 2005 showed that the European Board of Auditors and the Anti-Fraud Office were known to the majority of the interviewed; most considered these control institutions as very important (Haller and Ressler 2006a: 243ff.). However, there was much less trust in their efficiency; only about one third believes that there are good chances for the disclosure of fraud and corruption. The population estimates the financial losses associated with it much higher than the sums which are uncovered by these institutions. However, in this evaluation citizens may also include a substantial evaluation of misused financial means. An example is the fact that EU deputies could get the money for business-class flights irrespective of the fact if they did use such flights; since this is a legally correct account, the Court of Auditors or OLAF would not find any irregularity here. Finally, it was also found that people who were quite critical about corruption and fraud had a less positive attitude toward the EU. Thus, the problem of corruption is also quite important concerning the general legitimacy of the EU.

Is the EU Commission able to implement a bureaucratic cutback? Some surprising facts about recent reform efforts

The bureaucratic apparatus of the European Union has come increasingly under attack by politicians in recent times: They have been motivated to do so mainly by the decreasing legitimacy of the process of integration in the eyes of the general public. The Commission itself is well aware of serious problems in this regard. It is also the institution mainly responsible for the task of bureaucratic cutback. It is realistic to expect that it will able to achieve this aim? In order to answer this question, it is not enough to look at the reform proposals of the Commission (see, e.g., Egeberg 2003:134f.) but to investigate the concrete steps taken to this end.

The need for reform was felt quite early. Already in the 1970s, after the accession of Britain and Denmark, some officials from these countries articulated a number of criticisms (Stevens 2002:7). In 1985, the Commission proposed, in its White Paper on completing the internal market by 1992, to switch over from positive integration through common legislation toward negative integration by mutual recognition of national regulations (Attac 2006:75; Dinan 1999:109). They proposed to establish new EU regulations for only about 300 of the 100,000 existing national regulations. In recent years, leading politicians throughout Europe recognize a problem in this regard. Both the former German Chancellor Helmut Kohl, as well as the present Chancellor Angela Merkel, referred to it. The latter spoke even of a necessary "revolutionary step" concerning the necessary "*Bürokratieab-bau*."[38] In 1995, Commissioner Erki Liikanen introduced several management-reform programmes. They were concerned mainly with strengthening and "fraud proofing" of financial management; but the programmes were modest and progress slow. In 2002, a document was issued, entitled "Simplifying and Improving the Regulatory Environment."[39] Here, we read that the Commission is "aware that legislation has become increasingly detailed—which sometimes make it difficult to understand and put in practice—it intends to avoid making its legislative proposals unwieldy . . ." It is also recognized self-critically that "the body of Community law runs over 80,000 pages and already applies to operators and citizens." The general intent of the action plan is well-meant and accurate: It should make sure that EU regulations are written in a less complicated style, in order to help to save time and reduce costs for companies and public authorities; and to ensure a high level of legal certainty across the EU.

The Commission is highly proud of these efforts and praises itself in the following words: "On these web pages, you will find details of the most radical internal modernisation since the European Commission was established in 1958. . . . Over the past five years, the Commission and its staff have been engaged in the task of overhauling the administrative systems and procedures, the management of financial and human resources, and the way in which it plans and programmes its activities. The aim throughout has been to create a modern and efficient public administration based on the principles of efficiency, transparency and accountability."[40] Did the reform correspond to these grandiloquent words? Looking more closely at the content of the plan, it is difficult to recognize indications for a significant reduction and simplification of the EU regulations—rather the reverse seems to be true. Four characteristics of the plan stand out in this regard.

First, the causes for the proliferation and increasing complication of the EU legislation are sought more among other EU agents—the EP, the European Council, the member states—than among the Commission itself. Disguised in very polite language, the following demands are directed toward the EP and Council: In the monitoring of the adoption of legislative texts (which often takes too long a time), the Commission should give "the European Parliament and Council greater encouragement to come to an agreement quickly . . ."

In line with this tone is the second characteristic. The document makes it very clear from the beginning what the aim of the reform is not: "The aim is not to deregulate the Community or limit its scope for action." Action 2 proposes even a strengthening of theCommission in the common process of adoption of legislative measures with the EP and the Council: "The Commission will have to be more substantially involved in the early stages of the negotiation." Action 5 proposes that the community should make greater use of the opportunity to withdraw legislative proposals, especially if the amendments introduced by EP or Council "denature" a proposal by making it more complex. The following remarkable statement is added in this regard: " . . . of course, whether or not these measures are applied will be at the Commission's political discretion." The member states are sometimes addressed in a tone which seems to regard them not as the "masters of the

Treaties" but more as subservient local administrations. Action 12 proposes an improvement of national notifications of EU legislation: "The members states will provide modification of transposing measures electronically, using a standard form, proposed by the Council's information working party." Action 13 proposes an improvement in the consultations and impact assessments of legislation in the member states and prescribes to them that "the content or the act should . . . not be changed nor should there be any delay in the transposition of the act by the members states."

Third, many of the proposals will lead—when implemented—not to a reduction but to an increase in written output and even in tasks and personnel. Action 3 proposes to expand the explanatory memoranda, accompanying legislative proposals, including information on consultations held, impact assessments carried out, and the like. Action 4 proposes to include a review clause in legislative proposals, especially in areas of rapid technological change. Action 7 proposes to set up a loosely structured internal commission network for "better lawmaking," which should involve all DGs. Action 10 proposes to simplify and reduce the volume of common legislation; for this aim, interinstitutional ad hoc bodies should be created which have to specify responsibility for simplifying legislations. As a measure to improve the quality of legislative proposals, they should be reread by lawyer-linguists. Action 14 proposes to create a legislative network between the EU institutions and the member states and Action 15 an additional annual assessment of the quality of legislation.

How should these reforms be realized? The following is proposed: In order to achieve the bureaucratic cutback, a new staff unit will be established whose members will be appointed by the government of the member states. They should advise the commission, simplify or cancel existing rules, and cooperate in the formulation of new regulations![41] Thus, in order to achieve a bureaucratic cutback, a new bureaucratic unit and probably also new regulations shall be established and decreed. This is also the conclusion of a critical insider of the Eurocracy about the efforts of Commissioner Kinnock, responsible for bureaucratic reforms in the Prodi Commission: "It was a big mistake to appoint again the old Commissioner Neil Kinnock . . . because he had to implement reforms of a system whose part he himself was. Kinnock disregarded the fundamental message of the report of the experts [whose report had led to the demission of the Santer Commission]: Transparency and consciousness of responsibility. Kinnock's plans aimed at increasing bureaucracy" (van Buitenen 2004:227).

Very instructive is a more recent attempt at a reduction or streamlining of EU legislation. On July 22, 2005, Commissioner Verheugen announced in Berlin that hundreds of EU regulations would be cancelled and half of the current EU legislation plans relevant for business would be taken off. This purification should set "measurable positive impacts for growth and employment."[42] Here, probably for the first time, a high EU official stated that EU legislation is an economic stumbling block. Among existing EU legislation, 900 regulations should be abolished,[43] Verheugen added; the ultimate aim would be to reduce the 85,000 pages of valid community legislation to 35,000 pages. Regulations to be abolished belong particularly to the car industry. This is quite interesting since this commissioner stated in another context that the many regulations in this sector are of a purely technical character (Verheugen 2005:12).

Some further, recent events shed a surprising light on the willingness and ability of the Eurocracy to achieve a bureaucratic cutback. In a media report entitled "Commissioners told to 'speed up,'"[44] in mid-May 2006, Commission President Barroso's chief adviser, Jean-Claude Thébault, said that only eleven initiatives had been adopted to date from a total of ninety-six in the work programme for 2006; this was only a rate of 11% compared to 25% this time last year. He pointed to further obstacles against a faster progress in decision making. The report also finds—in an approving manner—that the Commission maintained a relatively high rate of adopting legislative proposals in 2005. An even more astonishing increase is noted concerning the proportion of legislative measures that were approved in first reading by the European Parliament: This rate was 18% in 2002, 38% in 2003, 47% in 2004, and 68% in 2005. In practice, this means that the number of legislations passed in a valid manner must have been increased considerably.

A clear conclusion emerges from this review of recent Commission efforts at a bureaucratic cutback. The good intent and the general aims of these efforts certainly cannot be questioned. Their success, however, is highly doubtful for several reasons: They concern only a tiny fraction of the huge body of EU regulations; often, they are connected with additional regulations and personnel; finally, parallel to them, demands for new tasks as well as concrete steps toward their bureaucratic implementation are continuing all the time. Thus, it would be a great illusion to believe that the Eurocracy will be able to de-bureaucratize itself in a significant way. This is so "not least because of inertia or even outright opposition to reform within parts of the bureaucracy itself" (Dinan 1999:223). The influential unions within the Eurocracy, for instance, resist reform processes because they consider "the statutory guarantees, career structures and emoluments of EU officials as intrinsic to their special status as guardians of the European project." (Stevens 2002:8). The hopes—also among social-scientific observers—that a serious and successful reform effort will come out of the commission itself seem rather naïve[45] (see also Dinan 1999:223).

CONCLUSION

The Eurocracy, as it came into being in 1957, is the main agency realising the famous "Monnet method," which implies that one goes on with continuing, often little steps of integration without having in mind a certain final outcome. In the Commission and its administration such steps are occurring daily and thousandfold without attracting much public attention—even in times of "Eurosclerosis." "Action must be taken all the time" is the unofficial motto of the Eurocracy, according to an anthropologist (Bellier and Wilson 2000:32). Thus, once established, the EU does not need any more energetic and charismatic personalities in order to grow further (Bellier and Wilson 2000:14). This growth is guaranteed, first, by the existence of a powerful Commission and General Directorates as collective bodies and, second, by the creation and growth of a vast bureaucracy and associated network of national and European politicians, officials, experts, and lobbyists. They all develop an interest in the preservation of their power, status, and privileges. In this sense, a truly new "European elite" has come into being—composed of all the people whose existence and future is closely connected with the EU. Even if they are not so closely integrated in social and cultural terms as to constitute a closed "power elite" (Mills 1959) or a dominant "social class" (Middlemas 1995:269f.), their lifestyles and value orientations are quite different from those of the members of the national elites.

6   One Union or Many?
Public Views of Integration in the Different EU Member States

INTRODUCTION

In chapter 1, we have seen that a considerable split exists between elites and citizens concerning the overall approval of the process of integration. In this chapter, we will investigate in more detail the perceptions and images, fears, and expectations concerning European integration in the different member states of the Union. We will focus on the views and expectations of the citizens but include also the aims and strategies of the elites and the historical background and structural situation of the different countries. By analysing these different views, we can also clarify the issue of the finality of integration. The thesis is that the continuation of the process of integration can only be successful in the long run if majorities in all countries of the Union share the general visions concerning this process and if these expectations are matched with the strategies of the political elites. If there are significant inconsistencies or discrepancies, integration will continue to experience setbacks, which will nourish the principal doubts about its aims and direction.

The first section of this chapter contains some considerations about the conditions which favour the integration or disintegration of a society and the importance for a society—and the European Union—to develop a clear identity. In the second and third sections, a typology of the relation of different countries to the process of integration is elaborated by including knowledge and data from many diverse sources. Seven different attitudes toward the European Union are distinguished here. In the fourth section we discuss if the EU can be considered a "community of values" based on Christianity or on a specific "European way of life" which transcends the differences and divergences in the views and evaluations of the EU. Also here, the answer is quite negative. All these findings point to the urgent need for finding some common vision for integration which can be shared by all citizens and social groups throughout all member states of the EU.

6.1 The integration and identity of societies and the case of the European Union

The integration of a society—a central but neglected problem of social-scientific analysis

It is a fundamental problem of any society how to achieve a satisfying amount of integration. However, this fundamental problem has disappeared from the agenda of social science and also of sociology—in contrast to the fact that it has been an issue of major concern among the rulers who "have always had a practical interest in the integration of their societies: they have invariably desired them to have more integration than they actually possessed . . ." (Shils 1982:52). Those who want to maintain their positions are also leaning toward the idea that a "good society" is one without conflict. What is a society? A society can be considered as a (relatively) large number of people, living on a certain territory, connected to each other by dense communication patterns and manifold, close relationships, and hold together also by social and political institutions. Usually, the nation-state has been considered the paradigmatic form of such a society. In the age of European integration and globalization, the nation-state becomes connected more and more with other states and the world as a whole. Therefore, it loses some of its autonomy (Luhmann 1975; Beck and Grande 2004). It still remains, however, the most important unit of societal integration (Weiss 1998; Haller and Hadler 2004/05). We must recognize, however, that higher-level (but also lower, subnational) units are coming into existence. Among these, one is the potential emergence of a European society. This is a fact due not only to the process of integration since the 1950s. It dates back several centuries and includes all countries on this continent (Friedrich 1969; Kaelble 1987; Busch 1991; Immerfall 1994, 2006; Mitterauer 2003). Before going on to the issue how far "Europe" is becoming a new society, let us discuss shortly what the factors are which lead to societal integration.

The integration of society is a highly variable fact. In the history of the last hundred years, there are many instances of societies which have disintegrated. Examples include the breaking apart of the Austro-Hungarian and the Ottoman empires after World War I; the numerous civil and tribal wars in postcolonial states in Africa and Asia; the disintegration of multinational states, such as Czechoslovakia, Yugoslavia, and the Soviet Union after the breakdown of Communist rule in 1989/90. Why did these societies disintegrate and collapse? What are the characteristics of a well-integrated, stable, and panic-proof society? Three issues are central in this regard.

First, integration does not presuppose that a society is free of conflict. The parties to a conflict reject the claims of their antagonists or refuse to accept their authority, but they "are not antagonistic with respect to every end they seek and every action in which they engage. Above all, they might be in agreement regarding the means which each may use . . . and they might equally respect a higher authority than either of them claims, for example, the authority of laws" (Shils 1982:45).

Second, the integration of a society includes "a number of different components and conditions, linked with each other in manifold and complex ways" (Shils 1982:9). Five dimensions are most relevant: a certain territory and attachment of the residents to it; a recognized name; a division of labour and a network of exchange of goods and services; a common culture and—maybe—language; a public image of the distribution of scarce and highly valued goods.

Third, integration is not an all-or-nothing but a highly variable phenomenon (Shils 1982:41ff.). What is most important in this regard: Integration as such is no positive aim in itself because it can also have negative consequences: "The increase in the integration of society occurs at the expense of the internal integration of parts of the society and some of the most important limits to the integration of society are thrown up by the exertions of the communities, corporate bodies, and social strata to maintain an internal integrity which would be lost by a fuller integration into society" (Shils 1982:41). The larger the size of a social unit (organization, state), the higher the distance between elites and people; the larger the bureaucratic apparatus, the lower "social efficiency" (Schumacher 1973; Kohr 1977, 1978).

The power of identity

Every social actor—be it an individual or a collective unit—needs an identity in order to be able to act in a coherent way (Mead 1934; Erikson 1980; Scheff 1990; Jenkins 1996; Haller 2003a:568ff.). Identity includes all those self-perceptions and evaluations which are central for a person and which determine his or her behaviours and actions within his or her social context. It includes also basic values (Taylor 1992) from which specific goals of action follow. Only if such values and goals are defined meaningful and coherent lines of action are possible. The effectiveness of a collective unit can only be evaluated at the background of these goals.

In modern societies, a high level of complexity in the division of labour and patterns of social organisation has developed. This structural change, on the one side, frees individuals and opens for them the possibility of choice between memberships in different social units. The position or status within one of them is in principle independent from that in others. The specific configurations of participation in different subsystems provide every person with a unique individual "personality" (Simmel 1971). On the other side, this change has led to the emergence of corporations as new and very powerful actors; in relation to them, individuals often feel powerless (Coleman 1982). A further new aspect, very important also in connection with European integration, is the central role of *law* in the rise of corporate actors.

Corporate actors are defined and come into existence by legal prescriptions. The most fundamental of these are called *constitutions;* they specify the basic rules for membership in and the workings and aims of corporations.

The concept of identity is crucial also for the understanding of corporate actors (Castells 1997). Firms and enterprises have long recognized the usefulness of a clear identity and culture. The concept of "national identity" captures this problematic area in the case of political communities. The identity of a political community such as the European Union must also include the three essential elements of any identity: knowledge, an emotional attachment of its members, and a readiness to act in a certain way (behavioural component). In the following analysis, concrete indicators for each of these three dimensions will be analysed as they relate to the people in the different member states of the European Union.

Out of these general considerations, we can now go on to discuss in a systematic way the problems of social integration and identity in the case of the European Union.

Factors of social integration and risks of disintegration in the European Union

Two topics shall be discussed in this section: The first concerns the factors which help to form an "integrated society" out of the people living in a certain territory and of the member states of a political community; the second concerns the factors which can lead to the disintegration and disruption of a society.

Four groups of factors may constitute *social structural limits for the extensive integration* in the case of the EU: its internal social and cultural structure; the absence of two important integrating factors; and the lack of a clear vision about the final goals of integration. The first factor, which casts into doubt all the efforts toward a far-reaching integration of the European Union, is the *consolidated character of its social structure.* A *consolidated structure* is one with a high degree of overlapping between the basic parameters of social structure in terms of ethnic, linguistic, religious, and socioeconomic differentiations. The United States is an example for the first type. The blacks, the immigrants from different countries, and so on, are not living on clearly circumscribed territories but are dispersed over the whole country; moreover, they are not differentiated from each other consistently in terms of language or religion. The opposite is true for the EU: Here, about two thirds of the member states have their own language; moreover, most of these states are homogeneous internally in terms of language, religion, and other cultural characteristics, in the level of socioeconomic development and in their whole institutional setup. Thus, rather compound countries or groups of countries exist which are differentiated from each other in more than one important criterion.

The probability that internal conflicts become enforced in such a situation is quite high. The reason is simple: In this type of society, any conflict—as trivial as its basis may be—can escalate because it always tends to take on a broader meaning and larger weight. Such constellations were obvious in the cases of Austria, Hungary, and, in more recent times, in those of Yugoslavia and the Soviet Union.

A breakup is a real possibility also for the European Union. Here, it would first occur in the form of secession of some of its members. The reason would not only be their consolidated structure but also the divergence about the fundamental values and principles guiding the process of integration. Therefore, the first member states to secede would probably not be the poor, peripheral countries in the South and East but rather the rich countries in the North and West. One political community has already seceded from the Union, the Danish autonomous province of Greenland.

Two further factors inhibiting a far-reaching integration of the European Union are obvious. One is the *lack of a common language.* This is one of the strongest factors making for the integration of a society (Deutsch 1966; Shils 1982). Throughout Europe, people consider language to be the single most important characteristic of national identity (Haller and Ressler 2006b). In terms of language, the European Union is—together with India—one of the two internally most differentiated political communities worldwide.

Another factor inhibiting a strong integration of the European Union as a society is its *weak central authority.* The Union lacks an apparatus of public agents (officers, policemen, etc.) who are present all over its territory. Thus, it lacks "the performance of acts of authority" (Shils 1982:33) as a means to strengthen integration.

The fourth factor inhibiting a continuous further integration of the EU is the lack of a clear identity. This fact will sketched out very clearly in the following analyses when we investigate the different views of and expectations on integration in the different member countries.

There are also factors which strengthen the integration of the European Union. We must mention at least four of them here as well in order to give a balanced picture.

First, the relations between the member states as a whole as between individual persons, firms, organisations, and associations throughout the Union are manifold and continue to increase. From this point of view, political scientists (Friedrich 1969) and social historians (Kaelble 1987) were right when they argued already some decades ago that a "European society" or a "European nation" is in the making. Second, with Brussels there exists a centre of the Union, albeit it is relatively weak in terms of its direct authority. But it is particularly strong in terms of enacting common laws valid throughout the community, laws which override national law. Third, given the dense interconnections between the member states, an exit would be costly, although it would not entail a total breakup of the existing manifold relations. As the cases of Switzerland and Norway demonstrate, a country can have very close relations with the Union even without being a member. The "power of habit" is very strong in all kinds of social relations which entail a multitude of interests, and it induces people to continue membership even if they are dissatisfied with many aspects of it. Fourth, a breakup of the Union is improbable as long as economic development looks favourable to most of its member countries and as long as the richer countries do not feel that the poorer ones are only a millstone round their neck.

The European Union in search of an identity

The concept of "identity" is of crucial importance also for the explanation of the origins and development of European integration. Three issues are relevant in this regard: Any social and political unit must ensure (1) a minimal degree of integration; (2) a certain degree of coherence in its relations to the outside world; and (3) if it is a unit *in nascendi,* it must know—at least in general terms—where its development will ultimately lead. Let us shortly discuss each of these issues.

The *lack of a clear identity,* of distinct aims and goals concerning the final state of European integration, has been noted by many social scientists as well as politicians. Already in 1958, Ernst Haas referred to the necessity of the EEC to develop a common ideology as a basis for further integration. Its lack is reflected in the ambiguity about the borders of Europe and in the divergent visions about its future (Oswald 2003:8ff.). The high and noble aspirations associated with European integration only hide the trouble with its identity (Kastoryano 2002:11). An increasing discrepancy exists between the Union as an economic-legal unit and the Union as a moral community (Ferry 2000:17).

The lack of a clear identity of the European Union has turned up most clearly in its efforts to develop a common "foreign policy." Some of the most spectacular failures of the Union occurred exactly in this regard. Examples have been the inconsistent, even contradictory position of different member states during the wars in Yugoslavia and in Iraq (König and Sicking 2004). It was no accident that the first mention of the issue of identity in official documents of the European Union has been in connection with foreign policy. In the Maastricht Treaty of the European Union, the necessity of developing an "identity" is mentioned explicitly in the preamble and in several paragraphs:

> *"The Union shall set itself the following objectives: To assert its identity on the international scene, in particular through the implementation of a common foreign and security policy including the eventual framing of a common defence policy, which might in time lead to a common defence"* (Art. 2).

In the Document on European Identity of 1973, core elements of a European identity are mentioned, such as its common heritage, its specific interests, and its particular obligations. Concerning the evolution of a European identity, the document states:

> *"The development of a European identity will follow the dynamics of the work of European unification. In their foreign relations, the Nine will be anxious to determine their identity in relation to the other political units step by step. In this way, they consciously strengthen their internal unity and contribute to the formulation of a truly European politics"* (Pfetsch 1997:98).

Finally, a clear identity is indispensable for *the continuation and accomplishment of the process of European integration.* This is true in particular for the EU because of its ambitious aim to create an ever closer union among the peoples of Europe (Schmidtke 1998:49). Also in this regard, a serious problem may be noted. The famous formula that European integration is an ongoing process whose final shape cannot be determined in advance has been coined already in the Treaty of Rome and recently incorporated into the preamble of Part II of the "Constitution for Europe": "The Peoples of Europe, *in creating an ever closer Union among them,* are resolved to share a peaceful future based on common values" (my emphasis). The factual development of integration since the early 1950s can in fact be described well under this title (Dinan 1999). The general idea behind this statement must be considered as rather problematic, however. A fully integrated society would in the last instance be a totalitarian society. But even in its milder forms a very high level of integration is hardly a sign for an open, liberal, and modern society. It could be characterized, with Alexis de Tocqueville (1947), as a "benevolent dictatorship." He notes—as other social scientists as well (Kohr 1977; Elias 1978; Dogan and Pelassy 1987)—a continuous trend toward higher levels of integration and centralization in Europe. A German economist has published a concise book with the accurate title *The Centralisation of Western Europe* (Vaubel 1995). The further development of the EU toward a closely integrated union would also abandon the secret of Europe's success in world historical comparison. This was the high level of creative competition between its different territorial-political units, resulting from the coexistence of economic integration and intense cultural exchange, with political fragmentation (Shils 1982:4; Swanson 1967; Baechler 1975).

Four theses concerning contradictions in the visions about European integration

Based on the foregoing considerations, we can now develop some general hypotheses concerning the finality of European integration and discrepancies between the different concepts and their supporters. Two dimensions are relevant in this regard: the variations between the different countries and macroregions of Europe and the differences between the opinions and aims of the elites and the citizens. This analysis will give us findings which help to delimit the potentials and viabilities of further integration. If a majority of the citizens in a member state are against a certain aim, it can hardly be realized (and probably also should not be realized). The same applies to the relation between the elites and citizens. Elites can push forward the integration process quite far without the consent of their populations. However, they can do so only at a considerable risk. Sooner or later, the lack of general support will become manifest and throw back on the process of integration. The opinions of the population should not be seen unconditionally as a final, irrevocable criterion. People's knowledge is limited, and opinions can be influenced by persuasion campaigns. However, if a clear majority of the public has a certain opinion it is probable that there is some truth behind it (Boudon 1999).

Let us now formulate the five sociological theses about the integration process and its finality.

1. *The widespread equalisation between the two terms "Europe" and "European Union" is misleading and can be seen as a part of an ideology legitimizing integration.* The European Union is also often described as the reconstitution of a "United Europe" as it should have existed in some former times. In post-Communist Eastern Europe, this idea is particularly popular when many speak of " 'a return to Europe' or the 're-uniting of Europe'" (Gasparski 1996:6). In geographic and sociocultural terms, however, Europe encompasses without any doubt also east Europe, including Russia. European society in this broader sense includes all parts of Europe which are connected with each other, where similar values and styles of life are endorsed, whose peoples feel that they share a common history, even if this history includes many tragic events and periods (Kaelble 1987; Jordan 1988; Mitterauer 2003).

2. *There exist far-reaching differences within the European Union concerning the ultimate aims of the integration process between countries and macroregions.* Economically strong and politically stable countries, as well as countries and nations with a high level of historical and political self-consciousness, will consider integration far more critical than countries with opposite characteristics. The latter see integration as a means to overcome and solve their long-lasting and deep-going national difficulties and problems. However, unification and integration out of weakness may constitute a problematic base for establishing a new political community.

3. *Significant differences and cleavages in the process of integration exist also between elites and citizens.* This fact has already been documented in Chapter 1. "Strong" or privileged social groups (in

terms of education and knowledge, occupational positions, financial resources) will favour integration much more than the population at large or "socially weak" groups in particular (such as women, old people, the uneducated and unemployed, persons handicapped in any form). To characterize the latter as "losers of modernization" is motivated by the ideological reason to characterize their deprivations as unavoidable and as only short-term consequences of progress. The group interested most in the process of integration, however, are the political and new European bureaucratic, political and professional elites proper who profit most directly from this process. These elites are trying to win the support of large groups of the population—or at least their passive consent—by the steering strategy of "persuasion" (Lindblom 1977), that is, by advertising the advantages of integration in propaganda campaigns.

4. *The definition of the European Union as a "Community of values" and the tendency to avoid a clear definition of territorial limits of expansion, following from this definition, must be seen very critical.* This tendency might also help elites to hide their economic and political interests connected with integration. If the idea of the EU as a "community of values" would be realized in a far-reaching way, it would lead to a stigmatisation or suppression of dissenting views and aims, not dissimilar to the situation which prevailed in the former Soviet Union (Boukovsky 2005). The relative distance to the process of integration of critical intellectuals can also be seen as an indication that the European Union is not, in the first instance, a community of values but an association based mainly on interests.

5. *The differences in the visions about the finality of European integration cannot easily be reconciled with each other.* As far as the issue of "finality" is concerned, quite different models can be distinguished. It will be argued, however, that these visions can be reconciled with each other if the EU is conceived as a "community of law." This conception shall be elaborated in detail in Chapter 8.

Based on these general considerations, we now go on to present empirical analyses on the view of the integration process and its final aims in the different countries and social groups in Europe.

6.2 The structural position of different countries and the attitudes of their populations toward integration: An inductive empirical typology

As pointed out in the first section, European integration fulfils different purposes for different nation-states, social groups, and actors. The first step towards an explanation is to conceptualize these different functions in a typology. In this chapter, two such typologies are presented; the first is a more an empirical-inductive one, based on statistical and survey data about the member states of the EU and their populations. The second has a more analytical or theoretical intent.

The empirical analyses presented in this and the following section include four kinds of data:

1. Structural data about the level of development and the relative position of the different countries within Europe;
2. Data on ideas, values and aims connected with integration as they can be inferred from the historical and cultural background of the countries;
3. Data on attitudes and emotions (expectations, fears, overall evaluations) of the elites and of the populations concerning integration and the European Union; here, Eurobarometer and ISSP surveys will be used.
4. Data on the values, aims, and behaviour of political elites. Here, we will include also materials about the historical background for present-day attitudes toward integration in the different countries.

As a first approximation to a sociological typology, the results of a cluster analysis are presented. Cluster analysis is a method which allows combining a high number of units into fewer but larger groups (clusters) by using knowledge about the characteristics of the basic units. Its principles are: (1) All those units are subsumed into one cluster which are similar to each other in the criteria selected. (2) This occurs step by step; in the first step, the two units most similar to each other are combined, in the second step, the next two units (one of them can also be the cluster formed before), and so on. In the context of this analysis, the method of hierarchical cluster analysis[1] has been chosen. Out of this analysis we can get (1) a measure indicating how distant the units at several steps are from each other (the agglomeration schedule); this helps to decide at which point the resulting number of clusters can be considered as "optimal"; (2) a dendrogram showing the several steps and the resulting clustering pattern; (3) a table with the mean values in all criteria used, describing the clusters.

Eight variables were used as input for the analysis. These variables include three structural and four attitudinal characteristics of the fifteen "old" EU member states and ten candidate countries (considering the situation in 2003).

The structural variables (taken from the Eurostat Web site) are: (1) GDP per capita (in PPS); (2) total unemployment rate in 2003 (%); (3) real GDP growth rate in 2003 (%); (4) forecasted contributions of the different member countries to the EU budget in 2005 (million euros).

Four attitudinal variables were taken from the Eurobarometer 60 and from the candidate countries Eurobarometer 2003.4 (autumn 2003). Out of the survey results, we calculated mean attitudinal values for each of the countries included. Thus, also the attitudinal variables are used here only as macrovariables, that is, by considering the mean or typical integration attitudes in the different countries. The variables used in this regard are based on the answers to the following four questions: (1) *Generally speaking, do you think that (your country's) membership of the EU is . . . a good thing, a bad thing, neither good nor bad, don't know?* (% good thing). (2) *Taking everything into consideration, would you say that (your country) has on balance benefited or not from being a member of the European Union? . . . benefited, not benefited, don't know* (% benefited). (3) *In general, does the EU conjure up for you a . . . very positive image, fairly positive image, neutral image, fairly negative image, very negative image, don't know?* (% very positive and fairly positive). (4) *Using this scale, how much do you feel you know about the European Union, its policies, its institutions? 1 (know nothing at all) . . . 10 (know a great deal)* (% categories 6–10). These data are reported for all countries in *Table 6.1*.

Figure 6.1 shows the dendrogram resulting from this analysis and *Figure 6.2* the mean values of these ten groups in six characteristics. The coefficients of distance between the clusters suggest that a distinction between ten clusters is most meaningful and produces relatively clear and homogeneous groupings. Let us look shortly at each of them, going down from the upper to the lower end of the dendrogram.[2]

The first group comprises the three countries that joined the Union in 1995, Sweden, Finland, and Austria. They are characterized by a relatively negative attitude toward the Union but a rather high knowledge about it; unemployment is clearly below the EU average, level of development is the highest, and all of them are net contributors to the EU budget (see *Figure 6.2*). Finland is somewhat distinguished from Austria and Sweden by its lower level of knowledge and higher unemployment.

In the second group, we find only Great Britain. This country is clearly differentiated from all other cases by the fact that for the British the EU has the lowest image; but they have also a rather low level of knowledge. The unemployment rate as well as GDP growth, however, compares well with the EU mean; net contributions to the EU are high but lower than those of Germany.

Group 3 includes the three large founding members, France, Germany, and Italy. The attitudes of their populations to the EU are comparable to the mean, with some slight variations. The general economic level is very high in these countries, and they pay the largest sums to the EU budget. However, economic performance (unemployment, growth) was rather poor in the early twenty-first century. Considering the fact that these three countries were the "founding fathers" of the EU, the similarity between them is not surprising. It would be a premature conclusion, however, to argue that they had the same motives for establishing the Common Market, or that the long common experience within this community has made them similar

Table 6.1   Cluster Analysis of the Twenty-Five EU Member States: Basic Attitudinal and Structural Data

Countries	EU membership is a good thing (%)	Country has benefited from being a member of the EU (%)	EU positive image (%)	High level of knowledge about the EU (%)	Total unemployment rate 2003	GDP per capita 2003 in PPS	Real GDP growth rate (%)	Forecasted contributions to the EU budget 2005 (million €)	EU-transfers 2004* Net payers (–)/receivers (+) (million €)
Sweden	40	31	33	36	5.6	114.4	1.5	2,817	–1.060
Austria	34	39	30	40	4.3	121.5	1.4	2,209	–365
Finland	38	40	32	30	9.1	113.2	2.4	1,512	–70
Great Britain	27	29	26	19	4.9	118.8(f)	2.5	12,339	–2.865
France	44	48	44	22	9.5	111.7	0.8	16,888	–3.051
Germany	47	37	40	35	9.0	109.1	–0.2	21,313	–7.141
Italy	58	49	60	29	8.4	106.1(f)	0.3	13,996	–2.947
Poland	52	56	47	29	19.2	45.6	3.8	2,367	+1.438
Slovakia	57	65	51	31	17.5	51.9	4.5	382	+169
Estonia	41	48	32	21	10.2	48.7	6.7	99	+145
Latvia	47	58	46	30	10.4	40.7	7.5	126	+198
Lithuania	59	66	53	26	12.7	45.5	9.7	211	+369
Spain	62	66	56	18	11.3	98.9(f)	2.9	8,901	+8.502
Portugal	54	65	61	14	6.3	77.2	–1.1	1,385	+3.124
Denmark	57	66	35	34	5.6	121.2	0.7	2,066	–225

Netherlands	62	54	39	31	3.7	125.9	-0.1	5,412	-2.035
Belgium	56	57	45	25	8.0	116.9	1.3	4,091	-536
Czech Republic	48	53	45	26	7.8	68.4	3.2	999	+272
Hungary	58	64	47	19	5.8	59.6	2.9	896	+193
Cyprus	58	69	53	34	4.5	81.6	2.0	157	+64
Slovenia	50	73	51	40	6.5	76.2	2.5	285	+110
Greece	62	75	58	32	9.7	80.6	4.7	1,848	+4.163
Malta	61	65	56	46	8.0	72.2	-1.9	51	+45
Ireland	72	81	68	20	4.6	135.7	4.4	1,366	+1.594
Luxembourg	77	69	57	24	3.7	213.2	2.9	238	-93
Grand Mean	53	57	47	28	8.3	94.2	2.6	4,078	

(f) = forecast. *Not used for cluster analysis.
Sources: Eurobarometer 60, CCEB 2003.4 (Autumn 2003); Eurostat, http://epp.eurostat.cec.eu.int (structural indicators).

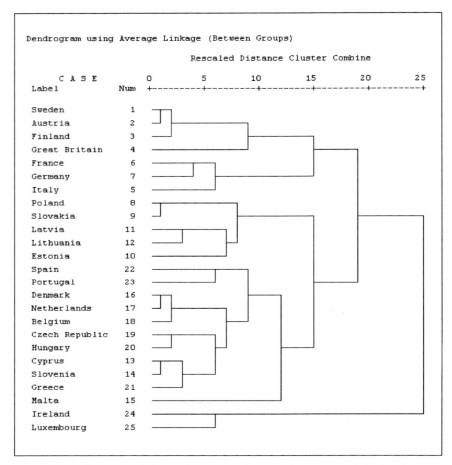

Figure 6.1   Cluster analysis of the twenty-five member states of the EU in terms of integration attitudes of their citizens: Dendrogram (average linkage—between groups method).

Source: Table 6.1.

to each other. The more refined sociological typology in the next section will show that there are significant differences between them.

Groups 4 and 5 comprise five East European countries from the former state-socialist bloc, Poland and Slovakia in the first, and the three Baltic states in the second group. These two groups of countries have been differentiated from all others mainly by their low level of development (in fact, the lowest among all); also, the unemployment rate is very high; however, economic growth was rather strong, particularly so in the Baltic states. In terms of attitudes toward the European Union, these countries show no great differences from the overall mean. All of these countries are net

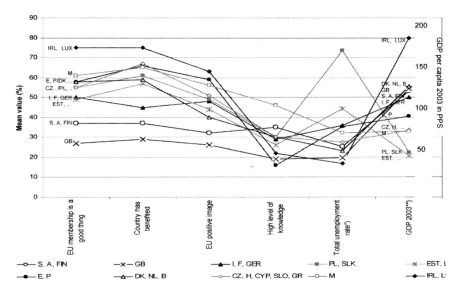

Figure 6.2   Typology of EU member countries: Mean values for ten clusters.

*Real total unemployment rate multiplied by 4 (PL, SLK: 18.4 × 4 = 73.6; IRL, LUX: 4.2 × 4 = 16.8).

**GDP standardised (IRL, LUX = 174.5; EST, LAT, LIT = 45.0).

Sources: Eurobarometer 60, CCEB 2003.4 (autumn 2003); Eurostat, http://epp.eurostat.cec. eu.int (structural indicators).

receivers of EU payments although the sums are more modest than those of the poorer old members.

In Group 6, we find the two countries on the Iberian Peninsula, Spain and Portugal. They have been singled out because of their rather positive attitude toward the EU but have the lowest level of knowledge about it. Both receive large sums from the EU. Spain, in fact, is the largest net receiver. The economic situation in these countries is mixed: high unemployment in Spain, negative economic growth in Portugal. Their level of development situates them between West and North Europe and the more advanced post-Communist countries.

Group 7 is quite homogeneous in geographic terms; it comprises two Benelux states (Belgium, Netherlands) and Denmark. This group is quite similar to cluster 1. These countries are among the most wealthy with low unemployment rates but also low rates of growth; they are net contributors to the EU budget. The attitude toward the EU, however, is more positive than in Group 1; knowledge is also quite high.

Group 8 comprises the three more advanced post-Communist, Central European countries (Czech Republic, Hungary, Slovenia) and two countries at the southern periphery of the EU (Greece, Cyprus). They have in common a rather low level of economic wealth but moderate levels of unemployment and considerable rates of growth. The attitudes toward the European Union are clearly more positive than the average (but somewhat less positive in the Czech Republic; while EU knowledge is quite low in Hungary). Malta is singled out as a separate case because of its negative economic growth and its low contribution to the EU budget; the attitudes to the EU are above the average.

Cluster 9 consists of only one case, the island state of Malta. However, it is singled out only because of its negative growth rate; in all other indicators, it is quite similar to cluster 8.

Group 10 includes only Ireland and Luxembourg. These two countries are among the richest in the EU, and their economic performance in the last years was excellent (low unemployment, high growth). Ireland does also receive considerable amounts of net transfers from the EU, while Luxembourg is a net contributor. The attitudes of their populations toward the EU are the most positive among all groups compared; interestingly, the level of knowledge about the EU is below the average.

This first glance over some of the main similarities and differences between the twenty-five EU member states shows three general facts. First, the attitudes toward the European Union vary strongly between countries. Only 27% of the British think that "membership is a good thing," but 77% of the citizens of Luxembourg do. Britons are on bottom also in regard to the perception that their country has benefited or that the EU has a positive image. Only about a quarter think this way, but 81% and 68%, respectively, of the Irish do. Second, we find a strong international variation in knowledge about the EU. It is lowest in Portugal and highest in Malta (14% versus 46%). Very remarkable is that knowledge is quite high in some countries characterized by rather critical attitudes (Austria and Sweden) but low in many of those with very positive attitudes toward the EU. Third, it is evident that the macrosocial and macroeconomic conditions in a country are correlated with the attitudes toward the EU. These attitudes are generally quite positive in the peripheral and poorer countries but much less so in the richer, West and North European countries.

In the following section, we will investigate how these attitudes toward European integration came into being and what the main aims connected with EU membership in the different countries are. For this aim, we have to look more closely at the historical backgrounds and the recent socioeconomic and political situation of the countries.

6.3 The seven faces of the European Union. A sociological typology of the meaning of integration among the different nation-states and their citizens

By developing the following typology, we assume that the attitudes of the different countries (or groups of countries) can be subsumed under a limited number of dominant orientations (see also Pfetsch 1997:70ff.). It is a basic insight of sociology that in every society there exists a specific dominant view, a *conscience collective*, as Durkheim (1965) called it (see also Haller, Mach, and Zwicky 1995; Boudon 1999). The aim of the typology is to elaborate the characteristic features of certain kinds of attitudes to the Union and their social context as sharply as possible. The resulting types cannot be considered as pure "ideal types" in the sense of Weber but only as empirically deduced, characteristic constellations (Hopf 1991) of the most important economic, social, and political values, interests, and forces in a country regarding its position in Europe. In order to get a comprehensive picture of the attitudes toward the European Union throughout Europe, we have to include also those countries which at some time considered becoming a member.

Seven "ideal types" of attitudes or positions toward the European Union are distinguished: (1) the EU as an undemocratic and bureaucratic Leviathan; (2) the EU as a necessary evil; (3) the EU as a prop or crutch; (4) the EU as a substitute for missing national identity; (5) membership in the EU as an end in itself ("It's taking part that counts"); (6) the EU as a means to (re-) gain global influence; (7) the EU as a "feeding dish." Let us look at each of them.

The EU as an undemocratic and bureaucratic Leviathan

In two West European countries, Switzerland and Norway, the citizens have repeatedly rejected membership in the European Union. *Switzerland* is an extremely informative case in this regard. On the one side, this nation of 7 million people can be considered as a role model for the Union. Despite its small size, it is internally one of the most variegated countries in Europe. It includes four linguistic groups (Italian, French, German, Rhaeto-Romanic); it is heterogeneous in religious terms, including Protestants and Catholics and—due to immigration—now also over 300,000 Muslims; it is probably the most open country in Europe both in terms of economic exchanges and in terms of having accepted the highest proportion of foreigners as residents (about 20%; probably some additional 10% are neocitizens); its political system has a strong federal character, and its politics has since long been neutral and able to keep itself out of wars for centuries; finally, Switzerland has a very slim federal government, leaving much room for local and private initiative both in economic and in social terms (Elsasser 1988; Bergier 1996)—also an aim for which the European Union is striving. Why did the Swiss, then, having so many characteristics in common with the European Union, reject participation in the integration process?

Two points have to be made clear before answering this question. First, the Swiss do not altogether reject the process of European integration; rather the opposite is true. Already in 1972, a bilateral agreement on free trade with industrial products was made with the European Economic Community; today, nine such agreements exist which establish very close relationships between Switzerland and the EU.[3] In 2000, 67.2% of the population accepted an extensive contract with the EU, including cooperation in seven areas; further agreements on judicial cooperation were signed in 2004 and accepted in two popular referenda in 2005 by 54% and 56% of the population. Switzerland even contributes 130 million euros per annum over five years to the social and economic cohesion in the enlarged EU; two thirds of Swiss exports and four fifths of its imports come from the EU.[4] In Chapter 4 it was shown that Switzerland is integrated strongly with the EU in terms of trade. Thus, in several of these regards Switzerland is in fact much more closely integrated with the EU than even some of its peripheral member states.

Second, we can observe in Switzerland, as in other parts of Europe, deep-going internal divisions concerning the attitudes to European integration. One is the split between the political elites and the population at large. On December 6, 1992, a referendum was held only about membership in the European Economic Area. This proposal was rejected by a small margin of 50.2% of the population, while an overwhelming majority of the political elites were in support of it. Eighty-five percent of the members of the *Ständerat* (the council of the cantons) and 62% of the deputies to the *Nationalrat* (parliament) voted in favour before the referendum was held. Second, within Switzerland a considerable split between the "German" and "Latin" areas could be observed; in the French and Italian cantons, the "pro" got large majorities while the "old" German-speaking cantons in the mountainous centre of the country were the bulwark of opposition against accession.

Why, then, does the majority of the Swiss people reject membership in the EU? There are six reasons for it.[5] The first three concern problems of internal democracy, the next two supposed negative economic effects of EU membership.

First, Switzerland would have to dispense with *political neutrality,* a factor which guaranteed peace and economic prosperity to this country for centuries. Since Switzerland contains German- and French-speaking population groups, neutrality was indispensable also for internal stability because most European conflicts involved France against German-speaking nations (Hirter 1993). By becoming a member of international organizations, this principle would be questioned (Jost 1999). This is a very important point, one which was a hotly debated issue also in other neutral countries like Austria and Sweden. Although the EU so far has no real common defence and military policy, it certainly expects from the members cooperation in this regard.

Second, Switzerland would have to dispense with its old and very well-established system of direct democracy which puts all main decisions to popular referenda. In fact, about ten nationwide referenda and dozens of referenda at the level of cantons are held every year (Kriesi 1998). These referenda would become obsolete, given the fact in the EU laws enacted by Brussels have to be taken over unconditionally by all member states. (In chapter 8, however, we will propose that the EU itself should introduce referenda).

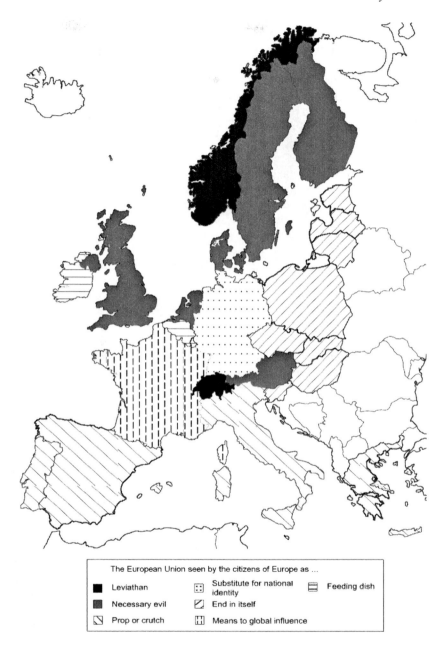

The European Union seen by the citizens of Europe as …

■	Leviathan	⬚	Substitute for national identity	⊟	Feeding dish
▓	Necessary evil	▨	End in itself		
◩	Prop or crutch	▥	Means to global influence		

Photo 6 Resistance to new European "Leviathan" in the Alps and in the North-western periphery: The attitudes of the citizens toward integration reflect deep-rooted social, cultural, and political cleavages in Europe.

Source: M. Haller and G. Kaup.

Closely correlated with this is the third argument, saying that also the strong federal political system of Switzerland would be undermined seriously. The autonomy of the cantons and the communes (which are also quite strong) would be abrogated by the principle of the preeminence of European law against national law because political decisions at the level of the Union could not be put any longer to an additional scrutiny and to the codecision of the cantons and the people. In this context it is interesting that in a survey of 6,000 persons in all 26 cantons a positive association was found between the level of direct democracy and life satisfaction of the citizens (Frei and Stutzer 2002). Thus, the resistance to the EC particularly of the population of the German-speaking rural cantons was not in the first instance (as many commentators would have it) an expression of backwardness but a well-founded fear that local democracy and national political autonomy would be significantly undermined by joining the EU. Survey data show that the Swiss—together with the Dutch—are at the top among 22 European countries as far as pride in their democracy is concerned. Eighty-four percent of the Swiss are proud in this regard, but only 56% of all Europeans (and even less than 30% in the post-Communist countries) represented in *Table 6.2*.

The next two arguments concern economic matters. The fourth was that the full inclusion of Switzerland into a socioeconomic area with a lower standard of living would be detrimental. Switzerland has a much higher level of income, a lower level of unemployment, and lower taxes than most member states of the EU. Fifth, it was argued that the higher level of value-added tax and the obligatory net contributions of Switzerland to the EU would contribute to a worsening of the economic situation of the country. The Swiss show also a very high level of pride in the economic achievements and the social security system of their country (*Table 6.2*).

The discussions before the referendum in 1992 showed many characteristics typical for similar discussions in other countries: Both the supporters (such as Pascal Delamuraz) and the opponents (such as Christoph Blocher) of the access used not only hard facts and sound arguments but also polemical overstatements.[6]

Turnout at the 1992 referendum about accession to the EEA was extraordinarily high (78%). The same was true for the degree of information of the population: 82% could be classified as well informed. Every citizen got an exemplar of the EEA contract five weeks before the referendum by post; in the media, the topic was discussed extensively. It is probably accurate to say that an average Swiss citizen knew more about the EEA contract than a member of the Swedish parliament who got the contract only one day before the parliamentary decision (Hirter 1993:11). This level of information and interest is an extreme contrast to the low participation levels at the referenda in Spain and many post-Communist countries. The opponents were also not "anti-Europeans," as they often are discredited in such cases: 78% of all voters and even 63% of the opponents said that Switzerland must show solidarity toward Europe. Thus, in 2005 the Swiss twice

Table 6.2 National Pride in Twenty European Countries in 2003

	Very proud/proud of ...			Very proud of ...		Overall national pride**
	Democracy	Economic achievement	Social security	[Nation's] History	being ... [Nation]	
Austria	72	79	76	31	50	20.7
Sweden	67	41	61	16	33	23.6
Finland	65	70	79	35	42	22.0
Great Britain	69	69	53	50	46	20.5
France	58	32	78	40	31	22.1
Germany/W	58	57	63	9	16	23.9
Germany/E	33	48	43	6	12	25.1
Italy	26*	40	28			
Poland	23	28	12	28	47	25.3
Slovakia	16	24	8	32	30	26.5
Latvia	33	23	9	15	34	27.5
Spain	66	72	69	24	45	21.5
Portugal	39	22	19	54	56	24.5
Denmark	82	68	77	31	34	21.6
Netherlands*	84	78	83			
Czech Rep.	28	15	20	38	22	25.7
Hungary	37	38	19	31	46	23.6
Slovenia	28	47	34	25	53	24.3
Ireland	65	87	64	51	74	18.9
Norway	67	72	64	22	35	22.9
Switzerland	84	71	71	22	36	21.4
Mean	56	52	47	29	34	23.2

*Data from ISSP 1995.
**Mean value from a summary score of 10 items on pride in different dimensions; 10 = very high, 40 = very low.
Source: ISSP 2003 "National Identity."

rejected referenda, initiated by right-wing forces, against the Schengen and Dublin system (free border crossing) and extension of the Swiss-EU agreement on the free movement of labour to the EU's ten new member states. Also, the forecasted negative economic consequences of nonmembership in the EU have not arrived in the last decade—contrary to what is often maintained in comparisons between the development of Austria and Switzerland in the last ten years. The Swiss Franc is still one of the strongest currencies in the world.[7] Table 6.2 shows also a high level of national pride among the Swiss.

Thus, seen from Switzerland, the European Union looks in fact like a huge, centralized superstate, where decisions are made by intransparent, bureaucratic procedures which can hardly be influenced by small states, not to speak of ordinary citizens.

This is a view not very different from that of *Norway*. Norwegians voted twice in referenda—1972 and 1994—against membership in the EEC and EU. One of the reasons was similar to Switzerland: Norway is one of the richest countries in Europe, it gets high revenues from the oil fields in the North Sea, and its economy is more dynamic than that of the Euro-zone. Also, its special interests in the fishing industry may have played a role: There is a "broad feeling that oil-rich, high-growth Norway does not need an economically stumbling European club."[8]

However, also in the case of Norway political matters were important but mainly those of social policy. An internationally renowned pioneer of computer science, Professor of Mathematics Kristen Nygaard, led the anti-EU campaign in 1994. He founded the "Nei til EU" movement, which became the largest political organisation in Norway (145,000 members in 1994). His main arguments against Norway's entry to the EU were:[9] To preserve the thousands of small villages and their economies of a country which extends itself in a narrow band 1,300 kilometres from south to north, interrupted by hundreds of fjords and mountains; they were seen as threatened seriously by the "four freedoms" valid in the EU; the insistence on state control for the exploitation of the Norwegian natural resources; the preservation of a special system of funds for the farmers which is settlement oriented; the securing of full employment (the Norwegian constitution includes the right to work for every citizen); the continuation of an egalitarian social and income policy. If Norway would join the Union, a "massive loss of sovereignty and independence" would take place; the EU Council is seen as "the only law generating institution in the Western world discussing and voting on laws in secrecy."[10] Data on national pride show that also the Norwegians score very high in all regards, but particularly so in regard to economic achievements and the welfare system (see *Table 6.2*).

The no-voters at the 1994-referendum were strongly concerned with these issues. They were concentrated in the areas outside Oslo; women, youth, old people and union members, farmers, and fishermen were over-represented. Turnout at this referendum was the highest in Norwegian history (88.8%). Polls also showed a high level of factual knowledge about the EU, and it was increasing—not decreasing—by geographical distance from the capital Oslo. Like Switzerland, Norway is also connected closely with the EU through many bilateral contracts.

Thus, four basic values and aims have led the Swiss and the Norwegians to their negative attitudes toward participation in European integration: (1) The love for peace which the Swiss see best guaranteed by political neutrality; (2) the preservation of grassroot democracy and autonomy of local and regional political communities; (3) the preservation of economic prosperity and growth; (4) the further securing of a well-balanced development in terms of welfare and social equality.

European integration as a necessary evil

There is one large nation-state where European integration is clearly not seen as a positive goal in and of itself but as something which nevertheless cannot be avoided in the long run because, in that case, negative consequences would result. This state is *Great Britain*; to a lesser degree, the Scandinavian states and Austria also fit into this category. There are at least three reasons for the very ambivalent attitudes of the British toward integration: (1) Historically, Britain was the centre of the huge British Commonwealth empire, and it still maintains close ties with the successor organization, the Commonwealth of Nations. This is not a powerful but a nevertheless rather vivid organization till today.[11] (2) Britain also maintains close ties with the United States, Canada, Australia, and New Zealand, which are based on a common cultural heritage and intensive economic, social, cultural-scientific, and political relations. (3) Britain has a strong tradition of economic and political liberalism, as well as an old and well-established democratic system; both make the Britons—like the Swiss—suspicious of a centralised political system and a comprehensive welfare state.

In Winston Churchill's speech at the University of Zurich in 1947, he asked for a United Europe but did not foresee Britain as a part of this alliance. Churchill also proposed only a rather limited form of integration, the "unionist model," in contrast to the much more ambitious federalist model which was highly in vogue in these times. So the foundation of the EEC in the mid-1950s took place without Britain. It was only in the 1960s that British European policy changed significantly. But even then, it was defined as "a policy of the last resort" (Pfetsch 1997:74). The European Community was seen as a necessary new partner for trade, since Britain's relationships with the former colonies had changed drastically, to the disadvantage of Britain. At the same time, the economic prosperity and increasing influence of the Community made it clear to the British that they would lose influence in Europe if they would remain outside. Thus, Prime Minister Harold Wilson "advocated British memberships for negative rather than positive reasons in 1961" (Dinan 1999:50). However, French President de Gaulle blocked the British request for membership.

In 1971, a new vote in the British parliament after the proposal of the conservative premier Edward Heath brought a majority in favour of joining the EC. As a consequence, Britain entered the Common Market on January 1, 1973. However, Britons continued to feel uneasy about their position in the EC. Therefore, the next government pledged itself to renegotiate better terms for Britain in the EC and then to hold a referendum. This took place in April 1975 and resulted in a surprisingly large proportion of "yes" (67.2%). Three factors were decisive for this high level of consent: First, the popularity of Harold Wilson only one year after he come to power; second, a massive propaganda campaign carried through by the leading government members, parties, and newspapers, with funding by banks and big

Photo 7   European integration and the media: A reflection of the highly different views but also of the critical attitudes toward integration in the different member states of the EU.

Source: Compilation by M. Haller and F. Haller.

industrial companies; third, a very low level of interest and information of the population about the EEC, which means that this was clearly a "second order election" (Reif and Schmitt 1980) where not European but national issues determined the outcome.[12]

But again in the 1980s, new objections were raised to British EC membership, this time by Margaret Thatcher. She argued strongly for Europe as "a family of nations" as opposed to an integrated federal state (Thatcher 1993:537, 548). Her vision was that the European Union should remain a large area of free trade, regulated only to a limited degree, and that it should not enter into a protectionist economic policy but fight for the establishment of free markets and trade all over the world (Thatcher 1993:537ff.). She achieved additional protocols in the Treaty of Maastricht with the consequence that Britain is not obliged to adhere fully to the integration process concerning social policy and the monetary union.

A more pro-European attitude seems to have been evident since 1997 with the new Labour government of Tony Blair. However, Britain's position towards integration did not change substantially. In his celebrated speech to the European Parliament on 26 October, 2005, Blair mentioned, for instance, the problem of unemployment in Europe. The solution proposed, however, could also have been made by Thatcher: "We must make

our labour markets less restrictive . . . , we have to make sure in research
and development, and innovation that we catch up with the best practice
in the world."[13] The proposals for the British presidency in the second half
of 2005 were hardly aiming at a serious strengthening of the EU (although
Blair frequently used the concept of the "European Social Model"): Promotion of research, development, and innovation; coordination of European
energy policy by creating a genuinely open energy market; making European universities competitive with the American ones; control of migration but also use it "to boost the effectiveness and competitiveness of the
European economy"; use the method of open coordination concerning the
demographic structure of Europe; create a "globalization fund" which
"helps people in circumstances where restructuring has made them redundant. . . ." After the rejection of the Constitution for Europe by the French
and the Dutch, Blair abandoned his plan to submit the constitution to a
referendum—an endeavour highly risky already earlier but probably leading to a clear rejection today.

Thus, EU membership is not something which Britons like (see also Coxall et al. 2003:269ff.). This is clearly reflected in survey data. Only about
one fourth of the population—the lowest proportion of all EU member
states—thinks that British membership in the EU is a good thing or has a
positive image and that Britain has benefited from membership. *Table 6.1*
shows that in autumn 2003, only one quarter of the Britons had a positive
image of the European Union. However, Britons seem also to be badly
informed about the EU—maybe because most consider it as irrelevant.
However, they are characterized by a rather high level of national pride,
both in general terms and in terms of pride in their history and armed
forces (*Table 6.2*). Britons feel much closer to their nation than to Europe;
the difference between high attachment to the nation and to the European
Union is highest in Britain, together with the Netherlands (*Table 6.3*). Only
16% of the British would be "very sorry" if the EU dissolved, but 30%
(against a mean of 15% in the EU) would be "very relieved." The same
negative view comes out in regard to the feelings associated with the EU in
British minds: Feelings of indifference, mistrust ,and anxiety are present
among sizable minorities (one fourth up to one third of the population;
see *Table 6.4*). Finally, we can also observe a considerable split between
the higher and lower, or privileged and less privileged, social classes and
groups: Slightly more than half of students and higher white-collar employees have a positive attitude toward the EU but only 29% of the skilled and
17% of the unskilled workers (*Table 6.5*).

It is an interesting question why the British have changed their opinions
so strongly since the referendum in 1975. There are at least four reasons
for this. First, the change may in fact not have been very strong. The high
consent in the 1975 referendum did not really indicate a positive attitude
toward integration as such as shown before. Second, Margaret Thatcher's
government (1979–1990) significantly changed the attitudes toward the EU

Table 6.3   Attachment to the Nation-State and to the EU and Attitudes toward the Dissolution of the EU (EU-15, 2003)

	Attachment to... own country (nation state)			Attachment to... European Union			Difference national-EU attachment	If the EU was dissolved, I would be... ...very sorry	...in- different	...very relieved*
	very strong	fairly strong	(Total)	very strong	fairly strong	(Total)				
Austria	59	33	(92)	23	43	(66)	(26)	34	36	18
Sweden	61	34	(95)	21	51	(72)	(23)	27	35	28
Finland	65	32	(97)	11	51	(62)	(35)	29	31	30
Denmark	75	22	(97)	22	51	(73)	(24)	44	27	18
Netherlands	44	40	(84)	6	23	(29)	(55)	40	34	17
Belgium	43	44	(87)	20	47	(67)	(20)	34	48	11
France	49	44	(93)	14	43	(67)	(26)	35	37	19
Germany/West	39	47	(86)	15	47	(57)	(29)	45	29	11
Germany/East	35	51	(86)	13	47	(60)	(26)	31	40	13
Italy	55	41	(96)	14	53	(68)	(28)	51	32	7
United Kingdom	47	41	(88)	7	34	(41)	(47)	16	44	30
North. Ireland	50	39	(89)	5	33	(38)	(51)	30	43	21
Spain	56	36	(92)	19	48	(67)	(25)	35	49	4
Portugal	63	34	(97)	16	47	(63)	(34)	49	33	6
Greece	87	10	(97)	16	34	(50)	(47)	44	45	6
Ireland	65	31	(96)	14	44	(58)	(38)	50	31	6
Luxembourg	57	35	(92)	32	44	(76)	(16)	63	27	6
Total	56	36	(92)	16	44	(60)	(32)	38	36	15

*Percent missing up to 100: "don't know."

Source: Eurobarometer.

toward a more critical stance. A similar change occurred among the press, particularly in the very influential tabloids owned by Rupert Murdoch (*The Sun* and *The News of the World*). Finally, also the European Union has changed its character significantly from that of a free-market area to that of an ever more encompassing political community (Alston and Weiler 1999:2). This fact may also explain why Margaret Thatcher had been among the strong supporters of the entry to the EEC in 1975 but later on became one of its most acute critics.

Somewhat similar attitudes toward the European Union can be seen among several Scandinavian countries. In economic terms, all of them are among the wealthiest countries in the world. At the same time, they are very proud of their welfare and social security systems, which have achieved a considerable equalization of life chances and the virtual elimination of open poverty.

Table 6.4   Feelings Associated with the EU in the Fifteen EU Member States (% Feeling Mentioned)

Country	(N)	Enthusiasm	Hope	Trust	Mistrust	Indifference	Anxiety	Rejection
Austria	(1,010)	4	32	16	27	21	29	10
Sweden	(1,000)	10	36	11	34	20	26	12
Finland	(1,018)	6	36	17	28	20	22	12
Denmark	(1,000)	6	35	27	23	19	14	3
Netherlands	(1,006)	5	30	32	24	20	8	12
Belgium	(1,022)	5	34	25	16	26	19	3
France	(1,015)	8	36	18	27	19	31	4
Germany/W	(1,016)	2	41	16	19	16	23	7
Germany/E	(1,023)	2	33	13	22	19	32	9
Italy	(1,008)	8	53	29	9	16	9	1
United Kingdom	(1,055)	7	23	7	26	34	19	12
North. Ireland	(307)	13	38	13	21	29	12	6
Spain	(1,000)	9	41	33	7	26	1	1
Portugal	(1,000)	9	44	21	15	16	3	2
Greece	(1,001)	5	50	27	10	15	17	2
Ireland	(1,014)	22	48	14	6	20	5	2
Luxembourg	(587)	6	44	28	13	15	19	1
Total	(16,082)	7	38	20	19	20	17	6

Source: Eurobarometer 60 (autumn 2003).

Table 6.5   Positive Attitudes toward the EU by Groups of Countries and by
Employment Status/Occupational Position.
(% EU membership is a good thing)

	Austria, Sweden, Finland, Denmark (5,123)	France, Belgium, Germany (4,100)	Italy (1,025)	United Kingdom (1,343)	Greece, Spain, Portugal, Ireland (4,006)	Luxem-bourg (619)
Professionals, managers, business owners	58	58	66	46	82	84
Middle managers	56	57	76	45	77	83
Routine white collar and service jobs	45	48	59	46	69	73
Skilled blue collar	42	39	48	29	62	63
Unskilled blue collar and service workers	45	36	38	17	59	66
Shop owners, self-employed craftsmen	48	50	56	55	70	(75)
Farmers	22	13	57	43	76	(100)
Students	60	68	61	54	73	89
Unemployed	38	36	36	25	54	(69)
Retired	39	44	49	28	61	80
Total	57	46	54	32	65	74
Difference between highest and lowest value	38	55	40	37	28	26

Source: Eurobarometer 61 (spring 2004); figure in parenthesis, if n < 30.

These facts are reflected in rather high levels of national pride (with the exception of Sweden; see *Table 6.2*). Scandinavians are also quite proud of their democracies and history, and they are much more attached to their nation-state than to Europe as a whole. Sizable minorities of the Scandinavians (20–34%) associate negative feelings (indifference, mistrust, anxiety) with the EU (*Table 6.4*). Only a minority of the farmers, but also of the unemployed and pensioners, have a positive image of the EU (*Table 6.5*).

Another factor which tended to make also Finland and Sweden sceptical for a long time about the European Union was their position of political neutrality in foreign affairs. It was thought, especially as long as Europe was divided into two hostile camps, that neutrality was not compatible with membership in the EC, as the EC member states maintained close ties with America and the military alliance NATO. A strong attachment to political neutrality was also one of most important reasons for the scepticism of many Swiss and Austrians about EC membership. The meaning and function of political neutrality has certainly changed since the collapse of the Iron Curtain and with globalization (Kriesi 1998: 27ff.). However, political neutrality is still valued highly among the general population in Austria and certainly because it is seen as the best guarantee for peace (Haller 1996b: 501ff.).

The EU *as a prop or crutch*

Several countries look to European integration primarily in the hope that through participation in this process domestic problems which these countries have been unable to solve by themselves in their postwar history can be solved. There are two main areas in which European integration is expected to serve as a panacea for nation-states. First, *in economic terms:* Countries lying behind the "European core" in terms of socioeconomic development (GNP/capita), and characterized by persistent socioeconomic problems, such as unemployment, high public deficits, and rates of inflation, expect that the process of economic integration will provide a spur to accelerated economic growth, ensure the economic catching-up, and the solution of the economic crisis phenomena. Second, *in political terms:* Countries lying behind in terms of "democratic maturity" expect that membership in the European Union will help them to establish firmly the democratic system and/or to improve the quality and efficiency of politics.

The country which fits best into this type is *Italy*. This country has been characterized throughout the postwar period by a rather unstable political situation. Italy has had over fifty governments between 1945 and 2000; the mean duration of a government in power was less than one year. Furthermore, Italy is characterized by high levels of "anticivilian" behaviour (including tax evasion, clientelism, corruption, and the like) among the elites as well as among the population.[14] In Italy, but also in Greece, the danger of a takeover of power by strong Communist parties was felt, particularly during the 1950s and 1960s. Also in economic terms, Italy was in serious crisis throughout much of postwar history in spite of its dynamic economic growth up to the 1980s. Here, we have to mention continuous high levels of unemployment, high public debts, and inflation rates connected with a badly regulated system of labour relations (e.g., very frequent strikes). Thus, it is understandable that Italy since the beginning was "a wholehearted champion of supranationalism." A paradigmatic example of the economic instability of Italy was its repeatedly devalued Lira (Reinhardt 2004:129). Therefore, Italians saw the introduction of the euro as the realization of plans (the introduction of a new currency called "gold lira") which they themselves have had since decades but were unable to realize. A very nice parody on the tendency of the Italians to expect the cure of all national ills from the European Union and the euro was made by the journalist Giorgio Bocca in his article "Santa Europa, Benedetto Euro."[15]

The peculiar situation of Italy reflects itself clearly in the attitudes of the general public. The overall attitude of the Italians toward the EU can be described as quite positive but not enthusiastic. The pride in national democracy, however, is extremely low (26% against a mean of 56%). Italians show the second-highest level of regret (51%) if the EU were to be dissolved; they also show the highest value of all concerning the feeling of "hope" associated with the EU (see *Tables 6.2* to *6.4*). Given the comparatively high level of corruption in this country,[16] it is not surprising that the EU is trusted very much (*Table 6.4*). Thus, all these indicators confirm clearly that membership in the EU is something which Italians strongly support, but primarily out of the negative evaluation of the institutions and politics in their own country. An additional reason could be the fact that Italians do not have any fear about German dominance in Europe, as some neighbour countries of Germany do. One study found that such fears are a significant determinant of attitudes toward European integration.

Also, the three Southern European countries which experienced dictatorial regimes in the postwar period, *Portugal*, *Spain* and *Greece*, fit into this type. In fact, it was a condition of the admission to the European Union that democratic political regimes were established in these countries. In all three countries, membership in the European Union was seen as a definite step toward ending socioeconomic and cultural backwardness and isolation and catching up with processes of modernization elsewhere in Europe (Diez Medrano 2003:159).

Thus, in the case of these four members of the European Union the main *motiv* for membership was the expectation that European integration would serve as an economic and political prop or crutch (see also Pfetsch 1997:77ff.). A similar factor might have been significant in the case of *Belgium*.[17] Also, Belgians exhibit a rather low attachment to their nation, but a rather positive one to Europe (see *Table 6.3*). Belgian internal politics has also been quite crisis-ridden and for a long time. Given the deep-going conflict between the Walloon- and Flemish-speaking national subgroups, even its existence as a state is somewhat in danger.

The economic motive was also important for all of these countries. In view of their relative economic backwardness up to the 1970s, with a high proportion of relatively poor agrarian populations, countries like Portugal, Greece, Spain, and Italy expected, and to a large degree obtained, economic support from the EC for their underdeveloped rural and peripheral areas. Considerable net financial transfers of the EU are going to Greece, Portugal, and Spain; Spain is the single largest net receiver (see *Table 6.1*).

The EU as a substitute for national identity

A very particular situation concerning the attitudes and behaviours of elites and citizens toward European integration can be observed in Germany, which was—together with France—one of the two "motors" of integration. We have seen that the general integration attitudes in these two countries are quite similar. A closer historical scrutiny, however, makes clear that there exist also some fundamental differences between them; they have to do with three facts (see also Gasteyger 1966; Loth 1996; Gillingham 2004).

First, French economy in the postwar time was less dynamic and strong than the German; this fact was clearly reflected in the relative strength of the respective currencies. The Deutsche Mark was one of the hardest currencies worldwide, and decisions of the *Bundesbank* were highly consequential also for France and Western Europe as a whole. Second, the two countries have different constitutional structures and histories. While France is one of the most strongly centralized countries in Europe, Germany has always had a pronounced federal system; in the constitution of the *Bundesrepublik*, this system was clearly strengthened. Third, and probably most important of all, is the fact that in Germany the most terrible version of a fascist regime, National Socialism, was in power for twelve years, a regime responsible for the Second World War and for the Holocaust. These historical experiences had a long-lasting influence on German public life and politics leading to deep-going feelings of national shame (Noelle-Neumann and Köcher 1987; Westle 1999; Buruma 1994; Elwert 1999; Haller 1999b).

The consequence is that Germans today are characterized by rather low levels of national identity, self-consciousness, and pride in their nation. It is, in fact, the lowest among the twenty-six countries examined in the study on national identity conducted by the International Social Survey Programme (ISSP) in 1995, and one of the lowest in the World Value Survey of 1990 (see also Westle 1992). *Table 6.2* shows that Germans in East and West have the lowest pride in their history (and armed forces, not shown in the table). Consciousness of the Holocaust, the systematic genocide of nearly six million Jews, remains a painful trauma for many Germans today. This issue continues to be debated hotly and strongly in the German public arena.[18] We must say, indeed, that Germany is still today an "ashamed nation." This thesis is supported by the fact that the Italians, who where also defeated in World War II, also have a low sense of pride in their army, but a rather high feeling of pride in their history; the same is true for Austria.

Looking at the data concerning the identification of Germans with Europe, we cannot say that they are as enthusiastic as the first group of countries discussed previously. Germans have the lowest level of attachment to their nation and only an intermediate level of attachment to Europe (*Table 6.3*). National and European identity are correlated with each other in a different way in Germany and Italy (Haller 1999b). German respondents who identify themselves in the first instance with "Europe" or with "the world as a whole" are characterized by a low level of national pride, but the same is not true for Italy. Thus, for many Germans, the identification with Europe constitutes a substitute for a low sense of national identity and pride.

This interpretation is confirmed by the study *Framing Europe* by Juan Diez Medrano. Summarizing his interviews with twenty-seven citizens in West and East Germany, the author concludes that "the 1933–45 period was, for most of the second half of the twentieth century, the main anchoring point of West German collective memory and identity." Moreover, the characteristics and behaviour of the Nazi regime were a major conditioning factor of West Germany national and foreign policies, and of foreign attitudes and behaviour toward Germany, during this same period (Diez Medrano 2003:179). Two thirds of his interview partners mentioned Germany's role in World War II when discussing European integration; hundreds if not thousands of novels have been written which try to come to grips with this period; also, official German foreign policy since 1945 has "conveyed a strong sense of dependence with respect to other countries' plans and international mistrust of FRG" (Diez Medrano 2003:181ff.).

This situation had a far-reaching consequence for German politics concerning European integration. Its population never got the chance to express their own view about the integration process. Many members of independent scientific and political elites have criticized this strongly, with an argument that can hardly be rejected, namely, that the basic constitution of Germany had been changed fundamentally by the gradual transfer of powers to the European Community. It is surprising that the same fact can be observed in most of the other member states which had experienced periods of fascism during the twentieth century (Portugal, Italy, and Greece). In the case of Germany, there exists a clear causal connection between these two facts. The German political elites not only considered it as superfluous to ask the citizens about their consent to integration; they found that this would even have been "dangerous." This might have been the reason why referenda are not foreseen in the constitution of the Federal Republic.[19]

This argument is directly relevant to the central question of this study, namely, the relation between the elites and the citizens. Implicitly, this argument contends that it was the German people who enabled the National Socialists to come into power, but not the elites. Since this is a very important issue, we shall investigate it more closely in the following section.

Historical excursus: Who enabled Hitler's takeover of power in Germany, the elites or the people?

First, let us look at some facts and figures about the situation in the early 1930s when Hitler and his National Socialists seized power in Germany.[20]

It seems in fact nearly incredible and shocking today that, in the two presidential elections of 1932, 11.5 and 13.5 million gave their vote to Hitler as a candidate for the position of *Reichspräsident* (in competition with the old President Hindenburg). However, in relative terms this was not more than 40% of all votes (the total electorate was over 30 million). The years 1930–1933 were extremely turbulent in German politics (most governments were in power only for a few months). In September 1930, the National Socialists for the first time became a large party with 18% of the votes. At the elections for the *Reichstag* (parliament) in November 1932, they got 33% of the votes; this was a loss compared with the last elections in July of the same year, when they had received already 37%. None of the *Reichskanzlers* in these years (Papen, Schleicher) was able to get a stable support in parliament. On January 30, 1933, Hitler was appointed as *Reichskanzler* by the eighty-six-year-old *Reichspräsident* von Hindenburg. The parliamentary elections in March brought 44% of the votes for the National Socialists. Thus, they got no absolute majority, as in the presidential elections the year before. This was even more remarkable because the elections took place in a situation of public terror by the quasi-military organization of the National Socialists, the SA (*Sturmabteilung*). In office, Hitler soon tried to enact a law, the *Ermächtigungsgesetz*, intended to suspend political freedom and parliamentary democracy. But Hitler had not the necessary two thirds majority in the *Reichstag*, necessary for such a constitutional change. However, all parties—except the Social Democrats and the Communists (which, however, were already excluded from the *Reichstag*)—agreed to his proposed law so that he got 441 out of 535. This means that 82% of the deputies consented to this law. Had all Social Democrats and also the Communists participated (with a negative vote), the proportion consenting would still have got a very strong majority, 69%. Thus, it is more than evident that the majority of the German people have never voted for Hitler, but that a large majority of its political representations has done so. It is incontestable to say that the German parliament eliminated itself in 1933.

This interpretation is corroborated if we look at the whole history of the Weimar Republic. The main reason for the instability of the period 1919–1933 was the unanimity among the political elites, their inability to put narrow party quarrels aside and to form stable governments. Thus, it were mainly the political elites who were responsible for the breakdown of democracy in Germany with its the fateful consequences: "The parliament removed itself more and more from the people because it was busy with itself and with the continuously changing governments, instead of caring for the interests of the state. More and more, a sense of irresponsibility against the people and democracy developed. This made it possible that the forces inimical to democracy could take over the power."[21] This elite-critical statement corresponds to extensive historical analyses (see, e.g., Schoenbaum 1967) as well as that of recognized social scientists. For Ralf

Dahrendorf (1962:247ff.), the rise of National Socialism must be understood as a coalition between the preindustrial, authoritarian elites that persisted into the Weimar Republic and the new, totalitarian elites. This alliance became successful because no "democratic coalition" was formed among the other parties, and elites were divided into three sharply separated hostile camps (the Conservatives, the Liberals, and the Social Democrats; see Best 1990).

There is a further argument among present-day elites against giving to the German people the possibility for referenda, namely, that Hitler used this instrument several times to get support for far-reaching political decisions. However, referenda under dictatorial political conditions cannot be equated with those under democratic conditions. Moreover, several referenda during the short-lived Weimar Republic (1919–1933) had shown a rather rational behaviour of the electorate; the radical, antidemocratic movements and forces had been given the brush-off (von Arnim 2000:179f.). Thus, it seems quite problematic to speak of National Socialism as a "catastrophe" and to characterize German history in the nineteenth and first half of the twentieth centuries as a *Sonderweg* (particular way), as was done by influential German historians (see the collection of essays in Weidenfeld 1983). Through such a characterization, the concrete responsibility of the political elites and leaders is dropped.

The two factors described before—the low level of national identity and pride and the fear of a reawakening of old demons—have also had definite consequences for the behaviour of the German political elites in the process of integration. This was most decisively so when the chance to reunify the country opened up after the Berlin Wall was torn down on November 9, 1989. The division into two parts, insulated from each other, was an old wound for Germans. Chancellor Kohl saw a historically unique chance, because with Gorbachev, a reformist leader, was on top of the Soviet Communist Party since 1985. However, some of the West European partners, in particular France and Britain, had severe reservations about German reunification. The same situation came to the fore as it had existed in the late 1940s and early 1950s, when the ECSC had been created: A united Germany with 80 million inhabitants would become much stronger than all the other member states of the Union. Thus, a new way of embedding and controlling this strengthened Germany had to be found. This position was taken particularly by France and its president, Mitterand. He found that the introduction of a common currency, controlled by the EU as a whole, would be the most efficient way to balance out the economic preponderance of Germany and its *Bundesbank* (Reimon and Weixler 2006:83ff.; Dinan 1999:130f.). Kohl agreed to this deal, ignoring the fact that many of the leading German economic and finance advisers, as well as a majority of the population, were against the substitution of the Deutsche Mark by the euro (see also Shore 2000:223).

Given these facts, it is not surprising that data on public attitudes show a particularly pronounced split between elites and citizens in Germany concerning European integration (see Chapter 1, *Table 1.3*). *Table 6.5* shows also that the difference between the well-to-do and the less privileged groups in the attitudes toward the EU is highest in the cluster of Germany, France, and Italy. Correlated with this split are the significant differences between West and East Germany (the former German Democratic Republic) concerning integration. In the east, the attitudes toward the EU are much less positive than in the west; 32% of the East Germans express feelings of anxiety in regard to European integration (*Table 6.4*). Two factors help to understand the difference: East Germans were incorporated into West Germany in the form of an *Anschluss,* that is, by having to accept all the conditions set by the Federal Republic. In spite of massive subsidies going from the west to the east, many of the provinces of East Germany are characterized today by high levels of unemployment and industrial stagnation.

In recent times, Germany more and more has itself become an autonomous driving force of European integration. In 1990/91, presidents Kohl and Mitterand made the proposal to accelerate the process of integration and to establish a European Defence Troop whose intent was also to include more closely Germany in terms of military and security policy.[22] These proposals led to the Maastricht Contract, which proposed the West European Defence Union as one of the pillars of European integration. This politics of integration has been continued by the government of Schröder; the speech of his foreign minister Joschka Fischer at Humboldt University in Berlin (May 4, 2000) was the last remarkable statement showing Germany's world-power ambitions in the context of the EU.

European integration as an end in itself

Many of the characteristics of the attitudes of the South European countries toward integration can also be observed in the ten *post-Communist Central and East European countries* that joined the European Union in 2004. Their situation was comparable to the South European countries, which had experienced fascist regimes for a considerable part of the history in the twentieth century. The post-Communist countries also had to solve two problems at once, the economic transition to market economies—a task which was much more difficult for them since private property and markets had been widely abolished—and the political transition from one-party authoritarian political systems to democracies. The population in some of these central East European countries (particularly in the German Democratic Republic and Czechoslovakia) had literately been caged for nearly half a century. The closure toward the West, openly visible in the *Iron Cage,* was a reaction of the ruling class backed by Soviet military power to the mass refugee movements and/or repeated political insurgences. The main motives for the high interest of the governments and peoples in the post-Communist states

234 Eurοpean Integration as an Elite Process

to become members of the European Union are obvious. Two groups of reasons can be mentioned.

The first has to do with the economic backwardness in which these countries found themselves increasingly during the 1970s and 1980s. This backwardness was certainly due to their fifty years' participation in a central command economy of Soviet type.[23] So, there were many economic gains to be expected from an opening toward the West. The access to the gigantic market of the European Union promised advantages and profits to several groups: Strong producers and consumers were eager to export products or to buy Western goods; mobile people of all social strata saw a chance to get access to work in Western countries which promised five to ten times higher wages than at home;[24] farmers expected new selling markets and subsidies from the EU. Among the political motives, two were the most important: Internally, the abolishment of the one-party system, the transition to democracy, and, externally, the liberation from the foreign rule (albeit it worked on only in indirect form) by the "great brother," the Soviet Union. As a member of the EU, national sovereignty and independence would be guaranteed best and forever. Especially for Poland, the largest among the Central East European countries, "the European Union was their *civilizational* choice, the *national patriotic duty*. Poland as a country chose the EU as its 'return to Europe,' because its history belonged to Europe . . ." (Guerra 2006:7). In this regard, Poles seem to echo Italian attitudes to integration—a comparison which also makes sense because in both countries Catholicism is the dominant religion.

However, there were also serious concerns about the access to the European Union, and they also involved quite diverse but significant groups of the population. First, the loss of power and influence of the old *Nomenclatura* and all their clienteles would be strengthened in this way; in fact, these groups are significantly less happy today than those in the middle strata of the post-Communist societies (Haller and Hadler 2006). Second, people employed in the public-service and in state-owned industries had to worry about the security of the jobs since all these sectors were overstaffed and quite unproductive, compared to their Western competitors. Finally, large segments of poorer people—working in blue-collar and service jobs, pensioners, people dependent on welfare, and so on—had to fear reduction of many kinds of public support and a significant increase of prices for basic goods (Szczerbiak 2001:114; Gasparski 1996). In Chapter 4, it was shown that the process of integration of these countries into Western capitalism in general and the EU in particular took place in a rather fast and painful way.

Given these contradictory facts, it is not so surprising that the consent to the access of these countries to the European Union was not as high as one might have expected or, as is often asserted in the West (when it is asserted), that these countries entered "enthusiastically" into the EU (Vetik 2003). One indicator is the rather modest turnout at the referenda in the different post-Communist countries—a fact which has been shown in Chapter 1 and which is usually shamefacedly concealed in reports about the outcome of these referenda. Turnout varied only between 45% in Hungary up to around 60% in the other countries. In the case of Poland and Hungary, this means that less than half (between 38% and 45%) of the elective adult population in fact voted for the access to the European Union. In several of these countries, preelection polls had even shown lower proportions of supporters than later came out. A very low level of interest turned out also at the elections for the European Parliament in June 2004: In Poland and Slovakia, only one fifth of the electorate participated; in Slovenia and Estonia, less than one third; and in all other post-Communist countries, less than half of the population. Such extreme low levels of turnout are hardly a sign of enthusiasm for the EU or for democracy in general.

This view is also confirmed by social surveys. The general attitude toward the EU is positive, but not extraordinarily so in central East Europe. The image of the EU is positive for a little bit over half of the respondents; most of the people think that their country has benefited. Knowledge about the EU is rather low in many countries (an exception is Slovenia; for Poland, see Guerra 2006; see also *Table 6.1*). Characteristic of most of these countries is also a low level of national pride in most dimensions (democracy, economic achievements, social security system; see *Table 6.2*). Nevertheless, people seem attached strongly to their nation, particularly so in Hungary and Poland.

Thus, a general interpretation valid for the overall attitude of the citizens in the post-Communist countries may well be captured by formulas such as "Membership as an end in itself" or "It's taking part that counts." In a study on attitudes toward the EU before the accession, it was found that most Poles were "Euroneutrals who *consent* to the idea of membership rather than being particularly *enthusiastic* about it" (Szczerbiak 2001:120). This attitude of a "passive participation" has been diagnosed also by well-informed analysts of the public mood in post-Communist East Europe today. According to Hungarian writer Peter Esterhazy, the word *freedom* in east Europe today does not mean liberty but just *survival;* as a consequence of centuries of foreign rule, "everywhere in these countries we have developed an incredible slyness to hide ourselves before the power."[25] Quite similar comments were given by Hungarian-Austrian journalist Paul Lendvai about the political situation in Hungary.[26] An outstanding example in this regard is Poland. The professor of history and editor of the magazine *Res Publica,* Marcin Krol, diagnosed a bad state of the health of democracy in Poland, indicated by the low turnout, high levels of political apathy, and a generally depressed mood of the population. Before the national election in 2005, 60% of the Poles said in a poll they did not expect an improvement of their life.[27] This is not surprising given the high unemployment rates at this time (20%), increasing inequality, and widespread poverty. A main reason for this development was the radical program of neoliberal reforms, which have been described in Chapter 4. In autumn 2003, a series of demonstrations of several groups (miners, health workers, farmers, and taxi drivers) took place in Warsaw against this kind of policy. However, among large parts of the population, especially the poorer and powerless ones (such as unemployed or pensioners), political apathy and frustration are spreading out; the lack of clear political programmes of the parties contributes to this depression. The reversal of the Polish political landscape toward the right with the victory of the rather conservative and nationalistic twin brothers Kaczynski as president and premier in 2005 is no surprise at this background.

A further interesting fact and indicator of a split between elites and citizens is that many of the leading politicians and economic advisers in these countries are supporters of a rather strict liberalist approach. A prominent representative of this approach is the present Czech president (an economist by profession), Vaclav Klaus. He argues that the European Union represents a model of a corporatist superstate, inspired by socialist ideas. In accordance with many Britons, he proposes that the Union should be expanded as far as possible, that it should include the Ukraine, Kazakhstan, and Morocco—"the more, the better"[28] (see also Strong 2006).

The liberalistic ideas and policies of the elites are not strongly supported among the broad new poor strata in Central East Europe. A survey in Estonia showed that 40% of the respondents considered the application of EU standards tantamount to the elite pursuing its own private interests (Vetik 2003). Within this group of the Union members, the split between the elites and the people is particularly pronounced. For East Germany it has been shown that managers were more oriented toward capitalist values, such as high profits and interests of owners, than their counterparts in West Germany (Best and Schmidt 2004). A study of the rich in Lithuania showed that they are more oriented toward Europe than the rest of society (Mathonyte and Gaidys 2004). All these findings indicate that new cleavages are developing in these societies which may contribute to the deepening of the conflict in the EU as a whole between supporters of the neoliberal model of integration and another model which also includes basic social rights and better opportunities for political participation of the citizens.

The EU as a means to (re-) gain global influence

Two main interests or motives played a central and "positive" role in European integration. The first is peace and security in Europe, the second the promotion of growth and prosperity. *France* is the country for which the European Union mostly constitutes a means to advance positive political interests (see also Siedentop 2001:140f., 223ff.). This is proved, first, by the fact that several of the most decisive political personalities in the European integration process—such as Jean Monnet, Robert Schumann, Jacques Delors, F. Mitterand, and G. d'Estaing—were French politicians.

But also Charles de Gaulle has been a decisive political personality for Europe (Dinan 1999:37). This thesis may appear as surprising at first sight since the name of de Gaulle is usually associated with the blocking of British entry to the EEC and the curtailing of the powers of the Commission and the European Parliament. However, de Gaulle accomplished the reconciliation between France and Germany and, thereby, established the "motor" for further integration. Furthermore, he proposed the Common Agrarian Policy (CAP), a central pillar of integration, and he achieved the retention and up-valuation of the council of government heads as the decisive political body in the EU.

Second, the French political elites as a whole were highly successful in shaping the process of European integration according to their own visions. They are the best educated and most determined in terms of their political aims: "Impatient of opposition once it has settled on a course of action as 'rational,' the French political class prizes outcomes, ends more than means" (Siedentop 2001:135). The strong centralization of the French state and the power of its bureaucracy have been crucial in this regard. In Chapter 5 we have seen that also high officers in the Eurocracy are composed to a large proportion by French persons. Siedentop (2001:136) goes so far as to argue that "the French political class was able to construct in Brussels a European edifice which reflected the French vision of Europe, French habits and French interests. In effect, the French political class become used to presiding over Europe."

Why was the French initiative for European integration so successful? France did not come out from the Second World War unhurt and as proud as Britain. It had been defeated disgracefully through Hitler's *Blitzkrieg* in 1940; the reputation of many politicians was damaged because of their collaboration with the Vichy regime, installed by Hitler (Wolton 2004). In economic terms, France was a weak nation, not only because of war damages but also because sharp restrictions on trade between the countries, a "strong pattern of bilateralism and autarky," existed in continental Europe (Milward 1992:6). Moreover, France had been in a weak situation already before the war, in its economy and military, but also in moral terms (Monnet 1988:297). Thus, a close cooperation at the European level, and in particular with the former old and strong enemy, Germany, could promise France the possibility to continue to play a significant role in world politics. This appeared as necessary because, with the Soviet Union, a new big power was on the rise which threatened Western Europe. The shadows of the coming "Cold War" were clearly visible at this time. The pivotal role of France in the early stages of the European integration process is also proved by the fact that several French politicians had proposed—already before the establishment of the ECSC—to establish a European Defense Community. A treaty about such a community was in fact signed in Paris in May 1952. However, the *Assemblé Nationale* rejected it in 1954 because it seemed to the deputies that it made too many concessions to the Federal Republic (Pfetsch 1997:32f.).

France also took a leading part in the economic integration process, which got a new push in the 1980s, when Jacques Delors became president of the EU Commission. In this period, the interests of large enterprises and multinational corporations have taken the lead in the integration process, as it was shown in Chapter 4. The next step when France pushed forward the integration process was in 1990, when President Mitterand proposed the common currency. Also in this proposal, concerns for France's national independence were of crucial importance; the euro and French codetermination of the common currency policy were conceived as a trade-off for the consent to German reunification in 1990.

However, if we look at public attitudes toward integration, also in France a clear split between elites and citizens emerges. While both national and European identity and pride are higher in France than in Germany, they are not exceptionally high. The French are very proud of their social security system and their history, but not very proud of the economic achievements of their country (*Table 6.2*). What is most significant: In France, there exist widespread feelings of mistrust (27% against a mean of 19%) and anxiety (31% against a mean of 17%) in connection with the EU. Also, the differences in the attitudes toward integration between social strata are considerable in France. This reserve toward integration among considerable sections of the French population has been a typical feature for some time. Other indications were the acceptance of the Treaty on the European Union (TEU) by only a very small margin of 50.7% in 1992, and the rejection of the Constitution for Europe in 2005 by a clear majority (54.8%) of the voters (see *Table 1.1*).

The European Union as a "feeding dish"

Cluster analysis has shown that two small countries—Luxembourg and Ireland—are set apart very clearly from all other member countries of the EU. Both can in fact be considered as constituting a specific type concerning their relation to European integration.

A particularly interesting case in this regard is the Grand Duchy of *Luxembourg*, in spite of its small size (about 460,000 inhabitants). Luxembourg is often quoted as being a paradigmatic example for the benefits of European integration. In fact, it is today one of the richest countries of the world, and a considerable part of this wealth is directly connected with European integration. It is also true that the people of Luxembourg, situated in a central position between the French- and German-speaking area, show a high level of openness toward other countries and cultures (indicated, for instance, by widespread knowledge of foreign languages); the Grand Duchy has also produced an overproportional number of outstanding European politicians (including two presidents of the commission,

Gaston Thorn and Jacques Santer). However, Luxembourg is also among the twenty-five member countries which profits most from its membership in the Union. This happens in four regards.

First, since the first beginnings of the integration process, Luxembourg hosts several EU institutions. In 1952, it became the seat of the High Commission of the ECSC. Later on, the offices of the European Court of Justice, the European Audit Court, and offices of the European Parliament and the Council of Ministers were added. About 6,500 EU employees may be working today in Luxembourg—a number which has a considerable weight in such a small country. Second, Luxembourg is the largest receiver of EU funds per capita of the population (Baldwin 2005:4). In 2004, it was 2.359 euros per person, including the administrative expenses; even considering only redistributive spending (mainly for agriculture and cohesion), Luxembourg was the fifth largest recipient per person. Third, also the private business sector (particularly banking) of Luxembourg can take advantages from its membership in the EU. The specific profitable conditions (in terms of taxes etc.) prevailing in this country attract many foreign companies. Facts like a proportion of 39% of foreigners and an absolute number of over 100,000 employed persons commuting daily into the grand duchy make this clear. Fourth, Luxembourg has a privileged position within the EU because of its small size. In the constitutional system of the EU, small countries have been granted an overproportional weight. Luxembourg has, for instance, six deputies in the European Parliament and Germany ninety-nine. This means that one MEP in Luxembourg represents about 70,000 voters, but one German MEP over 800,000. Thus, the vote of a single citizen of Luxembourg has a much higher weight than those of citizens in most other member states.

A similar situation of a direct advantage from the presence of European institutions exists in the Belgian capital, Brussels. The quantitative impact of this factor is even more important here; including the EU employees proper, the representatives of nation-states, provinces, and so on, the lobbyists of associations and firms, at least 50,000 persons are directly dependent of the EU in Brussels. This is certainly an economic factor of primary importance for the administration of the town. In addition, the orders for the building industries, the service sector, and others, coming from the European institutions, are quite important economically. In 1991, the EU was worth 10% of gross domestic product to Belgium (Shore 2000:159). Belgian authorities, therefore, are extremely sensitive about anything that could damage Brussels' reputation as the "capital of Europe."

The second country which belongs also to the type of the "EU as the feeding dish" is *Ireland*. Even after having gained its political independence, in 1922, this island remained strongly dependent on England and isolated from the rest of Europe. Only in the 1960s an economic opening was initiated, which culminated in the access to the EEC in 1973, together with Great Britain. While one reason for the access to the EU was to reduce dependence from Great Britain, the other was certainly to profit from EC structural funds and agrarian subsidies (Dinan 1999:67ff.). In fact, Ireland is—in relative terms (per capita)—the country which receives the largest amounts of subsidies (see *Table 6.1*). Both of these facts have certainly contributed to the fact that the Irish population shows rather positive attitudes toward European integration. In the several referenda about accession and institutional deepening (1972, 1987, 1992), clear majorities (70–80%) in favour of integration turned out (see Chapter 1). However, interest in these referenda was not very high, as shown in relatively low turnout rates. It seems that the Irish have rather utilitarian attitudes toward integration. This fact came out most clearly in the 2001 referendum on the Treaty of Nice, when a majority (54%) of the participants (only 35% of the electorate) rejected the treaty to the great surprise of the political elites. Ireland was seen as an ungrateful child and the replication of this referendum in 2002 brought the expected result.

Since its entry into the EC, Ireland underwent a very dynamic development: It was able—in contrast to the South European members Portugal, Spain, and Greece—to catch up fully with the richer members of the EU; since the mid-1990s, it has had strong economic growth and declining unemployment. In 2007, Ireland had the second highest level of GDP among the twenty-seven EU member states, surpassed only by Luxembourg.[29] In 1970, its mean income per capita had been only a half of the mean in the twelve EC member states. Thus, we must clearly speak of a "second economic miracle" in this case. This spectacular economic development has certainly contributed to the generally very positive stance of the Irish toward the EU: 81%—the largest proportion—think that the country has benefited from membership. The EU has a very positive image, but the level of knowledge is below average. Half of the Irish would regret very much if the EU were dissolved, and larger proportions than elsewhere associate feelings of enthusiasm and hope with the EU (*Tables 6.1* to *6.4*). However, it would be too simple to ascribe the success of Ireland mainly to the support received by the EU funds. One main factor for it has been massive foreign (mainly US-) investments which were attracted by the low corporate income taxes (10%) in Ireland; the language of the country has certainly facilitated it. So Ireland also constitutes a tax haven, like Luxembourg, Liechtenstein, and Switzerland (Huemer 1994; Sweeney 1998).

There is one conclusion that seems important in both these cases, particularly that of Luxembourg. It is the fact that it is quite misleading to see these countries as paradigmatic examples for the benefits of the integration process. Their prosperity is due to a considerable degree not to European integration but to special conditions, which are not given in the case of the poor countries of the EU periphery, in the south and east of Europe.

6.4 The European Union as a "Community of values"?

The foregoing analyses have shown that quite different interests, ideas, and expectations exist in regard to integration between the different member states and citizens of the EU. Given these divergences, one could argue that its unity and integration should be based less on short-term social and economic gains but more on general, common values. This is in fact an influential line of thinking and arguing. The European Union is ever more frequently characterized by politicians, intellectuals, and writers as a "Community of Values," such as freedom, human rights, democracy, and the like (see also Giorgi et al. 2006:135ff.). Also, in the basic treaties of the EU, the reference to such values plays an important role. In this section, we will investigate if this claim is true at all. The analysis is based on a content analysis of the proposed Constitution for Europe. This is the text best suited for this purpose since it incorporates all of the earlier basic treaties of the EC/EU into one single document. The EU Constitution shall also be compared with the constitutions of different EU member states and other democratic countries.

The claim of the EU to represent a Community of Values

If we look at the proposed EU Constitution, it is unquestionable that the EU sees itself as the guardian of the most basic and cherished human values (see also Giorgi et al. 2006:135ff.). At the very beginning (Art. I-2: "The Union's values"), not less than thirteen values are enumerated: "The Union is founded on the values of respect for human dignity, freedom, democracy, equality, the rule of law and respect for human rights, including the rights of persons belonging to minorities. These values are common to the Member States in a society in which pluralism, non-discrimination, tolerance, justice, solidarity and equality between women and men prevail."

Only in the next article, the Union's concrete objectives are defined. But also in this section, specific aims—economic growth, price stability, environmental protection, and so on—are intermingled with more general objectives, such as peace, the general well-being, and "the promotion of its values" (whatever this could mean). A reference to its basic values is also made concerning the acceptation of new members. Article I-58 states that the Union shall be open "to all European states which respect the values referred to in Art. I-2 . . ." A new clause (Art. I-59) states also that certain membership rights are suspended if "a clear risk of a serious break of a member state of the values" of the Union occurs.

This self-designation of the EU as a community of values is unique. A look at the constitutions of its twenty-seven member states shows that in none of them is an explicit and systematic listing of values contained.[30] Usually, the constitutions include two sections: One specifies the tasks and powers of the different political institutions (the largest part); the other one lists basic rights of citizens. The main document of the Austrian Constitution does not even contain a section on basic rights. The same is true for the French Constitution, although it contains—in the appendix—the relatively short Declaration of Human Rights of 1789. Is this a problem in the case of Austria? Since Austria has recognized—as all other EU member states—the UN Declaration of Human Rights of 1948 and the European Convention on Human Rights of 1950, this seems to be no problem. In fact, it is not known that human rights have been protected less in Austria than in any other European state. Only in the U.S., in the Preamble of the Constitution and in the Declaration of Independence, can something similar be found. But these texts speak not of "values" but of concrete aims which shall be promoted by the Union, or even of basic human "rights."[31] Maybe the Constitution of the Soviet Union was the only other one which was based on an explicit system of values (Boukovsky 2005).[32]

Thus, as far as Western democracies are concerned, the proposed EU Constitution has opened up a wholly new perspective by defining itself mainly as a community of values. The proposed Constitution has not introduced this self-image anew. Already in Article 2 of the Treaty of Rome (1957), a large number of basic, value-related aims (harmonious economic development, high level of employment and social protection, equality of men and women, enhancement of the quality of life, etc.) have been enumerated as tasks of the new community. Since then, the heads of states and governments have confirmed these noble values and aims of the Union over and over again in speeches and "solemn declarations." This is quite a different situation to that in the legal and social sciences, where little systematic analysis of the ideals connected with European integration has been carried out. We agree fully with Weiler (1999:240), however, that values are of central importance. (This argument was already set forth in Chapter 2.) The question is, however, if the values kept solemnly by the EU are really those which guide their institutional setup and political practice. This issue shall be taken up in the next chapter. Here, the question shall be discussed if the claim of the EU to constitute a community of values is substantiated from two other points of view. One of them relates to its "Christian" character, the other to the issue of a specific "European way of life."

The European Union as a political community based on Christian values?

European integration is often traced back to the empire of Charlemagne, who—so it is argued—united Europe for the first time under Christendom. During the work of the convention which elaborated the proposal for the Constitution, there was a hot debate going on about the inclusion of a reference to the Christian heritage of Europe and to God. Some Catholic member states, particularly Poland, asked for this, referring to the fact that Christianity had a deep impact on Europe and still is the "dominant" religion in all member states of the EU. This position was also supported by several bishops of the Protestant and Catholic churches. The final text found a solution to this thorny problem by referring only in general terms to the "cultural, religious and humanist inheritance of Europe" (preamble) without mentioning Christianity at all.

The issue if the EU can be considered as a "Christian" political community shall be discussed here, however, not only because it might come up on the table again (if the Constitution will be reworked), but also because it helps us to understand better the general issue of the role of values for a political community. The definition of the EU as a fundamentally "Christian" political community is inspired by the generally accepted fact that the Jewish-Christian heritage—besides Greek philosophy and Roman law—constitutes one of the historic-cultural foundations of Europe. Recently, Joseph Weiler (2003) proposed the idea that the EU Constitution should contain an explicit reference to Christianity. He bases his claim also on the argument that there exists a constitutional tradition in Europe and any constitution contains a transcendental core. This can again only be a Christian one because this upholds the principle of tolerance. The thesis proposed here is, however, that the understanding of the EU as a "Christian" political community would contradict the character of a modern, internally highly differentiated political community. There are three main reasons for this.

First, the idea of a "Christian, occidental Europe" is only one among at least three different models of social and political culture existing in the member states of the EU today (Antes 2005). Another one is that of the fully secular society, developed in the French revolution of 1789. The principle of the "laïcité culturelle" has been anchored in an irrevocable way since then in France (Dehove 2004:21ff.). A third one is the model of a "multicultural," pluralistic society which has relevance in countries such as the Netherlands and the UK. This model has also its historical precursor in the Roman Empire. Thus, the EU cannot privilege one of these models but must try to accommodate all of them.

Second, there exists a high diversity of religious attitudes and practices in present-day Europe. Large subsections of people within many European countries would directly feel alienated from a "Christian" Union because they cannot identify with Christianity. These include three groups: (a) People who are anticlerical because of the misbehaviour of the Christian churches in European history, up to the present time (we could think here of the suppressive and nationalistic role of some church representatives in countries such as Poland, Serbia, or Russia, or the moral misconduct of some very high church leaders), or because they personally experienced exclusion and suppression by the church. In France, this anticlericalism is quite strong. (b) The less militant, but quite large and growing sections of the populations which have consciously turned away from the churches for different reasons; in East Germany, the Netherlands, and England, these are already half or more of the population. (c) The growing number of people living in Europe who are not Christians; here, in particular immigrated Muslims and their children must be mentioned, whose number is estimated at 15 million. If Bosnia, Albania, and Kosovo will become members of the EU (which principle is not denied by anybody), also large native European populations will belong to Islam (a small one exists already in Bulgaria).

Finally, also Weiler's argument, that the European Constitution must be built upon existing constitutional traditions in Europe, cannot be sustained. The usual understanding of the process of constitution making has also in Europe been one in which the citizens and their political representatives themselves decide about their common institutional norms. By doing so, they are inspired by their traditions but not bound by them. The important principle of tolerance, stressed rightly by Weiler, can also be legitimized by reference to universal human values and traditions.

Thus, given the high internal variation of the EU also in religious terms, the only viable solution is that it remains fully neutral in this regard. Here, it can follow the example of other large or internally highly differentiated political communities. In fact it can be shown from the historical-sociological perspective that a clear separation between the church and the state also serves the interests of religion and churches. Religiosity is significantly higher today in those countries which have established a clear separation in this regard than in those where "state churches" have been established (Höllinger 1996). The United States is the paradigmatic example of the first, England and the Scandinavian countries for the latter case. In this regard, India might be considered as a particularly relevant positive case, from which the EU could learn quite a lot. In this very large and highly diversified country, the principles of multiculturalism and religious neutrality are an integral part of the constitution. India even tries to realize a model of *multicommunitarianism,* which combines a framework of equality, an explicit recognition of cultural diversity, respect for the sensibilities of others, and the sharing of social, cultural, and civic responsibilities and engagement (Momin 2006).

The third and most important reason why the EU should not be defined as a "Christian" political community is that there exists a fundamental difference between a religious and a political community. As witness for this thesis we can refer to Joseph Ratzinger, the present Catholic Pope Benedict XVI. In his booklet *Die Einheit der Nationen* (The Unity of the Nations), he argues, referring to the church fathers Origenes and Augustinus, that there exists a fundamental difference between God's empire of the church and the earthly empires of political communities and states. Only the first one encloses and integrates humanity as a whole and represents the highest and universal values; only God's empire is worth of our "highest concerns." A state, in contrast, represents only "relative" values; it secures the extrinsic (material and social) existence of humans. As such, it is also indispensable; we must not exaggerate it, however, and connect it with spiritual values which it does not represent (Ratzinger 2005). Also from this consideration, it follows quite clearly that the EU would be miscounselled significantly if it would define itself as a Christian-occidental community of values (see also Meyer 2004:229; Haller 2008).

Thus, it may be concluded from all these points of view that Christianity cannot be seen as a defining element of the EU. This is exactly the same conclusion which was drawn by Montesquieu (1965) when he wrote that patriotism, which in a republic is love of equality, is neither a moral nor a Christian but a *political virtue.* This does not mean that the legal regulations and the actual politics of the EU cannot be inspired by Christian values. These values to a large part are consistent with universal human values (Küng 1990; Khoury 1999), and Christianity contributed significantly to their enforcement (Siedentop 2001:193). Therefore, it certainly can be seen as positive if such an inspiration exists. From such a point of view, another approach promises to be more fruitful. Those who are convinced about the positive elements in the Christian tradition should concentrate their efforts to look critically at the substance of the Constitution and investigate if they correspond to those Christian principles which can also be considered as universal ethic-moral principles such as peace, social equality, tolerance, and the like (Belafi 2005).

The "European way of life"—an ambiguous concept without empirical substance

What remains of the peculiarity of Europe in terms of culture if its religious heritage does not provide an overarching value system able to overcome its internal divisions and providing the EU with a peculiar identity vis-à-vis other large political communities in the world? One other response to this question argues that there exists a particular "European way of life." This argument takes up a central position in Habermas's widely distributed plea for a European constitution. The project of a political union, of an "ever closer Union," the design "for a state of nation-states" demands, in his view, "the legitimation of shared values" (Habermas 2001): "The current lack of motivation for political union . . . makes the insufficiency of bare economic calculations all the more obvious. Economic justifications must at the very least be combined with ideas of a different kind—let us say, an interest in and affective attachment to a particular ethos: in other words, the attraction of a specific way of life." After decades of economic growth, Europeans have developed "a distinctive form of life based on, but not exhausted by, a glistening material infrastructure. Today, against perceived threats from globalization, they are prepared to defend the core of a welfare state that is the backbone of a society still oriented towards social, political and cultural inclusion." However, besides the reference to the "European welfare state," Habermas remains rather silent about the essence of this "much broader vision." Sociology, where the concept of the way of life is often used, does not inform us clearly about its meaning.

We can use empirical data to answer the question if such a specific "European way of life" exists at all. There exist two large, worldwide social surveys in which representative samples of the population are investigated regularly about a broad range of social and political values, attitudes, and behaviours. We can compare the attitudes of Europeans with those of persons in other nations and continents and see if Europeans are more similar to each other than to people in other world regions and cultures.

One analysis of this type has been carried out Ronald Inglehart, using the *World Value Surveys* (Inglehart and Baker 2000). He looks at the typical values and attitudes of people in a broad range of areas (marriage and family, work and leisure, educational values, attitudes toward minorities, toward the role of business and government, etc.). By comparing sixty-five societies all over the world, he finds that the European countries do not form one cluster, separated from the rest. Instead, he identifies the following groupings: (1) The catholic South European countries are very similar in their attitudes to all the East European (orthodox) countries; (2) Germany forms one cluster with the Scandinavian countries, but also Japan; (3) Ireland and Spain are most similar to the South European (Latin) American countries; (4) Great Britain is close to Canada, New Zealand, and Australia.

A similar analysis was been carried out in the context of the *International Social Survey Programme* (ISSP), which is a cooperation between about forty research institutes around the world which combine one of their annual surveys in order to produce high-quality, comparative survey data. These data have been used in order to show the variation between the social and political value orientations of the respondents within large countries (by subdividing them into three to five subregions) and between the different countries as a whole. In a cluster analysis of twenty-three indicators for attitudes to the nation-state and patriotism, the forty-six units (comprising twenty-three whole smaller countries, and twenty-three subregions of the larger countries (namely: Germany, Italy, Spain, GB, U.S., Canada, Russia, and Japan), two relevant findings turned out (Haller and Hadler 2004/05). First, in practically all cases the regional subunits of one country were clustered together in the very first steps. This implies that the value orientations between the different regions of one country are much less pronounced than those between the countries. Second, as far as the similarities between the different countries were concerned, four large groupings arose which in many regards are similar to those of Inglehart and Baker. (1) The Anglo-Saxon countries (Great Britain, Australia, and New Zealand); (2) Japan, Spain, and Ireland; (3) The Scandinavian countries (Denmark, Norway, and Sweden), Netherlands, Germany, and Canada; (4) South (Italy) and east European countries (Poland, Czech Republic, Slovakia, Slovenia, Hungary, Latvia, Bulgaria, and Russia) and the Philippines. Thus, among each of the four clusters some European countries were combined with non-European countries and again, no specific European cluster emerged.

The clusters empirically formed in both these analyses are consistent with a lot of knowledge about the dominant value orientations and the dominant religion (Protestantism vs. Catholicism and Orthodoxy), but also the systems of welfare, in the different countries and regions: In most countries of the Anglo-Saxon world—both in the UK and the U.S.—emphasis is laid on individual responsibility and achievement, freedom is preferred over equality, and the state is seen with suspicion by many. In the Scandinavian world and Germany, but also in Canada, the state plays a more central role in terms of welfare and of economic and social planning; in South and East Europe, as in Japan, the welfare state is less developed and integrated; familism is more important as a basic value (Haller and Höllinger 1990). Thus, the conclusion is unambiguous: In terms of people's social and political attitudes and styles of life, Europe does not form a "macrosociety" distinguished clearly from other macroregions or culture areas of the world, but it is highly differentiated internally. The different subregions of Europe are nearer to other culturally similar countries outside Europe than to the other European countries. This finding corresponds exactly to those concerning the international connections in terms of trade and business relations, presented in Chapter 4. It corresponds also to the fundamental differences in the kinds of welfare states within Europe, as they have been shown in G. Esping-Andersen's study on the *Three Worlds of Welfare Capitalism* (1990). The English welfare state, as it has developed recently, may be considered as being more similar to the American than to any of the European models. Therefore, also the thesis of the existence of a typical "European social model" is shaky; in most regards, the differentiation within the EU is more pronounced than the difference between Europe and the United States (Alber 2006).

6.5 Legitimacy through output? The modest socio-economic success of integration and its accurate perception by the citizens

We have seen that large variations exist in the perception and evaluation of European integration among the different member countries and their citizens. Consent to integration is much more limited among the citizens than among the elites, as shown in chapter 1. It is widely agreed that the European Union suffers from a democratic deficit or *input legitimacy,* that is, the possibility to participate in political decision-making and the selection of their representatives (*government by the people*). There seems to be one way out of all these dilemmas: If an institution works to the best of all participants, it may well be considered as possessing legitimation. Political scientists have developed the concept of "output legitimacy" (Majone 1996; Schimmelfennig 1996; Scharpf 1997, 1999; Crum 2003; Boedeltje/ Cornips 2005); *Output legitimacy* is given if this system works in an efficient manner (*government for the people*).[33] The public perception and evaluation of the integration process rightly gets increasing recognition today. Eichenberg and Dalton (1998:252) argue that a "Citizen's Europe" is on the rise in which the process of integration is accelerated if citizens are optimistic, and slowed down if they are sceptical. (See also Eichenberg/ Dalton 1993; Deflem/ Pampel 1996; Gabel/ Anderson 2002; Brettschneider et al. 2003).

Politicians and the representatives of the EU itself have a very positive view about the integration process and its achievements. Just a few examples: Romano Prodi said in 2001: "*Our present prosperity would not exist without the single market and the Euro. They have created an economic power of first range which can compete with the United States*"; Jacques Chirac (2000): "*The European Union today is world-wide the largest economic and trade power, a giant in the area of research and innovation*"; Tony Blair (2005): "*When the war was finished, Europe was in ruins. Today, Europe stands there like a monument for political accomplishments. Nearly 50 years of peace, 50 years prosperity, 50 years progress*"; Angela Merkel (2006): "*All positive turning points in German post-war history are connected inseparably with Europe. If it is the re-integration into the European Union or the re-unification of Germany: We awe to European integration an unparalleled time of peace, freedom and prosperity.*"[34] A vice president of the Commission: "*. . . There are no winners and losers in European integration. Integration benefits all. It creates a win-win-situation for all participants*" (Verheugen 2005:20).[35]

Also for many economists and social scientists (not to speak of business leaders), the economic advantages of integration are beyond all questions (Bornschier 2000b; Trichet 2001; Galati/ Tsatsaronis 2003; Bergsten 2005; Moussis 2006). However, there are also critical voices which point out less positive facts. These include persistent high rates of unemployment and modest economic growth in many EU-member countries; the hard currency policy of the European Central Bank is criticized for slowing down economic growth (Baader 1993; Friedman/ Mundell 2001; Gabel/ Anderson 2002; Eichengreen 2005; Caporale/ Kontonikas 2006; Wyplosz 2006).

Two issues shall be investigated here: The objective achievements of European integration and their perception among the citizens. Political elites often state that citizens' attitudes are mainly based on emotions, that they are unable to appreciate their effects in a rational way.

Socioeconomic developments in the EU-15 compared to the USA and Japan. The Euro Zone as the "red lantern" of the world economy?

How do objective developments in the European Union look like compared with the United States and Japan?[36] The EU is frequently compared with these countries and their achievements have often been taken as an occasion to ask for an enforced integration of Europe.[37] *Table 6.6* shows the developments in the period 1995–2004 in five central social and economic areas. The findings are rather clear and testimonialize not very positively for the European Union:

- In terms of economic growth, the United States had the best values in seven out of the ten years; the EU reached the growth level of the

US only in two years (1995 and 2000); in this regard Japan had the worst score.

- Concerning inflation, Japan showed the best achievement with the lowest rate in seven years (the extremely low growth of the Japanese economy is certainly the downside of this achievement); here, also the EU scored well in four years.
- In terms of unemployment and overall level of employment, the EU appears as a full failure: It shows the worst values in all ten years.

Two French authors (Fitoussi/ Le Cacheux 2005:41) draw a very critical conclusion from these facts:" The diagnostic is definitive: the Euro zone loses ground, it is the red lantern of the world economy (see also Lorentzen 1999).

Table 6.6 Indicators of Socioeconomic Development in the EU-15, USA and Japan, 1995–2004

		1995	1996	1997	1998	1999	2000	2001	2002	2003	2004
Real growth of GNP	EU-15	2,6	1,7	2,6	2,9	3	3,9	2	1,1	1,1	2,3
	USA	2,5	3,7	4,5	4,2	4,4	3,7	0,8	1,6	2,5	3,9
	Japan	2,0	2,6	1,4	-1,8	-0,2	2,9	0,4	0,1	1,8	2,3
Inflation rate	EU-15	2,8	n.a.	1,7[a]	1,3	1,2	1,9	2,2	2,1	2	2
	USA	2,8	3	2,3	1,6	2,2	3,4	2,8	1,6	2,3	2,7
	Japan	-0,1	0,1	1,8	0,6	-0,3	-0,7	-0,7	-0,9	-0,3	0
Unemploy- ment rate	EU-15	10,1	10,2	9,9	9,3	8,6	7,7	7,3	7,6	8	8,1
	USA	5,6	5,4	4,9	4,5	4,2	4	4,8	5,8	6	5,5
	Japan	3,1	3,4	3,4	4,1	4,7	4,7	5	5,4	5,3	4,7
Employ- ment rate[c]	EU-15	60,1	60,3	60,7	61,4	62,5	63,4	64	64,2	64,3	64,7
	USA	72,5	72,9	73,5	73,8	73,9	74,1	73,1	71,9	71,2	71,2
	Japan	69,2	69,5	70	69,5	68,9	68,9	68,8	68,2	68,4	68,7
Social spending in % of GNP	EU-15	28,2	28,4	27,9	27,5	27,4	27,2	27,5[b]	27,7[a]	28,3[a]	n.a.
	no comparable data for USA and Japan available										

Notes: (a) Estimated value; (b) Prognosis; (c) % employed among the work-age population 15–65; n.a.: not available.

Source: Eurostat 2005 (http://epp.eurostat.ec.europa.eu)

It is also of interest here to compare the EU-member countries which have introduced the common currency Euro in 2001 with those who did not; among the former, a distinction is made between the six founding members and the countries which became EU-members between 1973 and 1995. The countries which refused to become members of "Euroland"—Denmark, Sweden and the United Kingdom—had the best values in four indicators (unemployment, level of employment, inflation and level of welfare spending); only in economic growth, the new eastern EU-member states show a better record.

Looking at the different countries and regions within the EU, the general trend seems to be a change toward the mean. For some countries, this implied an improvement, for others, however, a relative (and often also absolute) deterioration. Economic weak member states and states with a poor welfare state could improve their situation considerably. This applies particularly to the peripheral cohesion countries in the south (Greece, Spain, and Portugal) and in northwest and northeast Europe (Ireland, Finland). It is probably that EU-membership has contributed in a significant, albeit weak way to this improvement (Bornschier et al. 2004). However, other countries, such as Austria and Germany, have experienced a relative deterioration: Economic growth decreased, and unemployment increased. The significant gains which enterprises in these countries could take out from the new business opportunities in East Europe, evidently have not benefited the populations as a whole (particularly in terms of employment and development of real wages). The Scandinavian countries and the Netherlands had to effectuate significant cuts in social expenditures. Criminality was on the rise in the majority of countries, particularly in those at the borderlines of the Schengen area. Thus, at the macro level, clear winners and losers of integration can be identified.

The perception of the recent socioeconomic developments among the populations

Let us now describe the perceptions and attitudes of the populations in the 15 EU-member countries toward specific areas of politics, and investigate systematically how these are related to objective developments.

Figure 6.3 present the results of the question on the general evaluation of the role of the EU in six selected, central areas of politics. They give no rosy picture: In three out of the five areas—inflation, unemployment and social standards—the percentage of respondents who see a positive role of the EU is lower than of those who see a negative role. In most areas, only about one fourth of the citizens in the EU-15 member states saw a positive role of the EU in 2004. Concerning economic growth and fight against crime, the proportion was around 41–44%, that is, even here less than half of the respondents see a positive influence of the EU. On the other side, negative effects of the EU-politics are felt by 20–30% of the respondents in the areas of preservation of social standards and fight against crime, and between 30% and 51% in all other areas.

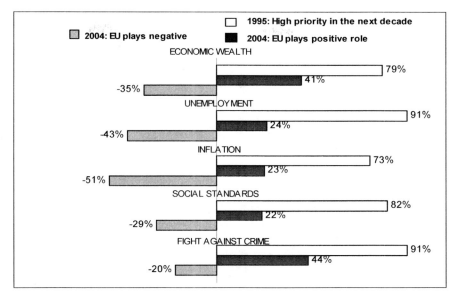

Figure 6.3 Attitudes of the population in the EU-15 concerning political priorities (1995), and evaluation of the actual role of the EU (2004) in five areas (in %)

Source: Eurobarometer 43.1, 45.1, 61.0, 15 EU-member states, n=16216; Question EU plays positive/ negative role: category "neither—nor" omitted.

Significant differences exist between countries in the evaluations of the political impact of the EU. Luxembourg is on top concerning the number of areas where its population sees a positive impact of the EU; but also in Spain, Greece and Ireland, positive evaluations are more frequent than in the EU-15 as a whole. Only in Denmark, positive and negative evaluations coexist. In all other countries, negative evaluations are widespread. This applies particularly to France, Germany and Austria, but also for Italy, Sweden and the United Kingdom. Thus, it seems that subjective perceptions of the citizens correspond quite well to objective developments.

This issue, however, can be investigated also directly by looking at the effects of individual and of macro-level characteristics on the perceptions of the achievements of the EU. Multivariate analysis enables us to check if there exists a significant effect of the objective developments, even if we control for other relevant factors. It is also of interest here which social groups see integration more positively, and which see it more negatively. We can assume that social groups who are able to utilize the new possibilities offered by the large free market will have more positive attitudes than those who may not be able to do so or who are affected negatively by integration.

In order to distinguish clearly between the effects of individual level and macro level characteristics, a multilevel regression analysis is carried out

Table 6.7 Effects of Country Characteristics on the Perception of the Role of the EU in Five Areas 2004 (0=negative; 1=positive influence of the EU); Logistic Multilevel Analysis

Predictors	Inclusion of single predictors			Cumulative models with all predictors				Min	Max	Mean-value	SD
	B-value	SE	Unexplained variance (Uo/SE)	B-value	SE	Unexplained variance (Uo/SE)	Corr[a]				
Model 1: Economic situation											
Adjusted model at micro level			0,11/0,04								
GNP/head (KKS) 2004 (low—high)	-0,00	0,00	0,10/0,03	0,00	0,00			73,1	216,8	114,7	25,1
Mean GNP-growth 1995–2004 (low—high)	0,16*	0,06	0,08/0.03	0,14*	0,06	0,08/0,03	0,18	1,21	6,6	2,5	1,4
Model 2: Labour market											
Adjusted model at micro level			0,11/0,04								
Rate of unemployment 2004 (low—high)	-0,03	0,04	0,11/0,04	-0,06*	0,03			4,5	11,0	7,3	2,3
Change in the rate of unemployment 1995–2004 (decrease—increase)	-0,04	0,03	0,09/0,03	0,02	0,03			-7,8	1,9	-2,2	3,2
Rate of employment 2004 (low—high)	-0,02	0,02	0,10/0,04	-0,02	0,01			57,6	75,7	66,0	5,3
Change in the rate of employment 1995–2004 (decrease—increase)	0,06*	0,02	0,04/0,02	0,07*	0,02	0,03/0,01	0,13	-1	14,0	4,8	4,0

Model 3: Inflation

Adjusted model at micro level			0,08/0,03								
Rate of inflation 2004 (low—high)	0,04	0,09	0,08/0,03	0,04	0,09			0,1	3,2	1,9	0,8
Mean rate of inflation 1995–2004 (decrease—increase)	0,06	0,04	0,07/0,03	0,06	0,05	0,08/0,03	0,08	-4,9	2,0	-0,7	1,6

Model 4. Social standards

Adjusted model at micro level			0,23/0,09								
Social spending 2002 (low—high)	-0,10*	0,02	0,07/0,03	-0,10*	0,02			16	32,5	26,8	4,3
Average growth of social spending 1995–2002 (low—high)	0,01	0,06	0,26/0,10	0,02	0,03	0,07/0,03	0,11	-5,3	4,3	-0,4	2,4

Model 5: Criminality

Adjusted model at micro level			0,08/0,03								
Crime rate 2004 (lowest—highest quartile)[38]	-0,19*	0,06	0,06/0,02	-0,19*	0,07			13,2 (1)	142,8 (4)	66,6	37,1
Change of crime rate 1995–2004 (decrease—increase)	0,00	0,00	0,10/0,04	0,00	0,00	0,06/0,02	0,08	-10	346,5	37,7	82,8

* Significant Beta-value

ᵃCorrelation between observed values and expected values

Guidance for the interpretation: Odds-ratios indicate the relative strength of the effect of an independent variable on the dependent variable. If it is 1, the values of the dependent variable are not affected by a change in the independent variable. If the value is above 1, it means that the value of the dependent variable is increased by this factor; if it is below 1, it decreases correspondingly.

Source: Eurobarometer 2004, EU-15, Basic data N = 16216

(Goldstein 1995). The dependent variables are the perceptions and evaluations of the achievements of the EU in the five different areas of policy discussed before. For reasons of space, not the whole results of this analysis can be presented in *Table 6.6,* but only those referring to the macro-level characteristics. In the statistical analysis, however, the individual and macro-level variables have been entered simultaneously into the regression.

How are the achievements of the EU evaluated among different social groups? Here, the data (not reported in the Table) show that women have a significantly less positive perception of the EU in most areas. The same is true for older, compared to younger people. Better educated people see a more positive influence of the EU than less well educated for economic growth and the fight against unemployment. Employed people see more frequently a positive influence of the EU than the non-employed; but they see also more frequently a negative influence of the EU on social standards. Concerning occupational position, one finding was clearly in contradiction to the expectations: Persons in white collar positions more frequently see a negative effect of the EU on economic growth and inflation than persons in other positions.

Let us now look at the effects of the macro-social characteristics, that is, characteristics of the 15 EU-member countries, on the subjective perceptions of the citizens about the effects of integration. Here, for the different dependent variables (the subjective evaluations concerning growth, unemployment etc.) only those sets of independent variables were considered which seemed to be of substantial relevance. So, for instance, the absolute level of economic wealth of a nation (GNP/ head) and growth of GNP in the period 1995–2004 has been considered as a determinant of the popular perceptions of the EU-effects on growth; for the evaluation of the EU-effects on inflation, the inflation rate in 2004 and the mean inflation rate 1995–2004 have been considered.

The findings in *Table 6.6* may be summarized as follows. (We must keep in mind, again, that the effects of individual characteristics have also been controlled for). First, we find a further confirmation of the thesis that the subjective evaluations of the people are based on the objective developments in their countries. In four out of the five dimensions, objective levels or changes in a specific aspect have a significant impact on the subjective evaluations of this aspect. If economic growth was high, the evaluation of the positive role of the EU in this regard is more positive; the same is true for the change in level of unemployment. In regard to social standards and level of crime, it is the actual level which is related significantly to the perception: If the proportion of social spending was low in 2002, the respondents see more frequently a positive influence of the EU (in fact, social spending in absolute terms has increased much more in such countries); if the level of crime was low, people see a more positive effect of the EU also in this regard.

Thus, we may conclude that critical public perceptions about integration are clearly based on objective socio-economic developments. It is simply wrong to state that the vast majority of the public "does not credit the EC/EU with a significant role in shaping those conditions." (Moussis 2006:189f.) Even in terms of output legitimacy, the EU enjoys a limited degree of consent among its citizens. One additional reason for this may also be the *overambitious, unrealistic target-setting* of the EU. The most obvious example was the *Lisbon process.* At their meeting in Lisbon in March 2000, the heads of the governments set very high targets for the development of the next ten years, which is until 2010. The main aims were to implement fully innovation as the motor of a more dynamic economic growth, create the "knowledge society," and further social cohesion and environmental consciousness throughout the Union; thereby, "the most dynamic and competitive know-ledge based economy in the world" should emerge. Already five years after the proclamation of these aims and strategies, their failure had become obvious. A high-level expert commission which evaluated the progress drew devastating conclusions:[39] "Over the last four years, the overall performance of the European economy has been disappointing . . . halfway to 2010 the overall picture is very mixed and much needs to be done in order to prevent Lisbon from becoming a synonym for missed objectives and failed promises."

What can we conclude from these findings concerning output legitimacy of the EU already here? (An additional examination of this issue shall be carried out in Chapter 8). First, we have seen that the output in fact was not very impressive—much more modest than usually praised by the elites. Second, output legitimacy is closely connected with input legitimacy: Deficits in the first may often contribute also to the low output performance in the multilevel government system of the EU. In areas like agricultural policy, regional development, science policy, EU programs may be much less effective as long as they do not involve a close cooperation of the relevant units and actors. Finally, a neglect of input legitimacy could become fatal for the overall and long-term legitimacy of the EU because here political movements and parties exist which are critical against the system as a whole. In such situations, decreasing performance can also lead to a withdrawal of basic trust and confidence in the system. (See also Weil 1989; McAllister 1994; Hooghe/ Marks 2002).

6.6 Strategies of the elites to win the consent of the citizens for integration

The data presented in this chapter have shown that the support of the citizens for European integration can at most be characterized as lukewarm: Over the EU as a whole, the percentage of those who have a definite positive attitude is not much more than 50%; in considerable subgroups of the populations, and in some member countries, a majority has a negative attitude; the EU seems to have no clear and generally accepted identity

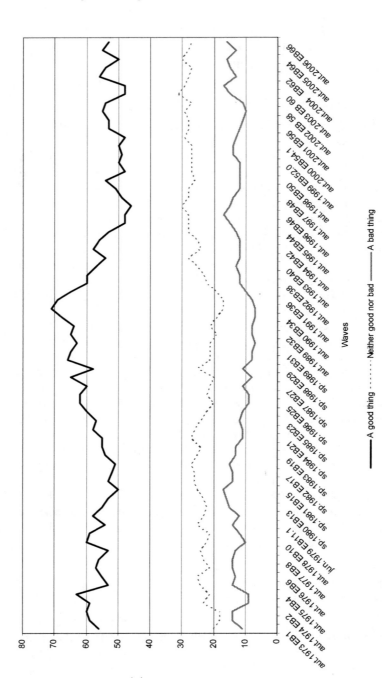

Figure 6.4   Evaluation of EU membership, 1973–2006.

[1] Generally speaking, do you think that (your country's) membership of the European Union is ...
Source: EB1 (1973) – EB66 (2006)

in the different member countries. One fact is very significant here: Over time, there is no trend toward a more positive attitude toward integration. From the early to the mid-1990s, approval was declining, and it has not gone up again since then (*Figure 6.4*). These sobering facts are well known to the "makers" of the EU. One could expect that the European elites will undertake definite efforts to come to grips with these sceptical attitudes and try to develop a more positive understanding of integration among the population. They will also make efforts to grasp continually the public mood of the citizens throughout the EU in order to be able to react to potentially dangerous negative attitudes.

Both these presumptions are true. It is probably safe to assert that no other modern political community invests so much into public relations efforts to improve its image and to justify its actions than the EU. It is probably that political community which uses most extensively the *strategy of persuasion* as an instrument of political steering (the other two strategies are steering through power centralization and through market mechanisms; see Lindblom 1977). There are two ways of persuasion: political indoctrination, used extensively by totalitarian regimes, and advertisement and public relations campaigns, typical for democracies. The cumulative effect of advertisement and public relations can be very successful if they are working over long periods of time. Thus, they lead exactly to *traditional legitimacy* in the sense of Weber (1978a: 226ff.), which consists in the taking for granted political institutions that are legitimate mainly because they are just in existence for a long time.

Three strategies of the EU in this regard shall be discussed shortly here: The continuous and recently intensified information and public relations efforts; the effort to grasp the opinion of the EU citizens through the regular, biannual Eurobarometer surveys; and specific information campaigns and public relations efforts before important decisions.

Marketing European integration and the EU

Public relations activities are a central concern of the European Union. For decades, the EU has distributed pamphlets and high-gloss brochures, organised visits to Brussels, and conducted tours through the EU buildings. The tone of these pamphlets reads as follows: "The European Union is in several regards a remarkable story of success. In more than 50 years it has raised the standard of living of its citizens to a level unmatched hitherto. It has created a single market without frontiers and a common currency, the Euro. It is an important economic power and leading world-wide in developmental aid . . ."[40] Everything which has been achieved in Europe seems to be credited to the EU. After the rejection of the Constitution for Europe in France and the Netherlands, these efforts have been intensified. A vice-president of the Commission (Margot Wallström) is in charge of the communication strategy. In a series of papers,[41] the Commission has declared its intent to enforce these activities in the EU and at the national levels. These include the creation of "European public spaces" where people can get information and discuss EU issues together with officials; a new Internet strategy for interactive discussion and a new audiovisual strategy to produce EU affairs programmes; more cooperation with the media and supply them with "high quality news and current affairs material"; visits of EU officials to member countries and instituting "European Goodwill Ambassadors" in them; holding "Round Tables for Democracy" in member-state cities. However, it is quite clear that all these efforts do not grasp the real problem of the low interest in and image of the EU among the citizens. This comes clearly out if we look more closely at the principles of this new "communication strategy."

First, it has an undoubted elitist character; even if it is argued that the representatives of civil society and even citizens shall be included and listened to, only a tiniest fraction of the nearly 500 million inhabitants can be reached by all these efforts. Margot Wallström reports on her homepage, for instance, that 305 visits of EU officials to member countries took place since Plan D was started in 2005, and 20,000 comments were posted on the online discussion forum Debate Europe. Second, instead of "a genuine dialogue" between citizens and officials, the whole communication strategy is clearly a one-way matter, transmitting information about the achievements of the EU to the citizens. Experiences with the concrete outcomes of many of the aforementioned round tables were quite disappointing. Third, the main problems of citizens' disenchantment are not tackled, namely, the democratic deficit of the EU and its focus on (neoliberal) market integration. All referenda about EU affairs have shown that when citizens really have the possibility to decide something by their votes, an intense public discussion is arising. The neglect of this aspect is clearly implied in the focus of the EU information campaign on "delivering results" and the aim "to clarify, deepen and legitimise a new consensus on Europe" (Plan D).

On special, important occasions and decisions, the EU carries out systematic *public relations campaigns* in order to get the approval of the citizens to their aims. One such campaign has been analysed in detail by Cris Shore (2000:97ff.). It was the campaign for the introduction of the euro in 1996; many of the features of this action can be found in other cases as well. This campaign, carried out by the EU Commission, involved the elaboration and distribution of policy documents; the commissioning of opinion polls; the provision of a budget, approved by the EP; the appointment of key personnel, including marketing specialists, and a bureaucratic infrastructure. At this time, the introduction of the euro was a very difficult and contested issue (in Germany, a majority of the citizens were against it). The EU elites, including leading member-state politicians, such as German Chancellor Helmut Kohl, saw in the common currency a grand political project, one helping on the process of integration strongly. However, this political aspect was downplayed and depoliticized by the European elites; the euro was presented to the people as "a safe and certain venture," with only positive consequences for all member states and citizens. A variety of strategies was used toward this aim, including "leaflets, glossy brochures, newsletters and 'information kits,' to conferences, round tables, radio and television broadcasting, videos at informing trade unions and businesses about the benefits the euro will bring to the world of work" (Shore 2000:103). Although the EU officials in public asserted that Europe cannot be built without the consent of the citizens, public attitudes in practice were considered as something which could and should be changed, according to the preconceived plan to introduce the euro. The Commission, in particular, tried to play down its political role, and to present itself as a nonpartisan broker of information; for this aim, even the word *campaign* was abandoned and displaced by *information activity*. A main reason for the banishment of the word *campaign* was that it implies that there is something to argue about; "'information action' not only construes the Commission's role as neutral and non-partisan, it also implicitly casts the single currency as an issue closed to debate, outside the realms of politics" (Shore 2000:106). In personal interviews, however, the Commission representatives were unable to conceal the ambiguity of this distinction. The negative findings of opinion polls were disregarded in this case; what the citizens thought was irrelevant to the outcome of the campaign.

Drawing upon public opinion democracy

A central element of the relation of the EU to its citizens has long since been the careful recording of public opinion. For this aim, the Eurobarometer (EB) has been established already in 1973 as a series of regular, representative population surveys, carried out two times a year.[42] In all member countries, 1,000 (or less in ministates) persons are interviewed about their general attitude toward European integration, and about specific, varying topics. The EU may be the first political community which has established such an instrument in order to get regular and reliable information about the political opinions of their citizens. It can also be considered as an instrument which helps to legitimize its actions (Bornschier 2000a:33), given the fact that direct democratic procedures (elections, referenda) are not highly relevant for its politics. The regular surveys on political opinions of the EU can be compared to the commissioners (*maitres des requetes*) of the French *Ancien Régime,* who had to visit and inspect the provinces and collect all kinds of data which could be relevant for the preservation of central power (Puntscher-Riekmann 1998:89ff.). The results from the Eurobarometer are published regularly and their data made available to the interested public (e.g., social scientists) without cost. In this regard, the implementation of this method cannot be considered as problematic from the viewpoint of normative democratic theory. In fact, the EB data are a very valuable source for social-scientific data analyses, particularly concerning long-term time trends. However, there are several aspects of the EB which are also problematic. These problems are now recognized also by the media.[43]

First, the sponsoring of the EB surveys by the EU is problematic. Methodological research has shown that the type of sponsor can have a significant effect on responses (Stocké and Becker 2004). If an interviewer introduces himself as carrying out a survey on behalf of the European Union, it is probable that the answers will be biased somewhat toward the positive side, although the effect may not be large.[44] Independent survey institutes often get much less positive answers to European integration than EB surveys. This fact has been documented for Germany (von Arnim 2006:100), and it is also evident if we look at the results of the EU-wide survey of Open Europe, reported in *Table 8.2.*

Second, the themes and questions included in the EB series are somewhat lopsided. Questions on critical issues, such as bureaucratism, waste, corruption, and the like, are not included at all. If questions on controversial topics are asked, often only the positive aspects are picked out and the negative ones omitted. The common agricultural policy is one of these controversial issues, as shown in Chapter 4. In EB 50/1998, it was asked: *"Twenty years ago, the member states of the European Community were trying to solve a certain number of common problems together. Here is a list of some of them. Could you please tell me which one of the problems, you think, is the most important at the present time?"* Among thirteen issues, the following was related to agriculture: *"Modernising European agriculture by encouraging the most productive farms and providing retraining people who leave agriculture."* None of the many fundamental problems and contradictions of this policy was mentioned. Frequently, issues are included in the EB on which the respondents cannot have an adequate level of knowledge; this is the case in the frequently asked question about trust in EU institutions, which includes not only the parliament and the Commission but also the European Court of Auditors, the Committee of the Regions, and the Economic and Social Committee; all of these are probably known only to a tiny fraction of Europeans, even among academics. Often, the formulation of the issues itself presupposes problematic theories or premises. This is the case in the following question: *"From the following list, who do you trust most to get the effects of globalisation under control? The (nationality) government; the EU, NGOs . . ."* (EB 55).

Third, a positive bias toward integration is often produced by the formulation of questions. Research on survey methods has also shown that the formulation of questions can have a significant impact on the responses (Rossi et al. 1983; Diekmann 1995). The suggestive character of some EB questions was evident already in the example about the agricultural policy mentioned before. It is even more so in this example: *"I'm going to read out a list of actions that the EU could undertake. For each one, please tell me if, in your opinion, it should be a priority, or not? Successful enlargement of the EU1 to include new member countries."* (EB 59). In the same EB, a battery of eleven items was asked concerning an EU foreign policy; all of them were positive, and none of the negative consequences of such a policy was mentioned. In EB 61 it is asked if *"the presidency of the [European Council] should be extended because six months is too short to achieve significant results."* A clever and candid respondent could only answer no because, if the statement were true, the EU would not have achieved significant results up the present day! Respondents are rather patient and ready to answer even questions which are rather meaningless to them; evidence for the relevance of this tendency in the EB series is the fact that the percentages of nonresponse usually are rather small. Combined with the tendency in favour of positive answers (if alone, in order to please the interviewer), this may explain the generally very positive picture about integration which comes out of the EB surveys

Finally, also the analysis of the data and the presentation of the findings from the EB surveys is problematic in several regards. First, the usual mode of presentation of the findings is by displaying the linear results for the member countries; mass media often report in headlines about these results. It is well known, however, that a comparison of marginal distributions between countries can often be highly misleading, since these distributions are also determined by differing sampling schemes, weighting of the data, and the like (Jowell et al. 2007) . Second, the interpretation of findings frequently is done in a rather naïve pro-EU way; often, the presentation of them alone suggests such a view. A few examples from EB 63 (spring 2005): It is reported that trust in "The European Union" is 44%, which is the third place after the United Nations and the national justice and legal systems, but clearly higher than trust in the national parliament and government. It is evident, however, that a main factor for respondents' positive evaluations of these political institutions was the distance of them from personal experience (as it is in the case in the UNO and the EU). Under the headline "But the quality of life in the European Union is deemed incomparable" it is reported that the majority of the respondents believe that the quality of life in Europe (not in the EU) is better than in the U.S. and Japan, not to speak of China and India. It is reported that the EU outperforms the U.S. in six out of ten areas (environment protection, healthcare, education, fighting social discrimination, disparities, unemployment); however, in fact many citizens believe—with good reasons—that European integration tends to increase social disparities and unemployment; moreover, the main actors in these areas are the member states, not the EU.

Inventing and nourishing myths about integration

All these strategies and actions can be summarized under the mechanism of the creation of "myths" about European integration. Political scientists have shown that the political process has two sides: (a) the real interests, fights, and outcomes and (b) the public presentation of these interests and the power structures behind them and the working of these processes by the elites (Edelman 1972; Schöpflin 2000:79ff.). Between these two aspects, often a remarkable discrepancy exists. Political myths are created about fundamental and contested issues which are complex and ambiguous; their creation is not necessarily a conscious camouflage by the elites, but it helps to provide a plausible interpretation for complex problems, to constitute coherence and moral integrity for a political community. Political elites tend to recapitulate these myths continuously and to legitimize their actions in this way. So they appear to be working for the best of all, while in fact they pursue also their own interests. In the case of European integration, quite a number of such myths have been created successfully (indicated by the fact that they are very seldom challenged; see also Hellström 2006):

- European integration has been the decisive process which secured peace in Europe since 1945.
- European integration is an irreversible process. If the integration process is delayed by some countries, the whole process of integration is endangered. Politicians who take actions which lead to such events—such as President Chirac when he announced a referendum about the Constitution for Europe—make a big mistake. A concomitant of this myth may be the thesis that 70–80% of all national laws are already determined by European institutions.
- European integration is necessary to control the economic dangers of economic globalisation. After its unquestioned popularity for over a decade and the appearance of hundreds, if not thousands of books on this term, it now becomes more and more clear that globalisation is only a catchword including a variety of very different processes and outcomes.
- European integration is necessary for continued economic growth in Europe, and it works to the benefit of all social groups, countries, and regions. It is also necessary in order to protect European agriculture and to assist in the development of the poorer countries and regions in South and East Europe.

Both of these last two assertions and the other myths have been discussed extensively in other chapters of this book, so there is no need to resume these discussions here.

CONCLUSION

The analyses of this chapter have shown: Among the different member countries, in different macroregions within the EU, and among elites and citizens, quite different interests, aims, and expectations are connected with European integration. For some of them, European integration is a means to achieve a new, powerful role in the world; for others, it is a means to overcome economic backwardness and political instability. For some, the EU should remain (or become again) a pure big market; others want it to develop further into a welfare state writ large. Also in terms of "output legitimacy," the socioeconomic achievements, an unisonous view about the EU can hardly develop. These achievements are much less outstanding than proclaimed by the elites and this fact is well recognized by the citizens. The self-conception of the EU as a community of values, or as a political institution designated to secure the typical "European way of life," do not offer promising ways out of these many contradictions. Also in cultural and religious terms, the EU internal differentiations (if not contradictions) prevail over commonalities; the "European way of life" is a dim phenomenon, hardly sufficient to build an encompassing new political community on. Is there at all a way out of this dilemma? A sustainable concept, on which the further development and finality of the European Union can be based, must certainly include values as Philip Alston and Joseph Weiler (1999:13) have written: "There is something terribly wrong with a polity which acts rigorously to realize its economic ambitions . . . but which at the same time, conspicuously neglects its parallel ethical and legal obligations to ensure that those policies result in the fullest possible enjoyment of human rights." However, there are two issues in this regard which have to be considered. First, it is the question what the values are to which European integration should be obliged first of all. We must also look at the relation between the formal declaration of values (which receives ample space in all basic EU documents) and their real embodiment in concrete institutions, norms, and political practices. Second, the reference to values alone is not enough. The European Union is not a religous community but a political community. As such, its main task is to look for the assertion and preservation of the interests of its citizens. How these two aspects can be reconciled is the topic of the next two chapters. In the following chapter, we discuss the issue of the ideas and values that have been connected with the "dream of Europe" for centuries. In the final chapter, the issues of the character and finality of the European Union and the question how values and interests can be reconciled with each other are taken up.

7 The Dream of Europe
Intellectual Ideas of Integration and their "Realization"

INTRODUCTION

In this first chapter, we will look at the ideas of European unification and integration as they have been developed through modern history. In this regard, intellectual elites have played the most important role. Intellectuals are persons who are concerned with social developments and problems from rational and moral points of view and who try to win recognition and influence among the public and in politics with their publications and writings (Shils 1982:179ff.). The notion of "intellectual" (intelligentsia) had been invented in countries like Russia, Poland, and France in the nineteenth century when they were fighting against totalitarian or foreign ruling classes or unscrupulous power elites; in these cases, they were also supporting revolutionary movements (Charle 2001; Winock 2003). In earlier times, intellectuals were often freelancing journalists or writers and living in precarious material and social circumstances; today, intellectuals are typically employed as public officials (such as university professors), commercially successful writers, and so forth. Intellectuals orient themselves (or claim to do so) toward universal human values, such as justice, rationality, and truth; because of this, they often tend to clash with the ruling elites. Intellectuals are chronically dissatisfied; they suffer from the state of society; and from this, utopian thinking emerges which designs a better world (Lepenies 1992). There are many different types of intellectuals, and their roles vary between epochs, societies, and cultures, depending on the character of the political regime (Münch 1986; Korom 2007). Intellectuals have not always been in opposition to the powerful; they can also serve as "ideologues," that is, providers of ideas and arguments for the governing political elites. Not thoroughness but sensibility is the virtue of intellectuals; their theoretical constructs are often wrong, but they always "see something very well" (Mannheim 1970:457).

Intellectuals have also thought quite early about European integration, and their thoughts have been interesting for the general public and useful for the political elites. Since the beginning of European integration in the early 1950s, the political elites claim that their strategy to integrate

Europe has been inspired by the ideas of great and respected intellectuals in history. Confronted with the concrete shape that European integration has taken since the early 1950s, we will show that several divergences can be observed. Among most historical thinkers, the formation of a political union among the states and peoples of Europe had one main aim: the creation and preservation of peace. They foresaw two strategies to secure this aim: the establishment of republican (democratic) constitutions in all European states and that of a loose confederation or league between them. The actual shape and development of unification since 1952, however, was toward *integration*—that is, the creation of a new political community which in some regards displaces the existing nation-states and takes over their competences. Among the present-day intellectual elites, many support this development; the academic profession of the jurists is even among its main promoters.

A further discrepancy is that there was not one unique but several different historical visions of an integrated Europe. The same was true for the movements for a United Europe after the Second World War. While the Federalists aimed at the creation of a true European federal state, the Unionists (represented by W. Churchill) aspired only to a loose cooperation modelled after the British Commonwealth. Some of them contained even quite problematic ideas from a present-day point of view. The positive among these visions are used and mentioned in solemn speeches and ceremonial addresses by the elites on many occasions; the less positive, however, are mentioned seldom or not at all.

This chapter is structured as follows. First, an overview is given on the historical visions of Europe. It will be shown that quite different visions have been developed in this regard—visions which hardly can be subsumed under one general topic of "European integration." Second, Kant's central idea in regard to the unification of European, the establishment of republican-democratic constitutions as a precondition for peace, is outlined. Third, the ideas of the intellectuals are confronted with the real aims and patterns of institutional development of the EC/EU since 1957 and with the content of the Constitution for Europe. Finally, the role of intellectuals and academic professions since 1945 is investigated.

7.1 The dream of Europe in history: A critical analysis of the ideas of European unification from the Abbé de Saint-Pierre (1713) until Richard Coudenhove-Kalergi (1923)

This short overview presents the ideas of European integration from the early eighteenth till the early twentieth century, not in a chronological order but according to the main topics and visions on which they rely. A distinction is made between positive and respected, universal aims connected with European integration which are still accepted today. However, there exist also less positive ideas which either are not any more acceptable today or

266 European Integration as an Elite Process

which are not expressed openly because they are related to a new kind of power politics. Second, we discuss in more detail the ideas of one outstanding figure in this regard, Immanuel Kant, and the ideas and the fate of the nineteenth-century national movements in Germany and Italy. These are paradigmatic cases for the fact that the ideas of national independence and freedom, democracy, and peace were considered as inseparable by the intellectuals but not by the ruling classes of the time. The latter realized only the ideas of national independence and power, often at the expense of freedom, democracy, and peace.

Comprehensive overviews on the idea of "Europe" have been given by many authors (see Foerster 1963; Tschubarjan 1992; Lützeler 1992; Wilson and van der Dussen 1995; Pagden and Hamilton 2002). Here, a systematic analysis is carried out from two sociological points of view. One is the concept of *sociology as science of social reality* in the sense of Max Weber (Weber 1973; Lepsius 1988). In this view, ideas have significant importance for human action and social processes; their relevance, however, can be evaluated only in connection with interests. The other approach is a critical *sociology of knowledge,* which looks at the practical and political use of ideas and the social and ideological backgrounds of their proponents (Mannheim 1970; Bouden 1986; Camic and Gross 2004). The task here is to "bring Europe down to earth" (Hellström 2006), that is, to investigate how the public language and speaking, influenced mostly by the political elites, determines what "Europe" is or should be. By these references, the elites want to give a kind of intellectual consecration or blessing to a political process which is guided to a large degree by mundane interests.

Three specific theses are proposed: (1) We cannot find a unique or consistent model of European integration among the historical authors. The frequent political reference to the "idea of Europe" suppresses the fact that very different models of an integrated Europe were proposed (see also Tschubarjan 1992; Joerissen 2001). (2) Most of the authors of books, essays, and pamphlets on the idea of Europe did not imagine an integrated Europe in the form as it has been founded by the Treaty of Rome and developed further since then. For many of them, the reference to Europe was just a strategy to mask the power interests of their own nation. Some of them have even envisioned an authoritarian, antidemocratic, and imperialistic "United Europe." (3) for many authors—as for the postwar makers of the European Community and Union—the unification and integration of this continent was a strategy to define and demarcate Europe form "others" seen as actual or potential hostile threats.

The general thesis is: We cannot say that the European Union "realises" a century-old dream of Europe, simply because there was no coherent, single dream of this sort. Rather, we must say that the makers of the EU use the intellectual ideas about "Europe" to justify and legitimate their own political ambitions. In this regard, they proceed in exactly the same way as all nation-states did when they tried to establish the historical legitimacy of their political aspirations (Faber 1979; Smith 1991; Swedberg 1994; Haller 1996a, b). In this regard, the present-day builders of "Europe" only continue a practice which originated already in the High Middle Ages. The concept of "Europe" was invented by the intellectuals of Charlemagne as a more respectable concept than that of *imperium occidentale*. In fact, however, his imperium and Charlemagne himself are quite mythical figures and entities (Segl 1993; Illig 2001).

In the following, we discuss, first, the positive views of European integration and their main components; and, second, we look at some of the less noble visions and proposals. Not only single intellectuals but also relevant social movements will be considered.

(a) Europe as a continent of democratic and peaceful nations

Four ideas have been central to the thinkers about Europe since l'Abbé de Saint-Pierre published his famous essay *Projet de paix perpetuelle entre les souverain chrétiens* in 1713: (1) The prevention of wars and the establishment of a stable peace in Europe; (2) the establishment of republican-democratic governments in all nations; (3) the preservation of the cultural richness and diversity of Europe; (4) the establishment of a European confederation or league of nations.

The prevention of wars and the securing of peace

This was a central aim of most authors who wrote about European integration. Let us discuss only three authors from the eighteenth, nineteenth, and twentieth centuries. The idea of the establishment of a "perpetual peace" was central in the influential work of Abbé de Saint-Pierre (1658–1743). Saint-Pierre was also a diplomat and is considered as a forerunner of the philosophy of Enlightenment. The intent of Saint-Pierre's proposal was to replace the thinking in terms of a power balance among the European princedoms by the idea of a peaceful federation or league of the twenty-four largest European states. The proposal foresaw also an economic integration by creating a free-trade area but did not think about any changes in the monarchical constitutions of the states.

The term "United States of Europe" was introduced for the first time in the mid-nineteenth century by the Scottish writer Charles Mackay, who had travelled extensively through North America and published books about its cultural history (Lützeler 1992:152ff.). The prevention of future wars in Europe was also his central idea. He considered also the liberal press, free trade, and the principle of the representation of the people of the United States as exemplary. Also, Mackay did not foresee a European government but only a federation in which all sovereign states with constitutional governments could become members.

An important element of the fight against wars in Europe was the *Peace Movement,* which was developing in the 1840s. Five large peace congresses took place between 1843 and 1851 (Tschubarjan 1992:67). This movement developed also the idea of European integration. As a consequence of the rise of nationalism in the second half of the nineteenth century, the peace movement lost its dynamic, however. An exception was the Austrian countess and writer Bertha von Suttner (1843–1914); her autobiographic and pacifistic novel *Die Waffen nieder* (Lay Down the Arms), first published in 1889, became a worldwide success (printed in nearly forty editions and translated into a dozen languages).[1] After World War I, these ideas appeared again. Peace on the European level was certainly an aim of Coudenhove-Kalergi, the founder of the Pan-Europa movement in the early 1920s. Yet I would argue, as most authors do, that this was not his primary aim (see, e.g., Wilson and van der Dussen 1993:99; see next).

The establishment of republican and democratic national constitutions and a European parliament

The most comprehensive plan for European unification of the nineteenth century was developed by the French social philosopher and publicist Saint-Simon (1760–1825) in his book *De la réorganisation de la société Européenne* (1814; Lützeler 1992:72ff.). Saint-Simon, of noble origin, participated actively in the American war for independence; during the French Revolution he worked as a businessman, but by the way also as a productive writer and journalist. He developed an early version of utopian socialism with Christian influences.

Saint-Simon criticized the Congress of Vienna, where many statesmen spoke of the necessity to create a new European order, which, in fact, however, foresaw only the reestablishment of the old dynastic system. As a consequence, he argued, also the wars associated with such an order would soon reappear. For Saint-Simon, the main precondition for the establishment of peace was the abolishment of absolutism and the introduction of parliamentarian systems throughout Europe. National parliaments should send delegates to a European parliament which should arbitrate conflicts between the states. Its tasks were to establish a European code of law, ensure peace, guarantee religious tolerance, develop and control education, and create an infrastructure for transport in Europe; all this should be guided by a new kind of transconfessional spiritual power. The European institutions should not replace the national political institutions; no centralized European state should be created but only a confederation of independent, sovereign states. In Saint-Simon's general view, however, government was less a matter of democratic election and decision procedures than one of skilful administration. The rhetoric of the politicians should be substituted by the positive knowledge and skill of bankers, industrialists, and scientists (Siedentop 2001:32). From this point of view, Saint-Simon was an important provider of ideas for the successful French model of European integration culminating in the famous "Monnet-method" (Swedberg 1994).

Saint Simon's model has in fact been realized to a considerable degree by postwar European integration with one important exception, however: There is no mentioning of a European public service at all in his thinking but only that of a European parliament. In the factual integration of Europe, however, the bureaucracy has been accorded the leading position from the beginning as shown in Chapter 5.

Probably the most important intellectual figure in the twentieth-century discussions about "Europe" was the Austrian count Richard Coudenhove-Kalergi (1894–1972). Also for Coudenhove-Kalergi, the prevention of wars and the establishment of a lasting peace in Europe was an important aim (Lützeler 1992:312ff.; Coudenhove-Kalergi 1953; 1958). He saw the reconciliation between France and Germany as the first step toward this aim. After the publication of his book *Pan-Europa* and the establishment of the Journal *Paneuropa* in 1923/24, Coudenhove-Kalergi contacted and won the support of many intellectuals and politicians throughout Europe. For Coudenhove-Kalergi, European unification was necessary in order to break with the past; he imagined this as a stepwise process, beginning with a pan-European conference, which had to adopt the statutes of a confederation; later on, a customs union and, finally, a fully integrated political union should be created. Coudenhove-Kalergi had no direct influence on the shape of European integration, as it developed from 1953 on; Jean Monnet even looked at him with some contempt. It is my thesis, however, that the idea of peace was only secondary in the visions of Coudenhove-Kalergi; his main motivation was to make Europe a new power in the world. (We will come back to this below.) In this regard, his vision did in fact influence the politics of European integration, although this point is much less emphasized in public.

The preservation of the cultural richness and diversity of Europe

This was also a recurrent topic of many writers focussing on Europe, particularly those of German romanticism in the early nineteenth century. One of the first representatives of it was the great German philosopher of history and culture Johann Gottfried Herder (1744–1803). Herder developed the forceful idea that a positive understanding of all cultures and languages of the different peoples of the world is necessary since all are highly valuable (Lützeler 1992:19ff.). Herder's concept of the "peoples" and their distinctive spirit (*Volksgeist*) was taken up by the German romanticist school and could be used as an intellectual weapon in the national independence fights against Napoleon. The national peculiarities should be preserved against the big equalizer, Napoleon, who "wanted to impose in too many areas (such as administration, military, judiciary, education) unification, rationalization, and centralization" (Lützeler 1992:21).

There were several further German authors writing about Europe in the spirit of Herder. One was the German poet Novalis with his essay "Die Christenheit oder Europa" (1799). This was more an apology against the new bourgeois materialism and a romantic plea for a renewed Christianity than a political manifesto (Wilson and van der Dussen 1993:69). Another one was Ernst Moritz Arndt. He was also an influential political writer for the insurgence against Napoleon and for German unification. In Germany, but also in England and France, several new journals were established around 1830 whose intent was to introduce foreign literature and arts to their compatriots. A German example was August Lewald's *Europa. Chronik der gebildeten Welt*, a French one *L'Europe littéraire* (Lützeler 1992:131). However, these journals had also a cosmopolitan orientation including, for instance, a critique of anti-Semitism. The "twin" of these German authors on the French side was Germaine de Stael, who wrote a very positive and influential portrait of Germany (*De l'Allemagne*, 1810). Similar intents—although with a more pragmatic and conservative undertone—were pursued by the Prussian (later Austrian) political philosopher and diplomat Friedrich Gentz in his *Fragments From the Most Recent History of the Political Equilibrium in Europe*. His basic aim was the restoration of the old dynastic order after its abolition by Napoleon.[2]

The establishment of a Confederation or League of Nations

The establishment of a European federation of nations was never seen as an end in itself. The main idea was that through such a federation trust and long-standing peaceful relations between the different nation-states could be established. This idea was clearly present in the first full text on Europe of the Abbé de Saint-Pierre. It is no surprise that a close political integration of Europe was no ideal of English or Scottish authors, as we have seen in the case of Charles Mackay. The same was true for the romantic thinkers and the supporters of the nationalistic movements in Germany and Italy. They all laid great emphasis on the uniqueness and preservation of the different cultures and societies and, therefore, also on the political autonomy and independence of the nation-states established on their basis. For many of them, the old Holy Roman Empire of German Nationality has been a model. This empire did not resemble a highly integrated modern state, even if we think only of large, federal states. It was rather a pre- or supranational entity, a political community based on feudal bonds, a kind of an umbrella organization which included many territories of differing size and legal status. The provincial rulers recognized the Kaiser, the imperial laws and courts, but codetermined the politics of the Reich. It was neither a federal state nor an association of states; its legal character was most of the time in dispute.

(b) Internal order and stability, national hegemony, and global power of Europe

The following ideas of Europe in history are less noble than those sketched out in the preceding section. Three themes can be found in this regard: European unification and integration as a means (1) to establish internal order and to suppress revolutionary movements; (2) to erect the hegemony of one's own nation; (3) as a step of Europe toward a global power.

European integration as a means to suppress internal revolutionary movements and to establish an elitist system

This least noble of all motives for European integration was already present in the path-breaking proposal of the Abbé de Saint-Pierre. He argued that a European federation made it possible to reduce the armies necessary for wars against each other; these forces could be concentrated, therefore, on the suppression and striking down of internal revolutions in the member states (Lützeler 1992:15).

An influential, more recent author in this regard is the German philosopher Friedrich Nietzsche (1844–1900). One of the main topics of this excentric, eloquent writer was the critique of religion and morale. He distinguished between a "masters" and a "slaves morale"; the first is typical for strong and powerful men and social groups, the latter for the poor and miserables. In their case, morale is also motivated by envy and resentment. Nietzsche coined the term *Übermensch* (overman)—a person in whom the will to power is concentrated and who is exempted from all moral restrictions. Nietzsche sees no progress in history—rather, everything which happens has already happened before and will return ever and ever. The radical and provocative but ambiguous concepts of Nietzsche provided inspirations for many later thinkers and movements. Fascism and National Socialism referred to his antidemocratic-elitist posture and his glorification of war even if Nietzsche himself disdained narrow-minded nationalism (which he criticized as German *teutonomania*) and anti-Semitism.

At several places in his work, Nietzsche refers to Europe (Lützeler 1992:190ff.; Bassina and Bas 2002). He argues that in the historical evolution of Europe, "the weak" and their political ideology, democracy, have gained more and more influence. The unification of Europe provides a possibility to overcome the nation-state system and democracy altogether although, in the first phase, Europeanisation will strengthen democracy. Later on, however, it will lead to a bifurcation: On the one side, among the masses, it will produce a human type "prepared for a new slavery." On the other side, "a 'strong man' will emerge—unprejudiced, of a dangerous and attractive character, a 'tyrant' unwittingly reared by the European democracy" (Bassina and Bas 2002:8) In Nietzsche's view, in the future a new pan-European mixed race and ruling caste will emerge. The rise of the latter will be furthered by an aristocratic education and a peculiar supranational aristocratic solidarism which will transcend national narrow-mindedness. A positive example for Nietzsche was France and Napoleon; the latter was the greatest symbol of his own ideal, the "good European."

Some of Nietzsche's ideas on Europe—the overcoming of narrow-minded nationalisms but also the striving toward power—remain influential till today.[3] An author congenial to Nietzsche in several regards was Oswald Spengler. His highly successful book *The Decline of the West,* published in 1918, propagated the rise of a heroic, action-oriented, and rational "faustic" type of man, a new "caesar" in Europe. Writers in the spirit of Nietzsche were also the elite theorists who saw the split between "elites" and "masses" and the power fights between elites as ever-recurring elements of human history.

European unification as a means to establish national hegemony

This idea was already present among one of the first authors who wrote about European integration. This was the Duke of Sully, a high officer during the Thirty Years' War. In his treatise *Grand Dessein,* he proposed a Christian-European federal republic with equal recognition of all Christian confessions, free trade, and the securing of peace through a common police force (Lützeler 1992:15ff.). The paradigm for his proposal was France under king Henry IV, who had freed the country from civil war, introduced religious tolerance, and furthered economic integration. However, an important part of his plan was the disempowerment of the Habsburgs as the dominant dynasty in Europe; the members of this family should not have been elected any more as emperors.

One of the most paradoxical representatives of this theme has been Napoleon Bonaparte. During his regime, he had no vision of an integrated Europe; his main objective was to establish the predominance of France over Europe (Lützeler 1992:70; Salvatorelli 1971; Tschubarjan 1992:37ff.). Napoleon, discovered the idea of Europe during the time of his last exile at the isle of St. Helena (1915–1821). The fact that his *Mémorial de Sainte Hélène* (1823) became one of the greatest best sellers of the nineteenth century shows that the intellectuals and educated strata of those times were fascinated by great personalities and empires (Sieburg 1971; Tschubarjan 1992:40). Even wars are often admired by contemporaries and later generations if they have been successful and have led to the establishment of large regimes (Hondrich 2002). Napoleon depicted the ideal constitution of Europe as a confederal system (Lützeler 1992:70ff.; Foerster 1963:167f.). In his memoirs, Napoleon tried to legitimize retroactively his regime as a logical continuation of the revolution. He wrote that it was his intention to realize such a system after the eventual successful campaign against Russia in 1812 (which failed dreadfully, however). Elements of this system should be a European congress, a European code of law and high court, uniform measuring units, free navigation, and the abolition of standing armies.

A conservative and restorative idea of Europe was also behind the loose union of the Holy Alliance, established after the defeat of Napoleon by the tsar of Russia, the emperor of Austria, and the king of Prussia (Wilson and van der Dussen 1993:70; Tschubarjan 1992:52ff.). This early supranational organization tolerated no interference into the alliance of throne and altar and cooperated in the suppression of national and liberal agitators. It was a kind of "international government of the great powers" (Morgenthau 1962:456ff.).

One of the more recent intellectuals belonging to this category was the German Friedrich Naumann (1860–1919). In his successful book *Mitteleuropa*, he proposed that Germany and Austria-Hungary should unite themselves into a great power state which would exert political leadership in central Europe (Wilson and van der Dussen 1993:90f.). Naumann could rely on ideas developed in 1879 by the historian Constantin Frantz in his book *Der Föderalismus*. Interestingly, Naumann's dreams of a great Germanic power were spread to a broad public through a crime novel of a British author (Henry Cord Meyer), *The Great Impersonation*, published in 1920 (Lützeler 1992:263). This book and with it the ideas of Naumann were received enthusiastically also by the National Socialists; until 1945, Meyer's novel was printed in forty-five editions.

Also several other authors used the idea of European integration mainly to legitimize a reestablishment of the predominance of their own nations over the rest of Europe. Among them was Mazzini's idea of democratizing and uniting Europe with Italy and Rome as its new spiritual centre. In 1821, the German Catholic writer *Joseph Görres* published his essay "Europe and the Revolution," in which he proposed a European federation of peoples as a kind of a renewed Holy Roman Empire, with a new German empire as its center. Miguel de Unamuno argued that the fundamentally Catholic Spain had no need to become "Europeanized" but rather the reverse was necessary, namely, a "Hispanisation" of Europe (Lützeler 1992:212).

The unification of Europe as a step toward a global power

This motive was clearly present already in the first proposal for a European federation of the Abbé de Saint-Pierre, discussed previously. For him, such a federation would provide a strong force against attacks from the Ottoman Empire. He thought in terms of a structuring of the world in large continental powers; so he also proposed an Asian federation of states (Lützeler 1992:15). The same idea was present in Schmidt-Phiseldeks's proposal of a European federation, published in 1821. This author saw two reasons for the necessity of such a federation: The increasing internal integration of the different parts of Europe and the rise of the United States to a new big power. More recently, this idea was central in the successful book *Le Declin de l'Europe* of the French geographer Albert Demangeon (1920). In this book, a precursor of Jean-Jacques Servan-Schreiber's postwar best seller *Le Dèfi Américaine,* the author documents with extensive statistics the economic and political backslide of Europe after the First World War compared with the United States; Europe, he argued, in some ways already appeared as a colony of the New World.

Photo 8a   Richard Coudenhove-Kalergi, 1953: "Europe marches with rapid steps toward its unification. In a few years, it will be a federal state which begins with Germany, France, Italy and the Benelux states, supplemented by the African colonial empires of France and Belgium . . . This federal state will be a powerful world empire, coequal to its British and American allies."

Source: Paneuropabewegung, Österreich.

The most influential author for whom the idea of Europe as a new world power was central, however, was Richard Coudenhove-Kalergi, the founder of the Pan-Europa movement (Wilson van der Dussen 1993:96ff.). Coudenhove-Kalergi is widely quoted by leading European politicians, and he was the first to be awarded with the Karls-Preis of the city of Aachen. In 1922, Coudenhove-Kalergi started his untiring propaganda campaign for a "United Europe." His writings continually blend the normative and empirical-factual perspective (in this way, they anticipate a typical kind of reasoning of European political elites today): "Continental Europe from Portugal to Poland will either amalgamate itself or already in the course of this century perish politically, economically, and culturally." In his book *The European Nation* (1953), published after World War II, he makes the accurate observation that most federations have originated in situations of external threats (see Chapter 2. Coudenhove-Kalergi sees European integration as a direct and necessary consequence of the new threat from the Bolshevik Soviet Union (see also Tschubarjan 1992:139ff.). He makes the following observations in this regard:

"*Since the revolution, a new elite stratum arose [in the Soviet Union] which included Russians and Ukrainians, Georgians and Armenians. The mother tongue did not play a role any more . . . all the republics felt bound together by a common patriotism, a common nationalism, the feeling of a community of culture and destiny, based on a common world view and style of life. This new-born Soviet Union created a danger of first order for Europe. It threatens it from within and from outside. Her aim is the annihilation of European culture and tradition and the liquidation of its bearers, as far as they do not join communism . . . The direct consequence of this threat is the unification of Europe, as a federal state and a nation*" (Coudenhove-Kalergi 1953:14) We will come back below to the several erroneous assumptions in these assertions.

Coudenhove-Kalergi argues that four large world cultures begin to form themselves: the European, the Islamic, the Indian, and the East Asian. In this spectrum, European culture includes also America, Australia, and South Africa. Europe should become a true federal state which comprises, in the first step, Germany, Italy, France, and Belgium, including "the African colonies of France and Belgium with its vast territories and its reserves in raw materials and mineral resources." This new federal state "will be a powerful world empire, coequal to his British and American allies" (Coudenhove-Kalergi 1953:142). In his 1923 book *Paneuropa,* he presents a map of the world divided into the five "global power fields" (Wilson and van der Dussen 1993:100). It is obvious that these ideas represent an early version of the controversial thesis of the Samuel Huntington (1996) that the world in the decades to come will be split along cultural or civilizational lines instead of political lines.

All the cited quotations from Coudenhove-Kalergi's writings make clear that his thinking was rather elitist and guided by great power aspirations for Europe. The term *democracy* does not appear frequently in his writings[4] as it does not come up among the four principles of the Pan-Europa movement, which are Christian, conservative, European, and liberal.[5] The aristocratic-elitist and power-inspired character of the Pan-Europa movement is indicated also by the fact that Otto von Habsburg, the son of the last Austro-Hungarian emperor, is the international honorary president, and his son, Karl Habsburg, the actual president of the Austrian Section of the Pan-Europa movement. Otto Habsburg has been an advocate of European integration since long (Habsburg 1965). As an active member of the European Parliament, he developed some pertinent critiques and ideas in regard to the reform of the EU institutions (Habsburg 1999).

7.2 Democracy and peace in Europe: Kant's universal dream and its political-practical relevance

The prevention of wars and the establishment of a lasting peace have been the main preoccupation of all thinkers about Europe since the early Modern Age. One author stands out among all others in this regard, the German Enlightenment philosopher Immanuel Kant. We will show in the first part of this section that his thinking is of high practical importance for a critical understanding of European integration. In the second part, we discuss the experiences and the fate of the nineteenth-century republican-democratic movements for national independence in Germany and Italy. Their failure shows in a dramatic way the negative consequences of the dissociation of the fights for democratisation and for national unification.

Immanuel Kant: The preconditions for eternal peace

Immanuel Kant (1724–1804) has been one of the most important figures in the historical discussions about peace in Europe. His philosophical works are regarded as a revolutionary breakthrough because they laid the basis for a philosophy based on pure reason, free of all speculative, metaphysical thinking.[6] In his essay "Perpetual Peace: A Philosophical Sketch" (1795), Kant has provided some very powerful ideas of political philosophy which are highly relevant today. Kant's essay was only one among many other proposals concerning the establishment of peace made in the eighteenth century (von Raumer 1953:127). Among them was also Abbé Saint-Pierre's "Projet pur render la paix perpétuelle," discussed previously. Another one was Rousseau, who discussed Saint-Pierre's ideas in an extensive essay of 1756 (von Raumer 1953:135; Foerster 1963:86ff.). Rousseau argued that peace was threatened by a dissatisfying internal political situation not guided by rational principles. The essay of Kant was not influential among academic circles after its publication; it was out of stock, however, within a few weeks and printed again in the same year.[7] Till today, this essay is his most famous work, translated into many languages of the world (von

Raumer 1953:162). In the twentieth century, his essay gains more and more prominence also in political philosophy.[8]

Kant's essay on peace consists of two sections. The first contains six preliminary conditions, which should be realized immediately; the second section enumerates three "definitive conditions" for peace. One of the basic assumptions behind the six preconditions for eternal peace is the principle of the sovereignty of nation-states. These preconditions are: (1) No treaty of peace shall be held valid in which there is tacitly reserved matter for a future war; (2) no independent states shall come under the dominion of another state by inheritance, exchange, purchase, or donation; (3) standing armies shall in time be totally abolished; (4) no national debts shall be contracted with a view to the external friction of states; (5) no state shall by force interfere with the constitution or the government of another state; (6) no state shall, during war, permit such acts of hostility which would make mutual confidence in the subsequent peace impossible. Kant gives also some "empirical justifications" for these principles, which seem

Photo 8b Immanuel Kant, 1795: " . . . a powerful and enlightened people can make itself a republic, which by its nature must be inclined to perpetual peace. This gives fulcrum to the federation with other states so that they may secure freedom under the idea of the law of nations . . . This league would not have to be a state consisting of nations. That would be contradictory since a state implies the relation of a superior (legislating) to an inferior (obeying), i.e., the people . . ."

Source: Wikipedia.

highly plausible from the viewpoint of present-day knowledge. Principle 3 is considered as necessary, for instance, because standing armies constitute a continuous menace to other states "by their readiness to appear at all times prepared for war; they incite them to compete with each other in the number of armed men, and there is not limit to this." Today, it is not the number of soldiers which is the crucial point but the amount of armaments; historical experience of the late nineteenth and the whole twentieth century has shown that there exists a strong competitive drive to increase one's military power, which, as a consequence, multiplies the risk of war (Singer 2004).

Most important for our discussion in this chapter are Kant's three "definitive articles" for the establishment and persistence of perpetual peace among states. They are quite short and state the following: (1) The civil constitution of every state should be republican; (2) the law of nations shall be founded on a federation of free states; (3) the law of world citizenship shall be limited to conditions of universal hospitality. Let us look at the grounds for each of these rules.

The first principle, the most important in the present context, states that all states should be republican by constitution. A state can be considered having a republican constitution, according to Kant, if it is characterized by three characteristics: (1) The freedom of all members of society; (2) the dependence of all upon a single common legislation (we could say the rule of law); (3) the law of equality between all citizens. What Kant says here in fact is that only a democratic constitution in the present-day meaning of this word within the single states, and the rule of law in the relations between the states, can be the basis for long-lasting, peaceful international relations.[9] A state is republican (or democratic, in present-day terminology) if the executive power is separated from the legislative and if the citizens have a possibility to codetermine all important political decisions; this includes in particular also the issue of wars (Rauch 2005:20). Kant sees a further favourable condition for the emergence of republican constitutions in a relatively small size of a political community and its government.

Very important are the reasons which make it more probable that republican-democratic states are more interested in peace than nondemocratic states. Kant writes in this regard:

> *"The republican constitution, besides the purity of its origin (having sprung from the pure source of the concept of law), also gives a favourable prospect for the desired consequence, i.e., perpetual peace. The reason is this: if the consent of the citizens is required in order to decide that war should be declared (and in this constitution it cannot but be the case), nothing is more natural than that they would be very cautious in commencing such a poor game, decreeing for themselves all the calamities of war. Among the latter would be: having to fight, having to pay the costs of war from their own resources, having painfully*

to repair the devastation war leaves behind, and, to fill up the measure of evils, load themselves with a heavy national debt that would embitter peace itself and that can never be liquidated on account of constant wars in the future."

Thus, pure rational considerations out of self-interest will lead the citizens of democratic nations not to consent that their government begins a war. This idea—that political rulers are responsible for wars—was also central in Bertha von Suttner's successful pacifistic novel, mentioned previously. The same is true for the famous French writer Victor Hugo, who is frequently quoted by present-day politicians as a witness for the idea of a united Europe. Although Hugo in fact used the concept of a new "Republic of Europe," his main aim connected with this concept was the preservation of peace. The main enemies of peace, in his view, were the kings, who "in order to defend themselves, need the soldiers who, on their side, must murder in order to survive. The kings need the armies, the armies need the war" (Hugo 1938:291). The abolition of the monarchical despotism will lead to welfare and peace throughout Europe. Victor Hugo supported also the peace movement of the 1840s (Benz 1988).

However, the establishment of a republican constitution in all nations around the world is not enough for the guaranteeing of peace, according to Kant. His second principle requires, in addition, that these nations form a "federation" or "league of free states." In the "state of nature," without such a federation, states would relate to each other as potential enemies. It is only through the regime of law that such an insecure situation can be overcome (von Raumer 1953:168). This is the same case as a constitution which eliminates the war of all against all within a single state. Such a league of nations, or "league of peace," Kant writes, *"would not have to be a state consisting of nations. That would be contradictory,* since a state implies the relation of a superior (legislating) to an inferior (obeying), i.e., the people, and many nations in one state would then constitute only one nation. This contradicts the presupposition, for here we have to weigh the rights of nations against each other so far as they are distinct states and not amalgamated into one" (my emphasis). The establishment of a peaceful league of nations would imply that each single state subordinates itself under a binding external legal authority, an international court of justice. As a consequence, also in the relations between the states the principles of law would rule and peace would result. For Kant, it is necessary in this regard to consider the world as a whole because only on that level can perpetual peace be guaranteed. A supranational Europe cannot be a surrogate solution.

The third basic precondition for peace mentioned by Kant was that "world citizenship" should be limited to conditions of universal hospitality. This article can be interpreted from two points of view. First, it was directed against the dominant praxis of colonialism at this time, when the large sea powers not only settled down in foreign countries but established a domination over those territories (von Raumer 1953:169). The second meaning of this rule may be seen as the "negative" side of the principle of the sovereignty of nation-states; it implies that one state cannot be made responsible for the fate of citizens of other states (with the exception of the case of refugees). This principle of Kant can also be interpreted as a clear refusal of a kind of utopian thinking which assumes that Europe can provide something like a "universal citizenship" (see Section 7.3c).

The fatal split between the fights for democracy and national unity in Germany and Italy

The experiences and fate of the movements for national independence and in nineteenth-century Germany and Italy are highly illuminating for the topic of this chapter: In these fights, the aim of democratization was also a central concern. However, democratization and nationalism were split apart quite soon—a fact which had fateful consequences not only for Germany and Italy but for Europe as a whole. A similar, although much less spectacular, splitting can also be observed in the present-day process of European integration. It seems appropriate, therefore, to take a look at the decisive social forces, personalities, and events in these fights.

After the Congress of Vienna, the political situation in central Europe appeared as more and more disappointing to many contemporaries: On the one side, the German-speaking countries were divided between Prussia and Austria; many of them constituted only miniprincipalities; large parts of Italy were under direct or indirect foreign rule. On the other side, the civil rights and constitutions which had been introduced under the influence of Napoleon became more and more restricted. From 1830 on, industrialization began to change the social structures, an independent public press started to form itself, internal political crises with political demonstrations broke out, and national consciousness began to grow. The revolution of February 1848 in France gave the final impetus for revolutions in several German principalities. In the following months, deputies were sent to Frankfurt, the old capital of the Holy Roman Empire. These deputies formed the famous *Paulsversammlung,* a "parliament" of 809 persons from all German countries, including Austria.[10] This parliament, consisting mainly of highly educated bourgeois intellectuals and liberally minded public officers, elaborated a constitution for Germany. It contained a catalogue of basic rights, provided for people's representation in two parliamentary assemblies, and a hereditary constitutional monarchy. This was a truly revolutionary constitution even if in some regards it had a "conservative" character (Palmade 1974:51); its implementation would have changed the course of German and European history in the nineteenth and twentieth centuries in a fundamental way. However, it was not realized for two reasons: first, because of the nearly insoluble problem of how to include the large, multinational Austrian empire into the new

German federation (as a whole or of only in its German-speaking parts?); second, because the ruling elites of Prussia and Austria did not accept the constitution and suppressed the revolutionary democratic movements in their home countries with military force.

The fight for national unity of Germany on the basis of democratic constitutional reforms was closely related to the idea of a "new Europe" (Franz 2004). Already at the patriotic meeting *Hambacher Fest* in 1832, the publicist Wirth had praised a "confederated republican Europe." In the parliament of the *Paulskirche*, the writer Arnold Ruge had characterized the political structure after the Napoleonic area (the Holy Alliance) as the "old Europe." The main witness for the thesis that the idea of a United Europe was closely related to that of the establishment of republican-democratic constitutions, however, is the ardent fighter for national independence of Italy, Giuseppe Mazzini (1805–1872). His political association *La Giovine Italia* (Young Italy), founded in 1831, and the *Risorgimento* movement aimed at the unification of "the many states and kingdoms of the peninsula into a single republic as the only true foundation of Italian liberty."[11] This new Italy and a "Third Rome" should become the center of newly ordered Europe (Tschubarjan 1992:59ff.; Plé 1993; Smith 1994; Lützeler 1992:118ff.). Later on, Mazzini founded similar organisations in Switzerland, Germany, and Poland, and an international one, called Young Europe. As a convinced adversary of the absolutist regimes, and in particular of the Austrian empire, which at this time possessed large parts of northern Italy, he soon was constrained to leave Italy. In successive periods of exile in Switzerland, France, and England, he continued not only with writing but also with organizing money and people for insurgences within Italy and for military campaigns into its northwestern frontier regions. All these attempts, however, failed. In the end Mazzini was isolated as a fighter because he was not ready to join the forces of Garibaldi, who had arranged himself with the princes of Savoy in order to effectuate Italian unity under monarchical rule.

But even if Mazzini's conspiracies failed, "they exerted constant pressure which in the long run was highly effective . . . He was an intrepid agitator and effective pamphleteer whose designs were feared by the leading politicians of Europe . . ." (Smith 1994:2). Mazzini was inspired by three sources: Saint-Simon's Enlightenment and his ideas that there exists a progress in history and that intellectuals have the task to educate and indoctrinate the people, the only true sovereign; the romanticist idea of the uniqueness and value of all cultures and nations; and Catholic social doctrine which motivated his engagement for the fate of workers and led him to combat Marxism and communism. Mazzini saw a close relationship between the fights for national independence and European unification. By supporting each other, the several European countries should help to establish democratic governments in all their own states. He did not foresee a close European integration, however, but only a loose confederation of independent, autonomous, and democratic nation-states. He was also against political centralization of nation-states but favoured local self-administration. From this point of view, he criticized the inflated civil service, which he saw as a major danger for Italy (Smith 1994:153). In general, his idea of patriotism was always subordinated to the far wider claims of general humanity.

A later author and politician congenial to Mazzini was Thomas G. Masaryk (1850–1937), the founding father of modern Czechoslovakia (Wilson and van der Dussen 1993:93ff.). He went into exile in 1914 to continue his fight for an independent Czechoslovakia. But he also embedded this claim into a proposal for cooperation at the regional and European level.

The failure of Mazzini's efforts to unite Italy under the banner of a democratic republic presents an obvious parallel to the fate of the fights for national independence and democratic reforms in Germany. Also here, the patriotic intellectuals and political idealists of the Paulskirche had failed in their effort to unite Germany under the auspices of a parliamentary constitutional monarchy. National unification was achieved three decades later, however, by Prussia and its "Iron Chancellor" Bismarck with the means of a successful army and under authoritarian monarchical rule. The same happened in Italy, where the king of Piedmont, Charles Albert, and his prime minister, Camillo di Cavour, saw the promising possibility to enlarge their dominion by supporting movements for Italian unification. The fact that in South Italy a considerable insurgence against unification under the banner of Piedmont-Savoy broke out and 1,000 revolters were shot proves that Italian unification was mainly a process from above. The ruling bourgeois liberal elites of North Italy were also unable to solve the pressing social problems of South Italy and to modernize Italy as a whole (Palmade 1974:262ff.; Procacci 1983). The devastating failure of the simultaneous establishment of national independence and democratic reform, which were intended by the members of the 1848 generation, however, "discredited the utopia, proved the incapability of the inferiors, and paved the way for relentless realism and realists" (Palmade 1974:67). Patriotism became reactionary and, in the name of freedom, the old despotism became sanctified anew (Salvatorelli 1971:200).

German and Italian politics in the next decades was a direct consequence of this unification from above, with military-authoritarian means. In the case of Germany, it led to longings of revenge in other countries (particularly in France, after Germany's occupation of Alsace-Lorraine), rearmament (increase of the standing army, upgrading of the fleet), and to colonial expansion in Africa. The most consequential of all was the development of plans for military invasions in the neighbour countries; the famous Schlieffen Plan, which foresaw an attack on Belgium, France, and, later, also Russia, was developed already at the end of the nineteenth century, furthered by the militaristic Kaiser Wilhelm II (Fischer

1979). In the case of Italy, similar expansionist adventures in Africa and other places were undertaken, although often with an embarrassing failure. Their main motivation was internal politics, that is, the securing of the power of the ruling-conservative elites (Procacci 1983:292ff.). In both countries, these developments and actions were the decisive preconditions which later led directly into the European catastrophe of the First World War. In the case of Italy, entrance to this war was not wished for by the majority of the population.

7.3 Historical visions and the "real Europe"

Let us now come back to the question raised at the beginning of this chapter: What does the concrete process of European integration since the 1950s look like in view of the ideas developed by intellectuals through the centuries? It must certainly be conceded that the concrete realisation of a political ideal can never be perfect or complete; it is the task of political skill to find acceptable compromises between an ideal and its realisation. However, if we do in fact find significant differences between ideal and reality, we have to investigate carefully what their character is. This examination of the relation between the historical ideas of "Europe" and real European integration gives us also significant insights into the reasons for the deep-going split between elites and citizens in the EU today. In the first part of this section, the declared aims of the political elites, but also their actual strategies and behaviours in the processes of political change and integration since 1945, are investigated; in the second part, a content analysis of the "Constitution for Europe" is carried out.

(c) Declared aims and concrete actions and achievements of the elites

Four topics shall be discussed in this section: (1) The reason for the establishment of peace in Europe; (2) the significance and role of democratization; (3) the question which kind of federation is adequate for Europe; (4) the role of the EU in the world.

The theory of democratic peace as a sufficient explanation for the end of wars in Europe

The main preoccupation of all authors concerned with the question of Europe was the securing of peace. It is now the place to reconsider the powerful thesis of Immanuel Kant (but also of Saint-Simon, Mazzini, and others) that there exists one central precondition for the preservation of eternal peace, namely, the establishment of democratic institutions and governments. How can we evaluate this thesis today, in light of the historical experience and empirical evidence of the twentieth century?

In the last decades, Kant's essay on perpetual peace has inspired a vast number of social and political studies. A few of them came to the conclusion that it has to be refuted. Critical arguments include logical flaws and contradictions in the theory (Koller 1996; Rosato 2003); empirical facts which seem to contradict it, such as that democracies have often waged wars against nondemocracies; that public opinion is not always against wars; that in particular the United States has often initiated wars, even against democratic states. A theoretical alternative to the theory of the democratic peace is *political realism* which holds that power is the primary determinant and end of politics (Morgenthau 1960; Waltz 1979). Strong nation-states will always enter into a war if they think this is the best means to assure or to enlarge their power. In the view of this theory, the absence of wars between advanced countries since 1945 is only an "imperial peace," based on an American military superpower. It is certainly a fact that wars have been a continuous concomitant of human history from the most ancient to the present times. Yet this theory neglects the fact that democracy is a wholly new phenomenon of modern times and this might bring with it a fundamental change. In fact, the vast majority of students found that Kant's theory of democratic peace is a valid theory. They have developed it further into the *theory of democratic peace* (Rauch 2005; see also Rummel 1995; Doyle 1996; Ward and Gleditsch 1998). Dozens of studies have investigated empirically the incidence and kinds of wars from the middle of the nineteenth up to the end of the twentieth century; they found strong support for the thesis that democracies do not wage wars against each other (Herman and Kegley 1996; Cederman 2001; Rosato 2003).

Recent studies have added some rationales for the theory of democratic peace (Rauch 2005:31ff.; Huth and Allee 2002). In democratic states, political leaders must try to get reelected, and therefore they will be attentive to the preferences of the citizens. They evaluate peace very high, clearly higher than the elites for which international power and influence is more important (CIRCAP 2006). Furthermore, cultural values are important: Democracies develop norms and ways of interaction which inhibit violence and favour peaceful solutions of conflicts. Democratic decision procedures are complex and take a lot of time; this leads to a cooking down of passions and to an avoidance of overhasty decisions. These facts are also known to the nondemocratic leaders and induce them to adapt their behaviour vis-à-vis democracies. Thus, also the *perception of an adversary* is of crucial importance: If he is perceived as nondemocratic, a war becomes possible. Finally, the connection between democracy and peace must be considered from a dynamic perspective: Democracy is a learning process both at the individual and the macrolevel. Thus, it can be expected that the behaviour of and against young democracies does not correspond fully to the theory (Cederman 2001).

What are the consequences out of this strongly corroborated theory for the problem of European integration? How much did integration itself contribute to the maintenance of peace? Officially, the preservation of peace has been one of the most frequently declared aims of the promoters of European integration since the Second World War, as we have seen at the beginning of this chapter. The political elites over and over again praise themselves for having achieved this aim; also many scientists accept this view (see, e.g., Schmidt 2000:34). A recent example was the speech of the German Chancellor Angela Merkel before the European Parliament in Strasbourg on January 17, 2007 (in her position as president of the European Council): "Looked from outside, the European Union is an unparalleled historical success story. The European Union is one of the most impressing peace works on the planet earth." My thesis is, however, that all declarations of this sort take the credit for integration for what has been achieved by something else. Three arguments support this thesis.

(1) There was no war between Western, democratic countries at all since World War II. This includes also all European countries which have not become members of the EC/EU but also all the democratic countries in North America, Australia, or Asia. (2) The bloody European and world wars of the twentieth century have been initiated by countries which were not democracies (such as Hitler's Germany in 1939) or could be considered as democracies only in a very limited sense (such as Austria-Hungary, Germany, and tsarist Russia before World War I). (3) The former European big powers, such as Great Britain, France, and Germany, have been relegated after World War II to second-order powers on the world level. A main motivation for the world wars provoked by European states was attempts to gain a dominant position not only in Europe but also in other parts of the world, particularly in the Third World. This argument has ceased to exist after the loss of the colonies outside Europe.

It might be true that after the Second World War a considerable level of distrust might have existed between France and Germany (Loth 1996). The idea seems absurd, however, that they would really have considered to enter into war against each other yet another time. In fact, a fundamental reconciliation between France and Germany could have taken place already after the First World War if Hitler would not have come to power in Germany. Many of the leading German and French politicians of that time (in particular foreign ministers Briand and Stresemann) aimed at reconciliation between the two countries (Wilson and van der Dussen 1993:101:ff.). In 1925, Aristide Briand used the notion "United States of Europe" and invited all European foreign ministers represented in the League of Nations to informal discussions about a closer economic and political cooperation.

Thus, we must conclude that the theory of democratic peace fully accounts for the absence of wars between the member states of the EC/EU since 1945. Changes of power distribution at the world level as well as the existence of atomic weapons (Thody 2000:3ff.) may have contributed to this peace. In Europe, also economic prosperity was important. However, the democratisation of all European countries was certainly the most important factor contributing to the maintenance of peace. The only large-scale war in Europe since 1945 broke out in the former Yugoslavia, which was no democracy at that time. Therefore, it was certainly not European integration in the first place which has established and secured peace in Europe. This argument has not only become obsolete in recent years (Offe 2003), but may have been so already since the beginning.

The ambivalent role of the EU in the establishment and securing of democracy in Europe

What was the role of European integration for the establishment and securing of democracy in Europe? The EU is very proud also in this regard. The progress of democracy is in fact one of the most spectacular and far-reaching changes of the last decades: After World War II, and far into post-war time, nondemocratic, autocratic political systems persisted in several countries of South Europe (Portugal, Spain, Greece) and in Communist Central East and Southeast Europe. At the beginning of the twenty-first century, most of these countries have been transformed into democracies and accepted as members of the EU. The EU praises itself for having contributed significantly to this change: First, by presenting a positive model to the countries with nondemocratic systems; second, by providing them financial and administrative-technical aid for institutional reforms; third,

Photo 9a   June 27, 1989: The "Reunification of Europe." Foreign Ministers Alois Mock (Austria) and Gylya Horn (Hungary) cut through the Iron Curtain at the Austrian-Hungarian border near Klingenbach.

Source: Bernhard J. Holzner/HOPI-MEDIA.

Photo 9b Toward a "Cosmopolitan Europe"? A new Iron Curtain was established around the Spanish enclave Melilla (Morocco), in order to prevent the influx of refugees and immigrants from Africa to Europe.

Source: PRO ASYL.

by supporting and safeguarding the functioning of the democratic institutions after their entrance to the EU.

These arguments are substantiated and shall not be put into question. The Copenhagen Criteria of 1993 define as one of the conditions under which a country is eligible to join the Union that it must have stable democratic institutions (Glenn 2003). However, did European integration really contribute to the implementation of democracy in the former nondemocratic countries and—moreover—is the EU able to inhibit nondemocratic tendencies within its own realm? Three theses are proposed in this regard: The democratic transitions in South and Central East Europe were mainly the result of internal revolutions and of changes in power relations at the world level; the EU has not been able to check efficiently nondemocratic tendencies in at least one of their own founding member states; the institutional development of the EU leads to an erosion of democracy at the member-state level which is not balanced out by a corresponding increase of possibilities for democratic participation at the level of the Union.

The *democratic transitions in Portugal, Spain and Greece* in the 1970s can be seen as a result of several factors: an increasing weakness of the internal ruling military and political elites and their authoritarian regimes which were engaged in unsuccessful foreign military adventures; an insurgence of younger, liberally minded, and progressive officers, as in the case of Portugal;[12] a social and economic backlash due to the encapsulation from the rest of Europe, which was increasingly felt by many as a chain inhibiting progress; the support of the population for the democratic transitions. In Communist Central East Europe, three factors were decisive. First, the internal democratic revolutions which were only the continuation of earlier uprisings against Soviet foreign rule in the GDR, Hungary, and Czechoslovakia. Second, the abolishment of the one-party system in the USSR and the collapse of the Soviet Union under Gorbachev. Third, the increasing retardation in the productivity of the economy and in standards of life, compared to the West, was of crucial importance. They were felt most acutely by the populations of the more advanced, Central East European countries, the German Democratic Republic, Poland, Czechoslovakia, and Hungary. The EU itself has contributed only in a modest way to these revolutionary transitions. In addition, southern enlargement of the EC was also seen as a strategy to reduce political instability there and as a means to detain the influence of Communist parties (Strezhneva 1991:84). These arguments are supported by the fact that Spain was for some time more welcome as a new member than England, and the EC did not consider, for a long time, that the Communist states of Central Europe would be able to transform themselves into democratic market societies.

The decisive factors for the democratic revolutions in south and east Europe were an increasing weakness of the internal ruling elites, but also the actions of oppositional elites and the broad support of them by the population at large. In this regard we have to mention the nearly ten million Polish workers who joined and supported the union *Solidarność;* the several hundred thousands of people who participated in demonstrations in Leipzig, Prague, and Budapest; and the intrepid and persistent actions of oppositional intellectual and political leaders such as the Poles and Czechs Adam Michnik, Jakek Kuron, Bronislav Geremek, Lech Walesa, Vaclav Havel, Petr Uhl, Jan Patocka, but also the Hungarian fighters for freedom from Soviet domination, executed after the abatement of the insurgence in 1956, Jozsef Szilagyi, Pál Maléter, Imre Nagy, and many others. All these men did not avoid prosecution and imprisonment in their fights for freedom and democracy. One could even say that it is an affront against these personalities to claim that the EU had contributed significantly to the overthrow of the autocratic political systems under Soviet rule in view of the position of many influential Western politicians at this time. Vladimir Boukovsky (2005:105) cites many statements which make clear that the Soviet system was largely accepted by leading West European politicians before 1989/90. They include the former French president and later president of the Constitutional Convention, Valery Giscard d'Estaing, who said in January 1989, visiting Gorbachev in Moscow: "We do not have the intention to 'spur on' the countries of the east, to convulse the base of their stability. We perceive the dangers of destabilization in the different states and this is not our interest." Henry Kissinger said that he and his colleagues "want to contribute in a constructive manner to the construction of this Europe for which the USSR and the United States have played the same positive role" (Boukovsky 2005:120).

What was the role of the EU concerning the securing of democracy within its own member states? Also in this regard, the answer is disappointing: The EU has, in fact, not been able to check nondemocratic tendencies at least within one of its member states, and, when it has tried to do so in another one, it has disgraced itself. These two cases are Austria and Italy.

In 2002, 14 member states of the EU imposed diplomatic sanctions against the member state Austria. The reason for these sanctions was that Wolfgang Schüssel, the leader of the Christian-conservative *Österreichische Volkspartei*, had formed a coalition government with the *Freiheitliche Partei Österreichs* (FPÖ) of *Jörg Haider*, throughout Europe known as an influential representative of the "new right" with a potential neo-Nazi orientation. However, both these parties had been elected by the Austrian citizens in a free election. The main voting motive for Haider's FPÖ was not nostalgia for the Third Reich but dissatisfaction with several decades of consensus government in Austria, dominated by the two large parties, which had led to political encrustation, clientelism, and incapacity for structural reforms (Haller 1996a). Later on, the EU installed a committee of three respected personalities who delivered a report on the political situation. It should clarify the support of European values by the Austrian government; the legal situation of minorities, immigrants, and refugees in Austria; and the political (democratic) character of the FPÖ. The committee found several problems connected with right-wing parties, unfair immigration laws, and the like, but they were not significantly different from those in other member states. Overall, the report states that the Austrian government respects European values, the legal situation corresponds to that in other EU member states, and the FPÖ is a right-wing party, but its ministers have observed all legal and governmental obligations. In retrospect, it is rather clear that the sanctions were not primarily the result of an apprehension for the stability of democracy in Austria but of several other factors. Among them were a special sensitivity against anybody who seems to be a neo-Nazi (for this reason, also the German government supported the sanctions); the feeling by French President Chirac of having been personally insulted by Haider;[13] the fact that the FPÖ was not a member of one of the two large party blocs in the European Parliament; and that Austria is only one of the smaller member countries of the EU. An American historian writes about this affair: "The bullying of the Alpine republic made Brussels look threatening as well as ridiculous and provided a *Paradebeispiel*—a convincing demonstration—of Commission arrogance and disregard for member state rights" (Gillingham 2003:315; see also Giorgi et al. 2006:58ff., 138).

The second case is the accession to government of Silvio Berlusconi in Italy in 1994 and 2001. In this case, an EU-member-state government has in fact launched laws and measures which are highly problematic from the democratic point of view. Berlusconi was an entrepreneur in the building trade, financed in a dubious way; later on, he became active in many other businesses and particularly in the media sector, where he bought the large private TV network Mediaset.[14] Very complex constructions of firms, located often in foreign countries, made the financing of his activities at all times quite intransparent; accusations of using black money, even from the Mafia, have never been disproved convincingly by Berlusconi. As a very able communicator in public, he used his vast media network to enter into politics and to support his own, newly founded party Forza Italia, in addition to massive public relations campaigns before elections. As prime minister, Berlusconi enacted a series of laws which protected him from judicial prosecution and which restricted media plurality (see Veltri and Travaglio 2001; Ginsborg 2004). In April 2004, the European Parliament released a critical report which stated that in Italy "a unique concentration of economic, political and media power in the hands of one man, the present prime minister Silvio Berlusconi, exists."[15] Then the EP, however, adopted, with only a small majority, a resolution formulated in very general terms without mentioning Berlusconi explicitly. The main reason for this handling of Berlusconi with kid gloves was the fact that his party, Forza Italia, was a member of the big conservative party bloc in the European Parliament.

The third aspect, which proves that democracy is not a basic dominant value of the EU, is its own institutional makeup and development. The structure of the European Union diverges from the normative principles of democracy in several regards, as will be shown in Chapter 8.

Which kind of integration for the "United Europe"?

Our review of the historical visions of European unification has shown that none of them envisaged a closely integrated new political community. Most of them thought only of a loose league of independent nation states, with some overarching common laws prescribing peaceful behaviour in the relations between the states. We could say they aspired only toward *European unification*, but not *integration*. Several authors have also thought of an economic integration of Europe, but mainly in terms of free trade between the states. Some, such as Saint-Simon, foresaw political integration and the establishment of a European parliament; also this, however, with only limited competences. None of the presented authors has thought of a European government and administration.

This, however, was the route on which the successful process of actual European integration since the early 1950s has proceeded. As we have shown in Chapter 5, Jean Monnet and Robert Schuman proposed to establish an independent bureaucratic body, the High Authority, whose task was to administrate the German and French coal and steel industry and pursue the process of their integration. This model was then taken over for the EEC in 1956/57. The Commission of the EEC—a bureaucratic-political hybrid—was equipped with far-reaching political competences, including legislative functions. History of European integration since then has shown that this Commission and its supporting and ever-growing bureaucratic apparatus were the main motor of integration. Today, even leading statesmen complain that this Commission has become an uncontrollable bureaucratic apparatus and has enacted regulations and decrees which narrow down the unfolding of economic entrepreneurship and activities.

However, it is not only the institutional model and practical method of integration which clearly diverges from the historical ideals about European integration; it is also its final aim. The founding document of the European Community, the 1957 Treaty of Rome, in the preamble states explicitly that the heads of the governments of the six founding states were "determined to lay the foundations of *an ever closer union* among the peoples of Europe." This is a famous formulation which is quoted frequently, and also used as book title (Dinan 1999). The development of the process of integration during the last half-century has shown that this far-reaching intent has in fact served as an effective guideline. The famous "subsidiarity principle" could not really restrain the growth of the competencies and power of the commission and the EU as a whole vis-à-vis the member states.

Thus, we can observe that the idea of "an ever closer Union" is becoming reality more and more. How will such a union look at the end? This central question, in fact, can be considered as one of the greatest mysteries of integration. In fact, the formulation does not specify a certain model of integration but only a *process*—and, what is more, an never-ending process. One could see this even as a kind of threat if one subscribes to the principle of definite restraint of governmental power as a principle of democracy and the division of power between different levels of government as a necessary specification of it.

Considering the central aims of integration—the preservation of peace and the furtherance of socioeconomic growth and welfare—it is far from evident why European integration should be aspiring toward an "ever closer

Union." This aim becomes clearer, however, if we look at visions about the role of Europe in world politics.

Europe as a new global power

For most of the historical authors, European integration was closely associated with changes in the relations of Europe to the rest of the world. Also in this regard, however, marked differences can be observed between the several authors. The idea of a new and powerful Europe was alien for all those who foresaw a kind of loose unification and the establishment of common institutions related primarily to issues of reconciliation, communication, and coordination. It was only in the first half of the twentieth century that this idea began to develop. The reason for it is obvious. Up to the First World War, the large European countries in fact have been or claimed to have become world powers. The experience of the World War and the rise of the United States and of the Soviet Union to economic and military superpowers relegated them to second-class powers. Thus, the idea of a United Europe as a new global power was born in this period. Its most professed advocate was the founder of the pan-Europa movement, Richard Coudenhove-Kalergi. Let us come back shortly to his ideas. First, he argues that also Europe can become a new "nation" in the sense a "community of culture and destiny." He also argues that Europe had been such a nation throughout the Middle Ages, when it was united under the Holy German-Roman Empire and the Catholic Church. The same argument comes out today among many politicians who refer to Charlemagne as the "father" of Europe (e.g., R. Prodi, F. Mitterand, H. Kohl). [16] However, the reference to Charlemagne as the "father of Europe" is highly questionable also because he created his empire in a series of aggressive bloody wars in which he subjugated under his rule the Bavarians, Saxons, and Lombards. Moreover, his empire enclosed only the territories of present-day France, Germany, and North and Central Italy, but not the large northwest, north, and eastern parts of the continent (see also Segl 1993).

Second, Coudenhove-Kalergi argues for the necessity of a new and powerful European suprastate because he sees a threat of Europe from the Soviet Union. We have seen before that he supposed that the Soviet Union was able to create a new "nation"—a thesis which has been disproved by history. Present-day Russia, however, does not and cannot aspire to attack Western Europe as a whole or even one of its countries for several reasons: It has not more a totally centralized, authoritarian system; it has its own interest in expanding peaceful economic relations with Western Europe; its huge geographic extension far into Asia and its borders with China and Japan make it very vulnerable in terms of security also from those large and rising nations (Habsburg 1965, 1999).

Which ideas were relevant in the real process of integration and how did they develop in regard to the role of the European Union in foreign and world politics? We can see a clear trend toward a deeper integration also in this regard. In the Treaty of Rome of 1957, issues of foreign policy were clearly subordinated to those of internal integration in economic and social terms. Only some marginal paragraphs were related to the external relations of the EEC. The situation changed basically with the Maastricht Treaty: Here, a Common Foreign and Security Policy (CFSP) was defined as the second pillar of the EU; its aim was "to develop a European security and defence identity"; to establish the Western European Defense Union as the European pillar of NATO; to increase cooperation between the member states in terms of defense and military; and to establish specific institutions for this aim, which has been realized (the European Defence Agency, the European Union Institute for Security Studies, and the European Union Satellite Centre now exist). This new pillar was taken over and strengthened in the Contract for a Constitution for Europe, signed by the heads of the member state and other European governments in 2004. Here, it is stated that CFSP shall be developed further into a common defense policy; that a "foreign minister" of the Union directs this policy; that this policy ensures the Union a capacity for worldwide operations, based on civil and military means (Art. I-41). All these characteristics make clear that the Union is aspiring now toward a full political community, a state in the proper sense if we follow the classical definition of Max Weber.[17]

In the official EU texts and in the proposed constitution, there is no definition of the substantive aims of this foreign policy—which is somewhat surprising given the rather extensive list of economic aims and rights. However, looking at the spirit of these paragraphs, and at other texts and speeches, it becomes evident that the European Union certainly aspires to become a strong player on the global scene. At the homepage of the Commission, the external relations and activities of the EU are described in the following way: "The sheer size of the European Union in economic, trade and financial terms makes it a *world player*. It has a web of agreements with most countries and regions of the globe . . . The European Union is putting in place a common and foreign security policy so that its members can act together on the world state as a united force for stability, cooperation and understanding. At the same time, the EU is developing a defence capability and has undertaken its first peacekeeping missions. It is also engaged in fighting terrorism"[18] (my emphasis).

Several concepts in this characterisation—security, stability, order, fighting terrorism—clearly indicate that the EU conceives itself now as a powerful actor that certainly can define by itself what kind of stability and order is necessary, which kinds of terrorisms have to be battled against and with which means. Among the leading politicians in Europe, it was probably the former German foreign minister, Joschka Fischer, who pronounced most clearly the idea of a powerful European state in his famous speech at Berlin's Humboldt University on May 12, 2000.[19] He gave a clear answer to the question: *Quo vadis Europa?* namely: "Forward until the completion of European integration." Starting from the well-known elite thesis that European integration has turned out as "phenomenally successful," he argued that the Schuman method—stepwise extension and deepening of the common institutions—had reached its limits. Now, it was time for a "full parliamentarization" and the establishment of a true "European federation" and European government.

(d) Content analysis of the Constitution for Europe

Another possibility to find out what the most important values and aims of the present-day EU are is to look at the content of the Constitution for Europe which was elaborated in 2003. This large text is well suited for this purpose because it includes all the earlier basic integration treaties into one comprehensive document. Even if this constitution was not put into practice, but substituted by the EU Reform Treaty, passed in Lissabon in 2007, it still is highly relevant today. This is so because the essence of the constitution, over 90% of its content, have been taken over in the Reform Treaty (see Chapter 8). The following analysis of the constitution is quantitative and qualitative. In addition, we compare the proposed EU Constitution with the constitutions of several member and nonmember states of the EU, including the United States.

What are these basic values of the EU when we consider this text as the most authoritative expression of these values? Looking at *Table 7.1*, we can say that three basic values stand out as the most important in quantitative terms (each mentioned more than 100 times): Security, freedom, and justice. The two values which were the most important ones for the intellectual writers about European integration, peace, and democracy appear very infrequently. This is quite a surprising result. In the following, let us discuss these five values in more detail.

Peace—a marginal value?

Peace is the value most often associated with European integration (see also Weiler 1999:240). The process of integration, so says the established narrative, has been necessary in order to prevent once and for all that self-destructive wars break out anew within Europe. Peace is also a central concern of people throughout Europe. We may assume, therefore, that the treatment of the issues of peace and war in the proposed EU Constitution has been a significant factor for its approval or rejection.

How relevant is the value of peace for the EU in the text of the Constitution for Europe? Hardly at all, one could conclude, at least in quantitative terms (see *Table 7.1*). The word *peace* is mentioned only nine times in the voluminous text comprising over 627 value-related words or concepts. It appears only at the end of the rank order of the words connected to basic values; the most frequently mentioned words, security and freedom, come up over 100 times. The low priority attached to the value of peace comes

Table 7.1 The Frequency of Words Indicating Basic Values in the Constitution for Europe

Basic words (word compositions)	Absolute frequency	% of all value-related words
Security	144	22.9
(National/international/member states; s. policy, social s., energy supply s., public order s.)		
Freedom	132	21.1
(Universal value; f. of arts, science, religion; choose occupation, of movement/establishment, of thought, of the media)		
Justice	126	20.0
(Social justice, solidarity, human rights, dignity, tolerance, rule of law, nondiscrimination)		
Employment	75	12.0
Equality, social exclusion, poverty	34	5.4
Competition	31	4.9
Progress, social progress	20	3.2
Territorial cohesion	16	2.5
Peace	11	1.7
Prosperity, welfare, well-being	10	1.6
Environment protection	10	1.6
Cultural diversity, national identity, pluralism	9	1.4
Democracy	9	1.4
Total number of words	(627)	99.7

Data basis: Treaty for a Constitution for Europe; method: counting of words without titles; program of analysis: ATLAS.ti; analysis carried out by Liria Veronesi.

up also if we look more closely at the content of the paragraphs where it is at stake. This is true in two regards.

First, the word *peace* is used either in very general terms (in the preamble and Art. I-3) or as a means for other aims. Article I-43 states first that the Common Foreign and Security Policy aims to provide a capacity to "carry out operations," which will help to establish peace and international security. Second, the concept opposite to peace, namely, war, appears two times in the text, but again not as an important issue of its own. It is only mentioned in connection with economic values: Article III-131 states that in the case of a serious international tension involving a war risk, the member states coordinate their activities in order to prevent derogations of the functioning of the free market. In the same vein, Article III-436 states that each member state is free in its measures for providing security as far as the production and trade of weapons is concerned; the only obligation is that these measures should not interfere with the rules of competition in the free market. This is evidently one of the several cases where a basic value is clearly subordinated to the principles of the free market! This marginal mentioning of the threat of war contrasts sharply with the constitutions of several EU member states wherein the prevention of war is mentioned explicitly in specific paragraphs. Two examples: "Italy discards war as a means of an attack to liberty of other peoples and as a means to the solution of conflictual international issues" (Art. 11). "The republic of Hungary overrules war as a means to solve conflicts between nations . . ." (Art. 6). The Austrian expert on constitutional law, Fried Esterbauer (1983), has proposed an EU Constitution which contains an article on "obligation to internal peace" and another one on "obligation of peace in relation to other states." In the latter, the states should promise not to enter into military attacks against other states. Another relevant aspect concerns the designation of the political bodies competent to declare a war. The constitution of France states that the parliament must authorize a declaration of war (Art. 35); the German constitution even states that the Bundestag must state if the state's territory is attacked militarily.

What does the European constitution say about peace and war? While it contains only few concrete statements about peace, the same is not true of security and defence. Eight issues are relevant here.

(1) The first and most important is the definition and implementation of the Common Foreign and Security Policy (CFSP), which includes "the progressive framing of a common defence policy" (Art. I-12). Here, the Union's competence shall cover all areas of foreign and security policy, and the member states shall support the Union's policy in this regard "actively and unreservedly" (Art. I-16). In this area, however, only a coordination and cooperation of the member states is foreseen so far, requiring unanimity in important decisions. This article implies, nevertheless, that the EU member states in such cases will be forbidden from pursuing an independent foreign policy.[20]

(2) The operations connected with the CFSP are not restricted to the territory of the Union: The CSFP "shall provide the Union with an operational capacity drawing on civil and military assets. The Union may use them on missions outside the Union for peace-keeping, conflict prevention and strengthening international security in accordance with the principles of the United Nations Charter" (Art. I-41).

(3) The constitution speaks only in a vague way about "tasks" or "missions" in this regard. The intent of these missions, however, goes far beyond peacekeeping, a kind of action which is approved by the UN. The constitution explicitly mentions also the "strengthening of international security." This is a very broad term under which many kinds of actions can be subsumed. Article III-295 includes also the use of military means for the fight against terrorism.

(4) One important further specification is that the member states "shall undertake progressively to improve their military capabilities" (Art. I-41). Thus, the constitution contains a commitment here for a concrete policy (increase of spending on defence) which is highly problematic from two points of view. First, a concrete political aim has no place in a fundamental text. Second, it seems very surprising that the constitution asks for an expansion of military expenses given the fact that the danger of wars has decreased significantly in Europe. Most EU member states have accommodated to this fact and reduced the size of their armed forces or abolished obligatory military service.

(5) In the same article, the foundation of the European Defence Agency is announced, which shall assist in the development of defence capabilities through research and strengthening of the industrial and technological base for the defence sector. The establishment of this autonomous body is a decisive step toward the development of an independent EU military policy.

(6) A very interesting point is the aim of international missions "to protect the Union's values." One could see here again a close parallel to the foreign and military policy of the Bush government of the United States, which has entered into war against Iraq in order to reestablish freedom and democracy there, neglecting the many negative concomitants of such a war. Many EU member states (including France and Germany) strongly opposed this intervention.

(7) The decision about missions or tasks concerned with issues of international security lies in the hands of the Council; it may entrust a group of member states with such tasks "in order to protect the Union's values and serve its interests." The European Parliament shall only be "regularly consulted" and kept informed about the choices of the common security and defence policy. Here, a much less transparent and democratic decision procedure is foreseen, as in many EU member states (see previous).

(8) Finally, a new position of a "foreign minister" of the EU is created whose tasks also include includes security policy; that is, he has to serve at the same time as foreign and as defence minister. In all modern states, these two functions have been divided for good reasons. In the case of a serious international conflict, the foreign minister must concentrate on all possibilities for a peaceful solution through negotiations, while the defence minister has to prepare the armed forces also for the eventual case of a war from the beginning.

Thus, in these paragraphs, the European Union clearly sets itself the task to develop a common security, defence, and military policy, to establish a common military force, and to use this force for "interventions" all over the globe. There are certainly sound arguments which can be brought forward in support of a common foreign and security policy. However, there exist several problems connected with the way in which the extremely important and delicate issue of the common foreign and security policy is treated in the constitution.

First, it is evident that the constitution is aiming primarily toward providing the EU with military capabilities; much less is said about possibilities to prevent war and to promote actively peace in the world. It says nothing about the necessity of nuclear and other disarmament; about the delimitation of the production of weapons and international arms trade, which are among the main reasons for the many bloody conflicts in the poor regions of the world; and about the containment and punishment of arms brokers and gunrunners. One reason for this may be that several EU member states are among the most potent producers of weapons in the world. Second, given the importance of the issue of a "European army," it should constitute a clearly separate part of the constitution but not be spread out (or even concealed) in different parts of the large text. Finally, it is a serious problem from the normative democratic point of view that many of the provisions of the constitution (the establishment of the defence agency, the battle groups, and the foreign and security "minister") have already been realized (Diedrichs and Wessels 2005:364). For the promoters of the Dutch no-campaign against the constitution, this "militarization" of the EU was a main argument (Giorgi et al. 2006:192ff.). The strengthening of its military power is an aim supported by 65% of EU officials and 71% of MEP's, but only 48% of citizens (CIRCAP 2006).

Security and global influence

Given these considerations, the very surprising result in *Table 7.1* can be understood much better: It shows, in fact, that *security* is the most frequently mentioned of all value-related terms in the constitution; it comes up 144 times, representing about one fourth of all value-related terms. This is astonishing because security is rather seldom mentioned as a basic value of the EU. However, from the viewpoint of the theoretical considerations and empirical facts presented in this book, this is not surprising at all. Four points can be made in this regard.

First, there is no doubt that security can be considered as a basic value of any human and society.[21] The provision of internal and external security is one of the central tasks of any political community. Security must, therefore, be of central concern also for the EU. This relates not only to aspects of defence and military but also to those of border control. The member states participating in the Schengen Treaty have removed their internal borders, which immediately makes necessary a strengthening of the new outside borders of this area. The securing of these foreign borders has taken on, particularly in the Mediterranean, the character of a military observation (Milborn 2006).

Second, the high relevance of security corresponds to our analysis of the origins and early development of the EU (see Chapter 2). By cooperating closely within Western Europe, the founding member states of the EEC wanted to gain security against the potential new threat from the Soviet Union (see also Swedberg 1994). In this endeavour, they were strongly supported (in some degree even pushed) by their mighty ally the United States. It may be noted here that the establishment of a common defence policy was among the first aims connected with European integration. French Prime Minister Pleven had launched a plan for a European Defence Community already in 1950; it was only because the French parliament rejected it, in 1954, that the Plan was not prosecuted further (Dinan 1999:26). After the breakdown of the Soviet system, a new foreign threat is seen in international terrorism, which is mentioned three times in the "solidarity clause" of the constitution (Art. I-43). Terrorism shall be combated mainly by military means, which is a rather dubious way and reiterates U.S. President Bush's "war against terrorism" (Strobe and Chanda 2002). Anders Hellström (2006:163ff.) diagnoses in this regard a process of securitisation of the EU, which implies to define also (illegal) immigration as a security problem.

Third, the high importance of the value of security is less surprising also when we look at the basic values and aims of the European welfare states. In fact, the provision of security may be their most important aim. Despite many assertions that the welfare state (particularly in its Scandinavian, social-democratic version) effects a significant redistribution and guarantees an equal and just society, its main task everywhere is a horizontal redistribution. This implies to care for the insecurities of life which arose as a consequence of the realisation of the universal market (including the labour market) and the dissolution of the family as provider of social assistance throughout the life cycle (Spieker 1986; Kirchhoff 2006). Thus, the term *security* in the constitution often refers to social security and social protection.

Fourth, security is also an aim quite relevant from the economic perspective. Economic transactions and international trade cannot be exercised without legal, political, and military security (Bornschier 1988). The revitalization of the process of European integration in the 1980s can be seen as a reaction to the increasing global competition between the triad Western Europe–USA–Japan. Transnational European corporations and the EU Commission formed an "elite pact" in order to strengthen the position of European transnational capital (Bornschier 2000a; Ziltener 2000). In this regard, also the germane concept of "stability" is relevant, which has also an important place in the constitutional text. The primary focus of politics of the European Central Bank on the goal of price stability, at the expense of other basic goals of economic policy (e.g., growth, creation of jobs), can also be seen as a reflection of this priority (Attac 2006:55).

From the foregoing considerations we can deduce, however, that an additional potential aim or value may lie behind the issue of security and defence. This is the striving of the European Union toward influence and power in the world. This *"imperial argument"* (Möschel 1994:126) says that the EU must develop a global political (and military) power which corresponds to its economic strength: "An economic giant, but a political-military dwarf." It does not come up openly in the constitution, however. This is probably so because the striving for influence and power is not so positive and noble as all the other basic values mentioned explicitly. In some texts of the EU Commission, however, it is expressed quite clearly: "The EU is a world player . . . as the Union expanded and took on more responsibilities, it had to define its relationships with the rest of the world . . . A major challenge now is to spread peace and security beyond the Union's borders."[22] Similar statements have been made by many leading EU politicians, such as J. Chirac, R. Prodi, and others. Finland's Prime Minister Lipponen expressed it most clearly: "The EU ought to develop into a great power in order that it may function as a fully fledged actor in the world"[23] (see also Attac 2006:254ff.).

In this regard, it is also interesting to remind that the aim of the European Union to develop its own "identity" has been motivated primarily by its aspirations toward prestige, power, and influence on the global scene. The Maastricht Treaty opens with the following assertions:

> "Preamble: The undersigned, resolved to implement a common foreign and security policy including the eventual framing of a common defence policy, which might in time lead to a common defence, thereby reinforcing the European identity and its independence in order to promote peace, security and progress in Europe and in the world, (. . .) have decided to establish a European Union (. . .).
>
> "Art. B: The Union shall set itself the following objectives: To assert its identity on the international scene, in particular through the implementation of a common foreign and security policy including the eventual framing of a common defence policy, which might in time lead to a common defence" (see also Pfetsch 1997:97ff.).

As we have already mentioned, the constitution says very little about alternative, nonmilitary means to solve conflicts and promote peace in the world (see also Attac 2006:263). The attractive idea of Europe as a *"civil power,"* proposed already by the Dutch Max Kohnstamm (1964), secretary of the High Authority of the ECSC, does not come up in the constitution. This idea would imply that the EU sets a clear priority on peacemaking activities instead of using military means in international relations (Ruf 2004). A central institution in this regard would be accorded to the UNO. The role of United Nations, however, is mentioned only in peripheral ways in the proposed EU Constitution; reference is made only to its charter, but nothing is said about EU efforts to support it actively (see Arts. I-3.4, I-41.7, III-292.1, etc.). It seems that the EU wants to develop parallel activities in this regard. In the media, it was rightly discussed if the EU does not appropriate tasks here which belong to the UNO.

It is also not surprising, from this point of view, that the constitution says nothing about the necessity of reducing the extremely asymmetric distribution of military power in the world today (with the U.S. as the new superpower) or about the present efforts of rearmament of rising world powers, such as China. Also here, economic interests of European corporations and member-state governments (selling of military products) may have inhibited any explicit, critical reference to the problem. These are certainly very hot potatoes, but a self-conscious European Union should be able to tell important truths also to a close ally as to any other state in the world. A relatively cautious statement relating to these issues could easily be incorporated into the constitution. A guideline for such a statement could be Article 7.2 in the constitution of Portugal, which states: "Portugal supports the abolishment of imperialism, colonialism and of any other form of aggression, domination and exploitation between the nations, as well as the general and balanced disarmament, the dissolution of military blocs and the establishment of an international security system for the creation of an international order which is able to guarantee peace and justice in the relations between the peoples."

In the objective for controlled disarmament, the EU would find a strong ally in Japan, which is economically one of the three strongest blocs in the world, but has consciously renounced to develop huge armed forces and weapons (including atomic weapons); it is never mentioned in the constitution. Interestingly, also for the French supporters of the constitution the argument of the strengthening of the EU was very important. The argument of Europe as a "world power in the making" is supported also by some social scientists (see, e.g., Weidenfeld 1991). Others, however, have recognized early and quite critically these tendencies. Johan Galtung (1973) characterized the EC in 1970s as a "superpower in the making." Recently, Joseph Weiler (1999:95) noted that "some of the harkening for a common foreign policy is the appeal of strength and the vision of Europe as a new global superpower."

Let us now consider the two other basic, value-related terms which come up very frequently in the constitution and which touch on the central self-definition of the EU.

Freedom and competition

Much less surprising is the fact that freedom is among the most important values of the EU if we measure it by the number of references to it in the constitution. It is the second in the rank order of basic, value-related terms, mentioned 132 times (see *Table 7.1*) This corresponds to the widely recognized fact that European integration was mainly a "negative integration" with the intent to reduce barriers for economic exchange between the member states. The term *freedom* is related mainly to economic freedom, the freedom of trade, the freedom to establish and conduct a business, and so on. If we include the term *competition,* which is also mentioned frequently (thirty-one times), the references to economic freedoms amount to 40% of all entries connected with the term *freedom.* However, it must be said that it is not only economic freedom which has importance in the text of the constitution. About one third of the entries refer to freedom in general terms, about one fourth to political and social freedoms (freedom of expression, of religion, to form associations, academic freedom, etc.), about one tenth to individual freedoms (freedom to choose an occupation, of movement and travel). Thus, we can say that here the constitution has in fact implemented an important basic value which can be considered, in principle, as rather positive.

However, there are three main problems in this regard: First, the principle of freedom is mainly applied to economic actors, much less to noneconomic collective and individual actors. One can say that the constitution, in fact, has codified a neoliberal model of the economy in its many detailed regulations in this regard (Attac 2006:53). Second, these principles are preferred in most cases over competing basic values (such as equality, national autonomy, etc.) in cases of conflict. Third, even in the field of culture, economic principles dominate. While the Union praises on every occasion the cultural diversity of Europe and the preservation of this heritage as a fundamental political goal, in its practical politics culture was instrumentalized: "The significance of culture for employment, export and economic added value was turned into a European Union doctrine" (Giorgi et al. 2006:151).

Justice, human rights, nondiscrimination, and social rights

In regard to this area, which covers a broad range of topics, a positive overall judgement can be given. Here we find references to justice as a universal value, and many references to the fight against discrimination (on grounds of nationality, gender, race, ethnic and social origin, discriminations in economic exchanges, etc.). These values are mainly contained in Part II of the constitution in the Charter of the Fundamental Rights. It contains sections on human dignity (personal integrity, the right to life, etc.), basic individual freedoms, social rights, equality and solidarity, political rights, and rights in judicial proceedings. References to solidarity include solidarity as a general value of the Union, solidarity between the member states and peoples, between the generations, and the like. The main problem with these rights, however, is that they are formulated in rather general terms. We will argue in the next chapter that the attractiveness of the constitution and the chance of its approval could be improved significantly if also the social rights would be formulated much more clearly. This applies also to the concept of *employment,* which comes up rather frequently in the constitution. Partly it is related to overall employment policies, to the labour market and different services, partly to conditions of employment (a fact quite relevant for the EU given its aim of increasing labour mobility throughout the Union), partly also to individual concerns in relation to employment (employment of children, employment opportunities, and discrimination). Here, we should also mention that the reference to terms related to social rights and problems in the widest sense occurs much less frequently than to those of "security" and "freedom" but still are mentioned quite often (thirty-four times). Problems in this regard, however, are that most of these rights are formulated only in a very general sense and in a rather nonbinding way. We will come back at this issue in the next chapter.

Employment

Employment is a term coming up very frequently in the constitution in fourth place, right after the three basic values. It seems somewhat strange to include it in the list of basic values. Yet this term testifies very clearly to the ambivalence and fuzziness of the constitution concerning the definition of basic values, legal prescriptions, and concrete political measures. Originally, the idea of the working group on "Social Europe" was to include the aim of "full employment." In this aim, it could rely on the "European employment strategy," established in anticipation of the European Monetary System by the Luxembourg Job Summit and incorporated into the Amsterdam Treaty of 1997. It foresees a coordination of employment and social policies in order to counterbalance the negative effects of economic and monetary integration (Giorgi et al. 2006:147ff.). However, the success of this strategy has been very modest. The thesis proposed here is that the aim of "full" or "high-level employment" is out of place in a list of fundamental social rights for two reasons: First, it does not denote an individual right, but a political aim. As such it may be contested for several reasons. Second, it is also out of place as a concrete political aim of the EU because the Union does not dispose of the means to implement such a policy. Thus, if it declares to achieve certain goals in this regard, it can only rouse disappointment among the public. The dramatic failure of the Lisbon Agenda is a main witness of this thesis. We will come beck to this issue in the next chapter.

Democracy—the forgotten basic value?

After peace, democracy is probably the value most often associated with European integration, and the political elites do not get tired of praising themselves for having secured this aim. In Section 7.3, we have already raised serious objections concerning the substance of these assertions. At the beginning of the process of integration, democracy was no main issue (Falkner and Nentwich 1995:5). It became more and more so, however, with the extension of the competences and tasks of the EC/ EU. Several measures—in particular the strengthening of the European Parliament— have been taken in order to make the Union more democratic. How does the EU perform today in this regard? The content analysis of the constitution only confirms the earlier negative judgement in this regard. With only nine entries, this is the value least frequently mentioned among all in the text (see *Table 7.1*). Three comments shall be made here in regard to this astonishing fact.

First, the constitution pays strong lip service to the value of democracy. A reference to it comes up right in the beginning, in the preamble, together with four other universal values (human rights, freedom, equality, rule of law) and in Article I-2, in which the Union's values are enumerated. However, it seems to take it as a matter of fact that the principle of democracy is fully realized in Europe. However, there are multiple assertions of political philosophers and scientists that democracy, as it has been realized also in the democratic nation-states in the present-day world, exhibits many and serious shortcomings. (See, for instance, Arendt 1963; Etzioni-Halevy 1993; Zürn 1998; von Arnim 2000; Siedentop 2001; Abromeit 2001; Offe 2003; Schmitter and Trechsel 2004; we will come back to this issue in the following chapter.) Empirical facts, like decreasing turnout at elections and the rise of distrust toward political institutions and personalities, confirm their judgements (Dogan 1997, 2001). None of these problems is addressed in the constitution.

Second, the constitution explicitly introduces the concept of "representative democracy" as its main and nearly unique principle (Art. I-46). The principle that citizens vote for their representatives, who then decide about the course of politics, is central to modern democracy, especially to large ones. Its main importance lies in the fact that it provides each citizen with an equal vote and ensures the democratic election and removal of political elites. However, the principle has also the shortcoming that citizens are not able to influence substantive politics in this way. The parties for which they vote usually have many different aims and hardly all of them are supported by a voter. Political representatives are elected for a period of four to six years; in the meantime, there is no direct control by the citizens. In the EU, an additional problem comes in, namely, the fact that the votes of citizens have a very unequal weight in different member states. In Luxembourg (the one extreme), one MEP represents about 70,000 voters, but in Germany about 800,000 voters.

Third, in the next article (I-47), the principle of "participatory democracy" is introduced by stating that the EU institutions "shall give citizens and representative associations the opportunity to make known and publicly exchange their view in all areas of Union action." This is certainly a positive commitment. It has two weaknesses, however. On the one side, associations, citizens' movements, and the like do not represent the whole population but typically those subgroups which are able to organize and express themselves well. This proposal fits in quite well with the development of the close relationships between the thousands of interest and lobby groups in Brussels which maintain regular and close contacts with the commission, as we have seen in Chapter 5. The intransparency of these groups and relations, however, is one of the main concerns with democracy at the European level.

On the other side, as far as the direct participation of individual citizens is concerned, the constitution specifies that at least one million citizens "of a significant number of Member states may take the initiative of inviting the Commission . . . to submit any appropriate proposal on matters where citizens consider that a legal act of the Union is required for the purpose of implementing the Constitution." It will be quite a strong barrier to organise a million signatures from citizens in several states. Moreover, this possibility provides only for a very weak direct influence of citizens because the proposed popular initiative includes no clear obligation for the EU institutions to take some concrete action. It is well known from member states (for instance, Austria), which foresee such nonbinding popular petitions that they usually have no political consequences.

7.4 Where have the critical intellectuals gone?

As mentioned at the beginning, it is the main intent of intellectuals to look critically at political and institutional developments by confronting them with basic human values. The analysis in this chapter has shown that there exists a considerable hiatus between the universal values that have inspired intellectuals in their thinking about Europe through the centuries and the concrete development of the European Union since 1945. One would expect, therefore, that contemporary intellectuals raise their voice and point to these discrepancies. However, the impression is that this is not the case (see also Narr 1989; Hornstein and Mutz 1993; König and Sicking 2004:7ff.). Three types of intellectuals may be distinguished here: radical critics, "progressive" intellectuals, and apologists of integration.

Radical critics of European integration

It cannot be said that the shortcomings of the "real Europe" have not found their critics. There are in fact many social scientists who, from different theoretical points of view, are quite critical about the "concrete Europe," the EU; their representatives have not become well known or influential to the public, however. These authors point to deficits of the European Union in terms of democracy, political-economic inefficiency, dominance of neo-liberal economic ideas, preponderance of economic interests, retrenchment of the welfare state, increasing inequality, red tapism and corruption in the European bureaucracies, and the like (Vaubel 1995; Ohr 1996; Hankel 1998; Chryssochoou 1998; Höreth 1999; Bach 2000a; Bieling and Steinhilber 2000; Siedentop 2001; Tausch 2001; Abromeit 2001; Sklair 2001; van Apeldoorn 2002; von Arnim 2006).

It is beyond question, however, that critical stances toward European integration are the exception in academia. A person who raises doubts in this regard is soon discredited as being "against Europe," as preferring the nation-state over the EU, and so on (see the nice example in Hellström 2006:18f.). There may be many reasons for this kind of *Gleichschaltung* (political phasing) of an institution and of professional groups which should be distinguished from other elites by their independent way of thinking. One might be their career interests which are closely connected with European integration in the case of the legal profession (see Chapter 3). Another one might be efforts of the EU to communicate its self-image as a unique achievement in world-historical terms. Such efforts may have some effect also in the area of academic teaching and research, through the research programmes, the sponsoring of Jean Monnet chairs, and similar activities of the EU Commission. It would be an interesting research topic to investigate, for instance, how many of the holders of these chairs (mainly jurists and economists) exhibit a critical stance toward the EU. (Since 1990, not less than 650 such chairs have been established.) Through their teaching and writing they will exert a considerable influence on opinion formation among young students all over the world. A short look at six large and comprehensive textbooks on the EU on my bookshelf shows that not less then five authors have close affiliations to the EU.[24] We must not discuss the arguments of the aforementioned critical academics here in detail, as we are referring to them in several places of this work.

Quite a number of critical books in the EU have been published by journalists and other writers.[25] It may be that some journalists become more aware of problems because they can often observe directly the concrete workings of the EU institutions in Brussels and elsewhere. That these journalists have been able to develop such a critical stance is quite remarkable given the constraints and pressures to which they are exposed. One is the fact that the media become more and more concentrated, and the influential media owners (Rupert Murdoch in Britain, Silvio Berlusconi in Italy, the former Axel Springer in Germany, Hans Dichand in Austria, Bernard Arnault and others in France) often determine a one-sided political view of the European integration process (although not always a positive one). The other is the fact that the EU has developed quite a lot of strategies to win the support of the media and the journalists.[26] Finally, we have to mention here also the EU-critical European movements, such as Attac or Newropeans, who are not only active politically but have also published EU-critical books (Attac 2006).

One outstanding representative of the group of critical intellectuals was the French sociologist Pierre Bourdieu (1930–2002). He was the holder of the prestigious chair of sociology at the Collège de France, a highly productive social researcher, but also engaged until the end of his life in political movements and actions, such as worker strikes and demonstrations, and in the movement against neoliberal globalization (as a member of Attac). In this context, he was very active in holding public speeches, giving interviews, and writing newspaper comments all over Europe. After his death, newspapers worldwide printed obituaries in a number as probably has never happened for an intellectual. Bourdieu's position in regard to European integration can be sketched out quite shortly; he published little on this topic (Bourdieu 2000). He saw European integration as part of worldwide processes of globalization, led by American neoliberalism and supported by transnational European capital and centre-right governments of member states. Neoliberalism, in his view, is not only a particular economic doctrine but a comprehensive *doxa,* a *Weltanschauung* which more and more pervades perceptions and thinking of people all over the world. Its central element is that the state has to be retrenched in favour of market and private activities. The EU is a strategy to implement this new system in Europe. Bourdieu's general critique of globalisation, the economic-liberalistic character of the EU, and the important role of ideas in political fights and transformations are certainly well taken. However, it shares with other critiques of this kind (e.g., Martin and Schumann 1997) a somewhat simplistic and one-sided picture of the world, although Bourdieu is far from being a narrow-minded Marxist. His critique of neoliberalism and its main agent, the U.S., offers little in terms of a concrete reform of the EU institutions.

"Progressive" intellectuals with little doubts about the merits of European integration

A second type of intellectual, more visible in the public than most of the aforementioned authors, at first sight seems to be quite critical about the EU in its present shape; it also aims at developing alternative visions. In the end, however, it seems that the proposals remain rather vague. A closer look often shows that the representatives of this group are quite supportive of the EU in its present shape or as envisioned by the elites. Let us present two prominent representatives of this type.

The German sociologist Ulrich Beck, widely known to the educated public, even outside of Germany, has published a book with the title *The Cosmopolitan Europe* (Beck and Grande 2004). Its main idea is that European integration needs a new conceptual basis, a "new narrative" which provides meaning to its evolution which has not been understood really by anybody. What is cosmopolitanism? It is a mentality and orientation which tries to develop a new form of the recognition of diversity within unity, which is the true achievement of Europe. It includes the principles of tolerance, democratic legitimacy, and efficiency and applies both to individuals and collective units. Central elements of this orientation are a superseding of the nation-state and its incorporation into a more complex system of multilevel political governing. National and European politics become closely intertwined to the advantage of both. European integration is—and should remain—a continuous process without a preformulated master plan. The EU can be described as a new kind of "empire" with constituent parts of differing size, power, and levels of integration but no dominance of any single of them; with a high level of internal differentiation in social, cultural, and political terms; with an efficient provision of welfare and security; with a differentiated internal network structure, no fixed external borders, and a new, complex "cosmopolitan sovereignty" which includes also nonmember states in the European neighbourhood.

As this short sketch shows, this work is full of interesting ideas and visions. It is also a rich guide to many problems and issues of European integration. However, it is hard to see if the idea of the "cosmopolitan Europe" leads us very far. The theses of Beck and Grande about the EU remain rather vague, indicated also by a continuous use of the concept of "Europe" instead of EU. It can be argued that the main principles of "cosmopolitanism" have been clearly formulated already by the thinkers which we have discussed in this chapter: freedom and democracy by Kant, the recognition of cultural diversity by Herder and others. The idea of a "cosmopolitan Europe" seems rather utopian in the escapist sense. It remains on a very general, abstract level so that little concrete consequences about institutional reforms of the EU can be deduced from it. One basic problem of the idea of the "cosmopolitan Europe" is that the role of the basic values remains unclear. According to Beck and Grande (2004:31, 163), European integration needs values and norms but their specification can remain open, or they have to be created anew. Which values could these be—in addition to freedom, democracy, and respect of basic human rights? In accordance with the EU official historical interpretation, Beck and Grande argue that the preservation of peace in Europe was due to integration but not—as we have argued before—to the establishment of democracies. As we have seen, they also subscribe to the "official" vision that European integration is an unfinished, never-ending process. Furthermore, the really influential social and political actors are not recognized in the idea of "cosmopolitan Europe." This applies both to the political elites (Beck and Grande usually write only about nation-states) and to economic interests and elites.[27] But also references to the citizens are hard to find, except on the concept of "civil society." It would be difficult to explain at the basis of Beck's concept to understand the rebellion of the French and Dutch citizens against such a noble vision. Beck and Grande give this: "It is not EU's failure but its very successes that trouble people."[28]

The other representative of this group is the German philosopher and sociologist Jürgen Habermas (born 1929), also an internationally widely known intellectual. Habermas was the holder of a prestigious chair at Frankfurt University and is considered as a late, important representative of the school of "critical theory." In addition to his comprehensive academic writings, Habermas has published continuously about politics in Germany and the EU in newspapers and magazines. Two documents of Habermas are relevant here. One is his essay "*Why Europe Needs a Constitution*," published in 2001 in many European languages. Therein he argues that new tasks arise for the European Union, after the post-war aims (peace and integration of Germany) have been realized; these are peacekeeping in the world and resistance to neoliberal globalisation, which threatens the European welfare states and the "specific European way of life." A strong Union is necessary to realize these aims (an argument echoing the statements of Jacques Chirac analysed in Chapter 1). Habermas's argument that political integration in Europe is "retarded" compared to economic integration reminds one clearly of the neofunctionalist theory of integration. The elaboration and ratification of a constitution would have a "catalytic effect"; if an EU-wide referendum were held, it would contribute to the emergence of a European public sphere (this is certainly a valuable idea). Finally, he argues, like Joschka Fischer, that the EU should move toward a full state, with financial autonomy, two parliamentary chambers, a specific political culture, and so on. The constitution itself is not discussed in any detail, in spite of the fact that it contains quite a lot of problematic aspects and lacks elements which would be essential from a democratic point of view (as Habermas claims to represent).

Another document relevant in this context is a manifesto against the second war in Iraq, which was published by Habermas on May 31, 2003, together with the French philosopher Jacques Derrida.[29] The occasion for it were the large demonstrations in Madrid, London, Berlin, and other European capitals against the participation in the Iraq war by European governments (in particular Spain and Great Britain). In this essay, the authors argue that the Iraq war had again brought to the fore the weakness and failure of European foreign politics. Therefore, it is necessary to develop a new and attractive vision for Europe—a vision which should help to overcome the memories of totalitarianism and Holocaust which stamped Europe in the twentieth century. Habermas and Derrida develop the vision of a future *Kerneuropa* (core Europe) which should have a coherent and strong common foreign and security policy; among the members of this group, "separatism should not be allowed." This new Europe would mark a turning away from earlier imperialistic thinking, and it could also foster Kant's hope for an "internal world politics."[30] In both of these essays, it clearly turns out that Habermas is strongly supporting the political elite's ambition to implement the Constitution for Europe as soon as possible. Problems and deficits of this constitution are hardly mentioned. Habermas—and his French coauthor Derrida—also seem to subscribe fully to the vision of the European Union as a future strong political (and military?) player on the world scene.

Europe—a dream nearly fulfilled. Apologists of integration

A third type of intellectuals can be called a convinced defender or even an apologist of the EU in its present shape. This attitude seems to be more pronounced in European countries which only recently became members of the EU or among intellectuals outside Europe. Their view is also quite relevant because the intellectuals of different societies also communicate with each other (Shils 1982:183).

An apologetic attitude to European integration is clearly present in post-Communist east Europe. "A united Europe and Poland in its center—this was the dream of my generation which was condemned to Soviet domination and the dictates of the communist party," said the Polish journalist and adviser of Lech Walesa, Adam Michnik, in an interview.[31] The Czech writer and diplomat Jiri Grusa, president of the international PEN club, expressed it even more hauntingly at a symposium in Vienna in 2006: He asked for a new kind of a biblical *Frohbotschaft* (blithe message), an *EUangelium* for the European Union, given its immense achievements.[32]

The most elaborated work of this type, *The Dream of Europe*, has been written by an American, Jeremy Rifkin (2004). Rifkin (born 1943) is considered as one of the most influential American *Popular Social Scientists* and intellectuals. He established the Foundation of Economic Trends, is a university teacher, an adviser of governments, including the EU Commission, and author of influential books. In the aforementioned, work, he compares Europe with the United States. Rifkin is the prime example of all those authors who present Europe as a kind of "USA plus" (Alber 2006). For them, "Europe" performs better in nearly every area: It has better educational and health systems, it favours public and communal over individual and private investments, and it weighs quality of life higher than economic growth; in Europe people are "working to live well," while the Americans live in order to work. The *European Dream* is so attractive because it proposes "a new history which is concentrating on life quality, sustainability, peace and harmony." In Europe, a "silent economic miracle" is on the way; a new kind of economic superpower emerges; an optimistic "atmosphere of departure" exists. European integration and the European Union are also highly praised in Rifkin's work: It is the third largest governmental institution in the world; it is a remarkable success and "condemned to further success." The EU is the first postmodern governmental institution, resurged from the ashes of history; the proposed basic human and social rights are highly progressive and comprehensive (he quotes Giscard d'Estaing as a witness for this); the proposed EU Constitution firmly establishes all the noble principles mentioned before; nearly everything done in Europe is "revolutionary" (for instance, that France and Italy establish a common natural park for Capricorns; p. 378); all this will have the consequence that the EU will function like a state. Rifkin admits that this *European Dream* sounds somewhat utopian; but, like the old "American Dream," it is a vision which can and does inspire real development.

It should have become quite evident from this short sketch that Rifkin continually confounds "Europe" and the "European Union"; that he ascribes to the latter aims and measures which have nothing to do with it; in some cases, the dominant orientation and politics of the EU are even clearly the opposite of the Rifkinian European Dream. The empirical data referred to are frequently interpreted very generously in favour of the EU. His characterisation of the proposed Constitution for Europe is a glorification hardly based on a systematic analysis of the text.

Résumé

What can we deduce from this short look at a few present-day intellectuals and their stances on European integration? Four general aspects seem remarkable.

First, it is evident that the visions of all these intellectuals have been influenced strongly by the respective national contexts. (See Münch 2008a for an extensive discussion of the quite different views of the intellectuals in France, Germany, and Britain on European integration.) It is no accident that one of the most fervent critics of the EU was the French Pierre Bourdieu. French intellectuals have historically been leftist (Boudon 2004), and the critique of Anglo-Saxon neoliberalism is an old tradition in France. Both the fervent argumentation of Beck against scientific and other forms of "nationalism," as well as Habermas's insistence that European integration is a result of the experience of totalitarian regimes and the Holocaust, are fully in accordance with the unique German understanding of European integration as we have outlined in Chapter 6. Even the relative absence of the British intellectuals from discussions on Europe is a national characteristic: British intellectuals do not claim such a special role as the French, and they share the general British scepticism against the EU (Münch 2008a).

Second, it seems to be true that no major present-day intellectual of international reputation has developed a critical stance toward the European Union and elaborated a systematic examination of its system. A rather positive attitude toward the "real Europe" seems to be the rule, in spite of the fundamental weaknesses of this project from several points of view. The fact that there is little effort among intellectuals to look closely at the institutional weaknesses of the EU, to denounce them, and to develop concrete proposals for reform is quite different from the situation of many intellectuals in the past who fought for their ideals and were persecuted by the power elites therefore. One reason for this situation might be that European integration is a process which was and is unfolding only gradually in a fully legal way, and with the consent of all participating nations, without the use of any open constraint or force. It is also a process which seems to avail all the participants, and the creeping hollowing out of the quality of the democratic life is not easily recognized. For the anthropologist Cris Shore (2000:xi), it is a principle of good science to be critical; but scepticism "is too readily castigated in the European Union. Sceptics are portrayed as somehow small-minded and anti-European. This is possible because European integration is connected with the modernist myth of rationalization and progress" (Hansen and Williams 1999).

Finally, many intellectuals at universities and other institutions, particularly those in the legal professions, have been directly co-opted by the EU as judges, experts, research directors, and so forth. We have given an indication for these facts in Chapter 3.

CONCLUSION

There is a large, unresolved dispute about the character of the European Union and the final aims of integration. This chapter started from the assumption that this dispute can be solved only if we look closely at the ideas of "Europe" as they have been developed through the centuries and as they are invoked by the present-day political elites to justify the process of integration. In this regard, the idea of the preservation of peace in Europe occupies a central place. We have shown, however, that this idea cannot really provide a basis for the far-reaching aim of an "ever closer integration." Peace between countries is preserved, first of all, if they have become democracies. The European Community and Union have only marginally contributed to the collapse of authoritarian regimes in South and East Europe since the 1960s. Besides the idea of peace, also other, less noble visions were connected with European integration already among many historical writers. The most important among them was that a united Europe should become a new global power. The content analysis of the Constitution for Europe has shown (as do recent surveys among the EU) elites that this idea is highly influential till today among the political makers of integration—even if only few of them admit this aim in public. This discrepancy between the officially declared and the actually pursued aims and goals may be the most basic reason for the increasing discrepancy in the evaluation of integration among elites and citizens. A solution of this contradiction is the precondition for a harmonization of the views and expectations of citizens and elites. It presupposes a new perspective on the character of the EU. Such a perspective shall be developed in the next chapter.

8 The European Union as a "Social Community of Law"
Proposals for Strengthening its Social and Democratic Character

INTRODUCTION

The analyses in the two preceding chapters have shown: There exist deep-going discrepancies between elites and citizens and between the different member states about the aims and visions concerning the EU; the real development of European integration is not inspired in the first instance by the positive values—democracy and peace—connected with the intellectual "dream of Europe" but more with those of Europe as a new economic and political power. We shall not end this study after having elaborated these contradictions but will try to deduce, in this final chapter, some practical-political conclusions about the reform and future institutional development of the EU. In our view, this is a very important task which is usually not recognized. It is certainly a task different from the analysis of the coming into existence and the workings of an institution. However, both approaches—the empirical-explanatory and the normative-constructivist—need each other. It is one of the weaknesses of the literature on European integration that such integrative analyses are missing. The first task, here, is to take up the fundamental issue of the character of the European Union. A clarification of this question is of fundamental importance for the debate about its further development. In order to find an answer to this question, we discuss first the rationales behind a constitution for the EU, the reason for its rejection by the French and Dutch people, but the attitudes of all EU citizens toward the idea of a constitution. Then, it is proposed to see the EU as a "community of law." Such an understanding, it is argued, makes possible a solution for most shortcomings of the present system of the EU, namely, its weak social orientation and its democratic deficit. It is shown that many EU member states have included strong social rights in their constitutions.

The third section takes up the issue of the democratic deficit of the EU. It starts from the general assumption that the EU should not see itself as a "governing" polity. The consequences which follow from such a view already eliminate many of the well-founded criticisms of its present-day workings. It is also proposed to enhance the transparency of the elite networks, to strengthen the personal responsibility of individual political actors, and to introduce strong elements of direct democracy. In the last section, it is proposed to take up again the process of a discussion and modification of the Constitution of Europe: the proposals developed in this regard are based on findings about the reasons for the rejection of the constitution in France and the Netherlands, as well as on a content analysis of the text of the present constitution.

8.1 Potentials and limits of the Constitution for Europe: The view of the citizens

A very decisive step forward in the process of institutional reform and development of the EU was the Treaty establishing a Constitution for Europe, signed by the government heads of member states in Rome on October 29, 2004.

As pointed out in Chapter 1, the negative outcomes of the referenda in France and the Netherlands about this constitution in May and June 2005 were felt as a kind of political earthquake. The citizens of two founding and influential member states of the EU had rejected a text which in many regards could rightly be considered as an advance: The constitution condenses the complex earlier treaties into one single text; it strengthens the role of the European and national parliaments, thus contributing to a reduction of the democratic deficit of the Union; it includes a section on basic human and social rights; it improves the transparency and efficiency of the political processes in the highly complex political system of the EU; and it introduces two new political top offices (president and foreign minister) in order to strengthen the efficiency of decision making and provide the EU with personal "faces."

It is not surprising, therefore, that the interpretation of these negative outcomes soon became the object of a heated debate. The political elites were eager to point out that aspects of internal politics had played a significant, if not the pivotal, role. In France, this was in the first instance the low popularity of President Chirac, the poor economic performance of the country (Perrineaux 2005:231), and the formation of an anti-EU alliance between right-wing nationalists and the left-wing anticapitalist political forces ("Left and Right United Against Europe"[1]). It is argued that no concrete lessons for the constitution can be drawn out of the negative results of the referenda (Kuhle 2005; Schildt 2005).

Yet these facts can also be seen in quite a different light. It is argued here that the results of these two referenda are highly relevant for the revision of the proposed constitution and that they do not imply a rejection of the idea of a constitution in general. Two specific theses are proposed: (1) The general attitudes of the French and Dutch voters are rather positive toward integration and a constitution in general, but critical about the concrete proposal. (2) Some concrete lessons about the constitution can be deduced from the results of the referenda, and these correspond very well to democratic elite theory proposed in this work. They throw also additional light on the split between elites and citizens.

The general relevance of a Constitution for the EU

Does the EU need a constitution at all? There are good arguments saying that the existing treaties in fact already constitute such a constitution (Griller and Müller 1995). Some argue that the EU is functioning quite well also without a formal constitution (Moravcsik 2006). These arguments are not wrong because of the thesis that the EU cannot have a constitution because it is no state (Stein 2001). The idea of enacting a constitution for the European Union is controversial also because in some way the EU then can be considered as a true political community of its own (Deloche-Gaudez 2005:27ff.). However, the case is made here that the elaboration and ratification of a formal, specific document called "Constitution for Europe" would be a major advance.

The importance of a constitution lies not only in the fact that it introduces new principles concerning the aims and institutions of the Union, but also in its symbolic nature (Fellmann 2003). In a real sense, every political community has a constitution—the sum of its valid laws. However, a formal, written constitution contains the most basic laws and ideals of a political community and defines them in a precise way (Kelsen 1925; Montesquieu 1955; Löwenstein 1957; Fioravanti 1999). "From the symbolic point of view, a constitution is a record of national experience and a symbol of the nation's aspirations. It serves the important function of articulating the ideals of the community, of stating its social and economic aims. It exerts a tremendous educational influence as a convenient, easily-read compendium of the nation's basic purposes and principles" (Fellman 2003:491). A constitution it is not subject to changes by ordinary legislative procedures, and it emanates directly from the citizens themselves; therefore, it is also contained in a specific written document and ratified in some special way (Fellman 2003:486). Two main principles underline all democratic constitutions: legal limits to arbitrary power and the responsibility of the government to the governed (Dippel 2001). For the groups competing for power, constitutions serve as a reservoir of political arguments (Adam and Heinrich 1987:41).

Five arguments have particular relevance for a European constitution (for overviews, see Timmermann 2001; Liebert et al. 2003; Jopp and Matl 2005; Wessels 2005; Stone Sweet 2005). First, a single constitutional text makes the institutional setup and the workings of the EU much clearer (Leinen 2001; Langen 2001; Pernice 2004:19; Bast et al. 2003; Fitoussi and Le Cacheux 2005). Second, the extension of the EU to twenty-seven member states makes reforms particularly urgent; this applies both to the growing inefficiency of its institutional bodies and to the necessity to revise the principles of agrarian support and structural redistribution. Third, citizen concerns throughout the EU can be met which relate to the growing intransparency and unsatisfying democratic quality of decision processes. Fourth, by installing a special convention, the legitimacy of the EU could be improved in a significant way. It will be proposed below that such a "constitutional moment" (Ackerman 1989; Grimm 2004) should be created once more. Fifth, the existence of a written, basic document which clearly delineates the competences of the EU institutions and their relations to the member states and other collective actors increases the security and stability of European law throughout the community (Siedentop 2001:178). It would also lead to a gradual adaptation of the presently diverging national legal cultures (Schneider 2000:178).

A community of law, however, is not a new superstate also if it has a constitution. Central elements of a state are missing in such a community. We do not expect, therefore, that people will ever develop a kind of deep-going attachment to the EU as they have done toward regions and nation-states (Haller and Ressler 2006b). A constitution alone is unable to cause "patriotism," as some German political theorists (Dolf Stemberger, Jürgen Habermas) expected (Nettesheim 2003; see also S. Obermeyer and J. Nielsen-Sikora in Heit 2005). All that can be expected is that a more realistic appraisal of the EU and its politics develops among the general population. As a consequence, however, also its legitimacy would be increased.

When discussing the strengths and weaknesses of the constitution, we should also include its evolution by the citizens. Let us consider, therefore, the reasons for its rejection by them. Three topics shall be dealt with in this regard: the determinants for participation in the referenda; reasons for accepting or rejecting the constitution; and the social characteristics of supporters and opponents. Two Eurobarometer surveys and a survey by the French JPSOS institute have been carried out after the referendum. [2]

Reasons for the rejection of the Constitution
in France and in the Netherlands

First, let us look at the determinants of the participation in the referendum and the characteristics of the voters participating or not. The main reasons for abstention in France were (Eurobarometer): personal circumstances at the day of the referendum (66%); the text was too complicated (60%); voters had not enough information (49%); the feeling that participation would not have made any difference and lack of political interest (each 30%); the wish to penalize President Chirac (27%). Nonvoters were overrepresented among the young and middle-aged, persons living in large towns, and persons without a party preference. In the Netherlands, the main reason for nonparticipation was lack of information (51%); then personal circumstances (41%); the feeling that participation would not have made a difference (26%); that the constitution was too complicated (26%); no interest in politics, in the constitution, and in EU affairs (each 23%); also here, the intent to penalize the government was rather seldom (14%). Nonparticipation in an election due to personal circumstances at the day of the election is a typical feature in any election. However, the other main reasons give important clues: the fact that the text of the constitution was too complicated; that there was not enough information; and the feeling that voting would not have made any difference.

Next, let us look at the reasons for the positive and negative votes in France. Among the yes-voters, one stands out among all: The expectation that the constitution will strengthen the global power and influence of France in comparison to the United States and China (64%). Moreover, 43% think that the constitution will strengthen French influence in Europe. (IPSOS survey). This popular opinion corresponds perfectly with the general findings in Chapter 6, that, for the French, European integration was primarily a means to regain and strengthen its influence in Europe and the world. Less important among the supporters of the constitution are other arguments, such as the improvement of the functioning of the EU-25 (44%) and the reinforcement of the "Social Europe." In the Eurobarometer surveys, the main reason for the supporters of the constitution was (both in France and the Netherlands) that it is essential for the further pursuing of European integration (39% and 24%); other reasons were much less frequent.

Among the people who refused the constitution, three main arguments can be discerned (IPSOS survey): (1) the dissatisfaction with the present economic and social situation in France, with the French political class and with President Chirac; (2) the fear that the constitution reinforces the market-liberalistic character of the EU; (3) fears about Turkey's entry into the EU and French national identity. The Eurobarometer survey in France showed similar results: economic concerns about negative effects on France (57%); the constitution is too liberal and not social enough (35%); opposition to President Chirac (18%). A somewhat different picture emerged in the Netherlands; most (32%) of the no-voters indicated a lack of information, 19% feared a loss of national identity, and 14% expressed an opposition to the government. Overall, for half of the French and Dutch voters the general opinion about integration and the constitution was the decisive factor!

Further insights into the reasons for the referendum outcome can be gained by looking at the social characteristics of the yes- and no-voters (IPSOS survey). Those who voted yes were overrepresented among the older age groups; the better educated; among students and pensioners, higher professionals and managers, and people with higher income (3,000 euros and more).[3] Those who voted no were more frequent among people with lower education, farmers, workers, and routine employees; and among the unemployed and—to some degree—public employees. Thus, it seems rather clear that the better-off social groups were the strongest supporters of the new constitution and those who are actually deprived (unemployed) or have to fear that their group could be affected negatively by further integration (public employees) were against it. A very significant fact is that the younger by no means were more in favour, as it is often argued. This appears plausible, however, given the fact that many of them are losers of recent socioeconomic developments in France with its rather high youth unemployment rate of 20% to 35%.

Highly important also were political factors for the decision for or against the proposed constitution. Party affiliation of the voters was the most important determinant of voting behaviour. Among persons sympathetic to the extreme left or right political spectrum, less than 10% voted in favour of the constitution. This has led to the thesis of some social scientific commentators to the problematic thesis "left and right united against Europe," discussed in the preceding chapter. But even between those sympathetic to the Socialist or Green parties and those near to the centre-right parties (UDF, UMP), a large split exists: 40–44% of the first, but 76–80% of the latter voted yes. Similar large differences existed in regard to union affiliation: Persons who tend toward the leftist unions (CGT, CGT-FO, SUD) were much less frequently voting yes than those who tend toward centrist unions (CGC, CFE, CFTC). These results, however, are not surprising given the fact that the extreme parties fully rejected the constitution, the Socialists and Greens were divided internally, and only the bourgeois centre parties were unequivocally in favour. Thus, it is evident that the position of the political elites is reflected strongly in the decisions of their respective voters or sympathizers. This fact can also be confirmed if we look at the results of EU-related referenda in other countries. It turns out that large majorities in favour of integration usually are obtained if the political elites are fully unanimous in this regard while the result is open in cases where this does not apply (Luthardt 1995).

What can we learn from these findings? Should we say that the vote of the citizens is mainly influenced by their political leaders and is not based on their own rational considerations? Such a conclusion cannot be made for two reasons. First, in the light of democratic elite theory such an outcome is not surprising at all. The "man on the street" is hardly able to develop alone a considerate and definite opinion on such a complex matter as European integration. Complex and far-reaching new ideas must always be developed and explained by the elites. In this regard, it is essential that also fundamental problems and flaws of certain political aims and measures are brought to public discussion by critical elites, intellectuals, and activists. Only then also the "normal" citizens will recognize the problematic aspects of an idea or proposal and consider them in his or her voting decisions.

Second, it is also unfounded to assert that a political position of a leader is problematic just because he wants to promote his own political career by elaborating an oppositional view. For a political leader both these motives— to be successful in the election and to promote a certain program—have equal importance; the one cannot be pursued successfully without the other. If there are no prominent oppositional intellectual and political leaders, the discontent among those groups of the population who are critical against certain lines of politics may accumulate over time and unload itself from time to time in unexpected and problematic forms; political dissatisfaction and alienation (*Politikverdrossenheit*) may be spreading out.

General attitudes toward the constitution and its content

A further, important aspect relates to the general support for integration and the idea of a constitution and the concrete text which was proposed. The question is here if the rejection of the constitution was an indication of a general critical stance toward European integration. This was evidently not the case. The attitudes toward European integration were rather positive in both countries. In the postreferendum Eurobarometer (June 2005), 88% of the French and 82% of the Dutch agreed that their country's membership is a good thing (see *Table 8.1*).

In France, also a large majority (75%) argued that "the European Constitution is essential in order to pursue the European construction." In the Netherlands, this percentage was lower (41% against 50% who disagreed). However, the concrete institutions of the EU have a much less positive image. Only for 53% of the French and 31% of the Dutch, the EU institutions "conjure up a good image." Highly relevant is the fact that the rejection of the proposed constitution did not imply a rejection of the idea of the constitution as such. This is particularly true for the French; 75% of them agreed with the statement that the European Constitution is essential

Table 8.1 Attitudes of the French and Dutch Toward the EU and the Constitution for Europe (2005)

Statement/question	France %	Netherlands %
[Country's] membership in the EU is a good thing	88	82
The constitution of the EU conjures up a good image for you	53	31
The European Constitution is essential in order to pursue the European construction	75	41
The no victory in the referendum will allow for a renegotiation of the constitution in order to come . . . . . . to a more social text	62	65
. . . to a text which will better defend [country's] interests	59	66

Source: Eurobarometer Postreferendum survey in France (May 2005, N = 2015) and in the Netherlands (June 2005, N = 2000).

in order to pursue the European construction. (Among the Dutch, this proportion was 41%.)

Finally, also the opinions about the further fate of the constitution in the case of its rejection are relevant. Two statements were presented to the respondents in this regard: "The No victory in the referendum will allow for the renegotiation of the Constitution in order . . . to come to a more social text . . . to better defend the interests of France/Netherlands." Clear majorities in both countries (60–66%) agreed to both of these statements. Thus, it is evident that voters wished that the constitution should be revised but not rejected altogether. It is remarkable that expectations for a renegotiation of the constitution for these two reasons were more frequent among the younger, the less well educated, workers, and those who said no to the constitution.

These findings can be summarized as follows: (1) There was a high interest in the referenda, particularly in France, and most of those who participated were well informed. Nonparticipants often felt that the outcome would not make any difference. (2) The attitude to European integration in general and to the constitution in particular were important positive factors for participation. (3) Three motives for the voting behaviour carried most weight: that one's own nation should remain independent and autonomous; that the text of the constitution was too long and complicated; and that the constitution is too liberalistic and does not care enough about social aspects.

At this point, it seems highly interesting to look at the results of another recent EU-wide survey on the attitudes of the citizens toward the constitution and a the EU institutions. This survey was carried out by the organisation *Open Europe*, an English "independent think tank set up by some of the UK's leading business people to contribute bold new thinking to the debate about the direction of the EU."[4] As we can expect, given the critical considerations about the client bias in European opinion surveys (see Chapter 6), it gives a much less positive view of integration than that known from the Eurobarometer surveys.

Two main topics were covered by the survey, the general attitude toward holding a referendum and that toward the division of power between the EU and the member states.

The first question asked if a referendum should be held about a treaty "which gives more power to the EU" (which the European Constitution doubtless would do). A large majority—75% in total—of the respondents answered yes to this question (see *Table 8.2*). A vast majority can be found not only in the EU-critical UK but also in the large founding member states France, Germany, and Italy; in the latter two, a popular referendum about integration was never held. Even in the countries with the lowest percentages of supporters of a general referendum—mostly the post-Communist, economically less developed Central East European countries—a clear majority (between 55% and 66%) is in favour of holding such a referendum.

Table 8.2 Attitudes toward a Constitution and European Integration in the Twenty-Seven Member States of the European Union (2007)*

Questions/ statements**	(1) People should be given a say on a new treaty	(2) Would vote for giving more powers to the EU	(3) The EU does not represent ordinary people
Country	%	%	%
All	75	41	56
France	81	50	59
Belgium	73	59	54
Luxembourg	74	58	35
Netherlands	62	41	51
Germany	77	40	56
Italy	70	60	49
United Kingdom	83	21	68
Denmark	73	31	36
Ireland	87	38	50
Portugal	64	44	46
Spain (ES)	73	60	47
Greece (EL)	83	40	59
Austria	71	21	65
Sweden	68	16	70
Finland	72	29	63
Slovenia	55	50	48
Hungary	66	28	70
Slovakia	64	17	62
Czech Republic	82	27	65
Poland	74	38	58
Estonia (EE)	74	31	60
Latvia (LV)	80	15	74
Lithuania (LT)	67	37	60
Cyprus	76	42	54
Malta	77	26	33
Bulgaria	71	29	58
Romania	66	25	47

Source: "Poll on the future of Europe," Open Europe (London). Total sample size: 17,443 (n = 500–1000 in the single countries).

**Full text of questions/statements: (1) "If a new treaty is drawn up which gives more powers to the EU do you think that people should be given a say on this in a referendum or citizen consultation or do you think that it should just be up to the national parliament to ratify this treaty?" (2) "If a new treaty is drawn up which would transfer more powers to the EU, would you vote for it or against it in a referendum or citizen consultation?" (3) "Which of the following comes closest to your own view? (i) The EU should have more powers than it has now and we should make more decisions at the European level; (ii) The EU should keep the powers it has now, but should not be given more; or (iii) The EU should have less powers than it has now and we should take more decisions at a national or local level."

The next question asked if the respondents would accept such a treaty, giving more powers to the EU. Here, opinions are divided: All in all, 41% say yes, and the same proportion no (the rest are "don't know" or "no answer"). There exists a high variation between countries in this regard, however: In south Europe (Spain, Italy) and in the countries which profit most from the EU (Belgium, Luxembourg), a clear majority is in favour (about 60%); 50% of the French and 40% of the Germans are in favour, but only 20% to 30% of the British, Swedes, Danes, and Austrians. Also in East Europe, consent to strengthen the EU vis-à-vis the member states is low; it varies from as little as 15% (Latvia, Slovakia) up to a maximum of 40%.

The final question concerned the perception of the influence of ordinary people in the EU. Here, we can see that a clear majority—56%—of the respondents think that "The European Union does not represent ordinary people in [our country]." These findings confirm the results of the small postelection survey presented in Chapter 4. Again, the differences between countries are very pronounced: In northwest Europe (UK, Finland, Sweden) and Austria, the majority (60% and more) is against transferring more powers to the EU. But also in many new member states in East Europe, about half of the population or more prefer this option. This finding again confirms that it is a myth that the populations in the post-Communist countries have voted "enthusiastically" for entry to the EU.

We can summarize the results of this section as follows: The citizens in France and the Netherlands, as well as those in the whole EU, have a rather positive attitude toward the idea of a constitution, and they strongly want to be involved in the decision about its shape. Yet they also have serious reservations about the content of the proposed Constitution for Europe. In the next two sections, the idea to understand the EU as a community of law will be proposed. Such a view understanding enables us to take seriously the reservations of the citizens and to reconcile different aims and expectations about integration in the different member states of the EU.

8.2 The EU as a "Social Community of Law" and its Charter of Fundamental Rights as an approach toward a *Social Europe*

In the following, we first elaborate the idea of the EU as a "Social Community of law (Soziale Rechtspemeinschaft). Then we show that such an understanding would enable the EU to develop its weak social elements without aspiring toward becoming a true (welfare) state.

The European Union as a "Social Community of Law"

There is a long discussion going on about the true "nature" of the European Union (Schneider 1992, 2000; Weiler 1999; Ferry 2000; Weiler and Wind 2003; Timmermann 2001; Griller 2005). Does it constitute only an association or confederation of independent states (*Staatenbund*) or already a federal state (*Bundesstaat*)? It is evident that both these characterizations are inappropriate. In at least three regards, the EU is much more than a mere confederation of independent nation-states: (1) The basic treaties between state governments include far more issues than an international treaty usually does; in fact, there exists practically no social or political issue which is excluded fully from their jurisdiction. (2) The EU has independent and strong permanent institutions whose exclusive task is to promote integration; in Chapter 5 it was shown that they were highly successful. (3) The interaction between the member states is regular, continuous, and intense, occurring on many different levels of politics and administration.

The European Union, however, can also not be conceived of as a federal state. The central element of a state is lacking, namely, the holding of "the monopoly of the legitimate use of physical force in the enforcement of its order" upon a specific territory (Weber 1978a:54). The European Union has no police and military force; it lacks a bureaucratic apparatus which directly interacts with citizens in the provision of services and the authority to collect its own taxes.

It seems that no adequate answer can be given to the question what kind of political community the EU constitutes. To denote it just as a new "political system *sui generis*" or to invent new concepts ("a new form of empire"; Beck and Grande 2004:97 ff.) is not convincing. Another possibility is to argue (or postulate) that the EU will develop further into a full federal state. Such a claim has been made in the famous speech of the German foreign minister Joschka Fischer at Humboldt University in 2000. Responding to his own question: Europe quo vadis? He stated: "Forward until the completion of European integration"[5] (see also Wind 2003). Full political integration, in his view, includes the establishment of a European parliament and government with full legislative and executive competences. This, however, would clearly imply the disempowerment of the member states, although their relevance would not be denied on paper. In recent articles, Fischer continues to argue for the necessity of the development of the EU toward a full state, particularly in terms of foreign and military policy. However, not only the critical responses of many leading EU statesmen on Fischer's speech confirm that such a solution is not feasible. It seems unnecessary, even undesirable, also from the viewpoint of historical and theoretical, legal, and social-scientific considerations.

Here, it is proposed to see the EU as a Social Community of Law. This designation means that the main principle constituting the unity and determining the working principles of the EU is the law in the widest sense. Such a comprehensive community of law is distinguished from more specific, narrow international treaties by the facts that (a) all areas of social, economic, and political life are or can be included; (b) the members of the community develop also a feeling of belonging together; a process of *Vergemeinschaftung* in the sense of Weber (1978a) is evolving. Let us look at some authors with a similar perspective and at some of the facets which it involves. We will see that many of them are fully congruent with the specific character of the political system of the EU.

From the side of legal science, Joseph Weiler (1999:91ff.) sees the EU at a crossroad between the model of "unity," with a full free market and economic liberalism as dominant value, and a "community model" wherein the member states remain autonomous and many more values are important. This model rejects the classical idea of international law, which "celebrates state sovereignty, interdependence and autonomy." "The idea of Europe as a community not only conditions discourse among states, but it also spills over to the peoples of the states, influencing relations among individuals" (Weiler 1999:93). Political scientists Alec Stone Sweet and Thomas Brunell (1998) have characterized the EU as a "transnational rule-of-law polity." In their view, European legal integration emerged out of three factors—transnational exchange between (mainly economic) actors, triadic dispute relations, and the production of legal norms to facilitate and institutionalize these relations. The driving forces for integration were private (mainly economic) litigants, national judges, and the European Court of Justice (ECJ), all interacting within the framework of the treaties. Since 1964 (Costa v. Enel case), the ECJ more and more assumed a central role in establishing the doctrine of the supremacy of community over national law. The "direct effect" principle empowers individuals and companies to sue national governments for not conforming to obligations contained in the treaties. Thus, it is rightly stated that the ECJ "constitutionalized" the treaties (Burley and Mattli 1993; Beck and Grande 2004:18 f.). Relevant in this regard is also a thesis of Marlene Wind (2003). She argues that most legal systems in history have been characterised by a great variety of coexisting legal orders at the national and international level, for private and state law, and so forth. From this point of view, the complex legal system of the EU is not new and unique. There was also a strong trend, however, that in modern societies, law assumes a central role not only as an expression of interests but also as a linkage to universal principles and as a source of identity for individuals and political communities (Boyle and Meyer 1998).

If we define the European Union as a "community of law," we can avoid the infelicitous decision between Scylla and Charybdis of *Staatenbund* against *Bundesstaat*. The essence of law is to provide a framework within which peaceful and beneficial reciprocal exchanges and cooperation can take place. This is possible without a central bureaucratic coordination of activities. Legal integration enables not only a far-reaching economic but also political and social integration. In legal theory, this thesis has been proposed most forcefully by Hans Kelsen (1925). In his "Pure Theory of Law," he argued that law is the main basis for political integration because of the sanctions associated with it. Insofar as a certain number of men and women are subjugated to a common legal order, they form a "people" or demos (*Staatsvolk*). A state is nothing else than a valid legal order. Kelsen's radical legal positivism was not generally accepted, particularly as it concerns the understanding of the state. However, when considering the European Union, his ideas appear as strikingly adequate. Recently, many authors have characterized the Union as a community of law, pointing to the fact that the main form of integration occurs through law since the beginning. Already Walter Hallstein (1979), the influential first president of the EC Commission, characterized the EC as a community of law (*Rechtsgemeinschaft;* see also Pernice and Maduro 2004:14). A. Stone Sweet (2005:28) denotes the EU as "a rule-of-law community"; law and legal regulations, however, are not independent from political processes and power relations but institutionalize these in a certain form.

An indication for the legal character of the EU is the central role of the European Court of Justice (ECJ). In fact, this court already in the 1960s clearly stated that the European Community constituted "a new legal order of international law in favour of which the member states have limited their own rights of sovereignty and whose legal subjects are not only the member states but also individual citizens" (Case van Gend and Loos 1969; see Langen 2001:382). Since that time, the ECJ has continuously and efficiently, without any serious objection from the member states, used its self-defined, far-reaching legal competencies to elaborate and strengthen the character of the EC/EU as an autonomous, new political community and the constitutional character of its legal system (Griller and Müller 1995:210 ff.). According to Bryde (1992) and Stone Sweet (2005), the ECJ transformed the EC treaties already since 1969 into a constitution and itself into a constitutional court. The preponderance of legal integration is further documented by the fact that the main activities of the large Euraucracy in Brussels are concerned with developing legal regulations and proposals. Recently, also the German sociologist Richard Münch (2008a) argues for such an understanding of the EU. This is so, first, because law is the basic structure of all modern societies; in this regard, Münch refers to Kant, who considered law as a main instrument producing societal integration. It is so, second, because in the most influential member states quite different semantics of integration prevail which can be integrated only through a common, overarching juridical-legal construction of the EU. In view of this fact, the democratization of law and of the legal institutions becomes a central issue, as already pointed out by Kelsen (see also Alliès 2005:50).

From the sociological perspective, the question is how far law is able to integrate a community. In one instance, law has very broad capacities in this regard. For Weber (1978a:333), "law guarantees by no means only economic interests but rather the most diverse interests ranging from the elementary one of protection of personal security to such purely ideal goods such as personal honour . . ." On the other side, sociologists of law point to the fact that the formal existence of a legal order must not correspond to its factual effects (Gephart 1992; Gessner 1992; Zürn and Wolf 2000). The factual recognition of a legal order by the people is covered by the concept of "legal culture" (*Rechtskultur*); its difference to the formal legal system is analogous to the distinction between a legal and a "real" constitution (*Realverfassung*).

As far as the EU is concerned, two problems exist in this regard. First, it is well known that in the different member states of the EU different legal cultures exist. These differences have a formal and a behavioural aspect. We may mention, in these regards, the difference between the tradition of Roman law in continental Europe and that of Common Law in Britain (Ebert 1978 distinguishes five *Rechtskreise* in Europe). Also, the differences in the attitudes toward state and law in the European north, particularly in Scandinavia, and in the south, the Mediterranean countries, are relevant in this regard, with much more trustful attitudes in the former than in the latter region. However, there exist also some common elements in the different constitutional principles in Europe (Dippel 2001:28ff.). Second, EU law is more remote from the concrete lifeworlds of people and their communities than is national law (Zürn and Wolf 2000). Breaches of EU law often do not arouse public scandals; contestable decisions of the European Court of Justice do not lead to EU-wide protests.

Notwithstanding all these problems, we would like to argue that the European Union can in fact be understood as a community of law. Such an understanding opens up far-reaching possibilities to accommodate the principles of unity and diversity, of centralization and decentralisation, as well as that of enhancing the social and democratic character of the Union. A clear self-concept of the Union opens a possibility to overcome the problematic understanding of European integration as a process without an end (Beck and Grande 2004:62). It would relieve it of the continuous unease and restlessness about its further development and the pressure to hasten from one reform to the next.

The fundamental rights in the Constitution— a sufficient basis for a "Social Europe"?

The one-sidedness of the EU in terms of its economic liberalistic orientation is one of two most problematic issues when it comes to a reform of the EU institutions in a way which could make it more attractive to its citizens, accord the project of "Europe" with a new spirit, able to arouse enthusiasm. The solution of this problem seems to be like trying to square the circle. The problem is that a reform of the EU which would provide it with extensive competences in the area of social and welfare policy would conflict sharply with the principle of subsidiarity. It would make little sense to endow the Union with far-reaching competences because social problems must be solved mainly at the national, regional, and local levels. A "Social Europe" in the sense envisaged by many Social Democrats would imply that the EU becomes a true federal superstate.

In the Constitutional Convention, there was general agreement that a better coordination of Union efforts to combat social exclusion and inequality are necessary. The majority of the members were not convinced—as are most social scientists—however, that this is best achieved by harmonization of social-protection systems (Giorgi et al. 2006:33; Liebert et al. 2003:119ff.). A European welfare state is impossible in the foreseeable future because there exists no European labour market, and geographic mobility between states is rather low (Leibfried 1996; Majone 1996a, b; Scharpf 2002; see also Chapter 4).

A solution of this problem can be found if the EU is understood as a Community of Law. Then, it will be its only task to define the most basic legal provisions in regard to social and welfare provisions. The concrete legal-normative dispositions and procedures of social administration are left wholly to the member states and their subunits. The proposed Constitution for Europe has already made a significant step toward defining such basic social rights in Part II (The Charter of Fundamental Rights of the Union). In the following, the strengths and weaknesses of this charter shall be discussed.

The *Charter of the Fundamental Rights* was developed by a special convention in 1999–2000 and approved in 2000 by the EU institutions and the European Council in Nice. This charter was included unchanged as a whole into the constitution. The explicit inclusion of such rights in a constitution is certainly important and well taken in principle (see also Contiades, cited in Pernice and Poiares Maduro 2004:59ff.). It happened only after decisive actions taken by several subgroups and members of the convention.[6] They are very proud of this achievement. According to the Austrian MEP Johannes Voggenhuber, who was leading in these efforts, the inclusion of these rights was a "revolutionary process"; it was "the first time in the history of human rights that social rights have been declared as classical, enforceable human rights."[7] Also, some analysts praise it as a basic text which "will make for legal clarity and security and strengthen the trust of citizens" (Liebert et al. 2003:154). A look at the substance of these rights, however, raises several doubts about these assertions in four regards (see also M. Opielka in Heit 2005:123).

First, several of these rights are self-evident, and one may ask why it is necessary at all to state them explicitly in the constitution. Examples include the right to freedom of thought (this "right" is hardly found in any other constitution), the prohibition of slavery, the right to establish a marriage and a family, the right to work. Some of these rights, however, are not trivial, and their inclusion really marks a unique European legal system based on specific values. Examples are the prohibition of the death penalty, of torture (a right quite actual if one looks at certain recent practices of the U.S. army), and of compulsory labour.

Second, many of the basic rights included are quite similar to those already formulated in existing national constitutions (e.g., right of dignity and life, equality before the law, etc.) or in the European Convention of Human Rights ratified by all EU member states. One could ask, in this case, why it is necessary to recapitulate them in the EU Constitution or what this inclusion adds to their relevance.

Third, the formulation of social rights or new rights—such as those relating to the environment—is rather weak concerning their degree of bindingness. Usually it is not stated that the EU will protect or enforce these rights but just that they have to be respected. Some examples: "The freedom and pluralism of the media shall be respected" (Art. II-71); "Everybody has the right to education . . . This right includes the *possibility* to receive free compulsory education" (Art. II-74); "The Union shall respect cultural, religious, and linguistic diversity" (Art. II-82). Sometimes even just factual statements are given: "Political parties at Union level contribute to expressing the political will of the citizens of the Union" (Art. II-72).

Fourth, the area of validity of these rights is very restricted. The general clause at the end of the constitution states that the provisions of this charter are addressed only to the institutions and bodies of the Union and to the member states only insofar as they implement Union law (Art. II-111). At several places, a clause is introduced stating that the rights are valid only to the degree that they correspond to existing national laws. Two examples: The freedom to found educational establishments "shall be respected in accordance with the national laws governing the exercise of such freedom and right" (Art. II-74). "Everyone has the right of access to preventive health care and the right to benefit from medical treatment under the conditions established by national laws and practices" (Art. II-95). All these rights could be formulated in a much more binding way. In the following, we give some detailed examples from two large member states and hint toward similar specifications in several others.[8] It may not be by accident that a firmer language is adopted only in two cases. They concern equality between men and women (Art. 83) and rights of workers (Art. II-7ff.). In both cases strong pressure groups—feminist organisations and unions—were supporting them. In only one case is positive action foreseen in order to enforce a right. Art. II-107 states that "legal aid shall be made available to those who lack sufficient resources . . ." Maybe the highly influential legal profession was behind this article, which ensures an important business area for their members?

A comparison with fundamental social rights in the constitutions of some EU member states

The constitution of Italy contains quite a lot of far-reaching social rights.[9] A considerable part of its relatively short constitution is devoted to them. Its first title contains civil liberties, the second "ethical-social relations," the third "economic relations," and the fourth "political relations." The section "ethical-social relations" contains also duties concerning marriage and family, such as the duty of parents to care for and to educate their children. It also states that the republic "facilitates by economic and other measures the establishment of a family and the fulfilment of the duties connected with it." This fact is quite relevant since a well-functioning social and political community presupposes that the citizens participate actively in public, societal, and political affairs. The EU Constitution contains no references to concrete duties or obligations of the citizens. The exception is a general remark in the preamble which states that the exercise of rights is also connected with obligations toward fellow human beings, the community, and future generations. This fact corresponds to a critical interpretation of the political system of the EU as a new kind of paternalistic "superstate" which cares for the well-being of its citizens in all regards but does not expect much activity from their side.

As far as the concreteness of social rights is concerned, the Italian constitution has adopted quite a different language. Let us give some examples. Quite at the beginning, it is made clear that equality is a similar basic right as freedom. Article 3 states that "all citizens observe the same respect and are equal before the law . . . It is the task of the Republic to eliminate all economic and social barriers which actually restrict freedom and equality of the citizens." In a similar vein, it states that the state protects health as a basic right of an individual and an interest of the community. Concerning education, it declares that gifted and deserving pupils have a right to achieve the highest levels of education, even if they are fundless; in this regard, the state supports them with stipends, family allowances, and the like. Concerning economic relations, the very first article of the constitution states: "Italy is a democratic republic, based on work," and it declares that each citizen has the right to work. In the section on economic rights and relations, it is determined that the republic protects work and that each working person has the right to a remuneration which corresponds to the quality and amount of his or her work; the income must be adequate to secure for him and his family a free and dignified life. Every citizen incapable to work has a right to subsistence and social welfare. Concerning property, it is stated that this can be "public or private"; for reasons of common welfare, law can declare that certain categories of enterprises or services can be assigned to public corporations; the state recognises and supports the social functions of nonprofit cooperatives. In the section on political relations, not only basic rights are formulated but it is also stated that everybody must contribute to the public expenses "according to his/ her tax power" and that the tax system has a progressive structure.

Another example that is relevant in this regard is the "Environment Charter of 2004," included as the first section with 10 articles in the French constitution. Also here, we find references both to rights and duties of citizens and to concrete obligations of the state. Articles 1 and 2 state that everybody has the right to live in a balanced and healthy environment, but also the duty to contribute to it and to avoid actions which could damage the environment. Politics has to control the state of the environment and further sustainable development; for this aim, it has to establish a balance between economic growth and social development, and it must promote environmental information, education, and research.

These two are not the only member states of the EU which formulate explicit social and environmental rights in their constitutions. The Belgian and Spanish constitutions establish the right to work. The Dutch and Greek constitutions declare the obligation of the state to care for "sufficient" employment; this seems a better aim (because it is related to the needs of the people) than the formulation in the EU Constitution, which promises to work for full employment; full employment is a rather contested and disputed statistical measure. In different states different measures concerning employment may be seen as adequate. In the UK (as in the U.S.), the focus is laid on ensuring the flexibility of the labour market, in Scandinavia on securing a high level of employment. Both models have their merits and shortcomings (Haller 1997; Haller and Heschl 2004). If the EU declares as its aim to achieve a certain level of employment, it encroaches on matters of national politics. Also, Alston and Weiler (1999:27) criticize the EU documents for their focus on "social policy," aims to overcome "social exclusion," and so on, instead of focussing on individual rights. Several states formulate the right of persons who are unable to work and care for themselves for state subsistence (Belgium, Spain). The Spanish constitution establishes the right to get a remuneration out of work which guarantees decent subsistence for the worker and his family (Art. 35). The Swedish constitution formulates concrete rights of foreigners residing in Sweden, including their access to education. In the section "Directive principles of social policy" in the Irish constitution, it is maintained that the state must prevent a destructive concentration of essential commodities in the hands of a few, that everyone has the right to an adequate occupation, and that the state must protect the vulnerable, such as orphans and the aged. Also, many of the new member states which formerly had state-socialist systems have included references to well-defined social rights; we cannot quote them all here.

Thus, it turns out quite clearly that many member states of the EU have gone much farther than the EU Constitution in defining concrete social rights and in placing an obligation to their realization both on individuals and the state. The same is partly true also for the European Charter of Human Rights of 1961 (Feldman 1993; Waldschmitt 2001). We can draw three general conclusions from these examples.

Three principles for the establishment of basic social rights in the EU Constitution

First, the constitution should also include basic social rights of individuals, as well as obligations, into its principles. This demand follows directly from the concept of democracy. Theorists from Aristotle to Rousseau have argued that democracy cannot work if social inequalities are too large (Graubard

1973). The recognition of basic social rights would do justice to the widespread demand that the EU should become more "social" (see, e.g., Falkner and Nentwich 1995; Ferry 2000:180ff.; Weiler 2002:56; Benz 2004; Attac 2006; Hermann 2006). It would also create more coherence and clarity in a field which up to now is characterized by a bewildering variety of principles and regulations (Waldschmitt 2001:77ff.). P. Alston and J. Weiler (1999:26) have expressed this point most succinctly: "The principle of the indivisibility of human rights is a keystone of EU policy. This means that economic, social and cultural rights should be accorded as much importance as civil and political rights." Up to now, social citizenship rights have been quite restricted. In the Maastricht Treaty, social rights were limited to employed people; the whole logic of these rights was market-oriented (Cole 1994). Such rights would also provide the concept of Union citizenship with more substance. Up to now it is more of a symbolic than a practical relevance, and it is only national citizenship which really counts (Dell'Olio 2005; Donati 2008; Nettesheim 2003; Dehove 2004:36ff.). These rights should be formulated in a way which specifies a clear obligation of politics to realize them. However, rights should not be granted without obligations (Giddens 1998). Increasing personal autonomy implies also that the individuals must contribute themselves when they draw on public support. Unemployment payments, for instance, must be coupled with individual efforts to look for a job.

The request to formulate basic social rights as concrete individual rights leads to a second postulate: The enactment and implementation of these rights should be left entirely to the member states and their competent subunits and associations. Even if the European Union will provide an important general frame for the basic rights, their concrete implementation must be left to the member states; we could say that *European citizenship* must be fulfilled with life by correspondingly adapted national citizenships (Miller 2000). Local, national, and EU citizenship together would constitute "nested membership rights" (Faist 2001; Lehning and Weale 1997). In this process, they could take into consideration their specific systems of welfare state and welfare provision and their level of socioeconomic development and also the preferences of their citizens (see also Pernice and Poiares Maduro 2004; Donati 2008). We have illustrated this principle already in regard to work and employment.

Another apt example where it can be shown how such a principle could work is that of the *minimum wage*. This idea has been discussed extensively also at the level of the EU (Dehove 2004:139). Certainly the same absolute minimum wage throughout the Union would be impossible. It would constitute an unacceptable interference and distortion of the process of wage formation, given the extreme differences in the level of wages between the member states. However, this problem could be perfectly avoided if the EU would restrict itself to establish as a rule that each member state has to declare a minimum wage which corresponds to the general income level of this country. In fact, twenty of the twenty-seven EU member states have already legally defined a minimum wage, including the United Kingdom (Dehove 2004:137). The significant variations in terms of general standards of living which presently exist between the member countries are clearly respected by defining the minimum wage.[10] In a rich country, a much higher level of public welfare provisions is possible than in a poor country. Not in all countries do the citizens wish a strong extension of social rights (Mau 2005). The granting of individual social rights would imply that he or she can sue his or her nation-state for them. This state then would have two choices: It could implement these rights or it could argue—against the EU Commission or the ECJ—that the level of provision which it offers is consistent with its financial possibilities, its own system of welfare, the wishes of most of its citizens, and the like.

There are several objectives which could be raised in this regard and which can be invalided quite easily, however. First, it would be central to establish the principle that only individual social rights should be laid down in the constitution for two reasons. First, individual rights are generally preferable to rights for groups and other collective units (Offe 2003). Second, European integration makes it particularly necessary that law is based on universal principles, which means in essence that social rights must refer to individuals (Münch 2008a).

Another objection to this proposal could be that the inclusion of these basic social rights in a constitution would not make much difference in practice. It is a matter of fact that already the existing EU law in the social area (e.g., labour law) is not implemented fully everywhere (Falkner et al. 2005). This is certainly true to some degree. However, all in all the bulk of EU law has in fact been implemented in the member states.

A third issue concerns the problem if the inclusion of basic social rights in the EU constitution would have a real effect on the policies of the member states and—in the end—on the improvement of the social situation and well-being of their less-well-to-do citizens. It can be argued that, in the middle and long term, these constitutional provisions could well become effective for three reasons. (1) The European Court of Justice would also have incentives to pronounce judgements which would enhance the realization of the basic social rights if these were specified as concrete individual rights in the constitution. Up to now, the ECJ has contributed little to the implementation of basic human rights (Stein 2001). Individual suits would induce the ECJ to specify and assert community law also in the area of basic social rights (as it did in the area of rights connected with economic liberty). (2) The inclusion of fundamental human and social rights would be "a decision of great symbolic significance" (Pernice and Poiares Maduro 2004:64) with important consequences. A Constitution for Europe can be considered as a far-reaching institutional invention, based on ideas and interests and respecting the differential tasks of individuals and collective units (Garrett and Weingast 1993:184). From this point of view, the

constitution as the basic set of rules of the community and the decentralized member and community enforcement of norms and concrete policies would be complementary. A constitution with concrete social rights
would be a normative system that translates the general idea of European
social integration into specific expectations and gains. In this regard, it
would also enhance significantly the trust in the political elites. Today,
these are "in danger of creating a profound moral and institutional crisis,"
just because "the public case for Europe is now being made almost exclusively in economic terms" (Siedentop 2001:216f.). (3) Also, the chances for
the implementation of these far-reaching principles into the constitution
should be given. It should be much easier to win the consent of elites and
citizens in the integration-sceptic countries (in particular the UK) for legal-
constitutional principles than for direct transfers of governmental welfare
functions to Brussels. If they do not wish to be subjected to a central EU
government, they could agree to submit themselves to the rule of European
law (Schneider 2000). This has happened in the case of Great Britain—as
in that of any other EU member state—already to a far-reaching degree.
Also in Britain a "new world of overlapping domestic and international
legal orders" exists as a consequence of its membership in the EU (Hunt
1997:3). Moreover, the focus on law which is individually centred should
also make it easier for the Britons to accept it given their liberal-individu-
alistic tradition (Ginsberg 1992:139ff.; Feldman 1993; Münch 2008a).

8.3 Enhancing of transparency and direct democracy: Consequences from the character of the EU as a consociational political system

The second main problem of the EU today concerns its democratic deficit.
In this section, we first discuss the character of this deficit and the solution for it proposed in the Constitution for Europe. Then, we look at the
Berlin Declaration of 2007—the response of the political elites to the crisis of integration after the rejection of the constitution in France and the
Netherlands. Our argument is that the EU will miss a historical chance if
it proceeds as it is foreseen in this declaration, that is, to implement it with
minor modification and only by the European Council. The next sections
discusses detailed problems and solutions for several aspects of the democratic deficit in the EU. In the concluding section, the proposal is made to
resume the constitutional discussion and to submit a new constitutional
text to the citizens throughout the EU.

Generic problems of present-day democracies and the democratic deficit of the EU

What is the nature of the "democratic deficit" of the EU? Some authors
argue that there exists no such deficit at all. Due to its character as an international community, standards of national democracy are not applicable to

the EU because there exist no "European people" and because the EU is a community of nation-states *sui generis*. Normative democratic requirements are met since the heads of the member-state governments in the European Council, the most powerful body of the EU, are elected by their respective citizenries, and the European Parliament is elected directly by the citizens; the sheer size and diversity of the EU precludes the development of the pre-conditions for democratic participation; finally, the success of integration proves that all this works very well and in the interest of the populations (Coultrap 1999; Dahl 2001; Moravcsik 2002; for an overview see Giorgi et al. 2006:34ff.). A main argument of these authors is the fact that the EU represents a very complex, multilevel system of governance which does not allow a simple application of nation-state principles of democracy. Some of these arguments may by sound. However, it is argued here that significant problems of democratic quality exist already at the level of the EU member states. Concerning the quality of democracy, European integration has aggravated these problems in a significant way.

We have already pointed in Chapter 3 to some of the most important present-day problems of democracy at the level of nation-states. They include (see Arendt 1963; Kelsen 1963; Pitkin 1967; Sartori 1968; Barber 1984; Held 1996; Höreth 1999, 2002; Norris 2005; Dalton 1999; Klingemann 1999; Siedentop 2001; Schmitter and Trechsel 2004a): commercialization of politics as a consequence of the spread of television and use of marketing methods; the rise of a "political class" with its own interests of self-preservation; growing entanglement between politicians and political parties as a consequence of the increase of public engagement in many areas; a tendency of party apparatuses to become self-interested and increasingly dependent on public financing; ideological deflation of political programmes; decline of turnout and decreasing trust in politics and politicians among citizens.

At the level of the EU (and in the globalised world as a whole), some of these problems are reiterated, some aggravated. The following are the most evident:[11]

- The European Parliament lacks the most central function of a parliament, that of enacting laws (Steffani and Thaysen 1995:36); within the parliament, no open competition between different political ideologies and camps exist. As a consequence, the parliament is overly busy in formulating resolutions on all major and minor problems around the world[12] but is often not able (or willing) to enforce its own standpoint against the other EU institutions.
- The European Commission, the "government" of the EU, consists of a body of appointed politicians who are not directly responsible to any electorate and cannot be removed from their offices; the same applies to the powerful high EU bureaucrats, the directors general of the commission.

- The European Council, the most powerful body, which decides collectively, is not responsible to any electorate in its decisions; its deliberations take place without publicity. Paul Alliès (2005:161ff.) calls this body a "cartel of the governments."
- The European Court of Justice, a body of independent professionals, acts as a kind of side parliament, also without any democratic control; its members are appointed by governments; its decisions are usually in favour of an extension of the free-market principle, at the expense of other considerations.
- The interaction patterns between the Commission, the European Parliament, and a myriad of lobby groups are highly intransparent; among the lobbyists, economically strong and self-articulated groups are overrepresented. In Chapter 4 we have seen that this situation is seen very critically by the public.
- Even from the viewpoint of a representative democracy, the EU scores poorly because representation in most cases is very indirect, with too many intermediate steps between the voters and their representatives (Pollak 2007).

The former German president and chair of the EU convention which elaborated the fundamental rights, Roman Herzog, has mentioned four reasons why competences are increasingly centralized in Brussels:[13] (1) The acting EU politicians are in fact bureaucrats and as such have an interest in establishing far-reaching regulations—independent of the fact if the EU has competences in a certain area or not; (2) A "cushion the ball" (*Spiel über die Bande*) is practised in the multilevel government system of the EU: National politicians or interest groups which are unable to implement a law or regulation encourage the Commission to establish it for the EU as a whole; in this way institutional reforms of the EU often do not weaken but strengthen member states' governments at the expense of their control through their parliaments and citizens (Weiler 1999:264ff.). (3) The adoption of "package deals" by the European Council: In order to arrive at majority decisions, the representatives of national governments form alliances and tie together issues which are unrelated in substantive terms; also in this way, centralization becomes stronger. In this way, it enables the member state governments to come home with a cornucopia of measures, particularly in the areas of agricultural and regional policy (Alliès 2005:174ff.). (4) The judicature of the European Court of Justice clearly privileges EU competences at the expense of national ones.

Democracy is closely connected with law (Skrapska 2001). Therefore, the Constitution for Europe has proposed a series of measures which would remedy some of the problems of the democratic deficit. They include: the strengthening of the competences of the European parliament by extending the power of codecision to most policy areas; public meetings of the European Council when it acts as a legislative body; the obligation of the Commission to inform national parliaments about new EU legislative proposals; the establishment of the principle of subsidiarity clarifying the division of competences between the EU and the member states; a possibility for direct involvement of citizens through the right of an initiative (by one million of citizens) which obliges the commission to reconsider a proposal for legislation. Considering the aforementioned deficits, it is evident, however, that these measures are insufficient. The Commission remains the sole initiator of legislative proposals; other bodies, as well as a citizens' initiative, can only require the commission to consider drafting or changing a proposal.

In this section, some concrete proposals for the reform of the EU institutions shall be made. They are informed by K. Popper's idea of "piecemeal engineering," which aims at clearly circumscribed, step-by-step reforms whose effects can be estimated and evaluated realistically (see also Griller and Müller 1995; Höreth 1999:309). Such a procedure is also demanded because the present institutional setup of the EU, with all its weaknesses, is the result of half a century of practical experiences whose value must not be underestimated. It represents a historically new and unique system "which in different aspects tries to guarantee a balance of equilibrium of power" (Poier 2004:1072; see also Lepsius 2000). The proposals concern four areas: Abandoning of governmental functions of the EU; enhancing transparency of elite networks; strengthening of personal responsibility of individual political actors; introducing elements of direct democracy.

Abandoning of governmental functions and democratising the legal functions of the EU

If we conceive the European Union as a community of law, it follows immediately that it is not and cannot act like a government, that is, carry out redistributive and steering politics which more or less directly intervene into social processes and the life of the citizens. Stefano Bartolini (2006) has shown . . . that a gradual "politicisation" of the EU could produce highly problematic consequences because it would destroy its finely balanced system. In the social scientific literature, the concept used in this regard is *governance* (Cameron 1998; Sandholtz and Stone Sweet 1998; Zürn 1998; Kohler-Koch 1999; Jachtenfuchs 2001; Held 2004; Jachtenfuchs and Kohler-Koch 2004; Axt 2005). This concept points to the fact that in the present-day world (1) a multiplicity of actors and levels and (2) several different models of coordination (hierarchic-bureaucratic, market-related, network-based coordination) are involved in the process of political regulation and steering. "Good governance" means that all these different mechanisms are integrated in an optimal way, combining transparency, openness to citizens' participation, and outcome efficiency. This concept is doubtless useful even if it has a strong normative component, particularly if applied to the EU. It should not be used, however, to obscure the fact that the EU in fact does and wants to act as a "government" in the classical sense. This applies, first of all, to the two main areas of its spending, the agrarian and the structural-regional policy. It is true also, however, for an increasing number of areas where the EU sets concrete political goals (e.g., in terms of certain levels of employment) or tries to implement specific kinds of policies throughout the Union (e.g., in the area of educational or family policy). The problematic aspiration of the EU to provide "concrete results" to the citizens, connected with its ambitions to governmental steering, has been clearly recognized also by Dimitris Chryssochoou et al. (1999): "Indeed, the largest deficit of both Amsterdam and Nice was their emphasis on policy rather than on politics, efficiency rather than democracy, distributive compromise rather than integrative accommodation, functionalistic structure rather than shored normative commitments . . ." (Chryssochoou et al. 1999:2002).

To argue that the EU should abandon all efforts to "govern" more or less directly seems to be a radical break with the self-image of the EU as well as its perception by the public. However, such a view is not so far from the real competences and functions that the EU has today. It is widely agreed that these are mainly of a legal and regulatory nature (Majone 1993, 1996 a, b). Recently the EU tends to switch over more and more to horizontal, "soft" methods of coordination and target setting (Mosher and Trubek 2003; Schäfer 2005). The success of these forms, however, remains contested (Schäfer 2005). Alec Stone Sweet (2005:55) draws the following conclusion in this regard: " . . . the EC governs principally through making rules (directives, regulations, decisions), drawing affected groups into deliberative procedures (Comitology and other modes of consultation); it has little capacity to govern through taxation, redistribution, and command-control. The EC has weak coercive capacities; the Commission succeeds by brokering interests, and arbitraging across domains and organizations; the administration and enforcement of EC law is typically left to national authorities. In consequence, modes of supra-national governance tend to be heavily norm-based: legalistic but incomplete" (Stone Sweet 2005:55).

This proposal makes it necessary to forbear the widespread expectation not only among EU politicians but also among political scientists that the EU can be "effective and democratic" at the same time (Scharpf 1999). As a community of law, it can provide only a framework within which effective economic and social politics can be carried out by political institutions and actors at the level of member states, provinces, and so on. If this politics is effective or not depends on many other factors in the first instance. The highly divergent political outcomes in the different member states of the EU, even within the Euro-zone, clearly prove this thesis. It has also been argued that a high "output legitimacy" of the EU can compensate for its low "input legitimacy," that is, the limited possibilities of citizens to influence the political process. If this assertion were true it would also provide an argument for relativising the democratic deficit of the EU. We have interpreted this issue already in Chapter 6 (p. 247ff). Since it is quite important, let us look again at it from some additional perspectives.

Excursus: Does and can the politics of the European Union generate a high "output legitimacy"?[14]

A high "output legitimacy" of a political system ("government for the people" instead of "government by the people") is given if it is efficient in its workings, in achieving its aims (Majone 1996a; Schimmelfennig 1996; Scharpf 1997, 1999; Crum 2003; Boedeltje and Cornips 2005). However, already this concept, developed by political scientists, is flawed from the viewpoint of the theoretical and sociological perspective developed in this book. First, it is problematic from the normative point of view. Efficient governing becomes a self-legitimizing quality, independent from its form and structure; a problematic reorientation occurs away from issues of political freedom and self-determination towards issues of welfare production (De Tocqueville 1947; Arendt 1963; Abromeit 2000). Second, it does not really capture the essence of the concept of "legitimacy," which is that a social or political system is actually seen as legitimate by the people (Weber 1978a:36). A mere positive output of a system can lead to an acceptance of that system, a high legitimacy, but it must not necessarily do so. We have to include the perceptions of the people about a certain system and its politics before we can say that it has a high or low legitimacy. We have to consider, therefore, also efforts of governments to induce a positive view about their politics among the electorate. This is quite necessary also in the case of the EU. Its leaders don't get tired of praising the positive outcomes of European integration and attributing to it all the positive developments that have occurred in Europe since 1945. They have also commissioned large scientific studies, such as the famous Cecchini Report (1988), to show these accomplishments and the potential gigantic losses in the case of an interruption of the integration process.

Two questions arise in this regard: Is it true that European integration has been so successful? How do the citizens throughout Europe perceive this success? It is well known that many citizens are quite critical in this regard. The political elites tend to argue that the population does not recognize the true achievements of integration. In order to get a comprehensive view about this situation, we have to look both at objective developments and their subjective perception by the populations.

Looking at objective developments in the last decade (1994–2005) and comparing the EU-15 as a whole with its three main "rivals," the United States and Japan, the European Union does not appear as having been particularly successful. As shown in Chapter 6, in terms of economic growth, the EU and Japan were far behind the U.S.; in terms of unemployment, development in the EU was a failure, showing the worst figures in all ten years; only in terms of inflation, the EU did quite well, but not as well as Japan. Within the EU, the countries of *Euroland* performed significantly worse than those outside of it (Denmark, Sweden, UK). There were big differences within the EU, however, in terms of success: The old and large member states, France, Germany, and Italy, were much less successful than the South European members, Luxembourg, Ireland, and Finland. In general, EU membership may have contributed to economic growth in the EU, although only in a moderate way (Bornschier et al. 2004).

What comes out if we look at the perception and evaluation of these trends among the citizens? Asked about the role and success of the EU in five central areas of politics, it turns out that the negative evaluations over-balance the positive ones in three of them: 43% say that "the EU plays a negative role" in the area of unemployment (24% see a positive role), 51% in inflation (23% a positive), and 29% in social standards (22% a positive).[15] Only in two areas, the positive evaluations are somewhat more frequent than the negative ones. (Economic growth and wealth: 41% positive, 35% negative; fight against crime 44% positive, 20% negative.) People in countries with objective positive developments evaluate them as more positive, those in countries with negative developments more critically and negative. Thus, citizens' perceptions are quite accurate if for them the achievements of the EU are not very noteworthy.

However, quite high proportions—between 40% and 80%—of the citizens have concrete "fears about the building of Europe" (see *Table 8.3*). Among six achievements mentioned, the majority sees a positive effect in only one area, namely, the perceived influence of one's own country in the EU. In two regards, the negative evaluations far outweigh the positive ones: One is the overproportional influence of the big countries; the other is the personal influence in the EU. Seventy-six percent of the respondents in the 15-EU member states feel that "the biggest countries have the most power in the EU"; but only 32% feel that "my own voice counts in the European Union." A breakdown of the results by countries shows that citizens have quite an accurate perception also in this regard: Most of the French and Germans (75–78%) feel that their country's voice counts in the EU, but less then 50% of the Finns, Portuguese, Italians, Britons, and Austrians. An even more negative picture of the consequences of integration comes out if we look at the concrete fears which the respondents associate with the EU. In most of the nine items asked, a majority of respondents are afraid of it. In four dimensions—job transfer to other member countries, drug trafficking, national payments to the EU, and difficulties for farmers—large majorities (between 62% and 74%) have fears in connection with European integration. Thus, among considerable sections of the population, a pervasive feeling of estrangement from the EU seems to be spreading out.

The fact that the subjective evaluations of the EU politics among the general public are closely related to objective developments is confirmed

Table 8.3   Perceived Achievements of the EU and Fears about the Building of Europe (2004)

Perceived achievements		Tend to agree	Tend to disagree*
I feel I am safer because (our country) is a member of the European Union	%	43.0	46.6
I feel we are more stable economically . . .	%	43.7	45.7
I feel we are more stable politically . . .	%	40.0	47.7
My voice counts in the EU	%	31.8	55.0
(Our country's) voice counts in the EU	%	62.8	26.9
The biggest countries have the most power in the EU	%	76.0	14.3
Fears about integration			
A loss of power for smaller member states	%	49.4	42.0
An increase in drug trafficking and international organized crime	%	68.2	27.2
Our language being used less and less	%	39.7	55.7
Our country paying more and more to the EU	%	64.4	26.5
The loss of social benefits	%	53.6	38.5
The loss of national identity and culture	%	42.2	52.3
An economic crisis	%	47.7	42.5
The transfer of jobs to other member countries which have lower production costs	%	74.1	19.9
More difficulties for (nationality) farmers	%	62.2	26.2

*Percentages missing up to 100% are "don't know."
Source: Eurobarometer 61 (Spring 2004). Questions 12 and 15; N = 16216.

by multilevel regression analysis as we have seen (Chapter 6). Positive developments in a country are significantly connected with positive, negative developments with negative evaluations in the several areas. If, for instance, jobs and the employment situation developed positively in a country, people recognize this in their evaluation of this sector. Thus, we may conclude that public opinions about integration are clearly based on objective socioeconomic developments. It is simply wrong to state that the vast majority of the public "does not credit the EC/EU with a significant role in shaping those conditions" (Moussis 2006:189f.). In terms of output legitimacy, the EU enjoys a limited degree of legitimacy among its citizens. This is based on the fact that the EU—at least in the last decade—was by far not as successful as it is often presented among politicians and business leaders, but also among economists and social scientists (Bornschier 2000b; Trichet 2001; Galati and Tsatsaronis 2003; Bergsten 2005; Moussis 2006). In fact, some social scientists have also pointed to the modest achievements or even failures of the EU (Baader 1993; Friedman and Mundell 2001; Eichengreen 2005; Caporale and Kontonikas 2006; Wyplosz 2006).

Let us summarize the judgements of experts in the evaluation of the success of EU policy in specific sectors. It turns out that they are also quite mixed and often negative. Agrarian policy, the area where the EU spends most, is nearly unanimously considered as an overall failure, despite some achievements. It has perverse distributional effects, as shown in Chapter 4; it produces excessive food prices; and the large sums involved cause wastage and corruption on a large scale (May 1985; Rieger 1996; Fouilleux 2003; El-Agraa 2004b:354ff.; Koland 2005; Wiggerthale 2005; Moussis 2006). A highly relevant conclusion has been deduced in this regard by Eve Fouilleux (2003:251 f) when she pointed to the powerful interest coalitions among big farmers, food producers, and national agrarian ministers which produced problematic political outcomes: "The CAP is an excellent example of what happens when there is no real link between the EU institutions and the EU's citizens. In such circumstance it is easy for governments to use the European Commission as a scapegoat for decisions that really do not want to take. The Commission is restricted in what it can do when this happens, and often ends up taking the blame for a policy it would like to see reformed" (Fouilleux 2003:25f.). Regional and structural policy of the EU has always been controversial, with contested positive effects in regard to its aims (Molle 2001); the political idea of a "Europe of the Regions" is far from any reality (Les Galès and Lequesne 1998; Armstrong 2004; Pollak and Slominski 2006:97ff.; Haller 2007). Economists question the positive effects of integration on economic growth, based on theoretical grounds and empirical data (Vanhoudt 1999; Sapir et al. 2003; Ziltener 2003, 2004; Aiginger 2004; Wyplosz 2006). As far as the common currency euro is concerned, many argue that its predominant policy as a hard currency may be a significant cause for the economic difficulties in Euroland (Lorentzen 1999; Cameron 1998; Ingham 2004; Wyplosz 2006). The industrial research and technology policy of the EU can be seen as positive if one subscribes to the aim of the EU to become a "global player." However, one can also say that this policy contradicts the free-market principle of the EU and constitutes an example of an interventionist policy; that the huge investments in this area (for instance, for the development of the Airbus industry) required massive state and EU support (Grande 1996b; Mussler and Streit 1996; Ziltener 2003; El-Agraa 2004b:236). No extensive comments are necessary concerning the achievements of the EU concerning common security and foreign policy; here, some of its most spectacular failures happened, based on the fundamental unanimity among its members, in the cases of war in Yugoslavia and in Iraq.

What can we deduce from these findings about the possibility to substitute the missing input legitimation by output legitimation? The answer seems straightforward: Such a substitution is not possible, both for normative and for empirical-factual reasons. A political system with little "input legitimacy" would be an "enlightened autocracy" (or dictatorship). The success of the EU in terms of policy has been rather mixed and modest, in some areas it was even quite negative. This fact is well recognized by the population at large and it contributes rather to a delegitimation of the EU.

———

The abandonment of governmental functions by the EU would have several immediate positive consequences: First, it would remove the many occasions for "bad government" in the widest sense, the wastage of money for the wrong purposes, unnecessary bureaucratic costs, and inclinations to clientelism and corruption. It is estimated that nearly three fourths of the EU budget and 80% of lawmaking are due to lobbying activities (Waldschmitt 2001:44). Second, it would supersede the "verbose rhetoric" of the EU leaders, the full-bodied promising of high achievements which cannot be fulfilled (Alesina et al. 2001). This rhetoric can be observed particularly in the area of economic policy but also in other areas, such as the common foreign and security policy. In this regard, one observer called the rhetoric of the EU as almost eldritch since behind it stands no single soldier (Stein 2001:50). The EU seems not to have learned much from the blatant failure of the Lisbon strategy, but it continues to insist on "output legitimacy." A recent statement of Commission President Barroso attests to this fact:

> *"Europe must do better. What we are proposing today is to release Europe's tremendous economic potential. This is needed to maintain the European model of society we value so much. This is the foundation for social justice and opportunity for all. Our ambition is undiminished. The overall Lisbon goals were right, but the implementation was poor . . . we must refocus this agenda to deliver results. The real issue is not about facts and figures on paper. It is about their impact on people's lives: how we pay for our education, pension, civil services and health care."*[16]

In the same press conference, it was told that the new strategy would boost GDP by 3% by 2010 and create over 6 million jobs. All the characteristics of the EU rhetoric are contained in these statements: The promise to achieve real improvements for people within a concrete period of time; the reference to the "European model of society" whose existence is doubtful, as we have shown in the last chapter; the reference to political issues (education, health, pensions) which belong to the competences of the member states. The same focus on concrete political achievements instead of democratic reforms is evident in the "Plan D for Democracy," which was issued by the Commission in October 2005, after the rejection of the constitution in France and the Netherlands. This plan proposed to initiate a broad dialogue and debate between the EU's institutions and the citizens and help to restore public confidence in the EU. The following passage makes clear that it is again more an exercise in public campaigning for the EU than an effort to look for substantive reforms of its institutional structure and lack of "input legitimacy":

> *"People need to feel that Europe provides an added value and they have the ability to affect the way decisions are taken . . . , the national debates should focus citizens' attention to the future of Europe, examining their expectations and discussing the added value and the concrete benefits of Community action. In this way, the debate should go beyond institutional questions and the Constitution. It should focus on how Europe is addressing issues such as jobs, the economy, transport, the fight against terrorism, the environment, oil prices, natural disasters or poverty reduction in Africa and elsewhere."*[17]

The negative effects of the continued use of such a rhetoric should not be underestimated. The split between promises and achievements may be one of the most significant causes for the flawed EU image among the public.

The focus of the EU on its central task as legislator would, thirdly, also remove one incentive for the excess activity of EU representatives of all sorts: Of the members of the national governments who meet regularly two times a years and, in addition, also in between; at these meeting often issues are debated which are topical at a certain moment but in which the EU has practically no influence; it would help to focus the activity of the European Parliament, which now is preoccupied around the clock with resolutions and statements to a myriad of issues of secondary importance; it could release national and EU bureaucrats who are busy with implementing overdetailed rules about the distribution, use, and control of the many funds through which the EU spreads its boons all over Europe. (In this case, the term *Europe* is adequate because the EU in fact distributes money also to many European states which are not EU members.) The aim of supporting less developed regions could be achieved much better by an autonomic financial redistribution (Haller 1995; Stiglitz and Schönfelder 1989:705ff.).[18]

A very important consequence of the focussing of the EU on its central tasks would also be a reduction of the high level of complexity of its institutions and workings. The competences of the different institutions and bodies could be defined much more clearly. This is the topic of the next section.

Enhancing transparency of elite networks and the workings of the EU institutions

From the viewpoint of democratic elite theory, the relations between the elites are of main concern. Two requirements are central in this regard:

The elites must be independent from each other, and the relations between them must be made transparent to the public (Etzioni-Halevy 1993). The existence of a democratic political elite structure is essential for the political system as a whole because it "minimizes the temptation for ordinary citizens to think of the political elite as *les autres,* as a privileged and remote group able to manipulate the machinery of the state for their own advantage" (Siedentop 2001:129). The European Union poses particular problems in this regard. We have seen that citizens are very critical in this regard (see Chapter 6). The structural institutional reason is that the EU is a very complex, multilevel system of government wherein many different institutional bodies are involved in political decisions. In this system, there exists a confusion, even dissolution of power, which no member state would tolerate within its own system (Alliès 2005:173). At the end, it is usually impossible to determine who was mainly responsible for the outcome. However, since the EU is a highly pluralistic and multilevel system, it cannot be dismissed altogether as undemocratic (Coultrap 1999; Fabbrini 2003). Three issues are relevant in this regard: The division of power and competences between the several EU institutions and actors; their relations to the member states and citizens; and the relations between the EU institutions and nongovernmental institutions. This is not the place to develop many detailed proposals. Some general comments can be made, however, concerning the main problems for the different EU institutions and actors.

The *European Council* occupies a central position in the decisional processes of the EU, and its role would even be strengthened by the constitution—a fact which confirms that the EU continues to constitute a cooperation of nation-states. Two aspects seem problematic as far as the Council is concerned. One is the limited transparency and publicity of its decisions; this would be corrected by the constitution to some degree. If the Council functions as legislator, the deliberations would have to be public. One could extend this requirement well to most of its deliberations. Another problem in the workings of the council is its tendency to hyperactivism. Its presidency changes every half year, and a new presidency is eager to put an ambitious agenda on the timetable. A pressure toward the proliferation of new proposals comes also from the many regular and exceptional meetings of the Council and its many different compositions throughout the year. Here, a focus on a fewer number of central problems and looser time schedules could often improve the quality of the decisions. Finally, the members of the European Council should be obliged to report regularly to their national parliaments about the working plans of the Council and about the decisions made.

The *European Parliament* (EP) would clearly be strengthened by the constitution. This is welcome since its competences up to now fall short of the competences of a full parliament. A strengthening of the parliament against the executive and bureaucracy is a general necessity in modern democracies (Weber 1978b). However, it would contradict the view of the

EU as a community of law to expect a solution of the democratic deficit by a full "parliamentarisation" alone. Parliamentary representation is only one (although a central one) among different forms of democratic participation. This applies particularly to the EU, where we have seen that people participate less and less in the elections to the EP.

In this regard, we have also to look at popular perceptions and behaviours. It seems that the European Parliament is not considered as an important institution by the citizens in the member states. Since the first elections in 1979, levels of turnout have been decreasing significantly from 75% to only 45.7% at the last elections in 2004 (see also Blondel et al. 1998). This is an astonishing trend, particularly in view of the fact that the competencies of the European Parliament have been extended considerably. Turnout at national elections is significantly higher (around 70% and more in most member states) and shows only a weak downward trend in some countries. In addition, in the European elections of 2004 political parties highly critically of the EU won large support, such as the United Kingdom Independence Party (16% of the votes in GB), or the lists of Hans Peter Martin in Austria and Paul Buitenen in the Netherlands. A special small study was carried out in connection with the European election of 2004 in nine member countries of the EU for the purpose of this book.[19] The results of this survey, as well as those of the Eurobarometer postelection survey 2004, showed that the first reason for nonparticipation in the European elections was general political disinterest. The findings showed also, however, that the influence of the MEPs was considered as being rather moderate and that their salaries and compensations were considered as being too high. Only 34% agreed to the statement that "the European political elites are responsible enough to their voters," but 74% agreed to the statement "clientelism and corruption are problems in the political institutions of the EU in Brussels." Less negative, however, were the judgements about the individual political deputies. A majority, for instance, thinks that they had been selected for the EP because of their political competence and not just because they have been influential politicians before and came to this office in order to get a good position. Quite significant were the results concerning a question about the groups which have a lot of influence in Brussels and which have a "too weak influence"; 75% and more considered the influence of large states, multinational corporations, and political elites as very strong. The reverse was true for workers, unemployed, and citizens; 73% and more considered their influence as too weak.

Nevertheless, the claim can hardly be disputed that the EP should get the right to codecide about all central political issues. However, it would also be necessary that the EP improves its working methods. It should focus more on central issues and be concerned less with purely technical matters of regulation, but also abandon the hyperactivity in terms of statements and resolutions concerning peripheral issues or issues on which the EU has no influence at all. At present, the parliament also often works in a quite obscure way, given the dominance of the two large party fractions

(Conservatives and Social Democrats) and their leaders. Their exist many possibilities to improve the transparency of its working both inside and in the relations between the EP and the public.

In Chapter 5 we have analysed the *European Commission* as that EU institution which is mainly responsible for the continuous expansion of the EU activities and competencies. A call for a significant retrenchment of the Commission's competencies and a dislocation of the EU institutions from Brussels to "European cities" in the member states (as some EU-critical movements do)[20] would constitute a radical change of the overall political system of the EU.

However, significant improvements in the control of the activities of the commission and in its public accountability are doubtless possible and necessary. The EU Commission could be obliged to disclose from where or from whom new proposals originated. The principle of discontinuity should be established which says that legislative projects which are not realized within one legislative period will expire.[21] At present, it is a typical practice of the Commission not to withdraw a rejected proposal but to modify it and to bring it repeatedly to the table so that it will be accepted at the end. Finally, also the role of the top Eurocrats, the Directors General, who are highly influential in the workings of the Commission, should be questioned. Why should they not, as it is more and more common for high-level bureaucrats at the level of the member states be appointed only for a limited period of time? Also, the process of the appointment of the GDs should become more transparent to the public.

Finally, very important would be reforms concerning the *European Court of Justice*, which has played a crucial role in the process of integration. Its independence is certainly out of question. Three problems exist in this regard where a reform seems necessary. First, we have, in Chapter 3, that the ECJ has arrogated for itself a central role in the process of integration. Its decisions have sometimes asked for more integration (and based on narrow economic-liberalistic principles) than the treaties have foreseen (Waldschmitt 2001:45). Thus, the first claim on the ECJ is that it limits itself to the role foreseen for it by these treaties. Second, the process of appointment of the judges of the ECJ should be made more transparent and submitted to democratic principles as far as they are applicable in such a case. Finally, also the national courts and parliaments should develop a more critical stance toward the decisions of the ECJ. They should not subordinate themselves uncritically to any decision of the ECJ. According to the Austrian constitution, the five most basic principles are superordinate also to European law. These principles are democracy, republicanism (federalism), rule of law, and division of political powers. It is quite evident that European integration is touching all of them.

An important aspect concerns the relations between EU institutions and actors and nongovernmental institutions. Here, mainly the problem of *lobbyism* comes up. One main demand in this regard would be that all lobbyists should have to register. Another one would be that the relations between the lobbyists and the EU institutions—mainly the Commission—should be made more transparent. In general, it is certainly a positive aspect that the EU tries to involve interests groups, citizens' associations, and so forth, extensively into its consultation processes. However, one must be aware that these groups and associations are no representative profile of the whole population (Etzioni-Halevy 1999). This fact is frequently overlooked by proponents of the idea of "civil society" (see, e.g., Beck and Grande 2004:195ff.). Better educated and financially more potent social groups are always overrepresented among them. Their success is also often due to clever methods of publicity and marketing. Thus, their influence in EU decision processes cannot compensate for direct and equal possibilities of participation of all individual citizens.

A further important issue concerns the relations between the central EU institutions in Brussels and the national governments, the division of competences between the EU and the member states. It can be seen as positive that the constitution explicitly enumerates the areas of exclusive competence of the Union, those of shared competence and those where the Union carries out supporting, coordinating, or complementary action. The definition of the cases where supporting action is necessary, and the degree to which such support should be given, however, remain vague. The same is true for the *principle of subsidiarity*, which states that the Union "shall act only if and insofar as the objectives of the proposed action cannot be sufficiently achieved by the Member states, either at the central level or at regional and local level, but can rather, by reason of the scale or effects of the proposed action, be better achieved at the Union level" (Art. I-11). Such a principle is "delusively simple" (Dehove 2004:75). It can be invoked for practically every area of politics to legitimate Union activity. The principle of subsidiarity alone is therefore toothless as an instrument to slow down the trend toward an increasing centralisation of politics at the level of the EU. It must be supplemented by strong, legally binding mechanisms by which the member states and regional and local authorities can question encroachments of the central EU institutions into their own competences. The possibility that the Committee of the Regions "may issue an opinion on its own initiative in matters where it considers that specific regional interests are involved" (Art. III-388) is certainly inadequate for this aim.

Strengthening the personal responsibility of individual political actors

Individual personalities play a decisive role in the political process, as outlined in Chapter 2 and shown in Chapters 3 to 5. This is so because politics is not only about interests and ideas, aims, and programmes but also about the personalities who propose and pursue those programmes. The personal authority, charisma, and trustfulness of political personalities are decisive both for the effectiveness of the political system as a whole and for the trust which citizens have in it. One reason why the EU looks so distant to citizens is that its institutions have no personal "faces," as national governments do. It is an built-in problem of the EU because the basic decisions taken in most of its decisive organs (European Council, Commission, ECJ) are the outcomes of collective decision processes, and no individual member can be made responsible for them. A solution of this problem at the level of the EU is not easy, particularly when we conceive it as a Community of Law. From this point of view, proposals like the election of the incumbents of high-profile EU offices (such as the Commission president or the president of the European Council) directly by the citizens are problematic because they would move the EU toward a true, supranational state. The constitution foresees the institution of a president of the European Council who should be elected by its members for a period of two and a half years. However, also such an office would be problematic if it is not connected with special competences. Also, the coordination with the president of the Commission would frequently create problems. However, there exist many other possibilities which could strengthen the aspect of personal responsibility of political actors at the level of the EU. They include:

- Obliging the members of the European Council to state and justify their individual positions concerning important decisions; obliging the Council to deliberate in public.
- Reform of the election procedures for the European Parliament. One problem of the EP, as direct representative of the European citizens, is the high number of voters (over 600,000 in the EU mean) which each MEP represents. Also in this regard, "it would be desirable that not only parties but also individual candidates play a major role in the relationship between politics and citizens" (Poier 2004:1077; see also Blondel et al. 1998). This could be achieved through majority systems in the member-state constituencies (one deputy represents one constituency) and a strengthening of the personality element in the election procedure.
- Appointment of the General Directors of the commission for only a limited period;
- Election of the judges of the ECJ by a public procedure. This happens in the United States, where their appointment must be confirmed by the Senate (Alliès 2005:121). This point is particularly important if we understand the Union as a Community of Law: The creation of new law cannot be left to (juridical) experts, appointed by governments without public control.

Introducing strong elements of direct democracy

A key element for strengthening the democratic character of the EU would be the introduction of effective elements of direct democracy. The rationale for this argument follows directly from the character of the EU as a consociational political system and its elitist character. The political processes and decisions in such a system need a corrective. The most effective corrective in this regard would be the introduction of elements of direct democracy. In this way, citizens could participate directly in substantive political decisions through initiatives (making proposals) and referenda, which can be consultative or binding for the legislators.

All arguments pointing to weaknesses of representative democracy and in favour of direct democracy are valid also for the EU (Pitkin 1967; Vaubel 1995):[22] Individuals elected to political offices are not representative of their constituencies in their social characteristics but come from more privileged classes and groups; they have their own interests and they develop practices of clientelism, patronage, and corruption; political parties are a "necessary evil" that intermediates between politics and citizens; governmental transitions often cause substantial disruption in long-term political goals; elections are very costly; once elected, political representatives often decide contrary to the wishes of their electorate. Therefore, many political and constitutional theorists (see, for instance, Kelsen 1963:38ff.; Arendt 1963; Barber 1984), as well as most of those authors who diagnose a democratic deficit of the EU, are unconditional supporters of direct democracy (Zürn 1996; von Arnim 2000:284ff.; Beck and Grande 2004:352f.; Giorgi et al. 2006).

One important further argument for Europe-wide referenda is that they could contribute significantly to the emergence of a *European public space*. The absence of a strong European public sphere, associated with the lack of a common language, differing political systems, and so on, could also be seen as an obstacle to direct democracy at the level of the EU. However, referenda could contribute to the emergence of such a sphere: "If people are given procedures that enable them to be genuinely citizens, then they will act as citizens and feel themselves to be truly members of a political community" (Giorgi et al. 2006:17). The proof of this is the fact of the intense public discussion about EU matters and the high levels of turnout when citizens' votes had a real impact, as it was the case in the referenda in Switzerland, Norway, Sweden, and France. There is some truth in the following arguments against direct democracy at the level of the EU but they are not convincing. The arguments say that referenda work only in small systems; that this form of political decisions is slow and inefficient; that demagogues can influence the outcomes; that voters decide mainly out of self-interest; that turnout is often low. Fully untenable is the argument that voters are not informed and knowledgeable enough to be able to decide about highly complex matters at the level of the EU (Höreth 2002; Seidenfaden 2005). This is the main thrust of elitist thinking which has informed European integration since the 1950s and which led to the present deep split between elites and citizens. There is one argument of these authors, however, which is quite relevant. The situation should be avoided that citizens vote on a complex proposal which has elaborated and agreed upon in a labour-intensive procedure. Therefore, a referendum should be arranged quite early in the process of reform, and the text should contain the main alternatives in a clear and compact form (Seidenfaden 2005).

Elements of direct democracy exist in many modern democratic nation-states. If they are not foreseen at the level of the central state, they exist at the lower levels of states or provinces, such as in Germany and the United States. In the age of the Internet and electronic democracy (Gibson and Rommele 2004), accomplishment of EU-wide referenda becomes easier and easier. Most relevant in our context are the experiences with referenda in Switzerland. This is an eminent example of a political community with strong elements of direct democracy from which the EU could learn a lot (Neidhart 1988; Linder 1999; Kriesi et al. 2005). In this country, democracy has been established earlier than in most other parts of Europe; the democratic system is anchored strongly among the population in spite of its high internal cultural (linguistic and religious) diversity; trust in the political system is higher than in most other European countries. Switzerland is comparable to the EU also because it constitutes a paradigmatic case of a consociational democracy, with continuous participation of the four large political parties in government. This system was introduced in the course of the nineteenth and twentieth centuries because deep-going internal ideological and political conflicts, together with a serious menace from outside (Nazi Germany), threatened to disrupt the nation. In the Swiss political system, there exists a close cooperation at the level of the elites: this is counterbalanced, however, by a strong system of direct democracy. Not only changes of the constitution, but also of other laws which are considered as of being importance by some group, must be submitted to a binding popular referendum. In fact, between 10% and 15% of all legal acts are put directly to the decision of the voter. In addition, if 50,000 citizens ask for it, any law must be submitted to a referendum; 100,000 citizens can ask for a change of the constitution. As a consequence, in some years about a dozen referenda are carried out in Switzerland. They have a high relevance for the emergence and clarification of political priorities. Even in the case of the rejection of a proposal (which happens frequently), the referendum activates large-scale discussions and contributes significantly to the formation of public opinion. It is also not true that citizens reject all proposals which are costly and require higher taxes. Most important in regard to Swiss direct democracy is the fact that it weakens the established actors, such as political parties, the parliament, and government compared to the direct influence of the citizens. This may also explain why participation in elections is rather low in Switzerland. It is estimated that more than half of these referenda concern issues which in the EU belong to the competence of Brussels.[23]

Also, the experience in the post-Communist democracies in Central East Europe is relevant here. Auer and Bützer (2001) have analysed referenda in these and other countries extensively. They found that participation in the referenda was very high when they concerned vital issues of the countries. In the independence referenda, carried out in fourteen countries in 1990–1991, turnout was 90% and more in six cases, and over 80% in five cases. Most of these countries included the possibility of referenda into their new constitutions. For Italy, these authors found that popular involvement did not complicate political processes but actually strengthened parties and legislatures in putting through important reforms (Auer and Bützer 2001:307ff.). Even in the United States, where participation in referenda often is low, they are reasonably effective in making sure that government policies conform with citizens' preferences.

Given the importance of the principle of direct democracy, it was a progress that the definition of the political system of the EU, as based on the principle of representative democracy, has been supplemented with a further article on participatory democracy in the proposed constitution (Art. I-47). However, it is evident that the authors of the constitution had not a real "participatory democracy" in mind as it exists in Switzerland but just something like "consultative democracy." The main objective of people's participation, as expressed in this article, is to "give citizens and representative associations the opportunity to make known and publicly exchange their view in all areas of Union action" and to oblige the Union institutions to "maintain an open, transparent and regular dialogue with representative associations and civil society." The new possibility of a "citizens' initiative" remains within this framework; it states that one million citizens from a significant number of member states may submit to the commission "any appropriate proposal on matters where citizens consider that a legal action of the Community is required for implementing the Constitution." The Commission must then deliberate on this initiative, but it is left fully to its discretion which consequences it will draw from it. These are all very modest obligations and they do in fact not oblige the EU institutions to do anything more than what it is already being done today. The impression one gets from this new "right" is that it fits in very well into the image of the EU as an enlightened, but in fact quasi-authoritarian *Obrigkeitsstaat* whose political leaders are open to the needs and wishes of their subordinates but decide by themselves if these should be fulfilled or not.

8.4 A proposal for the generation of a renewed "constitutional moment"

In this final section, the proposal is made to revitalize the Constitution for Europe. Four issues are discussed: (1) Some formal problems of the present text of the constitution; (2) the way of elaboration and implementation (ratification) of it; (3) the Berlin Declaration of March, 2007, which was the decisive outline of the further proceedings of the EU with the constitution; (4) an alternative strategy.

Formal deficits of the Constitution: Excessive length and complexity, and blending of general rules and concrete political prescriptions

All commentators of the constitution agree that it is a rather long and complicated text. This is not a minor issue since a constitution represents the basic written document of a political community which should be well readable and understandable by the citizens. Only then can it unfold its symbolic and educative meaning and influence. In the preceding section, we have seen that the complexity of this text was among the main reasons for not participating in the referendum. From this point of view, it makes sense to compare the Constitution for Europe with the constitutions of several nation-states. *Figure 8.1* shows clearly that the length of the EU Constitution far exceeds that of the constitutions of eight member states and of the United States. With about 414,000 words, it constitutes a voluminous, nearly 500-page bulky book. It is 2.6 times as long as the German constitution (the longest among the other nine constitutions), and 8.4 times as long as the American one. The EU Constitution contains 448 articles, the German 149, the Italian 139, and the French 89. The reason why the EU Constitution is so long is clear: 43% of it concerns detailed regulations about the different areas of politics (contained mainly in Parts III and IV). If we consider only the general sections concerning the fundamental principles of the working of the institutions and the section on basic rights (Parts I and II), the difference from national constitutions is not so large. These parts include about 128,000 words in the EU Constitution and 159,000 words in the German and 43,000 in the U.S. constitution.

Length per se, however, is certainly not a criterion for discrediting the constitution outright. The reason for this length is that it is also a contract of international law which contains all the earlier treaties of the European

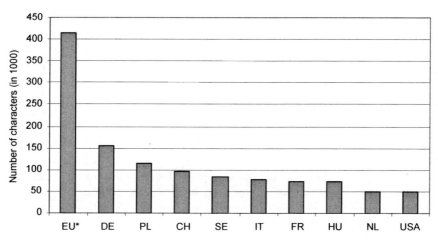

Figure 8.1. The length of the European Constitution and of selected national constitutions (total number of words).

*"Treaty establishing a Constitution for Europe" as signed in Rome on Oct. 29th, 2004, Part I-III; Part I-III plus part IV (General and Final Provisions and Final Act).

Sources: EU member states: *Verfassungen der EU—Mitgliedsstaaten* (2005); Switzerland, U.S.: Internet.

communities now in force. Most of these are highly complicated juridical texts, containing a myriad of internal references to other parts or to earlier treaties so that they are accessible only to juridical experts. From this point of view, the constitution constitutes a real progress (Deloche-Gaudez 2005:28). It was also a "victory of the integrationist" over the sceptics of further integration that the concept of "constitution" was introduced at all (Jopp and Matl 2005:16). This has also motivated many member-state governments to put the text to a popular referendum. However, the simplification of the treaties in the constitution "stopped halfway": Many of the detailed provisions in Part II "were simply taken over from the existing treaties. The 465 Articles and several protocols should be consolidated and simplified following the basic topic of Part I" (Pernice 2004:19).

This problem of length is closely related to a formal-substantive problem, its intermixing of general rules and concrete political prescriptions (Fitoussi and Le Cacheux 2005:26). By establishing fundamental, unchangeable rules about concrete political issues, the constitution undermines a generally respected principle that concrete politics can and must be decided by the government in power but not fixed in the constitution. By codifying concrete policies, the constitution imposes very specific kind of politics on diverging minorities and future generations. This concerns in particular the economic sphere where a model of (neo-) liberal policy is clearly dominant. A case in point is the currency policy where the constitution definitely states: "The primary objective of the European System of Central Banks shall be to maintain price stability" (Art. III-185). This contradiction reflects another fundamental paradox of the constitution: While it is liberal in economic terms, it is anti-liberal, or even antidemocratic, in political terms (Fitoussi and Le Cacheux 2005:27). Another example is foreign and defence policy, where also very concrete policy prescriptions are contained in the constitution.

The process of elaboration and ratification of the Constitution

The idea of a Constitution for the European Community was not new. It was supported quite early by the federalists, who envisaged the development of a European federal state. Already at the Hague Congress in 1948, and again at the assembly of the ECSC in 1952, proposals for a European Political Community were presented (Jopp and Matl 2005: 20). Later on, the Italian MEP Altiero Spinelli elaborated a concrete proposal which was supported by the European Parliament in 1984 but rejected by the heads of the national governments (Lafan 2005). During the 1999 elections to the EP, the idea was revived by some political parties (Socialists, Greens, UDF). Further impetus was given by the speech of German Foreign Minister Joschka Fischer at Humboldt University in Berlin in 2000. A general loss of legitimacy of the integration process occurred in the sequence of the Maastricht Treaty and the negative Irish vote on the Treaty of Nice (Wehr 2004:15). At the background of the failure of the heads of the governments in Nice to find a compromise for a reform which became necessary before the EU enlargement in 2004, they installed a convention with the task to elaborate a new reform proposal (Liebert et al. 2003:6; Alliès 2005:65). It was only during the first meetings of this convention that its president, Giscard d'Estaing, began to use the concept of "constitution." Surprisingly, the heads of the member states—including the UK—did not oppose it (Duhamel 2005:VIIIff.; Deloche-Gaudez 2005:27; Jopp and Matl 2005:28).

The Constitutional Convention itself—with 105 full, in all 207 members—was composed of representatives of the member-state governments, national and European parliaments, and of the European Commission; parliamentarians were the majority (68%). In addition, representatives of the candidate member countries and of the Council of Regions and the Economic and Social Council participated in the discussions (Fischer 2003:27f.; Lafan 2005). The convention chairmanship was composed of three experienced and respected European politicians, all former prime ministers of their states (Giscard d'Estaing, Luc Dehaene, and Giuliano Amato). This broad representation of countries and different groups was a positive aspect, as was the fact that all members participated intensively during the short period of the working of the convention (little more than a year, from 28.2.2002 until 10.7.2003). It can also be said that the convention overall was quite successful since it was able to elaborate a full constitutional document. The chronological division of its work into three stages—one of hearing, one of reflection, and one of elaboration of proposals—turned out as appropriate. The convention tried also to include the public throughout Europe through the Internet (a special homepage was established); all plenary meetings were public, and many non-governmental organisations were informed and consulted regularly.

However, there were also significant shortcomings of this "convention method." First, the members of the Constitutional Convention were appointed from above but not elected by the citizens, as it would be self-evident given the far-reaching importance of its task (Giorgi et al. 2006:192). In terms of political orientation, the composition was one-sided insofar as deputies of the two large political camps (Conservatives and Social Democrats) were over-represented; among them, the Conservative Party dominated (Wehr 2004:23; Alliès 2005:67). Second, the discussions and workings of the convention were controlled strongly by the presidium and the president, with very limited discussion time for participants, no votes taken, and many long texts presented at the last minute so that practically no discussion was possible (Efler and Rhode 2005). Third, the strict time deadline set by the European Council became a straightjacket and made it impossible—particularly in the third phase—to discuss and elaborate in detail and in the plenary the proposals. Particularly at this stage, the convention chairmanship worked in a rather autocratic way, looking more for developing proposals which would be accepted by the European Council than for new path-breaking principles (Alliès 2005:71).

Thus, the citizens of the member states were not really involved. The routine and special Eurobarometer surveys carried out in parallel to the meetings of the convention showed a very low public knowledge about and interest in its workings and outcomes throughout the EU member states. In spring 2003, at the peak of the convention's work, EB 59 showed that 57% of the interviewed 16,410 person knew nothing about the convention; 53% did not know that their own government was represented in it (Fischer 2005:54ff.). In July 2003, 45% knew about the work of the convention, but 40% had no interest in the text of the proposed constitution; 38% wanted to read only a summary. As to the results of the work of the convention: Only 30% declared satisfaction with it, 20% were not satisfied, but 50% had no opinion. Even in November 2003, only 39% knew about the work of the convention; 41% believed (erroneously) that a referendum about it was imperative for all member states. Nevertheless, throughout this period, a clear majority (about two thirds of the respondents) approved the idea of a constitution. Also, the convention of the youth which was called up in order to present the visions of the European youth to the constitutional convention was not representative and successful (Liebert et al. 2003:205ff.; Wehr 2004:27).

The process of ratification is of high relevance from the central perspective of this book, the relation between the elites and citizens. It is a widely agreed principle that a new constitution should be submitted to a popular referendum. A referendum about the new EU Constitution was obligatory only in Denmark and Ireland, while in other countries (Germany, Belgium, the Netherlands, Malta, and Cyprus) the constitutions do not foresee any referendum. However, about half of the member countries announced plans to carry through a referendum. In France and the United Kingdom a referendum was announced, but mainly after increasing pressure from the public and from several political groups. After the French and Dutch no, the British premier Blair, however, revised his opinion and declared to abandon the idea of a referendum altogether. It seems that the decision to hold a referendum in many of those cases was based more on short-term considerations of internal politics than on the desire to get a true response of the citizens concerning the constitution. In many countries where only the parliament decided about the referendum, population surveys showed that large majorities were in favour of holding a popular referendum.

The conclusion from all these facts is quite clear: The process of elaboration and ratification of the constitution was steered to an overwhelming degree by the political elites; the citizens were never involved in a systematic way, and in only a few countries could they really decide about it. In all these regards, the proceeding did hardly correspond to democratic principles (Asbach 2002).

The Berlin Declaration and the Reform Treaty of 2007.
How the political elites have missed a chance of the century

On March 25, 2007, at the occasion of the fiftieth anniversary of the Treaty of Rome, the leaders of the EU, under the chairmanship of German Chancellor

Angela Merkel, launched the "Berlin Declaration" about the future of the constitution and the EU. This text is highly relevant here because it marks the official "response" of the top EU leaders to the integration crisis (after two years absence or *Denkpause*). The job of Angela Merkel as president of the European Council was certainly difficult at this moment of a deep EU crisis and that it was already an achievement that this text could be adopted (Schulmeister 2007). The way in which this declaration was elaborated, its content, and the further proceedings it proposes, however, make it appear as a document which perfectly reiterates the elite-driven way of integration of the last decades. The Portuguese presidency of the EU in the second half of 2007 continued the style of Germany. It pressed on a "highly ambitious" time schedule for a fast ratification of the "Reform Treaty" (as it is now called), and tried to avoid any further discussions about its content.[24] On December 13, 2007, the heads of the EU member state governments have signed the revised constitution, now called *Reform Treaty*, in Lisbon. In this way, they have missed a unique chance to put trough a fundamental reform of the EU institutions which would strengthen in a significant way the acceptance of integration among the citizens (see also Wehr 2004:140ff.). Let us shortly look at these two steps.

The short *Berlin Declaration* consists of three parts: In the first, the positive achievements of integration (peace, freedom, democracy, prosperity, etc.) are praised; the second part focuses on the strengths and objectives of integration; the third contains future intentions. The following five aspects, however, make this declaration a very poor achievement if one hopes for a substantial progress of the EU reform process: (1) The declaration continues with the typical "verbose rhetoric" of the EU (Alesina and Perotti 2004; Weiler 1999), praising its high success in many areas. We have shown in several chapters of this book that it is simply not true that European integration has been the main factor for certain achievements (peace) and that the success in other regards (economic growth, employment) has been quite modest. (2) The declaration includes many empty clichés ("The European Union is our response to these challenges") but proposes no single concrete solution about the further reform process, except a single one. This is the time deadline that the EU shall be placed "on a renewed common basis before the European Parliament elections in 2009."[25] This is quite problematic, however, because it again puts high time pressure on all efforts to revise the constitution. The opposition of the Czech government against the declaration was directed particularly to this point.[26] (3) One of the two central problems of the EU, its democratic deficit, is not addressed. The only reference to democracy is that the Union wants to promote democracy "beyond its borders." Even the constitution is not addressed at all in the declaration, after objections by the Czech, UK, and Polish governments. Thus, the declaration represents nothing more than the "lowest common denominator" about the further integration process. (4) The missing sense of an EU democratic deficit among the authors of the declaration is proven

Photo 10a Back to elitist political decisions: (From left to right) Hans Gert Pöttering (president, European Parliament), Angela Merkel (chancellor of Germany), José Manuel Barroso (president, EU Commission) signing the Berlin Declaration, March 25, 2007.

Source: Auswärtiges Amt, Berlin and Kühler.

by the way in which the declaration was elaborated. This was a classical instance of *Geheimdiplomatie:* The text of the declaration was elaborated by a small body, based on separate individual consultations of the German presidency with the member states; the text was published at the very last minute; and only three high representatives of the EU, the president of the European Council (Angela Merkel), of the commission (J. Manuel Barroso), and of the EP (Hans-Gert Pöttering) signed the declaration (see photo 10a).[27]

All these criticisms get support by the fact that the evaluation of this declaration is completely different from the side of EU insiders and outsider. The representatives of the EU praise it as a very important achievement, well suited to stop "the days of elite-driven integration with no participation from Europe's citizens."[28] Independent observers see it much more critically: "The recent Berlin declaration offers few grounds for optimism. It reads like a liturgy learned by rote, offering a paean of praise to universal values in language belonging to a quasi-religious ceremony in the Church of St. Charles de Gaulle."[29]

After hectic negotiations about some special objections from some countries (especially Poland and Italy), the Portuguese presidency was able to present a new, revised version of the Constitution and get it accepted by the European Council on December 13, 2007. The new Treaty of Lisbon keeps practically all of the institutional innovations that were agreed upon in the European Constitution, such as a permanent EU president, a foreign minister (renamed "High Representative of the Union for Foreign Affairs and Security Policy"), the same distribution of parliamentary seats, a reduced number of Commissioners, a clause on withdrawal from the EU and a full legal personality (currently held only by the European Community) allowing it to sign international agreements.[30] In addition many of the political changes and substantial amendments to the old treaties in the European Constitution have also been kept. The following points are the major changes: (1) The name "Constitution" is dropped from all parts of the text. (2) All references to state-like symbols—flag, anthem, motto—were dropped. (3) The treaty does not include and integrate—as the Constitution did—all earlier treaties into one text; rather, it consists of two different texts, the "Treaty on the European Union" (the Maastricht Treaty) and the Treaty on the Functioning of the European Union" (the Treaty of Rome); it is considered only as an amendment of the older treaties. (4) Practically all other important new elements of the old Constitution have been incorporated into the new treaty. This fact was confirmed in public by all leading politicians throughout Europe; a detailed analysis shows that only ten out of 250 proposals in the new treaty are different from those in the Constitution; this means that 96% are the same.[31] The Charter of Fundamental Rights is not part of the treaties, but a legally binding reference to them is made. Thus, all the analyses carried out in this and the foregoing chapter about the Constitution are fully valid also for the Reform Treaty. (5) In order to become valid in 2009, the constitution must be ratified by the member states till the end of 2008; this shall be done in most countries only by a parliamentary voting.

From the viewpoint of the normative democratic theory which was hold throughout this work, this procedures and characteristics must be considered as being extremely problematic; let us discuss each of them shortly. Changes (1) and (2)—the dropping of the term Constitution and the reference to state-like symbols—have only symbolic value; moreover, the flag and anthem of the EU will continued to be used; the EP even declared that it will use them more in the future. (3) The waiving of the elaboration of a single, comprehensive text has not changed the fact that the EU treaties are extremely complicated and unreadable even for an educated reader. Thus, a main objection against the Constitution in the French and Dutch referenda—that it was complicated (although it was much less so than the Reform Treaty)—has been aggravated. (4) The fact that the new treaties are equivalent to the Constitution makes the call for referenda in this case as equally justified as in the case of the Constitution. In reality, high pressure was and is exerted on those governments (e.g., the Portuguese) who promised to carry out referenda on the treaty. British premier Gordon

Brown has great difficulties to explain to his electorate why there should be no referendum now—which was promised for the Constitution by his predecessor Tony Blair.

At the present moment it seems rather utopian to argue for a reformed constitution. I will do so, nevertheless, in the following section. Social science cannot look only at today and tomorrow but must have a longer time perspective. From such a point of view, it is highly probable that the EU will slide again into a new crisis of identity and legitimation.

A proposal to resume the constitutional discussion and a revised strategy for the ratification of a new Constitution

After having shown the shortcomings of the development of the proposed constitution, and its replacement, the Treaty of Lisbon, we will deduce quite shortly a proposal for a renewal of the constitutional debate. First, a new constitutional convention should be convoked whose task would be to revise the existing texts. The selection of the members of the convention should be highly transparent and follow rigorous democratic principles. There should exist no time straitjacket for the workings of the convention, although a certain (not too long) deadline should be specified.

For many of those who did not participate in the referendum about the constitution or who rejected it, the reason was that is was too long and complicated. This issue must be taken seriously. We propose that the constitutional text should be divided into two parts: Only the first and basic part (corresponding roughly to parts I and II) should be submitted to a referendum (see also Leinen 2001). The other parts, concerned with the specific areas of politics and working of the Union (parts III and IV), should be scrutinized carefully by politicians and experts to make sure that they correspond to the general principles laid out in the basic parts. Also in these parts, however, no concrete political aims and strategies and measures should be included.

The constitution (first part) should then be submitted to a popular referendum at the same day in all EU member states. Such a referendum would not work wonders as far as the development of a European public sphere and democracy is concerned (see several contributions in Timmermann 2001; Pernice and Maduro 2004). It would constitute one important step in this regard, however. It should be specified clearly in advance when the constitution will be considered as accepted. A clear majority of both countries and citizens would certainly be necessary.

CONCLUSION

Did European integration fulfil a century-old dream? It seems to be true if we believe the political elites, and if we look only superficially at developments since 1945. Half a century long, there was no major war between European countries, economic growth was spectacular over the long run, dictatorial regimes have been overthrown, the Iron Curtain has fallen down, and the Central East European countries became members of the Union. Yet there is also another point of view. In the old member countries, integration has been accompanied with modest growth, massive employment problems, and a significant rise of inequalities; declining birthrates and badly integrated immigrants are destabilizing socioeconomic development and cultural integration; the quality of democracy has been seriously undermined. A clear majority of the citizens of France and the Netherlands have also seen serious problems in these regards when they rejected the new Constitution for Europe. It is quite probable that the main postwar European achievements, the securing of peace and the establishment of democracy, have not been a consequence of integration but of worldwide changes in power structures and of autonomous revolutions in the former nondemocratic countries. For the elites, however, integration has evidently become an aim of its own as expressed in the aim to become "an ever closer Union."

When the intellectuals in the last centuries dreamed of "Europe," they in fact had in mind the world since Europe was its unchallenged centre. Today, in the era of globalisation, it is ever more evident that peace and democracy are problems of the world. At this level, they are far from having been realized. Also from this point of view, achievements in Europe look much less impressive. Europe has become an island of wealth amidst a world still troubled with extreme poverty, insecurity, and military violence. A new Iron Curtain has been established at the outside frontiers of the EU Schengen area, in particular in the Mediterranean, in order to shield this island from unwelcome, poor immigrants and refugees. Not a few among the political elites seem to follow that other old dream which wishes Europe to become one of the new world players in political and military terms. Such a dream, however, is hardly reconcilable with another vision of Europe which hopes that it grows as a democratic and just community of nations, that it develops trustful and friendly relations to its still powerful neighbour in the east, which helps efficiently the peoples living in its poor neighbour continent in the south, and which contributes significantly to effective disarmament and the enforcement of the rule of law on the world scale. Is it just wishful thinking to dream of such an alternative Union? It might be so as long as the present elitist pattern of integration continues which aims not only to integration, but also toward centralisation (Vaubel 1995). It may, however, become reality if the peoples and citizens of the EU get more influence on the shape of this process. There are two main preconditions for such a process: that the elites trust more in their people and that the citizens are ready and willing to engage themselves actively for such an aim.

Notes

NOTES TO CHAPTER 1

1. R. Augstein, L'Europe Oui, Maastricht non, Der Spiegel, 14.9.1992.
2. Flash Eurobarometer "The European Constitution: Post-referendum survey in Spain." European Commission, 2005, pp. 4, 19.
3. http://www.wikipedia.org/wiki/Spanish_European_Contitutions_referendum.
4. Ibid.
5. Flash Eurobarometer on the Spanish referendum, p.32 (see footnote above).
6. News Welt, 14.7.2007.
7. http://www.wikipedia.org/wiki/Spanish_European_Contitutions_referendum.
8. Democracy International, press release (called up July 27, 2007); see http://democracy-international.org/bestseller.html.
9. See the CAP Web page, quoted in the foregoing footnote.
10. Pierre Hausemer (Department of Government, LSE), Luxembourg's referendum on the European constitutional treaty, July 2005. See http://www.sussex.ac.uk/sei/documents/epern-rb_luxembourg_2005.pdf.
11. Hausemer, ibid., p. 5.
12. The parliamentary votes on the Maastricht Treaty in the countries with no referendum have not been included in the table. They were all quite positive.
13. See http://de.wikipedia.org/wiki/Gr%C3%B6nland.
14. Eurobarometer 65, January 2007; European Commission, Brussels, p. 149.
15. In 1993, a group of German academics, led by the economist Renate Ohr, published a memorandum against the introduction of the Euro (Nollmann 2002:233). See http://www.ifd-allensbach.de/news/news/.
16. Somewhat different results, however, are reported in the *Eurobarometer* according to which the majority of Germans (60%) in autumn 2001 were in favour the *Euro* (see *Eurobarometer 56*).
17. Report in FISCHER WELTALMANACH 1995, p. 213.
18. German Constitution, Art. 29 (Verfassungen der EU-Mitgliedsstaaten 2005, p. 66f.).
19. Survey by the Forsa-Institute, June/July 2004. See ngo-online, 31.5.2007.
20a. Unfortunately, the CIRCAP study came to my knowledge only after having finished the manuscript. 205 members of the European Parliament and 50 top level officials of the EU Commission were interviewed between May and July 2006 in 9 EUP member countries, as well as 1000 citizens in each of these countries. Also this study showed large differences in the opinions of the elites and the citizens, the first feeling "extremely positive about EU growth and leadership", expressing more enthusiasm about European integration than the citizens; the latter also see less global threats and are much more sceptical against the EU access of Turkey than the elites (CIRCAP 2006).

20. The European Union "A View from the Top." Top Decision Makers and the European Union, Report prepared by Jacqueline M. Spence, Conducted by EOS Gallup Europe, Wavre (Belgium); the report is available at internet: http://ec.europa.eu/public_opinion/archives/top/top.pdf

21. Beatrice Gorawantschy, Frankreich vor dem Referendum, Konrad-Adenauer-Stiftung, Bonn, April 2005. See http://www.kas.de/db_files/dokumente/7_dokument_dok_pdf_6703_1.pdf.

22. The analysis is based only on the transcription of the text. However, the text also contains some informations concerning the dynamics of the discussion; it is marked, for instance, if a speaker was interrupted. The text has been made available on Web by the office of the French president (http://www.elysee.fr); the printout was made and transmitted to me by Laurent Tessier, Paris. Translations from the French by M. Haller, with the assistance of Laura Perres (Graz/ Paris).

23. Gorawantschy 2005; see footnote 22 above.

NOTES TO CHAPTER 2

1. Some recent general introductions to sociological elite theories include Scott 1990; Dogan 2003; Hradil and Imbusch 2003; Coenen-Huther 2004; Wasner 2004. The most informative book on the comparative study of elites still is Putnam 1976.

2. The concept of elites is more useful for studying European integration than that of "classes" because this concept also presupposes the existence of social and cultural commonalities (patterns of intergenerational reproduction and marriage, lifestyles); there are no European "upper" or "dominant classes" in the making in this sense. The (neo-) Marxist concept of the capitalist class underestimates the role of politics and bureaucrats, as well as that of ideas and institutions, such as democracy. In practice, however, the perspectives of elite and class theory might not be very different. Bastian van Apeldoorn, for instance, who works in a neo-Marxist, Gramscian perspective, frequently also uses concepts such as "class-elites," "Europe's corporate elite," and the like (see van Apeldoorn 2000).

3. For useful introductions and overviews, see Putnam 1976; Etzioni-Halevy 1993; Coenen-Huther 2004; Wasner 2004.

4. This approach has been developed by classical authors such as Mead, Weber, Popper, Elias, and others. For a short presentation of this approach, see Haller 2001; for an extended discussion see Haller 2003a.

5. For further sociological works on European integration, see Bryant 1991; Münch 1993; Bach 2000; Immerfall 1994, 2000; Rumford 2002; Nieminen 2005.

6. From such a perspective, there is no danger that they are "idealized" or their steering power is overestimated, as Pelinka (2005:151f.) warns.

7. There exists an abundance of literature on the political system of the EU. Some standard works include Jachtenfuchs and Kohler-Koch 1996; Pfetsch 1997; Dinan 1999:205ff.; Hartmann 2001; Nicoll and Salmon 2001:79ff.; Cini 2003; Neisser 1993; Moussis 2006; Pollak and Slominski 2006.

NOTES TO CHAPTER 3

1. At this time, Cologne belonged to Prussia, the largest and dominant subunit within the Weimar Republic.

2. See http://de.wikipedia.og/wiki/KPD-Verbot.

3. See also "Jean Monnet, die Montannion und die Anfänge der Europäischen Gemeinschaft," *Neue Solidarität* 51/2000 (available on the Web).

4. The following biographical informations are taken from Monnet's autobiography (1988) and *Duchene, Jean Monnet: The Statesmen of Independence* (1994); see also Dinan (1999:11–35).
5. The term "Schuman Plan" was invented because the French foreign minister Schuman—himself a fascinating "European personality" (see this chapter)— presented the plan to the public; but the ideas have been developed mainly, if not exclusively, by Monnet.
6. See "Europa im Sumpf der Korruption" by Olivia Schoeller, http://www. toni-schonfelder.com/print.asp?idte=129
7. Fischer Weltalmanach 2001:301.
8. Fischer Weltalmanach 2002:303.
9. Fischer Weltalmanach 1996:631.
10. Fischer Weltalmanach 2001:259.
11. *Der Spiegel*, No.12, 18.3. 2002. According to this report, the number of corruption procedures because of bribery increased fivefold between 1994 and 2000 (from 258 to 1,243).
12. Commission of the EC, Report from the Commission to the EP and the Council: Protection of the Communities' Financial Interests—Fight against fraud— Annual Report 2005. (Available on the Web site http://ec.europa.eu.)
13. Report in Der Standard (Vienna), 10.7.2007, p.15.
14. In a scattergram showing the position of the countries in a field with the two axes satisfaction with national democracy/satisfaction with EU democracy.
15. http://en.wikipedia.org/wiki/Nile.
16. The countries covered were Austria (9 interviews), Italy (6), Germany (2), France (2), Czech Republic (1), Lithuania (1), and Hungary (1).
17. In the German Bundestag, for instance, the proportion is similar. See www. bundestag.de/.
18. From the homepage-information, it is often not clear if some other function is still exercised or not.
19. See http://www.europarl.europa.eu/oeil/file.jsp?id=5254742, Statute for Members of the European Parliament.
20. For this section, a report by Albert Reiterer, Vienna (Europäische Identität und "europäische" Eliten), elaborated for this publication, was very useful.
21. *Frankfurter Allgemeine Zeitung*, July 1, 2004.
22. Reports by the German public television network ZDF (Tagesschau. de of May 13, 2006) and the newspaper *Die Welt* (http://www.welt.de/ data/2005/04/706154.html).
23. *Der Standard*, 29.5.2006, p. 11.
24. http://core.try.org.uk/publications/proeuropeanpolicy.html.
25. Interview with the title "To the EU must be set limits" in *Der Standard*, 25./26.6.2005, p. 28.
26. Interview with the title "Otherwise the system explodes" in *Der Standard*, 30.6.2005, p. 19.
27. See http://curia.europa.eu/en/instit/presentationfr/cje.htm.

NOTES TO CHAPTER 4

1. See Forbes, *World's Business Leaders 2000*, http://www.forbes.com.
2. In the comprehensive study of Pollack (2003), for instance, concepts like corporations, firms, enterprises, economic elites, and the like appear neither in the content nor in the index.
3. Communication from the Commission to the Council and the European Parliament, SEC (2005) 981 of 20.7.2005 (COM (2005) 330 final), p. 4.

4. See http://www.klaus.cz/klaus2/asp/clanek.asp?id=zWV7JeVDR33K.
5. Due to lack of space, we cannot present here the detailed table which was elaborated for the first version of the manuscript.
6. Vladimir Spidla, "Lob der Arbeitsmobilität," *Der Standard* (Vienna), 26.9.2006.
7. Findings from the Eurobarometer, quoted in Mayes and Kilponen 2004:325.
8. "The rise of corporate power," Institute for Policy Studies, Dec. 2000; available at: http//:www.ips-dc.org/downloads/Top_200.pdf.
9. Paul de Grauwe and Filip Camerman, "How Big are the Big Multinational Companies?" University of Leuven and Belgian Senate 2002; available at: http:www.econ.kuleuven.ac.be/ew/academic/intecon/Degrauwe/.
10. In the following, I am relying on van Apeldoorn and Horn 2005.
11. *Süddeutsche Zeitung* (Munich), 1.6.2005, p. 25. The U.S. had subsidized Boeing since 1992, according to EU sources, with $29 billion.
12. European Affairs Consulting Group, Interessensvertretungen in Brüssel. Die Arbeiterkammer und ihr Umfeld in der Europahauptstadt, Brüssel 2005 (unpublished report).
13. It might be mentioned that Schrempp was also the architect of the "elephant marriage" between Daimler-Benz and Chrysler which later (2006/07) turned out as a gigantic wrong decision. Schrempp had to abdicate his office in 2005.
14. The survey covered 300 persons in the province of Styria, carried out in spring 2006 (Haller and Ressler 2006a).
15. *La Stampa* (Torina), 15.6.2004, p. 15.
16. André Sapir et al. (2003), A New Agenda for a Growing Europe. Making the EU Economic System Deliver, Report of an Independent High-Level Study Group, July 2003.
17. Such efforts were the Brussels Sugar Convention of 1902, the establishment of the International Institute of Agriculture in 1905, and the International Wheat Agreement of 1933 (Tracy 1989:139ff.).
18. In the UK, the strongest was the NFU—National Farmers Union; in France the FNSEA—Fédération Nationale des Syndicats des Exploitants Agricoles; in Germany the DB—Deutscher Bauernverband.
19. See also the concise summary in http://wikipedia.org/wiki/Common_Agricultural_Policy, and http://wikipedia.org/wiki/Agricultural_subsidy.
20. Four denote internal market prices (target price, guide price, norm price, and basic price), three internal price supports (intervention price, withdrawal price, minimum price), and three to exports and imports (threshold price, sluice-gate price, and reference price; see Fennell 1987:99).
21. See www.farmsubsidy.org.
22. Information has been taken from the homepages of these firms.
23. See http://www.oxfam.org/en/news/pressreleases2005/pr051107_france_eu.
24. See http://en.wikipedia.org/wiki/Common_Agriculture_Policy.
25. For informative general accounts of the enlargement process from the economic point of view, see Glenn 2003; El-Agraa 2004b:494ff.; Ingham 2004:243ff.
26. Klaus Morischat, Handelsblatt 7.4.2004.
27. See the reports of the Dresdner Bank, "Investieren in Mittel- und Osteuropa," Oct. 2005; http://www.dresdner-bank.de/kontakt/ (9.12.2006); and the report of Price Waterhouse Coopers: "Fördermöglichkeiten in Mittel- und Osteuropa," von Grit Bugasch, fax.net (5.6.2003).
28. Data of the Board of Bank Regulation at the Ukrainian Central Bank, reported in *Kyiv Weekly*, June 14–20, 2007, p. 2.
29. *Der Standard*, 12.7.2007, p. 24.

30. This resulted, among others, from a personal interview with the head of the Polish delegation to the EU in the accession negotiations.
31. Eurostat, Statistik kurz gefasst. Bevölkerung und soziale Bedingungen, No. 7/2006.
32. *Der Standard* (Vienna), September 22, 2006, p.24.
33. *Die Kleine Zeitung* (Graz), September 23, 2006, p.12–13.
34. CBOS, Polish Public Opinion (Newsletter), February 2003; see also http://www.cbos.pl. I am grateful to the director of CBOS, Krzysztof Zagórski for making available these data to me.
35. See Eurobarometer 63, May–June 2005, European Commission, Directorate General Press and Communication. http://europa.eu.int/comm/public_opinion/index_en.htm.

NOTES TO CHAPTER 5

1. In the comprehensive works on the European Union, such as Dinan (1999), Nicoll and Salmon (2001), Pollack (2003), Cini (2003a), and Moussis (2006), the concept of "bureaucracy" does appear neither in the table of contents nor in the index.
2. For critical accounts on these approaches, see Schmid and Treiber 1975; Würtenberger 1977; Pierre 1995:xv.
3. See, for instance, Mayntz (1985) and Parsons and Smelser (1984).
4. There are many descriptions of the European Commission, most of which, however, are focussing on their formal structure. For more informative treatments and special studies, see Edwards and Spence 1994; Wessels 1996; Dinan 1999:205ff.; Nicoll and Salmon 2001:129ff.; Egeberg 2003; Pollack 2003:75ff.
5. Commission of the EC, "Action Plan: Simplifying and Improving the Regulatory Environment," Doc. Com (2002) 278 Final.
6. Address of Walter Hallstein at the British Institute of International and Comparative Law in London on 25 March 1965; Commission of the EC, Doc. 3574/X/65-E.
7. One of the few who recognizes this clearsightedness of Weber is Bruno Bandulet (1999:82).
8. See the informative report "Die Diktatur der Bürokraten" in *Der Spiegel*, No. 23, 2005, pp. 106–19.
9. Address of Walter Hallstein in London, 1965, quoted in footnote 6 above.
10. For interpreters, see http://europe.eu.int/languages/de/chapter/40; data for translators have been provided for by the single EU institutions.
11. ILO Yearly Data. Tables 2B and 2E; for the USA: ILO-Public Sector Data (for both see http://laborsta.ilo.org); see also Dogan and Pelassy 1987.
12. *Sources:* Wirtschafts- und Sozialstatistisches Taschenbuch der AK, Austria; Statististisches Jahrbuch 2005, p. 596 (Federal Republic); www.civil.service.gov. uk/management/statistics/publications/; U.S. Census Bureau, federal government employment and payroll data (www.census.gov/govs/www/apesfed.html).
13. See http://europe.eu/agencies/index_de.htm (7.5.2007).
14. See also OECD, Historical Statistics 1960–1990, Paris; Table 2.13, p. 42; Haller 1997, p. 401.
15. This relative decrease, however, probably has not implied an increase in absolute numbers, since the total number of employed people increased strongly in this period.
16. These collaborators were Liria Veronesi (Italy), Bernadette Müller (Austria), Reinhard Blomert (Germany), and Anders Hellström (Sweden).

17. Quoted from the report of Anders Hellström: The number, size and composition of the EU bureaucracy in Sweden, November 2006, p. 10.
18. The full title is "Staff Regulations of Officials of the European Communities. Conditions of Employment of Other Savants of the European Communities" (2005).
19. Staff Regulations of Officials of the European Communities (2005), Title 5, pp. I-31–34.
20. Due to reasons of space, we cannot present these data in detail. For the first version of the book manuscript, several detailed tables have been elaborated.
21. European Commission, Comparative Study of the Remunerations of Officials of the European Institutions, June 2000, pp. 15ff. Available at: http://ec.europa.eu/reform/pdf/salaries_study-eu.pdf (13.6.2006).
22. Interview carried out by the author in March 2006 in Brussels.
23. "Staff Regulations" 2005, Chapter 4 (I-25–27), Annex V (pp.I-70–81).
24. "Goldener Handschlag für EU-Beamte," *Der Standard* (Vienna), 18.8.2005, p. 5.
25. So it was told that a car mechanic did not repair the car of a customer in a reliable way after having recognized that the customer was an EU official.
26. *European Voice*, 3–30 August, 2006, p.14. In this letter, the author criticizes an earlier article by a Finnish EU civil servant who had complained that "the salaries are too low" and he suffered "from continuous work overload due to structural lack of manpower."
27. See http://europa.eu/comm/reform/2002/selection/chapter1-en.html.
28. The results of this survey are summarized in a report entitled "The General Directors of the European Commission—Lines of Life and Visions of a European Elite" (see http://www.euro.de/europa/studie_eur_kommission/studie.html) and in a press information by Prof. Eugen Buss and Ulrike Fink-Heuberger in: www.soziologie.uni-hohenheim.de/C4_presse_presse-meldungen.htm) and in the extensive report of the Identity Foundation (2003).
29. These data are taken from the curricula vitae of the GDs, available at http://europa.eu.int/.
30. In the comprehensive introduction to the system of the EU by Dinan (1999), the terms *corruption* and *clientelism* appear neither in the contents nor in the index. The topic is also not treated in quite critical studies on the EU bureaucracy, such as Puntscher-Riekmann (1998) and Bach (1999). An exception is von Arnim (2006).
31. "Report From the Commission to the European Parliament and the Council" on "Protection of the Communities' Financial Interests—Fight Against Fraud—Annual report 2005; available on the Internet.
32. See, for instance, Rechnungshof—Jahresbericht zum Haushaltsjahr 2003, Amtsblatt der Europäischen Union, 47. Jd., 30. November 2004 (Document C 293).
33. See http://www.icg.org/downloads/Corruption ... (downloaded Aug. 1, 2006).
34. See also "Corruption in Central and Eastern Europe," http://www.eumap.org/topics/corruption.
35. Personal communication by MEP Herbert Bösch, reported in Haller and Ressler 2006a, p. 253.
36. See the above-quoted Commission report on "Protection of the Communities' Financial Interests—Fight Against Fraud—Annual Report 2005."
37. The number of interpreters was about 3,200 in 2005; 500 had fixed contracts, and the rest were accredited freelance interpreters; the number of translators was at least 2,000 (every office has its own staff in this regard).

See EU Commission, Directorate for General Interpretation: Interpretation: Where Do We Stand After One Year of Enlargement? Brussels 2005 and several Internet pages of the EU.

38. Speech before the German Parliament (Bundestag), Plenary protocol 15/35 of 11/5/2006; see also the report in *European Voice*,18–23 May 2006, p. 8.
39. Commission document COM (2002) 278 Final: http://ec.europa.en/governance/law_making/law_making.eu.htm.
40. See http://ec.europa.en/reform/intdex_en.htm (4.6.2006).
41. Communication of the German government: http://www.bundesregierung.de/E-Magnzin-Beitrag/,-977865/dokument.print.htm.
42. Report on the homepage of the German government www.staat-modern.de.
43. According to other sources 1,400 regulations.
44. *European Voice*,24–31.5.2006,p.2.
45. Desmond Dinan (1999:223), for instance, writes in this regard quite realistically: "It is impossible for even the most zealous president . . . to suddenly and successfully reform the Commission, not the least because of inertia or even outright opposition to reform within parts of the bureaucracy." Yet, then he goes on to comment on the reform efforts of the Santer Commission that these are "serious and substantively important" and most of the blame for not achieving reforms must go to the member states because they keep a stranglehold on the Commission's structure.

NOTES TO CHAPTER 6

1. Two methods of clustering cases have been used: the *Average Linkage— Between groups* method (graph 2) and the *Complete linkage* method (graph 4); data have been standardized (converted to *Z scores);* the distance considered is the *Squared euclidean distance.*
2. The data used are not the most recent ones (they are from the years 2003–2005). This is not a problem because the structural differences between the countries on which our analysis is focussed did not change substantially since then.
3. See the information on the EU page: http://europa.eu.int/external_relations/sweitzerland/index.htm.
4. See www.eda.admin.ch/eda/g/home/foreign/eu.html.
5. A succinct statement of these reasons is given in the homepage of the regional newspaper *Mythen-Post* of the Canton Schwyz: http://mythen-post.ch/themen_uebersicht/eu_ewr.htm (3.2.2006) at the Web site of the Swiss parliament, Jean-Francois Aubert, "Switzerland's Political Institutions": http://www.parlament.ch/e/homepage/sv-services-dummy/sv-ch-schweiz-kurze/sv-ch-staat.htm (3.2.2006). See also Hirter 1993 and Kriesi 1998.
6. H. P. Kriesi et al., Analyse des votations fédérales du 6 décembre 1992, GFW Institut de Recherche, Université de Genève 1993.
7. It must be admitted, however, that its stability has also to do with the fact that Switzerland is used by very rich and corrupt people around the world as a haven for depositing black money. This sector has also been involved in several scandals (Ziegler 1998).
8. Ivar Ekman, "In Norway, EU pros and cons (the cons still win)," *International Herald Tribune,* October 27, 2005.
9. Kristen Nygaard, "We are not against Europe. We are against Norwegian membership in the European Union," available at the homepage of Oslo University: http://heim.ifi.uio.no/~kristen/POLITIKKDOK_MAPPE/P_EU_Munchen_eng.html.
10. Ibid.

11. See http://en.widipedia.org/wiki/British_Commonwealth.
12. See: Wikipedia, United Kingdom referendum 1975.
13. Http://www.number10.gov.uk/output/page8384.as.
14. However, I would not like to discredit the Italians in general as being dishonest, inefficient, and so on. Rather, as Victor Willi (1983) has shown, most Italians are characterized by high levels of responsibility and efficiency in carrying through their activities, even in spite of adverse circumstances. In my view, the main reason for the high instability of Italian postwar governments, as well as for the high levels of corruption, was the fact that the large Communist Party was not considered as a "constitutional party" which could be included into a government coalition. This had the consequence that the coalitions which were only formed between Christian-conservatives, social democrats, and a few other small centre parties had a monopoly on government and used this for clientelistic and corruption purposes.
15. See: Il Venerdi della Repubblica, Supplemento del giornale La Repubblica, Roma, 27.2.1998, p. 38.
16. In the ranking of Transparency International, Italy is ranked at the forty-second place among 145 ranking places; this is far worse than most West European countries, and worse than countries such as Uruguay, Bahrain, Malaysia, and Costa Rica.
17. Therese Jacobs (University of Antwerp) suggested in a lecture at the University of Graz (14.4.1998) that the internal ethnic-national conflict between the Flemish and Walloon groups is the main factor for the low national pride. Belgians, particularly French-speaking Belgians, might greet European integration as a means of overcoming this division of the country.
18. One of the most recent instances was the widely discussed publication of Daniel Goldhagen's book on the attitudes and behaviour of ordinary Germans concerning the Holocaust (Goldhagen 1996; see also Noelle-Neumann 1987; Scheff 1994).
19. Here is one exception, namely, the case of the split-up of an existing or the formation of a new Bundesland. However, this constitutional fact would not forbid to hold a referendum in Germany; also in many other EU member states referenda have been held without a constitutional obligation.
20. See the concise description of the events by the Oxford historian Parker (1967). Detailed figures on the outcomes of the elections to the Reichstag 1919–1933 are given in http://st-franziskus.region-kaiserslautern.de/projekte/Projst.text23.htm.
21. http://st-franziskus.region-kaiserslautern.de/projekte/projst/text23.html.
22. Bundeszentrale für politische Bildung, 13.2.2006, "Europapolitik" (Michael Woyke), http://www.bpb.de/wissen/
23. This thesis applies certainly more to the most advanced Central East European countries, such as the Czech Republic or Slovenia (see Haller and Höllinger 1995), and to those which followed the Soviet model, but less to those in which not the whole economy was nationalized (such as in Poland, Hungary, and Yugoslavia) or to those which still were on a rather low level of development before the Communists took power (such as Romania or Bulgaria).
24. A Polish survey in the 1980s showed that for a vast majority of Poles at that time the best way "to get ahead in life" was "to emigrate" (compared to getting a good education, working hard, and so on).
25. Interview with the Italian newspaper *La Repubblica*, 18.4.2004.
26. See, for instance, his comment "Warnsignale aus Wien und Warschau" in *Der Standard*, 27.10.2005, p. 35.
27. Marcin Krol, "Der polnische Patient,,"= article in the Austrian newspaper *Der Standard*, 21.10.2005, p.35

28. Interview with the German newspaper *Frankfurter Allgemeine Zeitung*, 15.3.2005.
29. Data from Eurostat, reported in http://wko.at/statistik/eu/europa-BIPjeEinwohner.pdf.
30. See Verfassungen der EU-Mitgliedsstaaten (2005).
31. In the preamble, it is stated: "We the people of the United States . . . establish justice, insure democratic tranquillity, provide for the common defence, promote the general welfare, and secure the blessings of liberty . . ." In the Declaration of Independence, annexed to the Constitution, we read: "We hold that . . . all men are endowed by their Creator with unalienable Rights, that among these are Life, Liberty and the pursuit of Happiness."
32. See Verfassung der Union der Sozialistischen Sowjetrepubliken vom 7.10.1977; http://www.verfassungen.de/su/udssr77.htm. The new Russian constitution of 1993 has explicitly broken with the earlier tradition. It states: "Ideological plurality shall be recognized in the Russian Federation. No ideology may by instituted as a state-sponsored or mandatory ideology." See http://www.departments.bucknell.edu/russian/const/ch1.html.
33. The concept of output legitimation has problems of its own, however. The essence of legitimation is that an order *is actually seen as legitimate by the participants.* (Weber 1978:36) Thus, it relates exclusively to the acceptance and support that people confer to this system. However, it is not necessarily the case that a positive output leads to high and a negative output to low legitimacy. A seemingly successful government is often deselected in spite of an objectively quite positive output; and an elite (and the system it represents) can continue to enjoy trust and support in spite of very hard times for the citizens (this is typically so in the case of a war).
34. All quotations are taken from Konrad Adenauer Stiftung, Europäische Grundsatzreden von 1946–2006; see: http://www.europa-union.de.
35. Fakten und Zahlen über Europa und die Europäer, Europäische Kommission, Brüssel, May 2005 (see europa.eu.int/comm/publications); translation from German M.H.
36. In these analyses, we consider only the twelve "old" member states of the EU because only in their case does it make sense to investigate the effects of EU-membership. The ten-year period 1995–2004 seems adequate to get at a conclusion about the effects of integration and their public perception.
37. See Servan Schreiber's widely discussed book *The American Challenge*, published in 1968.
38. Unrecoded values of the crime rate 2004 are also significant, but the effect is not so clearly.
39. See "The Lisbon strategy for growth and employment," Report from the High Level Group, chaired by Wim Kok, November 2004, Luxembourg: Office for Official Publications of the European Communities (also available in Internet)
40. Facts and Figures about Europe and the Europeans, Luxembourg, Office for Publications of the EC 2006.
41. Plan D for Democracy, Dialogue and Debate, Brussels 13.10.2005; White paper on a European communication policy, Brussels, 1.2.2006; Communicating Europe in Partnership, Brussels 2007. See also the homepage of Commissioner Margot Wallström.
42. A comprehensive information on the EB is given in http://www.gesis.org/en/data_service/eurobarometer/standard_eb/index.htm.
43. See, for instance, the article "What does a poll really tell to you?" by Herb Ladley in *European Voice*, 5–11 July, 2007, p.13.

44. We inserted the EB general question on the attitude toward the EU into the Austrian Social Survey 2003, and found no difference in the answers. However, differences were found between proportions preferring the two largest Austrian parties, depending on the fact if the survey institute was the main contractor of the one or the other party.

NOTES TO CHAPTER 7

1. See the essay by S. and H. Bock in Suttner 2006:405ff.
2. See http://de.wikipedia.org/Friedrich_Gentz.
3. See Pavel Kouba," 'Die guten Europäer.' Friedrich Nietzsches Beitrag zur gegenwärtigen Diskussion über die europäische Integration," Transit 31/2003. Patrick Horvath ("Friedrich Nietzsche. Der Philosoph mit dem Hammer" (http://members.surfeu.at/4all/nietz.htm, 2002) calls him a "far sighted visionary of a United Europe."
4. In his book, Coudenhove-Kalergi (1953:120) reports that in 1946 he made a postal survey among 4,256 parliamentary deputies of all free European nations which was answered by 1,818; 97% of them said yes to his question "Are you for a European Federation in the context of the United Nations?" From this result, he immediately concludes that "not only the parliaments but also the peoples of Europe were ripe for a solution of the European question."
5. See the Web page of the pan-Europa movement: http://www.paneuropa.or.at/index2.html.
6. For a short introduction, see Bernhard Plé, "Immanuel Kant. Einführung in seine Philosophie," University of Bayreuth (2005).
7. Sigrid Pöllinger, "Immanuel Kant's Kampf um den,Ewigen Frieden' bleibt aktuell," *Die Presse*, 27.12.2006 (available under http://www.diepresse.com/Artikel.aspx?channel=m&ressort=g&id=607618.
8. See Georg Zenkert, Kants Friedensschrift in der Diskussion, http://www.information-philosopie/kantfrieden.htm.
9. Kant himself distinguishes the *republican constitution* from a *democratic* one. He argues that the latter is a kind of despotism, because it establishes—through the "will of the people"—in fact the domination of a majority over minorities. If we argue that in democracies, the respect for minorities has to be considered also a fundamental principle, this problem disappears. I think it is not necessary, therefore, to go more in detail into this terminological differentiation.
10. See the concise summary in: http://de.wikipedia.org/wiki/Frankfurter_Nationalversammlung.
11. Quoted from http://enwikipedia.org/wiki/Giuseppe_Mazzini.
12. Here, even a high officer, General A. de Spinola, had laid the foundation for the breakdown of the authoritarian regime by publishing the critical book *Portugal e o Futuro*. Furthermore, a critical *Movement of the Armed Forced* existed.
13. In his usual aggressive form of verbal behaviour, Haider had argued on public television that Chirac himself was guilty of corruption and was, therefore, not legitimized to accuse him.
14. See, for instance, http://de.wikipedia.org/Silvio_Berlusconi.
15. Gian Enrico Rusconi, "Die Mediendemokratie und ihre Grenzen—am Beispiel von Berlusconis Italien," in: Aus Politik und Zeitgeschichte B35–36/2004.
16. See K. Adenauer Stiftung, Europäische Grundsatzreden, http://www.karl-spreis.de/portrait/1988_3.html.

17. He defines as its basic characteristic the control of physical violence within a certain territory, also by means of armed force (see Weber 1978, vol.II, Ch. 8).
18. http://ec.europa.eu/publications/booklets/move/47/index_en.htm.
19. http://zope.hu-berlin/presse/veranstaltunge/reden
20. See "EU Foreign Security and Military Policy," TEAM—The Alliance of EU-Critical Movements, Fact Sheet No.6, 1994; http://www.teameurope.info/FSno6-militarization-FINAL.pdf.
21. In the famous hierarchy of values, proposed by A. Maslow (1987), security is considered as one of the essential "social values," equally as important as love, belongingness, or recognition by others.
22. European Commission, "A World Player. The European Union's External Relations," Brussels 2004; http://ec.europa.eu/publications/booklets/move/47/index_en.htm.
23. Team Fact Sheet 6, 1994; see footnote 20 above.
24. The books and their authors: Dinan (1999); Desmond Dinan, Professor at the College of Europe (Bruges and Natolin), financed mainly by the EU; Nicoll and Salmon (2001): Sir William Nicoll, Honorary Director General of the EU Commission; Trevor C. Salmon , J. Monnet Professor, Aberdeen; Cini (2003a): Michelle Cini: J. Monnet Lecturer, Bristol; Moussis (2006): Nicolas Moussis, worked for the EU Commission 1967–2000 (this book, which appeared in the 15th edition, contains the highest praise of the EU: "An experience which will change the history of mankind," etc.). The only textbook whose author seems not to be affiliated with the EU is El-Agraa (2004).
25. Some German and English books include: Baader 1993; Newhouse 1997; Bandulet 2000; Wehr 2004; Oldag and Tillack 2005; Reimon and Weixler 2006; Milborn 2006.
26. In April 2006, newspapers reported that the EP pays about 60 journalists each month travel, accommodations, and board costs to attend the EP session in Strasburg (*New Herald Tribune*, 5.4.2006, p. 1). When Austria held the EU presidency in this period, it invited and took over the travel costs for 60 international journalists (*Der Standard*, 4.5.2006, p. 35). According to the U.S. handbook *Ethical Journalism*, such practices are forbidden.
27. See also Frieder Otto Wolf, "Europe neu denken," Freitag 24. Die Ost-West-Wochenzeitung, 17.6.2005 (available also on the Internet).
28. Ulrich Beck and Anthony Giddens, "Nationalism has now become the energy of Europe's nations," *The Guardian*, October 4, 2005, p. 24.
29. Jürgen Habermas and Jacques Derrida, "Nach dem Krieg: Die Wiedergeburt Europas," *Frankfurter Allgemeine Zeitung*, 31.5.2003 (available at www.faz.net).
30. It is hard to see from which writings of Kant Habermas and Derrida deduce this assertion.
31. Adam Michnik, "L'accomplissement d'un reve," *Le Figaro*, 28./29.5.2005, p. 18.
32. *Der Standard*, 25.11.2005.

NOTES TO CHAPTER 8

1. This was the title of a public lecture by the internationally known Austrian political scientist Anton Pelinka in Graz, May 7, 2007.
2. European Commission, the European Constitution: Postreferendum survey in France, Flash Eurobarometer 171, 2005. European Commission,

the European Constitution: Postreferendum survey in the Netherlands, Flash Eurobarometer 172, 2005. IPSOS, postreferendum survey; N = 3355. Nationwide representative quota survey by telephone. Client: Le Figaro. Data available at: http://www.ipsos.fr/CanalIpsos/poll/8074.asp (6.6.2005).

3. Similar findings from a survey of SOFRES are reported in Perrineaux 2005:241f.

4. See http://www.openeurope.org.uk/about%2Dus/board.aspx (17.4.2007).

5. Joschka Fischer, "Vom Staatenbund zur Föderation; Gedanken über die Finalität der europäischen Integration," speech on May 12, 2000, at Humboldt University, Berlin; see http://www.auswaertiges-amt.de/6_archiv/2/r0005512a.htm (15.5.2000).

6. In particular, members of social-democratic and green parties.

7. Interview with MEP Voggenhuber in Vienna on July 21, 2005 (interviewer: M. Haller).

8. Most texts of the national constitutions are available through the Internet. In the German version, they are contained (in German) in the collection *Verfassungen der EU-Mitgliedsstaaten* (München 2005).

9. One could ask why just the Italian constitution contains such far-reaching social rights. The explanation is probably that in 1947, after the Second World War and the end of the fascist period, leftist political forces were rather strong; in fact, also the Communist Party was at this time part of government and the constitutional convention.

10. Presently, the monthly minimum wage is 1,570 euros in Luxembourg and 92 euros in Bulgaria, the two extremes in the EU. See http://de.wikipedia.org (Mindestlohn).

11. Kielmannsegg 1996; Weiler 1999; Chryssochoou 1998; Giddens 1998; Chryssochoou at al. 1999; Bach 2000a; Abromeit 2001; Courable 2001; Siedentop 2001; Höreth 1999, 2002; Rumford 2002:209ff.; Held 2004; Wehr 2004; Efler and Rhode 2005; Oldag and Tillack 2005; Alliès 2005; Giorgi et al. 2006; Attac 2006:40ff.; von Arnim 2006; Griller and Müller 1995; Pollak 2007.

12. An Italian MEP expressed this in a quite direct way in the interview: "It is enough that somewhere in the world somebody urinates in the wrong way and the EP will pass a resolution . . ."

13. Roman Herzog and Lüder Gerken, "Europa entmachtet uns und unsere Vertreter," *Die Welt*, 13.1.2007.

14. In the original manuscript, this topic was treated extensively in a whole chapter.

15. Results from the Eurobarometer 61.0, spring 2004.

16. EAEA News 2.3.2005; see http://www.eaea.org/news.php?k=5604&aid=5605.

17. Commission of the European Communities. The Commission's contribution to the period of reflection and beyond: Plan-D for Democracy, Dialogue and Debate, Brussels, 13.10.2005.

18. This idea has also been proposed by James Buchanan in a lecture at the University of Graz, 29.9.1994.

19. Countries covered were Austria, Germany, France, Italy, UK, Sweden, Spain, and Poland. The total sample size was 244. The questionnaire covered 40 closed and 10 open questions. The study was carried out by young social scientists in the respective countries (see Preface).

20. See *Newropeans'* 16 proposals for rendering the EU more democratic (www. Newropeans.eu) and Attac's 10 principals for a democratic EU treaty (www. attac.at).

21. See Herzog and Gerken, footnote 12, above.

22. See also the summary in "Direct democracy," http://en.wikipedia.org/wiki/Direct_democracy (29.4.07).
23. Andreas Kellerhals et al., Fragen einer Mitgliedschaft in der EU, Gutachten für den Schweizerischen Bundesrat 1999. See www.crossnet.ch/europe-magazin.
24. *Der Standard*, 12.7.2007, p. 5.
25. The influential prime minister of Luxembourg, Jean-Claude Juncker, has even gone further and proposed that a revised text of the constitution should be prepared until the end of 2007. *Kurier* (Vienna), 25 March 2007, p. 6.
26. *European Voice*, 15–21 March, 2007, p. 2
27. An interesting rationale was given for this procedure: Getting 30 politicians to sign the text would have taken around 90 minutes and would not be followed on television by the general public at whom it was aimed (*European Voice*, 22–28 March 2007, p. 2).
28. Margot Wallström (EU commissioner for communications), "What to do after the birthday party," *European Voice*, 4–11, April 2007, p. 14.
29. John Wyles, "Europe must be united or be irrelevant," European Voice, 4–11, April 2007, p. 12.
30. See http://en.wikipedia.org/wiki/Treaty_of_Lissabon. The text of the treaty can be found at http://bookshop.europa.eu/uri?target=EUB:NOTICE:FXAC07306:DE:HTML; http://www.openeurope.org.uk.
31. OpenEurope, A guide to the constitutional treaty, London 2007; available at http://openeurope.org.uk

References

ABBREVIATIONS

JCMS—Journal of Common Market Studies
KZFSS—Kölner Zeitschrift für Soziologie und Sozialpsychologie

Abbott, Andrew. (1988). *The System of Professions*. Chicago and London: University of Chicago Press.

Abromeit, Heidrun. (2000). "Kompatibilität und Akzeptanz—Anforderungen an eine integrierte Politik," in Grande and Jachtenfuchs, *Wie problemlösungsfähig ist die EU*, pp. 59–75.

Abromeit, Heidrun. (2001). Ein Maß für Demokratie. Europäische Demokratien im Vergleich, Institut für Höhere Studien. Wien: *Reihe Politikwissenschaft 76*.

Ackerman, Bruce. (1989). "Constitutional Politics and Constitutional Law," *Yale Law Journal* 99: 453–547.

Adam, Antail, and Hans-Georg Heinrich. (1987). *Society, Politics and Constitutions. Western and Eastern European Views*. Wien, Köln. and Graz: Böhlau.

Aiginger, Karl. (2004). "The Economic Agenda: A View From Europe." *Review of International Economics* 12:187–206.

Aiginger, Karl, and Gunther Tichy. (n.d.). *Die Größe der Kleinen. Die überraschenden Erfolge kleiner und mittlerer Unternehmungen in den achtziger Jahren*, Wien: Signum.

Ajzen, Icek, and Martin Fishbein. (1980). *Understanding Attitudes and Predicting Social Behavior*. Upper Saddle River, NJ: Prentice Hall.

Alber, Jens. (2006). "Das 'europäische Sozialmodell' und die USA." *Leviathan* 34:208–41.

Albrow, Martin. (1972). *Bürokratie*, München; List (engl.: Bureaucracy. London: Pall Mall Press 1970).

Alesina, Alberto et al. (2001). What Does the European Union Do? NBER Working Paper 8647. Cambridge, MA: National Bureau for Economic Research.

Alesina, Alberto, and Roberto Perotti. (2004). *The European Union: A Politically Incorrect View*. Unpublished paper, NBER and CEPR, Harvard University and IGIER–Università Bocconi, Milan.

Alf, Sophie. (1977). *Leitfaden Italien. Vom antifaschistischen Kampf zum historischen Kompromiss*. Berlin: Rotbuch.

Alliès, Paul. (2005). *Une Constitution contre la Démocratie? Portrait d'une Europe depolitisée*. Castelnau-le-Lez, France: Climats.

Alston, Philip, and Joseph H. H. Weiler. (1999). *An 'Ever Closer Union' in Need of a Human Rights Policy: The European Union and Human Rights*.

Howard Jean Monnet Working Paper 1/99 (http://www.jeanmonnetprogram. org/papers/99/990105.html).

Anderson, Peter J., and Aileen McLeod. (2004). "The Great Non-Communicator? The Mass Communication Deficit of the European Parliament and Its Press Directorate." *JCMS* 42:897–917.

Antes, Peter. (2005). "Christentum und europäische Identität." In Heit, *Die Werte Europas*, pp. 49–56.

Ardi, Brian, and Ali El-Agraa. (2004). "The General Budget." In El-Agraa, *The European Union*, pp. 343–53.

Arendt, Hannah. (1951). *The Origins of Totalitarianism*. New York: Harcourt, Brace.

Arendt, Hannah. (1963). *On Revolution*. New York: Harcourt, Brace Jovanovich.

Armstrong, Harvey. (2004). "Regional policy." In El-Agraa, *The European Union*, pp. 401–20.

Arndt, Helmut. (1980). *Wirtschaftliche Macht. Tatsachen und Theorien*. München: Beck.

Arnold, Hans. (1993). *Europa am Ende? Die Auflösung von EG und NATO*. München and Zürich: Piper.

Arnull, Anthony. (1999). *The European Union and Its Court of Justice*. Oxford: Oxford UP.

Arnull, Anthony. (2003). "The Community Courts." In Cini, *European Union Politics*, pp. 179–91.

Asbach, Olaf. (2002). "Verfassung und Demokratie in der Europäischen Union." *Leviathan* 30:267–97.

Attac, ed. (2006). *Das kritische EU-Buch. Warum wir ein anderes Europa brauchen*. Wien: Deuticke.

Auer, Andreas, and Michael Bützer. (2001). *Direct Democracy: The Eastern and Central European Experience*. Aldershot, UK: Ashgate.

Axt, Heinz-Jürgen. (2005). *Konkordanz als governance*. Unpublished paper, University of Duisburg, Essen, Germany.

Axt, Heinz-Jürgen, and Frank Deppe. (1979). *Europaparlament und EG-Erweiterung. Krise oder Fortschritt der Integration?* Köln: Pahl-Rugenstein.

Baader, Roland. (1993). *Die Euro-Katastrophe. Für Europas Vielfalt—gegen Brüssels Einfalt*. Böblingen, Germany: Anita Tykve Verlag.

Bach, Maurizio. (1992). "Eine leise Revolution durch Verwaltungsverfahren. Bürokratische Integrationsprozesse in der Europäischen Gemeinschaft." *Zeitschrift für Soziologie* 21:16–30.

Bach, Maurizio. (1999). *Die Bürokratisierung Europas. Verwaltungseliten, Experten und politische Legitimation in Europa*. Frankfurt/New York: Campus.

Bach, Maurizio. (2000a). "Die europäische Integration und die unerfüllten Versprechungen der Demokratie." In Hans-Dieter Klingemann and Friedhelm Neidhardt, eds., *Zur Zukunft der Demokratie*. Berlin: Edition Sigma, pp. 185–213.

Bach, Maurizio, ed. (2000). "Die Europäisierung nationaler Gesellschaften." Special Issue No. 40, *KZFSS*.

Bach, Maurizio, Christian Lahusen, and Georg Vobruba, eds. (2006). *Europe in Motion. Social Dynamics and Political Institutions in an Enlarging Europe*. Berlin: Edition Sigma.

Baechler, Jean. (1975). *The Origins of Capitalism*. Oxford: Basil Blackwell (French ed.: *Les Origines du capitalisme*. Paris: Gallimard 1971).

Balànyá, Bela, et al. (2000). *Europe Inc. Regional and Global Restructuring and the Rise of Corporate Power*. London: Pluto Press.

Baldwin, Richard. (2005, June). "The Real Budget Battle. Une crise peut en cacher une autre." Brussels: *CEPS Policy Brief* 75 (available at http://www.ceps.be).

Bandulet, Bruno. (1999). *Tatort Brüssel. Das Geld, die Macht, die Bürokraten.* München: Wirtschaftsverlag Langen Müller and Herbig.

Barber, Benjamin. (1984). *Strong Democracy. Participatory Politics for a New Age.* Berkeley: University of California Press.

Bartolini, Stefano. (2006). "Mass Politics in Brussels: How Benign Could It Be?" *Zeitschrift für Staats- und Europawissenschaften* 1:28–56.

Bassina, Irina, and Marcel Bas. (2002). "The United Europe as an Antidote to a Democratic Nation State in the Ideas of F. Nietzsche" (http://www.roepstem.net/nietzsche.html).

Bast, Jürgen et al. (2003). Der Verfassungsentwurf des Europäischen Konvents. *Integration* 24(4).

Bauer, Michael, and Bénédicte Bertin-Mourot. (1999). "National Models for Making and Legitimating Elites. A Comparative Analysis of the 200 Top Executives in France, Germany and Great Britain." *European Societies* 1:9–31.

Beck, Ulrich. (1986). *Risikogesellschaft. Auf dem Weg in eine andere Moderne.* Frankfurt: Suhrkamp.

Beck, Ulrich, and Edgar Grande. (2004). *Das kosmopolitische Europa. Gesellschaft und Politik in der zweiten Moderne.* Frankfurt am Main: Suhrkamp.

Belafi, Matthias. (2005). "Christliche Werte und europäische Verfassung." In Heit, *Die Werte Europas*, pp. 70–84.

Bell, Daniel. (1999). *The Coming of Post-Industrial Society. A Venture in Social Forecasting.* New York: Basic Books.

Bellier, Irène, and Thomas M. Wilson, eds. (2000). *An Anthropology of the European Union. Building, Imaging and Experiencing the New Europe.* Oxford and New York: Berg.

Bendix, Reinhard. (1960). *Max Weber. An Intellectual Portrait.* London: Methuen.

Beninger, Werner. (2004). *Beamtenrepublik Österreich. Die unglaublichen Privilegien unserer 'Staatsdiener.'* Wien: Ueberreuter.

Benz, Bemjamin. (2004). *Nationale Mindestsicherungssysteme und europäische Integration.* Wiesbaden, Germany: VS Verlag für Sozialwissenschaften.

Benz, Wolfgang, ed. (1988). *Pazifismus in Deutschland. Dokumente zur Friedensbewegung 1890–1939.* Frankfurt: Fischer.

Bergier, Jean-François. (1996). *Europe et les Suisses.* Genève: Ed. Zoé.

Bergsten, Fred. (2005, April 27). *The Euro and the World Economy.* Paper delivered at the conference The Eurosystem, the Union and Beyond: The Single Currency and Implications for Governance, Frankfurt, Germany.

Berthold, Norbert, and Jörg Hilpert. (1996). "Wettbewerbspolitik, Industriepolitik und Handelspolitik in der EU." In Ohr, *Europäische Integration*, pp.77–109.

Best, Heinrich. (1990). "Elite structure and regime (dis)continuity in Germany 1867-1933: The case of parliamentary leadership groups", *German History* 8:1-27.

Best, Heinrich, and Rudi Schmidt. (2004). "Caders into Managers: Structural and Attitudinal Changes of East German Economic Elites." Second Workshop on Elites and Transformation in East Europe, Budapest, Hungary.

Bieler, Andreas. (2002). "The struggle Over EU Enlargement: A Historical Materialist Analysis of European Integration." *Journal of European Public Policy* 9:575–97.

Bieling, Hans-Jürgen, and Jochen Steinhilber, eds. (2000). *Die Konfiguration Europas. Dimensionen einer kritischen Integrationstheorie.* Münster: Westfälisches Dampfboot.

Blondel, Jean, Richard Sinnott, and Palle Svensson. (1998). *People and Parliament in the European Union. Participation, Democracy, and Legitimacy.* Oxford: Clarendon Press.

Bockstette, Carsten. (2002). *Konzerninteressen, Netzwerkstrukturen und die Entstehung einer europäischen Verteidigungsindustrie.* Hamburg, Germany: Verlag Dr. Kovac.

Boedeltje, Mijke, and Juul Cornips. (2005). *Input and Output Legitimacy in Interactive Governance.* https://ep.eur.nl/bitstream/1756/1750/2/NIG2–01.pdf.

Bohle, Dorothee. (2000). "EU-Integration und Osterweiterung: die Konturen einer neuen europäischen Unordnung." In Bieling and Steinhilber, *Die Konfiguration Europas,* pp. 304–30.

Böhm-Amtmann, Edeltraud. (2003). "Entstehung, Grundzüge und Entwicklungstendenzen des Konzepts 'European Governance' und die Rolle der EU-Mitgliedstaaten." In E. Bohne, Hrsg., *Ansätze zur Kodifikation des Umweltrechts in der Europäischen Union.* Berlin: Duncker & Humblot, pp. 85–97.

Bonde, Jens-Peter, ed. (2005). *The Proposed EU Constitution—The Reader-Friendly Edition.* Brussels: European Parliament.

Bornschier, Volker. (1988). *Westliche Gesellschaft im Wandel.* Frankfurt and New York: Campus.

Bornschier, Volker. (2000a). *State-Building in Europe. The Revitalization of Western European Integration.* Cambridge: Cambridge University Press.

Bornschier, Volker. (2000b). "Ist die Europäische Union wirtschaftlich von Vorteil und eine Quelle beschleunigter Konvergenz? Explorative Vergleiche mit 33 Ländern im Zeitraum von 1980 bis 1998." In Bach, *Die Europäisierung nationaler Gesellschaften,* pp. 178–204.

Bornschier, Volker, Mark Herkenrath, and Patrick Ziltener. (2004). "Political and Economic Logic of Western European Integration. A Study of Convergence Comparing Member And Non-Member States, 1980–98." *European Societies* 6:71–96.

Borrmann, Axel, et al., eds. (1995). *Regionalismus-Tendenzen im Welthandel.* Baden-Baden, Germany: Nomos.

Boudon, Raymond. (1986). *L'idéologie. L'origine des idées recues.* Paris: Librairie Arthème Fayard.

Boudon, Raymond. (1999). *Les sens des valeurs.* Paris: Presses Universitaire de France.

Boudon, Raymond. (2004). *Pourquoi les intellectuels n'aiment pas le Libéralisme.* Paris: Odile Jacob.

Boukovsky, Vladimir, avec Pavel Stroilov. (2005). *L'Union Européenne, une Nouvelle URSS?* Monaco: Èditions du Rocher.

Bourdieu, Pierre. (1999). *Language and Symbolic Power.* Cambridge, MA: Harvard University Press.

Bourdieu, Pierre. (2000). "Die Durchsetzung des amerikanischen Modells und die Folgen." In *Loccumer Initiative, Europa des Kapitals oder Europa der Arbeit?* pp.171–89.

Bourricaud, Francois.(1958), "France," in: Arnold M. Rose, ed., *The Institutions of Advanced Societies,* Minneapolis: University of Minnesota Press.

Boyle, Elizabeth Heger, and John W. Meyer. (1998). "Modern Law as a Secularized and Global Model: Implications for the Sociology of Law." *Soziale Welt* 49:213–32.

Bozóki, Andràs. (2003). "Theoretical Interpretations of Elite Change in East Central Europe." In Dogan, *Elite Configurations at the Apex of Power,* pp. 215–47.

Braun, Neville L/ Francis G. Jacobs, eds. (1989), *The Court of Justice of the European Communities,* London: Sweet & Maxwell.

Brechon, Pierre. (2004). "Crise de confiance dans les elites politiques." In Cautrés and Mayer, *Le nouvau désordre électoral,* pp. 47–69.

Brettschneider, Frank, Jan van Deth, and Edeltraud Roller. (2003). *Europäische Integration in der öffentlichen Meinung.* Opladen, Germany: Leske und Budrich.

Breuss, Fritz. (2002). "Benefits and Dangers of EU Enlargement." *Empirica* 29:245–74.

Brinkmann, Gerhard. (1981). *Ökonomik der Arbeit.* Vol. 2: *Die Allokation der Arbeit.* Stuttgart, Germany: Klett-Cotta.

Brinkmann, Gerhard. (1984). *Ökonomik der Arbeit.* Vol. 3: *Die Entlohnung der Arbeit.* Stuttgart, Germany: Klett-Cotta.

Brunn, Gerhard. (2002). *Die Europäische Einigung von 1945 bis heute.* Stuttgart, Germany: Reclam.

Bryant, Christopher G. A. (1991). "Commentary: Europe and the European Community 1992." *Sociology* 25:189–207.

Bryde, Brun-Otto. (1992). "Europarecht in rechtssoziologischer Perspektive." In Schäfers, *Lebensverhältnisse und soziale Konflikte im neuen Europa,* pp. 79–88.

Buckwell, Allan, et al. (1982). *The Costs of the Common Agricultural Policy.* London and Canberra, Australia: Croom Helm.

Burgess, Michael. (2003). "Federalism and Federation." In Cini, *European Union Politics,* pp. 65–79.

Burley, Anne-Marie, and Walter Mattli. (1993). "Europe Before the Court: A Political Theory of Legal Integration." *International Organization* 47:41–76.

Buruma, Jan. (1994). *The Wages of Guilt. Memories of War in Germany and Japan.* London: Vintage/Random House.

Busch, Klaus. (1991). *Umbruch in Europa. Die ökonomischen, ökologischen und sozialen Perspektiven des einheitlichen Binnenmarktes.* Köln, Germany: Bund-Verlag.

Cameron, David R. (1998). "Creating Supranational Authority in Monetary and Exchange-Rate Policy: The Sources and Effects of EMU." In Sandholtz and Stone Sweet, *European Integration and Supranational Governance,* pp. 188–216.

Camic, Charles, and Neil Gross. (2004). "The New Sociology of Ideas." In Judith R. Blau, ed., *The Blackwell Companion to Sociology,* pp. 236–49. Malden, MA, Oxford, and Carlton, UK: Blackwell.

Cancian, Francesca. (1975). *What Are Norms? A Study of Beliefs and Action in a Maya Community.* London: Cambridge University Press.

Caporale, Guglielmo Maria, and Alexandros Kontonikas. (2006). *The Euro and Inflation Uncertainty in the European Monetary Union.* Economics and Finance Discussion Papers, No. 06–01, Economics and Finance Section, Brunel University (available online).

Carrubba, J. Clifford, et al. (2004). "A Second Look at Legislative Behaviour in the European Parliament. Roll-Call Votes and the Party System." Political Science Series, No. 94, Institute for Advanced Studies, Vienna, Austria.

Castells, Manuel. (1997). *The Power of Identity, Vol. II of the Information Age. Economy, Society and Culture.* Oxford: Blackwell.

Castells, Manuel. (1999). *The Information Age: Economy, Society and Culture. Vol. 1, The Rise of the Network Society.* Cambridge, MA: Blackwell.

Cautrès, Bruno, and Nonna Mayer. (2004). *Le nouveau désordre electoral. Les lecons du 21 avril 2002.* Paris: Presses de Sciences Po.

Cecchini Report. (1988). *Europe 1992: The Overall Challenge.* European Communities, Document SEC (88) 524 Final.

Cederman, Lars-Erik. (2001). "Back to Kant: Reinterpreting the Democratic Peace as a Macrohistorical Learning Process." *American Political Science Review* 95:15-???.

Chalmers, Damian. (2004). "The Legal Dimension in EU Integration." In A. M. El-Agraa, *The European Union,* pp. 57–75.

Chandler, Alfred. (1977). *The Visible Hand: The Managerial Revolution in American Business.* Westport: Greenwood.

Charle, Christoph. (2001). "Intellectuals: History of the Concept." In Neil Smelser and Paul Baltes., eds., *International Encyclopedia of the Social and Behavioral Sciences,* pp. 7627–7631. Amsterdam: Elsevier.

Chryssochoou, Dimitris N. (1998). *Democracy in the European Union.* London and New York: Tauris Academic Studies.

Chryssochoou, Dimitris N., et al., eds. (1999). *Theory and Reform in the European Union,*.Manchester and New York: Manchester University Press.

Chubb, Judith, and Maurizio Vanicelli. (1988). "Italy: A Web of Scandals in a Flawed Democracy." In Markovits and Silverstein, *The Politics of Scandal,* pp. 122–50.

Cini, Michelle, ed. (2003a). *European Union Politics.* Oxford and New York: Oxford University Press.

CIRCAP. (2006). *European Elites Survey 2006.* Siena, Italy: Centre for the Study of Political Change (Research Report; available on Internet).

Coen, David. (1997). "The Evolution of the Large Firma as a Political Actor in the European Union." *Journal of European Public Policy* 4:91–108.

Coenen-Huther, Jacques. (2004). *Sociologie des elites.* Paris: Armand Colin.

Cole, Phillip. (1994). "Towards a Citizens' Europe?" In Paul Gilbert and Paul Gregory, eds., *Nations, Cultures and Markets,* pp. 153–64. Aldershot, UK: Avebury.

Coleman, James S. (1982). *The Asymmetric Society.* Syracuse, NY: Syracuse University Press.

Coleman, James S. (1990). *Foundations of Social Theory.* Cambridge, MA, and London: The Belknap Press.

Collins, Randall. (2005). *Interaction Ritual Chains.* Princeton, NJ: Princeton University Press.

Coser, Lewis. (1956). *The Functions of Social Conflict.* New York and London: The Free Press and Collier Macmillan.

Coudenhove-Kalergi, Richard. (1953). *Die Europäische Nation.* Stuttgart, Germany: Deutsche Verlags-Anstalt.

Coudenhove-Kalergi, Richard. (1958). *Eine Idee erobert Europa. Meine Lebenserinnerungen.* Wien, München, and Basel: Verlag Kurt Desch.

Coultrap, John. (1999), "From Parliamentarism to Pluralism. Models of Democracy and the European Union's 'Democratic Deficit.' " *Journal of Theoretical Politics* 11:107–35.

Courable, John. (2001). "The Death of Democracy: A View From the Left." *The European Journal* 8:19–21.

Coxall, Bill, Lynton Robins, and Robert Leach. (2003). *Contemporary British Politics.* Houndmills, UK, and New York: Palgrave Macmillan.

Crozier, Michael. (1967). *The Bureaucratic Phenomenon.* Chicago: University of Chicago Press.

Crum, Ben. (2003). *Output Legitimacy of European R&D-Policy.* Paper prepared for the EUSA 8th International Biennial Conference, Nashville, Tennessee (available online).

Cutler, Tony, et al. (1989). *1992—The Struggle for Europe. A Critical Evaluation of the European Community.* New York: Berg.

Dahl, Robert A. (2001). "Is Post-National Democracy Possible?" In Fabbrini, *Nation, Federalism and Democracy,* pp. 35–46.

Dahrendorf, Ralf. (1962). *Gesellschaft und Freiheit. Zur soziologischen Analyse der Gegenwart.* München: R. Piper.

Dahrendorf, Ralf. (1965). *Gesellschaft und Demokratie in Deutschland.* München: Piper.

Dahrendorf, Ralf. (1968). *Gesellschaft und Demokratie in Deutschland.* München: Deutscher Taschenbuch Verlag.

Dalton, Russel J. (1999). "Political Support in Advanced Industrial Democracies." In Norris, *Critical Citizens,* pp. 57–77.

Debus, Karl Heinz, ed. (1995). *Robert Schuman. Lothringer, Europäer, Christ.* Speyer, Germany: Pilger.

Deflem, Mathieu/Pampel, Fred C. (1996): The Myth of Postnational Identity: Popular Support for European Unification. *Social Forces* 75:119-143.

Dell'Olio, Fiorella. (2005). *The Europeanization of Citizenship: Between the Ideology of Nationality, Immigration and European Identity.* Ashgate, UK: Aldershot.

Dehousse, R. (1994). *La Cour de Justice des Communautés européennes,* Paris: Montchrestien.

Dehove, Mario, ed. (2004). *Le nouvel état de l'Europe. Les idées-forces pour comprendre les nouveaux enjeux de l'Union.* Paris: La Découverte.

Deloche-Gaudez, Florence. (2005). *La Constitution Européenne. Que faut-il savoir?* Paris: Presse de la Fondation Nationale des Sciences Politiques.

Delors, Jacques. (1993). *Das neue Europa.* München: C. Hanser.

De Tocqueville, Alexis. (1947). *Democracy in America.* New York: Oxford University Press (here quoted after German edition: Über die Demokratie in Amerika. München: Deutscher Taschenbuch Verlag 1976).

De Tocqueville, Alexis. (1988). *L'ancien régime et la révolution.* Paris: GF Flammarion.

Deutsch, Karl W., et al. (1957). *Political Community and the North Atlantic Area: International Organisation in the Light of Historical Experience.* Princeton, NJ: Princeton University Press.

Deutsch, Karl. W. (1966). *Nationalism and Social Communication. An Inquiry Into the Foundations of Nationality.* Cambridge, MA, and London: MIT Press.

Diedrichs, Udo, and Wolfgang Wessels. (2005). "Die Europäische Union in der Verfassungsfalle? Analysen, Entwicklungen und Optionen." *Integration* 4:287–306.

Diekmann, Andreas. (1995). *Empirische Sozialforschung. Grundlagen, Methoden, Anwendungen.* Reinbeck, Germany: Rowohlt.

Diez Medrano, Juan. (2003). *Framing Europe. Attitudes to European Integration in Germany, Spain, and the United Kingdom.* Princeton, NJ, and Oxford: Princeton University Press.

Dinan, Desmond. (1999). *Ever Closer Union. An Introduction to European Integration.* Houndmills, Basingstoke, UK: Palgrave.

Dippel, Horst. (2001). "Warum Verfassung? Der Gedanke der Verfassung in der europäischen Rechtskultur" In Timmermann, *Eine Verfassung für die Europäische Union,* pp. 13–40.

Docksey, Christopher, and Karen Williams. (1994). "The Commission and the Execution of Community Policy." In Edwards and Spence, *The European Commission,* pp. 117–45.

Dogan, Mattei, ed. (1975). *The Mandarins of Western Europe. The Political Roles of Top Civil Servants.* Beverly Hills, CA: Sage.

Dogan, Mattei. (1997). "Erosion of Confidence in Advanced Democracies." *Studies in Comparative International Development* 32.

Dogan, Mattei. (2001) "Deficit of Confidence Within European Democracies ." In Haller, *The Making of the European Union,* pp. 241–61.

Dogan, Mattei, ed. (2003). *Elite Configurations at the Apex of Power.* Leiden and Boston: Brill.

Dogan, Mattei, ed. (2005). *Political Mistrust and the Discrediting of Politicians.* Leiden and Boston: Brill.

Dogan, Mattei, and Dominique Pelassy. (1987). *Le Moloch en Europe. Etatisation et Corporatisation.* Paris: Economica.

Domhoff, G. William. (1990). "Social Clubs, Policy-Planning Groups, and Corporations: A Network Study of Ruling-Class Cohesiveness." In Scott, *The Sociology of Elites I,* pp. 173–82.

Donati, Pier Paolo. (2008). "Quale cittadinanza europea? Costruire una fortezza o creare un nuovo modello di cittadinanza aperta?" In Haller, *Identität und Grenzen Europas/Identitá e Confini dell'Europa* (in press).

382   *References*

Donges, Jürgen, and Andreas Schleef. (2001). *Die EU-Osterweiterung—gesamtwirtschaftliche und unternehmerische Aspekte.* Berlin: Verlag GDA.
Donnelly, Martin, and Ella Ritchie. (1994). "The College of Commissioners and Their Cabinets." In Edwards, Geoffrey, and David Spence, eds., *The European Commission,* pp. 31–61. Harlows, Essex, UK: Longman.
Downs, Anthony. (1967). *Inside Bureaucracy.* Boston: Little, Brown.
Doyle, Michael W. (1996). "Reflections on the Liberal Peace and Its Critics." In Michael Brown et al., eds., *Debating the Democratic Peace—An International Security Reader,* pp. 358–363. Cambridge, MA: MIT Press.
Draxler, Gudrun. (2002). *Das Europäische Amt für Betrugsbekämpfung OLAF,* Wildon
Duchene, F. (1994). *Jean Monnet: The Statesman of Independence.* London: Norton.
Duhamel, Olivier, ed. (2005). *La Constitution Européenne. Les principaux textes présentés par O. Duhamel.* Paris: Armand Colin and Éditions Dalloz.
Durkheim, Emile. (1965). *Die Regeln der soziologischen Methode.* Neuwied and Berlin: Luchterhand (first French edition 1895).
Ebert, Kurt Hanns. (1978). *Rechtsvergleichung. Einführung in die Grundlagen.* Bern, Switzerland: Stämpfli.
Ebner, Michl. (2004). *Mein Rechenschaftsbericht. Zehn Jahre im Einsatz für Südtirol in Europa.* Bozen, Italy: Athesia.
Edelman, Murray. (1972). *Politics as Symbolic Action. Mass Arousal and Quiescence.* Chicago: Markham.
Edwards, Geoffrey, and David Spence, eds. (1994). *The European Commission.* Harlows, Essex, UK: Longman.
Efler, Michael, and Percy Rhode (2005). "Critical Analysis of the Democratic Aspects of the EU." Online at www.mehr-demokratie.de/eu-kritik.html.
Egan, Michelle. (2003). "The Single Market." In M. Cini, *European Union Politics,* pp. 28–45.
Egeberg, Morten. (2003). "The European Commission." In M. Cini, *European Union Politics,* pp.131–47.
Eichenberg, Richard C./Dalton, Russell J. (1993): Europeans and the European Community: the dynamics of public support for European integration. *International Organization* 47:507-534.
Eichengreen, Barry. (2005). "Europe, the Euro and the ECB: Monetary Success, Fiscal Failure." *Journal of Policy Modeling* 27: 427–439.
Eising, Rainer. (2004). "Der Zugang von Interessengruppen zu den Organen der Europäischen Union: Eine organisationstheoretische Analyse." *Politische Vierteljahresschrift* 45:494–518.
El-Agraa, Ali (2004a), "General Introduction: the EU within the global context of regional integration," in: El-Agraa, *The European Union Economics and Politics,* pp. 1–22.
El-Agraa, Ali M., ed. (2004b). *The European Union. Economics and Policies.* Harlow, UK: Pearson Education and Prentice Hall.
Elias, Norbert. (1978). *The Civilizing Process.* New York: Uritzen Books.
Elias, Norbert. (1985). *Humana Conditio. Beobachtungen zur Entwicklung der Menschheit am 40. Jahrestag eines Kriegsendes (Mai 1985).* Frankfurt: Suhrkamp.
Elsasser, Hans, et al. (1988). *Die Schweiz.* Stuttgart, Germany: Kohlhammer.
Elwert, Georg. (1999). "Deutsche Nation." In B. Schäfers and Wolfgang Zapf, eds., *Handwörterbuch zu Gesellschaft Deutschlands.* Opladen, Germany: Westdeutscher Verlag.
Engelmann, Bernt. (1993). *Wir Untertanen. Ein deutsches Geschichtsbuch.* Göttingen, Germany: Steidl.
Erhard, Ludwig. (1957). *Wohlstand für alle.* Düsseldorf: Econ.

Erikson, Erik H. (1980). *Identity and the Life Cycle.* New York: Norton.
Esping-Andersen, Gøsta. (1985). *Politics Against Markets. The Social Democratic Road to Power.* Princeton, NJ: Princeton University Press.
Esping-Andersen, Gøsta (1990). *The Three Worlds of Welfare Capitalism.* Cambridge: Polity Press.
Esterbauer, Fried. (1983). "Die institutionelle Sackgasse der Europäischen Gemeinschaft auf dem Wege zur Föderation." In Fried Esterbauer et al. , eds., *Von der freien Gemeinde zum föderalistischen Europa,* pp. 603–27. Berlin: Duncker & Humblot.
Etzioni, Amitai. (1988). *The Moral Dimension. Toward a New Economics.* New York and London: The Free Press and Collier Macmillan.
Etzioni, Amitai. (2001). *Political Unification Revisited. On Building Supranational Communities.* Lanham, MD: Lexington Books.
Etzioni-Halevy, Eva. (1990). "Comparing Semi-Corruption Among Parliamentarians in Britain and Australia." In Else Oyen, ed., *Comparative Methodology. Theory and Practice in International Social Research,* pp. 112–33. London: Sage.
Etzioni-Halevy, Eva. (1993). *The Elite Connection. Problems and Potentials of Western Democracy.* Cambridge: Polity Press.
Etzioni-Halevy, Eva. (1999). "Elites, Inequality and the Quality of Democracy in Ultramodern Society." *International Review of Sociology* 9:477–93.
Eyal, Gil, Iván Szelenyi, and Eleanor Townsley. (2000). *Making Capitalism Without Capitalists. Class Formation and Elite Struggles in Post-Communist Central Europe.* London and New York: Verso.
Fabbrini, Sergio, ed. (2001). *Nation, Federalism, and Democracy. The EU, Italy and the American Experience,* Bologna, Italy: Editrice Compositori.
Fabbrini, Sergio. (2003). "Bringing Robert A. Dahl's Theory of Democracy to Europe." *Annual Review of Political Science* 6:119–37.
Faber, Anne. (2005). *Europäische Integration und politikwissenschaftliche Forschung. Neofunktionalismus und Intergouvernementalismus in der Analyse.* Wiesbaden, Germany: VS Verlag für Sozialwissenschaften.
Faber, Richard. (1979). *Abendland. Ein 'politischer Kampfbegriff.'* Hildesheim, Germany: Gerstenberg Verlag.
Faelcker, Margot. (1991). "Demokratische Grundhaltungen und Stabilität des politischen System: Ein Einstellungsvergleich von Bevölkerung und politisch-administrativer Elite in der Bundesrepublik Deutschland." *Politische Vierteljahresschrift* XXXII:71–91.
Faist, Thomas. (2001). "Social Citizenship in the European Union: Nested Membership." *JCMS* 39:37–58.
Falkner, Gerda, et al., eds. (2005). *Complying With Europe. EU Harmonisation and Soft Law in the Member States.* Cambridge: Cambridge University Press.
Falkner, Gerda, and Michael Nentwich. (1995). *European Union: Democratic Perspectives After 1996.* Wien: Service Fachverlag.
Farmer, Karl, and Thomas Vlk. (2005). Internationale Ökonomik. Eine Einführung in die Theorie und Empirie der Weltwirtschaft. Wien: Lit.
Farr, James. (1985). "Situational Analysis: Explanation in Social Science." *The Journal of Politics* 47:1085–1107.
Fehr, Helmut. (2004). "Eliten und Zivilgesellschaft in Ostmitteleuropa." Beilage zur Wochenzeitung *Das Parlament,* B 5–6/2004.
Feldman, David. (1993). *Civil Liberties and Human Rights in England and Wales.* Oxford: Clarendon Press.
Feldmann, Horst. (1993). "Europäische Industriepolitik." In ORDO. *Jahrbuch für die Ordnung von Wirtschaft und Gesellschaft,* Struttgart: Lucius & Lucius Vol. 44, pp. 139–68.

Fellman, David. (2003). "Constitutionalism," pp. 485–92, in *Dictionary of the History of Ideas*, Vol. 1. Charlottesville, VA: Electronic Text Center of the University of Virginia.

Fennell, Rosemary. (1987). *The Common Agricultural Policy. Its Institutional and Administrative Organisation*. Oxford: BSP Professional Books.

Fennema, M. (1982). *International Networks of Banks and Industries*. The Hague, Boston, and London: M. Nijhoff.

Feron, Elise, John Crowley, and Liana Giorgi. (2006). "The Emergence of a European Political Class." In Giorgi et al., *Democracy in the European Union*, pp.79–114.

Ferry, Jean-Marc. (2000). *La question de l'ètat européen*. Paris: Gallimard.

Fioravanti, Maurizio. (1999). *Costituzione*. Bologna: Il Mulino.

Fischer, Fritz. (1979). *Griff nach der Weltmacht. Die Kriegszielpolitik des kaiserlichen Deutschland 1914/18*. Frankfurt: Fischer Taschenbuch Verlag.

Fischer, Klemens H. (2003). *Konvent zur Zukunft Europas. Texte und Kommentar*. Baden-Baden, Germany: Nomos.

Fischer, Klemens H. (2005). *Der Europäische Verfassungsvertrag. Texte und Kommentar*. Baden-Baden, Wien, and Bern: Nomos, Manz, and Stämpfli.

Fischer Weltalmanach. *Zahlen—Daten—Fakten*, Frankfurt: Fischer Taschenbuch Verlag (appears annually).

Fischer Weltalmanach. (2006). *Zahlen—Daten—Fakten*. Frankfurt: Fischer Taschenbuch Verlag (appears annually).

Fitoussi, Jean-Paul, and Jacques Le Cacheux. (2005). *L'État de l'Union Européenne 2005*. Paris: Fayard et Presses de Sciences Po.

Fix, Elisabeth. (1992/93). "Integration als,Vernunftehe' im Spannungsfeld zwischen ‚loyalty,' ‚voice' und ‚exit'—Zu den Rahmenbedingungen der Genese und des Fortbestandes von Föderationen." In *Jahrbuch zur Staats- und Verwaltungswissenschaft*, 6, ed. by T. Ellwein u.a., Baden-Baden, Germany: Nomos, S.113–61.

Fligstein, Neil. (2001). *The Architecture of Markets. An Economic Sociology of Twenty-First-Century Capitalist Societies*. Princeton, NJ, and Oxford: Princeton University Press.

Foerster, Rolf Helmut. (1963). *Die Idee Europa 1300–1946. Quellen zur Geschichte der politischen Einigung*. München: Deutscher Taschenbuch Verlag.

Fontaine, P. (2000). *Una proposta nuova all'Europa. La dichiarazione Schuman, 1950–2000*. Luxembourg, Luxembourg: Ufficio delle Publicazioni Ufficiali delle Comunità Europee.

Forder, James. (1999). *Is European Integration Really the Friend of Free Trade?* London: Politeia.

Fouilleux, Eve. (2003). "The Common Agricultural Policy." In Cini, *European Union Politics*, pp. 246–63.

Franz, Monika. (2004). "Fundamente europäischer Identität. Teil II." BLZ-Report 03/2004 (Beilage der Bayerischen Staatszeitung; available online).

Frei, Bruno, and A. Stutzer. (2002). *Happiness and Economics. How the Economy and Institutions Affect Well-Being*. Princeton, NJ, and Oxford: Princeton University Press.

Friedman, Milton, and Robert Mundell, (2001). "One World, One Money?" *Policy Options* 10–30.

Friedrich, Carl J. (1969). *Europe. An Emergent Nation?* New York and Evanston, IL: Harper & Row.

Fuhrmann, Nora. (2005). *Geschlechterpolitik im Prozess der europäischen Integration*. Wiesbaden, Germany: VS Verlag für Sozialwissenschaften.

Gabel, Matthew J./ Christopher J. Anderson (2002), "The Structure of Citizen Attitudes and the European Political Space", *Comparative Political Studies* 35: 893-913.

Gabriel, Oscar. (2000). " 'It's time for a change.'—Bestimmungsfaktoren des Wählerverhaltens bei der Bundestagswahl 1998." In Fritz Plasser et al., eds., *Das österreichische Wahlverhalten*, pp. 333–92. Wien: Signum.

Galati, Gabriele, and Kostas Tsatsaronis. (2003). "The Impact of the Euro on Europe's Financial Markets." *Financial Markets, Institutions and Instruments* 12:165–221.

Galtung, Johan. (1973). *The European Community. A Superpower in the Making.* Oslo and London: Universitetsforlaget.

Garrett, Geoffrey, and Barry R. Weingast. (1993). "Ideas, Interests, and Institutions: Constructing the European Community's Internal Market." In Judith Goldstein and Robert O. Keohane, eds., *Ideas and Foreign Policy. Beliefs, Institutions, and Political Change*, pp. 173–206. Ithaca, NY, and London: Cornell University Press.

Gasparski, Wojciech, ed. (1996). *The Political Economy of EU Enlargement. The Polish Report.* Warsaw: Institute of Philosophy and Sociology, Polish Academy of Sciences.

Gasteyger, Curt. (1966). *Einigung und Spaltung Europas 1942–1965. Eine Darstellung und Dokumentation über die Zweiteilung Europas.* Frankfurt: Fischer Bücherei.

Gatnar, Lumir. (2004). "Czech Political, Economic and Cultural Elites. Structural Relationships During the EU Entry Process." In Lengyel, *Cohesion and Division of Economic Elites in Central and Eastern Europe*, pp. 63–72.

Gellner, Winand, and Hans-Joachim Veen, eds. (1995). *Umbruch und Wandel in westeuropäischen Parteisystemen.* Frankfurt am Main: Peter Lang.

Gephart, Werner. (1992). "Einführung." In Schäfers, *Lebensverhältnisse und soziale Konflikte im neuen Europa*, pp. 55–59.

Gerhards, Jürgen. (2000). "Europäisierung von Ökonomie und Politik und die Trägheit der Entstehung einer europäischen Öffentlichkeit." In Bach, *Die Europäisierung nationaler Gesellschaften*, pp. 277–305.

Gessner, Volkmar. (1992). "Wandel europäischer Rechtskulturen." In Schäfers, *Lebensverhältnisse und soziale Konflikte im neuen Europa*, pp. 68–78.

Gibson, Rachel K. and Andrea Rommele, eds. (2004). *Electronic Democracy: Mobilisation, Organisation and Participation via New Icts*, London/ New York: Routledge.

Giddens, Anthony. (1998). *The Third Way. The Renewal of Social Democracy.* Cambridge: Polity Press.

Gillingham, John. (1985). *Industry and Politics in the Third Reich. Ruhr Coal, Hitler and Europe.* Stuttgart, Germany: Franz Steiner.

Gillingham, John. (1986). "Zur Vorgeschichte der Montan-Union. Westeuropas Kohle und Stahl in Depression und Krieg." *Vierteljahresheft für Zeitgeschichte* 34:381–405.

Gillingham, John. (1987). "Die französische Ruhrpolitik und die Ursprünge des Schuman-Plans. Eine Neubewertung." *Vierteljahreshefte für Zeitgeschichte* 35:1–24.

Gillingham, John. (2004). *Coal, Steel, and the Rebirth of Europe, 1945–1955: The Germans and French from Ruhr Conflict to Economic Community.* Cambridge and New York: Cambridge University Press.

Ginsberg, Norman. (1992). *Divisions of Welfare. A Critical Introduction to Comparative Social Policy.* London: Sage.

Ginsborg, Paul. (2004). *Silvio Berlusconi. Television, Power and Patrimony.* London: Verso.

Giorgi, Liana, Ingmar von Hohmeyer, and Wayne Parsons, eds. (2006). *Democracy in the European Union. Towards the Emergence of a Public Sphere.* London and New York: Routledge.

Glenn, John K. (2003). "EU Enlargement." In Cini, *European Union Politics*, pp. 211–28.

Goldhagen, Daniel. (1996). *Hitler's Willing Executioners: Ordinary Germans and the Holocaust.* New York: Knopf.

Goldscheid, Rudolf. and Joseph Schumpeter. (1976). *Die Krise des Steuerstaates.* Frankfurt am Main: Suhrkamp.

Goldstein, H. (1995), *Multilevel Statistical Models*, London: Edward Arnold.

Grande, Edgar. (1996a). "Demokratische Legitimation und europäische Integration." *Leviathan* 24:339–60.

Grande, Edgar. (1996b). "Das Paradox der Schwäche. Forschungspolitik und die Einflußlogik europäischer Politikverflechtung. In: *Jachtenfuchs/ Kohler-Koch*, eds., Europäische Integration, pp.373–399.

Grande, Edgar, and Markus Jachtenfuchs, eds. (2000). *Wie problemlösungsfähig ist die EU? Regieren im europäischen Mehrebenensystem.* Baden-Baden, Germany: Nomos.

Grant, Charles. (1994). *Delors. Inside the House that Jacques Built.* London: Nicholas Brealey Publishing.

Graubard, Stephen R. (1973). "Democracy." In Philip L. Wiener, ed., *Dictionary of the History of Ideas,* Vol. 1, pp. 652–67. New York: Charles Scribner's Sons.

Green Cowles, Maria. (1995). "Setting the Agenda for a New Europe: The ERT and EC 1992." *JCMS* 33:501–26.

Greenwood, Justin, ed. (1998). *Collective Action in the European Community. Interests and the New Politics of Associability.* London: Routledge.

Greib, Harald. (2006). *Berlin, mit der Bitte um Weisung.* Mitteldeutscher Verlag.

Greiffenhagen, Martin and Sylvia. (1979). *Ein schwieriges Vaterland. Zur politischen Kultur Deutschlands.* Frankfurt: Suhrkamp.

Greschat, Martin, and Wilfried Loth, eds. (1994). *Die Christen und die Entstehung der europäischen Gemeinschaft.* Stuttgart, Berlin, and Köln: W. Kohlhammer.

Griller, Stefan. (2005). "Die Europäische Union—ein staatsrechtliches Monstrum?" In Gunnar Folke et al., eds., *Europawissenschaft*, pp. 201–272. Baden-Baden, Germany: Nomos.

Griller, Stefan. and Barbara Müller. (1995). "Demokratie-, Institutionen- und Grundrechtsreform der EU." In Anton Pelinka et al., eds., *Europa 1996. Mitbestimmen, Menschenrechte und mehr Demokratie,* pp. 21–104. Wien: Verlag Österreich.

Grimm, Dieter. (2004). "Integration durch Verfassung. Absichten und Aussichten im europäischen Konstitutionalisierungsprozess." *Leviathan* 34:448–63.

Guerra, Simona. (2006). *Polish Public Opinion Before and After Accession: Is Something Changing?* Paper presented to the Third International Conference "Elites and EU Enlargement," 17–18 February 2006, Prague.

Guttsman, W. L. (1990). "Social Stratification and Political Elite." In Scott, *The Sociology of Elites,* pp. 137–99.

Haas, Ernst B. (1958). *The Uniting of Europe. Political, Social, and Economic Forces 1950–1957.* Stanford, CA: Stanford University Press.

Haas, Ernst B. (1964). *Beyond the Nation State. Functionalism and International Organization.* Stanford, CA: Stanford University Press.

Habermas, Jürgen. (2001, September/October). "Why Europe Needs a Constitution." *New Left Review.*

Habsburg, Otto. (1965). *Europa—Großmacht oder Schlachtfeld.* Wien and München: Herold.

Habsburg, Otto von. (1999). *Die paneuropäische Idee. Eine Vision wird Wirklichkeit.* Wien and München: Amalthea.

Hadler, Markus. (2005). *Die Qual der Wahl: Eine Überprüfung unterschiedlicher Wahltheorien anhand einer Panelstudie zur steiermärkischen Landtagswahl 2000.* Wien: LIT-Verlag.

Hadler, Markus. (2006). "Intentions to Migrate Within the European Union: A Challenge for Simple Economic Macro Level Explanations?" *European Societies* 8:111–40.

Hakim, Catherine. (2001). "Alternative European Models of Women's Roles in the Family and the Labour Market." In M. Haller, *The Making of the European Union*, pp. 265–86.

Halberstam, Daniel. (2003). *From Competence to Power: Bureaucracy, Democracy, and the Future of Europe.* Jurist EU, Paper 7/2003 (http://www.fd.unl.pt/je/edit_pap2003–07.htm).

Haller, Max. (1987). "Soziale Normen und Gesellschaftsstruktur." In T. Meleghy u.a. (eds.), *Normen und soziologische Erklärung*, pp. 39–64. Innsbruck and Wien: Tyrolia.

Haller, Max. (1990) "The Challenge for Comparative Sociology in the Transformation of Europe." *International Sociology* 5:183–204. .

Haller, Max. (1995). "Das Vereinte Europa als demokratisch-föderalistische Staatenunion. Soziologische Überlegungen zu Grundlagen und Funktionsprinzipien einer neuen 'Verfassung' der EU." In Josef Langer and Wolfgang Pöllauer, Hrsg., *Kleine Staaten in großer Gesellschaft*, pp. 196–232. Eisenstadt, Austria: Verlag für Soziologie und Humanethologie.

Haller, Max. (1996a). "The Dissolution and Building of new Nations as Strategy and Process Between Elites and People. Lessons From Historical European and Recent Yugoslav Experience." *International Review of Sociology* 6:231–47.

Haller, Max. (1996b). *Identität und Nationalstolz der Österreicher. Gesellschaftliche Ursachen und Funktionen–Herausbildung und Transformation seit 1945–Internationaler Vergleich.* Wien, Köln, and Weimar: Böhlau.

Haller, Max. (1997). "Klassenstruktur und Arbeitslosigkeit—Die Entwicklung zwischen 1960 und 1990." In Stefan Hradil and Stefan Immerfall, eds., *Die westeuropäischen Gesellschaften im Vergleich*, pp. 377–428. Opladen, Germany: Leske + Budrich.

Haller, Max. (1999). "Voiceless Submission or Deliberate Choice? European Integration and the Relation Between National and European Identity." In Hanspeter Kriesi et al., eds., *Nation and National Identity. The European Experience in Perspective*, pp. 263–96. Chur, Switzerland, and Zürich: Rüegger Verlag.

Haller, Max. (1999b). "Effizienter Staat, beschämte Nation—ineffizienter Staat, stolze Nation? Befunde über nationale Identität und Nationalstolz der Deutschen und Italiener." In H. von Meulemann and R. Gubert, eds., *Gesellschaftsvergleich Deutschland-Italien. Annali di Sociologia/Soziologisches Jahrbuch.* Trento, Italy: Università degli studi.

Haller, Max. (2001a). *Sociology as a Science of Social Reality. Elements of an Integrative Theoretical Approach.* Paper presented at the 5th European Conference of Sociology, Helsinki, Finland.

Haller, Max. (2001b). "The Model of Science and Research Policy of the European Union in Perspective." In M. Haller, *The Making of the European Union*, pp. 363–92.

Haller, Max. (2003a). *Soziologische Theorie im systematisch-kritischen Vergleich*, 2nd ed. Wiesbaden, Germany: VS Verlag für Sozialwissenschaften.

Haller, Max. (2003b). "Die Europäische Einigung als Elitenprozess." In Stefan Hradil and Peter Imbusch, eds., *Oberschichten—Eliten—herrschende Klassen*, pp. 337–67. Opladen, Germany: Leske + Budrich.

Haller, Max. (2003c). "Europe and the Arab-Islamic World. A Sociological Perspective on the Socio-Cultural Differences and Mutual (Mis-) Perceptions Between Two Neighbouring Cultural Areas." *Innovation* 15: 285–311.

Haller, Max. (2007). "A 'Europe of Regions'—Myth and Reality." In Josef Langer, ed., *Euroregions—The Alps-Adriatic Context*, pp. 47–63. Frankfurt am Main: Peter Lang.

Haller, Max, ed. (2001). *The Making of the European Union. Contributions of the Social Sciences*. Berlin, Heidelberg, and New York: Springer.

Haller, Max, ed. (Forthcoming). *Identität und Grenzen Europas*. Jahrbuch für Soziologie/Annali di Sociologia. Trento, Italy: University of Trento.

Haller, Max, and Markus Hadler. (2004/05). "Ist der Nationalstaat überholt? Überlegungen und Fakten über die sinnvollste Einheit bzw. Analyseebene in der international vergleichenden Sozialforschung." *AIAS-Informationen* 23:141–61.

Haller, Max, and Markus Hadler. (2006). "How Social Relations and Structures Can Produce Happiness and Unhappiness: An International Comparative Analysis." *Social Indicators Research* 75:169–216.

Haller, Max, and Franz Heschl. (2004). " 'Der Staat sollte einen Arbeitsplatz für jeden bereitstellen, der arbeiten will . . . ' Einstellungen zu arbeitsmarkt- und beschäftigungs-politischen Maßnahmen in 24 Ländern." *Arbeit. Zeitschrift für Arbeitsforschung, Arbeitsgestaltung und Arbeitspolitik* 13:368–98.

Haller, Max, and Franz Höllinger. (1990). "Kinship and Social Networks in Modern Societies: A Cross-Cultural Comparison Among Seven Nations." *European Sociological Review* 6:103–24.

Haller, Max, and Franz Höllinger. (1995). "Zentren und Peripherien in Europa. Eine Analyse und Interpretation der Verschiebungen zwischen dem ersten und dritten Viertel des 20. Jahrhunderts." In Stefan Immerfall and Peter Steinbach, eds., Historisch-vergleichende Makrosoziologie, Historical Social Research—Historische Sozialforschung, Köln, Germany: Quantum, Vol. 20/2, pp. 4–54.

Haller, Max, Franz Höllinger, and Martin Gomilschak. (2000). "Attitudes Toward Gender Roles in International Comparison. New Findings From Twenty Countries." In Rudolf Richter and Sylvia Supper, eds., *New Qualities in the Life Course. Intercultural Aspects*, pp. 131–52. Würzburg, Germany: Ergon Verlag.

Haller, Max, Bogdan Mach, and Heinrich Zwicky. (1995). "Egalitarismus und Antiegalitarismus. Zwischen gesellschaftlichen Interessen und kulturellen Leitbildern. Ergebnisse eines internationalen Vergleichs." In Hans-Peter Müller and Bernd Wegener, eds., *Soziale Ungerechtigkeit und soziale Gerechtigkeit*, pp. 221–64. Opladen, Germany: Leske + Budrich.

Haller, Max, and Regina Ressler, eds. (2006a). *Wir da unten—Die da oben. Die Europäische Union aus der Sicht von BürgerInnen und Eliten*. Graz, Austria: University of Graz, Department of Sociology.

Haller, Max, and Regina Ressler. (2006b). "National and European Identity. A Study of Their Meanings and Interrelationships." *Revue Française de Sociologie* 47:817–50.

Haller, Max, and Rudolf Richter, eds. (1994). *Toward a European Nation? Political Trends in Europe. East and West, Center and Periphery*. Armonk, NY, and London: M. E. Sharpe.

Haller, Max, and Peter Schachner-Blazizek, eds. (1994). *Europa wohin? Wirtschaftliche Integration, soziale Gerechtigkeit und Demokratie*. Graz, Austira: Leykam.

Haller, Max et al. (1990), "Leviathan or Welfare State? The Role of Government in Six Advanced Western Nations", in: D. Alwin et al., eds. *Attitudes to Inequality and the Role of Government*. Rijswijk, NL: Social en Cultureel Planbureau/ CIP-Gegevens Koninklije Bibiotheeek, pp.33-62.

Hallstein, Walter. (1979). "Die EWG—eine Rechtsgemeinschaft." In W. Hallstein, *Europäische Reden*, pp. 341–48. Stuttgart, Germany: Deutsche Verlags-Anstalt.

Hancock, Donald, et al. (1993). *Politics in Western Europe*. Houndmills, UK, and London: Basinstoke.

Hankel, Wilhelm. (1993). *Die sieben Todsünden der Vereinigung. Wege aus dem Wirtschaftsdesaster*. Berlin: Siedler.

Hankel, Wilhelm. (1998). *Die Euro-Klage: Warum die Währungsunion scheitern muss*. Reinbek bei Hamburg, Germany: Rowohlt.

Hansen, Line, and Michael C. Williams. (1999). "The Myths of Europe: Legitimacy, Community and the 'crisis' of the EU." *JCMS* 37:233–49.

Hartley, Trevor C. (1998). *The Foundations of European Community Law*. New York: Oxford University Press.

Hartmann, Heinz. (1999). "Auf dem Weg zur transnationalen Bourgeoisie? Die Internationalisierung der Wirtschaft und die Internationalität der Spitzenmanager Deutschlands, Frankreichs, Grossbritanniens und der USA." *Leviathan* 27:113–41.

Hartmann, Heinz. (2002). *Der Mythos von den Leistungseliten. Spitzenkarrieren und soziale Herkunft in Wirtschaft, Politik, Justiz und Wissenschaft*. Frankfurt and New York: Campus.

Hartmann, Heinz. (2003). "Nationale oder transnationale Eliten? Europäische Eliten im Vergleich." In Stefan Hradil and Peter Imbusch, eds., *Oberschichten—Eliten—herrschende Klassen*, pp. 273–97. Opladen, Germany: Leske + Budrich.

Hartmann, Jürgen. (2001). *Das politische System der Europäischen Union. Eine Einführung*. Frankfurt and New York: Campus.

Hartmann, Michael. (1999). "Auf dem Weg zur transnationalen Bourgeosie? Die Internationalisierung der Wirtschaft und die Internationalität der Spitzenmanager in Deutschland, Frankreich und den USA." *Leviathan* 27:113–41.

Hartmann, Michael. (2002). "Die Spitzenmanager der internationalen Großkonzerne als Kern einer neuen 'Weltklasse.' " In Rudi Schmidt et al., eds., *Managementsoziologie*, pp. 184–208. München and Mering, Germany: Rainer Hampp.

Hauser, Richard. (1949). *Autorität und Macht*. Heidelberg: Lambert Schneider.

Heidenreich, Martin, ed. (2006). *Die Europäisierung sozialer Ungleichheit. Zur transnationalen Klassen- und Sozialstrukturanalyse*. Frankfurt and New York: Campus.

Heismann, Günter. (1999). *Die entfesselte Ökonomie. Ein Standort-Report*. Berlin: Rowohlt.

Heit, Helmut, ed. (2005). *Die Werte Europas. Verfassungspatriotismus und Wertegemeinschaft in der EU?* Münster: Lit.

Held, David. (1996). *Models of Democracy*. Stanford, CA: Stanford University Press.

Held, David. (2004). *Global Covenant. The Social Democratic Alternative to the Washington Consensus*. Cambridge amd Malden, MA: Polity Press.

Hellström, Anders. (2006). "Bringing Europe Down to Earth." *Lund Political Studies* No. 144. Lund, Sweden: Lunds Universitet, Department of Political Science.

Hentschel, Volker. (1996). *Ludwig Erhard. Ein Politikerleben*. München and Landsberg, Germany: Olzog.

Herman, Margaret G., and Charles W. Kegley. (1996). "Ballots, a Barrier Against the Use of Bullets and Bombs." *Journal of Conflict Resolution* 40:436–59.

Hermann, Peter. (2006). *Politics and Policies of the Social in the European Union: Looking at the Hidden Agenda*. New York: Nova Science Publishers.

Heschl, Franz. (2002). *Drinnen oder draußen? Die öffentliche österreichische EU-Beitrittsdebatte vor der Volksabstimmung 1994*. Wien, Köln, and Weimar: Böhlau.

Heschl, Franz. (2003)."Der Europäische Rat und die europäische Realität. Zur Wahrnehmung sozialer Ungleichheit durch den Europäischen Rat." *SWS-Rundschau* (2)256–76.

Hirter, Hans. (1993). *Die schweizerische Abstimmung über den EWR*. Tübingen, Germany: Eberhard Karls-Universität.

Hofbauer, Hannes. (2003). *Osterweiterung. Vom Drang nach Osten zur peripheren EU-Integration*. Wien: ProMedia.

Hoffmann-Lange, Ursula. (1992). *Eliten, Macht und Konflikt in der Bundesrepublik*. Opladen, Germany: Leske + Budrich.

Holland, Stuart. (1980). *Uncommon Market. Capital, Class and Power in the European Community*. London and New York: Macmillan.

Höllinger, Franz. (1996). *Volksreligion und Herrschaftskirche. Die Wurzeln religiösen Verhaltens in westlichen Gesellschaften*. Opladen, Germany: Leske + Budrich.

Holman, Otto. (1992). "Introduction: Transnational Class Strategy and the New Europe." *International Journal of Political Economy* 22:3–22.

Holmes, Dougas R. (2000). "Surrogate Discourses of Power: The European Union and the Problem of Society." In Irène Bellier and Thomas M. Wilson, eds., *An Anthropology of the European Union. Building*, pp. 93–115. Oxford and New York: Berg.

Hondrich, Karl Otto. (2002). *Wieder Krieg*. Frankfurt: Suhrkamp.

Hooghe, Lisbeth and Gary Marks (2005), "Calculation, Community and Cues: Public Opinion on European Integration", *European Union Politics* 6: 419-443.

Hoover, Kenneth, et al. (1997). *The Power of Identity. Politics in a New Key*. Chatham, NJ: Chatham House.

Hopf, Christel. (1991). "Regelmäßigkeiten und Typen. Das Durchschnittshandeln in Max Webers Soziologie." *Zeitschrift für Soziologie* 20:124–37.

Höpner, Martin. (2003). *Wer beherrscht die Unternehmen? Shareholder Value, Managerherrschaft und Mitbestimmung in Deutschland*. Frankfurt and New York: Campus Verlag.

Höreth, Marcus. (1999). *Die Europäische Union im Legitimationstrilemma. Zur Rechtfertigung des Regierens jenseits der Staatlichkeit*. Baden-Baden, Germany: Nomos.

Höreth, Marcus. (2002). "Das Demokratiedefizit lässt sich nicht wegreformieren. Über Sinn und Unsinn der europäischen Verfassungsdebatte. *Internationale Politik und Gesellschaft* (4)11–38.

Hörmann, Günter. (1997). "Wie ein Gesetz entsteht—oder: The fine art of lobbying." In Ludwig Krämer et al., eds., *Law and diffuse Interests in the European Legal Order*, pp. 905–11. Baden-Baden, Germany: Nomos.

Hornstein, Walter, and Gerd Mutz u.a. (1993). *Die europäische Eignung als gesellschaftlicher Prozess. Soziale Problemlagen, Partizipation und kulturelle Transformation*. Baden-Baden, Germany: Nomos.

Hradil, Stefan, and Peter Imbusch, eds. (2003). *Oberschichten—Eliten— Herrschende Klassen*. Opladen, Germany: Leske + Budrich.

Huemer, Ulrike. (1994). *Der keltische Tiger: Irlands Transformation vom Armenhaus zum Musterland für Aufschwung und Konsolidierung*. Diploma thesis, University of Graz. Graz, Austira.

Hugo, Victor, *Actes et Paroles*, Vol.1 (1937); Vol. 2 (1938); Vol. 3 (1940). Paris: Albin Michel.

Hunt, Murray. (1997). *Using Human Rights Law in English Courts*. Oxford: Hart Publishing.

Huntington, Samuel P. (1996). *The Clash of Civilisations and the Remaking of World Order*. New York: Simon & Schuster.

Hunya, Gábor. (2006). Increasing Significance of Repatriated and Reinvested Earnings, WIIW Database on Foreign Direct Investment in Central, East and Southeast Europa. Vienna: The Vienna Institute for International Economic Studies.

Huth, Paul K., and Todd L. Allee, eds. (2002). *The Democratic Peace and Territorial Conflict in the Twentieth Century*. Cambridge: Cambridge University Press.

Hyde-Price, Adrian. (2006). "'Normative' Power Europe: A Realist Critique." *Journal of European Public Policy* 13:217–34.

Identity Foundation. (2003). *Quellen europäischer Identität. Die Generaldirektoren der Europäischen Kommission.* Düsseldorf: Identity Foundation.

Illig, Heribert. (2001). *Das erfundene Mittelalter. Die größte Zeitfälschung der Geschichte.* Düsseldorf and München: Econ.

Ilzkovitz, Fabienne, and Roderick Meiklejohn, eds. (2006). *European Merger Control. Do We Need an Efficiency Defence?* Cheltenham, UK, and Northampton, MA: Edward Elgar.

Immerfall, Stefan. (1994). *Einführung in den europäischen Gesellschaftsvergleich. Ansätze—Problemstellungen—Befunde.* Passau, Germany: Wissenschaftsverlag Rothe.

Immerfall, Stefan. (2000). "Fragestellungen einer Soziologie der europäischen Integration." In Bach, *Die Europäisierung nationaler Gesellschaften,* pp. 481–503.

Immerfall, Stefan. (2006). *Europa—politisches Einigungswerk und gesellschaftliche Entwicklung: Eine Einführung.* Wiesbaden, Germany: VS Verlag für Sozialwissenschaften.

Ingham, Barbara. (2004). *International Economics. A European Focus.* Harlow, UK: Prentice Hall.

Inglehart, Ronald. (1977). *The Silent Revolution. Changing Values and Political Styles Among Western Publics.* Princeton, NJ: Princeton University Press.

Inglehart, Ronald. (1997). *Modernization and Postmodernization. Cultural, Economic and Political Change in 43 Societies.* Princeton, NJ: Princeton University Press.

Inglehart, Ronald, and Wayne E. Baker. (2000). "Modernization, Cultural Change, and the Persistence of Traditional Values." *American Sociological Review* 65:19–51.

Jachtenfuchs, Markus. (1996b). "Regieren durch Überzeugen: Die Europäische Union und der Treibhauseffekt." In Jachtenfuchs and Kohler-Koch, *Europäische Integration,* pp. 429–54.

Jachtenfuchs, Markus. (2001). "The Governance Approach to European Integration." *JCMS* 39:221–40.

Jachtenfuchs, Markus, and Beate Kohler-Koch. (2004). "Governance and Institutional Development." In Wiener and Diez, *European Integration Theory,* pp.97–115.

Jachtenfuchs, Markus, and Beate Kohler-Koch, eds. (1996). *Europäische Integration.* Opladen, Germany: Leske + Budrich.

Jackall, Robert. (1989). *Moral Mazes: The World of Corporate Managers.* New York: Oxford University Press.

Janssen, Joseph H. (1991). "Postmaterialism, Cognitive Mobilization and Public Support for European Integration." *British Journal of Political Science* 21:443–68.

Jaques, Elliott. (1967). *Equitable Payment. A General Theory of Work, Differential Payment, and Individual Progress.* Harmonsworth, Middlesex, UK: Penguin Books.

Jarass, Hans D. (1975). *Politik und Bürokratie als Elemente der Gewaltenteilung.* München: Beck.

Jaspers, Karl. (1966). *Wohin treibt die Bundesrepublik? Tatsachen, Gefahren, Chancen.* München: R. Piper.

Jenkins, Richard. (1996). *Social Identity.* London and New York: Routledge & Kegan Paul.

Jensen, Carsten Stroby. (2003). "Neo-Functionalism." In Cini, *European Union Politics,* pp. 80–92.

Joerissen, Britta. (2001). *Europa-Ideen in Deutschland und Frankreich.* Master's thesis, Fachbereich Politikwissenschaft, University of Trier, Trier, Germany.

Jopp, Mathias, and Saskia Matl, eds. (2005). *Der Vertrag über eine Verfassung für Europa. Analysen zur Konstitutionalisierung der EU.* Baden-Baden, Germany: Nomos.

Jordan, Terry G. (1988). *The European Culture Area. A Systematic Geography.* New York: Harper & Row.

Jost, Hans-Ulrich. (1999). *Europa und die Schweiz 1945–1950. Europarat, Supranationalität und schweizerische Unabhängigkeit.* Lausanne, Switzerland: Ed. Payot.

Jowell, Roger, et al., eds. (2007). *Measuring Attitudes Cross-Nationally: Lessons From the European Social Survey.* Thousand Oaks, CA: Sage.

Kaelble, Hartmut. (1987). *Auf dem Weg zu einer europäischen Gesellschaft. Eine Sozialgeschichte Westeuropas 1880–1980.* München: Beck.

Kant, Immanuel. (1795). *Zum ewigen Frieden. Ein philosophischer Entwurf.* Königsberg, Germany: Friedrich Nicolovius.

Kanter, Rosabeth Moss. (1995). *World Class.* New York: Simon & Schuster.

Kastoryano, Riva, ed. (2002). *Quelle identité pour l'Europe? Le multiculturalisme à l'épreuve.* Paris: Presses des Sciences.

Katz, Richard S., and Bernhard Wessels. (1999). *The European Parliament, the National Parliaments, and European Integration.* Oxford: Oxford University Press.

Kelsen, Hans. (1925). *Allgemeine Staatslehre.* Berlin: J. Springer.

Kelsen, Hans. (1963). *Vom Wesen und Wert der Demokratie.* Aalen, Germany: Scientia.

Khoury, Adel Theodor, ed. (1999). *Die Weltreligionen und die Ethik.* Freiburg, Basel, and Wien: Herder.

Kielmannsegg, Peter Graf. (1996). "Integration und Demokratie." In Jachtenfuchs and Kohler-Koch, *Europäische Integration,* pp. 47–71.

Kirchhoff, Paul. (2006). *Das Gesetz der Hydra. Gebt den Bürgern ihren Staat zurück!* München: Droemer.

Kirchner, Emil Joseph. (1977). *Trade Unions as a Pressure Group in the European Community.* Westmiad: Hunts, UK: Saxon House.

Kirchner, Emil Joseph, and Konrad Schwaiger. (1981). *The Role of Interest Groups in the European Community.* Aldershot, UK: Gower.

Klages, Helmut. (1993). *Häutungen der Demokratie.* Zürich: Ed. Interfrom.

Kleinert, Jörn. (2004). *The Role of Multinational Enterprises in Globalization.* Berlin, Heidelberg, and New York: Springer.

Kleinsteuber, Hans J. (1994). "Kommunikationsraum Europa—Europa als ein Raum verdichteter Kommunikation." In Haller and Schachner-Blazizek, *Europa wohin,* pp. 337–49.

Klingemann, Hans-Dieter. (1999). "Mapping Political Support in the 1990s: A Global Analysis." In Norris, *Critical Citizens,* pp. 57–77.

Kluckhohn, Clyde. (1951). "Values and Value-Orientations in the Theory of Action: An Exploration in Definition and Classification." In Parsons and Shils, *Toward a General Theory of Action,* pp. 388–433.

Koester, Ulrich. (1977). *Agrarpolitik in der Sackgasse. Divergierende Interessen bei der Verwirklichung der EWG-Agrarpolitik.* Baden-Baden, Germany: Nomos.

Koester, Ulrich. (1996). "Gemeinsame Agrarmarktordnungen der EU." In Ohr, *Europäische Integration,* pp. 141–72.

Koester, Ulrich, and Ali El-Agraa. (2004). "The Common Agricultural Policy." In A. El-Agraa, *The European Union. Economics and Politics,* pp. 354–90.

Kohler-Koch, Beate. (1996). "Die Gestaltungsmacht organisierter Interessen." In Jachtenfuchs and Kohler-Koch, *Europäische Integration,* pp. 193–222.

Kohler-Koch, Beate. (1999). *Europe in Search of Legitimate Governance.* ARENA Working Paper 99/27.

Kohnstamm, Max. (1964). *The European Community and Its Role in the World.* Columbia, MO: University of Missouri Press.

Kohr, Leopold. (1977). *The Overdeveloped Nations. The Diseconomies of Scale.* New York: Schocken Books.

Kohr, Leopold. (1978). *The Breakdown of Nations.* New York: Dutton.

Koland, Olivia. (2005). *Landwirtschaft auf neuen Wegen. Die Agrarpolitik der Europäischen Union im Spannungsfeld zwischen Osterweiterung und Internationalisierung.* Diploma thesis, Department of Economics, University of Graz, Graz, Austria.

Koller, Peter. (1996). "Frieden und Gerechtigkeit in einer geteilten Welt." In Reinhard Merkel and Roland Wittmann, eds., *Zum ewigen Frieden. Grundlagen, Aktualität und Aussichten einer Idee von Immanuel Kant*, pp. 213–39. Frankfurt: Suhrkamp.

König, Helmut, and Manfred Sicking, eds. (2004). *Der Irak-Krieg und die Zukunft Europas.* Bielefeld, Germany: transcript.

König, Johann-Günther. (1999). *Alle Macht den Konzernen. Das neue Europa im Griff der Lobbyisten.* Reinbek, Germany: Rowohlt.

Korom, Philipp. (2007). *Öffentliche Intellektuelle in der österreichischen Presse.* Diploma thesis, Department of Sociology, University of Graz, Graz, Austria.

Kovách, Imre, and Eva Kucerová. (2006). "The Project Class in Central Europe: The Czech and Hungarian Cases." *Sociologia Ruralis* 46:3–21.

Krämer, Manfred. (1973). *Kirche kontra Demokratie? Gesellschaftliche Probleme im gegenwärtigen Katholizismus.* München: J. Pfeiffer.

Kriesi, Hanspeter. (1998). *Le Système Politique Suisse.* Paris: Economica.

Kriesi, Hanspeter, et al., eds. (2005). *Contemporary Switzerland.* Hampshire, UK: Palgrave.

Kristóf, Luca, and András Csite. (2004). "Firm Networks and Growth Strategies in the Hungarian Large Company Population." In Lengyel, *Cohesion and Division of Economic Elites in Central and Eastern Europe*, pp. 73–91.

Kronbichler, Florian. (2005). *Was gut war. Ein Alexander-Langer-ABC.* Bozen, Italy: Edition Raetia.

Krugman, Paul. (1994). "Competitiveness—a Dangerous Obsession." *Foreign Affairs* 73:29–44.

Kübler, Hans-Dieter. (2005). *Mythos Wissensgesellschaft. Gesellschaftlicher Wandel zwischen Information, Medien und Wissen. Eine Einführung.* Wiesbaden, Germany: VS Verlag.

Kuhle, Gesa S. (2005). "Schlussfolgerungen aus den gescheiterten Referenden zum Europäischen Verfassungsvertrag." Berlin, Germany: Institut für Europäische Politik, IEP Policy Brief 20/2005.

Kühnhardt, Ludger. (2005). "Quo vadis Europa?" *Aus Politik und Zeitgeschichte* 36, 3–7.

Küng, Hans. (1990). *Projekt Weltethos.* München and Zürich: Piper.

Kuzmics, Helmut. (2001). "(Europäische) Regionen zwischen (Des-) Integration und Identität." In Erhard Busek, Hrsg., *Europa—Vision und Wirklichkeit. Europäisches Forum Alpbach 2001*, pp. 259–80. Wien: Verlag Österreich.

Lafan, Brigid. (2005). "Der schwierige Weg zur Europäischen Verfassung." In Jopp and Matl, *Der Vertrag über eine Verfassung für Europa*, pp. 473–92.

Lane, David. (1997). "Russian Political Elites, 1991–1995: Recruitment and Renewal." *International Politics* 34:169–92.

Langen, Werner. (2001). "Das Europäische Parlament und die Verfassungsdebatte der Europäischen Union." In Timmermann, *Eine Verfassung für die europäische Union*, pp. 373–86.

Lasch, Christopher. (1995). *The Revolt of the Elites and the Betrayal of Democracy.* New York and London: Norton.

Le Galès, Patrick, and Christian Lequesne, eds. (1998). *Regions in Europe.* London and New York: Routledge.

Lehning, Percy B., and Albert Weale, eds. (1997) *Citizenship, Democracy and Justice in the New Europe*. London and New York: Routledge.

Leibfried, Stephan. (1996). "Wohlfahrtsstaatliche Perspektiven der Europäischen Union: Auf dem Weg zu positiver Souveränitätsverflechtung?" In Jachtenfuchs and Kohler-Koch, *Europäische Integration*, pp. 455–77.

Leinen, Jo. (2001). "Eine europäische Verfassung—Grundlage einer föderalen und demokratischen Ordnung der EU." In Timmermann, *Eine Verfassung für die europäische Union*, pp. 57–66.

Lengyel, György, ed. (2004). *Cohesion and Division of Economic Elites in Central and Eastern Europe*. Corvinus University of Budapest, Department of Sociology and Social Policy.

Lepenies, Wolf. (1992). *Aufstieg und Fall der Intellektuellen in Europa*. Frankfurt and New York: Campus.

Lepsius, M. Rainer. (1988). *Ideen, Interessen und Institutionen*. Opladen, Germany: Westdeutscher Verlag.

Lepsius, M. Rainer. (2000). "Welche Verfassung für Europa?" *Gegenwartskunde* 49:269–74.

Leydendecker, Hans. (2003). *Die Korruptionsfalle. Wie unser Land im Filz erstickt*. Reinbek, Germany: Rowohlt.

Leydendecker, Hans, Michael Stiller, and Heribert Prantl. (2000). *Helmut Kohl, die Macht und das Geld*. Göttingen, Steide.

Lieberman, Robert C. (2002). "Ideas, Institutions, and Political Order: Explaining Political Change." *American Political Science Review* 96:697–712.

Liebert, Ulrike, et al., eds. (2003). *Verfassungsexperiment. Europa auf dem Weg zur transnationalen Demokratie?* Münster: Lit.

Lindblom, Charles. (1977). *Politics and Markets. The World's Political-Economic Systems*. New York: Basic Books.

Linder, Wolf. (1999). *Schweizerische Demokratie. Institutionen—Prozesse—Perspektiven*. Bern, Stuttgart, and Wien: Verlag Paul Haupt.

Lipgens, Walter (1974), "Europäische Integration," in: Richard Löwenthal/ Hans-Peter Schwarz, eds., *Die zweite Republik. 25 Jahre Bundesrepublik. Eine Bilanz*, Stuttgart: Seewald, pp. 519–553.

Lipset, Seymour M., and William Schneider. (1983). *The Confidence Gap. Business, Labor, and Government in the Public Mind*. New York and London: The Free Press and Collier Macmillan.

Lipsey, Richard G. (1972). *An Introduction to Positive Economics*. London: Weidenfeld and Nicolson.

Lorentzen, Jochen. (1999). "Who Loses? Economic integration, unemployment and inequality", in: Ronald Tiersky, ed., *Europe Today. National Politics, European Integration, and European Security*, Lanham, Boulder etc.: Rowman & Littlefield, pp.337–367.

Loth, Wilfried. (1996). *Der Weg nach Europa. Geschichte der europäischen Integration 1939–1957*. Göttingen, Germany: Vandenhoeck & Ruprecht.

Loth, Wilfried et al. (1995). *Walter Hallstein—der vergessene Europäer?* Bonn: Europa Union Verlag.

Löwenstein, Karl. (1957). *Political Power and the Governmental Process*. Chicago: University of Chicago Press (German: Verfassungslehre, Tübingen: Siebeck 1975).

Lucks, Kai, and Reinhard Meckl. (2002). *Internationale Mergers & Acquisitions. Der prozessorientierte Ansatz*. Berlin: Springer.

Luhmann, Niklas. (1975). "Die Weltgesellschaft." In Niklas Luhmann, *Soziologische Aufklärung 2*, pp. 51–71. Opladen, Germany: Westdeutscher Verlag.

Luthardt, Wolfgang. (1995). "Die Referenda zum Vertrag von Maastricht. Politikmanagement und Legitimation im Europäischen Integrationsprozess." In Steffani and Thaysen, *Demokratie in Europa*, pp.65–84.

Lutz, Burkhart. (1984). *Der kurze Traum immerwährender Prosperität. Eine Neuinterpretation der industriell-kapitalistischen Entwicklung im Europa des 20. Jahrhunderts.* Frankfurt and New York: Campus.

Lützeler, Paul Michael. (1992). *Die Schriftsteller und Europa. Von der Romantik bis zur Gegenwart.* München: Piper (new edition: Baden-Baden 1998).

Luxemburg, Rosa. (1923). *Die Akkumulation des Kapitals. Ein Beitrag zur ökonomischen Erklärung des Kapitalismus.* Berlin: Vereinigung Internationaler Verlags-Anstalten (reprinted by Verlag Neue Kritik, Frankfurt 1966).

Maier, Hans. (1983). *Katholizismus und Demokratie.* Freiburg, Basel, and Wien: Herder.

Majone, Giandomenico. (1993). "The European Community Between Social Policy and Social Regulation." *Journal of Common Market Studies* 32:153–70.

Majone, Giandomenico. (1996a). "Redistributive und sozialregulative Politik." In Jachtenfuchs and Kohler-Koch, *Europäische Integration*, pp. 225–47.

Majone, Giandomenico, ed. (1996b). *Regulating Europe.* London: Routledge.

Malgeri, Francesco. (1982). *Alcide De Gasperi.* Rome: Il Poligono Editore.

Mannheim, Karl. (1970). *Wissenssoziologie. Auswahl aus dem Werk.* Neuwied, Germany, and Berlin: Luchterhand.

Manow, Philip, Armin Schäfer, and Hendrik Zorn. (2006). "Europäische Sozialpolitik und Europas parteipolitisches Gravitationszentrum in den Jahren 1957–2003." *Zeitschrift für Internationale Beziehungen* 1:77–112.

Markard, Morus. (1984). *Einstellung. Kritik eines sozialpsychologischen Grundkonzepts.* Frankfurt and New York: Campus.

Markovits, Andrei S., and Mark Silverstein. (1988). *The Politics of Scandal. Power and Process in Liberal Democracies.* New York and London: Holmes & Meier.

Martin, Hans-Peter, and Harald Schumann. (1997). Die Globalisierungsfalle. Der Angriff auf Demokratie und Wohlstand. Reinbek bei Hamburg, Germany: Rowohlt.

Maslow, Abraham H. (1987). *Motivation and Personality.* New York: Harper & Row.

Mathonyte, Irmina, and Vladas Gaidys (2004). *The Lithuanian Rich and Their Attitudes Toward the EU and the State.* Paper presented at the second Workshop on Elites and Transformation in East Europe, Budapest, 2–4 September 2004.

Matthews, Alan (2004). "The EU and the developing world." In A. El-Agraa, *The European Union*, pp. 471–92.

Mau, Steffen. (2005). "Democratic Demand for a Social Europe? Preferences of the European Citizenry." *International Journal of Social Welfare* 14:76–85.

May, Bernhard. (1985). *Kosten und Nutzen der deutschen EG-Mitgliedschaft.* Bonn: Europa Union Verlag.

Mayes, David, and Juha Kilponen. (2004). "Factor Mobility." In A. El-Agraa, *The European Union Economics and Politics*, pp. 311–32.

Mayntz, Renate. (1985). *Soziologie der öffentlichen Verwaltung.* Heidelberg: C. F. Müller Juristischer Verlag.

Mazey, Sonia. (1992). "Conception and Evolution of the High Authority's Administrative Services (1952–1956): From Supranational Principles to Multinational Practices." *Jahrbuch für europäische Verwaltungsgeschichte* 4:31–47.

Mead, George H. (1934). *Mind, Self and Society From the Standpoint of a Behaviorist.* Chicago: University of Chicago Press.

Mearsheimer, John J. (2001). *The Tragedy of Great Power Politics.* New York and London: Norton.

Meiklejohn, Roderick. (2006). "M&A Activity and Merger Control Since 1991." In Ilzkovitz and Meiklejohn, eds., *European Merger Control*, pp.10–42.

Meleghy, Tamas. (2001). *Soziologie als Sozial-, Moral- und Kulturwissenschaft.* Berlin: Duncker & Humblot.

Mendras, Henri. (1988), *La seconde Révolution française 1965–1984.* Paris: Gallimard.

Meyer, John W., and Ronald L. Jepperson. (2000). "The 'Actors' of Modern Society: The Cultural Construction of Social Agency." *Sociological Theory* 18:100–20.

Meyer, Thomas. (2004). *Die Identität Europas. Der EU eine Seele?* Frankfurt am Main: Suhrkamp.

Michalowitz, Irina. (2004). *EU—Lobbying—Principals, Agents and Targets. Strategic Interest Intermediation in EU Policy-Making.* Münster: Lit.

Middlemas, Keith. (1995). *Orchestrating Europe. The Informal Politics of the European Union 1973–95.* London: Fontana Press.

Milborn, Corinna. (2006). *Gestürmte Festung Europa. Einwanderung zwischen Stacheldraht und Ghetto. Das Schwarzbuch.* Wien, Graz, and Klagenfurt: Styria.

Miller, David. (2000). *Citizenship and National Identity.* Cambridge: Polity Press.

Mills, C. Wright. (1959). *The Power Elite.* London: Oxford University Press.

Milward, Alan. (1992). *The European Rescue of the Nation State.* London: Routledge.

Mitchell, G. Duncan, ed. (1968). *A Handbook of Sociology.* London: Routledge & Kegan Paul.

Mitterauer, Michael. (2003). *Warum Europa? Mittelalterliche Grundlagen eines Sonderwegs.* München: Beck.

Molle, Willem. (2001). *The Economics of European Integration.* Aldershot, UK: Ashgate.

Momin, A. R. (2006). *India as a Model for a Multiethnic Society.* Unpublished Manuscript.

Monnet, Jean. (1988). *Erinnerungen eines Europäers.* Baden-Baden, Germany: Nomos (French ed.: *Mémoires.* Paris. Ed. Fayard 1976; English ed.: *Memoirs.* Garden City, NY: Doubleday 1978).

Montesquieu, Charles de Secondat, Baron de. (1965). *Von Geist der Gesetze,* Stuttgart: Reclam (first published in French 1748).

Moore, Barrington (1978), *Injustice: The Social Bases of Obedience and Revolt,* White Plains, N.Y.: M. E. Sharpe.

Moravcsik, Andrew. (1998). *The Choice for Europe. Social Purpose and State Power From Messina to Maastricht.* London: UCL Press.

Moravcsik, Andrew. (2002). "In defence of the 'Democratic Deficit': Reassessing Legitimacy in the European Union." *Journal of Common Market Studies* 40:603–24.

Moravcsik, Andrew. (2006). "What Can We Learn From the Collapse of the European Constitutional Project?" *Politische Vierteljahresschrift* 47:219–41.

Morgan, Roger. (1992). "Jean Monnet and the ECSC Administration: Challenges, Functions and the Inheritance of Ideas." *Jahrbuch für europäische Verwaltungsgeschichte* 4:1–9.

Morgenthau, Hans J. (1962). *Politics Among Nations. The Struggle for Power and Peace.* New York: Alfred A. Knopf.

Morgenthau, Hans J. (1960). *Politics Among Nations. The Struggle for Power and Peace.* New York: Knopf.

Mörz, Johanna. (2007). *Personalrekrutierung in der Europäischen Union.* Diploma thesis, Department of Sociology, University of Graz, Graz, Austria.

Mosca, Gaetano. (1966). *La Classe Politica.* Bari, Italy: Editori Laterza (English: *The Ruling Class.* New York: McGraw-Hill 1939).

Möschel, Wernhard. (1994). "Europäische Integration am Wendepunkt? Perspektiven nach Maastricht." *Wirtschaftswissenschaftliches Studium* 23:123–31.

Mosher, James S., and David M. Trubek. (2003). "Alternative Approaches to Governance in the EU: EU Social Policy and the European Employment Strategy." *JCMS* 41:63–88.

Mouffe, Chantal. (2005). *On the Political*. London and New York: Routledge.

Moussis, Nicholas. (2006). *Access to the European Union. Law, Economics, Politics*. Rixensart, Belgium: European Studies Service.

Moxon-Browne, Edward, ed. (2004), *Who Are the Europeans Now?* Aldershot, UK: Ashgate.

Müller, Günther. (1994). *Faß ohne Boden. Die Eurokratie von Brüssel und unser Geld*. München: Wirtschaftsverlag Langen Müller und Herbig.

Müller, Jan-Werner. (2002). *Memory and Power in Post-War Europe. Studies in the Presence of the Past*. Cambridge: Cambridge University Press.

Münch, Richard. (1982). *Theorie des Handelns. Zur Rekonstruktion der Beiträge von Talcott Parsons, Emile Durkheim und Max Weber*. Frankfurt: Suhrkamp.

Münch, Richard. (1986). *Die Kultur der Moderne. 1. Ihre Grundlagen und Entwicklung in England und Amerika. 2. Ihre Entwicklung in Frankreich und Deutschland*. Frankfurt am Main: Suhrkamp.

Münch, Richard. (1993). *Das Projekt Europa. Zwischen Nationalstaat, regionaler Autonomie und Weltgesellschaft*. Frankfurt am Main: Suhrkamp.

Münch, Richard. (2008a). *Die europäische Gesellschaft. Wirtschaft, Recht und Verfassung jenseits des Nationalstaats*. Frankfurt and New York: Campus.

Münch, Richard. (2008b, forthcoming). "Christentum oder Zivilreligion als Grundlagen der europäischen Identität?" In M. Haller, *Identität und Grenzen Europas*.

Münz, Rainer, and Wolfgang Seifert. (2001). "Immigration to Europe and Its Consequences for the Host Societies." In M. Haller, *The Making of the European Union*, pp. 309–29.

Mussler, Werner, and Manfred E. Streit. (1996). "Integrationspolitische Strategien in der EU." In Ohr, *Europäische Integration*, pp. 265–92.

Narr, Wolf-Dieter. (1989). "Von den kommenden Segnungen der europäischen Gemeinschaft—Ansichten eines provinziellen Weltbürgers", *Leviathan* 17:574-595.

Nassmacher, Karl-Heinz. (1982). "Öffentliche Parteienfinanzierung in Westeuropa." *Politische Vierteljahresschrift* 28:101–25.

Nassmacher, Karl-Heinz. (1992). "Parteifinanzen im westeuropäischen Vergleich." *Zeitschrift für Parlamentsfragen*, H.3, 462–88.

Neidhart, Leonhard. (1988). "Die Schweizer Konkordanzdemokratie." In Hans Elsasser et al., *Die Schweiz*, pp. 128–55. Stuttgart, Germany: W. Kohlhammer.

Neisser, Heinrich. (1993). *Das politische System der EG*. Wien: Holzhausen.

Nettesheim, Martin. (2003). "Die Unionsbürgerschaft im Verfassungsentwurf—Verfassung des Ideals einer politischen Gemeinschaft der Europäer?" *Integration* 26:428-39.

Newhouse, John. (1997). *Europe Adrift*. New York: Pantheon Books.

Nicoll, William, and Trevor C. Salmon. (2001). *Understanding the European Union*. Harlow, Essex, UK: Pearson Education.

Nieminen, Ari. (2005). "Toward a European Society? Integration and Regulation of Capitalism." *Research Report* N. 245, University of Helsinki, Department of Sociology, Helsinki, Finland.

Nippel, Wilfried. (2000). *Virtuosen der Macht. Herrschaft und Charisma von Perikles bis Mao*. München: Beck.

Niskanen, William. (1971). *Bureaucracy and Representative Government*. Chicago and New York: Aldine-Atherton.

Nissen, Silke. (2006). "European Identity and the Future of Europe." In Bach et al., *Europe in Motion*, pp. 155–174.

398   References

Noelle-Neumann, Elisabeth, and Renate Köcher, eds. (1987). *Die verletzte Nation. Über den Versuch der Deutschen, ihren Charakter zu ändern.* Stuttgart, Germany: Deutsche Verlags-Anstalt.

Nollert, Michael. (2000). "Lobbying for a Europe of Big Business: The European Round Table of Industrialists." In Bornschier, *State Building in Europe*, pp. 187–209.

Nollert, Michael. (2005). *Unternehmensverflechtungen in Westeuropa. Nationale und transnationale Netzwerke von Unternehmen, Aufsichtsräten und Managern.* Münster: Lit.

Nollmann, Gerd. (2002). "Die Einführung des Euro. Vom Edelmetall zum reinen Beziehungsgeld." *KZFSS* 54:226–45.

Norris, Pippa, ed. (2005), *Critical citizens. Global Support for Democratic Government*, Oxford etc.: Oxford University Press.

Nugent, Neill, ed. (2002). *At the Heart of the Union. Studies of the European Commission.* London and New York: Macmillan and St. Martin's Press.

Offe, Claus. (2003). *Herausforderungen der Demokratie. Zur Integrations- und Leistungsfähigkeit politischer Institutionen.* Frankfurt and New York: Campus.

Ohr, Renate, ed. (1996). *Europäische Integration.* Stuttgart, Berlin, and Köln: W. Kohlhammer.

Oldag, Andreas, and Hans-Martin Tillack. (2005). *Raumschiff Brüssel. Wie die Demokratie in Europa scheitert.* Frankfurt: Fischer Taschenbuch Verlag.

Opp, Karl-Dieter. (1994). "The Role of Voice in a Future Europe." *Kyklos* 47:385–402.

Oswald, Bernd. (2003). *Europa. Wissen 3000.* Hamburg: Europäische Verlagsanstalt.

Pagden, Anthony, and Lee H. Hamilton. (2002). *The Idea of Europe: From Antiquity to the European Union.* Cambridge: Cambridge University Press.

Page, Edward C., and Linda Wouters. (1995). "The Europeanization of the National Bureaucracies?" In Jon Pierre, ed., *Bureaucracy in the Modern State*, pp. 185–204. Aldershot,UK: E. Elgar.

Palmade, Guy, ed. (1974). *Das bürgerliche Zeitalter*, Fischer Weltgeschichte, Vol. 27. Frankfurt am Main: Fischer Taschenbuch Verlag.

Parker, R. A. C. (1967). *Das Zwanzigste Jahrhundert I*, Fischer Weltgeschichte, Vol. 34. Frankfurt am Main: Fischer Taschenbuch Verlag.

Parkinson, C. Northcote. (1957). *Parkinson's Law.* Boston and Cambridge: Houghton Mifflin and The Riverside Press.

Parsons, Talcott. (1951). "Systems of Value Orientations." In Parsons and Shils, *Toward a General Theory of Action*, pp. 159–89.

Parsons, Talcott and Edward A. Shils, eds. (1951). *Toward A General Theory of Action.* Cambridge, Mass.: Harvard University Press.

Parsons, Talcott, and Neil J. Smelser. (1984). *Economy and Society. A Study in the Integration of Economic and Social Theory.* London: Routledge & Kegan Paul.

Pelinka, Anton. (2005). *Vergleich politischer Systeme.* Wien, Köln, and Weimar: Böhlau.

Pernice, Ingolf. (2004). "The Draft Constitution of the European Union: A Constitutional Treaty at a Constitutional Moment?" In Pernice and Poiares Maduro, *A Constitution for the European Union*, pp. 11–22.

Pernice, Ingolf, and Miguel Poiares Maduro, eds. (2004). *A Constitution for the European Union: First Comments on the 2003-Draft of the European Convention.* Baden-Baden, Germany: Nomos Verlagsgesellschaft.

Perrineaux, Pascal, ed. (2005). *Le vote européen 2004–2005. De l'élargissement au referendum français.* Paris: Presses des la Fondation Nationale des Sciences Politiques.

Peters, B. Guy. (1995). *The Politics of Bureaucracy.* White Plains, NY: Longman.

Pfetsch, Frank R. (1997). *Die Europäische Union. Geschichte, Institutionen, Prozesse.* München: W. Fink.

Pierre, Jon, ed. (1995). *Bureaucracy in the Modern State. An Introduction to Comparative Public Administration.* Aldershot, UK: E. Elgar.

Pitkin, Hannah Fenichel. (1967). *The Concept of Representation.* Berkeley: University of California Press.

Planitz, Ulrich. (1975). *Konrad Adenauer. Eine Biografie in Wort und Bild.* Bergisch-Gladbach, Germany: G. Lübbe.

Plé, Bernhard. (1993). "Giuseppe Mazzini." In *Biographisch-Bibliographisches Kirchenlexikon,* pp. 1118–1143. Nordhausen, Germany: Traugott Bautz.

Poferl, Angelika. (2006). "Solidarität ohne Grenzen? Probleme sozialer Ungleichheit und Teilhabe in europäischer Perspektive." In Heidenreich, *Die Europäisierung sozialer Ungleichheit,* pp. 231–52.

Poier, Klaus. (2004) "In Search of the 'Ideal' Electoral System for the European Union." In Hedwig Kopetz et al., eds., *Soziokultureller Wandel im Verfassungsstaat. Phänomene politischer Transformation,* pp. 1059–1099. Wien, Köln, and Graz: Böhlau Verlag.

Pollack, Mark A. (2003). *The Engines of European Integration. Delegation, Agency, and Agenda Setting in the EU.* Oxford and New York: Oxford University Press.

Pollak, Johannes. (2007). *Repräsentation ohne Demokratie. Kollidierende Systeme der Repräsentation in der Europäischen Union.* Wien and New York: Springer.

Pollak, Johannes, and Peter Slominski. (2006). *Das politische System der EU.* Wien: Facultas and WUV (UTB 2852).

Popper, Karl R. (1972). *Objective Knowledge.* Oxford: Clarendon Press (German ed.: *Objektive Erkenntnis. Ein evolutionärer Entwurf,* Hamburg: Hoffmann und Campe, 1973).

Procacci, Giuliano. (1983). *Geschichte Italiens und der Italiener.* München: C. H. Beck.

Puntscher-Riekmann, Sonja. (1998). *Die kommissarische Neuordnung Europas. Das Dispositiv der Integration.* Wien and New York: Springer.

Putnam, Robert D. (1976). *The Comparative Study of Political Elites.* Englewood Cliffs, NJ: Prentice Hall.

Rasmussen, Hjalte. (1986). *On Law and Policy in the European Court of Justice.* Dordrecht, Leiden, the Netherlands, and Boston: M. Nijhoff.

Ratzinger, Joseph. (2005). *Die Einheit der Nationen. Eine Vision der Kirchenväter.* Salzburg and München: Anton Pustet.

Rauch, Carsten. (2005). *Die Theorie des demokratischen Friedens. Grenzen und Perspektiven.* Frankfurt and New York: Campus.

Reichel, Peter, ed. (1984). *Politische Kultur in Westeuropa. Bürger und Staaten in der Europäischen Gemeinschaft.* Frankfurt and New York: Campus.

Reif, Karl, and Hermann Schmitt. (1980). "Nine Second-Order National Elections." *European Journal of Political Research* 8:3–44.

Reimon, Michel, and Helmut Weixler. (2006). *Die sieben Todsünden der EU. Vom Ausverkauf einer großen Idee.* Wien: Ueberreuter.

Reinelt, Elke. (1998). *Die EG-Bankbilanzrichtlinie und der Lobbyismus der Banken.* Frankfurt am Main:

Reinhardt, Nickolas. (2004). "Pecuniary Identity and European Integration." In Moxon-Browne, *Who Are the Europeans Now?* pp.112–35.

Rieger, Elmar. (1996). "Agrarpolitik: Integration durch Gemeinschaftspolitik?" In Jachtenfuchs and Kohler-Koch, *Europäische Integration,* pp. 401–28.

Rifkin, Jeremy. (2004). *The European Dream.* New York: Jeremy P. Tarcher and Penguin (German ed.: *Der Europäische Traum. Die Vision einer leisen Supermacht,* Frankfurt am Main: Fischer Taschenbuch Verlag).

Rikin, Hanna Fenichel. (1967). *The Concept of Representation.* Berkeley, Los Angeles, and London: University of California Press.

Risse-Kappen, Thomas. (1996). "Exploring the Nature of the Beast: International Relations Theory and Comparative Policy Analysis Meet the European Union." *JCMS* 34:53–80.

Roesler, Jörg. (1999). *Der Anschluss von Staaten in der modernen Geschichte. Eine Untersuchung aus aktuellem Anlass.* Frankfurt am Main: Peter Lang.

Roland, Gèrard. (2001). "Ten Years After . . . Transition and Economics." *IMF Staff Papers*, Vol. 48 (special ed.), pp. 29–52.

Roniger, Luis, and Ayse Günes-Ayata. (1994). *Democracy, Clientelism, and Civil Society.* Boulder, CO: L. Rienner.

Rosamond, Ben. (2000). *Theories of European Integration.* Basingstoke, UK: Palgrave.

Rosato, Sebastian. (2003). "The flawed logic of Democratic Peace theory." *American Political Science Review* 97:585–602.

Ross, George. (1995). *Jacques Delors and European Integration.* Cambridge: Polity Press.

Rossi, Peter H., James D. Wright, and Andy B. Anderson, eds. (1983). *Handbook of Survey Research.* New York: Academic Press.

Rouban, Luc. (1995). "Public Administration at the Crossroads: The End of French Specificity?" In Jon Pierre, ed., *Bureaucracy in the Modern State,* pp. 39–63. Aldershot, UK: E. Elgar.

Roy, William. (1997). *Socializing Capital. The Rise of the Large Industrial Corporation in America.* Princeton, NJ: Princeton University Press.

Rudzio, Wolfgang. (1995). "Der demokratische Verfassungsstaat als Beute der Partien? Parteienkritik als Krisenelement." In Gellner and Veen, *Umbruch und Wandel in westeuropäischen Parteisystemen,* pp. 1–15.

Ruf, Werner. (2004). "Die Finalität Europas—Ende des Traum von der Zivilmacht?" Unpublished Lecture at the Summer Academy Stadtschlaining, Austria.

Rumford, Chris. (2002). *The European Union. A Political Sociology.* Malden, MA, and Oxford: Blackwell Publishing.

Rummel, Rudolph J. (1995). "Democracies ARE less warlike than other regimes." *European Journal of Industrial Relations* 1:457–79.

Sainsbury, Diane. 1999. *Gender and Welfare State Regimes.* Oxford etc.: Oxford University Press.

Salmon, Pierre. (2002). *Accounting for Centralisation in the European Union: Niskanen, Monnet or Thatcher?* Unpublished paper, Bougogne, France: Université de Bougogne, Faculté de Science Economique , LATEC.

Salvatorelli, Luigi. (1971). "Napoleon und Europa." In Heinz-Otto Sieburg, ed., *Napoleon und Europa,* pp. 171–200. Köln and Berlin: Kiepenheuer & Witsch.

Sandholtz, Wayne, and Alec Stone Sweet, eds. (1998). *European Integration and Supranational Governance.* Oxford: Oxford University Press.

Sapir, André, et al. (2003). *An Agent for a Growing Europe. Making the EU-System Deliver.* Report of an Independent high-level study group established on the initiative of the president of the European Commission, Brussels.

Sartori, Giovanni. (1968). "Democracy." In David L. Sills, ed., *International Encyclopedia of the Social Sciences,* Vol. 3, pp. 112–21. New York: Macmillan & Free Press/London: Collier-Macmillan.

Savary, Gilles. (2004). *L'Europe va-t-elle démanteler les services publics?* La Tour d'Aignes, France: Éditions de l'Aube.

Schäfer, Armin. (2005). *Die neue Unverbindlichkeit. Wirtschaftspolitische Koordinierung in Europa.* Frankfurt and New York: Campus.

Schäfer, Armin. (2006). "Die demokratische Grenze output-orientierter Legitimation." Köln: Max-Planck-Institut für Gesellschaftsforschung (available online).

Schäfers, Bernhard, ed. (1992). *Lebensverhältnisse und soziale Konflikte im neuen Europa. Verhandlungen des 26. Deutschen Soziologentages in Düsseldorf 1992.* Frankfurt and New York: Campus.

Scharpf, Fritz. (1997). Demokratische Politik in der internationalisierten Ökonomie, Max Planck Institut für Gesellschaftsforschung, Working Paper 97/9, Cologne.

Scharpf, Fritz. (1999). *Governing in Europe: Effective and Democratic?* Oxford: Oxford University Press.

Scharpf, Fritz W. (2002). "The European Social Model: Coping With the Challenges of Diversity." *JCMS* 40:645–70.

Scheff, Thomas. (1990). *Microsociology. Discourse, Emotion and Social Structure.* Chicago and London: University of Chicago Press.

Scheff, Thomas. (1994). *Bloody Revenge. Emotions, Nationalism and War.* Boulder, CO: Westview Press.

Scheingold, Stuart A. (1965), *The Rule of Law in European Integration. The Path of the Schuman Plan,* New Haven/ London: Yale University Press

Schepel, Harm/ Rein Wesseling (1997), "The legal community: Judges, lawyers, officials and clerks in the writing of Europe," *European Law Journal* 3:165–188.

Scheuch, Erwin K. and Ute. (1992). *Cliquen, Klüngel und Karrieren. Über den Verfall der politischen Parteien— eine Studie.* Reinbek, Germany: Rowohlt.

Schildt, Joachim. (2005). "Ein Sieg der Angst—das gescheiterte französische Verfassungsreferendum." *Integration* 1:187–200.

Schimmelfennig, Frank. (1996). *Legitimate Rule in the European Union. The Academic Debate.* Tübinger Arbeitspapier zur internationalen Politik und Friedensforschung 27 (http://tobias-lib-ub.uni-tuebingen.de/volltexte/2000/150/index.htm).

Schmid, Günther, and Hubert Treiber. (1975). *Bürokratie und Politik. Zur Struktur und Funktion der Ministerialbürokratie in der Bundesrepublik Deutschland.* München: Wilhelm Fink Verlag.

Schmidt, Manfred G. (2000). "Der konsoziative Staat. Hypothesen zur politischen Struktur und zum politischen Leistungsprofil der europäischen Union." In Grande and Jachtenfuchs, *Wie problemlösungsfähig ist die EU,* pp. 33–58.

Schmidtke, Oliver. (1998). "Obstacles and Prospects for a European Collective Identity and Citizenship." In Ulf Hedetoft, ed., *Political Symbols, Symbols Politics. European Identities in Transformation.* Aldershot, UK: Ashgate.

Schmitt, Hermann, and Jacques Thomassen, eds. (1999). *Political Representation and Legitimacy in the European Union.* Oxford: Oxford University Press.

Schmitter, Philippe C. (2004). "Neo-Neofunctionalism." In Wiener and Diez, *European Integration Theory,* pp. 45–74.

Schmitter, Philippe C., and Alexander H. Trechsel, eds. (2004). *The Future of Democracy in Europe. Trends, Analyses and Reforms.* Strasbourg, France: Council of Europe Publishing.

Schneider, Heinrich. (1992). "Europäische Integration: die Leitbilder und die Politik." In Michael Kreile, ed., *Die Integration Europas,* pp. 3–35. Opladen, Germany: Westdeutscher Verlag.

Schneider, Heinrich. (2000). "Alternativen der Verfassungsfinalität: Föderation, Konföderation—oder was sonst? *Integration* 23:171–84.

Schneider, Heinrich. (2001). *Jacques Delors: Mensch und Methode.* Vienna: Institute for Advanced Studies, Political Science Series 73.

Schoenbaum, David. (1967). *Hitler's Social Revolution. Class and Status in Nazi Germany.* London: Weidenfeld & Nicholson.

Scholz, Reiner. (1995). *Korruption in Deutschland. Die schmutzigen Finger der öffentlichen Hand.* Reinbek, Germany: Rowohlt.

Schöpflin, George. (2000). *Nations, Identity, Power. The New Politics of Europe.* London: Hurst & Co.

Schroeder, Wolfgang. (2006). "Change and Continuity of Industrial Relations in Central and Eastern Europe." In Bach, Lahusen, and Vobruba, *Europe in Motion*, pp. 97–117.

Schulmeister, Paul. (2007). "Wohin führt Angela Merkel die EU? Die deutsche Ratspräsidentschaft: Möglichkeiten und Grenzen." *Europäische Rundschau* 35:31–47.

Schumacher, E. F. (1973). *Small Is Beautiful. A Study of Economics as if People Mattered.* London: Blond & Briggs.

Schumpeter, Joseph A. (1962). *Capitalism, Socialism, and Democracy.* New York: Harper.

Scitovsky, Tibor. (1962). *Economic Theory and Western European Integration.* London: Unwin University Press.

Scoppola, Pietro. (1991). *La Repubblica dei Partiti. Profilo storico della democrazia in Italia (1945–1990).* Bologna, Italy: Il Mulino.

Scott, John, ed. (1990). *The Sociology of Elites*, Vol. I. Aldershot, UK: E. Elgar.

Scully, Roger, and David M. Farrell (2003). "MEPs as Representatives: Individual and Institutional Roles." *JCMS* 41:269–88.

Segl, Peter. (1993). *Karl der Große und die Grundlegung Europas im Mittelalter.* Abensberg, Germany: Verlag der Weltenberger Akademie.

Seidenfaden, Toeger. (2005, Spring). "Saving Europe From the Tyranny of Referendums." *Europe's World*, pp. 65–75.

Seldeslachts, Jo. (2005). "Warum Fusionen scheitern. Von Informationen und Integrationsanstrengungen." *WZB-Mitteilungen* 108:16–19.

Servan-Schreiber, Jean-Jacques. (1968). *The American Challenge.* London: Hamilton (Le défi Americaine, Paris: Denoel, 1967).

Shils, Edward. (1982). *The Constitution of Society.* Chicago and London: University of Chicago Press.

Shore, Cris. (2000). *Building Europe. The Cultural Politics of European Integration.* London and New York: Routledge.

Shore, Cris. (2001). "European Union and the Politics of Culture." Talk given to the Bruges Group; available at http//:www.brugesgroup.com/mediacentre/index.live?article=13.

Sieburg, Heinz-Otto. (1971). *Napoleon und Europa.* Köln and Berlin: Kiepenheuer & Witsch.

Siedentop, Larry. (2001). *Democracy in Europe.* New York: Columbia University Press.

Siedschlag, Alexander. (2006). "Neorealist Contributions to a Theory of ESDP." Paper presented at European Security Conference II, Innsbruck, Austria (www.esci.at/papers/NR-ESDP.pdf).

Siegwart, Hans, and Gregory Neugebauer, eds. (1998). *Mega-Fusionen. Analysen—Kontroversen—Perspektiven.* Bern, Stuttgart, and Wien: P. Haupt.

Simmel, Georg. (1971). *On Individuality and Social Forms. Selected Writings.* Chicago: University of Chicago Press.

Singer, Peter Warren (2004), *Corporate Warriors. The rise of the Privatized Military Industry*, Ithaca, NY etc.: Cornell University Press.

Sklair, Leslie. (1991). *Sociology of the Global System.* New York: Harvester Wheatsheaf.

Sklair, Leslie. (1997). "Social Movements for Global Capitalism. The Transnational Capitalist Class in Action." *Review of International Political Economy* 4:514–38.

Sklair, Leslie. (2001). *The Transnational Capitalist Class.* Oxford: Blackwell.

Skrapska, G. (2001). "Law and Democracy." *International Encyclopedia of the Social and Behavioral Sciences*, pp. 8839–8842. Amsterdam: Elsevier.

Smeets, Heinz-Dieter. (1996). "Grundlagen der regionalen Integration: Von der Zollunion zum Binnenmarkt." In Ohr, *Europäische Integration*, pp. 47–75.

Smith, Anthony D. (1991). *National Identity*. London: Penguin Books.

Smith, Denis Mack. (1994). *Mazzini*. New Haven, CT: Yale University Press.

Spence, David. (1994). "Staff and Personnel Policy in the Commission." In Geoffrey Edwards, Geoffrey and David Spence, eds. Pp. 62–96,*The European Commission*. Harlow, Essex, UK: Longman.

Spieker, Manfred. (1986). *Legitimitätsprobleme des Sozialstaats. Konkurrierende Sozialstaatskonzeptionen in der Bundesrepublik Deutschland*. Bern and Stuttgart: Paul Haupt.

Spierenburg, Dirk, and Raymond Poidevin. (1994). *The History of the High Authority of the European Coal and Steel Community: Supranationality in Operation*. London: Weidenfeld & Nicolson.

Steffani, Winfried, and Uwe Thaysen, eds. (1995). *Demokratie in Europa: Zur Rolle der Parlamente*. Opladen, Germany: Westdeutscher Verlag.

Stein, Thorsten. (2001). "Europas Verfassung." In Timmermann, *Eine Verfassung für die Europäische Union*, pp. 41–56.

Stevens, Anne. (2002). "Europeanisation and the Administration of the EU: A Comparative Perspective." Queen's Papers on Europeanisation, No. 4, Aston University, Birmingham, UK.

Stiglitz, Joseph E., and Bruno Schönfelder. (1989). *Finanzwissenschaft*. München and Wien: Oldenbourg.

Stocké, Volker, and Birgit Becker. (2004). "Determinanten und Konsequenzen der Umfrageeinstellung." *ZUMA-Nachrichten* 54:89–116.

Stone Sweet, Alec. (2005). *European Integration and the Legal System*. Reihe Politikwissenschaft 101. Wien: Institut für Höhere Studien.

Stone Sweet, Alec, and Thomas Brunell. (1998). "Constructing a Supranational Constitution: Dispute Resolution and Governance in the European Community." *American Political Science Review* 92:63–81.

Stone Sweet, Alec, Wayne Sandholtz, and Neil Fligstein, eds. (2001). *The Institutionalization of Europe*. Oxford and New York: Oxford University Press.

Strezhneva, Marina. (1991). "Lessons of the European Community." *International Affairs* 12:83–91.

Strobe, Talbott, and Nayan Chanda, eds. (2002). *Das Zeitalter des Terrors. Amerika und die Welt nach dem 11. September*. München and Berlin: Propyläen.

Strong, Carol. (2006). "Vaclav Klaus, Lech Kaczyński, and the Future of the European Union." Paper presented at the Third International Conference "Elites and EU Enlargement," 17–18 February 2006, Prague, Czech Republic.

Stürmer, Michael. (1977). "Gesellschaftskrise und Bürokratie in Preussen-Deutschland seit 1800." In T. Leuenberger and K.-H. Ruffmann, Hrsg., *Bürokratie. Motor oder Bremse der Entwicklung*. Bern: Peter Lang.

Suttner, Bertha von. (2006). *Die Waffen nieder! Eine Lebensgeschichte*. Husum, Germany: Verlag der Nation.

Swanson, Guy. (1967). *Religion and Regime. A Sociological Account of the Reformation*. Ann Arbor: University of Michigan Press.

Swedberg, Richard. (1994). "The Idea of 'Europe' and the Origin of the European Union—A Sociological Approach." *Zeitschrift für Soziologie* 23:378–387.

Swedberg, Richard. (1998). *Max Weber and the Idea of Economic Sociology*. Princeton, NJ: Princeton University Press.

Sweeney, Paul. (1998). *The Celtic Tiger: Ireland's Economic Miracle Explained*. Dublin: Oak Tree Press.

Szczerbiak, Aleks. (2001). "Polish Public Opinion: Explaining Declining Support for EU Membership." *JCMS* 39:105–22.

Tausch, Arno. (2001). "The European Union: Global Challenge or Global Governance?" In Gernot Köhler and Emilio J. Chaves, eds., *Globalization: Critical Perspectives*, pp. 93–197. Huntington, NY: Nova Science Publishers.

Taylor, Charles. (1992). *The Sources of the Self*. Harvard, MA: Harvard UP.

Taylor, Paul. (1993). *International Organization in the Modern World. The Regional and the Global Process*. London and New York: Pinter.

Thatcher, Margaret. (1993). *The Downing Street Years*. London: HarperColllins.

Therborn, Göran. (1995). *European Modernity and Beyond. The Trajectory of European Societies, 1945–2000*. London: Sage.

Thody, Philip. (2000). *Europe Since 1945*. London and New York: Routledge.

Tichy, Gunther. (1994). "Geliebte Vielfalt in der nötigen Einheit. Zur Langsamkeit des europäischen Integrationsprozesses." In M. Haller, *Europa wohin?* pp. 49–64.

Tichy, Gunther. (2002). "What Do We Know About Success and Failure of Mergers?" *Journal of Industry, Competition and Trade* 1:347–94.

Tiersky, Ronald, ed. (1999), Europe Today. National Politics, European Integration and European Security, Lanham, Boulder etc.: Rowman & Littlefield

Timmermann, Heiner, ed. (2001). *Eine Verfassung für die europäische Union. Beiträge zu einer grundsätzlichen und aktuellen Diskussion*. Opladen, Germany: Leske + Budrich.

Tocqueville, Alexis de. (1976) *Über die Demokratie in Amerika*. München: Deutscher Taschenbuch Verlag (First French ed. 1835).

Tracy, Michael. (1989). *Politics and Agriculture in Europe 1889–1988*. New York: Harvester Wheatsheaf.

Trichet, Jean-Claude. (2001). "The Euro After Two Years." *Journal of Common Market Studies* 39:1–13.

Tsatsos, Dimitris T., ed. (1992). *Parteifinanzierung im europäischen Vergleich*. Baden-Baden, Germany: Nomos Verlagsgesellschaft.

Tschubarjan, Alexander. (1992). *Europakonzepte von Napoleon bis zur Gegenwart*. Berlin: Edition Q.

Van Apeldoorn, Bastian. (2000). "Transnationale Klassen und europäisches Regieren: Der European Round Table of Industrialists." In Bieling and Steinhilber, *Die Konfiguration Europas*, pp. 189–221.

Van Apeldoorn, Bastian. (2002). *Transnational European Capitalism and the Struggle Over European Integration*. London and New York: Routledge.

Van Apeldoorn, Bastian, and Laura Horn. (2005). *The Marketisation of European Corporate Control: A Critical Political Economy Perspective*. Paper presented at the seventh Conference of the European Sociological Association, Torun, Poland.

Van Buitenen, Paul. (2000). *Unbestechlich für Europa*. Basel-Gießen, Germany: Brunnen Verlag.

Van Buitenen, Paul. (2004). *Korruptionskrieg in Brüssel. Kampf um mehr Transparenz für Europa*. Basel-Gießen, Germany: Brunnen Verlag.

Van der Pijl, Kees. (1989). "Ruling Classes, Hegemony, and the State System." *International Journal of Political Economy* 193:7–35.

Vanhoudt, Patrick. (1999). "Did the European Unification Induce Economic Growth? In Search of Scale Effects and Persistent Changes." *Welt-Wirtschafts-Archiv* 135:193–20.

Van Miert, Karel. (2000). *Meine Erfahrungen als Kommissar in Brüssel*. Stuttgart, Germany: DVA.

Várhegyi, Éva. (1998). "A Magyar banktulajdonosi szerkezet sajátos vonásai." *Közgazdasági Szemle* XLV:906–22.

Vaubel, Roland. (1995). *The Centralisation of Western Europe. The Common Market, Political Integration and Democracy*. London: Institute of Economic Affairs (IEA).

Veltri, Elio, and Marco Travaglio. (2001). *L'odore dei soldi*. Rome: Editori Riuniti.

Verfassungen der EU-Mitgliedsstaaten. (2005). With an introduction by A. Kimmel and C. Kimmel. München: Deutscher Taschenbuch Verlag.

Verheugen, Günter. (2005). *Europa in der Krise. Für eine Neubegründung der Europäischen Idee.* Köln: Kiepenheuer & Witsch.

Verschave, Francois-Xavier. (2002). *Noir Chirac. Secret et impunité.* Paris: Les Arènes.

Vetik, Raivo. (2003). "Elite vs. People: Eurosceptic Public Opinion in Estonia." *Cambridge Review of International Affairs* 16:257–71.

Vobruba, Georg. (2005). *Die Dynamik Europas.* Wiesbaden, Germany: VS Verlag für Sozialwissenschaften.

Von Arnim, Hans Herbert. (2000). *Vom schönen Schein der Demokratie. Politik ohne Verantwortung—am Volk vorbei.* Frankfurt am Main and Wien: Büchergilde Gutenberg.

Von Arnim, Hans Herbert. (2006). *Das Europa-Komplott. Wie EU-Funktionäre unsere Demokratie verscherbeln.* München and Wien: Carl Hanser.

Von Beyme, Klaus. (1993). *Die politische Klasse im Parteienstaat.* Frankfurt am Main: Suhrkamp.

Von Raumer, Kurt. (1953). *Ewiger Friede. Friedensrufe und Friedenspläne seit der Renaissance.* Freiburg and München: Verlag Karl Alber.

Waffenschmidt et al. (1979). *Erstickt der Bürokratismus unsere Demokratie?* Schriftenreihe des Deutschen Städte- und Gemeindetages, H. 35. Göttingen, Germany: O. Schwartz.

Waldschmitt, Elmar. (2001). *Die europäische Sozialunion. Ordnungspolitischer Prüfstein des europäischen Integrationsprozesses.* Frankfurt: Peter Lang.

Wallace, Helen, and A. Young, eds. (1997). *Participation and Policy Making in the European Union.* Oxford: Clarendon Press.

Wallerstein, Immanuel. (1974). *The Modern-World System. Capitalist Agriculture and the Origins of the European World-Economy in the Sixteenth Century.* New York: Academic Press.

Waltz, Kenneth N. (1979). *Theory of International Politics.* Reading, MA: Addison-Wesley.

Wagner, Anne-Catherine. (2004). «La mondialisation des dirigeants économiques», in : Paul Bouffartigue, ed., *Le Retour des Classes Sociales*, Paris : La Dispute/ SNÉDIT, pp.125-139

Ward, Michael, and Kristian S. Gleditsch. (1998). "Democratizing for Peace." *American Political Science Review* 92:51–61.

Wasner, Barbara. (2004). *Eliten in Europa. Einführung in Theorien, Konzepte und Befunde.* Wiesbaden, Germany: VS Verlag für Sozialwissenschaften.

Weber, Max. (1973). *Soziologie. Universalgeschichtliche Analysen, Politik.* Stuttgart, Germany: Kröner.

Weber, Max. (1973a). "Die 'Objektivität' sozialwissenschaftlicher Erkenntnis." In M. Weber, *Soziologie*, pp. 286–62.

Weber, Max. (1973b). "Der Beruf zur Politik." In M. Weber, *Soziologie*, pp.167–85.

Weber, Max. (1978a). *Economy and Society. An Outline of Interpretative Sociology*, 2 vols. G. Roth and C. Wittich, eds. Berkeley, Los Angeles, and London: University of California Press.

Weber, Max. (1978b). "Parliament and Government in Reconstructed Germany." In M. Weber, *Economy and Society*, Vol. 2, pp.1381–1469.

Weber, Max. (1988). *Gesammelte politische Schriften.* Tübingen, Germany: Mohr.

Wehr, Andreas. (2004). *Europa ohne Demokratie? Die europäische Verfassungsdebatte—Bilanz, Kritik und Alternativen.* Köln: PapyRossa Verlag.

Weidenfeld, Werner, ed. (1983). *Die Identität der Deutschen.* Bonn: Bundeszentrale für Politische Bildung.

Weidenfeld, Werner, ed. (1991). *Wie Europa verfasst sein soll. Materialien zur Politischen Union.* Gütersloh, Germany: Bertelsmann.

Weil, Frederick D. (1989), "The sources and structure of legitimation in western democracies: A consolidated model tested with time-series in six countries since World War II," *American Sociological Review* 54:682-706.

Weiler, Joseph H. H. (1999). *The Constitution of Europe, "Do the New Clothes Have an Emperor?" and Other Essays on European Integration.* Cambridge: Cambridge University Press.

Weiler, Joseph H. H. (2002). "A constitution for Europe? Some Hard Choices." *JCMS* 40:563-80.

Weiler, Joseph H. H. (2003). *Un' Europa Cristiana.* Milano, Italy: Biblioteca Universale Rizzoli.

Weiler, Joseph H. H., and Marlene Wind, eds. (2003). *European Constitutionalism Beyond the State.* Cambridge: Cambridge University Press.

Weiler, Joseph H.H., Ulrich R. Haltern, and Franz C. Mayer. (1995). "European Democracy and Its Critique." *West European Politics* 18:4-39.

Weiss, Linda. (1998). *The Myth of the Powerlessness of the State. Governing the Economy in the Global Era.* Cambridge: Polity Press.

Weiss, Linda. (2002). *How to Argue With an Economist. Reopening Political Debate in Australia.* Cambridge: Cambridge University Press.

Wendt, Ingeborg. (1973). *Freiheit, du bist ein böser Traum. Die amerikanische Tragödie.* München: Kindler.

Wesolowski, Wlodzimierz. (2004). "Evolution of the Polish Economic Elite Since 1989." In Lengyel, *Cohesion and Division of Economic Elites in Central and Eastern Europe*, pp. 35-62.

Wessels, Wolfgang. (1996). "Verwaltung im EU-Mehrebenensystem: Auf dem Weg zur Megabürokratie?" In Jachtenfuchs and Köhler-Koch, *Europäische Integration*, pp. 165-92.

Wessels, Wolfgang. (2005). "Die institutionelle Struktur des Verfassungsvertrags; Ein Meilenstein der Integrationskonstruktion." In Jopp and Matl, *Der Vertrag über eine Verfassung für Europa*, pp. 45-85.

Westin, Charles. (1998). "On migration and Criminal Offence Report on a Study From Sweden." *IMIS-Beiträge*, H. 8:7-29.

Westle, Bettina. (1999). *Kollektive Identität im vereinten Deutschland: Nation und Demokratie in der Wahrnehmung der Deutschen.* Opladen, Germany: Leske + Budrich.

Wiener, Antje, and Thomas Diez, eds. (2004). *European Integration Theory.* Oxford: Oxford University Press.

Wiggerthale, Marita. (2005). *What's Wrong With EU Agricultural Subsidies?* www.attac.de/agrarnetz/dokumente/marita_eusubsidies.pdf.

WIIW Handbook of Statistics. (2005). Central, East and Southeast Europe. Edited by the Vienna Institute for International Economic Studies, Vienna.

Willi, Victor. (1983). *Ueberleben auf italienisch.* Wien: Europaverlag.

Willke, Gerhard. (2003). *Neoliberalismus.* Frankfurt and New York: Campus.

Wilson, Kevin, and Jan van der Dussen. (1995). *The History of the Idea of Europe.* London: Routledge.

Wimmer, Hannes. (2000). *Die Modernisierung politischer Systeme. Staat. Parteien. Öffentlichkeit.* Wien, Köln, and Weimar: Böhlau.

Wind, Marlene. (2003). "The European Union as a Polycentric Polity: Returning to a Neo-Medieval Europe?" In Weiler and Wind, *European Constitutionalism Beyond the State*, pp.103-31.

Windolf, Paul. (1992). "Mitbestimmung und 'corporate control' in der Europäischen Gemeinschaft." In Michael Kreile, ed., *Die Integration Europas*, pp. 120-42. Opladen, Germany: Westdeutscher Verlag.

Windolf, Paul. (1994). "Die neuen Eigentümer. Eine Analyse des Marktes für Unternehmenskontrolle." *Zeitschrift für Soziologie* 23:79–92.

Winock, Michel. (2003). *Das Jahrhundert der Intellektuellen*, Konstanz, Germany: UVK.

Wolfe, Alan. (1989). *Whose Keeper? Social Science and Moral Obligation.* Berkeley: University of California Press.

Wolf-Phillips, Leslie. (1972). *Comparative Constitutions.* London and Basingstoke, UK: Macmillan.

Wolton, Thierry. (2004). *Brève Psychoanalyse de France.* Paris: Plon.

Würtenberger Jr., Thomas. (1977). "Bürokratie und politische Führung." In T. Leuenberger and K.-H. Ruffmann, Hrsg., *Bürokratie. Motor oder Bremse der Entwicklung*, pp. 99–116. Bern: Peter Lang.

Wyplosz, Charles. (2006). "European Monetary Union: The Dark Sides of a Major Success." *Economic Policy*, April, pp. 207–61.

Zapata-Barrero, R. (2006). "The Muslim Community and Spanish Tradition: Maurophobia as a Fact and Impartiality as a Desideratum." In Tariq Modood et al., eds., *Multiculturalism, Muslims, and Citizenship: A European Approach.* London: Routledge.

Zapf, Wolfgang. (1987). *Individualisierung und Sicherheit. Untersuchungen zur Lebensqualität in der Bundesrepublik Deutschland.* München: Beck.

Zarek, Brigitte. (2006). "Die Osterweiterung der Europäischen Union: Auswirkungen auf die Handelsstrukturen zwischen der EU-15 und den Ländern Mittel- und Osteuropas." *Osteuropa-Wirtschaft* 51:107–26.

Zenkert, Georg. (n.d.). "Kants Friedensschrift in der Diskussion." http://www.information-philosophie.de/kantfrieden.htm.

Ziegler, Jean. (1998). *The Swiss, the Gold, and the Dead.* New York: Harcourt Brace.

Ziegler, Jean. (2003). *Die neuen Herrscher der Welt und ihre globalen Widersacher.* Gütersloh, Germany: Bertelsmann.

Ziltener, Patrick. (2000). "Regionale Integration im Weltsystem. Die Relevanz exogener Faktoren für den europäischen Integrationsprozeß." In Bach, *Die Europäisierung nationaler Gesellschaften*, pp. 156–77.

Ziltener, Patrick. (2003). "Hat der EU-Binnenmarkt Wachstum und Beschäftigung erbracht?" *WSI-Mitteilungen* 4:221–27.

Ziltener, Patrick. (2004). "The Economic Effects of the European Single Market Project: Projections, Simulations—and the Reality." *Review of International Political Economy* 11:953–79.

Zingerle, Arnold. (1981). *Max Webers historische Soziologie.* Darmstadt, Germany: Wissenschaftliche Buchgesellschaft.

Zschiedrich, Harald. (2004). "Ausländische Direktinvestitionen: Segen oder Fluch?" *Wirtschaft und Gesellschaft* 30:45–71.

Zürn, Michael. (1996). "Über Staat und Demokratie im europäischen Mehrebenensystem." *Politische Vierteljahresschrift* 37:27–55.

Zürn, Michael. (1998). *Regieren jenseits des Nationalstaates. Globalisierung und Denationalisierung als Chance.* Frankfurt: Suhrkamp.

Zürn, Michael, and Dieter Wolf. (2000). "Europarecht und internationale Regime: Zu den Merkmalen von Recht jenseits des Nationalstaates." In Grande and Jachtenfuchs, *Wie problemlösungsfähig ist die EU?* pp. 113–40.

Zweifel, Thomas D. (2003). "Democratic Deficits in Comparison: Best (and Worst) Practices in European, US and Swiss Merger Regulation." *JCMS* 41:541–66.

Name Index

412   *Name Index*

Subject Index

The future of Northern Ireland

A paper for discussion

NORTHERN IRELAND OFFICE

HMSO price 20p

THE FUTURE OF NORTHERN IRELAND

A paper for discussion

London   Her Majesty's Stationery Office   1972

SBN 11 700498 7

CONTENTS

FOREWORD

The British Government have a clear objective in Northern Ireland. It is to deliver its people from the violence and fear in which they live today and to set them free to realise their great potential to the full.

We want to help them to draw together; to find a system of government which will enjoy the support and the respect of the overwhelming majority. If it is to do so, such a system must emerge in large measure from the ideas and the convictions of the Northern Ireland people themselves. This is why there has to be a lengthy process of consultation, which I started on arrival, have been continuing ever since, most recently at the Darlington conference for Northern Ireland parties, and which I shall now seek to bring to fruition over the coming weeks.

But the stage has now been reached at which we must take a step forward in shaping the future. This is the purpose of this Paper for Discussion. It does not set out any single cut and dried scheme for the future but sets out some fundamental conditions (including the clear pledges of successive British Governments) which any settlement must meet. It places the Northern Ireland situation in the wider context of certain unalterable facts of life—political, economic and military—which must fundamentally influence any settlement.

This Paper is intended to provide a comprehensive basis for further discussions which I now propose immediately to put in hand. These must go ahead with the utmost urgency. What is at issue is the future of Northern Ireland, and I have set out in the first paragraph of this Foreword what the Government aim to achieve for its people. But the future of any community depends upon the will of its own people to live, to work and to make progress together; in the last resort responsibility for bringing about a peaceful future lies with them. This Paper seeks to provide, as its title and sub-title indicate, a basis for discussion as to how that may best be achieved.

WILLIAM WHITELAW
Secretary of State for Northern Ireland.

October, 1972.

PART I HISTORICAL BACKGROUND

1   For more than 50 years, between 1921 and the enactment of the Northern Ireland (Temporary Provisions) Act, 1972, Northern Ireland was governed under the scheme of devolution embodied in the Government of Ireland Act, 1920. That scheme remains today the basic constitutional document for Northern Ireland, since the Act of 1972 did not replace it, but rather superimposed upon it certain temporary provisions, in particular the prorogation of the Northern Ireland Parliament and the assumption by the Secretary of State for Northern Ireland of those executive powers hitherto discharged by the Government of Northern Ireland.

2   Annex I summarises the principal provisions of the Government of Ireland Act, 1920 (hereafter referred to, for the sake of brevity, as 'the Act of 1920') as it came into force in Northern Ireland. It is important to remember, however, that the Act was intended to establish a scheme of devolution not just for Northern Ireland, but for Ireland as a whole. In an attempt to reconcile the conflicting views of the majority in Ireland, who sought Home Rule, with those of a minority, largely concentrated in the North, who wished to preserve the Union with Great Britain, the United Kingdom Government introduced a compromise, providing for the establishment in Northern Ireland and in Southern Ireland of subordinate legislatures and governments within the United Kingdom, and also for specific machinery (the Council of Ireland) to promote co-operation and encourage ultimate union within the United Kingdom by agreement. In the event Southern Ireland did not operate the institutions established by the Act of 1920. The scheme of devolution for which that Act provided came into force in Northern Ireland alone, subject to such modifications as were made necessary by the subsequent changes in the status of the rest of Ireland; and although the subsequent course of North-South relations (of which a summary is given in Annex 2) did not preclude a degree of practical co-operation, the formal joint institutions envisaged by the Act of 1920 were stillborn.

3   Although the Northern Ireland Parliament (subsequently to become widely known as 'Stormont' from its eventual location) was endowed with quite extensive lawmaking powers, it became apparent at an early date that the exercise of these powers in practice would be tempered by the realities of the financial situation. The Parliament and Government of Northern Ireland were from the outset in the anomalous position of having responsibility for a wide range of public expenditure without any comparable responsibility for raising the major part of the revenue to finance it, since those 'transferred' taxes which the Northern Ireland Parliament had power to levy were at no time adequate to finance more than a minor proportion of 'transferred' expenditure. The rates of those

1

'reserved' (or Westminster controlled) taxes from which the greater part of Northern Ireland expenditure had to be met fluctuated in response to economic, financial and budgetary circumstances of the United Kingdom as a whole; hence Northern Ireland was unable to engage in those aspects of economic management which are central to the concerns of modern democratic governments.

4   On the contrary, there steadily evolved a relationship based upon the principle of 'parity', by which citizens of the United Kingdom living in Northern Ireland paid the same taxes and enjoyed a similar standard of public sector services as their fellow-citizens in Great Britain, achieved by payments to the Northern Ireland Exchequer, to Northern Ireland statutory funds (such as the Northern Ireland National Insurance Fund), and direct to individual citizens in Northern Ireland.

5   Thus, as a part of the United Kingdom, Northern Ireland has not been held back by inadequate tax resources from the development of services to standards acceptable in Great Britain. But the arrangements designed to secure this end have inevitably meant that the ability of the Northern Ireland Parliament to create, by legislation, distinctive policies of its own, has been severely inhibited. In the specific areas covered by the various 'parity' agreements, the Northern Ireland Parliament bound itself of its own choice, and in order to secure substantial benefits for the Northern Ireland community, to legislate virtually in parallel with Great Britain. Nor was the effect of Northern Ireland's financial dependence confined to those areas covered by specific parity arrangements. Because public expenditure in Northern Ireland exceeded public revenue raised there, virtually all Northern Ireland's policies involving significant new expenditure had to be agreed in advance with HM Treasury; so that even in fields where the distinctive traditions and needs of Northern Ireland led to the provision of distinctive programmes and policies, the Northern Ireland Parliament's freedom of legislative action was limited by the constraints of United Kingdom public expenditure. In fields such as industrial development the need to take account of additional factors such as international obligations and consequential effects in Great Britain both for individual companies and particular regions meant that more detailed consultation with Whitehall was necessary.

6   The Northern Ireland Parliament has nevertheless enacted in many fields legislation specially adapted to the local situation. For example, Northern Ireland legislation on industrial development at various times and in various ways provided for a level of inducements to industry intended to offset as far as possible Northern Ireland's geographic and other disadvantages. Specialised agencies established by the Northern Ireland Parliament, such as the Northern Ireland Tuberculosis Authority and the Northern Ireland Housing Trust, made a most significant contribution towards the betterment of life in the Province.

7   Because the Northern Ireland Parliament lacked real economic or financial independence the area of its genuinely and wholly independent legislative action tended to be concentrated on the social and regulatory fields, on changes in distinctive codes of law, and on measures which were significant for other reasons than their expenditure implications.

8   Of particular importance was that wide area of public policy which may be described as 'law and order and security'. On the one hand the Northern Ireland Parliament's general grant of powers charged it with responsibility for peace and order, as well as for good government; on the other, the United Kingdom Parliament reserved to itself responsibility for the defence of the realm and for the raising of any kind of military force. In practice, however, this division of power was not easy to observe in the face of developments in Northern Ireland itself. Although the Act of 1920 by no means envisaged the Irish border as an international frontier, it steadily assumed that character as Southern Ireland became first the Irish Free State and ultimately the Irish Republic. The partition of Ireland was deeply resented, and the new institutions of Northern Ireland were opposed; militant elements of the republican tradition launched violent attacks upon the Province and its institutions both from within Northern Ireland and across the border.

9   In response to this threat (from time to time dormant, but periodically renewed) the Northern Ireland Parliament used its legislative powers to enact measures and to establish institutions without equivalent in Great Britain, although by no means without precedent or parallel in Ireland. The Civil Authorities (Special Powers) Act (Northern Ireland), 1922 conferred upon the executive wide powers to make regulations for the protection of the State, under which provision was made, *inter alia*, for detention and internment without trial. The Royal Ulster Constabulary, established in 1922, inherited from its predecessor, the Royal Irish Constabulary, distinctive traditions and functions which themselves originated in the special public order problems of Ireland. The Northern Ireland Parliament also voted moneys for the maintenance of the Ulster Special Constabulary, which was an armed force most of whose members had been trained to carry out patrols of a varying nature and guard duties, rather than to reinforce and assist the Royal Ulster Constabulary in the performance of police duties as generally understood in the rest of the United Kingdom.

10   There were also important areas of policy in which Northern Ireland legislation diverged from that in force in the rest of the United Kingdom, not because the Northern Ireland Parliament enacted specifically different legislation, but because it did not make changes comparable with those made in Great Britain by the United Kingdom Parliament. Certain of these areas involved sensitive issues on which there were

distinctive Northern Ireland points of view. Some, however, involved important questions of citizens' rights. In particular, the Northern Ireland Parliament did not, for many years, follow the example of the United Kingdom Parliament in moving from a ratepayers' franchise at local government elections to a basis of universal adult suffrage.

11 Section 75 of the Act of 1920 saved the sovereign authority of the United Kingdom Parliament over all matters in Northern Ireland. In practice, however, this reserve of power came to be used only in the most limited way. In general the view prevailed that, having established responsible if subordinate institutions in Northern Ireland with certain powers, the United Kingdom Parliament and Government should not lightly supersede or override those powers. Thus there developed a convention that the United Kingdom Parliament would legislate within the field of Northern Ireland's 'transferred' powers only by invitation. This convention merely reflected the general view of the sovereign Parliament as to the prudent exercise of its powers; it did not, and could not, override the clear and unambiguous wording of the Statute.

12 The most striking feature of the executive government of Northern Ireland throughout this period of more than half a century was its virtually complete concentration in the hands of a single political party, the Ulster Unionist Party. At every General Election from 1921 to 1969 this Party secured an absolute majority of the seats in the Northern Ireland Parliament. Thus, following the general convention governing such matters in the United Kingdom, successive leaders of that Party were invited by the Governor to form an Administration, and did so almost entirely from fellow members of the Party in one or other House of the Northern Ireland Parliament, (two of the three notable exceptions being appointed in 1971—Mr. Bleakley, and Dr. Newe, a Roman Catholic).

13 The unbroken dominance of the Northern Ireland House of Commons (and thus of the Government) by the Ulster Unionist Party was based upon an authentic electoral mandate. Although the franchise up to 1968 included provision for a business vote, and electoral boundaries of the Stormont constituencies were not reviewed for many years, neither of these factors had any major bearing on the balance of the parties in the Northern Ireland Parliament.

14 The alternation of governing Parties which has for so long been a characteristic of the British political system, and which has undoubtedly contributed in a marked degree to the stability of Parliamentary Government in Great Britain, accordingly did not exist in Northern Ireland. It is true that there are other democracies, whether sovereign States or self-governing areas within them, of which this can also be said. The

4

special feature of the Northern Ireland situation was that the great divide in political life was not between different viewpoints on such matters as the allocation of resources and the determination of priorities, but between two whole communities. The 'floating vote' for which rival parties would normally compete was almost non-existent. Thus the relationship between the parties was not fluctuating and uncertain, but virtually fixed from one Election to another. Such a situation was unlikely to foster either sensitivity on the part of the permanent majority, or a sense of responsibility on the part of the permanent minority.

15   It would be quite wrong to infer that, in spite of this fundamental defect at the heart of the system, successive Governments of Northern Ireland did not achieve—with the co-operation, financial and otherwise, of successive United Kingdom Governments—substantial advances in many important fields of vital concern to the individual citizen and the whole community. In 1921 Northern Ireland, in many of its public services, shared with the rest of Ireland lower standards than Great Britain. Over the half century which followed, schools, hospitals, roads and many other services were developed to levels fully comparable with those of any area of Great Britain. Energetic industrial development policies achieved great economic diversification and a marked increase in real wealth, though, as in certain regions of Great Britain, this failed to bring unemployment percentages down to the national average in the face of contracting employment in certain basic industries.

16   There were, however, persistent protests on behalf of the Roman Catholic minority that they were being excluded by deliberate policy from their fair share of the benefits of increasing prosperity, and from that legitimate political influence which would permit their claims to be more effectively advanced. While some of these complaints were undoubtedly justified, in some cases opportunities to participate were not taken up, and in others the minority, detecting an unfavourable position resulting from other circumstances, genuinely believed that there had been bias or malice where none existed. Thus a higher rate of unemployment in a comparatively remote area which had a predominantly Roman Catholic population could be attributed by that population to governmental bias against it; but could also result from the real practical problems of promoting new economic development in a remote area. What is incontestable is that the continuous and complete control of central government by representatives of the majority alone was virtually bound to give rise to such suspicions.

17   Moreover, since the Report in 1969 of the Commission headed by Lord Cameron there has been on record an account of deliberate policies of discrimination, particularly in relation to housing and public employment by some though not all of the local authorities in Northern Ireland,

5

and of a toleration of local government electoral boundaries in some areas which produced wholly artificial results.*

18   When the 1920 Act was passed, there had been a clear intention to prevent discrimination whether in legislation or in executive acts. Section 5(1) of the Act prohibited the making of laws interfering with religious equality, while section 8(6) prohibited the use of the executive power so as to give a preference, privilege or advantage, or impose a disability or disadvantage on any person on account of religious belief. Whether because of doubts about the application of section 8(6) to local authorities and public bodies as distinct from central government or because of the difficulty of proving actual bias in an individual case, these provisions were not in practice invoked by persons seeking redress before the Courts. Thus many members of the minority felt that they could not expect redress of grievance through Parliament or through the constitutional safeguards which had been written into the Act of 1920.

---

*Disturbances in Northern Ireland (Cmd. 532 of 1969).

The Commission concluded that the general causes of the disorders which began in October 1968 were (paragraph 229(a)):

(1) A rising sense of continuing injustice and grievance among large sections of the Catholic population in Northern Ireland, in particular in Londonderry and Dungannon, in respect of (i) inadequacy of housing provision by certain local authorities (ii) unfair methods of allocation of houses built and let by such authorities, in particular, refusals and omissions to adopt a 'points' system in determining priorities and making allocations (iii) misuse in certain cases of discretionary powers of allocation of houses to perpetuate Unionist control of the local authority.

(2) Complaints, now well documented in fact, of discrimination in the making of local government appointments, at all levels but especially in senior posts, to the prejudice of non-Unionists and especially Catholic members of the community, in some Unionist controlled authorities.

(3) Complaints, again well documented, in some cases of deliberate manipulation of local government electoral boundaries and in others a refusal to apply for their necessary extension, in order to achieve and maintain Unionist control of local authorities and so to deny to Catholics influence in local government proportionate to their numbers.

(4) A growing and powerful sense of resentment and frustration among the Catholic population at failure to achieve either acceptance on the part of the Government of any need to investigate these complaints or to provide and enforce a remedy for them.

(5) Resentment, particularly among Catholics, as to the existence of the Ulster Special Constabulary (the 'B' Specials) as a partisan and para-military force recruited exclusively from Protestants.

(6) Widespread resentment among Catholics in particular at the continuance in force of regulations made under the Special Powers Act, and of the continued presence in the statute book of the Act itself.

(7) Fears and apprehensions among Protestants of a threat to Unionist domination and control of Government by increase of Catholic population and powers, inflamed in particular by the activities of the Ulster Constitution Defence Committee and the Ulster Protestant Volunteers, provoked strong hostile reaction to civil rights claims as asserted by the Civil Rights Association and later by the People's Democracy which was readily translated into physical violence against Civil Rights demonstrators.

19   By 1968 there had emerged an active and articulate movement demanding changes in the area of civil rights, such as the acceptance of universal adult suffrage as the basis for all elections, the redrawing of electoral boundaries, and the ending of discrimination in employment and housing. From the start this movement was largely (though not exclusively) Roman Catholic, and although it undoubtedly attracted support from militant republicanism, its declared aim was to achieve the objectives by non-violent means. On 5 October 1968, however, a violent confrontation with the police occurred when a Civil Rights march took place in Londonderry in defiance of an Order made by the Minister of Home Affairs for Northern Ireland.

20   The reactions and counter-reactions which followed led in August 1969, to widespread inter-communal disorders at a number of places in Northern Ireland. These were subsequently to be described in the report of the Scarman Tribunal* as follows:

'Neither the IRA nor any Protestant organisation nor anybody else planned a campaign of riots. They were communal disturbances arising from a complex political, social and economic situation. More often than not they arose from slight beginnings: but the communal tensions were such that, once begun, they could not be controlled'. (Paragraph 24).

Even with the commitment of members of the Ulster Special Constabulary in conditions for which their training had in no adequate way prepared them, the 'law and order' resources of the Government of Northern Ireland were stretched to breaking point. First in Londonderry, and then in Belfast, requests were made and granted for the deployment of the Army in aid of the civil power. This turn of events inevitably had profound effects upon the conventional relationship which had hitherto existed between the Parliament and Government of the United Kingdom and the authorities in Northern Ireland. The practice that Parliament did not discuss, except in the most general way, matters within the 'transferred' responsibility of Northern Ireland Ministers was discarded by general consent. The United Kingdom Government, widely supported in this respect by Members of all parties, concluded that a much deeper involvement in the domestic affairs of Northern Ireland was now inescapable.

21   On 19 August the Prime Minister (Mr. Wilson) and a number of his senior colleagues met Major Chichester-Clark and other Northern Ireland Ministers at 10 Downing Street. The practical results of this meeting included giving the General Officer Commanding (Northern Ireland) overall responsibility for all security operations throughout Northern Ireland, with full command of the Ulster Special Constabulary

---

*Violence and Civil Disturbances in Northern Ireland in 1969—Cmd 566 of 1972

and with control of the deployment and tasking of the Royal Ulster Constabulary for all matters relating to security operations; withdrawing the Ulster Special Constabulary from riot or crowd control duties and strictly controlling their arms; and the appointment for the first time of a senior official as United Kingdom Representative in Northern Ireland. The meeting also produced the Downing Street Declaration*, embodying a re-affirmation of the pledge by successive United Kingdom Governments that Northern Ireland should not cease to be a part of the United Kingdom without the consent of the people of Northern Ireland, and a commitment to the principle that 'in all legislation and executive decisions of government every citizen of Northern Ireland is entitled to the same equality

---

*Cmd. 4154 of 1969. The full text is:

1   The United Kingdom Government reaffirm that nothing which has happened in recent weeks in Northern Ireland derogates from the clear pledges made by successive United Kingdom Governments that Northern Ireland should not cease to be a part of the United Kingdom without the consent of the people of Northern Ireland or from the provision in Section I of the Ireland Act, 1949, that in no event will Northern Ireland or any part thereof cease to be part of the United Kingdom without the consent of the Parliament of Northern Ireland. The border is not an issue.

2   The United Kingdom Government again affirm that responsibility for affairs in Northern Ireland is entirely a matter of domestic jurisdiction. The United Kingdom Government will take full responsibility for asserting this principle in all international relationships.

3   The United Kingdom Government have ultimate responsibility for the protection of those who live in Northern Ireland when, as in the past week, a breakdown of law and order has occurred. In this spirit, the United Kingdom Government responded to the requests of the Northern Ireland Government for military assistance in Londonderry and Belfast in order to restore law and order. They emphasise again that troops will be withdrawn when law and order has been restored.

4   The Northern Ireland Government have been informed that troops have been provided on a temporary basis in accordance with the United Kingdom's ultimate responsibility. In the context of the commitment of these troops, the Northern Ireland Government have reaffirmed their intention to take into the fullest account at all times the views of Her Majesty's Government in the United Kingdom, especially in relation to matters affecting the status of citizens of that part of the United Kingdom and their equal rights and protection under the law.

5   The United Kingdom Government have welcomed the decisions of the Northern Ireland Government relating to local government franchise, the revision of local government areas, the allocation of houses, the creation of a Parliamentary Commissioner for Administration in Northern Ireland and machinery to consider citizens' grievances against other public authorities which the Prime Minister reported to the House of Commons at Westminster following his meeting with Northern Ireland Ministers on 21 May as demonstrating the determination of the Northern Ireland Government that there shall be full equality of treatment for all citizens. Both Governments have agreed that it is vital that the momentum of internal reform should be maintained.

6   The two Governments at their meeting at 10 Downing Street today have reaffirmed that in all legislation and executive decisions of Government every citizen of Northern Ireland is entitled to the same equality of treatment and freedom from discrimination as obtains in the rest of the United Kingdom, irrespective of political views or religion. In their further meetings the two Governments will be guided by these mutually accepted principles.

7   Finally, both Governments are determined to take all possible steps to restore normality to the Northern Ireland community so that economic development can proceed at the faster rate which is vital for social stability.

of treatment and freedom from discrimination as obtains in the rest of the United Kingdom, irrespective of political views or religion'.

22   In order to prevent direct confrontation between the communities in those sensitive areas of West Belfast where they lived in homogeneous districts contiguous to each other, one of the Army's first major acts after its involvement in August 1969 was to build the so-called 'Peace Line' along the sensitive inter-face. To a considerable extent peace was kept, but as the Army stood between the communities it was drawn into conflict at different times with first one and then the other. The earliest serious confrontation, in October 1969, was between the Army and Protestant elements on Belfast's Shankill Road affronted by the Northern Ireland Government's acceptance of the changes in police organisation recommended by the Hunt Committee;† but as time elapsed the Provisional wing of the Irish Republican Army (consisting broadly of the more traditionally militant elements of that organisation after a split in its leadership) emerged in 1970 as a most serious threat to security and public order. Because it was in the Catholic areas of Belfast that the main brunt of the destruction of August 1969 had been borne, the local IRA elements were able—as they had not been between 1956–62—to project themselves as the defenders of the wider Catholic community, and thus to win substantial numbers of recruits and a considerable degree of mass support. At first encouraging and manipulating civilian rioters (using such weapons as stones or petrol bombs) but gradually developing direct action with firearms and explosives against the security forces and the wider community, the IRA (largely locally recruited, but to an increasing extent under the influence of the movement's national leadership in the Republic) steadily stepped up its efforts, requiring in response a growing commitment of troops to Northern Ireland.

23   Neither the increasingly tight security policy, involving the presence of the Army in increasing strength and the use of parts of the Special Powers Act, nor the implementation or announcement of a number of radical reforms (see Annex 3) prevented the IRA from extending its campaign of violence. This led the Northern Ireland Government, after consultation with the United Kingdom Government, to introduce internment; one consequence of this was to reinforce Roman Catholic leaders in the decision they had already taken a month earlier, on other grounds, to withdraw from the Northern Ireland Parliament. As both the IRA campaign and this political rift continued, the growing inter-communal bitterness steadily reduced any realistic hope of political progress.

24   Faced by this evident impasse the United Kingdom Government came to the conclusion that it was necessary to remove from the Parliament

---

†See Annex 3, para. 2.

and Government of Northern Ireland their responsibilities for law and order. The Northern Ireland Government felt unable to accept this transfer of functions, and indicated their intention to resign instead. The United Kingdom Parliament enacted the Northern Ireland (Temporary Provisions) Act, 1972 in March 1972 which effectively vested in the Secretary of State for Northern Ireland the powers formerly exercised by the Northern Ireland Government.

25   Following the introduction of direct rule, the Secretary of State for Northern Ireland has been involved in intensive discussions with all shades of opinion in Northern Ireland, and has in addition invited and received many written suggestions from individual citizens of Northern Ireland. In August 1972 it was announced that a conference would be held to which each of the seven parliamentary political parties of Northern Ireland was invited to discuss suggestions for the future of Northern Ireland: the conference was held at Darlington from 25–27 September and representatives of the Unionist, the Alliance and the Northern Ireland Labour Parties were present. Parts II and III of this Paper take account of the many views which have been represented to the Secretary of State both during this conference, and in his other consultations.

PART II   PROPOSALS AND POSSIBILITIES

Proposals by Political Parties in Northern Ireland

26   It is appropriate to begin a review of the possibilities of future political development in Northern Ireland with a brief analysis of the proposals made by Northern Ireland political parties and interests, some of which were discussed at the Darlington Conference. Paragraphs 27–31 accordingly provide a brief summary of the proposals of political parties; but since any process of compression may involve the omission of points considered important by those who put them forward, the published views of the various parties are, with their permission, reproduced in full in Annexes 4 to 9. Paragraphs 33 to 35 concern the proposals of other organisations and of individual members of the public. This section concludes with a brief reference, in paragraph 36, to the views of United Kingdom political parties.

27   **Proposals of the Ulster Unionist Party*** (32 Members in the Northern Ireland House of Commons before prorogation: Leader, Mr Brian Faulkner).

(i) A unicameral Northern Ireland Parliament of 100 Members elected by simple majority vote; five Parliamentary Committees, each covering the activities of a department, plus a Public Accounts Committee. Membership of Committees to reflect the strength of parties in Parliament and at least three to be chaired by Opposition Members.

(ii) An Executive to consist of a Cabinet comprising a Prime Minister and five or six Ministers each heading a department.

(iii) The Royal Ulster Constabulary and its Reserve to continue to be answerable to the Northern Ireland authorities, and to be responsible for intelligence gathering and the control of subversive activities (as far as possible) as well as for ordinary civil policing.

(iv) The Special Powers Act to be replaced by alternative emergency legislation, excluding the power to intern, with its operation dependent upon the declaration by the Northern Ireland Parliament of a state of emergency, and renewable for six months at a time by resolution of that Parliament. A system of Special Courts to deal with cases involving either widespread sectarian violence or widespread terrorist activity.

---

*The Unionist Party's publication 'Towards the Future' is reproduced in full in Annex 4.

(v) A precise and comprehensive Bill of Rights, to equalise and safeguard citizens' rights, with provision for judicial review and enforcement.

(vi) A tripartite Declaration, analogous to the Agreement of 1925, by the Governments in London, Dublin and Belfast affirming the right of the people of Northern Ireland to self-determination. Intergovernmental discussion about co-operation in ending terrorism in Ireland, and review of extradition arrangements or declaration of a Common Law Enforcement Area in Ireland. If such action is taken, the formation of an Irish Intergovernmental Council, with equal membership from the Northern Ireland Government and the Government of the Republic of Ireland, to discuss matters of mutual interest, particularly in the economic and social fields.

28 **Proposals of the Alliance Party*** (Three Members in the Northern Ireland House of Commons before prorogation. Leader, Mr Phelim O'Neill.)

(i) A unicameral Northern Ireland Assembly elected by the Single Transferable Vote (STV) system of proportional representation at maximum intervals of four years, and divided into Committees according to the main functions. Chairmen of Committees to be elected by the Assembly by proportional representation.

(ii) The Assembly itself to oversee executive functions through its Committees with management functions exercised by a Committee consisting of the chairman of the Assembly and the chairmen of its Committees.

(iii) The Royal Ulster Constabulary to be concerned only with serious crime and any police functions affecting security, and to be under Westminster control. An ordinary Police Force, to deal with parking, traffic control and offences, vandalism and minor crime, to be under the control of the Northern Ireland Assembly.

(iv) The Special Powers Act to be phased out as soon as possible, and the new Assembly to have no powers to enact any similar legislation. All security legislation (as also all legislative powers in relation to electoral matters) to be a Westminster responsibility.

(v) A Bill of Rights, guaranteeing to all citizens their fundamental human rights, and based on the Universal Declaration of Human Rights.

(vi) The Irish Republic not to be represented at talks on the political future of Northern Ireland but should accept a fair settlement. Extradition arrangements to be re-negotiated, to provide for ex-

*The Alliance Party's proposals are reproduced in full in Annex 5.

tradition of persons charged with crimes of violence of a political nature. The formation of an advisory Anglo-Irish Council with representatives from Westminster, the Dail and the new Northern Ireland Assembly.

29 Proposals of the Northern Ireland Labour Party* (One Member in the Northern Ireland House of Commons before prorogation, Mr F. V. Simpson).

(i) A unicameral Northern Ireland Assembly of 100 Members, elected by proportional representation at maximum intervals of four years, with dissolution also possible by simple majority vote. A system of Departmental Committees of the Assembly elected on a proportionate basis.

(ii) Each Departmental Committee to constitute the legal entity formerly constituted by a departmental Minister.

(iii) Westminster to be responsible for the courts and judiciary, legislation on and licensing of firearms, emergency powers (which should accord with international obligations and conventions) and the power to raise, disband, arm, or control the criteria for recruiting of, any police force. The Northern Ireland Assembly, however, to retain management powers in relation to the police, including power to increase its strength and review the exercise of its functions.

(iv) Anything in the nature of Special Powers legislation to be a Westminster matter, but full account to be taken of the existence of a serious emergency in Northern Ireland.

(v) A Bill of Rights to give statutory expression to the Downing Street Declaration of August 1969 and acknowledge the Westminster Parliament's role as guarantor of civil, religious and political liberty in Northern Ireland. The position in Northern Ireland on such matters as the death penalty, race relations, homosexual practices, termination of pregnancy and divorce to be brought into line with that in the rest of the United Kingdom; all future legislation in the field of civil (and individual citizens') rights enacted at Westminster to be applied to Northern Ireland unless the Westminster Parliament determines otherwise; and the Westminster Parliament to reserve expressly the right to annul any provision made by the Northern Ireland Assembly which it resolves to affect adversely citizens' rights.

(vi) A consultative and deliberative Council of Ireland to be established.

---

*The Northern Ireland Labour Party's proposals are reproduced in full in Annex 6.

30 **Proposals of the Social Democratic and Labour Party*.** (Six Members in the Northern Ireland House of Commons before prorogation: Leader, Mr. Gerard Fitt).

(i) An immediate declaration by the United Kingdom that it would be in the best interest of all sections of the communities in both islands (i.e. Great Britain and Ireland) if Ireland were to become united on terms which would be acceptable to all the people of Ireland, and that the United Kingdom will positively encourage such a development.

(ii) Pending the achievement of unity, the establishment of an interim system of government for Northern Ireland under the joint sovereignty of the United Kingdom and the Irish Republic, who would reserve to themselves all powers relating to foreign affairs, defence, security, police and financial subventions and would be represented in Northern Ireland by Commissioners who would sign all legislation of a Northern Ireland Assembly or, if one or both considered it necessary, refer it for determination by a joint Constitutional Court.

(iii) The Assembly to consist of 84 Members elected by the STV system of proportional representation, with power to legislate in all fields including taxation, except those matters reserved to the joint sovereign powers.

(iv) An executive of 15 Members to be elected from the Assembly by proportional representation and to hold office through the duration of an Assembly except in the case of a 75 per cent adverse vote. A chief executive, elected by the executive, to allocate departmental responsibilities subject to the approval of both Commissioners.

(v) No representation for Northern Ireland in either the Westminster or the Dublin Parliament.

(vi) All powers of security to be under the direct control of a department headed by both Commissioners.

(vii) Creation of a new national Senate for the whole of Ireland, with equal representation from the Dublin Parliament and the Northern Ireland Assembly, the Parties from each being represented according to their strength, to plan the integration of North and South and agree on an acceptable constitution.

---

*The Social Democratic and Labour Party's publication 'Towards a New Ireland' is reproduced with their permission in full in Annex 7: it was not submitted to the Darlington conference.

31   Proposals have also been sent to the Secretary of State by the **Ulster Liberal Party***, which was not represented in the Northern Ireland House of Commons at the time of prorogation. The main features are as follows:

   (i) A unicameral Northern Ireland Assembly of 75 Members elected by the STV system of proportional representation, with a system of Departmental Committees.

  (ii) The main policy-making body to be a Finance Committee. Its chairman, who would in effect be head of the Government, to be the member of the Assembly receiving most first-preference votes in an election of a panel of chairmen by STV. Other members to be the chairmen of the other Committees and three persons appointed by the Secretary of State for Northern Ireland from outside the Assembly.

 (iii) All members of the judiciary to be appointed by the Lord Chancellor. Matters affecting security and civil rights to remain for the time being under the control of the Secretary of State, with power to delegate to relevant departments.

 (iv) Westminster to have overriding responsibility for fair and proper standards of government.

  (v) A consultative Joint Council to be set up by the Northern Ireland Finance Committee and the Dublin Government, to investigate the necessity for joint Commissions upon which powers could be conferred by the Dail and the Assembly for specific purposes.

32   To complete this account of the views of the Northern Ireland political parties, mention must be made of the general position of those parties which were not represented at the Darlington Conference and which have not sent to the Secretary of State any detailed, formal proposals for the future:

   (a) the **Nationalist Party** (four Members at Stormont before prorogation) and

   (b) the **Republican Labour Party** (one Member) have consistently seen the future of Northern Ireland in an all-Ireland context.

   (c) the **Democratic Unionist Party** (four Members, two of whom resigned their seats immediately before prorogation) have adopted the general attitude that, since the restoration of the Northern Ireland Parliament with its former powers and status is extremely unlikely Northern Ireland should cease to have any separate legislature or executive of its own, but be fully integrated with the rest of the United Kingdom.†

---

*Reproduced in full in Annex 8.
†The Democratic Unionist Party intend to present their proposals to the Prime Minister. They were not ready in time for inclusion in this Paper.

Other Proposals

33   There are in addition to the political parties in Northern Ireland, other organisations, both inside and outside the Province, which have from time to time expressed views about the future, and accounts have been taken of these views in the analyses in paragraphs 37–64.

34   Some of these organisations have sent specific proposals to the Secretary of State. The **New Ulster Movement** advocates*:

(i) A unicameral Northern Ireland Assembly elected by the STV system of proportional representation, with six or seven Members returned for each of the 12 Westminster constituencies, giving a total of 72–84. A committee system.

(ii) Executive decisions to be made by Committees, with co-ordination through chairmen (posts held in proportion to party strength). Also scope for decentralisation of control to local authorities and delegation to statutory bodies.

(iii) Control of the police to remain in Northern Ireland, provided it is made a fully civilianised force, totally unarmed, clearly separated from the political arena and subject to an effective Police Authority and inspection by the Chief Inspector of Constabulary.

(iv) An Act of Human Rights, to provide for access of aggrieved persons and organisations to a Tribunal modelled on Industrial Tribunals, with a minimum of rules of procedure and an ultimate appeal to a Tribunal made up of Judges drawn equally from Northern Ireland and the Irish Republic.

(v) Recognition by the Irish Republic of the political status in international law of Northern Ireland as a region of the United Kingdom and its right to remain such until a majority of its citizens decide otherwise. Machinery for North-South co-operation and consultation.

35   Nor have the suggestions for the future government of Northern Ireland come only from Northern Ireland parties and organisations. Following an appeal to the people of Northern Ireland by the Secretary of State that they should write to him putting forward their own views, some 2,500 (of which 200 were anonymous) have been sent to him by **individual citizens.** The views expressed in those letters are taken into account in the analyses in paragraphs 37–64.

36   Views have of course also been expressed by parties and interests outside Northern Ireland. The attitude of the **Government** has been consistently to seek by inter-party discussion the widest possible measure

---

*The New Ulster Movement's publication 'A new Constitution for Northern Ireland' is reproduced in full in Annex 9.

of agreement as to how Northern Ireland should in future be governed and how in particular the minority as well as the majority may be assured of an active, permanent and guaranteed role in its life and public affairs. The **Labour Party** have made their own specific proposals for consideration in that context, based on the 15-point plan put forward by the Leader of the Opposition in his House of Commons speech on 25 November 1971 (House of Commons Official Report Vol. 826, No. 18. Columns 1571–1593). Mr. Thorpe, leader of the **Liberal Party** has endorsed the views of the Ulster Liberal Party (which are summarised in paragraph 31, and set out in full in Annex 8).

The Theoretical Possibilities

37   At this stage it is possible to set out the range of possibilities theoretically open before firm decisions on detailed policy are taken. In setting this out account is taken not only of the great volume of specific proposals already published but of parliamentary and constitutional development in other countries, where this appears to be even potentially useful or illuminating.

38   The following paragraphs accordingly set out the major components from which the detailed form of an ultimate settlement will have to be constructed. Paragraphs 39–42 relate to questions of sovereignty and citizenship, paragraphs 43–45 to possible forms of Government of Northern Ireland within the United Kingdom, paragraphs 46–49 to the division of power between United Kingdom and Northern Ireland institutions; and paragraph 50 to the supervision of the exercise of powers by Northern Ireland institutions. Paragraphs 51–63 deal with details of possible Northern Ireland institutions. The proposals for a Bill of Rights are dealt with in paragraph 64.

Sovereignty and Citizenship

39   First there are issues of sovereignty and citizenship concerned with Northern Ireland's status as part of the United Kingdom and its relationship with the rest of Ireland. United Kingdom policy on this matter is governed by the solemn and binding pledges given by successive governments since the decision of what is now the Irish Republic to sever its connections with the Crown and Commonwealth. The pledge was originally expressed by Mr. Attlee as Prime Minister on 28 October 1948 in the words:

> 'The view of HM Government has always been that no change should be made in the constitutional status of Northern Ireland without Northern Ireland's free agreement.'

The pledge was given the form of a statutory declaration by Section 1(2) of the Ireland Act, 1949:

'It is hereby declared that Northern Ireland remains part of His Majesty's dominions and of the United Kingdom and it is hereby affirmed that in no event will Northern Ireland or any part thereof cease to be part of His Majesty's dominions and of the United Kingdom without the consent of the Parliament of Northern Ireland.'

This commitment has since been repeated by all successive Governments and as already noted was incorporated in the Downing Street Declaration* of 20 August 1969. On 15 November 1971 speaking at the Mansion House in London the present Prime Minister used the following words:

'Many Catholics in Northern Ireland would like to see Northern Ireland unified with the South. That is understandable. It is legitimate that they should seek to further that aim by democratic and constitutional means. If at some future date the majority of the people in Northern Ireland want unification and express that desire in the appropriate constitutional manner, I do not believe any British Government would stand in the way. But that is not what the majority want today'.

40   It has been argued that consideration might be given to a partial or incomplete transfer of sovereignty either in geographical terms (ie by transferring to the Irish Republic those parts of Northern Ireland where a majority in favour of such a transfer exists) or in jurisdictional terms (eg by adopting a pattern of joint sovereign responsibility for Northern Ireland as recommended by the Social Democratic and Labour Party or by a scheme of condominium for which there are such precedents as the New Hebrides and Andorra). However neither of these courses if adopted without consent, would be compatible with the express wording of Section 1(2) of the Ireland Act, 1949. Moreover the exponents of a united Ireland all demand a unity of the whole island and show no sign of settling for less: they might well regard the establishment of a predominantly Protestant state as an obstacle to unity.

41   In announcing Direct Rule the Prime Minister stated that in the future periodic plebiscites would be held to allow the people of Northern Ireland to declare their views on the Border issue. Within the context of this general decision, specific decisions will have to be made as to how frequent the plebiscites are to be; what should be asked; and what procedures are to be followed in the event of a majority vote at a future plebiscite in favour of constitutional change.

42   Such then is the present position. The United Kingdom Government is bound both by statute and by clear and repeated pledges to the people of Northern Ireland. It is only in this context that the following selection

---

*See paragraph 21 and footnote.

of theoretically possible courses of action, not all of which are mutually exclusive, can be examined:

(a) Simply to affirm that Northern Ireland is part of the sovereign territory of the United Kingdom and will remain so: and not even to admit the possibility of change at any time. This course is not without its advocates, who argue that Northern Ireland cannot achieve stability as long as its constitutional future appears to be open-ended; but it is difficult to sustain the argument that Northern Ireland is to remain part of the United Kingdom while that is the wish of a majority, if it must also so remain even if a majority wish otherwise.

(b) To admit the possibility of change, either towards Irish unity or some form of condominium; but not specifically to provide for it. This could take the form either of a 'neutral' declaration ('It is for Northern Ireland to make up its mind what it wishes to do, but the United Kingdom Government would not stand in the way in the event of a wish for change') which has, indeed, already been made in substance by United Kingdom Ministers, or of a 'positive' declaration ('The United Kingdom Government would welcome the achievement of Irish unity, but this cannot come about unless and until the people of Northern Ireland freely consent to it').

(c) To admit the possibility of change, and also to provide specific machinery by which it could be achieved in an orderly way, subject to consent. It would be possible, for instance, to lay out a theoretical path towards closer integration, and possible ultimate unity in Ireland, subject to the consent of the people of Northern Ireland as expressed by plebiscite before advancing from one stage to another.

(d) To legislate for future change, either gradual or rapid. It can be argued, however, that it would be wrong to do so if the demand for such change did not first come from a majority of the people in Northern Ireland; and while there has been much discussion of the possibility one day of an all-Ireland State, there are many conflicting ideas as to its form and constitution, and the need for a continuing devolution of powers to Northern Ireland within such a State.

(e) Whether or not any change is made affecting sovereignty or citizenship, nevertheless to recognise that, because of the existence of common problems, some form of joint machinery, either at inter-parliamentary or at inter-governmental level, should be established. There is now much common ground between a number of the Northern Ireland parties on the need for some form of joint Council, although some wish to see a consultative and deliberative Council alone, while others envisage a joint discharge of executive functions. It would be possible to start on the more limited basis and subsequently broaden the powers of a Council by mutual agreement.

Form of government of Northern Ireland within the United Kingdom

43   It is noteworthy that even amongst those who advocate the earliest possible achievement of Irish unity there is a wide measure of agreement that this could not come about for some considerable time. If a plebiscite or other means of determining the wishes of the people of Northern Ireland shows that they wish to remain within the United Kingdom then the question does not arise unless and until a further expression of view shows a different result; but if a desire for unity were to be made manifest at the first plebiscite there is a general recognition that a lengthy process of discussion and negotiation would inevitably follow. Therefore whatever assumption is made about the longer term the immediate question to be determined is how Northern Ireland should be governed so long as it remains a part of the United Kingdom.

44   Insistence upon Northern Ireland as a part of the United Kingdom, involves accepting unequivocally the ultimate sovereign authority, in all circumstances, of the United Kingdom Parliament over Northern Ireland as over all other parts of the country. The question then posed is, what law-making and executive powers (if any) should be devolved upon specifically Northern Ireland institutions?

(a) 'Total integration'

This would mean that laws for Northern Ireland, as for Great Britain, would henceforth be made by the Westminster Parliament, and the prorogued Stormont Parliament would be abolished. Northern Ireland business in the House of Commons might well be dealt with by a Northern Ireland Grand Committee, analogous to the Scottish Grand and Standing Committees. It would follow that there would be no separate Northern Ireland executive, and that all services of central government in Northern Ireland would be the responsibility of the United Kingdom Government. While, in theory, separate departmental structures in Northern Ireland could be abolished and the functions redistributed amongst appropriate United Kingdom Departments, the more promising course would be to entrust the administration of Northern Ireland services to a Secretary of State and subordinate Ministers on a Scottish Office pattern. This course would afford the best opportunity of preserving the considerable administrative benefits of devolution.

In the event of a solution along these lines, it would have to be borne in mind that, when the changes stemming from the Macrory Report are complete, responsibility for certain public services which in the rest of the United Kingdom will continue to rest with local authorities will in Northern Ireland be the responsibility of central government (ie Westminster). In such circumstances, strong arguments would no doubt be advanced for the restoration in Northern Ireland of responsibility for those services to local government and hence for a different pattern of local authorities. However, a re-opening of this issue would not only involve further confusion and uncertainty, to the detriment of services and personnel, but might also involve consideration of further changes, such as the division of Northern Ireland into comparatively few areas, within which elected authorities would exercise quite wide powers. Indeed it has been argued that the problem of participation of the minority in the exercise of power could more realistically be solved by giving control of services to the overall minority in areas where they are a local majority, rather than by seeking to give them a share of power at the centre. In considering the possibility of 'total integration' account must also be taken of the fact that the majority of parties in Northern Ireland are opposed to it, that it would represent a complete reversal of the traditions of half a century, that it would impose a substantial new legislative burden on the Westminster Parliament, and that it would be unacceptable to the Republic of Ireland and would make cooperation with the Republic more difficult.

(b) A purely executive authority (a 'Northern Ireland Council')

This would mean that, while all power to **legislate** for Northern Ireland would be retained at Westminster, as many **executive** functions as possible would be carried out by an elected regional authority for the whole of Northern Ireland. Such an authority might have powers to introduce Private Bills at Westminster. Powers hitherto exercised under the Act of 1920 by the Northern Ireland Government, but considered to be unsuitable for exercise by the authority, would for the most part be exercised by a Secretary of State, though some (such as those connected with social security) might be transferred to appropriate United Kingdom Departments and Ministers. As a minimum the powers of the new authority would extend to the 'top-tier' of services transferred from local authorities to the centre in accordance with the Macrory Report.

(c) A limited law making authority (A 'Northern Ireland Convention')

This would involve the establishment of a Northern Ireland Assembly, which might well have (as in pattern (b) above or otherwise) executive functions, but would also play a part in the making of laws relating exclusively to Northern Ireland. This could involve procedures similar to those contemplated by Sir Alec Douglas-Home's Scottish Constitutional Committee, under which Bills would start and finish their legislative process at Westminster but be taken through intervening stages in a local Convention. Such a Convention could also question a Secretary of State and subordinate Ministers in relation to the exercise of powers reserved to them.

(d) A powerful Legislature and Executive (a Northern Ireland Parliament or Assembly)

This would involve either the restoration of a full-scale Parliament and system of Cabinet government with powers comparable with those

21

hitherto exercised at Stormont, or the creation of a new Assembly and Executive capable both of enacting laws and of administering the public services within the powers devolved upon them.

45 With the exception of Course (a), each of the solutions discussed in paragraph 44 has certain elements of 'integration' (reservation of power to the United Kingdom Parliament and Government) and certain elements of 'devolution' (grant of power to Northern Ireland institutions)—but the balance between reservation and devolution of power differs from one model to another.

Division of powers between United Kingdom and Northern Ireland institutions

46 The division of powers is clearly bound up with the view taken on the question of forms of government (paragraphs 44 and 45), but it also involves the separate consideration both of the extent of powers (which functions should be allocated to Northern Ireland institutions?) and the degree of supervision of them by Westminster (how genuinely autonomous ought the exercise of the devolved powers to be?).

Extent of powers.

47 There are a number of different aspects from which this problem has been considered by interests in Northern Ireland:

(a) There is first, what may be described as the **'argument from Macrory'**, which proceeds from the contention that the entire scheme of reorganisation of local government recommended by the Macrory Report assumed the existence of Stormont as a top-tier authority in relation to services transferred from local government, and that therefore any new institutions should as a minimum have power to deal with those services as Stormont would have done.

(b) There is the **'argument from social values'**, which maintains that Northern Ireland ought to have the power to preserve conditions of social behaviour generally acceptable to its own citizens, even where these are different from those in Great Britain (so that laws relating to issues such as abortion or divorce could reflect local religious or other standards): however, it may be noted that the Northern Ireland Labour Party, in its published proposals, took precisely the opposite view.

(c) There is the **'argument for the preservation of distinctive patterns of administration'**, which proceeds from the contention that in Northern Ireland many services, because of special local conditions or special efforts to overcome local problems, have been developed along distinctive lines and that the ability to do this, and to preserve such advantages as Northern Ireland may gain thereby, should not be lost.

(d) There is, as a converse, the **'argument against the retention of meaningless powers'**, based on the view that it is pointless for Northern Ireland to retain notional powers to do something different from Great Britain (eg in relation to the cash social services) while in practice to have to do very much the same things because Northern Ireland alone does not have the economic or other resources necessary to follow a different and autonomous policy.

48   Much the most difficult decisions relate to the issues of finance and of what might be called **divisive powers**: part I of this Paper has sought to illustrate how, in practice, the operation of certain powers in Northern Ireland proved controversial and divisive. The matters involved included electoral law and boundaries, the courts and the general administration of justice, security and public order, emergency powers and the police. This cannot be an exhaustive list, for in a divided and tense society almost any matter can be made an occasion of conflict, but it does include those matters which have occasioned much bitterness. Strong arguments have accordingly been advanced either that all or most of these powers should be excluded from the responsibilities of any new institutions in Northern Ireland, or that at the least their exercise should be subject to the most stringent controls and safeguards against any possible abuse. It is argued that, if any new constitution for Northern Ireland permits majority government, the majority may use such powers oppressively or discriminatorily; and that if, on the other hand, a new constitution seeks to promote broadly-based government, the exercise of the divisive powers would submit such a government to intolerable strains. On the other hand, there are those who argue, in relation to the 'law and order' powers in particular, that these are fundamental to the operation of anything which can be characterised as a government; or, that the more real and pressing problems are, the more important it is to force representatives of the community concerned to face up to them. It is not the purpose of this Paper to strike a balance now between these conflicting arguments; but in considering questions of security, the overall responsibility of the central government for the defence of the realm and the operation of the armed forces must be taken fully into account.

49   Finally, there is the question of **finance**. Here there is a strong theoretical argument that any Northern Ireland institutions with appreciable functions will not be capable of developing real political responsibility, imagination and courage unless they also have to provide the resources for carrying them out. But the hard logic of the situation must be faced. To meet this requirement it would be necessary either to supplement Northern Ireland's own resources with large unconditional grants (and it may be questioned whether any United Kingdom Parliament

could or would provide additional assistance on a massive scale automatically and without conditions), or to reduce Northern Ireland's expenditure to relate it to the area's true means involving radical reduction in all public expenditure and a failure to maintain parity of standards with the rest of the United Kingdom. As an alternative to either of these radical courses, it would be possible to continue to provide assistance to Northern Ireland for the financing of agreed programmes and to explore the scope for giving the Northern Ireland institutions the power to make their own decisions within defined financial limits.

Supervision of powers

50   It should be appreciated that the devolution of powers to subordinate institutions does not leave these institutions completely free to exercise such powers as they wish. Under the Act of 1920 as it stands, the sovereign authority of the Westminster Parliament is expressly saved by Section 75, the courts may review the validity of Acts of the Northern Ireland Parliament, and certain constitutional questions may be referred to the Judicial Committee of the Privy Council. Under his Instructions the Governor may reserve the Royal Assent to a Northern Ireland Bill, and there was one such case, although the Bill in question was eventually allowed to become law. There are other possible patterns of supervision. Any Acts passed by the legislatures of the Channel Islands and the Isle of Man are subject to the approval of Her Majesty in Council and the Crown acts through the Privy Council on the recommendation of United Kingdom Ministers. This might be described as 'governmental supervision'. Another theoretical device would be 'parliamentary supervision' by which the legislation of a Northern Ireland Parliament or Assembly (or defined categories thereof, possibly within the fields described earlier as 'divisive') would either require an affirmative resolution at Westminster to be given the force of law, or could be 'prayed against' within a prescribed time. (These parliamentary sanctions at present exist in relation to Northern Ireland legislation during the currency of the Northern Ireland (Temporary Provisions) Act by way of Orders in Council.) Other theoretical possibilities indicate supervision by some form of joint United Kingdom/Northern Ireland Parliamentary Commission, or by a 'Council of State' of Northern Ireland notables appointed by the Crown or United Kingdom Government.

Northern Ireland Institutions

51   The complex question of the form, structure, composition and functioning of a Northern Ireland Parliament or Assembly and executive is again inter-related with the questions already discussed. Separate analysis is, however, required of four distinct but related questions—the form, etc., of any representative assembly in Northern Ireland; the form, etc., of the executive in Northern Ireland; the form of local government in Northern Ireland and its relationship to the Assembly and the Executive; and the implications of these three questions for the relationship

between the Assembly and the Executive on the one hand, and Westminster on the other.

52   **A Representative Assembly: Form of Assembly.** It will be seen from the submissions of some of the parties that there is a view that any new legislature should not be called a Parliament. It is argued that the title and the adoption of elaborate Westminster procedures have not only been out of proportion to the real functions independently performed and to the size of population covered by them, so that these arrangements have led to what may be described as 'over-government', but also have promoted a false view of 'Stormont sovereignty' which has been positively harmful. Amongst those who hold this view there is strong support for the title of 'Assembly'. The Ulster Unionist Party does not share this view, and its proposals call for the continuation of a Northern Ireland Parliament. They share with others, however, the opinion that there should henceforth be a **single chamber legislature,** with membership of the order of 72–100. There appears to be comparatively little support for a second chamber in a new structure although, in considering the range of theoretical options, it should be appreciated that the second chamber is used in a number of jurisdictions to give particular interests a weight they would not achieve through a popular-elected chamber based on universal suffrage, and/or to allow measures to be blocked by the second chamber so weighted. A second chamber is also frequently used to introduce into parliamentary life the representatives of certain broad 'interests' (as, indeed, is the case in the Senate of the Republic of Ireland). It would also be possible, though some would object in principle to the dilution of the popular mandate, to nominate to a single chamber Assembly (or to its Committees) representatives of important interests or of communities under-represented following an election.

53   The nature of an Assembly may also be influenced by the basis and method of **elections** to it; and it is apparent from the submissions of the political parties that there is a good deal of support for the use in Northern Ireland of the Single Transferable Vote (STV) system of proportional representation (although the Ulster Unionist Party, in recommending a chamber of some 100 members, notes that this increase 'would reduce the need for proportional representation since there would be fewer wasted majorities'). Another theoretical possibility is the use of separate or multiple voting rolls. This mechanism assures a minority community of adequate representation, but it does so at considerable risk of entrenching divisions and encouraging polarisation.

54   As to the **method of working** of an Assembly, again there is considerable agreement amongst the Northern Ireland political parties that there should be a highly-developed system of functional Committees, and some have advocated that the chairmanships of such Committees should be shared amongst the parties, rather than concentrated in majority hands. While the post of chairman is obviously one of real influence and impor-

tance, and the more so if Committees have really significant executive as distinct from advisory or consultative responsibilities, the establishment of a committee system does not of itself assure the participation of minorities in the exercise of power. It is the normal practice, both in parliamentary and local government, that Committees should constitute a microcosm of the whole body, with the majority of the whole constituting also a majority of each Committee. Thus, the application to Northern Ireland of a system of committee government would make the application of executive power less concentrated, but in the last resort matters put to a vote would be carried by the elected majority. This would be true whether the Committees served as a check on the executive (as the Ulster Unionist Party proposes) or themselves constituted the executive (as proposed by other parties).

56   There are various forms of blocking mechanism inside or outside an Assembly, some of which (such as a Council of State or a degree of supervision by the Sovereign Parliament or Government) have already been mentioned. There are also a number of overseas precedents. Thus, in Belgium, with its problem of linguistic divisions, three-quarters of either language group in Parliament can cause any draft legislation to be referred back to the Council of Ministers if it is considered harmful to intercommunal relations. In Switzerland, any law passed by the Federal Assembly may be made the subject of a national referendum if 30,000 eligible voters so request within 90 days.

57   **The Executive.** Here the crucial question is whether, in addition to any heightening of their influence, it is desirable and possible to secure the participation of the Northern Ireland minority in the actual exercise of executive powers. On the one hand, it can be argued that in Northern Ireland, as in many other democracies, those who represent a majority in the legislature should have the right to form the government; that any form of coalition tends to provide weak and indecisive government, and all the more so if it comes about artificially, rather than by the voluntary collaboration of parties with real mutual interest; that the underlying problem of Northern Ireland can only be solved by the slow and steady evolution of new party structures rooted in both communities: and that, bearing in mind the real practical problems which must be solved in Northern Ireland, it would be dangerous to make complex arrangements which can be manipulated to produce deadlock and frustration.

58   On the other hand, it can be argued that the British democratic system only works where a regular alternation of parties is possible; that the real test of a democratic system is its ability to provide peaceful and orderly government, and that by that standard the existing system has failed in Northern Ireland; that other countries with divided communities

have made special constitutional provision to ensure participation by all; that a number of these countries have had stable and successful coalition governments over many years; and that there is no hope of binding the minority to the support of new political arrangements in Northern Ireland unless they are admitted to active participation in any new structures.

59   If the need for actual participation is accepted, there are a number of ways in which it might in practice be achieved. Reference has already been made to the proposal that executive powers in Northern Ireland should be exercised through a structure of Committees, and of the difficulty that, while this would increase the active part played by minority interests, it would not in the last resort prevent decisions being taken on a majority vote, if in the event decisions developed along party lines. If, on the other hand, Northern Ireland were to continue to have Cabinet Government, other considerations would apply. In other jurisdictions, a broad basis of government is sometimes achieved by convention and sometimes by formal constitutional provision.

60   Apart from what may be described as 'committee government', which has already been discussed, there are at least four theoretical means of securing a broadly-based administration in Northern Ireland.

(a) 'Entrenched government', whereby certain minority elements must by constitutional requirement be included in a government. This course could present very difficult problems of definition, and impede the development of non-sectarian party structures.

(b) 'Proportional Representation government', whereby all substantial elements elected to the legislature would, in proportion to their representative strengths, secure representation in a government. This course could, however, exclude the possibility of any Opposition as currently understood in the legislature and would not be made easier by the very broad range of political opinion.

(c) 'Bloc government', whereby the party or parties commanding a majority in the legislature would be required to coalesce with the party or parties commanding a majority of the minority. This would ensure some residual opposition, and make possible the exclusion of small irresponsible groups on the extreme wings of politics, but it in practice would be apt to prove a somewhat complex, inflexible and artificial device.

(d) 'Weighted majority government', whereby an incoming government would require the endorsement of the legislature not by a simple majority, but by a majority so weighted as to make necessary a broad range of support. In order to ensure that support would not come from representatives of a single community, the percentage required could hardly be less than 75. The requirements of a weighted majority could be applied solely to the endorsement of a government and subsequent votes of confidence, or to a wider range of parliamentary business.

61   It must be recognised that there is, in the use of any of these devices, an inherent danger that any major political element could choose, for its own purposes, to bring the system to a standstill. Any such system would therefore have to be under-pinned by clear, swift and efficient procedures for the resolution of disputes and the exercise of reserve powers: and such procedures carry the dangerous dilemma that if the political groupings are deadlocked, the holder of reserve powers must either override them or allow the deadlock to persist.

62   **Local Government.** In the context of any system of administration in Northern Ireland, account must clearly be taken of the 'Macrory' re-organisation of local services. The restructuring of local government in Northern Ireland, as in many other cases, proved a difficult and time-consuming affair: there were a number of false starts before the Macrory review body completed its report* in 1970. This scheme of local government adopted on the basis of this report was to reduce the existing, basically two-tier structure of local government to a single-tier system of 26 elected district councils exercising local environmental powers: while large scale regional services were to be transferred to the central government, to be managed either directly (eg water, sewerage, roads, electoral arrangements) or through Area Boards (personal social services, education and libraries). Plans had already been made to transfer housing administration to a statutory body, the Housing Executive. When the Northern Ireland Parliament was prorogued some of the measures necessary to carry these reforms into effect had already been enacted, some were in the process of passing through that Parliament, and others had still to be introduced. Planning for the detailed implementation of the new structure was far advanced and the uncertainty about local government could not be allowed to persist for much length without serious risk to its future viability. In these circumstances, the United Kingdom Government decided that the reorganisation programme should continue, and be carried through to completion, under the temporary powers granted by Parliament. While it would be theoretically possible, after the reorganisation takes full effect next year, to 'unscramble' it again, there are extremely strong arguments against doing so, if the efficiency of the public services and the morale of those 60,000 people involved in the operation of them are not to be impaired. It was an inherent part of the 'Macrory' structure that the Northern Ireland Parliament would constitute a top-tier authority of democratic scrutiny and control of services to be managed henceforth

---

*Report of the Review Body on Local Government in Northern Ireland 1970—Cmnd. 546 of 1970.

on a Province-wide basis; and there is a need for a central body capable of carrying out that particular function.

63　**Representation of Northern Ireland interests in the United Kingdom Parliament and Government.** Consideration of the number of Members sent by Northern Ireland to the Parliament at Westminster would rest on a number of factors including the extent of powers devolved upon Northern Ireland; the basis of election to Westminster (whether the same as for the rest of the United Kingdom, or the same as at other Northern Ireland elections even if these are conducted on a different basis); and the nature and extent of Westminster involvement in matters covered by devolved powers. Taking into account the nature of any institutions proposed for Northern Ireland and of the powers to be given to them, arrangements will also have to be made to ensure the continuing effective representation of Northern Ireland interest within the United Kingdom Government. Moreover, the United Kingdom Government will clearly have a major continuing interest in Northern Ireland which must be recognised by suitable machinery of government in Belfast.

Bill of Rights

64　Finally there is a wide body of opinion that a **Bill of Rights** should be enacted in Northern Ireland. There is much to commend this suggestion but in devising any Bill of Rights certain fundamental problems must first be faced, such as what rights are to be enshrined; whether they should be protected through the Courts or by a body specially set up for that purpose; how to secure practical, effective and speedy means of redress and compensation; and how to deal with those who consistently and deliberately infringe the rights of others. What is essential is that any provisions which might be incorporated in legislation should have a practical and not just a declaratory effect.

PART III   TOWARDS A SETTLEMENT

Some Basic Facts

65   Part I has dealt with the development of the present situation, and Part II with the proposals and possibilities available to those who must determine the way forward. This part of the Paper, while not setting out to pre-judge the ultimate form of a settlement, places on record some unalterable facts about the situation, and some vital conditions which must be met.

66   **The financing of services in Northern Ireland.** Northern Ireland contains 35 per cent of the population of the whole of Ireland, and 2·5 per cent of the population of the British Isles. Average earnings per head in April 1971 were only 85 per cent of the average in Great Britain, and unemployment percentages have also consistently been higher than in Great Britain.

67   Such a community has required, and has received in common with other less prosperous areas substantial material support from the United Kingdom as a whole. This has taken many different forms: details of the financial arrangements are given in the White Paper 'Northern Ireland: Financial Arrangements and Legislation' (Cmnd. 4998), in paragraph 15 of which it is demonstrated that special payments and subsidies amounted to some £125 million in 1971/2, while loan advances to the Northern Ireland Government amounted to £65 million, and both sums were expected to increase. The combined total of special payments, subsidies, and loan advances from the National Loans Fund, is estimated to amount to around £300 million in the current year, of which loan advances represent an amount of the order of £100 million. In addition, industries vital to Northern Ireland, particularly shipbuilding and aircraft, have been given financial support by Westminster. It must, of course, be remembered that the people of Northern Ireland bear tax obligations virtually identical with those borne by their fellow-citizens in Great Britain, and have made their own distinctive contributions in peace and in war to the progress, life and survival of the whole nation.

68   **The Armed Forces.** More recently, the assistance has gone far beyond the provision of financial and economic aid. Since August 1969, when it became apparent that the existing forces of law and order were unable (for whatever reasons) to control a deteriorating security situation, an increasing military commitment became inevitable. On the eve of the disorders in August 1969 the strength of the Army in Northern Ireland stood at some 3,000 men; on 12 July 1970, at 13,000; on the day of internment, 9 August 1971, at some 14,000; and on the day of Operation

Motorman on 31 July 1972, at about 21,000 men. This very large increase is indicative of the determination of successive United Kingdom Governments to provide the security forces with sufficient strength to deal with violence and the threat of violence from whatever quarter, despite the penalties which this carries in terms of cost and the stretching of the Army's resources (to the extent that it has been necessary on occasions to deploy temporarily in Northern Ireland units which form part of the United Kingdom's NATO commitment): and the cost is not confined to penalties of this kind—by 1 October 1972, Regular Army casualties in Northern Ireland stood at 132 dead and 880 wounded.

69   It may be argued by some people in Northern Ireland that the situation could, and should, have been dealt with by security forces responsible to the Northern Ireland Government. It should be remembered in this context that the commitment of the Army in aid of the civil power came about only at the request of the Northern Ireland Government and after the civil power in Northern Ireland had failed to contain the situation by use of the regular and reserve forces available to it. It must also be emphasised that this commitment preceded the Hunt Report and the subsequent reorganisation of the police. Nor could the situation as it has since developed have been met other than by the raising of a local full-time military force, which is outside the constitutional competence of the Parliament and Government of Northern Ireland.

70   As in the financial and economic fields, so in the security field the support accorded to Northern Ireland is what its inhabitants (many of whom have themselves served with distinction in the Armed Forces) have a right to expect as citizens of the United Kingdom; but its extent is not always adequately appreciated.

71   Moreover, it is quite apparent that, once peace and stability in Northern Ireland have been restored, its rehabilitation and the restoration of its full potential for social and economic growth will involve an invest-ment of national economic resources on a very substantial scale. The mere task of replacing and compensation for what has been damaged or destroyed will be enormous, but beyond this lies the still more demanding work of recreating confidence and the capacity to attract new investment at the high rate required. These tasks will demand an effort not just by Northern Ireland but by the United Kingdom as a whole.

72   **The interdependence of Northern Ireland.** Any proposed political settlement which considered Northern Ireland in isolation would be unrealistic. In a world of growing inter-dependence, where even the aspirations of major sovereign powers can only be fully met by their participation in wider associations and communities, a small area such as Northern Ireland cannot, without the gravest consequences for its own citizens, make its way alone. Even if it were feasible for Northern Ireland

so to reduce its expenditures as to be able to live within its own real means—and such a reduction would greatly lower the standards of life and of services enjoyed by the whole community—it would remain dependent upon external investment and external trade, and upon its standing and credit-worthiness in the European and the wider international communities.

73   Northern Ireland cannot expect a form of independence which would guarantee substantial continuing financial, economic and military aid from the United Kingdom but which would otherwise confer upon it virtually sovereign status. No United Kingdom Government could be a party to such a settlement. It may be argued by some that if Northern Ireland was prepared to accept a drastic fall in the standards of living and services it could in that sense be viable though at a very high cost to all its people; but that is too limited a view. Such a form of government could not be viable in a much more fundamental sense, that of being a state commanding the loyalty of the overwhelming majority of its own citizens and the acceptance and respect of the international community.

The United Kingdom Interest

74   Division and disorder in Northern Ireland are liabilities both to that Province and to the United Kingdom as a whole; and in seeking to restore order and resume progress there the United Kingdom Government are serving both the national interest and the true interest of all the people of Northern Ireland. The United Kingdom Government has three major concerns in Northern Ireland. First, that it should be internally at peace— a divided and strife-ridden Province is bound to disturb and weaken the whole Kingdom. Second, that it should prosper, so as to contribute to and not detract from the prosperity of the whole. Third, that Northern Ireland should not offer a base for any external threat to the security of the United Kingdom. In pursuing these objectives, the Government will wish to consider at all times the views and interests in Northern Ireland and to take them as fully as possible into account. So long as Northern Ireland remains part of the United Kingdom, the United Kingdom Parliament must be the sovereign authority over all persons, matters and things in Northern Ireland, and the ultimate acceptance of that authority must be a necessary condition of the financial, economic and military assistance from which Northern Ireland benefits as a part of the United Kingdom. While such assistance continues, or may be required in the future, no Government could recommend a settlement to Parliament which did not give the Government an effective voice in the use to which it is put.

75   A recognition of the right of self-determination of the people of Northern Ireland does not exclude the legitimate interest of other parties.

To say that it would be wrong to terminate the relationship between Northern Ireland and the rest of the United Kingdom against the wishes of a majority in Northern Ireland is not to say that it is for Northern Ireland alone to determine how it shall be governed as a part of the United Kingdom, since its association with Great Britain involves rights and obligations on both sides; it is to say that insistence upon membership of the United Kingdom carries with it the obligations of membership including acceptance of the sovereignty of Parliament as representing the people as a whole.

The Irish Dimension

76   A settlement must also recognise Northern Ireland's position within Ireland as a whole. The guarantee to the people of Northern Ireland that the status of Northern Ireland as part of the United Kingdom will not be changed without their consent is an absolute: this pledge cannot and will not be set aside. Nevertheless it is a fact that Northern Ireland is part of the geographical entity of Ireland; that it shares with the Republic of Ireland common problems, such as the under-development of western areas; and that, in the context of membership of the European Communities, Northern Ireland and the Republic will have certain common difficulties and opportunities which will differ in some respects from those which will face Great Britain. It is also a fact that an element of the minority in Northern Ireland has hitherto seen itself as simply a part of the wider Irish community. The problem of accommodating that minority within the political structures of Northern Ireland has to some considerable extent been an aspect of a wider problem within Ireland as a whole. Even if the minority had themselves been more disposed, and more encouraged than they were, to accept the settlement of 1920, they would still have been subject to those powerful influences which regard the unification of Ireland as 'unfinished business', declined to accept the institutions of Northern Ireland as legitimate, and were made manifest in the Irish Constitution of 1937. As long as such influences continue to exist they are bound to be a powerful factor to be taken into account in the search for stability in Northern Ireland. Moreover the problem of political terrorism, which has reached such proportions in Northern Ireland today, has always had manifestations throughout the island (although, of course, the great majority of those who wish to see the unification of Ireland do not advocate or approve of the use of violence to achieve it).

77   No United Kingdom Government for many years has had any wish to impede the realisation of Irish unity, if it were to come about by genuine and freely given mutual agreement and on conditions acceptable to the distinctive communities. Indeed the Act of 1920 itself, which has for so many years been the foundation of Northern Ireland's constitutional status, explicitly provided means to move towards ultimate unity on just

such a basis; but the will to work this was never present. It is a matter of historical fact that this failure stemmed from decisions and actions taken, not only in Great Britain and Northern Ireland but in the Republic of Ireland also.

78 Whatever arrangements are made for the future administration of Northern Ireland must take account of the Province's relationship with the Republic of Ireland: and to the extent that this is done, there is an obligation upon the Republic to reciprocate. Both the economy and the security of the two areas are to some considerable extent inter-dependent, and the same is true of both in their relationship with Great Britain. It is therefore clearly desirable that any new arrangements for Northern Ireland should, whilst meeting the wishes of Northern Ireland and Great Britain, be so far as possible acceptable to and accepted by the Republic of Ireland which from 1 January 1973, will share the rights and obligations of membership of the European Communities. It remains the view of the United Kingdom Government that it is for the people of Northern Ireland to decide what should be their relationship to the United Kingdom and to the Republic of Ireland: and that it should not be impossible to devise measures which will meet the best interests of all three. Such measures would seek to secure the acceptance, in both Northern Ireland and in the Republic, of the present status of Northern Ireland, and of the possibility—which would have to be compatible with the principle of consent—of subsequent change in that status; to make possible effective consultation and co-operation in Ireland for the benefit of North and South alike; and to provide a firm basis for concerted governmental and community action against those terrorist organisations which represent a threat to free democratic institutions in Ireland as a whole.

PART IV   THE WAY FORWARD

79   What conclusions may be drawn from the foregoing review of fact or opinion about the future shape of the administration of Northern Ireland? In general, there are widely-differing views about the desirable functions, powers and form of an assembly or authority, and its precise relationship with the sovereign Parliament and Government of the United Kingdom. At the one extreme, the argument is for a substantial form of regional authority; at the other, for a Parliament which would not only have the existing powers of the Northern Ireland Parliament but would be in a position to exercise them more freely. This is not the appropriate stage at which to form a final judgment on these matters, but in the view of Her Majesty's Government any firm proposals must meet the following criteria:—

(a) In accordance with the specific pledges given by successive United Kingdom Governments, Northern Ireland must and will remain part of the United Kingdom for as long as that is the wish of a majority of the people; but that status does not preclude the necessary taking into account of what has been described in this Paper as the 'Irish Dimension'.

(b) As long as Northern Ireland remains part of the United Kingdom the sovereignty of the United Kingdom Parliament must be acknowledged, and due provision made for the United Kingdom Government to have an effective and continuing voice in Northern Ireland's affairs, commensurate with the commitment of financial, economic and military resources in the Province.

(c) Any division of powers and responsibilities between the national and the regional authorities must be logical, open and clearly understood. Ambiguity in the relationship is a prescription for confusion and misunderstanding. Any necessary checks, balances or controls must be apparent on the face of a new constitutional scheme.

(d) The two primary purposes of any new institutions must be first to seek a much wider consensus than has hitherto existed; and second to be such as will work efficiently and will be capable of providing the concrete results of good government: peace and order, physical development, social and economic progress. This is fundamental because Northern Ireland's problems flow not just from a clash of national aspirations or from friction between the communities, but also from social and economic conditions such as inadequate housing and unemployment.

(e) Any new institutions must be of a simple and businesslike character, appropriate to the powers and functions of a regional authority.

(f) A Northern Ireland assembly or authority must be capable of involving all its members constructively in ways which satisfy them and those they represent that the whole community has a part to play in the government of the Province. As a minimum this would involve assuring minority groups of an effective voice and a real influence; but there are strong arguments that the objective of real participation should be achieved by giving minority interests a share in the exercise of executive power if this can be achieved by means which are not unduly complex or artificial, and which do not represent an obstacle to effective government.

(g) There must be an assurance, built into any new structures, that there will be absolute fairness and equality of opportunity for all. The future administration of Northern Ireland must be seen to be completely even-handed both in law and in fact.

(h) It is of great importance that future arrangements for security and public order in Northern Ireland must command public confidence, both in Northern Ireland itself, and in the United Kingdom as a whole. If they are to do so they must be seen in practice to be as impartial and effective as possible in restoring and maintaining peace and public order. In any situation such as that which obtains at present, where the Army and the civilian police force are both involved in maintaining law and order and combating terrorism, it is essential that there should be a single source of direct responsibility. Since Westminster alone can control the Armed Forces of the Crown this unified control must mean Westminster control. For the future any arrangements must ensure that the United Kingdom Government has an effective and a determining voice in relation to any circumstances which involve, or may involve in the future, the commitment of the Armed Forces, the use of emergency powers, or repercussions at international level.

80   The objective now must be to advance as rapidly as possible towards the preparation of a comprehensive new scheme for the government of Northern Ireland which will satisfy these fundamental conditions.

81   The period of one year for which, unless extended, the Northern Ireland (Temporary Provisions) Act 1972, remains in force, comes to an end on 30 March 1973. While it is possible to extend its application for a further limited period until more permanent arrangements are made, there are strong grounds for keeping such a period to a minimum. The temporary arrangements for the discharge of both law-making and executive responsibilities are not suitable for long-term use. In particular, it would be unsatisfactory to continue indefinitely making important legislative provision for Northern Ireland by way of Orders in Council. Moreover, continuing uncertainty about the future is unsettling to the public service, and can feed the fears and suspicions of a wider public.

82 As the Government move towards a settlement they will of course wish to continue to take Northern Ireland opinion fully into account. The wishes of the people of Northern Ireland on their relationship to the United Kingdom and to the Republic will be ascertained by a plebiscite early in the New Year. But it will be essential for the formulation of new arrangements to hold further and separate consultations on the issues and options set out in this Paper, with the object of discovering how far the various strands of opinion can be brought together into a broad consensus. Such a process must of its nature be pragmatic and must take a form which permits those who accept the need for peaceful discussion to take part.

83 When the process of consultation has been completed, the United Kingdom Government have the responsibility of putting forward proposals, and of recommending them to Parliament. They will do this in the knowledge that there is no definite answer to questions as difficult and long-standing as these; no panacea which can transform strife into harmony. Whatever the constitutional arrangements may be, many difficult practical problems will remain. There is not least the great need to rid Northern Ireland of the presence and threat of violence. Both political theory and practical experience show that no scheme of government, however carefully drawn, can do more than present an opportunity for progress. It is in the hearts and minds of the people of Northern Ireland, and not just in the aims of Government or the words of Acts of Parliament, that the capacity for working and living together must flourish. For the ultimate truth is that the people of Northern Ireland need each other, and that to squander their great talents in bitter conflict is to diminish the prospects of them all. It is the profound wish and hope of the United Kingdom Government that this fundamental truth will be recognised, and will be the basis on which all concerned will take part in the further consultations for which this Paper is intended to provide a basis.

ANNEXES

THE GOVERNMENT OF IRELAND ACT, 1920: THE ORIGINAL SCHEME OF GOVERNMENT

1   The main points of the Act of 1920 as it came into force in Northern Ireland were as follows:—

  (i) It provided for the establishment in Belfast of a bicameral Parliament, consisting of a 52 member House of Commons elected by Proportional Representation, and a Senate of 26 Members, 24 elected by the Members of the Northern Ireland House of Commons and two (the Lord Mayor of Belfast and Mayor of Londonderry) sitting ex officio.

 (ii) This Parliament was given a general power to make laws for 'the peace, order and good government' of Northern Ireland, subject to certain specific reservations, conditions and safeguards. In particular:—

    (a) The Act specifically reserved to the Parliament of the United Kingdom certain powers principally relating to the Armed Forces, the Crown, and international matters.

    (b) The fiscal powers of the Northern Ireland Parliament were severely restricted by the reservation to the Parliament of the United Kingdom of power to levy income tax and customs and excise duties.

    (c) The Northern Ireland Parliament was specifically prohibited from making laws and the Northern Ireland Government from taking administrative action other than on a basis of religious equality.

    (d) Section 75 of the Act provided that:

        'the supreme authority of the Parliament of the United Kingdom shall remain unaffected and undiminished over all persons, matters and things in [Northern] Ireland and every part thereof'.

(iii) The Governor of Northern Ireland, in whom the executive powers of the Northern Ireland Parliament were vested, was 'aided and advised' by the executive committee of the Privy Council, or Cabinet consisting of Ministers of Northern Ireland.

 (iv) Northern Ireland was to be represented in the Parliament of the United Kingdom by 12 Members for territorial constituencies and one for the Queen's University of Belfast.

  (v) Northern Ireland was to make towards 'Imperial liabilities and expenditure, a 'just' contribution having regard to the relative taxable capacities of Northern Ireland and the United Kingdom as a whole.

2   The Act also made provision for a Council of Ireland, whose purpose was

defined in the Explanatory Memorandum to the Government of Ireland Bill in the following terms:—

> 'Although at the beginning there are to be two Parliaments and two Governments in Ireland, the Act contemplates and affords every facility for union between North and South, and empowers the two Parliaments by mutual agreement and joint action to terminate partition and to set up one Parliament and one Government for the whole of Ireland. With a view to the eventual establishment of a single Parliament, and to bringing about harmonious action between the two Parliaments and Governments, there is created a bond of union in the meantime by means of a Council of Ireland, which is to consist of 20 representatives elected by each Parliament, and a President nominated by the Lord Lieutenant. It will fall to the members of this body to initiate proposals for united action on the part of the two Parliaments and to bring forward these proposals in the respective Parliaments.'

The Act reserved certain specific but limited matters to the Council, provided that the Belfast and Dublin Parliaments might confer additional functions upon it by identical legislation, and charged it with the specific duty of considering what further matters might, in the general interest of the whole of Ireland, best be administered on a central basis rather than by the two separate administrations.

DEVELOPMENTS IN NORTH-SOUTH RELATIONS

1   As noted in Annex 1, the Government of Ireland Act, 1920 included provisions to establish a Council of Ireland as a means to facilitate unity between the Parliaments and Governments to be set up with equal powers and status, both within the United Kingdom.

2   The Act came into force in May 1921, but the Parliament of Southern Ireland never effectively met, because of the massive swing of public opinion in the South behind the much more radical separatist aims of Sinn Fein. As a result, the Southern membership of the Council of Ireland was never elected.

3   The 'truce' of July 1921 was followed by further discussions between British representatives and the representatives of Sinn Fein, leading eventually to the conclusion of the treaty which received parliamentary confirmation in the Irish Free State (Agreement) Act 1922. This agreement granted dominion status to the whole of Ireland, but allowed to Northern Ireland the option (which was swiftly exercised) of remaining outside the new Irish State and retaining the system of government established by the Act of 1920, including the provisions relating to the Council of Ireland, slightly amended to take account of the constitutional changes in the South. However, although the Parliament of Northern Ireland appointed its representatives to the Council as early as June 1921, the new Parliament or Oireachtas of the Irish Free State never reciprocated. Thus the Council did not function, and the matters specifically reserved to it by the Act of 1920 were for a time exercised in Belfast by a United Kingdom official known as the Imperial Secretary.

4   The treaty had also provided for a Boundary Commission to consider adjustment of the border between North and South, taking account as far as possible of the wishes of the inhabitants; and the parties to the agreement appear to have had somewhat different impressions of the likely outcome, with the Irish representatives apparently anticipating, or at least hoping for, a substantial contraction of the area and population of Northern Ireland. The establishment of the Commission was attended by various difficulties, but eventually it carried out its work and completed its award under the Chairmanship of the South African judge, Mr Justice Feetham. The nature of the award (which transferred to the Irish Free State some comparatively limited areas of Northern Ireland, but which also transferred to Northern Ireland less extensive areas of the Free State) was a grave disappointment to the Dublin Government and in the event it was agreed between the British, Northern Irish and Irish Free State Governments that the Report should not be published, but that the existing boundary should be re-affirmed. This agreement (endorsed by the Ireland (Confirmation of Agreement) Act, 1925) also pledged the two Irish Governments to a friendly and neighbourly relationship to be underpinned by regular cross-border meetings.

5   The expectations prompted by this agreement were not fulfilled, and in 1937 there was promulgated a new Irish Constitution, which proclaimed that the 'national territory' consisted of the whole island of Ireland. The growing gulf between North and South was further accentuated when the Irish Government remained neutral throughout the Second World War. In 1948 that Government decided to sever its links with the Crown and Commonwealth and to establish an Irish Republic. In the subsequent United Kingdom legislation made necessary by these developments (the Ireland Act, 1949), Parliament affirmed that Northern Ireland remained part of the United Kingdom, and that neither Northern Ireland as a whole nor any part thereof should cease to be part of the United Kingdom without the consent of the Northern Ireland Parliament.

6   While the progressive withdrawal of what had been the Irish Free State from its formal associations with the British Commonwealth and the Crown inevitably changed the nature of partition, this did not prevent in the post-war era the development of certain measures of practical co-operation between the Governments in Ireland—as, for example, in the establishment of the Lough Foyle Fisheries Commission, the Erne drainage and hydro-electricity scheme, and joint action to save the Great Northern Railway. In 1965 meetings took place between the Prime Ministers of Northern Ireland and of the Irish Republic leading to a closer co-operation in tourist promotion and other areas and to the establishment of an inter-connector between the two electricity systems.

7   Relations between Northern Ireland and the Irish Republic were affected by the periodic activity of militant republican elements. At its inception Northern Ireland had suffered the impact of a major terrorist campaign; the threat of renewed violence was felt to be ever present, and indeed became a reality at different times, as for example between 1956 and 1962. Frequently this activity took the form of armed raids across the border, and the headquarters of the Irish Republican Army was throughout based in the South. Although firm action (including, for instance, the use of internment powers between 1957 and 1961) was from time to time taken in the Republic, the IRA remained a continuing threat. In the current troubles in Northern Ireland, terrorists based in the Republic, some of them fugitives from Northern Ireland, have continued to make armed raids across the border.

THE REFORM PROGRAMME 1968-72

1   A five-point reform programme was announced by the Prime Minister of Northern Ireland on 22 November 1968. Successive Northern Ireland Governments have been firmly committed to the implementation of this programme and indeed expanded it as time went on. The initial proposals were:—

(i) the substitution of a broadly-based Development Commission for elected local government in the Londonderry area—implemented by the establishment of the Londonderry Development Commission on 5 February 1969;

(ii) the future allocation of public authority housing on a points system—implemented on the basis of the model points scheme referred to in the Commission of 29 August 1969;

(iii) new methods of investigating citizens' grievances—implemented by the appointment of a Parliamentary Commissioner for Administration and a Commissioner for Complaints under two new Acts of Parliament which became law on 24 June 1969 and 25 November 1969 respectively; (the statutory limit of the Parliamentary Commissioner being subsequently extended to cover, in addition to the functions discharged by his Westminster counterpart, the investigation of matters of personnel administration; and by arrangement to cover certain matters arising out of the anti-discrimination clause in Northern Ireland Government contracts).

(iv) the abolition of the Business Vote at elections for Stormont, extended in March 1969 to include the substitution of universal adult suffrage for the ratepayers' franchise at local government elections—implemented in the Electoral Law Acts of 1968 and 1969;

(v) a promise to review the Civil Authorities (Special Powers) Act and Regulations as soon as the situation permitted.

2   Further reforms followed. The Northern Ireland Government accepted the recommendations of the Hunt Committee that the Royal Ulster Constabulary should become a normally unarmed force and that defence of Northern Ireland against armed terrorists should be a military responsibility. Thus a new structure for the police force was embodied in the Police Act of 1970 and the Ulster Special Constabulary was replaced by the RUC Reserve established under that Act. In addition the part-time Ulster Defence Regiment which was established by the United Kingdom Government to assist the Army in its security role became operational on 1 April 1970.

3   Provision for a central housing authority to be responsible for all public authority house building, management and allocation was made in the Housing Executive Act which became law on 25 February 1971.

4   Following the decision to centralise responsibility for housing, a committee under the Chairmanship of Mr Patrick Macrory was set up to review the then existing plans for the reorganisation of local government.

5   In the context of local government reorganisation an interim Staff Commission was established in June 1970 on a non-statutory basis to assist central and local government with the complex staffing difficulties of reorganisation. Provision for a permanent and statutory local government Staff Commission was made in the Local Government Act (Northern Ireland), 1972.

6   The Ministry of Community Relations was established under legislation which became law on 28 October 1969. Among other things the Ministry was charged with the responsibility for obtaining declarations of equality of employment opportunity from public bodies and local authorities and of ensuring that the same employing authorities devolved and adopted acceptable codes of employment procedure. In addition, a Community Relations Commission was appointed under the Community Relations Act (Northern Ireland), 1969.

7   The Northern Ireland Government also made proposals for the reform of the Stormont Parliament. On 22 June 1971 Mr Faulkner, then Prime Minister, announced that the Government intended to recommend to Parliament a new committee system. In addition to the Public Accounts Committee, there would be three new functional Committees covering the fields of social services, environmental services and industrial services. It was intended that the Committees should be representative of party strength in the House and that members of the Opposition should chair at least two. These proposals were later incorporated in a Green Paper on the Future Development of the Parliament and Government of Northern Ireland published in October 1971 (Cmd 560 of 1971) which canvassed, *inter alia*, the possibility of introducing proportional representation, of increasing the size of the House of Commons and of widening the basis of the Senate. They were developed in correspondence between the Governments of Northern Ireland and the United Kingdom, referred to in the Northern Ireland Government's White Paper 'Political Settlement' (Cmd 568 of 1972).

ULSTER UNIONIST PARTY

TOWARDS THE FUTURE

Foreword

By Rt. Hon. Brian Faulkner, M.P.
Leader of the Unionist Party

Northern Ireland is facing the greatest crisis in the 50 years of its existence, a crisis which will determine not simply the future forms of Government in Northern Ireland, but whether or not the people of Ulster are to continue to determine their own destiny.

It is a time of change and challenge; a time for new and original ideas rather than the digging of old trenches. We must not allow bitterness about the past or the present, to cloud our judgments about the future.

The Unionist Party has attempted to meet this challenge by producing a constructive and comprehensive blue-print for the future institutions of government in this part of the United Kingdom. The people of Ulster have been confused and uncertain about the future for too long. We have, I believe, produced a set of proposals which can point the way firmly to the future. **THEY ARE PROPOSALS WHICH COMBINE REALISM WITH IDEALISM, WHICH CAN PROVIDE DURABLE STRUCTURES ALLOWING FOR FULL PARTICIPATION BY ALL REASONABLE MEN.**

The Unionist Party has frequently been accused by its enemies of being a party which refuses to face up to change. I hope these plans will finally demolish the credibility of such accusations. We have never claimed that the system provided for in the 1920 Act was perfect; **BUT WE HAVE TRIED TO MAKE IT WORK.** Some of the ideas in this blue-print have already been put forward for discussion by a Unionist Government. We have also included many new ideas; a small executive in a large unicameral Parliament, a radically expanded committee system (which would be a central feature of the new Parliament), the replacement of the Special Powers Act, and a comprehensive Bill of Rights. These and many other ideas should be honestly studied by all the people of Ulster.

We have judged our proposals by two criteria; the safeguarding of the union, and the creation of structures which would permit all reasonable people to play their part in public life. Surely the problems of our community can only be solved by Ulstermen themselves, meeting, talking and debating, in their own institutions.

Brian Faulkner.

1   Background

Our object in producing this blue-print for the future is to provide institutions that will attract, or, failing that, persuade, all reasonable sections of the community, apart from the irredeemable hard core, towards an acceptance of and a participation in the public life of Northern Ireland. This has not happened to a completely satisfactory extent during the 50 year existence of Northern Ireland. The Northern Ireland Parliament started its career amidst boycott and it was suspended in March against a background of boycott.

Now is not however a time for looking back. Northern Ireland has seldom had a more difficult situation to face militarily and politically. In producing this document we have tried to face up squarely to our problems and produce a system that will both safeguard the Union and permit all reasonable people to play their part.

This is not the first time Unionists have put forward constructive—and detailed—proposals for the future. As early as June 1971, the Unionist Government of Northern Ireland produced proposals for the development of a system of Committees in the Parliament of Northern Ireland.

In October 1971, the Government produced proposals for discussion on the future development of the Parliament and Government of Northern Ireland. As late as February of this year, further proposals were made to the United Kingdom Government. For a variety of reasons these proposals have at no time been allowed to be the subject of discussion with the other Northern Ireland political parties.

At all times, therefore, the leader of the Ulster Unionist Party and his colleagues have been ready to join at the conference table with all the elected representatives from the other parliamentary parties in Northern Ireland in discussions with regard to the future government of the province. If such discussions can now take place they will be welcomed by Unionists who, for their part, would have preferred them to have taken place 12 months ago.

While we would not agree to any departure from established constitutional practices, our proposals are open for discussion by party and country alike.

2   A Regional Parliament

We are convinced that, whatever else may be left open for discussion, there must be a strong regional parliament and government in Northern Ireland. We are not so concerned about the structure of this parliament as about its role in the community and its powers.

It is absolutely clear that if Northern Ireland were governed entirely from London, a significant minority of the population would remain totally opposed to the administration. It is equally clear that if Government were centred in Dublin, a majority of the citizens of the province would owe the administration no allegiance. These things being so, the basic tension and division of the community can only be resolved inside a parliament of Northern Ireland.

The geographical isolation of the province from the rest of the United Kingdom, the dangers of impersonal administration from a distant capital and the general movement of opinion in favour of devolution to the regions within the United Kingdom all argue for a separate parliament in Northern Ireland.

The province has a number of problems which are unique in the Kingdom: several of these such as education arise from community divisions; others arise from acute economic problems, for example, lack of raw materials, dependence on imported animal foodstuffs, high unemployment; others arise from locally developed structures—for example, the legal system and parts of the law concerning land tenure are substantially different; others from matters of conscience and morality which affect legislation.

Finally local government in the province is being reorganised in accordance with a set of proposals which depend on the existence of a strong regional legislature. Elected representatives have a smaller range of powers in the new district councils and only a limited proportion of the seats on the several new area boards. Only in a regional parliament would they have the predominant role and it is here that major problems have to be dealt with.

In a community which has very high political involvement, it is essential to have plenty of roles for political activists to play and we believe these roles must be ones which involve the exercise of real influence. These roles could not be found at Westminster and in any case it is most unlikely that Westminster will want to be involved in the minutiae of housing and other local government problems for more than the most limited period.

3   A Unicameral Parliament

We can see no reason to advocate a two chamber system on the Westminster model. Indeed any shortcomings in the Northern Ireland Parliamentary system hitherto may have been due to too slavish an imitation of the Westminster model in circumstances which that model was not evolved to meet.

The Senate served four main purposes. First, it provided a constitutional safeguard, since its composition only reflected that of the House of Commons after a period of time. Consequently it gave time for second thoughts in the event of any extreme swing at a general election. Second, it had power to check House of Commons legislation—a power rarely, if ever, used. Third, it scrutinised and revised the drafting of legislation. Fourth, it provided a forum for general debates. The third and fourth of these tasks would be undertaken by the new committees (see below).

It was suggested in 1971 that the Senate might be expanded to include a number of able people from outside the purely political sphere. However, if the single chamber is expanded along the lines advocated later, there should develop an able and professional cadre of politicians including specialists in most significant fields.

The single chamber should be larger than the present House of Commons in order that there are sufficient members to staff the Executive and Committees and still have a sizeable back bench. The ideal number might be about 100. This increase in the number of M.P.s would reduce the need for Proportional Representation since there would be fewer wasted majorities.

There must in the new Parliament be a recognised opposition with a salaried leader supported by appropriate facilities.

4   The Executive

This we propose should be smaller than the Cabinet and Government heretofore. We suggest five or six major departments in addition to that of the Prime Minister, each being headed by a Minister.

These would be the Departments of Home Affairs; Development, Health and Social Services; Commerce and Finance; Education and Community Relations; and Agriculture. The Ministers could, if necessary, be supported by junior Ministers in the more important departments. This distribution of responsibilities would of course be the prerogative of the Prime Minister, but regard should be had to keeping the numbers of salaried ministerial posts to a minimum. The benefit of a strong back bench is one asset that should be maintained in the new Parliament.

The Executive would be obliged to work very closely with the new committee system and the chairmen of committees, of whom there would be six.

5   A Committee System

This is the kernel of our proposals for a new Regional Parliament. It would involve far greater direct participation in Government by every parliamentary party, opposition parties as well as government, than was ever possible before. We propose the establishment of a system of six Committees covering the main departments of government. These would be:—

The Home Affairs Committee. This would effectively have within its terms of reference the functions of the Department of Home Affairs: Police, Prisons, Courts, Licensing and so on.

The Committee on Development and the Environment. This would cover the responsibilities of the Departments of Development and Health and Social Services. It would include such functions as Local Government, Sewerage, the Hospital and Welfare Services, Housing and Roads within its terms of reference.

The Committee on Education and Community Relations. Again, this would cover the affairs of the Department concerned.

The Committee on Commerce and Finance. This Committee would look after a wide range of fiscal and commercial matters including industrial incentives, tourism, the budget and whatever forms of taxation are to be decided locally (for example Rates).

The Committee on Agriculture. Since this is so central to the life and well being of our community, it is thought that there should be a separate Committee covering agricultural matters.

The Public Accounts Committee. This would be similar to and perform the same function as did the present Public Accounts Committee.

Structure of the Committees

Committee membership would be drawn from Parliament and should reflect party strength there. Of the six committees at least three would be chaired by members of opposition parties. This gives a good opportunity to ensure that chairmanships of committees are reasonably spread among the political parties in Parliament.

The Chairman's role would be vital to the working of the Committee. He should be given a substantial salary, would have access to the Executive by memoranda or invitation on Committee matters and could be considered for membership of the Privy Council. His function would be not only to chair the Committee but to draw up the agenda and determine the order of business. Such a person must be experienced, respected and capable, since a great part of the value of the Committee's work will depend on the ability and personality of its chairman. For this reason the post, which in practice would be full time, should be made as attractive as possible.

We propose that the Committees should employ their own staff and independent specialists.

Size of the Committees: Bearing in mind the size of the new Parliament and the need to represent Party strength there adequately, we believe the optimum number of committee members should be seven to nine. It is desirable that the Committees should be small enough to permit a good close working relationship between members.

Selection of Committees: We propose that the members of Committees be appointed by the Prime Minister after consultation with the leaders of all parliamentary political parties. Membership would then be ratified by Parliament as a whole. This would avoid an excessive power of patronage and permit the evolution of strong parliamentary conventions about manner of appointment.

Consideration should be given to attendance allowances for members of Committees in order to differentiate somewhat between Committee members and the rest of the members of Parliament. This incentive would ensure that membership of Committees is attractive to all the members of Parliament.

Powers and Functions of Committees: All legislation would pass through the relevant Committee in a similar method to the present committee stage of Bills at Westminster. Since these Committees will be closely concerned with a specialist field, and because of the intimate working relationship that will result between members of a Committee, the review of legislation by Committee would be much more effective than it was in the whole House of Commons.

Their influence, considerable anyway, will obviously depend on the development of a committee as opposed to a party approach to issues. This in the smaller, more intimate conditions provided by the committee system should be more easily achieved than it was in the House of Commons. The Committees will very rapidly develop their own esprit de corps and sense of independence.

As well as considering the legislation sponsored by the executive, the Committee would have power to sponsor its own. Obviously in its role of considering and formulating policy it would have the power to promote its own ideas. As a result the Committees occasionally would clash with the Executive on such matters, but we strongly feel that the very process of working out solutions to these problems would be part of the new techniques in co-operation that would have to be learnt. All legislation would of course have to be finally approved by the House.

Apart from the consideration of policy and legislation a major function of each Committee will be to review Executive action and the Administration's implementation of both policy and legislation. Here the Committees would have power to invite Ministers and Civil Servants to appear before them. In all these matters they would have their own independent sources of advice.

Hearings would be in public or in private at the discretion of the committee.

Benefits of a Committee System. Some of these we have already mentioned above.

The Committee system is designed to allow the maximum minority influence commensurate with majority government. The Committees will, by their role and their prestige, exert considerable influence and will be somewhat removed from party politics. The specialist nature of the Committees will not only ensure this is so but will result in the raising of the general standard of policy discussion.

Following a referendum on the constitution and with the establishment of a Bill of Rights, we hope these Committees will open the way for a co-operation in government and a participation in public life by the minority that has not yet been seen in Northern Ireland.

The powers of the Executive are not substantially reduced except in on sphere. The Executive is now smaller, the Parliament larger. The responsibility for getting a legislative programme implemented would still be with the Minister for the Department, but now he would have to work through a powerful Committee with considerable influence in the House. There can be no doubt that Government is not made easier by such a system. The Executive does not control the Committee in the same way as it could control a House of Commons. Every department's actions will therefore be closely scrutinised by a Committee.

The Committees would offer considerable advantages. They would greatly broaden political participation while blunting political controversy in policy making. This would allow a double check on legislation that removes the necessity for an Upper House and because of their power to amend all legislation, they answer the demands made for a power of veto or inbuilt blocking mechanism.

6 Powers

Given that there now exists an opportunity to recast the powers of the Northern Ireland Parliament to take account of the changes in the past 50 years, we should not be bound by the division in the Government of Ireland Act, 1920.

In that Act the division was roughly as follows:

WESTMINSTER	NORTHERN IRELAND
Crown	Internal Security
Armed Forces	Prison and Legal Systems
Foreign Relations	Agriculture
Major Taxation	Education
Post Office	Regional Economic Development
Coinage	Health and Social Services
External Trade	Local Government
	Rating and Valuation

The powers we would advocate should be given to the local Parliament would be basically those listed above, but it should have adequate powers to apply financial measures to further the regional economy. Such powers would have to be subject to EEC scrutiny but might include special rates of VAT, for example, on animal foodstuffs and regional employment premiums.

There is need for a closer liaison with Westminster with respect to EEC matters and external relations generally.

Internal and external security is dealt with in a separate section.

7 Finance

The arrangements under which the province has been financed have become unsatisfactory not least because of the heavy burden of Social Security benefits. It is easy to extract figures from published accounts to show that expenditure in Northern Ireland is very much greater than the tax revenue raised here and the difference would still be large, even if account is taken of the many hidden reverse payments. This would apply to many other areas of the United Kingdom if separate accounts were available for them. The payments to Northern Ireland represent common citizenship not subsidy.

New financial arrangements are in any case necessary as referred to in the recent Westminster White Paper on Northern Ireland Finance. Furthermore, accession to the European Economic Community may cause a revision of existing financial arrangements depending on the many special local problems which are likely to arise because of Common Market membership.

Such problems must be fully debated in the local Parliament and the necessary financial arrangements entered into as a result of these debates.

8 Security

However one might wish it otherwise, the most crucial element in providing stable government for the province will revolve round the control of law and order, both internal and external. There is a cult of violence in the community which leads to periodic outbreaks of violent political activity. No administration, whether Westminster based, Belfast based or Dublin based would be safe without adequate means to contain these outbreaks.

In maintaining peace one can identify the following tasks:

(a) **The defence of the province** in the context of Western Europe—a task to which Ulster contributes through recruitment to the Army and through the Territorial Army.

(b) **The defence of the border** and guarding of installations during periods of disturbance—a task now done by the UDR.

(c) **The gathering of intelligence** locality by locality which enables the violent element to be watched and contained. This is a job for police rather than the Army because it requires continuous local involvement in an area.

(d) **The control of subversive activities,** riots and dealing with outbreaks of shooting, arson or bombing. This is a task which is at present being done by the Army but which in normal times could be handled by police at least up to a certain level of intensity.

(e) **Normal civilian policing**—detection and prevention of crime, traffic control, etc.

(a) has always been a matter for the Army and should remain so. We advocate (b) remaining with the UDR. We think (c) should be added to the duties of the RUC Reserve, as well as being a prime job of the RUC. We think (d) should be handled by a specially trained riot police, part of the RUC, with Army held in reserve as long as possible. (e) is the task of the RUC, supported by the Reserve.

We do not advocate special police forces for special areas. There is an urgent need to build up the RUC, both in numbers and morale, so that it can relieve the Army of work which no Army is trained or equipped to do. The Army is a blunt instrument for dealing with crisis situations and cannot provide the sensitive approach to maintaining order which would be provided by a cadre of localised men, familiar with terrain and clientele, essential to a good police reserve.

As far as political responsibility for security forces is concerned, the United Kingdom should retain responsibility for (a) and (b). (c), (d) and (e) should be the responsibility of the Northern Ireland Government.

We are assuming that in the event of the Army being called to the aid of the civil authority there would be close liaison between the two governments because the Northern Ireland Government would continue to control the police while the United Kingdom Government would control the Army.

Special Powers Act

We propose that the Special Powers Act should be replaced by alternative emergency legislation which would not include the power to intern. The operation of this legislation would be dependant on an emergency being declared by the Northern Ireland Parliament and would be renewable for six months at a time as determined by resolution in that Parliament.

The Alternative System

SPECIAL COURTS: If the Northern Ireland Parliament is to be without an interning power, then some system of Legal Procedure involving modification of the ordinary criminal law would be necessary to meet the peculiar security problems of Northern Ireland. Although only to be used under emergency powers, we propose that this machinery be kept available.

We see this as necessary

— To meet widespread intimidation of witnesses

— To protect those who give information to the authorities in areas where terrorists are strongly entrenched

- To prevent intimidation of juries
- To safeguard identity of Police Special Branch members
- To ensure speedy trials
- To modify the present exacting Criminal Law standards of evidence and proof
- To allow convictions to be more easily obtained.

At present the ordinary courts are neither equipped to deal with emergency situations, nor do they adopt a uniform approach on such matters (e.g. bail in charges involving possession of weapons).

We propose the appointment of a **Chief Magistrate** who can give general directions on what courts will sit and also on principles to be followed in such matters as the granting of bail in cases involving terrorist activity.

We propose the setting up of a **Special Court System** to deal with cases involving either widespread sectarian violence or widespread terrorist activity. This court would have two levels. The first tier would deal with committals and all minor cases such as are at present dealt with by Magistrates' Courts. The second tier would deal with those more serious cases committed for trial by Magistrates.

This court could well have direct appeal to the Privy Council or House of Lords. Serious cases would be heard before three judges.

In order to ensure the speedy and effective operation of such a system it would be necessary to amend some of the rules of evidence. We recommend the rules concerning the admission of hearsay evidence should be relaxed. The court must have power to exclude from its consideration obviously prejudicial evidence but it should be put before the court. The standard of reasonable probability or balance of probabilities could be substituted for the present requirements of proof beyond reasonable doubt. We say this in the belief that this interference with the traditional liberty of the subject is a minimal substitute for the more drastic power of internment.

Other recommendations we make are:

- That Special Courts do not have Jury Trial
- That hearings be in camera and if good cause be shown, police evidence could be by affidavit subject to examination by the judges.

This system would be the responsibility of the Northern Ireland Parliament. Review would be provided by the judicial committee of the Privy Council or the House of Lords.

9 Safeguards for Minorities

A Bill of Rights

We propose the introduction of a precise and comprehensive Bill of Rights. This would include Rights as follows:

Freedom of Speech. This would not only include the spoken word but also the written word.

Freedom of Political Association.

Freedom of Practice of Religion.

Freedom from discrimination on religious grounds.

Freedom of the person and the right to trial.

Careful attention would have to be given to the content of such a Bill. It could be made very comprehensive and precise—with specific Rights for Education, Rights of Employment and so on. We are aware that there are also problems about whether the Rights listed be absolute or qualified, how they will be drafted, whether they will be used and how they will be interpreted by the courts.

Will it be used? It has often been overlooked, but we have had in Northern Ireland a comprehensive Bill of Rights concerning religious discrimination, contained in Sections 5 and 8(6) of the Government of Ireland Act. The fact is that these have existed for over 50 years without being resorted to (for instance, alleged acts of housing discrimination could easily have been tested in court as could the validity of endowing Church schools or RI in State Schools). The answer may be that those who complained were not anxious to have their claims legally examined or that they found it difficult to do so by reason of lack of means or evidence.

In either case, we would argue that the precise nature of a Bill of Rights— its comprehensive coverage of issues—combined with the availability of judicial remedies or legal aid should ensure that public pressure is put on those complaining to seek recourse to the law. The dramatic nature of a Bill of Rights would give this incentive.

The Drafting of a Bill of Rights. The extent of the Rights listed is a crucial matter. We believe it is important that they be more than mere standards by which to judge executive and legislative action; yet if the Rights are expressed in absolute terms, we realise they considerably restrict the powers of Government.

The restriction of over wide legislative and executive action in these matters is an important safeguard.

A Bill of Rights also can expose not only maladministration or abuse of legislative powers but also weak and contrived allegations of discrimination by demonstrating them to be unfounded. In this sense a Bill of Rights would be a good complement to the existing machinery.

Availability of Review and Enforcement. We would propose legal aid to be made available to suitable applicants. This would be decided by the normal process—the Legal Aid Committee.

Enforcement would be by the normal judicial remedies of injunction, mandamus and declaratory judgment though some procedural amendments might be necessary here. It would not be necessary to set up a new Court for judicial review but more desirable to rely on the existing Supreme Court of Northern Ireland with direct appeal to the House of Lords.

Other Safeguards

In addition to the guarantees contained in the Declarations of Equal Employment Opportunity by public bodies and in the nondiscrimination Clauses in Government Contracts, other measures would be initiated to ensure the minority satisfactory guarantees of fair treatment. In this we believe it is not a matter of securing fair treatment for the minority but of making certain that the minority can see that that is what they are in fact getting.

PUBLIC EMPLOYMENT GENERALLY. While the Local Government Appointments Commission and the Civil Service Commission are, we believe, satisfactory safeguards against any possible discrimination in public employment, generally THERE MIGHT STILL BE SOME MERIT IN GIVING THE MINISTRY OF COMMUNITY RELATIONS A SUPERVISORY ROLE IN MINOR APPOINTMENTS. THE OBJECT AGAIN WOULD BE TO REVIEW THE GENERAL BALANCE OF SUCH APPOINTMENTS.

In both of the above, however, we feel it is vital that there be no attempt to regulate by numerical quota of Roman Catholics to Protestants.

There can be no substitute for merit and experience as considerations for employment in public office and it would be invidious to have any hard and fast rule based on religious considerations. Any attempt to secure a fixed numerical balance would only serve to accentuate community divisions.

10 Relations with Southern Ireland

Relationship with Southern Ireland. In our opinion the task of securing a stable and lasting political settlement in Northern Ireland can be made significantly easier by the co-operation of the Government and people of Southern Ireland. To give any system that may prove acceptable to the majority of Unionist and Nationalist minded people in Northern Ireland a good chance of success will require several major contributions from the South.

The first contribution which must be made is the acceptance by the South of the right of the people of the North to self-determination. The obvious advantages— of calming the fears of the Northern majority and of isolating those who believe in physical force—would be enormous. In reality this means asking Southern Politicians to translate their verbal commitments to the idea that force will not be allowed to bring about a United Ireland into political and constitutional action.

WE PROPOSE THIS DECLARATION BE IN THE FORM OF A SOLEMN AND BINDING AGREEMENT BETWEEN THE THREE GOVERNMENTS CONCERNED AS IN 1925.

The second contribution must be a greater commitment of the Southern Government to co-operate in ending terrorism here. We propose that several basic steps be taken immediately. FIRSTLY INTER-GOVERNMENT DISCUSSIONS SHOULD BE UNDERTAKEN CONCERNING POSSIBLE MEASURES. SECONDLY THE POSITION ABOUT THE RETURN OF CRIMINALS MUST BE REVIEWED. So long as extradition agreements exclude offences of a political character, this will be used to justify the non-return of many of those responsible for the murder of innocent citizens. Either the extradition treaty should be re-negotiated or the British Isles made a Common Law enforcement area. The latter would be preferable. A warrant issued in Belfast would be executed in Dublin in the same way as it would be in Sheffield.

SUCH ACTION WOULD ENABLE A JOINT IRISH INTER-GOVERNMENTAL COUNCIL TO BE FORMED WITH EQUAL MEMBERSHIP FROM THE GOVERNMENTS OF NORTHERN IRELAND AND THE IRISH REPUBLIC. SUCH A COUNCIL COULD DISCUSS MATTERS OF MUTUAL INTEREST, PARTICULARLY IN THE ECONOMIC AND SOCIAL FIELD.

ALLIANCE PARTY

The Alliance Party is fully committed to the establishment of a regional parliament or assembly in this province. The structures and powers of a regional assembly need to be clearly defined. Alliance is not demanding the restoration of an unreformed Stormont but a new form of democratic structure with legislative powers.

We are convinced that the basic problems of sectarianism and division can only be solved by the people of Northern Ireland within a Northern Ireland context. The fact that these problems were not solved during 50 years of Stormont or during the previous 120 years of 'direct rule' does not mean that the problems are insoluble.

The exact powers, structure and method of electing such regional assembly are something which we believe can and should be negotiated with political parties in Northern Ireland even if total agreement is not possible.

In the enclosed document, Alliance has put forward its views on the type of political settlement which would be most acceptable to the majority of the people of Northern Ireland. It goes without saying that on most of the points raised, we as a party, would be prepared to negotiate. We must, however, make it clear that there are matters upon which Alliance would not be prepared to make any compromise. These are:—

(1) That there must be no severing of the link between Great Britain and Northern Ireland without the full and free consent of the majority of the Northern Ireland people.

(2) That defence of the realm is and must remain the sole responsibility of Westminster.

(3) That all people in Northern Ireland without distinction of political or religious belief must be guaranteed equality of rights.

(4) A system must be designed to ensure that all sections can play a responsible role in running the country but we are against any system which provides for inbuilt sectarian representation.

Proposals for a political settlement in Northern Ireland

The Border

Alliance is not interested in participating in any sterile arguments about the rights or wrongs of the decision to partition Ireland in 1920. The basic fact is that for over 50 years there has been an independent 26 County state by the clear wish of the majority in that area and a six county Northern Ireland which is part of the United Kingdom because of the clear desire of a majority of its people. Alliance demands as an absolute commitment that the British Government will not make any change in the position of Northern Ireland as part of the United Kingdom without the clear consent of the people of this province as determined by referenda. We do not accept that there can be any compromise on this principle.

Regional Legislative Assembly

We are in favour of the establishment of a regional assembly in Northern Ireland with certain legislative powers and in particular powers to deal with Education, Development, Agriculture, Housing, Commerce and Health and Social Services, which should be comparable to the powers of the previous Parliament with the limitations mentioned below. Such an assembly in our view should conform to the following standards:—

(a) It should be entirely elected by adult suffrage on the basis of PR (STV).

(b) Westminster shall remain the Sovereign Parliament in relation to the powers transferred to the new Assembly.

(c) The new Assembly should have no powers transferred to it in relation to the defence of the realm including the security of the province. This point will be discussed in more detail hereafter.

(d) Westminster should retain the legislative powers in relation to all matters pertaining to elections.

Consideration might be given to the following method of operation:—

(a) The assembly could conduct its business on a Committee system rather than an executive system. The assembly could divide itself into a number of Committees for each of its major functions. The Chairman of each Committee would be elected by PR by the assembly.

(b) Such an assembly would have technically no executive in the sense of a body accepting cabinet responsibility. Management functions would be exercised by a Committee consisting of an assembly Chairman and the Chairmen of Committees.

(c) We feel that there is a good argument for re-election to the assembly being held every four years at the maximum.

Relations with Republic

We are in favour of the creation of machinery to achieve not only better understanding between Northern Ireland and the Irish Republic but also to achieve joint planning for common economic, social and agricultural problems facing the whole island, now even more important with the advent of the Common Market.

We have examined the idea of a Council of Ireland as originally envisaged in the Government of Ireland Act. We believe, however, for a variety of reasons, that the structure should be an Anglo-Irish Council with representatives from political parties at Westminster, the Northern Ireland Assembly and the Dail.

We envisage such a Council having advisory powers only but its scope should not be of a static or rigid nature.

We are opposed to the government of the Republic being represented as a participating body in any talks on the political future of Northern Ireland. We hope, however, that when, after consultation with the parties in Northern Ireland, the British Government produces a blueprint for the future government of the province that this blueprint will be accepted by the Republic, as representing a fair solution to a problem which also affects the South. The IRA and gun politics are as much a threat to democracy in the Republic as they are in the North.

Condominium

We reject the idea of a condominium. We think that it is divisive in concept and would not work in practice.

Extradition

Alliance is in favour of every effort being made to re-negotiate extradition with the Irish Republic so as to include persons to be charged with crimes of violence of a political nature. We do not believe that relations between different parts of the British Isles should be based strictly on treaties of an international nature.

The Economy

Alliance will be pressing for massive financial aid for Northern Ireland to re-construct the economy of the province and to rapidly tackle bad housing, unemployment and poor environmental factors.

Security

Alliance is totally committed to all security powers being retained by Westminster. This not only includes the control of and legislation relating to the army and the UDR but also certain police functions and all security legislation.

We wish to see the new assembly having no powers to enact legislation such as the Special Powers Acts. This legislation in our opinion, should be phased out as soon as possible.

Police

While we have said we believe that defence of the realm and the security of the province should be a Westminster matter, this throws up a question with regard to responsibility for the police. The simplest way to deal with this is to reserve all police matters to Westminster. It will, however, be argued that even County Councils in England are police authorities. It must be appreciated that the RUC is grossly undermanned and appallingly overworked. This arises partly out of having to cope with a unique situation of violence. But there is another contributory cause and that is the substantial increase in minor police duties brought about by the development of modern society and the increased traffic on our roads.

One method of resolving the difficulty may be to have in effect two police bodies as follows:—

(1) A Police Force to deal with parking, traffic control and offences, vandalism and minor crime. This Force to be under the control of the new assembly.

(2) Royal Ulster Constabulary to be relieved of the workload of petty crime, and to be upgraded to a Scotland Yard type force, to deal only with serious crime and any police functions affecting security. This force to be under the control of Westminster.

While there would undoubtedly be difficulties in drawing up lines of demarcation for these two forces, we believe that there is no solution to this problem of responsibility which is without difficulty. In many other countries such as Canada there is already the division between the Federal and State Police.

Internment and Special Powers

We oppose internment. We wish to see all internees and detainees either charged or released as soon as is humanly possible.

We also consider that permanent Special Powers legislation is totally repugnant. We wish to see this legislation repealed quickly while realising that it may be necessary in exceptional circumstances for Westminster to enact temporary special legislation.

Private armies such as the IRA and UVF must be rigorously dealt with under the law but we see no justification for a blanket ban on purely political activity whether republican or otherwise.

Human Rights

Alliance considers that in any legislation passed at Westminster to set up a new structure of government for the province there should be incorporated a Bill of Rights, guaranteeing to all citizens their fundamental Human Rights based on the Universal Declaration of Human Rights.

NORTHERN IRELAND LABOUR PARTY

PROPOSALS FOR THE FUTURE GOVERNMENT OF NORTHERN IRELAND

Part A. Introduction

1   The Labour Party earnestly desires that this Conference should result in a useful and constructive exchange of views among the parties represented and that Her Majesty's Government will be assisted in their deliberations by the exchange which takes place. The success of the Conference depends upon the attitudes adopted by all concerned. In a situation where daily more and more innocent lives are being lost with men and women and children being maimed (some to suffer grave handicaps for life) and incalculable economic destruction is being wrought it would be nothing less than contemptible that any single Party should seek to jeopardise the Conference and thus exacerbate the situation.

The Labour Party does not suggest that a frank exchange of views at this Conference taking place in an atmosphere of mutual respect in itself would end the deaths and the destruction or eradicate speedily the widespread distrust and hostility. But the participants should not for partisan reasons act or continue to act so as to make the present grave situation worse. To those evil forces in Northern Ireland whose campaign of violence continues unabated we hope a simple unified message will emanate from this Conference:—

'You have nothing to offer the people of Northern Ireland but horror and destruction. Whatever division of views may exist among us at this Conference we are at one in our determination to see your defeat. With your defeat hope could replace fear.'

All participants will recognise that it will be the intention of the IRA to create a climate of affairs in which constructive discussion and exchange is made very difficult. The participants, however, must not let themselves be used as pawns in that scheme.

2   It is equally relevant in our view to recognise not only the possible dangers surrounding but also the limitations of this Conference. It is not designed to reach decisions. It is more significant that no firm indication has been given by Her Majesty's Government as to how matters are to proceed subsequent to the Conference and in particular whether the people of Northern Ireland or their elected representatives are to be consulted about the acceptability of either the principles underlying or the institutional means utilised in the 'settlement' which is ultimately unveiled. Unhappily we feel obliged to record that the lack of this clearly announced strategy on the part of the Government

in itself serves to undermine the significance of this conference; more disturbing in some quarters it has increased already considerable anxiety and hostility.

3   In this paper we enumerate first those *principles* which we believe are fundamental to any settlement worthy of support. Within the confines of those principles we enumerate secondly Labour's proposals for the future government and institutions of Northern Ireland. It should be understood that the proposals of modification (but not the principles) are not regarded by us as inviolate or incapable of modification or improvement. The proposals, however, represent a considered, workable and a fair basis for the future (and better) government of Northern Ireland. We trust we will have the opportunity to expand upon our reasons in advancing them. We take our place at this Conference with an open mind, genuinely prepared to consider each alternative presented on its merits. We are convinced that this attitude offers the most promising basis for participants entering these discussions.

Part B   Principles

Labour regards the following as the basic principles which must be honoured in any settlement:

(1) That the constitutional status of Northern Ireland as an integral part of the United Kingdom can in no event be altered without the consent of the majority of the people of Northern Ireland.

(2) That all the citizens living in Northern Ireland regardless of race, religion or belief are entitled to equality of treatment, freedom from discrimination, and equality of opportunity. That violence as a political method is not acceptable and those who perpetrate same in the present Northern Ireland situation must have no share in dictating the course of events.

(3) That any settlement must be designed to bring about not only the necessary consent of a majority of the people of Northern Ireland but also to provide opportunities for a new degree of harmony between both the Protestant and Catholic communities within Northern Ireland.

Part C   Divisive and Unifying Issues: Institutionalised Sectarianism or Social Harmony?

1   It is crucial to seize the opportunity to rebuild a system free from the divisive issues which have crippled Northern Ireland for so long. It is important to realise it has been clearly established that there are areas where people, irrespective of their religious background, will work together. The trade union movement and many social services are eloquent testimony to this fact. In another sphere the Derry Commission with its long record of unanimous decisions is another. In 1968 National Opinion Poll Surveys showed that religious background had in no way prevented a substantial (and hitherto disregarded)

consensus of view on a wide range of social and economic issues ranging from integrated education to licensing laws.

2   There will be those who will argue the case for institutional devices to be built into the new Northern Ireland Assembly to take account of the fact that we are a divided community. Thus for example the proposal that we should have government on the basis of compulsory religious or political quota. This we feel would do nothing to help us create an integrated community in the long term.

3   Labour recognises, however, that if all the citizens of Northern Ireland are to have a 'guaranteed' role in the public life of the province then the terms of any settlement must provide in addition to enacted legal equality careful checks against the abuse of power. If our view is accepted that the arguments against 'institutionalised sectarianism' are overwhelming, then we consider one of the most fruitful areas for discussion, requiring careful examination, must be the character of any checks to prevent the possible abuse of power. By the term 'abuse of power' we mean something very much more comprehensive than that phrase is accorded in legal decisions in administrative law.

4   The first objective against which Northern Ireland institutions should be planned is the highlighting of unifying areas of decision-making. By this we mean areas of social and economic policy vital to the reconstruction of Northern Ireland society.

5   There are administrative features of Northern Ireland which are conducive to aid any settlement. It must be conceded that Northern Ireland is an appropriate size as a modern area for regional government. Administratively it forms a readily delimited area. Thus major services for an area the size of Northern Ireland, in particular housing, health, environmental control, industrial development, transport and education, are only effective if centralised. The re-organisation of local government, a re-organisation which accorded with Labour's proposals to the McCrory Commission, assumes the existence of a regional authority in these areas and a number of other spheres as well, e.g., fire services, welfare, electricity supply and so on. For these reasons alone, a measure of regional administration is clearly desirable in Northern Ireland and if there is to be regional administration then it must be democratically accountable to the population. In addition there is a demonstrable desire for some local self government.

6   The constraints upon any settlement must include recognition of the overwhelming (Catholic and Protestant) support for the present constitutional position of Northern Ireland as part of the United Kingdom without losing sight of the position of those who wish to see Ireland united. Within the ambit of the principles enumerated above there must be freedom to advocate constitutional change by peaceful legal means. We must recognise the grave dangers inherent in the existence of any group which finds itself in a political minority and with little apparent likelihood in the alteration of that position. Thus by stressing (a) the need for jurisdiction in the unifying areas for a Regional Assembly, (b) the value (psychological as much as legal) of an enacted Bill of Rights, (c) the logic and value of the reservation of citizens rights and the major security functions to Westminster and (d) the case for providing a worthwhile constitutional check

against the abuse of power without overlooking the legitimate claims of a majority, we believe greater confidence can be engendered within both communities.

Part D   Proposals

1   Constitutional Status and the Referendum

The status of Northern Ireland as part of the United Kingdom should not be capable of alteration without the consent of the majority of the people of Northern Ireland freely expressed in a referendum. Labour has pressed for the early holding of such a referendum believing that the result would give an important perspective to the present attitudes held in Northern Ireland. As to the suggestion for the conduct of a referendum at set and pre-determined intervals, e.g., each 10 years or 15 years, we believe this would be counter-productive in that it would serve to keep alive and heighten in the intervening intervals the importance of such political division.

However, serious study should be given to the mechanics of holding subsequent referenda, if this should be desired, in the future. A way must be found which leaves open democratic means of securing Irish unification to those who will continue to aspire to Irish unification, but which also prevents the issue being repeatedly used as a sectarian ploy for perpetuating fundamental divisions within our community.

2   Electoral Law and Franchise

All laws governing elections and the franchise in Northern Ireland should be reserved to the Westminster Parliament.

3   Representatives at Westminster

Northern Ireland citizens should be accorded full parity of representation at Westminster with the people of Great Britain. There are two reasons for this. First, parity of representation reinforces Northern Ireland's status as an integral part of the United Kingdom. Secondly, as Northern Ireland citizens will no longer be able to determine their rights as citizens locally, full British citizenship requires that they be accorded equality of influence in determining the basic terms of citizenship by equality of representation at Westminster.

In order to help contribute to the breakdown of sectarianism, to improve the quality of membership and to ensure the return of members to both sides of the House of Commons, we advocate the use of Proportional Representation for the election of Northern Ireland members to the House of Commons at Westminster. It would be quite appropriate to treat Northern Ireland as one constituency. It should be remembered that two systems of electing members have until very recent times been regarded as quite acceptable to the Westminster Parliament.

4 Citizens Rights Laws

It is Labour's view that British citizenship should carry with it for all the people of Northern Ireland guarantees of an equality of rights not only *inter se* but also an equality with the rights of our fellow citizens who live in other parts of the United Kingdom. Thus we desire to see the reservation of legislative power in this area to the Westminster Parliament. We recognise however that there will be disagreement on the scope of the concept of citizens rights. We suggest there be (a) enactment at Westminster of a Bill of Rights giving statutory expression to the Downing Street Declaration and acknowledging the West-minster Parliament's role as guarantor of civil, religious and political liberty in Northern Ireland. The legislation should incorporate those measures which bring into line the position of Northern Ireland with the rest of the United Kingdom on such matters as the death penalty, race relations, homosexual practices, termination of pregnancy and divorce. All future legislation in the field of civil (and individual citizens) rights enacted at Westminster should be applied to Northern Ireland unless the Westminster Parliament otherwise determines. The Westminster Parliament should reserve expressly the right to annul any measure (or part of a measure) otherwise properly passed by the Northern Ireland Assembly in the exercise of its powers which the Westminster Parliament resolves adversely affects citizens rights. The parties at this Conference should discuss at length their respective definition of the term 'citizens rights'.

5 Security and Law and Order

The Security of Northern Ireland should be a matter for the Westminster Parliament not only in relation to the Armed Forces but also as regards the power to raise, disband, arm or control the criteria for recruiting any police force. We are satisfied that such a position serves to emphasise the constitutional relationship of the two parts of the United Kingdom, rather than as some suggest, weakens our defences. The reservation of such security (including law and order) functions to Westminster must however, be accompanied by a genuine acceptance of responsibility and accountability at Westminster to the people of Northern Ireland in these fields. The vast majority of the people of Northern Ireland are basically not concerned with the issue of who controls security; but with how secure they actually are. It does not and ought not to follow that the reservation of such security functions should operate to the complete exclusion of the Northern Ireland Assembly.

Labour proposes the Northern Ireland Assembly retain *management* powers in relation to the police force, including power to increase its strength and review the exercise of its functions.

The exercise of these powers in Northern Ireland should not operate to exclude members of the Westminster Parliament asking questions in the House on any aspect of police affairs.

6 The Courts and the Judiciary

At present the Supreme (High) Court of Northern Ireland is a function reserved to Westminster. The distinction between the Supreme Court and the inferior (Magistrates and County Courts) is ultimately administrative and *all* these courts should come within the Westminster jurisdiction. Accordingly all judicial appointments should also rest with Westminster. These appointments must be made on merit alone. While it is not necessarily a part of any settlement Labour suggests that there would be value in attempting to integrate more closely the various levels of courts operating in Northern Ireland.

7 Emergency Legislation

It should be a term of the settlement that all 'Special Powers' legislation should be a matter for the Westminster Parliament. The derogation from normal process involving as it may departure from international standards must only be sanctioned by our superior parliament. Equally the context of the settlement must clearly recognise that there is a serious emergency in Northern Ireland which requires the exercise of emergency powers and that Her Majesty's Government will not shrink from taking any proper powers which may be required.

Emergency powers should accord with our international obligations and conventions which do not prevent appropriate powers being taken in a public emergency.

8 Firearms and Explosives: Legislation and Licensing

We consider that these are fields in which the Westminster Parliament should have specific responsibility.

9 Secretary of State for Northern Ireland

The increase of functions of the Westminster Parliament points to the need for a Minister at Westminster, preferably of Cabinet rank.

10 Northern Ireland Office

A Northern Ireland office at Westminster outside the Home Affairs is needed.

Acceptance of proposal (9) above would make this proposal (which can be judged on its own clear merits) even more cogent.

11 A Northern Ireland Assembly

Northern Ireland should have a regional parliament (hereinafter called 'the Northern Ireland Assembly') elected on a liberal, (i.e. genuinely proportionate) basis of proportional representation. The Northern Ireland Assembly should have 100 members. It should have power to dissolve itself by a simple majority vote and elections should be held at least every fourth year.

The Northern Ireland Assembly's jurisdiction must be concentrated upon social (including welfare), economic and cultural features which can most readily be operated regionally and are unifying rather than divisive in their impact upon the community.

The Assembly should have legislative powers (but see paras. 13 and 14 re the exercise of executive and prerogative and the procedure governing Royal Assent to Bills.)

Labour favours an elected unicameral Assembly rather than the present bicameral system which is unduly cumbersome for such a small region. The Northern Ireland Assembly should be modern in character and the pomp of English historical features such as Black Rod, Sergeants at Arms, etc., should be abandoned.

Members should be paid expenses and a sufficient remuneration as to encourage a high calibre of member, prepared to devote himself to full-time involvement in the duties and responsibilities of membership.

12 Northern Ireland departments and the exercise of Executive Functions

In the past self government in Northern Ireland has meant there were Ministers in charge of the executive functions of the several functional Departments (e.g. Home Affairs, Finance, Commerce, etc.). These Ministers combine in Cabinet as the Executive. With three limited, and very unusual exceptions, all Ministers have been members of the Unionist Party.

Whilst it is essential that there be efficient and continuous control of the work of the Departments by those elected to the Assembly we recognise that one party rule has resulted not only in political frustration for non Unionist voters but at executive level has also contributed to distrust and abuse of powers.

We propose that Departmental Committees elected on a proportionate basis among members of the Northern Ireland Assembly should become the legal entity formerly constituted by each Minister. Thus say the Northern Ireland Departmental Committee for Commerce would collectively become in law the entity formerly constituted by a Ministry thereby giving access to elected members from both sides of the Assembly to the day to day information within each Department and allowing for joint supervision of the exercise of powers.

We emphasise, however, that if there is to be social progress definable policies must be able to be formulated and pursued. Thus it is essential that Departmental Committees should not be able to stultify development. There is no reason why they should. Each Committee will elect its own Chairman/Vice-Chairman from among its own members and will, of course, reflect the composition of the Assembly itself.

Whilst new legislative measures would technically (apart from Private Members Bills) emanate from each Departmental Committee the existence of a majority party or majority coalition within Committees would allow for the social and economic policies of the majority administration to be carried into effect.

13 Royal Assent, the Prerogative and a Northern Ireland Council of State

By the Government of Ireland Act, 1920, the executive power is vested in Her Majesty and in relation to transferred functions the Governor of Northern Ireland has delegated to him the executive and prerogative power vested in Her Majesty, the present Ministers being in technical constitutional terms appointed by the Governor. The Governor also exercises the function of according Royal Assent to Bills passed by the Northern Ireland Parliament and takes the chair at meetings of the Northern Ireland Privy Council. We have dealt with the discharge of executive functions by Departmental Committees. We propose that Royal Assent to Bills should require as a condition precedent the approval of a Northern Ireland Council of State which shall be the body consulted in relation to the exercise of those prerogative powers, thus taking the place of the present Northern Ireland Privy Council. The Northern Ireland Council of State should be composed of 15 members, of whom 10 should be elected members of the Northern Ireland Assembly representing proportionately the position of the political parties in the Assembly. The remaining members of the Council should be nominated by Her Majesty on the advice of the Government at Westminster. The Secretary of State for Northern Ireland should be entitled to attend ex-officio at the Council's meetings, and if he so desires, convene meetings of the same. Royal Assent to Northern Ireland Bills should require a positive vote of the Council.

Royal Assent to Northern Ireland Bills should require a positive vote of the Council but this should be qualified by the need to withhold Assent should a substantial number of the Council (to be determined) resolve that the granting of Royal Assent would result in the enactment of a measure calculated to impair or endanger community harmony and development.

Where a resolution has been passed within the Council resulting in the withholding of Royal Assent then since the resolution is dependent upon the notion of endangering of community harmony the issue should be referred for the determination of a Commission (or other mechanics) appointed in that behalf by the Secretary of State. Thus no caucus should be able, for ulterior motives, to defeat the expressed wish of the Northern Ireland Assembly unless the view of that group, which is required to be grounded on vital social considerations, is upheld on reference of the issue.

14 Inter-Parliament Consultative Committees

The division of responsibility for Northern Ireland between Westminster and the Northern Ireland Assembly suggests the need for one or more working inter-parliamentary groups whose functions would be consultative but which could undertake a continuous review of how the system is operating. We are satisfied that the existence of such a Committee (or possibly more than one

Committee established on functional criteria) could aid not only the harmonious development of government within Northern Ireland but operate to evolve meaningful conventions whereby Northern Ireland would not, as in the past, derogate from general British standards.

15   The Northern Ireland Attorney General

There would be value in having the Northern Ireland Attorney General acting as the Chief Law Officer of the Northern Ireland Assembly also working with a Departmental Committee and clearly appointed as a servant of the whole Assembly not simply as the recipient of the favours of a majority group.

16   Economic Developments

In the general sphere of economic development Northern Ireland's record, while not nearly so good as it should have been, has been better than other depressed regions of the United Kingdom. This is due to the ability of Northern Ireland through the generosity of the British Government, to offer better inducements to industry, to devote more resources to improving its infrastructure and to follow up by a better 'after sales service'. It is probable that a degree of devolution provides a community with the kind of leverage which is required to obtain financial aid from a central government. This will be more important once we are inside the European Economic Community.

As Northern Ireland's major problem in the years ahead will be the need to strengthen her economy it is important to establish institutions which will provide the people of Northern Ireland with effective economic tools. If Westminster is to be guarantor in the political sphere we need an active and radical local agency in the economic sphere. Northern Ireland cannot be allowed to die by neglect as parts of Scotland have. Conversely we must not be bullied into thinking that Northern Ireland can, unaided, conquer the underlying structural economic problems. The British Government and Westminster must acknowledge overall responsibility assisting in the attainment of full economic development, notwithstanding any devolved power.

We should propose that the regional Assembly which will be established in Northern Ireland should be equipped with a wide array of economic and fiscal powers but so that any exercise of powers of taxation should be capable of being effected with the express approval of the Westminster Parliament which parliament would also have powers of revocation.

The challenge which will unite the people of Northern Ireland is the challenge to build a prosperous society. A strong regional authority with legislative as well as administrative powers is essential if that is to be achieved.

17   Ratification by Westminster Political Parties

In addition to ratification by the British Parliament we believe that public opinion in Northern Ireland would welcome the endorsement of the ultimate settlement, provided it is based on the above principles, by each of the political parties separately. This would go a long way to alleviate the deep suspicion of all people in Northern Ireland of the good faith of all of the parties at Westminster.

18   A Council of Ireland

Serious (and realistic) consideration must be given to the relations between the two parts of Ireland. The existence of the Republic of Ireland as a separate sovereign state need not of necessity serve to prevent sensible, friendly and beneficial relations, and widening areas of joint development between Northern Ireland and the Republic. It must be noted, however, that the claim of jurisdiction over the whole of Ireland made by the Republic of Ireland acts as a major irritant to the present situation, giving offence to those who cannot and ought not to be compelled to give allegiance to the Republic. The territorial claim creates the atmosphere in which a terrorist nationalistic organisation can operate. The Republic of Ireland must be asked to review again its attitude to the rights of the people (all the people) of Northern Ireland. It may be that the present review of the Constitution of the Republic of Ireland will prove helpful in this context. There ought not to be re-enacted in the new Northern Ireland Act a power similar to section 4(7) which prevents the Northern Ireland Parliament enacting measures which affect many aspects of trade or social relations with the Republic of Ireland.

If the Republic of Ireland is prepared to recognise its role in the matter joint negotiations should be commenced to establish a new Council of Ireland as a consultative and deliberative body charged with the task of exploring areas of mutual co-operation for the benefit of all who live in Ireland.

SOCIAL DEMOCRATIC AND LABOUR PARTY

TOWARDS A NEW IRELAND

An Examination

Any proposals which are put forward as a solution to the present serious difficulties of the North of Ireland must be proposals which will provide permanent peace, and stability so that the people of Ireland of all traditions, can come together on a basis of harmony and justice, ending for all time the unjust domination of any one Irish tradition by another. They must be proposals which are put forward without taking into account any sectional or party advantage and which are arrived at by a genuine analysis of the constitutional and institutional difficulties which have led to the present situation.

The first unchallengeable fact which we face is that the area which has come to be known as 'Northern Ireland' is inherently unstable. While many people, including ourselves, will react with horror to the terrible atrocities and violence of which all our people have been victims, the fact remains that any Society which has been the subject of periodic and sustained political violence is inherently unstable, and it is this basic truth which is the underlying cause of all our difficulties.

The last attempt to find a settlement to the problems of this country was **THE GOVERNMENT OF IRELAND ACT, 1920.** It was an imposed settlement which was at the time, unacceptable to all sections of the people of this Island. It has failed. One of its essential elements, The Stormont Parliament, has recently disappeared and it is necessary to realise that its failure does not simply represent the failure of the Northern System of Government but the failure of the 1920 Irish Settlement of which it was a part.

Any re-examination must therefore take place, not on a purely Six County context, but in an Irish context.

Secondly, the means whereby the original settlement was arrived at—the threat of violence by a minority of the people not only of this Island but of the United Kingdom as well and its refusal to accept the democratic decision of the elected representatives of the British and Irish peoples at the beginning of the century—were means which were essentially undemocratic and placed a serious question mark over the legitimacy of the Northern Ireland state—a recipe for periodic political violence.

Thirdly, the means whereby the area of the State was decided—the necessity through a deliberate sectarian headcount of providing permanent sectarian domination was a further recipe again for permanent instability which will frustrate in the future, as it has done in the past, all genuine attempts to destroy sectarianism as a force in Irish Politics.

Fourthly, those who object to Catholic ascendancy, particularly in the religious field, in the Republic of Ireland are in effect, objecting to the effects of the partition settlement which effectively institutionalised the differences between the two main traditions creating a Protestant ascendancy in the North and a Catholic one in the South, thereby preventing the positive interaction of one tradition on the other, which a unified state would have provided. Normal politics has thus become impossible in both parts of this Island ever since the preventing of the essential debate on what politics should be about—the conflict between capital and labour interests on issues affecting a fairer distribution of the country's income and wealth and a fuller use of its natural resources.

Finally, we are now in the second half of the twentieth century, at a time when the whole of Europe is looking to the future with a vision to end the old quarrels. Old and bitter enemies are settling their differences and are working together in a new and wider context of a United Europe. We in this Island cannot remain in the seventeenth century. We cannot participate in this vision while at the same time continuing our outdated quarrel. It is not beyond the wit and ingenuity of the Irish people—all its sections—to devise amongst themselves a means whereby they can live together in peace and harmony. To do so requires no further imposed settlements but agreements freely arrived at amongst ourselves without any outside interference.

A Declaration

It follows from all of this that Britain must not again attempt to impose a settlement on this country. The key to her role now lies in her making an immediate declaration that she believes that it would be in the best interests of all sections of the Communities in both Islands, if Ireland were to become united on terms which would be acceptable to all the people of Ireland. Such a declaration should contain no hint of coercion but should make it abundantly clear that this is Britain's view and it is the one that she will positively encourage. No one in Ireland has demanded that such a declaration be translated into immediate Irish Unity. There are too many problems inherent in its implementation which will take time to resolve and which will require the setting up of democratic machinery for their resolution. In the meantime an interim system of Government for Northern Ireland should be set up which is fair to all sections.

The Proposals

The basic proposals of the Social Democratic and Labour Party therefore fall into three parts:

(1) An immediate declaration by Britain that she believes that it would be in the best interest of all sections of the Communities in both Islands, if Ireland were to become united on terms which would be acceptable to all the people of Ireland and that she will positively encourage the prosecution of this viewpoint.

(2) The creation of an interim system of Government for Northern Ireland which will be fair to all sections of the people of Northern Ireland.

(3) The creation of Democratic Machinery in Ireland to implement the terms of the above declaration by the agreement and consent of the people of Ireland, North and South.

The interim system of Government

It is both fair and reasonable to assume that until a new system of Government is created in Ireland, democratically agreed to by all sections of the people of Ireland, North and South, that neither section of the population of the North will abandon immediately their present basic loyalties. Any interim system of Government for Northern Ireland which is devised must take those basic loyalties into account, and must give fair expression to them. It must also provide an acceptable Police and Security system. The recognition of these two factors is essential to providing a peaceful interim settlement and to removing the possibility of political violence.

In the absence of a settlement which they will regard as better than their present position Protestant loyalty in general will remain partly to Britain, partly to themselves as a people, to their way of life and to a British link as a safeguard of that way of life. On the other hand Catholics in general will continue to give their loyalty to Ireland. Immediate unity therefore means defeat of Protestants and victory for Catholics, and the continuation of the present constitutional relationship with Britain means victory for Protestants and defeat for Catholics. Either would mean the continued existence of political violence by dissident minorities.

We would therefore make the following proposals designed to create an interim system of Government which will take into account the need to give fair expression to the present basic loyalties of both sections of the people of the North. They will also create an acceptable system of security and policing which will ensure an effective end to political violence. The provision of the latter is a key to success of any interim proposals and it should be emphasised that one of the main weaknesses of Stormont or any of the more civilised versions of it now being proposed by other parties (such as NILP and ALLIANCE) is that they fail to give full expression and protection to the basic Irish aspirations of the Catholic community.

We would propose that Britain and the Republic of Ireland agree on the treaty accepting joint responsibility for an interim system of Government for Northern Ireland to be known as the Joint Sovereignty of Northern Ireland, reserving to themselves all powers relating to foreign affairs, defence, security, police and financial subventions and setting up the following institutions:

(1) Two Commissioners to act jointly as the Representatives of the Sovereign powers who must jointly sign all legislation passed by the Northern Ireland Assembly unless either or both Commissioners are of the opinion that any legislation is an infringement of the treaty between Britain and the Republic of Ireland, in which case they may refer the legislation to the

Constitutional Court which must decide whether the Assembly has exceeded its powers.

(2) An Assembly consisting of 84 members and elected by the people of Northern Ireland for a period of four years on a basis of proportional representation (the single transferable vote) to legislate in all fields including taxation except those reserved to the Sovereign powers.

(3) An executive of 15 members elected by proportional representation from the members of the Assembly, exercising executive powers for the duration of the Assembly, and holding Office throughout its duration except through an adverse vote of 75 per cent of the Assembly.

(4) A Chief Executive elected by the Executive to allocate departmental responsibilities subject to the approval of both Commissioners.

(5) A Constitutional Court of three judges, one appointed by each Commissioner in addition to the Chief Justice of Northern Ireland. The functions of this Court would be to hear appeals on Constitutional law from the Northern Ireland Court of Appeal and to pronounce on the constitutionality of legislation referred to them by the Commissioners.

(6) All legislation to require the signature of each Commissioner.

(7) Flags of both Sovereign States to have equal status.

(8) No representation in either Westminster or Dublin Parliament is envisaged.

The treaty should also guarantee normal civil liberties to all citizens and should allow complete freedom of political expression. All powers of security should be under the direct control of a department headed by both Commissioners. The creation of an acceptable security system is the crucial key to providing peace and order and must include a new unarmed police force or forces jointly recruited by both Governments to maintain peace and order. The area should normally have no military presence but if necessary both Commissioners should be able to call on the Defence Forces of both Sovereign Governments to enter the area.

A National Senate of Ireland

It must be clear that the translation of the declaration by the British Government on the question of Irish Unity into a reality is the most difficult and delicate of all our proposals to implement. The very mention of Irish Unity creates the impression of the Catholic victory with which it has come to be associated. It is necessary therefore to make clear from the outset that the unity that we seek is an entirely new concept and that the New Ireland that should evolve will be one that will still Protestant fears and will have the agreement and consent of all sections of opinion in Ireland. To achieve this the machinery which will bring it into being, must be such as to give full confidence to the Protestant Community in the North, that the kind of Ireland that will emerge will be one, in which their rights are fully and adequately protected and in which, they would be subjected to no sectional or sectarian domination and in which they would play a full role.

Accordingly we would propose the creation of a NATIONAL SENATE OF IRELAND which would have equal representation (elected by PR) from both the Dublin Parliament and the New Northern Assembly. The basic function of the Senate should be to plan the integration of the whole island by preparing the harmonisation of the structures, laws and services of both parts of Ireland and to agree on an acceptable constitution for a New Ireland and its relationships with Britain. We would visualise that no preconceived concept should be placed before the Senate but that a new concept of a New Ireland should evolve from the genuine discussions of the elected representatives of all sections who comprise its membership, although we would envisage the emergence of a Parliament for the whole of Ireland directly elected.

THE NATIONAL SENATE would also plan and implement initially, harmonisation of policies in all fields in which there is already an obvious common ground and a necessary common interest such as regional planning in the context of EEC electricity and power, tourism and all social and economic matters that common sense demands should be pursued in the context of the whole Ireland.

The arrangement for the Constitution, Functions and Finance of the NATIONAL SENATE must be a part of the treaty between Britain and the Republic of Ireland.

Summary of Proposals

1   A Declaration by Britain that it would be in the best interests of all sections of the communities in both islands if Ireland were to become united on terms acceptable to all the people of Ireland, North and South, and that she will positively encourage such a development.

2   A treaty between Britain and the Republic of Ireland:—

(a) Accepting joint interim responsibility for the administration of Northern Ireland through certain institutions including two Commissioners, an Assembly and an executive, and reserving to themselves all powers of security defence, policing, foreign affairs and financial subventions.

(b) Setting up of a National Senate drawn equally from the Northern Assembly and the Dublin Parliament to plan the integration of the whole island and the harmonisation of structures, laws and services in both parts of the island.

3   These proposals are to be taken as Unified and Interdependent.

Appendix

We recognise that these proposals will involve certain legal problems and in this appendix we give our suggestions as to how some of these problems should be dealt with as well as outlining the institutions that we envisage for the Joint Sovereignty.

A   The Treaty

1   The basic and fundamental document would be a treaty between Great Britain and the Republic of Ireland who would, after the treaty had been ratified by the respective jurisdictions in Dublin and London, constitute the Joint sovereignty of Northern Ireland.

2   Once the treaty has been ratified, legislation in Westminster and Dublin would have to be passed. Westminster is the legal sovereign over Northern Ireland at present and only the British parliament could surrender the sole and exclusive power to exercise jurisdiction in, over and under Northern Ireland and its territorial waters. Westminster would also have to pass consequential legislation to enable the troops to be placed under the command of the joint sovereigns, to enable payments of subventions to the Commissioners, etc. Finally, the Republic of Ireland would also have to amend a number of its laws but the effect would be more far-reaching. Various parts of the 1937 Constitution would have to be amended or repealed, in particular article 3 which limits the applicability of the laws passed by the Parliament of the Republic to the 26 Counties area.

3   Because of the fact that Northern Ireland would not form part of the land territory of either Great Britain or the Republic, the treaty would have to lay down that both states would enter into negotiations with the EEC, the United Nations and other international agencies to apply trade, economic, monetary and telecommunications agreements, amongst others to Northern Ireland. As far as the EEC is concerned, this would provide an added impetus to the demands for a regional development programme, which would embrace areas which have national affinities of geography and economy and which were artificially sundered in 1920.

4   In the event of a dispute between the Republic of Ireland and Great Britain as to the interpretation of the treaty (as distinct from whether a matter falls to be determined by the Constitutional Court), both parties will undertake under the treaty to accept as compulsory the jurisdiction of International Court of Justice at The Hague and will further undertake to accept the judgment of the Court.

5   Nearly all the provisions of the treaty can only be operative if both the sovereign powers carry out their obligations in good faith. Since good faith is a requirement of International Law in the observance of treaties, either party would be breaking its obligations under International Law (which neither the Republic nor Great Britain would do lightly, in the current international atmosphere) if it created difficulties or placed obstacles in the way of implementing the machinery anticipated in the treaty, e.g., by not appointing the Commissioner or by refusing to appoint a Judge of its nomination to the Constitutional Court. If this situation did arise and since it is desirable that the treaty provisions should not be negated, it is possible to include a provision in the treaty that in the event of one of the parties failing to carry out a particular duty in the treaty, e.g., non-appointment of a Commissioner, that such an appointment might be made by an external agency.

6   The treaty would contain a general preamble which would embrace the intentions of the state parties to the treaty. The object of the preamble is that it sets down the political aims and aspirations of the parties and relates them to the context in which the treaty provisions will operate.

7   Although the kind of declaration envisaged in the Party's proposals concerning the reunification of the country will normally be found in the preamble to the treaty, it is suggested that such a declaration should form Article 1 of the treaty. In this way the declaration should not only include the legally binding provisions of the treaty (preambles are not binding—in the event of ambiguity they are guides to interpretation) but the status of the Declaration is raised to a more solemn and serious plane.

8   Since this treaty would be between two states, it would be necessary for the purposes of protecting the human rights provisions, to implement the treaty within Northern Ireland. In other words to have the force of law in Northern Ireland, the present legal sovereigns would have to pass legislation implementing the treaty within Northern Ireland at the same time as Great Britain ratifies the treaty. Otherwise, it would be necessary for the Assembly of Northern Ireland to do so which is neither desirable nor legally possible since the Assembly would not have competence to legislate on certain matters covered by the treaty.

9   In addition to the declaration of unity, the treaty will contain the following matters:

   (a) An acceptance by both state-parties of joint sovereignty which will constitute their interior responsibility for the administration of Northern Ireland.

   (b) A recognition of the national identities of both communities in Northern Ireland.

   (c) Specific guarantees of the rights of the individual in Northern Ireland cognisable in courts of law;

   (d) The establishment of the institution of the interior system of government.

   (e) The constitution, powers and duties of the National Senate of Ireland.

   (f) The constitution, duties and powers of a Community Relations Board.

B   National Identity

10   The treaty shall recognise the right of inhabitants of Northern Ireland to claim either Irish or British citizenship, to hold either a British or Irish passport, to use the facilities provided abroad by British or Irish consulates and embassies. It shall be unlawful to discriminate against a person who holds a particular citizenship for the purpose of any form of public or private employment or the conferment of any benefit.

11   The treaty shall recognise the right of Northern Ireland to have a flag and an anthem which would enable the people to have a focus of loyalty. The British and Irish flags shall have official status and shall be flown on public occasions together with the Northern Ireland flag.

C   Individual Rights

12   The treaty shall guarantee the normal and accepted civil liberties already accepted by the Joint Sovereigns. Such rights as the right to free speech, publication and peaceful assembly, equality, before the law, freedom from arbitrary arrest, freedom from imprisonment or other forms of punishment without trial, freedom from cruel or unusual punishments shall be protected by the courts of law. To establish the integrity of such rights and to permit the derogations accepted in a democratic state, the European Convention on Human Rights and Fundamental Freedoms shall become part of the internal law of Northern Ireland.

13   In addition to the above rights included in the European Convention the right, peacefully to advocate change to or retention of the status of Northern Ireland shall be specifically guaranteed.

14   The Republic of Ireland and Great Britain shall agree to permit the right of individual petition to the European Commission on Human Rights to holders of their passports where it is alleged that the provisions relating to human rights have been violated.

D   The Commissioners

15   Each Government shall appoint a Commissioner whose duties shall be general overseeing of the powers and duties specifically reserved to the Joint Sovereigns. Any power not reserved to the Commissioners shall be exercisable by the Assembly and any dispute as to whether a particular function is a reserved function or not shall be determined by the Constitutional Court.

16   Legislation shall be jointly signed by the Commissioners. In the event of a refusal to sign a law because of any possible infringement of the treaty, a Commissioner shall refer the matter to the Constitutional Court whose decision shall be final and binding.

17   The Commissioners shall have the authority to establish advisory committees to assist them in the execution of their reserved functions.

18   In order to assist the Commissioners in the exercise of police and security matters, they shall have authority to appoint a Security Council. The Commissioners shall be responsible for the recruitment and administration of police forces in Northern Ireland. In the event of any outbreak of political violence, the Commissioners shall have the authority to declare a State of Emergency. In such a situation, units of the armed forces of the Republic of

Ireland and Great Britain may enter Northern Ireland to deal with such violence. The commanding officers of such forces shall be under the authority of and shall be responsible to the Commissioners. Such forces shall leave Northern Ireland at the end of any state of emergency.

19 The appointment, terms of employment and other conditions of service of all levels of the judiciary shall fall under the jurisdiction of the Commissioners. The administration of justice, including the office and functions relating to the Director of Public Prosecutions, shall fall under the jurisdiction of the Commissioners. Senior judges of the High Court and the Court of Appeal and the Director of Public Prosecutions shall not be dismissed or disciplined by the Commissioners without the consent of the Constitutional Court.

E   The Assembly

20 The Assembly shall have the power to legislate on all matters not expressly reserved to the Joint Sovereigns by the treaty. It shall also have the power to levy taxes in Northern Ireland for expenditure on functions not reserved to the Joint Sovereigns. Besides this limitation on the legislative competence of the Assembly, the only further limitation on the competence of the Assembly in the interim period will be the Bill of Rights provisions. No legislation shall violate the provisions of the Bill of Rights and every person residing in Northern Ireland or affected by legislation passed by the Assembly shall have the right to contest the validity of such legislation in the High Court. The Commissioners shall have the right to refer legislation which might violate the provisions of the Bill to the Courts for an advisory opinion.

21 The 84 members of the Assembly shall be elected under a system of proportional representation, in multi-member constituencies with a single transferable vote. There will be an Electoral Commission comprising three members, one each appointed by the Commissioners and the third by the Chief Justice of Northern Ireland. The Commissioner shall be charged with the duty of dividing the territory of Northern Ireland into appropriate constituencies, bearing in mind the principle that one vote shall have an equal value in all parts of Northern Ireland. Hence, there shall be no discrimination in favour of or against any particular part of Northern Ireland.

F   The Executive Council

22 The Executive Council shall be elected by the Assembly on the basis of the proportional representation of the parties and groups in the Assembly. The Executive Council members shall elect a Chief Executive whose function shall be to preside at meetings of the Executive Council and to allocate or distribute departmental responsibilities. The treaty shall fix the maximum and minimum number of departments. The allocation of departments to individual council members shall require the consent of the Commissioners. In the event of inability to reach an agreement between the Chief Executive and the Commissioners, the Commissioners shall allocate the departmental responsibilities.

Each member of the Executive Committee shall be responsible for the department allocated to him.

23   The life of the Executive Committee shall coincide with the life of the Assembly. In other words, although the Executive Committee shall report to the Assembly and be answerable to it, it will not be removed save in a situation where three quarters of the total membership of the Assembly pass a motion of no confidence in the Executive Committee. In such a situation, the Executive Committee shall resign and fresh elections to appoint a new Executive Committee by the Assembly shall take place. If the Assembly is unable to make such an appointment or if another vote with the majority of three quarters of the members of the Assembly pass a further vote of no confidence, the Assembly shall be dissolved and elections for a new Assembly shall take place.

G   The Constitutional Court

24   The Constitutional Court shall consist of three judges one each appointed by the Commissioners, the third being the Chief Justice of Northern Ireland. The Courts' jurisdiction shall extend to the cases (i) where the Commissioners have referred legislation to test the legislation's validity to the treaty and (ii) on appeal from the Northern Ireland Court of Appeal on points of constitutional law and violations of the Bill of Rights.

H   Community Relations Board

25   The treaty shall make provision for the appointment by the Commissioners of a Community Relations Board, responsible to the Commissioners. The powers of the Board shall be similar to those of the Race Relations Board and shall include the powers of prosecution but the Board shall have further and more precise powers in the field of employment.

I   The National Senate of Ireland

26   The National Senate shall be constituted on the basis of provisions of the treaty between the Republic of Ireland and Great Britain. It will be comprised of 50 members—25 appointed by the Assembly of Northern Ireland and 25 appointed by Dail Eireann on the basis of parity of group strength.

27   The National Senate shall meet at least four times a year, and its sittings shall alternate between Dublin and Belfast.

28   Initially, the National Senate would plan and propose the harmonisation of policies in areas of common interest such as regional planning in the context of the EEC, electricity and power, tourism and certain aspects of social and economic policy.

29   Besides providing a forum of discussion on matters of common interest, the National Senate shall plan the integration of the whole island by preparing

the harmonisation of the structures, laws and services of both parts of Ireland and it would keep, as an urgent task, the perspective of an acceptable constitution for the new Ireland. During the interim period, it would also turn its attention to the provisions of the 1937 Constitution which provides the constitutional framework for the Republic of Ireland.

J Representation

30 There should be no representation of Northern Ireland in Dail Eireann or in the House of Commons.

K Subventions

31 The subvention should be paid by Britain and the Republic of Ireland in proportion to their Gross National Product and should be the subject of annual negotiations between Northern Ireland, Britain and the Republic of Ireland. The subvention will be partly used to defray the expenses of the High Commission and those departments subject to the High Commission control and partly placed at the disposal of the Assembly to enable it to maintain an adequate level of social services etc., within Northern Ireland.

ULSTER LIBERAL PARTY

PROPOSALS FOR PARLIAMENTARY REFORM IN NORTHERN IRELAND

Introduction

We refer to our proposals published in September 1971* in which we urged that all elections in Northern Ireland should be by proportional representation; that there should be a proportionately elected Government; and that permanent consultative machinery should be set up between Northern Ireland and the Republic to deal with matters of common interest. What follows is an amplification of those proposals.

Basic Principles

We repeat our assertion that two basic principles must be recognised:

1   That there can be no change in Northern Ireland's position as part of the United Kingdom without the consent of a majority of the people of Northern Ireland.

Such consent is obviously not forthcoming at the present time. The views of the people must be respected. Any attempt to force unification would, in our view, be doomed to failure. We say this notwithstanding that we believe in the ultimate unity of Ireland, and notwithstanding our conviction that the Northern Protestant would be far better able to achieve his full potential as a fully-fledged Irishman rather than in the ambiguous position in which history has left him.

2   Northern Ireland cannot function properly without the full participation of the two religious communities. There can be no going back to the system of majority domination which obtained for the last 50 years.

We do not accept that no solution exists, in the Northern Ireland context, which could resolve the tragic conflict that threatens to destroy us. The solution lies in the creation of a community which cherishes all people equally, and which earns and obtains the respect and support of all its members. Structures of government must be designed to ensure that this aim cannot be frustrated by those who cling to the old divisive attitudes.

---

*Copy appended hereto.

Restoration of Self-Government

We believe that self-government must be restored to Northern Ireland, subject to the United Kingdom's overall responsibility for ensuring fair and proper standards of government. We urge the establishment of a new type of Legislative Assembly, elected by proportional representation and with a built-in system for the sharing of power as widely as possible. It should have a minimum of 75 Members.

Instead of the former Cabinet system, with Ministers chosen by a Prime Minister, there should be a system of Departmental Committees, elected by the Assembly on a proportional basis as follows:

1 Chairmen of Committees

The first task of the newly-elected Assembly would be to elect a Panel of Chairmen using the single transferable vote. The Chairman receiving the greatest number of first preference votes would have first choice of Department, the second would have next choice, and so on, subject to the proviso that no Member could hold the office of Chairman of the Finance Committee for more than the life of one Assembly, or five years, whichever period shall be the longer.

2 Finance Committee

The Finance Committee would be the main policy making body and its Chairman would be, in effect, the Head of Government. The Committee would consist of the Chairman of the other Committees and three persons appointed by the Secretary of State for Northern Ireland from outside the membership of the Assembly.

3 Other Departmental Committees

Each would consist of its Chairman and eight proportionately elected Members. No person would be eligible to be elected to more than two Committees. The Chairman of each Committee would be the link between the Assembly and the Department, but decisions, other than on matters of routine administration, would be taken by the Committee. In the event of a clash between a Chairman and his Committee, the matter would be referred to the Finance Committee which would have power to overrule any other Departmental Committee.

4 Legislation

Legislation would normally be conducted through the Assembly by the Chairman of the relevant Committee but he could, if he so wished, appoint any Member of the Committee to act on his behalf, or, if the Committee agreed, could ask a Civil Servant to conduct some specific piece of legislation. For this purpose Civil Servants would have a right of audience in the Assembly, and possibly also for the purpose of answering Members' questions. They would, of course, attend Committee meetings as required.

RELATIONS BETWEEN THE NORTHERN IRELAND ASSEMBLY AND WESTMINSTER

There should continue to be a Secretary of State for Northern Ireland who would exercise overall supervision of Northern Ireland affairs on behalf of the Westminster Parliament. For the time being at any rate he should retain control over all matters affecting security and civil rights, but he should have power to delegate his authority in respect of these matters to the relevant Department.

The former convention that matters within the transferred field could not be discussed at Westminster must on no account be revived. Westminster's power to legislate for Northern Ireland should continue undiminished and there should be no necessity for parity legislation—social security, etc.,—to be duplicated by the Assembly.

We believe that there could be advantages in giving the Northern Ireland Members at Westminster the right to sit and to be heard in the Assembly. They should not, however, have the right to vote or to be elected to Committees unless the method of their election to Westminster were changed to PR. As we have stated before we would favour the whole of Northern Ireland being treated as one constituency for the purpose of electing the Westminster Members.

All members of the judiciary (including county court judges and resident magistrates) should be appointed by the Lord Chancellor. While security remains in the hands of the Secretary of State the British Attorney-General should continue to hold the same office in Northern Ireland. Thereafter the Attorney-General should be appointed by the Secretary of State, preferably, but not necessarily, from the membership of the Assembly. If not a Member he would have a right of audience in the Assembly but not a right to vote.

Senate

We doubt the necessity for a second chamber but if it were to be retained it would have to be reformed and its membership reconstituted to include representatives of interest groups such as industry, farmers, trades unions, tenants associations, sport, etc.

RELATIONSHIP WITH THE REPUBLIC OF IRELAND

Permanent consultative machinery should be set up between Northern Ireland and the Republic to deal with matters of common interest. It should take the form of a Joint Council whose members would be appointed in equal numbers by the Northern Ireland Finance Committee and the Government in Dublin. It would have no executive powers, but one of its functions would be

85

to investigate the necessity for joint Commissions upon which powers could be conferred by the Dail and the Assembly for specific purposes.

One such specific purpose which requires urgent attention is the economic development of the Foyle valley. There should be immediate negotiations between the Governments at Westminster and Dublin with a view to the setting up of a Commission with very wide-ranging powers for the joint development of the area comprising the new local government districts of Londonderry and Strabane and that part of north-east Donegal which, were it not for the Border, would naturally centre on Derry.

Because of the seriousness of the security situation in Derry and its drastic effect on the economy, negotiations should also take place with a view to instituting a special joint force of RUC and Garda to patrol the Commission's area and to initiate a recruitment drive specially focussed on that area. One of the aims would be to enable the Army to withdraw from Derry as soon as possible.

Stormont never had power to legislate for matters affecting trade, commerce, etc., outside its own jurisdiction. If useful co-operation is to be achieved with the Republic in economic matters it is eminently desirable that the new Assembly should have all such powers as may be necessary to implement recommendations of the Joint Council.

Fundamental to the success of the Joint Council would be a statement by the British Government—which undoubtedly would have the backing of Parliament—that it wished to see increased co-operation between Northern Ireland and the Republic. There should therefore be an undertaking that every possible backing, financial or otherwise, will be given to any reasonable project for which Northern Ireland and the Republic put forward joint plans.

We regard the establishment of structures for co-operation between Northern Ireland and the Republic as being vital to the development of effective co-operation between the two sections of the community in Northern Ireland.

APPENDIX TO ANNEX 8
PROPOSALS FOR PARLIAMENTARY REFORM IN NORTHERN IRELAND

Introduction

In the present tragedy of Northern Ireland it is absolutely vital that all those who believe in parliamentary democracy should try to give a constructive lead to the people, rather than pour petrol on an already inflamed situation. The torrents of abuse and hatred must eventually stop and the sooner the better. We re-affirm our belief that talks among all interested parties are an imperative first step.

Basic Principles

Two basic principles must be recognised:

1   There can be no change in Northern Ireland's position as part of the United Kingdom without the consent of a majority of the people of Northern Ireland. Any worthwhile re-unification of Ireland can only be brought about by agreement of the two parts of Ireland.

2   Northern Ireland cannot be made to work without the full participation of the two religious communities. There can be no going back to the system of the last 50 years.

Elections by Proportional Representation

An electoral system in Northern Ireland must give fair representation to all sections of opinion. Voters must also be allowed to express preferences for candidates outside their own political or religious group. These aims can only be achieved by the use of the Single Transferable Vote in multi-member constituencies. The arguments in favour of the re-introduction of Proportional Representation are now well known and have the support of an ever-increasing body of opinion both within and outside Northern Ireland.

We commend the recent report of the Electoral Reform Society on the re-introduction of Proportional Representation for a Parliament of 52 members.

Increased Size of Stormont

The Government's proposed re-organisation of local Government means that many of the former local authority functions will in future be centralised. Thus the amount of work and the responsibility of the Stormont Parliament will be increased. To meet this new situation and to allow a greater choice of ministerial candidates we advocate an increase in the size of the House of Commons to 75 members. Our enclosed scheme for the election of 75 MP's is mainly based on the county boundaries and the new Westminster constituencies in Belfast. Because of the small size of the electorate in Fermanagh it has been necessary to include the Trillick and Fivemiletown areas of Co. Tyrone which fit geographically.

The same system of Proportional Representation must be used in all elections in the Province.

(a) Westminster General Elections

Northern Ireland ought to have at Westminster a team of MP's fairly representing the various sections of opinion, rather than particular geographical areas. We believe that the best method of doing this would be to treat the province as one constituency electing its 12 Westminster MP's by the Single Transferable Vote. This would be the best possible test of public opinion.

(b) Local Government

The present re-organisation of Local Government could greatly be speeded up by the introduction of Proportional Representation, as the multi-member wards would require much less drawing of boundaries.

The Senate

If the Senate is to act as an effective second chamber there is a need to reform the present system whereby it merely reflects the political composition of the Commons. We feel there is a need to greatly broaden its membership to include representatives of sectional interests such as farmers, trade unions, sport, etc. The former University representation in the Commons could be given voice in the Senate.

Provision for Constitutional Referendum

The Government of Ireland Act should be amended to make provision for a referendum to be held before any change is made in the constitution of Northern Ireland. This would effectively take the 'border issue' out of parliamentary elections.

Co-operation within Ireland

Permanent consultative machinery should be set up between Northern Ireland and the Republic to deal with matters of common interest. This will be all the more necessary within the European Economic Community.

Partnership in Government

Many countries in the world have had to face the problem of a divided community. The solution has been to give all sections a direct sense of involvement in government. The recent history of Switzerland is worthy of consideration. Within the last century friction between Protestants and Catholics led to disturbances involving loss of life at several elections. This has been overcome by the introduction of Proportional Representation right up to Government level.

We therefore believe that the Swiss system could well be adopted in Northern Ireland.

Undiluted one party Government has proved an abject failure in Northern Ireland. The Westminster model is satisfactory when it is possible to change the Party in power. This is not successful where parties are based on a permanent majority—minority division, as it leads to arrogance on one side and frustration on the other.

We therefore believe that the Swiss system could well be adopted in Northern Ireland and we recommend that the proportional principle is extended beyond the election of Parliament to the formation of the Government. A team of ministers would, therefore, be elected by the Members of Parliament using Proportional Representation, instead of being nominated by the Prime Minister from his own party as at present.

PROPORTIONAL REPRESENTATION IN NORTHERN IRELAND

SCHEME OF PROPOSED CONSTITUENCIES

Fermanagh

3 seats   38,823 electorate (12,941 per member)

Co. Fermanagh plus the neighbouring Tyrone electoral divisions of Fivemiletown, Dromore, Rahony, Tattymoyle, Drumharvey, Greenan, Moorfield, Kilskeery, Lifford and Trillick.

Tyrone

6 seats   87.022 electorate (14,504 per member)

Co. Tyrone excluding the area added to Fermanagh.

Londonderry

8 seats   114,109 electorate (14,264 per member)

County and City of Londonderry.

Armagh

6 seats   88,600 electorate (14,767 per member)

County Armagh.

North Antrim

7 seats   93,336 electorate (13,334 per member)

The present Stormont constituencies of North Antrim, Bannside, Mid Antrim and Larne.

South Antrim

8 seats   113,329 electorate (14,166 per member)

The present Stormont constituencies of South Antrim, Antrim, Newtownabbey and Carrick.

South Down

7 seats   95,738 electorate (13,677 per member)

The present Stormont constituencies of South Down, West Down, Iveagh, Mourne and East Down.

North Down

6 seats   76,668 electorate (12,778 per member)

The present Stormont constituencies of Ards, Bangor, North Down, Mid Down and Lagan Valley excluding the Dundonald-Castlereagh-Newtownbreda area inside the new Belfast UK constituencies.

North Belfast

6 seats   83,065 electorate (13,844 per member)

The new UK constituency including the present Stormont constituencies of Duncairn, Clifton, Oldpark, Shankill and Dock.

East Belfast

6 seats   82,162 electorate (13,694 per member)

The new UK constituency including the present Stormont constituencies of Pottinger, Victoria and Bloomfield as well as parts of North Down, Mid Down and Lagan Valley.

South Belfast

6 seats   79,312 electorate (13,344 per member)

The new UK constituency including the present Stormont constituencies of Willowfield, Ballynafeigh, Cromac and Windsor as well as parts of Lagan Valley and Larkfield.

West Belfast

6 seats   80,066 electorate (13,344 per member)

The new UK constituency including the present Stormont constituencies of Woodvale, Falls, Central and St. Anne's as well as part of Larkfield.

NEW ULSTER MOVEMENT

A NEW CONSTITUTION FOR NORTHERN IRELAND

1   The proposals contained in this publication should be read as the fourth in a series of linked papers. In the first of these, 'THE REFORM OF STORMONT' (June 1971), we analysed the weakness of the existing Northern Ireland political structure and suggested this could be summed up as being 'that the Westminster model of government has been applied in a society to which it is not suited'. We went on to say: 'The Westminster model works well only in rather special circumstances. It is a system which can easily lead to tyranny, because it produces a remarkable concentration of power in the government of the day. To avoid this risk, the system requires the existence of two strong parties, competing with each other at elections on fairly even terms. Where this happens, power is not monopolised by a single team of ministers, but alternates between two teams, which between them have the support of the great majority of the electorate . . . . In such circumstances the government will treat the opposition with respect, and will even consult it on matters of policy, because ministers know that their own turn in opposition may come soon, and that they will then be glad of considerate treatment from their successors in government. It is easy to see that, in Northern Ireland, the conditions for working the Westminster model have not been attained . . . . This means that one section of the community has monopolised power, with consequent tendencies to complacency, arrogance and at times injustice; while another section has been excluded from power, with consequent tendencies to frustration, irresponsibility and at times a hankering after violent solutions. The political structure of the province, instead of assuaging community discord, has been so designed that they increase it'.

2   On this basis we then proceeded to outline those constitutional devices open to government and parliament of Northern Ireland so as to introduce a degree of power sharing and participation into the then existing devolved parliamentary structure of Stormont. One of these—proportional representation on the basis of the 'single transferable vote'—has been accepted for the forthcoming Local Government elections in principle and should be extended to the Regional Assembly referred to below. The other devices—the use of parliamentary committees, an enlarged parliament, the reconstruction of the senate, power sharing in the cabinet and the use of weighted majorities—have not received due consideration prior to the prorogation of Stormont in March 1972.

3   'THE WAY FORWARD', although published in November 1971, was based upon a memorandum sent to the Home Secretary in November 1970 and circulated privately in Northern Ireland. Whilst advocating the suspension of Stormont by our sovereign authority at Westminster, we nonetheless regarded suspension as an unfortunate but necessary **temporary** decision. Indeed we said then: 'The right to the principle of devolved government is the bedrock

of our proposals. This principle is inviolate . . . . We favour the retention under the sovereign authority of Westminster, of the principle of devolved government in Northern Ireland'. We advocated suspension because we could see no prospect of 'good government for all our people' evolving out of a parliamentary structure dominated by sectarian politics.

4   Our third publication 'TWO IRELANDS OR ONE?' analysed the problems in the way of any plans for the unification of Ireland. We posed the question that if justice for all our citizens in Northern Ireland could be obtained 'by a restructuring of institutions in the North so as to guarantee a sharing of power' the strength of the case for a United Ireland would be altered. Finally we asked in that publication: 'Provided a just re-structuring can be achieved in the North would it not be better for all of us if you (the Republic of Ireland) went your way and we (Northern Ireland) went ours—two states acknowledging their different traditions but ready to co-operate in all matters of common concern?'.

5   The points raised in the preceding paragraphs remain the policy of NUM. Recent tragic events have, if anything, strengthened them. Before outlining the constitutional changes which we believe ought now to follow suspension, there are two further points to be noted. Firstly, we subscribe fully to the 1969 'Downing Street Declaration' which designated 'equality of citizenship' as the only proper basis for the administration of our country.

6   Secondly, we believe that all citizens, whether they be Unionists, Nationalists, Republicans, Communists, or whatever, have the right to hold their political opinions and to advance their cause by every means within the rule of law. In particular those who aspire to a United Ireland have been promised periodic referenda which is the only feasible, legitimate way of testing public opinion to have been advanced so far. The first referendum should be for a period of 10 years.

Recommended Constitutional Changes

7   Before outlining the changes we advocate, we would record that we do not seek the return of either the old Stormont or indeed of any structure resembling a 'Parliament'. Many of our current divisions have their roots in the erroneous belief that Stormont was a sovereign authority. That contention is untenable. Nonetheless, it is easy to understand that 50 years of acquaintance with an institution which, by Westminster design, appeared in its external symbols to resemble so closely that sovereign Parliament, would lead many of our people to believe those who, for political reasons, chose to argue that Stormont was a sovereign authority. One in fact, which could not be changed, let alone suspended, except it agreed to any such change itself. The trappings of sovereignty, which included not only a representative of the Queen, a Privy Council and a Prime Minister, but also a Cabinet and a Senate, a Speaker and Black Rod, Sergeant-at-arms and Gentlemen ushers, encouraged people to believe that Stormont represented something it was never intended to be. We do not wish to return to those days. The symbolism of the new structure should match the realities. Therefore:

A Regional Assembly

8   There should be elected on the basis of Proportional Representation (STV) a Regional Assembly to administer Northern Ireland as a region of the United Kingdom. The administrative arguments for having our own limited autonomy are still valid (THE WAY FORWARD p 7/8). Indeed the Macrory reform of local government, which has our support, makes some kind of regional authority essential.

9   The Assembly should be larger in size than the old Stormont (REFORM OF STORMONT p8 para. 3). However, elections should be based on the 12 existing Westminster constituencies. That number should not be increased as has been suggested elsewhere. It would seem that the boundaries of all, or some, of the constituencies would need to be redrawn. The number of seats in each of these 12 constituencies for election to our Regional Assembly should be either 6 or 7 (i.e. a total of 72-84 members). This formula should provide Northern Irish citizens with the same degree of participation in the government of their country as obtains elsewhere in the Kingdom. Under this arrangement Westminster MP's will be able to liaise closely with the Regional Assembly representatives of their own constituency. Citizens themselves will have the opportunity, for the first time, of identifying their constituency with both Westminster and the Regional Assembly. We recommend that dual membership (of Parliament and the Regional Assembly) should be forbidden. The salary of a member of the Regional Assembly should be sufficient to attract competent candidates and to encourage them to devote the maximum of their time to the work of the Assembly.

10   The Regional Assembly should not include a second chamber. The former Senate was an unnecessary piece of pretentiousness which added nothing to the quality or efficiency of the administration but did help to inflate the image of Stormont. We would prefer to see decisions and participation in the decision making machinery directed downwards towards the people and not elevated upwards, away from the people. Although we considered the argument which favours a second chamber if it is composed of special interest groups e.g. Trades Unions, Universities, Farmers' organisations, etc. (REFORM OF STORMONT p9 paras. 1-4), we believe that this principle can best be attained, as outlined below, without recourse to such a second chamber.

The Authority of the Regional Assembly

11   Substantially this should be the same as that enjoyed by the Northern Ireland Parliament from 1921-72, provided it is made legally and explicitly clear that the Regional Assembly is, in every respect, subordinate to the Westminster Parliament. The retention of the scale of authority vested in the old Stormont is only advocated in conjunction with the keystone to these proposals which is concerned with the 'power-sharing' devices outlined below. Control of the police would remain in Northern Ireland provided that it is made a fully civilianised force, totally unarmed, clearly separated from the political arena and subject to an effective Police Authority and inspection by the British Inspector General of Police.

12   Although we recommend that the control of the police be retained in the hands of an independent Police Authority, we believe that the functions and responsibility of this body require to be re-emphasised so that matters other than those of a purely administrative nature, e.g. working conditions and public relations, are given the top priority they deserve. To make the Police Authority more of a reality to the community, we recommend the setting up of area committees throughout the country to act as local police liaison committees. Such committees would send representatives to the central authority which in turn would have an executive of its own.

The Sharing of Power

13   This is the most important, and, heretofore, the most intractable problem. In the past the difficulty was increased by the fact that Northern Ireland followed the Westminster pattern of concentrating power in a strong cabinet. This meant that schemes for power-sharing tended to turn into schemes for choosing the cabinet in some new way. We suggested for instance in 'THE REFORM OF STORMONT', that it be chosen by PR and should be based on the Swiss model. A Cabinet drawn from different parties could work only if the parties shared a minimum common purpose, and there was no sign in Northern Ireland of this minimum being reached. The suspension of Stormont, however, has cleared the ground. There is now no Cabinet, strong or otherwise, and a wider range of options comes into view. A number of devices exist for diffusing power, and different ones can be used in different fields of government. The following paragraphs will identify some of these devices, and suggest where they might be useful in the special circumstances of Northern Ireland.

14   **Decentralisation of control to local authorities.** This means that each community at least has control in the areas where it is in a majority and it is a device widely used in other divided countries. In Northern Ireland, however, the Macrory report—which the opposition supported—went decisively the other way. There is no point at this stage in attempting any general reversal of the Macrory proposals—local government has been in the melting pot for far too long already. But there may be particular subjects for which this device would be appropriate or even necessary. The use of this device will be more apposite when, as Macrory envisaged, greater power returns eventually to local government.

15   **Delegation of control to statutory bodies,** on which the different strands of opinion in the province would be represented roughly in proportion to numerical strength. This is the device already adopted in Northern Ireland for managing housing, and the Community Relations Commission. To some extent, when the new area boards come into operation, it will be used for health, education and social services. There have been complaints about the way in which particular members of statutory bodies were chosen, and it will be necessary to find a formula acceptable to the members of the Assembly in future which is fair and reasonable for the nomination of members to such bodies. But in principle the device seems a sensible one.

16   **The use of Parliamentary committees** (REFORM OF STORMONT p6/7/8 section 2). The British Parliament, and the parliaments modelled on it, like Stormont and Dail Eireann, are exceptional in that they use committees so little. In many democratic countries the bulk of the work of parliament is done by committees, each specialising in a different subject. The full parliament meets only to scrutinise bills, etc., which have been reported to it by the various committees. This arrangement is not peculiar to countries with community problems—indeed it is also the basis on which local authorities in Britain are run. But it does have an additional advantage in countries with such problems. This arises from the nature of committee work. In a committee, working away from the glare of publicity, and with its members getting to know each other very well, influence becomes increasingly detached from party labels. Men with a real knowledge of their subject tend to win the respect of other members of their committee, regardless of party allegiance. Thus a member of a minority party may, in committee, wield an influence that he is unlikely to have in the Assembly as a whole. As proposed later these committees would replace the Cabinet system. Therefore each committee should be linked with the relevant civil service department(s). Each committee should have a limited power to consult or employ specialists or experts.

17   **The distribution of committee chairmanships among members of different parties in proportion to party strength in the Assembly.** It is a fact of observation that committee chairmen can be influential people. By their handling of a discussion they can make a considerable difference to its outcome. In some parliaments they are given additional powers. They may determine the committees' agenda, and they may engage the specialist staff on which it depends for an independent estimate of the case put up to it by government departments. If committee chairmanships are divided between parties in proportion to their parliamentary strength, then this is an important further means for diffusing power. As it is one already proposed by the Unionists in their Green Paper of last year, there should be no difficulty in getting it accepted.

18   **The weighted majority.** This means arranging that, in controversial areas, e.g. the police, planning, etc., decisions must be taken by more than a bare majority.

19   The adoption of these devices would make possible a still more radical departure: **the abolition of the Cabinet.** If decision-making were diffused on the lines suggested above there would be no longer any need for a Cabinet. Decisions which have hitherto been made in the Cabinet would be made by committees of the Assembly. Co-ordination is obtained by committee chairmen consulting and effecting necessary liaison with each other. By adopting this technique Proportional Representation in government is achieved.

The Chairman of the Assembly

20   The Chairman of the Assembly would be elected annually by the committee chairmen from among their own members. He should not be eligible for re-election for three years.

The Secretary of State

21   We wish to retain the presence of the Secretary of State for Northern Ireland. He should be a member of the Westminster Cabinet, open the Regional Assembly and act as the link between Northern Ireland and Great Britain.

North/South Relations

22   This subject is bound to arise in considering the constitution of Northern Ireland (but see 'TWO IRELANDS OR ONE?'). Since the creation of the Irish Free State/Republic and Northern Ireland, the relationship between the two has never been satisfactory and most of the time has been distinctly unfriendly. The paramount aim must be to reconcile the two communities in Northern Ireland and the Republic, at all levels, The first prerequisite is clearly recognition by the Republic of the political status in international law of Northern Ireland as a region of the United Kingdom and its right to remain such until a majority of its citizens decide otherwise. Meanwhile our parameters are clear. On the one side there can be no question of coercing Unionists into a United Ireland. Successive British governments of both parties are pledged against this. We should also note that the Dublin government, supported by the opposition parties, the SDLP and Nationalist parties all subscribe to the principle that a United Ireland should not and must not be obtained under duress, by force or without the freely given consent of the majority of the citizens of Northern Ireland. On the other hand Nationalists and Republicans must be assured that there is absolutely no impediment in any new administrative structure, directly or indirectly, preventing social, economic, cultural and political exchanges—even if these might ultimately lead to agreed changes in political relationships.

23   These requirements are not incompatible. Mr Faulkner and leading Unionist spokesmen have accepted that Republicans have equal rights with Unionists to express their viewpoint or canvass their political creeds without interference. These rights, in both cases, exclude recourse to violence or other illegal methods.

24   Our immediate aim, therefore, should be the establishment of a permanent policy of good neighbourliness between North and South, to increase, where mutually beneficial, areas of co-operation and joint action. The particular devices or structures we advocate are:

25   **An Act of Human Rights** in specific detail. The Act would provide for access of aggrieved persons **and organisations** to a Tribunal modelled on Industrial Tribunals, with a minimum of rules of procedure and with an ultimate appeal to a Tribunal made up of Judges drawn equally from Northern Ireland and the Irish Republic.

26   **The creation of an all Ireland Standing Committee to keep the laws of Northern Ireland and the Irish Republic under constant review** and to keep divergencies to a minimum. In our opinion, having regard to their common

obligations and commitments in the EEC this Standing Committee might well include Great Britain.

27   **The sharing of power through a system of Parliamentary Committees in the Dail,** so as to enable meetings on matters of common interest between the committees of the Northern Ireland Assembly and committees of the Dail.

28   **The establishment of a standing committee of educationalists and others** to study and advise on all aspects of education in Ireland with immediate reference to the study and teaching of Irish history and the promotion, by means of schools curriculae, of better community relations.

29   **Administration of matters of joint interest by joint statutory bodies.** Precedents for this already exist in the Foyle Fisheries Commission and similar structures. Tourism, trade and agricultural interests clearly lend themselves to similar structures.

30   **Joint Development Commission.** Ireland, North and South, lies well outside the 'Golden Triangle' of the EEC. Many of us have grave doubts as to the effectiveness of the Community's policies on Regional Development. There is, therefore, a common task facing both Northern Ireland and the Irish Republic—to improve the economic lot of all our people. A joint Industrial Development Commission could, in particular, study the development of areas with a natural and common link such as Derry and Donegal, South Down (Newry) and Louth (Dundalk).

31   To remove the political question of the border from the work of administering the region it is imperative that the people of Northern Ireland, rather than the Regional Assembly, must have the sole right to recommend any alteration in the new constitution to the sovereign parliament, in so far as any such alteration might substantially affect the constitutional link with Great Britain.

32   Although the structures advocated in this publication would provide, in our judgment, a substantially better political framework for our community than that obtained under the 1920 Government of Ireland Act, it is clear that ultimately neither the law nor the political framework can bring peace, justice or prosperity to all our people. These conditions can only obtain in the ultimate if sufficient citizens have the will and the determination to live at peace with each other. Patently this demands a radical change of heart in many of us and a determination to work for reconciliation and justice through **all** our institutions—not least the Christian Churches.

Printed in England for Her Majesty's Stationery Office
By Brown Knight & Truscott Ltd. London and Tonbridge

Dd. 505636 K400 10/72

HER MAJESTY'S STATIONERY OFFICE

Government Bookshops

80 Chichester Street, Belfast BT1 4JY
49 High Holborn, London WC1V 6HB
13a Castle Street, Edinburgh EH2 3AR
109 St Mary Street, Cardiff CF1 1JW
Brazennose Street, Manchester M60 8AS
50 Fairfax Street, Bristol BS1 3DE
258 Broad Street, Birmingham B1 2HE

*Government publications are also available
through booksellers*

SBN 11 700498 7